Search Engine Marketing, Inc.
Third Edition

Search Engine Marketing, Inc.

Driving Search Traffic to Your Company's Website

Third Edition

Mike Moran

Bill Hunt

IBM Press
Pearson plc
Upper Saddle River, NJ • Boston • Indianapolis • San Francisco
New York • Toronto • Montreal • London • Munich • Paris • Madrid
Cape Town • Sydney • Tokyo • Singapore • Mexico City

Ibmpressbooks.com

IBM Press Program Managers: Steven M. Stansel, Ellice Uffer

Cover design: IBM Corporation
Editor In Chief: Bernard Goodwin
Marketing Manager: Dan Powell
Publicist: Lisa Jacobson-Brown
Editorial Assistant: Michelle Housley
Managing Editor: Kristy Hart
Designer: Alan Clements
Project Editor: Andy Beaster
Copy Editor: Keith Cline
Indexer: Christine Karpeles
Compositor: Nonie Ratcliff
Proofreader: Kathy Ruiz
Manufacturing Buyer: Dan Uhrig

Published by Pearson plc
Publishing as IBM Press

For information about buying this title in bulk quantities, or for special sales opportunities (which may include electronic versions; custom cover designs; and content particular to your business, training goals, marketing focus, or branding interests), please contact our corporate sales department at corpsales@pearsoned.com or (800) 382-3419.

For government sales inquiries, please contact governmentsales@pearsoned.com.

For questions about sales outside the U.S., please contact international@pearsoned.com.

To my wife, Linda, and my children, David, Madeline, Marcella, and Dwight,
with great appreciation for their support for me.
—Mike Moran

To my wonderful wife, Motoko, and my children, Mariko and William,
for their tremendous patience, encouragement, and support.
—Bill Hunt

Contents

Part I: Understand Search Marketing

Preface

Search marketing demands a curious mix of business, writing, and technical skills. No matter which skills you have, you probably have *some* of the skills needed to succeed, but not *all* of them. This book will fill those gaps.

If you possess marketing skills, or you have a sales or other business background, you will quickly see the ways that search marketing draws on your previous experience, but you will also learn how it is different. Like any form of marketing, you will focus on the target markets you want to reach—in this case, searchers looking for certain words. You will segment those markets. You will realize that your web pages are your marketing communications materials. You might see parallels to direct marketing as you relentlessly measure your success, or perhaps you will see the possibilities for search marketing to burnish your brand image. Regardless, like all marketing, you will learn to design your search marketing program to meet your company's larger goals. Unlike other forms of marketing, search marketing is not designed to interrupt people with an advertising message. Successful search marketing meets people at their point of need. When searchers want something, you must be ready to satisfy them with what they want, even if you would prefer to sell them something else.

As critical as marketers are to success, search marketing is, at its core, a writer's medium. Like direct marketing, a well-crafted message is critical to enticing a searcher to click your page. Once at your site, the words on your page also influence whether the prospective customer buys your product or abandons your site. But search marketing relies on skilled writing to an even greater extent than that, because the search engines choose the pages they show based on words. You will learn how to write the words that your customers and the search engines are looking for. If you are a writer, you will find search marketing a challenge like none you have ever seen, but one that can reward your company richly.

If you have technical skills, you are needed, too. Search marketing depends on your website's design and operation. Many commonly used web technologies stop search marketing cold. You will find that search marketing is similar to other technical projects; you must understand the requirements so that you can develop the solution. You need to develop a business case to see the value so the work can be prioritized and funded for your busy IT team. You will need a project plan to execute on schedule. You will have standards and operational procedures that keep the system running smoothly. If you are a webmaster, a web developer, or any kind of technologist, your skills are vital to search marketing success.

If you are looking for a book about the secrets of search marketing, this book does have a few. However, they might be secrets of a surprising kind. Some people think of search marketing as an arcane pursuit where you need to know the "tricks" to get search engines to show your site. But those tricks are *not* the secrets of search marketing; you do not need tricks to succeed. What you really need is a firm understanding of how search marketing works, a methodology to plan your search marketing program, and the information required to execute it. The biggest secret of search marketing is that knowledge, hard work, and flawless execution are all you need. This book shows you how to get all three.

Part I covers the basics of search marketing: how search marketing works, how searchers work, and how search itself works, operationally. Marketers and writers will learn more about search technology. Technologists will be exposed to the opportunity search marketing offers your company. You will learn how to segment searchers based on their behavior, so you will know what they want from your site. Part I will teach you all the background you need to formulate a custom search marketing program for your company—which is what you will do in Part II.

Part II takes you step by step through developing a proposal for your own search marketing program. You will learn how to identify the goals of your website and measure your current success in meeting them. You will learn how well you are doing at search marketing today and how much it is worth to do better. We show you how to estimate your costs, choose your strategy, and get your proposed program approved by your executives and by all the folks in your company who you need on your side. Because search marketing demands cooperation from so many people in your company, we show you proven ways to get each kind of person to work hard on your program.

Part III explores all the details you need to execute your program. Every website poses different challenges to a search marketing program. You will learn how to diagnose problems on your site and correct them. We teach you methodologies for every part of the search marketing process that you can apply to your own business. And we explain how to measure everything in your program so that you can improve the operation of your program every day.

 Throughout the book, you will see icons that signify special material on two important subjects. The first, shown at the left, is the *spam alert* icon, which warns you about overly clever tricks that pose a real danger to your search marketing campaign. You are probably familiar with email spam, when you get unwanted messages in your inbox, but search marketing has its own meaning for spam: any technique that is designed mainly to fool the search engines to gain an untoward advantage. That is an overly broad definition, but we explain exactly where the ethical lines are drawn every time you see this icon. Spam can be hazardous to the health of your search marketing program, because search engines have rules to control search marketing behavior.

When you break the rules, the search engines might take action to hide your content from the search results. Whenever you see this icon, you will know that there is a line that you cross at your own peril.

 You will also see, shown at the left, the *global tip* icon, which alerts you about techniques that are especially relevant to international search marketing campaigns. Most of the advice in this book is pitched to an audience of U.S. companies and companies using Google and other English-language worldwide search engines. You will learn, however, that searchers in many countries use search engines specific to that country, and that your non-English content sometimes has special issues that must be addressed. We highlight those areas in the book for you. Whether your website serves international visitors now, or you are considering doing so in the future, these tips are important for you.

New for our third edition, we've created a companion website at SEMincBook.com, containing tools and deeper information requiring faster update than we can do with a published book. Throughout the book, we provide references to the website that you can follow for more information.

No matter what your background, you are already partially prepared to become a search marketer. In this book, you will learn why it is so important to form a team of skills outside your own. Marketers, writers, technologists, and folks from other fields must collaborate to make search marketing work. You will find out why it is that the larger your website, the harder that collaboration can be—but you will also learn how to pull it off. Your business can coordinate these diverse skills to create a successful search marketing program. You just need to know how.

Whether you have been turned off in the past by experts selling quick-fix voodoo or you have just found search marketing too complicated or too intimidating, put that behind you. This book explains everything you need to know in simple terms that you can understand no matter what your experience. If you can use a web browser, you can learn search marketing.

Every day, more and more business is done on the web. And, increasingly, people looking to do business start with a search. Remember, if they can't find you, they can't buy from you. Discover how your company can be found.

Acknowledgments

Acknowledgments from Mike

Leading my list of people to thank is Bill Hunt, my co-author. When I first met Bill, I was an expert in search technology, but knew almost nothing about search marketing on the web. To me, if there was a problem with a search engine returning the wrong results, then we should dive in and tweak the ranking algorithm until it worked. Uh, right. Bill quickly showed me the rules of the search marketing road, and I started to learn search from the outside in—how to change our site to get what we want. In our work together at ibm.com, Bill helped me through every difficult problem and has made it fun. Since retiring from IBM, I have relied on Bill's advice and help so often that I have lost count. Working on a book is never easy, but working with Bill made it as easy as possible.

I would like to thank my former IBM management team, including John Rosato and Lee Dierdorff, for their encouragement to complete the first edition of this book. (I want to stress that the opinions expressed in this book are mine alone and do not necessarily reflect those of the IBM Corporation or IBM's management.) I also want to thank Doug Maine, David Bradley, and Jeanine Cotter, other former managers at IBM, who were willing to take a chance on search marketing at IBM. This book is a compilation of what worked, but I want to thank them for riding out the things that did not work out as well. I want to thank Jeff Schaffer from my old IBM team, a good friend with a wonderful mind, who worked with me to develop many of the original ideas in what we called the "wheel of fortune" that the industry now calls the Buyer's Journey. I'd also like to thank Rob Key, who has given me numerous opportunities to help clients of both Converseon and Revealed Context, thus developing even more of the ideas explained herein. (And I have always wanted to write the word *herein*.)

The team at IBM Press, especially our editor Bernard Goodwin, was very helpful, especially as we blew deadline after deadline on this third edition. Thanks to all of you for putting up with us. I hope it was worth the wait.

Great thanks are also due to our technical reviewers on this third edition, Hamlet Batista, Mona Elesseily, Andreas Ramos, and Matt Van Wagner, who slogged through the entire manuscript and found numerous errors and suggested critical improvements. We're indebted to them. If you do spot any remaining errors, blame us, not them. They found the vast majority of the mistakes we made.

I also want to thank my sister, Eileen Cosenza, who takes on every tough job at Mike Moran Group, so that I am free to do the things I am really good at. Without Eileen, I'd still be sending out invoices and updating my website, instead of working on this book.

Most of all, I want to thank my wife, Linda, and my children, David, Madeline, Marcella, and Dwight, who made so many sacrifices so "Daddy could write the book," being patient while I spent many hours writing on top of an already heavy workload from my day job. Without their love and support, I certainly could never have completed this book. I have read many acknowledgments of authors thanking their families for the heavy burdens they carried while the book was written, and I now understand what those other authors were saying. My family deserves every accolade for helping me complete this. I love them very much.

For this third edition, my daughters, Madeline and Marcella, also did a lot of legwork in helping to get the book whipped into shape. This book is better because of what they did.

But my wife, Linda, requires a special acknowledgment for her work on this book, because it goes so far beyond anything an author would ever expect of a spouse. Before this book ever went to the publisher, Linda proofread it. And copyedited it. And the publisher was very pleased with how clean it was (crediting Bill and me far too much). But even those exhausting tasks do not scratch the surface of what Linda put into this book.

Linda is herself a writer, thus bringing a level of professionalism and experience to the craft of writing that she painstakingly taught me throughout the writing of this, my first book. Moreover, Linda has worked as a programmer in a large company and has been the webmaster of three websites, so she is actually the perfect audience for this book. Her keen technical mind and corporate experience made her the ideal reader.

Even though this is the third edition of our book, it was a nearly complete rewrite that took as long to write as the first edition. Linda and I spent hours brainstorming ideas for the book, honing them until we agreed on the best way to explain them. As Bill and I "completed" each chapter, I would present it to Linda to see whether it made any sense to her, as someone who should understand it perfectly. And occasionally it did. But more often, Linda pointed out a critical flaw in terminology, a better organization for the same information, an improvement to an exhibit, or simply a technical error that we had overlooked. It sounds trite to say that this would not be the same book without Linda, but it is true. You would not believe how much harder to understand it would be. Linda did not just proofread or copyedit the words, she inspected the ideas. She judged the nomenclature, the style, the consistency, the flow; she worked over every thought and every word. Linda was truly our editor, in every sense of the word.

—Mike Moran

Acknowledgments from Bill

I would like to thank Mike Moran, my co-author on this book, for his encouragement, vast knowledge, and willingness to partner with me to write and rewrite the third edition this book while managing an already heavy workload.

Without Mike's encouragement, gentle nudges, constant pacing, occasional kick in the backside, and, of course, his sense of humor, I could never have started this book, let alone generate three editions. I am indebted to Mike for his writing style, which has given my rants a consistent voice to raise their value to the reader.

Furthermore, Mike continues to be my mentor, teaching me how to effectively navigate the complex maze of large companies to demonstrate search engine marketing as the ultimate marketing tool.

A very special thank you and debt of gratitude goes out to Linda Moran for her continued support of Mike and me on this book. Linda's assistance in reading and critically reviewing each iteration of this book was helpful beyond belief. In addition, thank you, Linda, for sacrificing your time with Mike to allow him to work with me on this demanding project and pick up the slack when I fell behind on my chapters. I would also like to thank the rest of the Moran family for their various efforts on the project.

I want to give special thanks to my wife, Motoko, and to my children, Mariko and William, for their tremendous support and encouragement for each of the versions of this book. I need to thank my son William for challenging the old man's knowledge as he grows in his own search career. I am indebted to my daughter Mariko for helping me understand the nuances of social media especially how to talk to creative types to get them to optimize as they create.

I need to offer a heartfelt thank you to Motoko, not only for her support on this book, but also for her dedication to my career, often at the sacrifice of her own, for the past 30 years. It is so true that behind every successful man is a strong woman, and Motoko is just that woman! Without her tremendous support, love, and understanding, this book and my overall success would not have been possible.

I further need to thank her for allowing me to become the expert in Japanese and Asian search marketing by keeping me current and providing many deep insights that I could have never realized alone. Thank you!

Thank you also to the content reviewers, Hamlet Batista, Andreas Ramos, Mona Elesseily, and Matt Van Wagner, who kept us honest and ensured accuracy and relevancy resulting in a quality product.

The team at IBM Press was invaluable to this process, especially our editor Bernard Goodwin, who was very helpful and patient as we tried to deliver this edition with our many logistical and time challenges.

Many others provided assistance, examples, and encouragement along the way. Most of all, they validated some of these crazy enterprise search theories. I'd like to specifically thank Marshall Simmonds, Derrick Wheeler, Jeremy Sanchez, Mike Grehan, Cindy Yerkie, Vicqui Chan, Fredrik Thorsen, Eva Sjokvist, Danny Sullivan, Chris Sherman, Lee Moore, Eddie Choi, and many others to whom I apologize for not listing here.

—Bill Hunt

About the Authors

Mike Moran has worked on the web since its inception, in both marketing and technical roles, including eight years at IBM.com, IBM's customer-facing website. In 2008, Mike retired from IBM to pursue speaking, writing, and consulting at Mike Moran Group, and also serves as a senior strategist for both the social media consultancy Converseon, and its spin-off social analytics company, Revealed Context. He's twice been named one of the top 50 Internet marketers and regularly consults for Fortune 500 companies around the world.

Mike is also the author of *Do It Wrong Quickly: How the Web Changes the Old Marketing Rules*, perhaps the first book on agile marketing. He writes regular columns on digital marketing at WebProNews and Search Engine Guide, and is the founder and senior author at Biznology (www.biznology.com).

He's a Senior Fellow of the Society for New Communications Research and an Open Group Distinguished IT Specialist. Mike is a frequent keynote speaker on digital marketing at events around the world, serves as a Visiting Lecturer to the University of Virginia's Darden School of Business, works as an instructor for both Rutgers University and the University of California at Irvine, and holds an Advanced Certificate in Market Management Practice from the Royal UK Charter Institute of Marketing.

Mike also has a broad technical background, with over 30 years of experience in search technology, working at IBM Research, Lotus, and other IBM software units. He led the product team that developed the first commercial linguistic search engine in 1989 and has been granted 11 patents in search and retrieval technology. He led the integration of ibm.com's site search technologies as well as projects in content management, personalization, and web metrics. Mike led the adoption of search marketing at ibm.com back in 2001 and pioneered product search facilities that dramatically raised conversion rates. Mike was named an IBM Distinguished Engineer in 2005.

Mike can be reached through his website (www.mikemoran.com).

Bill Hunt has been a pioneer in search marketing, first optimizing pages in 1994. He is considered the top thought leader on enterprise and global search engine marketing and is an internationally recognized search marketing expert who has spoken at conferences in over 30 countries.

Press, industry analysts, and corporate leaders frequently seek Bill's advice to help them effectively leverage enterprise and global search marketing. Bill is the CEO of Back Azimuth Consulting. Through Back Azimuth, Bill provides cutting-edge keyword data-mining models to identify missed opportunities and increase revenue based on understanding consumer needs. Bill is also responsible for Back Azimuth's search marketing thought leadership and for developing global search marketing strategic roadmaps for multinational corporations such as Absolut Vodka, Cisco, HP, MGM, and Pernod-Ricard.

Bill is a veteran of the U.S. Marine Corps, and he earned a B.A. in Asian Studies/Japanese from the University of Maryland, Tokyo Campus, and a B.S. in International Business from California State University, Los Angeles. Bill can be reached through his company website (www.back-azimuth.com) or his blog (www.whunt.com).

PART I

Understand Search Marketing

You are ready to go. You are motivated. You are just itching to dive into search marketing. But where do you start? Understanding, that's where.

First, in Chapter 1, "How Search Marketing Works," we examine what search marketing is all about. We look at the different kinds of search marketing and why search marketing is so valuable to your organization—how it can drive visitors to your website. You will be convinced that your company cannot ignore searchers any longer. But before being overcome by irrational exuberance, we also take a cold look at why some companies find search marketing so hard to do—for companies both large and small. And we provide practical advice on how to get started.

Building on that overview, we peek inside the mind of the searcher in Chapter 2, "How Searchers Work." Find out what these folks are really looking for when they type in one or two words. Understand how the same searcher might behave differently in different situations, such as searching from a computer or from a mobile device. Learn to use your knowledge of searchers to your advantage.

We wind up Part I with Chapter 3, "How Search Works," where we dive into the ins and outs of what Google and friends actually do: what happens when someone is looking for a word, where the results on the screen come from, and how your content can show up right on that search results page. We will look at different types of search marketing so that you can start thinking of how you can compete with every other company out there fighting for those same searchers. We'll also help you think through the proper philosophy as you approach your search marketing program.

Regardless of what job you have now, by the time you complete Part I, you will have all the background needed to be a search engine marketer. You will know the terminology and the concepts. You will be ready to learn how to create your very own search marketing plan.

CHAPTER 1

How Search Marketing Works

Search marketing. Perhaps you've heard this term kicked around, but you don't know what it means. Or, if you do know, you don't know where to start. As with anything new, if you take it step by step, you can learn it. A systematic approach can lead to search marketing success in any organization.

When someone types a word into Google (or another search engine), sees a page listed from your site, and clicks through to visit your site, you have attracted a searcher. If you do nothing at all, searchers will still find your site—sometimes. To maximize the number of searchers coming to your site, however, you must take specific actions to attract visitors to your site from search sites. That's search engine marketing (or search marketing, for short). This book shows you how to become a search marketer. This chapter covers the following topics:

- **Why search marketing is important:** You are probably not reading this book as an academic exercise; instead, you want to know how to get more visitors to your website. You already spend your marketing budget on other ways to entice people to visit. This chapter explains why search marketing in many ways is the best kind of marketing there is. And some of it is free.

- **Why search marketing is difficult:** Attracting searchers to your site is appealing, but it's harder to do than you might think. As search marketing becomes more and more widespread, your competition is increasing. What's more, small companies have different challenges than big companies—and it isn't easy for either one. This chapter explains why so many websites struggle to attract search visitors. But don't worry. The rest of this book shows you how to overcome these challenges.

- **What search marketing is:** When a search site responds to a searcher, many types of search results show up on that screen. We explain where those results come from and how Google and Bing decide what to show.

- **How to get started in search marketing:** When a search site responds to a searcher, many types of search results show up on that screen. We explain where those results come from and how you, as a search marketer, can influence your content to show up on that result screen. You can get started today if you just know how to approach search marketing. And you'll learn more and more as you move deeper into this book.

Let's get started now! First up, we'll look at why search marketing is so important to any marketer with a website.

Why Search Marketing Is Important

Unless you've been under a rock since the late 1990s (and maybe even then), you know that search marketing is important, even if you might not have done much about it up until now. You know it's important because you likely use search yourself, probably every day, and you're not alone; 91% of online adults used search engines to find information on the web in 2012, up from 84% in 2004. But you might not be focusing on all of the reasons that search marketing can be critically important to your **marketing mix**.

Searchers Are Highly Qualified Prospects

You know that potential customers are out there that you want to reach and that search is one important way to do it. But it goes deeper than that.

Any form of marketing can reach potential customers; that's why marketing exists. Search marketing is unique among marketing techniques in that searchers are out there raising their hands saying, "Please sell to me now!" When searchers belly up to Google and type something into the search box, they are begging to receive marketing messages. Now, not every search revolves around a potential purchase, but many do, and your company can be in the middle of those sales possibilities.

But it's even better than that.

Not only are many searchers potential customers, but the very words that they type into the search box reveal where they are in their purchase process. Someone who enters *hair loss remedy* is not ready to buy, but someone who enters *rogaine* might be. You'll want two very different marketing messages in response to these two different searches, with the first one focusing on alternative treatments for baldness and the second maybe offering a coupon. What other form of marketing is so tuned to the customer's readiness to buy?

That readiness to buy is one of the most basic reasons to spend your scarce marketing budget on search: 89% of those online use search engines to look for information about brands and products. Lest you think that not enough people are online for search marketing to be worth your while, note that total Internet users passed the seven billion mark worldwide in 2012. As simple as it sounds, your customers are online, and they use search to buy. Your site must be found by these searchers who are ready to buy.

Think about the new way that people purchase products. They no longer call your company to have you mail them a brochure. They "Google" your offering (*verizon wireless*). Or maybe they look for your competitor's (*sprint*). Or they search for its generic name (*cell phone service*).

If your company's website is not listed in the first few search results for these searches, you're out! You are out of the customer's **consideration set**—the group of companies that will be considered for the customer's purchase. If you are not in the customer's consideration set, you have no chance to make the sale to that customer.

Even if the goal of your website is not online purchase, your customers must find you to learn about your offerings, download information, or find the location of a retail store. Searchers are far more qualified visitors to your site than someone who clicks a banner ad, for example, so attracting search visitors is just good business.

And search volume is growing dramatically, due to the explosion in the use of mobile devices. If you stop to think about it, these small screens with ubiquitous wireless access to the web are tailor-made for a more search-centered user experience. There is no room to look at long web pages with lots of links to navigate; searching using the keyboard or voice recognition is much easier. There's always enough room for a search box.

The main reason to make search part of your marketing mix is that that's where your customers are, but there are other reasons.

Search Marketing Is Cost-Effective

Beyond your customers' use of search, the case for including search in your marketing mix is compelling for another reason: Search marketing expenditures are a good value compared to other forms of marketing. We've already talked about how searchers are more qualified than others you market to, because the act of searching is an expression of interest. That alone saves money wasted in other forms of marketing. But there are more reasons that search is a good buy.

Some search tactics require no payment to the search engine for **traffic**, so it can be among the most cost-effective forms of marketing, especially if your website is already well designed with high-quality content. Even with the costs of search advertising, you pay only for the people who actually click through to your site, unlike other forms of advertising where you pay for each ad impression shown. Marketing software company HubSpot has found that search engine optimization (SEO) has the highest lead-to-customer close rate of any form of generation marketing at one-third lower cost than outbound marketing tactics, such as advertising and direct mail.

Why is this important? Because if you want to start spending money on search, you need to stop spending on something else. When you understand that search is the most effective way to spend your scarce marketing dollars, you should be able to easily reduce some existing budgets (direct mail, perhaps?) to find the money for your new search expenditures. An Advertising.com survey found over 35% of marketers indicated paid search is their most cost-effective lead generation method, nearly twice as effective as other forms of marketing.

Search Marketing Is Big Business

You can tell a new marketing technique is taking off by noticing the number of consultants who hang out their shingles to help you do it! Several kinds of firms are involved in search marketing:

- **Search consultants:** A brand new kind of consultancy has sprung up in the past several years; these new firms handle search marketing and nothing else.

- **Traditional advertising agencies:** At the other end of the spectrum are the old-line advertising agencies that have been around for years. Just as firms such as Young & Rubicam and Ogilvy & Mather handle TV, radio, and print advertising, in recent years they have taken on web advertising. Starting with banner ads, they have now moved into search marketing, too.

- **Interactive advertising agencies:** In between the two extremes, interactive agencies handle anything online, ranging from search marketing to social media to email campaigns. Sometimes these agencies are subsidiaries of the traditional ad agencies, whereas others are smaller, independent firms.

All of these firms are competing for your growing interactive marketing budget. Your organization might already work with one of these companies, or might be looking for a search marketing partner. What is most important at this point is your interest in allocating part of your marketing budget to search, because you will soon see that achieving success is rather challenging.

Why Search Marketing Is Difficult

Because you bought this book, you probably were already convinced that search is a big marketing opportunity, but it's time for a reality check: Search marketing is *not* easy to do.

Although every company differs, large and small companies typically face different challenges in search marketing. (If your organization is medium sized, you might have some problems of each.) Because these are generalizations, your company might have some differences from its stereotype, but understanding what can go wrong can help you analyze your own situation.

Normally, large organizations have the advantage in marketing, but small companies sometimes have the upper hand in *search* marketing. Big companies still have some advantages, but it is a much more level playing field than with other areas of marketing. Let's investigate the success factors for search marketing and see how they relate to company size.

You Need Flexibility

Smaller companies are generally "light on their feet"—more flexible than their larger counterparts. This flexibility provides small companies with fundamental advantages in search marketing, starting with a basic willingness to pursue search marketing in the first place.

Large companies are often "stuck in their ways": They execute the same kind of marketing programs year after year, and it can take them a long time to even try search marketing. Some corporate types are risk-averse, not wanting to go out on a limb for the new thing. Small companies are often more willing to take a chance on an unproven approach and are more likely to raise investment in search marketing quickly when they see it is working.

Large companies are often slower than small ones, which hurts search marketing in several ways. First, search marketing inevitably requires changes to your website. The faster you can make those changes, the faster your search success can begin. Moreover, continuing success depends on frequent fine-tuning. Smaller companies tend to be able to make changes with more speed and less bureaucratic wrangling.

You Need Coordination

As you'll learn, search marketing requires many little things to be done properly in order to succeed. For small companies, this isn't that hard; sometimes everything can be done by a handful of people, or even one individual. But large companies usually have daunting coordination challenges that can hamstring their search marketing programs. At large companies, you often hear some telltale conversations about splitting up the web team or even dividing the website into multiple parts, which makes search marketing a lot tougher:

- **We need multiple teams of specialists:** "The copy writers and the HTML coders really should be in different departments...."

- **We need multiple product sites:** "Each product line should really run its own separate website...."

- **We need multiple audiences:** "We should really have different user experiences for consumers than for our business customers...."

- **We need multiple countries:** "It is really easier for everyone if the Canada and the U.S. sites are separate...."

- **We need multiple technologies:** "We decided to keep using the Apache server for the marketing information, but we are putting all of the commerce functions into WebSphere...."

Each time a large company starts separating itself in these ways, it makes the coordination for search marketing more difficult. In Chapter 10, "Make Search Marketing Operational," we'll offer some ways to help, but this need to work together across business units is more difficult for search marketers in large enterprises. And, the bigger the company, the harder it is.

You Need Name Recognition

Small companies often have the advantage in search marketing, but not here. Large companies have a big edge in publicity. Searchers know their names and the names of their products.

Searchers are more likely to include those names in searches, a big edge for the large companies that own those names.

But it does not end there. The bigger and more well-known the website, the more other websites will link to it and the more social media activity will mention that site—both of these are indicators to Google of a site's importance. Big sites get links and social media activity for whatever they do without even asking. Because everything that big companies do seems newsworthy, they attract news coverage for every tiny product announcement (which means links from news organizations and other well-respected sources). Customers, suppliers, and resellers cozy up to large companies to bask in their reflected glory. Large corporations often have multiple sites that are interlinked, adding to their link advantage. The link popularity and social media activity that large sites enjoy helps their search rankings immeasurably.

Because of all of these factors, large brands have an advantage in search marketing. Studies show that content from large brands often outranks content from smaller brands that could be of higher quality. You can think of this as a "trust factor." Just as a traveler might be more likely to stay at a name brand motel chain rather than the locally owned inn, and just as someone passing through a new neighborhood might opt to eat at McDonald's (a known quantity) rather than the unknown local burger joint, search engines have shown a bias to large brand content, other things being equal.

On the flip side, these large brand names can be attacked in social media by pressure groups, disgruntled employees and customers, and anyone with an axe to grind. Because social media is so important to search success, big brands are big targets that can make search marketing more difficult. On balance, however, search marketing is easier when you are well-known.

Small companies can sometimes attract the out-sized attention of big brands, but it takes a lot more work—and often a good bit of luck.

You Need Resources

Larger organizations typically have a huge edge in marketing resources, but they are often slow to devote them to something new, such as search marketing. So, although larger budgets can be an advantage, sometimes small companies spend more than big companies do.

In addition, the largesse of big companies sometimes gets in their own way. Small companies are much quicker to seek outside expertise, and might get better advice from consultants than corporations get from their less-experienced internal personnel who are not search marketing experts.

When it comes to money, more is better than less. But most big companies squander this advantage with the overly complex design of their websites. Search engines greatly prefer simple sites without expensive technical gimmickry that small companies typically cannot afford. There are often good reasons to use these fancy techniques, but when they are overused or used

incorrectly, they quash search marketing. Small companies tend to have simple, clean designs
that search engines love.

You Have Lots of Competition

Each of the preceding obstacles to search success is important, but the toughest roadblock to your success is your competitors. You are not the only person joining the search marketing game. So the good news is that you are catching the wave, but the bad news is there are a lot of other surfboards out there to contend with.

Not too many years ago, small companies had search marketing to themselves, because many large corporations were oblivious to the importance of search marketing, or had experimented and failed. Today, large organizations are becoming formidable search marketing competitors. They are using their superior resources to address the other weaknesses outlined earlier so that they can leverage their brand names for their natural advantages.

Big business is not the only source of new competition. As a search marketer, you might already be doing battle in global markets, and you see that competitors seem to be getting more sophisticated about search marketing, lessening your advantage. Or, worse, you do business in just a few local markets and you are starting to face competition from other regions or countries that could never do business in your territory before the Internet, but now they can.

Before the web, companies seeking to enter foreign markets used exporters, licensees, joint ventures, or wholly owned subsidiaries to create a local presence in each market. Although these techniques still have their place, the web allows businesses to sell directly to a customer, no matter what country each one is in. The rise of global search engines helps a business from across the world seem just as "local" as one a block away. It's likely that your business will be competing with new entrants around the world, if it is not doing so already.

Even more competitors are out there, and they are right in your own backyard—local small businesses. Search engines can personalize results by location, so millions of local businesses whose ad budgets are spent on Yellow Pages advertising are now able to profitably engage in search marketing. If you work for a large company, such as Home Depot, you might have had search marketing to yourself, but will soon face increased competition from local hardware stores.

What happens as more and more marketers realize how well search marketing works? As changes in search marketing make it profitable for more and more businesses? The simple answers are that it makes it tougher to rank at the top of the organic search results, and it also makes paid search marketing more expensive because more companies are bidding the price up. So what do you do about that? That's what the rest of this book is about.

Before leaving the topic of competition, we should point out that the changes leading to more competition offer opportunities, too. Just as your business might face competitors from new places, your business can seek customers in new markets that were not cost-effective in the past. If you can become efficient enough, you can become a feared competitor in any market using search marketing and the web.

What Search Marketing Is

Search marketing is a form of digital marketing (or Internet marketing) that consists of a variety of tactics to promote your business by increasing visibility of your content to searchers. Search marketing usually begins when a searcher enters a **keyword** into a search engine, such as Google or Bing, and sees a **search engine results page** (**SERP**) that contains a series of **search results**.

Each country in the world has a set of search engines that attract the bulk of the searchers in that market. We talk mostly about Google Search and Microsoft's Bing search because they are by far the two most important search engines in the United States. (Yahoo! continues to operate a search site, but Microsoft technology engine powers Yahoo! results in most countries.)

If you engage in search marketing outside the United States, Google and Bing might still be the most important search engines to you in those countries, but you'll want to investigate their market shares to be sure. In the Nordic countries, for example, Google has nearly a 100% market share. In China, Baidu is the leading search engine. In Russia, it's Yandex. For some up-to-date information about which search engines matter in various country markets, check out our website (SEMincBook.com/country-search-engines).

You might never have paid attention to all the different kinds of search results on a page, but search marketers distinguish between two main kinds, **organic search** and **paid search**. Exhibit 1-1 shows which results on the screen are organic results and which are paid.

Organic search is also called **search engine optimization** (**SEO**) or, less commonly, **natural search**. Organic search results are typically on the left side of the page, often below a paid search ad or two. Organic search results consist of a title and a preview of the content—text from web pages and blog posts, or photos for images and videos.

Search engine marketing (**SEM**) is a broader term than SEO that encompasses any kind of search results (organic and paid). Some people, however, use the term *search engine marketing* to refer to paid search only, contrasting SEO with SEM, so you need to judge its meaning from context.

Paid search goes by other names, such as **pay per click** (**PPC**), **cost per click** (**CPC**), **paid placement**, or sometimes **search engine advertising**, but we stick with the name *paid search* in this book. Paid search results tend to be at the top and on the right side of search result pages, but you can find them at the bottom of the page sometimes, too. Paid search ads have traditionally consisted of a title and a description—all words—but search engines are beginning to experiment with bolder forms of advertising that include images.

Exhibit 1-1 A search results page. Search engines show paid and organic results on the same page, but do identify the "sponsored results" as being paid for by advertisers.

Let's look at a partial list of the different kinds of search results and where they come from, as shown in Exhibit 1-2. You can see a mixture of these result types on the page, and some have tabs that searchers can press to isolate to a specific type (all images, for example).

- **Web pages:** "Web pages" takes in a lot of ground, everything from eCommerce sites to message boards, blog posts, and anything that doesn't fall into one of the other categories below. You'll see them on the results page with a link to the web page (drawn from the **title** on the web page) and a **snippet** of text from the page that usually contains the search keywords, as shown in Exhibit 1-3.

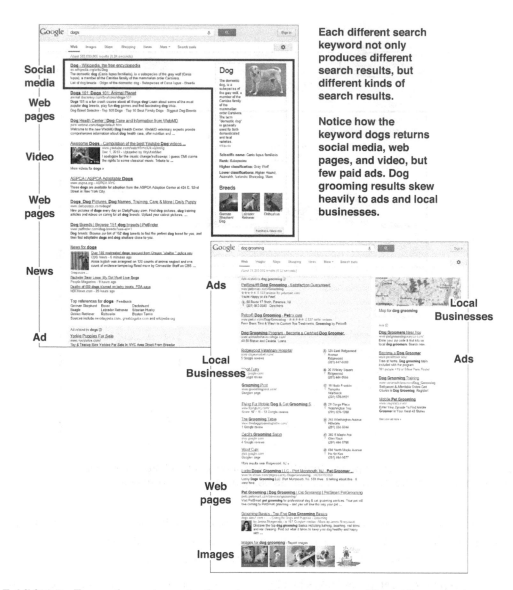

Each different search keyword not only produces different search results, but different kinds of search results.

Notice how the keyword dogs returns social media, web pages, and video, but few paid ads. Dog grooming results skew heavily to ads and local businesses.

Exhibit 1-2   Types of search results. Search results come in many different flavors and are drawn from many different places.

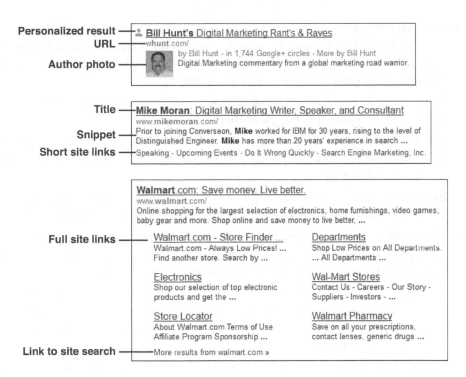

Exhibit 1-3 Organic search results. Organic search results usually contain a title, URL, and snippet, but can also include other items.

- **Ads:** Paid search results are ads that you create, consisting of a **headline** and a **description** that each provides details on the offer, as you can see in Exhibit 1-4.

Exhibit 1-4 Paid search results. Paid search results include a headline, description, and display URL, but sometimes have more.

- **Products:** When the search is for a retail item, a picture and price of the item is displayed with a link to the store that sells it. These products are drawn from Google Product Search or Bing Shopping from product listings submitted by retailers; you can see an example of dog grooming supplies pictured in Exhibit 1-1.

- **News:** Some keywords match breaking news stories drawn from known news sources that have been approved by Google or Bing.

- **Local businesses:** If a search seems to be looking for a nearby location, such as a store, the search results include a map with "pins" for locations near the searcher, or a merely a text list of nearby places.

- **Images:** A search might include a gallery of photographs or other pictures, sometimes from image sites such as Flickr, but they can be drawn from any site on the web.

- **Videos:** More and more, search results include videos that can play right from the search result page. Google mostly shows videos from YouTube (which is owned by Google), while Bing shows videos from both YouTube and other video sites.

- **Social media:** Some people consider video and image content to be social media, but there is a lot more social content in the search results. Wikipedia, blog posts, and content from other social venues such as Twitter, Facebook, LinkedIn, and Pinterest have all begun showing up in search results.

- **Direct answers:** Some specialized searches produce results designed to provide the answer right on the search result page, obviating the need to click through to a new page to get the answer. You'll see this for searches as varied as the weather, stock ticker symbols, airline flights, events, and anything famous enough for a Wikipedia entry. Google provides some direct answers through its Knowledge Graph, which it has been rolling out in multiple languages in recent years.

In recent years, both Google and Bing have aggressively integrated these different types of search results onto their main search result pages, referring to this approach as **blended** search (or in Google's case, **Universal Search**). Some of these different kinds of search results can be isolated from the rest, as you can see in Exhibit 1-5.

It was once commonplace to use entirely separate search engines to look for these kinds of results. **Product search engines**, also known as **shopping search engines**, such as Shopzilla and NexTag allow searchers to shop for products across retailers, comparing prices and shipping times to make their purchase. **Internet Yellow Pages (IYP) sites**, such as Superpages and YellowPages.com allow you to find local businesses. Nowadays, many of these so-called **vertical search** sites are fading in importance, as Google and Bing invest in integrating these specialty types of searches into their own mainline search results. In fact, some verticals have very little independent competition these days; Google and Bing show the lion's share of video and image searches, for example.

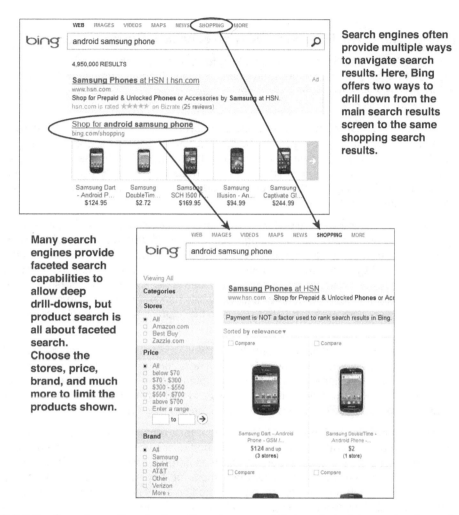

Search engines often provide multiple ways to navigate search results. Here, Bing offers two ways to drill down from the main search results screen to the same shopping search results.

Many search engines provide faceted search capabilities to allow deep drill-downs, but product search is all about faceted search. Choose the stores, price, brand, and much more to limit the products shown.

Exhibit 1-5 Search result navigation. Searchers can drill down to isolate results of a certain type in various ways.

Not all vertical search sites are fading. Travel sites, such as TripAdvisor, Kayak, and Expedia, still receive lots of traffic. Yelp provides reviews of local businesses. Some searchers head straight to these sites to do their searches, whereas others may stumble across them in the mainstream engines' search results. But clearly Google and Bing have such sites in their sights, so to speak, and they come under more pressure every year.

FACETED SEARCH: THE POWERFUL WAY TO NAVIGATE SEARCH RESULTS

When searchers don't find what they are looking for at the top of the search results, they typically won't page forward through more search results. Instead, they search again for something else. But what happens when what you are looking for can't be easily described using more search words?

Some call it **faceted search**, others **multifaceted search**, and still others **faceted browsing**. No matter what you call it, there's no denying that it is becoming an increasingly important way for searchers to drill down into search results to find what they are seeking more quickly and easily. Product search engines, such as Shopzilla, have been built on this capability, and Google Product Search employs faceted search. Exhibit 1-5 shows how Bing uses faceted search for products.

Product search is a natural application for the multifaceted search approach, because some products, such as digital cameras, are bought based on the facets (features) of the product. Shoppers care about price, brand, resolution, and other facets of a camera. As they choose the facets they want (such as "more than 16 megapixel resolution" or "between $150 and $250 in price," and so on), unwanted choices disappear, so shoppers never get a "not found." But it can be used in other places, as Bing shows with its video search; you should expect to see more uses of faceted search in the future, because searchers find it so easy to use.

If you've taken for granted that search marketing revolves around keywords, faceted search gives you some more ideas to think about. Yes, searchers continue to enter keywords to isolate products or videos, to name just two examples, but the facets that searchers drill down with are just as important in determining what they click on. For product search, you must be prepared to compete against other merchants on price, shipping speed, and reliability.

If shoppers are choosing between multiple cameras, for example, each camera might be listed in the search results (along with a picture, a short description or feature list, customer reviews, and the price range). As shoppers hone in on particular models of digital cameras, the websites (often called *stores*) that offer the camera are displayed in the search results. Each store might show its logo, merchant rating (voted on by its previous customers), price for the camera, and other distinguishing information to coax shoppers to click through to the store's site. When shoppers click results, they are taken to websites (stores) to complete their purchases.

Faceted search is prized by searchers because they can isolate products by features or price without knowing the exact prices or features names. Similarly, if you are looking for a short video or one from a particular source, faceted search does the job. You might call faceted search the *antisearch* because it's often used without entering any keywords at all. In actuality, however, faceted search technology is just a more powerful addition to traditional text searching that allows searchers to restrict the search results by responding to choices offered by the search engine. Peter Morville believes faceted search capability provides users the "illusion of getting started quickly," comparing that style with drivers who get in their car and start driving, only consulting a map when lost, just as we enter a few search words and then navigate from the search results page. Faceted search allows searchers to continually narrow down their results by clicking another constraint on their search.

Other specialty searches are under attack, too. Try searching for an airline flight and you might see flight choices displayed right on the search results page. You can still use travel search sites, such as Kayak, but Google and Bing will be happy to book your reservation for you with their own proprietary reservation facilities. A few years ago, the searcher might have been sent to Expedia or Priceline.

When the mainstream search engines have not been able to co-opt the search results of vertical search engines, they've bought them. Google owns YouTube, the largest video search facility. Microsoft owns Travelocity, the travel search and booking site.

Google has been under pressure lately from government regulators for favoring its own properties in its search results, but as of this writing, no changes have been forced. Google does favor its own video results from YouTube, for example, but that isn't any different from what Microsoft does with Travelocity results in Bing.

Social media items have become more prominent in the search results, including multi-media (images, audio, and video), social network conversations, and blog posts. Microsoft has a deal with Facebook to show results, and you'll sometimes see results from Twitter and LinkedIn. Google, of course, will show results from its Google+ social network when relevant. One of the most interesting aspects of social media results is that they are often **personalized**—not every searcher sees the same results.

Although many websites, led by Amazon, have personalized their user experience, until the last few years search engines have been decidedly retro. Different searchers, by and large, were getting the exact same results when they type the same keyword into a search engine.

A quick review of the history of search technology reveals that the vast majority of improvements have been based on the content: analyzing it better, understanding it more deeply, and assessing its quality. But what about applying the same kind of thought to the searcher? After all, what makes a successful search is the best match between the content and searcher, so why have search engines focused on analyzing the content so much and ignored the searcher?

In part, the maniacal focus on content stems from the fact that understanding the content is easier than understanding people. However, despite the inherent difficulty, search engines are increasingly emphasizing personalized search results based on several factors, including the following:

- **The searcher's location:** As we saw with **local search** results, search engines already try to show results from companies nearby, often by picking out place names within the keywords. The search engines also use the **IP address** of the searcher's device to approx-imate location. With the rise of GPS capabilities in mobile devices, search engines can sometimes pinpoint location with startling accuracy. When GPS data is less accurate or unavailable, WiFi hotspot locations can also help identify searcher locations.

- **The searcher's device:** Closely related to location, search engines are increasingly showing search results differently on phones, tablets, and computers. Google in particular has been experimenting with a "tablet" interface that shows fewer ads—often at the bottom of the screen. Mobile searchers tend to click on fewer paid search ads than computer users, so expect the search engines to continue to try new approaches to appeal to mobile searchers.

- **The searcher's interests:** Could search results be improved if search engines knew searchers' interests? When searchers enter "jaguar," are they looking for the car, the animal, the football team, or the Apple operating system? If search engines understood the searchers' interests, they might be able to take a better guess. Google, especially, is mining information from searcher's Gmail discussions and from where they navigate on the web to determine which sites might be of more interest than others. Data collected by Google Analytics and Google Wallet might someday allow Google to show results based on previous purchases.

- **The searcher's friends:** As noted earlier, Bing sometimes personalizes results based on what a searcher's Facebook friends like, as shown in Exhibit 1-6. Expect Google to do the same with its Google+ social network.

Now that you know more about what search marketing is, it's time to begin exploring what you can do about it.

How to Get Started in Search Marketing

Wait, you aren't learning about search engines as an academic exercise? Okay, then, let's talk about the business of search—how you can get started in making your search program a success. We'll look at organic search, paid search, and the steps for search success with both. Let's dig into organic search first.

Getting Started with Organic Search

Organic search refers to the way search engines find the most relevant match to a searcher's keyword. You can think of it as the librarian's answer to the question. Organic search results are driven purely by the **relevance** of the matches to the keyword that the searcher entered, and are not influenced by any payments made to the search engine by search marketers.

In contrast with paid search, where you must pay the search engines whenever someone clicks on your ad, organic search is free—kind of. It's free the way that public relations is free: You don't have to pay the *New York Times* to print your story, but you might have to pay your PR person to get the newspaper to print your story. Similarly, although sometimes it is inexpensive to get your content shown in organic search, there are other situations where it is a lot of costly work.

Bing has a deal with Facebook that allows it to show results based on what your Facebook friends like.

Bing also shows results from blogs, social networks, Klout, Quora, and many other social media venues.

Exhibit 1-6 Social media search results. Social media can show up in the search results, sometimes personalized based on searchers' friends.

Search marketers use many techniques to improve their site's organic search results. As mentioned earlier, these techniques are often referred to as search engine optimization. Later in this book, we explore these approaches in depth so that you can decide which ones are right for you. For now, let's just look at how different options have different price tags.

Why It Works

Despite the wide range of cost, no search marketer can skip organic search. Organic search is critical to any search marketing program, even if you also use other search marketing techniques.

In recent years, organic search marketing is commonly part of a larger **content marketing** program. In content marketing, you use your web pages, blog posts, videos, and other content to solve your customer's problem. Your content might include do-it-yourself ideas, how-to instructions, or common customer problems and solutions. Often, content marketing begins as a social media campaign of some kind, such as the do-it-yourself videos that Home Depot uses to explain how to use the materials and tools sold there.

Organic search marketing is a critical part of any content marketing campaign. Here's why. When you invest the kind of time and money into creating great content, the way Home Depot has in our example, of course you'll use social media to promote it. Each time Home Depot creates a video, they post it to YouTube, they tweet it, they link to it from their Facebook fan page, they create a blog post around it, and any other way they can think of. With that social media attention, the content marketer hopes that others will also share the content so that even more people will be exposed to it. Even under the best of circumstances, it's hard to hope that social media will get exposure for your content for more than a few days. For the rest of the life of that content, its exposure hinges on organic search marketing.

For your content to rank highly in organic search, it must be perceived as being of high quality. Perhaps this is obvious, but the simplest way for your content to be perceived as high quality is to actually *be* of high quality. Search engines have different ways of ascertaining your content's quality, which we explain in detail in Chapter 9, "Prove Your Content's Quality."

Organic search marketing has several specific benefits for your overall marketing:

- **Highly qualified searchers discover your content:** Organic searchers who click your content from the search results are *highly qualified* as prospective customers. They are much more likely to make a purchase than people exposed to your content in social media or who might otherwise visit your website. To understand why, think about the motivation of visitors reaching your site from a successful banner ad. Those visitors set out to find some information (possibly on a subject wholly unrelated to your site), and while reading that article, spot your ad. Intrigued, they click through to your site. These visitors are far less qualified than searchers because they did not start out with interest in your products. You can build the interest and still make the sale, but that is a lot harder to do than to sell to someone already interested. In contrast, searchers initiate their search on a subject related to your business. That's why the search engine shows *your* content in the results. Those searchers want to learn. You are far more likely to sell to searchers than to someone who clicks a banner ad, simply because searchers might intend to buy, whereas banner visitors were doing something else when you caught their eye. People using product search engines, as you might expect, are *especially* likely to buy.

- **You can do it on a budget:** Although some websites suffer from expensive-to-fix problems (which we talk about in the next section), most websites find organic search to be a fairly inexpensive kind of marketing. Your site probably has many pages that already show up in the search results, and you can tune your content to rank higher and draw more traffic—all without breaking the bank.

- **Your efforts work across all search engines:** Unlike paid search, where an ad listed with Microsoft does not appear in Google, most organic search techniques work across all search engines. Whatever you do to improve your results in Google will probably also help your content in Bing. Just by its nature, organic search success tends to require the same techniques for all search engines.

- **Your efforts can last for a long time:** In contrast to paid search, where the benefits end the moment you put away your credit card, organic search marketing efforts usually last much longer. For example, if you discover the techniques that cause a page to be found by and be persuasive to searchers, you can reap the benefits until a competitor discovers a better formula. Nothing lasts forever, but organic search success can continue even after you stop working on it.

This is an impressive list of benefits, but we wouldn't blame you if you want to know what you need to spend to get them. That's up next.

What It Costs

Organic search is an interesting search marketing technique, because utilizing the technique can cost next to nothing, or it can be expensive, depending on the situation you are in and what you decide to do about it.

It's possible that your site might already be well represented in search and might already rank well in organic search for many keywords. If so, it might be inexpensive to improve your results even more, by choosing more keywords to sprinkle into your content, for example. If your site is missing in action in the search results, however, optimizing your content for organic search can be a daunting prospect; it can be complicated and expensive to make the changes required.

The costs for organic search come from making changes to your content and to your website technology. At this point in your search marketing knowledge, it's natural for you to believe that you don't know enough to make these content and technology changes yourself. You might even think you'll never learn enough to tackle this work on your own.

Because a lot of marketers are in that same situation, they hire SEO consultants. If you need expert advice on choosing keywords, optimizing your content, or measuring your business results, it does not come cheap. If you want to start small, you might find some search marketing firms that will help you optimize a few pages for important keywords for between $5,000 and $20,000. Conversely, you should expect to pay hundreds of thousands per year for a consultant to thoroughly address problems in a large site.

If your budget allows it, you can benefit greatly from hiring an expert to jump-start your organic search marketing program. Your site's problems in search are lowering your revenue, and each day they are not fixed is more money down the drain. It can be cost-effective to accelerate your efforts by using an expert who gets more visitors coming to your site quickly. It is a big decision to hire (or decide not to hire) a search marketing consultant. Chapter 5, "Create Your Search Marketing Program," walks you through the process.

Happily, under normal circumstances it is not absolutely necessary to use consultants. You and your team can learn enough to do it yourself. Just keep in mind that it will take you considerably longer than a consultant to identify solutions for your problems, which might not be cost-effective based on your available budget and the business opportunities that you are losing each day.

Regardless of how you determine the solutions, you'll find that the technology and content changes that you make to *implement* those solutions are your biggest organic search expense. Those costs vary widely from website to website, but Part III of this book is devoted to diagnosing search problems and helping you correct them.

Although you are unsure of exactly what it will cost, it doesn't have to be scary. You probably do not know how much it costs to update your site to introduce a new line of products, or to acquire another company, or to support a new advertising campaign, but these are business decisions that are made every day in every company. The web team knows that it is part of its job to support these initiatives; whatever it takes is just a cost of doing business. Your biggest job will be to make search marketing just another part of the web team's job—just another everyday cost of running your website. Chapter 5 tackles how you convince the web team to take that on. After you are successful, and the web team makes search-related changes every day, you *still* will not know how much it costs, but at least it will be happening.

Organic search success sometimes requires changes to your technology so that the search engines can discover your content. If your site has a small number of pages, updating the technology is probably not very pricey. If you have a huge technically complex site, however, it can be expensive to fix. Chapter 3, "How Search Works," explains how search engines discover your content.

Many websites inadvertently make it difficult for spiders to index their pages. In Chapter 7, "Get Your Content Listed," we work through the most common site design problems and the technology changes required to correct them. Usually, they require some kind of technology change, as the following examples demonstrate:

- We must change the commerce URLs so that they do not have so many dynamic parameters.
- We have to update the content management system so that writers can modify the titles and descriptions for every page.
- We have to modify the metadata template for all HTML pages so that we do not block the spider from crawling each page.
- We need to change the menus in the left navigation bar so that they do not require JavaScript.
- We must remove session identifiers from the URLs.

Don't worry if you don't understand the list. That's the point, actually. Every item in that list is something that your technology folks might need to do to fix your site so that search engines can discover the content on your website. (And we cover many more, too.)

If your site suffers from some of these problems, it can be expensive to get them fixed. Technology projects can be costly, hard to manage, and slow to complete. It is not unheard of for a large company to spend millions of dollars over several years to eradicate all of these organic search problems.

Content changes are typically less costly and easier to manage than technology changes. It is expected that content will be constantly created and updated, so if you can convince your web team to write with search engines in mind, they will do that as a matter of course. It is not any more expensive to write a new page that includes mentions of the important search keywords for that page. Technology changes, however, are not so easy.

You don't need to optimize every page on your site (although that is great to do); you need optimize only the pages that you want returned for the keywords you are targeting. One reason you might shy away from optimizing every page is that it can be expensive to do. Estimates vary, but some studies show that optimizing each web page costs between $100 and $200, on average. Most modern websites use templates so that optimizing one template can improve many pages at once, which greatly lowers the costs.

Organic search marketing is usually the least expensive form of digital marketing, despite these costs, which is why almost all websites depend on it. But paid search can bring great business results, too.

Getting Started with Paid Search

"Money is better than poverty, if only for financial reasons," Woody Allen reminds us. So too, search marketers who are flush with cash have the advantage, but only if their money is spent wisely. We all know that a fool and his money are soon parted, but with paid search you might be shocked as to how quickly they are parted. Paid search is deceptively simple in concept, yet never mastered. The paid search programs are constantly changing, and your competition is always on the move. However, you can succeed in paid search if you learn some basic principles and stick to them.

Paid search has been described as a cross between day trading and direct marketing. Most paid search requires bidding against other search marketers to win the top spot for your site. Bidding can be intense, changing every second as companies jockey for position. Every word in your listing matters—making the difference between an ad that gets clicked and one that does not. Besides paid search ads, we've also talked about product search (shopping search), but paid search ads are the most popular form of paid search marketing.

One difference between paid and organic search is that you list your ad separately for each search engine. So, listing your ad in Google AdWords (the paid search program for Google's search engine) won't get your ad into Bing Ads (the corresponding program for Bing and Yahoo!). Despite that difficulty, paid search is still easier to get started with than organic search.

Google and Bing are the leaders, but you can get a more complete list of the more minor players at our website (SEMincBook.com/ppc-vendors).

By now, you have gotten a taste for the difficulty of revamping your site to garner organic search traffic. Although it pays off handsomely, organic search success takes skill, effort, and time. Paid search seems far easier. Select a keyword, plunk down your credit card, and overnight you have the #1 search position! It *can* work that way—*if* you know what you are doing. Let's explore paid search, the fast (and sometimes easier) method of paying your way to the top.

Why It Works

Paid search offers a proven way to attract visitors to your website, but put that credit card away for a minute. For all of the benefits of paid search, you can quickly burn through your budget, getting few sales, if you are not careful. Managed well, paid search is an indispensable part of a search marketing plan for lots of reasons—if you know what you are doing.

Every search marketer ought to at least consider paid search opportunities. For some, paid search will not be cost-effective, but many search marketers find paid search to be more valuable than organic search. It all depends on your site and your situation. We will help you decide

CONTEXTUAL ADVERTISING: DISPLAY ADVERTISING MEETS SEARCH

Paid search vendors offer a form of marketing known as **contextual advertising**, where marketers bid to place ads on the pages of websites that have articles about subjects related to your ads. For example, if your company runs a hotel in Philadelphia, you might want to display an ad for your hotel on a travel site's pages about Philadelphia tourist attractions.

In its most basic form, contextual advertising depends on the paid search vendor striking a deal with an information site to show ads on the information site's pages. Any site that draws heavy traffic is a strong candidate to display contextual ads—think CNN or ESPN or weather.com or CNET. Every article on these sites offers possibilities for contextual ads.

Paid search vendors already know how to display different ads depending on what the searcher enters, so why not apply that same technology to rapidly changing information sites? Google's AdSense program was the first major example of contextual advertising, but Microsoft's Content Ads have their own network of information sites to display ads.

Contextual ads rely on the search engine examining the words on a page in its ad network, and selecting ads related to that subject to be displayed alongside the story. Readers then click the ad to go to the advertiser's URL, just as with paid search. The advertiser pays for the click and the search engine and the owner of the ad network site both take a cut. Each information site might place the ads in different spots on their pages, but they all attempt to drive qualified visitors to the advertiser's site.

Contextual advertising programs work like any other paid search program in which you pay for each person who clicks your ad, but it isn't really search marketing, because the person who clicks on the ad has not searched for anything. For that reason, we won't spend any whether paid search is right for you, and, if it is, how to make the most of it. Check out all the reasons paid search might be an important addition to your digital marketing mix:

- **Highly qualified visitors will come to your site:** Just as with organic search, paid search attracts visitors who are already interested in what your site does. If they weren't, they would not have been searching in the first place. So it makes sense that searchers who click paid search listings are more likely to buy than visitors arriving at your site from clicking a banner ad, for example. But paid search listings get lower clickthrough rates than organic search, and searchers say that they trust them less, so organic search might still have the edge in converting searchers into buyers.

- **You see immediate results:** As you have seen, organic search success requires painstaking attention to detail to get your site discovered and to optimize its content for both search engines and for visitors—all of which can take months. Paid search, conversely, can require up-front work on landing pages and with trusted feeds for shopping engines, but often it can be initiated in a few days with an instant impact on your site. The biggest difference between paid search advertising and organic search is that paid search offers

more time on it in this book, but we mention it because it is similar to paid search in every way except how well it works. Because the ads are not clicked by people searching for something, they are less qualified than actual searchers and tend to have much lower conversion rates.

Most contextual ad programs allow you to make separate (usually lower) bids from the paid search bids for those same keywords, reflecting their lower conversion rates. Some also give you some control over what kind of stories your ad can be placed next to—so that you won't be seen sponsoring content that might prove embarrassing to your brand image. Contextual ad programs also often allow you to bid higher for certain reader demographics.

One technique many successful search marketers use in conjunction with contextual ads is called **retargeting** (Google calls it **remarketing**), in which previous visitors to your website are shown your contextual ads when they visit other websites; you hope that they are reminded of what they almost purchased from you and that they reconsider.

To see whether contextual ads are cost-effective for your keywords, you can run a test with one campaign that uses your keywords in the traditional search paid search and a second campaign with the same keywords enabled for contextual placement only. The search engine vendor will report each campaign separately, and you can compare to see whether the contextual campaign delivers enough value to be worth your while. Some search marketers report that contextual advertising has been a gold mine, whereas others have been disappointed; so, test it for yourself. In spite of some challenges, contextual advertising continues to grow each year and might be appropriate for your digital marketing mix. But it isn't search marketing and you shouldn't treat it that way.

near instantaneous traffic to your site. You can launch a campaign immediately by paying your money, writing your ads, and bidding your way to the top of the paid results—all without changing a line of code on your website. Organic search, in contrast, takes much longer to kick in.

- **It's inexpensive to get started:** Unlike organic search, where your site might need expensive changes, paid search requires low up-front costs. For as little as $50 and a credit card, you can open a paid search account. In addition, compared to organic search, paid search requires less expertise, so it is more likely that you can get started without engaging an expert consultant.

- **You pay only for visits to your site:** Many advertisers prefer paid search's fee structure—you typically pay only when searchers click your ad, not when they view your ad. With banner ads and other types of paid advertising, you are charged for impressions; you pay every time your ad is shown. If you design your site to efficiently persuade those paid searchers to buy, your return on your investment can be very profitable.

- **You can target your audience:** Whereas keyword planning enables you to target searchers by their interests (for both organic and paid search), paid search provides more pinpoint precision. Product search isolates transactional searchers ready to buy, and paid search ads can identify searchers by characteristics such as geographical location—both of which might be important to your business and well worth paying for.

- **Near-total message control:** Paid search provides near-total control over what your listing says, allowing you to further qualify searchers so that only the "right" ones click through. In organic search, although you can pick your page's title, the snippet that appears below the title is chosen by the search engine from the words that appear on your page. Paid search offers far more message control because the message can be directly targeted at searchers, with little concern about what the search engines want. Your ability to control your message is unmatched by any other advertising medium.

- **Unequalled adjustability:** You have learned how difficult it can be to make changes to your website to support organic search, especially if you have a medium to large site. If your inventory runs low on your best-selling product, your organic search results will keep pouring visitors into your site. If you reduce your product's price, it could take days for the organic search results to reflect it. Paid search, however, can adapt to these changes as they occur. You can stop buying the keyword for an out-of-stock item in paid search, and you can remove the item from product search. You can reflect price changes as they happen. You can ratchet up your investment during your busy season and taper it off at other times. What's more, you can constantly monitor the return on your investments and make changes each day to increase profitability. Paid search is probably the most flexible form of advertising available today.

- **Unlimited keyword targeting:** Organic search has a natural limit in the number of keywords that can be targeted. Although it is best to use existing pages on your site as search landing pages for both organic and paid search, inevitably you will find the need to add new landing pages as your keywords become more obscure. Because organic search landing pages must be deeply linked into the navigation of your site, there is a natural limit of how many landing pages (and therefore how many keywords) you can target. Because paid search landing pages need not be part of the site's navigation, you can target as many paid search keywords as you can justify the investment for.

Despite all these advantages, paid search is not for everyone. If you sell low-priced, low-margin products, you might find that the cost of advertising is more than you can justify in return. If you are unable to place any monetary value on visitors to your website, it will be hard to justify paid search spending. Many noncommercial and nonprofit sites find that paid search does not help them sustain their operations. For businesses, however, especially businesses that are trying to attract prospective customers to their site, paid search increasingly has a place in even the smallest marketing budgets.

What It Costs

One of the best things about paid search is that you can control the costs. You can buy as many or as few keywords as you want, and you decide how much you are willing to pay for each click. And you can adjust anything at a moment's notice, so you can control your budget.

As you embark on a paid search program, here are the kinds of costs to keep your eye on:

- **Creative costs:** Whether you do it in-house or you hire a consultant or ad agency to do it for you, it costs money to create the titles and descriptions that display onscreen. Remember, the number of searchers who click through to your site depends completely on the killer title and description you write, so this is no place to skimp on the budget. Agencies can usually do three or four new ads an hour, charging anywhere from $50 to $200 an hour to do so.

- **Management costs:** Tracking and adjusting your bids can be a lot of work, but it is the key to maximizing the return on your paid search investment; these campaigns do not run well on autopilot. You also need to keep track of your creative changes and deadlines, reconcile your bills, and verify your clickthroughs. You can hire an ad agency or search consultant to manage your paid search campaign for you. Conversely, if you manage it in-house, budget at least one full-time person to manage a highly competitive or large campaign (more than a thousand keywords).

- **Per-impression fee:** Usually referred to as CPM (cost per thousand—M is the Roman numeral for 1,000), you pay each time your ad displays onscreen, whether a searcher clicks or not. Typically, CPM pricing is used only for fixed-placement advertising, not bid-based advertising, and it varies from $10 to $30 per thousand impressions (or about 1¢ to 3¢ per single impression). Some obscure search engines charge per impression, but mainstream search engines do not.

- **Per-click fee:** Often called CPC (cost per click), it refers to the fee charged by the search engine each time a searcher clicks your advertisement. Typically, you open an account for a set amount and start bidding for placement. Whenever a searcher clicks your ad, the current bid (per-click) fee is deducted from your account, with your ad disappearing if your account reaches zero. CPC prices range from about 10¢ (usually the lowest bid allowed) to $30 or sometimes more, with the average around $1. The vast majority of paid search ads are charged per click.

- **Per-action fee:** Also known as CPA (cost per action), you pay only when the searcher takes "action"—typically a purchase of your product. Some paid search engines are beginning to experiment with CPA pricing, so you might have a choice between CPC and CPA pricing for your keywords. In addition, a new kind of action, a phone call, is also becoming a popular pricing model; it's called pay-per-call pricing.

KEYWORD BATTLES: HOW TO BLOW YOUR BUDGET IN ONE EASY LESSON

Because paid search has increased in popularity among search marketers, it is rare to find a popular keyword phrase without any bidders. It is also increasingly likely that bidders are using bid management software to control constant changes to their bids to maintain their place as #1, for example.

When two or more sites decide to be #1 for a particular keyword, a keyword battle ensues. Each time one site raises its bid, another increases its bid to leapfrog the original site. Unless one side eventually reaches its bid limit, the bidding can escalate dramatically. That's good for the search engines, but not for search marketers.

Sometimes these battles are fought intentionally, with each side consciously raising its bids, but all too often the battle is a mistake. The typical keyword battle arises between two sites with bid management software instructed to always be #1 for that keyword. As you might expect, neither site's software can succeed at being #1 for long—just the length of time in between bids. In this situation, the dueling software keeps bidding higher until one side exhausts its budget, usually within a couple of days.

It doesn't have to be that way. When you set up your bid management software, you can still request that it be #1, but also set a limit of the highest bid you are willing to pay. That way, your bid management system stops escalating its bid when it reaches the limit you set, defusing the battle, and saving your budget for opportunities with higher return on your investment. Even better, you could base your bidding on something smarter than being #1, which we discuss in Chapter 8, "Optimize Your Content."

CPM, CPC, and CPA fees are usually mutually exclusive; you pay only one of them on any particular ad. Exhibit 1-7 shows what a paid search campaign might cost when priced according to each method. Some advertisers prefer one method over another, but there is no surefire way to pay less on a consistent basis. It all depends on how many searches, clickthroughs, and purchases there are.

Method	Searches	Clicks	Actions	Rate	Total Cost
CPM	1,000,000			1¢ per impression	$10,000
CPC		50,000		20¢ per click	$10,000
CPA			1,000	$10 per action	$10,000

Exhibit 1-7 Comparing pricing formulas. What you pay depends on the activity multiplied by the rate, but no magical method will always save money.

Every pricing method has advantages and disadvantages. Chapter 8 reviews bidding strategies in more detail, and provides examples to help you choose the best option for your objectives.

The Steps to Search Success

Despite the differences between organic and paid search, the basic steps to success are the same:

1. **Choose your target market segments.** To get serious about search marketing, you need to focus on the keywords that searchers use that should find your site. Many of the keywords are the same between organic and paid search, but some marketers find that they can target more keywords for paid search or that some keywords are too expensive to be targeted outside organic search. We explore this step in detail in Chapter 6, "Choose Your Target Market Segments."

2. **Get your content listed.** Nothing else you do will matter if you don't even appear in the search results. For organic search, you must ensure that your content is discoverable by the search engines. For paid search, you must work with each search engine individually to get your ads listed for the keywords you have targeted. In Chapter 7, we examine the various techniques required to ensure your content is in the game.

3. **Optimize your content.** To rank well for popular keywords, you need to ensure that your paid search ads and your landing pages contain those words sprinkled in the right places. For paid search, you must also optimize your per-click bids to earn as much profit as possible. Chapter 8 walks you through what you need to know.

4. **Prove your content's quality.** Search engines are demanding; they don't show their searchers low-quality content. For your content to make the grade, you need to create content that searchers like. Search engines look at links to your content and social media activity for organic search, and they check your clickthrough rate and other factors. We look at all the ways that search engines judge your content's quality in Chapter 9.

If it sounds a bit overwhelming, fear not! That's what the rest of this book is for. We'll take you step by step to a successful search marketing program.

Summary

You are on your way as a search marketer! You have learned the two basic techniques in search marketing: organic search and paid search. Each technique proves advantageous under the right circumstances, but each one must be handled with care to avoid the pitfalls. Exhibit 1-8 summarizes the strengths and weaknesses of each technique.

Search Marketing Technique	How Much Expertise Is Required?	How Many Keywords Can You Target?	How Quickly Do You See Results?	How Long Do Results Last?
Organic search	High	Moderate	Slow	Lengthy
Paid search	Moderate	High	Fast	While paying

Exhibit 1-8   Search marketing techniques comparison. Organic is hard to do but yields high reward, whereas paid happens quickly but requires higher investment.

Paying attention to searchers takes more work than you might expect. Large sites and small sites have different issues in search marketing, but those problems must be overcome to achieve search marketing success.

Since the rise of the web in the 1990s, more and more of your customers have turned to the web, and more specifically to web search, to find what they are looking for. What's more, these searchers are among the most highly qualified visitors to arrive at your website. By focusing on searchers as part of your marketing plans, you *will* raise your sales.

In the next chapter, we examine why searchers behave the way they do—critical information for you, the search marketer. If you do not understand searchers, you cannot predict which keywords they will use, nor what content will strike their fancy. Let's examine the research into searcher behavior in Chapter 2, "How Searchers Work."

How Searchers Work

Management Would Be Easy... If It Weren't for the People is the whimsical title of Patricia J. Addesso's excellent book (American Management Association, 1996). Similarly, search marketing would be a lot easier if we did not have to worry about those pesky searchers.

You know the best search words to use to find your hit product, but searchers might not. Searchers might not know your product's name, or might not be able to spell it. Or they might not know that you call them *notebook computers* because they think of them as *laptops*. If you optimize your pages for *notebook computers*, you sure are going to miss a lot of those *laptop* searchers.

Searchers are not experts. They are not experts in your content. They are not even experts on how to search. If you are expecting them to be, then they will continue to use search to find their answers; they just will not find them from you! One of the hardest things about any kind of marketing (and search marketing is no different) is to put yourself in your customer's shoes. *You* might know how to find the information on your website, but searchers do not. Your searchers are probably not like you, because you know a lot more than they do about searching, and you especially know more about your content.

Now that you've learned how search marketing works, it's time to examine how *searchers* work: how they think, what they do, and what you can do about it. Not surprisingly, any effective search marketing program requires a solid understanding of the web searcher. This chapter covers the following topics:

- **Website visitor behavior:** Before we look at the particulars of how searchers behave, we need to take a look at some general findings on the behavior of visitors to websites.

- **The searcher's intent:** When formulating the keyword, every searcher has some objective in mind. Understanding the searcher's intent helps you provide the right information for the search engine to return. We will categorize search keywords into several distinct types.

- **The searcher's device:** Searcher behavior differs based on which device is used to enter the keyword. Desktop computers, tablets, and phones are used differently.

- **The searcher's typing:** As the searcher enters his search keyword, the search engines respond in ways that alter searcher behavior.

- **The searcher's click:** Which links on the search results page do searchers click? We review the research into why searchers click where they do.

- **The searcher's follow-through:** Getting the searcher to visit your site is only half the battle. You need to develop your model of visitor activity on your site after they search to be sure that they will follow through—to buy your product, or sign up for your newsletter, or vote for your candidate.

- **How to work the searcher:** All this information is nice, but what does it mean to you as a search marketer? Find out how to use what you now know to improve your search marketing results.

Anyone who spends time studying people realizes that they interact with the world in unexpected and complex ways, and searchers are no exception. Let's start by examining the basic principles of how website visitors behave.

Visitor Behavior

No matter what you want your website visitors to do, they have goals of their own. They might be figuring out why their geraniums keep dying, or choosing which cell phone service to switch to, or checking their doctor's advice about their high cholesterol. You must start with an understanding of what visitors to your website are trying to accomplish before you can help them reach their goals.

For some of you, thinking about visitor behavior is second nature; you might be a product marketer, or maybe you are responsible for voter research in a political campaign. If you are in a more technical role, however, such as a webmaster or a Java programmer, you might not have thought much about this subject at all. Before we examine how to track visitor behavior, you need to understand some of the basic principles.

Fortunately, all the complex factors that affect visitor behavior have been studied for many years, because before they were "web visitors" they were just plain folks—and research scientists have studied people's behavior for decades. If you are selling something, there is a wealth of information on **buyer behavior**. There is also plenty of research on other kinds of behavior. (Political scientists regularly research **voter behavior**, for example.) No matter who your visitors are, there is probably a lot of information you can learn about their motivations, their beliefs, and their thinking—all of which help predict their likely behavior.

Because many of you are using search marketing to sell something, this chapter focuses mainly on sales examples, but we also examine the behavior of visitors with other goals (such as attracting votes for a candidate) so that you discover the underlying principles.

Buyer Behavior

Each of us buys things often, but somehow we forget our own experiences when we start selling things to other people. If your site's goal is to sell something, you need to be attuned to exactly what your prospective buyers are looking for. There is no shortage of terms used to describe buyer behavior, but one important way to differentiate buyers is by the type of information they are seeking.

Some buyers are in the early stages of consideration of a purchase. Some marketing gurus call this **primary demand**, using the economic term *demand* to indicate when a buyer feels a need for something. Buyers experiencing primary demand have a problem, but they might not know whether there is any solution for it. Or they do not know which of several types of solution to choose. Contrast this with **selective demand**, where the buyer wants a particular brand of product or even a specific model.

If this is all you ever understand about buyer behavior, you will still be miles ahead of some of your search marketing competitors. You can imagine how a primary demand buyer might need a lot of education about various solutions to his problem before he is ready to hear about different products, whereas a selective demand buyer would be bored by such information and just wants to get detailed product information. For search marketers, these differences can mean the difference between success and failure.

Consider someone who needs the snow shoveled from her driveway, which you can now identify as a primary demand situation. This buyer does not know whether she wants to hire a snow removal service or buy a snow blower, an electric snow shovel, or just a new shovel. How would you pitch what you are selling to such a person? If you happen to sell snow blowers, telling this buyer that your snow blower is the highest rated in the industry and it is on sale this weekend is pointless. She does not even know if she *wants* a snow blower. An article that shows the pros and cons of the various ways to remove snow, on the other hand, is exactly what the buyer wants to read. Here is where your powers of persuasion come in handy. Does your article point out the benefits of snow blowers as opposed to other methods? Because buyers are distrustful, your article should be sure to point out the legitimate situations in which other solutions are worthwhile, but you can certainly favor snow blowers as the solution of choice in most situations.

Your goal is to *inform* the primary demand buyer, allowing her to *become* a selective demand buyer. Notice that only when the buyer is convinced that she needs a snow blower does it make sense for you to extol the virtues of your snow blower over your competitor's. At that point, all the information deemed inappropriate earlier (its high rating and its sale price) might become important to that same buyer.

Human beings are complex creatures, and many different factors go in to decision making. The more that you know about what drives your visitors' buying behavior, the more easily you can tailor your website to address their needs—and the more easily you can tailor your search marketing efforts.

Other Visitor Behavior

Just as businesses pursuing search marketing must understand buyer behavior, organizations whose website visitors are not buyers must understand other kinds of behavior. Maybe your web visitors are not buyers at all. Perhaps yours is a persuasion site trying to elect the next governor, in which case you need to consider everything you know about voter behavior when designing your site—and designing your search marketing. You need to understand how voters decide whom to vote for and you must decide what motivates voters to go to the polls rather than sitting the election out at home. (It is of no use to persuade those who do not actually cast their vote.)

Different voters make different decisions in the same situation. Some political scientists believe that it is important in close elections to appear to be the front-runner, because "bandwagon behavior" causes undecided voters to go with the apparent winner. Other experts note that the leader often struggles to get supporters to the polls, because of the perception that the candidate is going to win anyway. Do voters look at your candidate differently because he is the challenger and not the incumbent? Regardless of what your pollster is telling you about your voters, you want voters exposed to certain themes and specific messages, and your understanding of voter behavior is a key part of deciding what your website says. It is also a key part of deciding which search keywords those prospective voters might enter.

The same principles apply to visitors to other kinds of persuasion websites. In the medical field, it is increasingly recognized that **patient behavior** is important to any successful outcome, especially when it comes to so-called high-risk behaviors such as smoking, drug taking, or sexual promiscuity. But patient behavior often rules much more mundane situations, too—such as whether a medication will get a chance to work, based on whether the patient actually takes her pill when required. These so-called compliance issues are crucial in designing some pharmaceutical websites—and can drive the selection of content and search keywords for side effects and other factors that lead to ignoring the doctor's instructions to take a prescription.

Regardless of the type of web visitor—buyer, voter, patient, or someone else—your understanding of the behavior of your site's target audience helps you design the messages that persuade them to your point of view.

The Searcher's Intent

Now that you understand the basics of web visitor behavior, let's talk specifically about search. Web searchers have behaviors all their own that start with the search keyword itself.

Throughout history, human beings have sought to bring order to information by sorting and grouping documents to find them when they need them. The advent of computer **information retrieval** (that is, search) made possible a massive increase in the number of documents available to find the needed information. And mostly, that's good. The problem arises when we expect those poor human beings to know how to find information in a whole new way. Folks who are comfortable using library card catalogs, book indexes, and other paper techniques find that none of those skills translate into using web search.

So, although searchers are growing more sophisticated each year, the task of actually *choosing* the keyword is one of the most difficult parts of searching. A few years ago, searchers mostly entered one- or two-word search keywords, and although keywords are getting longer each year, it is still hard for search engines to know exactly what the searcher intends by a keyword.

It's actually a simple question: What does the searcher really want when he enters a keyword? The answer is hardly as simple as the question. When a searcher enters "home improvement," is he remodeling his bathroom or interested in Tim Allen's old TV show? Researchers from top search engines say one of their biggest frustrations is making sense of the searcher's keyword. Despite this, it is not a hopeless cause. You *can* dramatically improve your search marketing by thinking about the need behind the keyword. This knowledge helps you deliver the best possible content to your visitors when they search.

Our former IBM colleague Andrei Broder, now a Distinguished Scientist at Google, segments searchers into three categories:

- **Navigational searchers** want to find a specific website (perhaps because they do not know the exact URL or don't want to type it), and use keywords such as *irs website* or *valley hospital*.

- **Informational searchers** want information to answer their questions or to learn about a new subject, and use keywords such as *what is scuba* or *hard water treatments*.

- **Transactional searchers** want to do something (buy something, sign up, enter a contest, and so forth), and use keywords such as *coldplay tickets* or *chase visa card activation*.

We need to examine each kind of searcher so that you can reach them with your content. Understand that real people shift roles all the time; the same searcher might enter informational keywords to learn about a new product and suddenly decide to use a transactional keyword to buy it. A clear understanding of the types of searchers and their respective intent will help you reach more searchers with less effort.

Navigational Searchers

Navigational searchers are looking for a specific website, perhaps because they have visited it in the past, or someone has told them about it, or because they have heard of a company and they just assume the site exists. Unlike other types of searchers, navigational searchers have just one right answer in mind. Exhibit 2-1 shows some examples of navigational searches.

Search Keyword	Probable Destination
greyhound bus	www.greyhound.com
internal revenue service	www.irs.gov
jetblue airlines	www.jetblue.com
toys are us	www.toysrus.com
barnes and noble	www.bn.com

Exhibit 2-1   Examples of navigational keywords. Searchers expect a single correct result from any navigational keyword, often the home page of the site they are looking for.

Even when they use the same keyword, navigational searchers might not have the same destination in mind, as Exhibit 2-2 shows.

Search Keyword	Probable Destinations	Organization
delta	www.delta.com	Delta Airlines
	www.deltafaucet.com	Delta Faucets
usc	www.usc.edu	University of Southern California
	www.sc.edu	University of South Carolina
cardinals	www.stlcardinals.com	St. Louis Cardinals baseball team
	www.azcardinals.com	Arizona Cardinals football team
hoover	www.hoovers.com	Hoover's Online
	www.hoover.com	Hoover Vacuums

Exhibit 2-2   Confusion with navigational keywords. Searchers expect a single correct result from any navigational keyword, but exactly which result is not always clear.

Although it might be unclear what the navigational searchers want, it is clear what they do *not* want. They do not want deep information from a website; they want the home page. They know what site they want, and only that site will do. And, in most cases, they want just the home page for that site—no other pages.

AFFILIATE "SPAM" FRUSTRATES NAVIGATIONAL SEARCHERS

At a standing-room-only session on Internet travel deals at a popular New York City tourism conference, one woman stood up after a panel discussion and launched into a complaint about a particular hotel chain. She was furious that this hotel had hundreds of websites, each offering different prices and conflicting information. Not one of them showed the phone number so that she could actually call the hotel and book a reservation directly. This rant elicited cheers of support and sympathy.

The session moderator calmly tried to retake control of the session by explaining that those sites were affiliate sites and they did not actually belong to the hotel chain. Each site was a legitimate affiliate marketing partner of the hotel chain that gets a small commission for every reservation it books on behalf of the hotel. Unfortunately, some of these sites use unethical techniques (spam) to get top search rankings, frustrating navigational searchers who find these affiliate sites rather than the official site for the actual hotel.

This explanation did not make the attendees any happier, but at least they now understood what they were seeing. Another woman in the audience made the suggestion that searchers add the word *official* to their search keyword. For example, the keyword *official hilton hotel* actually returns the "official" Hilton website high in the results list in the major search engines, avoiding the spam.

Often, novice search marketers find navigational searchers the hardest to fathom; this type of search does not make any sense to them. "Why would someone go to a search engine to search for my company when the URL is our name?" they ask. But veteran web surfers know that they do this all the time. One reason is that it's easier to type everything into one box. In the Chrome browser, for example, there is just one box that takes URLs or searches.

You might be wondering what you can do to make sure those searchers find your site. Usually, you do not need to do much. Most navigational keywords don't have a lot of competition; when someone enters the name of your company into the search box, your website should show up. As Exhibit 2-2 shows, if your company's name is shared by other companies, there might be some competition, but there is much less competition than for other kinds of keywords. Most corporations should be in the top few results of most search engines for searches on their company name or their popular brand names.

Take steps now to make sure your website ranks well for navigational keywords:

- Ensure that your site is in the major search engines' indexes. Most organizations are already indexed, but see Chapter 7, "Get Your Content Listed," if yours is not.

- Make sure that the search engines show a good description for your home page for searches on your company name. If you do not like what you see, add a strong sentence with your company name to your page; the search engines will take that information and show it in the results.

- When running advertising campaigns, anticipate navigational searches based on your ad copy. Consider critical words in your slogan, product names, problems identified, and any other words that are emphasized in your TV commercials, radio spots, or print ads. These words usually become the navigational keywords that searchers enter.

- Remember that hate sites (yoursite-sucks.com) and negative social media content often rank close to (or occasionally higher than) your website and your other content. See Chapter 5, "Create Your Search Marketing Program," for ideas about increasing the search exposure of your site and limiting the visibility of your detractors.

Because people often use navigational keywords to locate a company when they cannot figure out how to type the URL directly, you might also consider registering domains for common misspellings of your company name. That way, people might find your company without resorting to navigational searches at all.

Informational Searchers

Informational searchers want to find deep information about a specific subject. Informational searchers believe this deep information exists, but they don't know where it's located. Unlike navigational keywords, informational keywords do not have a single right answer. The best search results are a mixture of content that all shed some light on the subject.

Almost every web user is an informational searcher at one time or another. Most searchers start with a simple search keyword, refining it until they locate good answers (or give up). The intent of informational searchers proves the most difficult to deduce because their keywords can mean so many things. Many informational searchers enter only a single phrase, such as *new york*. Whether that searcher meant New York City or the state of New York, and whether she wants to visit New York or learn about its history, discerning her intent is next to impossible.

The informational searcher is the mainstay of any search marketing program. Informational searchers have not yet chosen the product they want to buy (for example), so they are still "up for grabs." Informational searchers allow you to present your products before they have chosen a specific product.

The key to satisfying informational searchers is to provide clear "learn about" content related to your products or services. If you are selling riding lawnmowers, explain why riding lawnmowers are superior to the hand-push kind. If you offer a smoking-cessation program, why does yours work while others fail? No matter what your website sells, why is yours better? Whatever your website does, why do you do it better?

By researching the informational keywords that searchers use (explained in detail in Chapter 6, "Choose Your Target Market Segments"), and by optimizing your pages to meet those information needs (covered in Chapter 8, "Optimize Your Content"), you can attract informational searchers to your site.

CASE STUDY: IS THE SEARCHER'S INTENT INFORMATIONAL OR TRANSACTIONAL?

At the peak of the dotcom boom, a leading art and print site was spending millions of dollars on paid search placements for art-related search keywords. The marketing manager knew that *monet* was one of its most heavily trafficked keywords, but recently the visits from Yahoo! for *monet* had decreased significantly. What had changed?

Examining the Yahoo! search results for *monet* revealed a new site in the organic listings offering the complete history of Monet. Apparently, many searchers were looking for information on Monet and were probably heading to that new site, instead of the art and print site.

In response, the marketing manager placed more historical information about Monet on his site and soon found his Monet page ranked highly in the Yahoo! organic listings. As expected, he began to see the traffic to this new Monet page increase significantly from the organic listing. The surprise was in the paid search clicks; they dropped even further. Worse, there were no more buyers of Monet prints even though overall traffic had doubled when you added up both paid and organic referrals. Why?

The marketing manager decided to perform a test. He added a survey to the new Monet page offering a drawing for a free print for those who would reveal their purpose in coming to the site. Of the survey respondents, 95% indicated that they were students simply looking for biographical information on Monet and information about his paintings. These were informational searchers who had no desire to ever buy a Monet print.

Armed with this information, the marketing manager switched his paid placement buys from an informational keyword (*monet*) to specific transactional keywords (the names of Monet paintings such as *water lilies*). This strategy not only increased traffic but also increased sales, by capturing people who were not entering *monet* as their search keyword, but were truly ready to buy a specific print.

As you can see, careful study of the searcher's intent pays off in more visitors who are focused on your site's goal. It can be just as important to avoid the wrong traffic as to get the right traffic, because every art student who clicked the paid placement page cost the art and print site a few cents in pay-per-click fees that were completely wasted. By focusing on keywords that real purchasers use, the art and print site reduced the art students and attracted more art buyers at the same time, thus selling more while paying less.

Transactional Searchers

Transactional searchers make things happen. They are not looking for information; they want to *do* something. Transactional keywords cluster around specific tasks, such as buying products, accessing databases, and downloading various types of files (images, software, or songs). When searchers enter the name of a book, or the model number of a digital camera, they are intending to make a transaction, namely to buy the item. But there are many other kinds of transactional keywords. Anyone trying to download a fix for a computer, or signing up for a newsletter, or donating to a charity is a transactional searcher.

Transactional searches are the hardest of all keywords to incorporate into an optimization program. Transactional keywords are often related to specific products, and should return product catalog pages, which often have little content on them and do not rank well in search engines. The text-rich informational searcher pages that solved shoppers' problems with your products are gone, replaced by barren catalog pages with model numbers, specifications, and a picture. It is hard work to dress up these catalog pages for search engines.

What's more, transactional searches are the biggest moneymaker for the search engines themselves. They command the highest paid search ad prices, are the most suitable for lucrative product search results, and increasingly allow search engines to siphon off the actual commerce for itself. Check out Exhibit 2-3, where Google Flight is "taking off" by booking the airfare itself, without sending you to any other website.

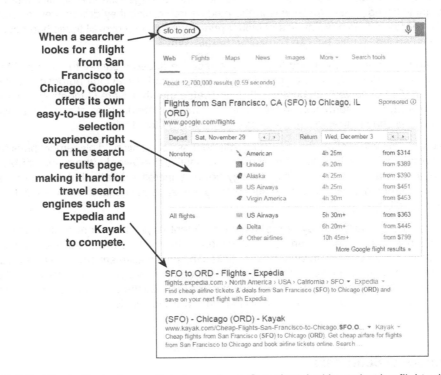

When a searcher looks for a flight from San Francisco to Chicago, Google offers its own easy-to-use flight selection experience right on the search results page, making it hard for travel search engines such as Expedia and Kayak to compete.

Exhibit 2-3   The battle for transactional searchers. Searchers looking to book a flight might not even leave the search result page to do it, using Google Flight.

The most important goal for improving these catalog pages is to make the search result's snippet relevant to the keyword. You improve your chances of both being found by the search engine and being clicked by the searcher if you incorporate the keyword into the title and other parts of the page. In addition, you should feature any special pricing or other offer prominently on the page to catch the attention of the searcher. If your page can reassure searchers that it is a good choice, even better.

The Searcher's Device

Search marketers must now consider the device their prospects are using to search. In the old days, we had to think only about desktop and laptops but this has shifted dramatically with new worlds of smartphones and tablet computers. Mobile search has grown to 31% of the total search volume in early 2014 according to Rimm-Kaufman Group.

Smartphones and tablets differ from desktops in one obvious way: Their screens are smaller. Some believe that those smaller screens lead to more searching. Why? Because it is harder to click on links on web pages with our fat fingers, so we are more likely to search.

The difference between computers and mobile devices that most people focus on is that mobile devices move around. But that can lead us astray in our thinking.

You see, when we say that over 10% of searches are *mobile*, it might make you think about people walking down a city street or riding a bus—and many of those searchers are indeed out and about. But many of them are actually surfing the web with an iPad on their living room couch; those searches are counted as *mobile* searches but they are likely looking for very different kinds of content. Fifty percent of mobile searches have local intent (as you would expect from people out and about), but 50% do not. Seventy percent of mobile searches lead to action within an hour (as you would also expect of people on the go), but 30% don't.

The bottom line is not to assume that all so-called mobile searchers are locating restaurants or gas stations while on the go. Many of them are couch surfers on a tablet looking for things that might be more similar to desktop searches. In addition, laptops with mobile broadband access might lead to more of those so-called nonmobile (stationary?) searches—the ones from computers—really coming from people on the go.

One thing that seems to be true of smartphone and tablet searchers is that they use fewer individual words within their keywords. This makes sense, because it is harder to enter text on a phone than to type words on a computer keyboard. Search marketers should expect that mobile searchers are more likely to take advantage of search suggestions—choosing a popular keyword suggested by the search engine rather than continuing the laborious act of typing. This might lead mobile searchers to employ less variation in their use of keywords than desktop searchers.

Perhaps the most-discussed aspect of mobile searching is **showrooming**, where consumers go to a retail store to touch and feel the product while using their phones to find a lower price to buy it online. Research from InsightExpress found that 59% of smartphone users have used their mobile phone to help them find a cheaper product while actually in a retail store.

Major online retailers such as Amazon even offer barcode scanner "comparison apps" that allow a user to scan a product in the store to make it easier to match the exact product online. In response, retailers such as Best Buy have removed bar codes from product boxes. For online retailers, it's important to include model numbers in your pages as well as noting stock levels to attract searchers looking for a specific model product in your city.

But mobile searchers are not just looking for a lower price. More than half of all consumers surveyed by MediaPost say that they would research products on their phones before asking a salesperson. InsightExpress found that 43% of in-store shoppers looked for reviews of products.

These statistics point to an underlying shift in the locations and the devices that many customers use, creating new challenges for you the marketer. Not only should you make sure that relevant product attributes are included but also that your website is mobile friendly. Several options exist for mobile-friendly websites, ranging from a completely separate mobile version of the site to one that adapts by expanding or shrinking appropriately for each device's proper screen size.

The Searcher's Typing

Since the advent of text search in the 1960s, one problem has bedeviled searchers and continues to haunt them to this day: Searchers often do not know the best words to use in their keywords. Over time, search engines have introduced new techniques to help searchers pick the right words.

One innovation is a unique form of spellchecking that doesn't correct what the searcher types, but rather shows search results (or asks to show them) when the keyword seems like a variant of a much more likely keyword. Exhibit 2-4 shows how Google handles misspellings without slowing down the searcher; Bing's approach is similar.

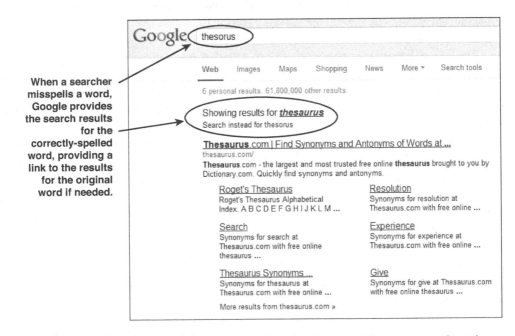

Exhibit 2-4   Handling spelling errors elegantly. Google substitutes the correct words and prompts the searcher to click on the results for the original words if desired.

More recently, the major search engines have begun offering **keyword suggestion**, which provides a drop-down menu underneath the search box showing popular keywords that others have entered which start with the same letters. Exhibit 2-5 shows how the suggestions change as each letter of a keyword is entered. As *dig* is entered, the suggestions keep changing, and range from *digestive system* to *digital cameras*.

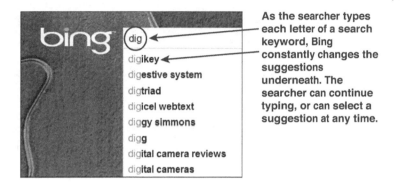

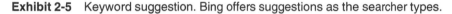

As the searcher types each letter of a search keyword, Bing constantly changes the suggestions underneath. The searcher can continue typing, or can select a suggestion at any time.

Exhibit 2-5   Keyword suggestion. Bing offers suggestions as the searcher types.

Keyword suggestion features have probably changed searcher behavior, but theories abound as to nature of these changes. Do searchers use fewer misspellings? Do they use longer keywords, such as *digital camera reviews*, because they did not have to think up the words and type them in? Have the most popular keywords become even more popular, with fewer variations in wording?

Because search keyword usage changes all the time, there is no way to conduct a proper study because there is no control group. In addition, keyword suggestion affects only some search keywords—searches typed directly into some browser address bars don't see any suggestions, or don't see the same suggestions. Moreover, search engines try to personalize the suggestions based on what searchers have looked for in the past, so the suggestions that one person gets aren't the same as what others receive.

Regardless, simple keyword suggestions are not enough for Google, who upped the ante with its Google Instant, which goes beyond merely suggesting searches to executing them. Unless the searcher explicitly turns off the capability, any searcher using Google's website search box at Google.com can watch as search results appear and disappear on the screen as each letter is typed in the search keyword, as shown in Exhibit 2-6.

As the searcher begins to type *d* and then *i*, Google constantly changes the search results below, including both paid and organic results. The searcher can continue typing, choose suggested keywords below, or accept the results on the screen, in this case for *digital cameras*.

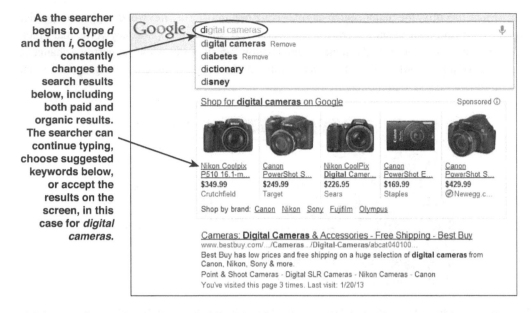

Exhibit 2-6   Google Instant speeds things up. Google executes searches as searchers type.

As these seemingly simple changes by the search engines show, search marketers must evolve as search technology evolves, because searcher behavior changes with each technology update. Lacking usability studies, search marketers must cast a watchful eye on trends in search keyword usage that affect their search marketing results.

The Searcher's Click

Now that we understand why searchers enter the keywords they do, we need to learn what they do with the search results. We already learned that searchers have *different* needs motivating their search keywords, but now we will see that searchers *share* certain behaviors when dealing with search results.

Just because your site ranks at the top of the results does not mean that searchers will view your page. You need to give them a reason to click.

Searchers see only a few things about your page on the search results page: the title, the snippet, and the URL. Your copy writer selects the title, and your webmaster chooses the URL, but the *search engine* picks the snippet from your page based on the searcher's keyword.

Let's take a deeper look at how searchers look at search results, why they click where they do, and what is happening when searchers do *not* click a result at all.

How Searchers Look at Results

People do not *read* content when they use the web—they *scan*. So it is no surprise that web searchers also scan a search results page, instead of starting in the upper-left corner and reading each word.

Searchers seem to use some common approaches when they scan, as revealed by **eye-tracking analytics** studies, in which test subjects' eye movements are tracked as they look at a computer screen. Exhibit 2-7 shows what a typical searcher actually looks at on a search results page.

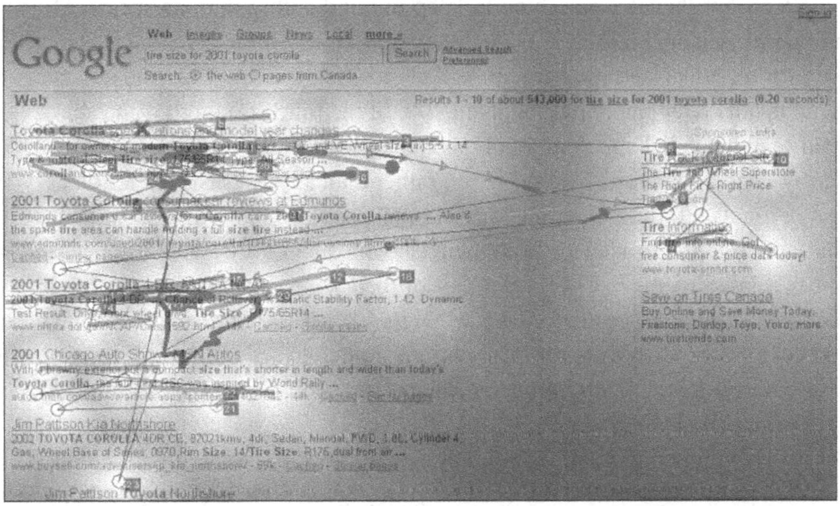

Exhibit 2-7   What searchers see on the results page. Each dot shows where searchers' eyes track.

Source: Mediative

Eye movement studies (and other studies) disclose what searchers scan for the following:

- Searchers "mentally divide" the page into sections and focus on the organic results the most. Four out of five searchers ignore the sponsored links (**paid listings**).
- Nearly all users look at the first two or three organic search results.
- Searchers spend less time looking at organic results ranked below #3, and far less time scanning results that rank seventh or lower, possibly because these results require scrolling down on the page. Eighty-eight percent of searchers report scrolling down only when there is no relevant result in the top three.
- Within each result, searchers spend 44% of the time viewing the snippet, followed by 39% reviewing the title.

If you did not realize it already, you can see that high rankings for search keywords are the key to getting noticed. The first hurdle to being clicked by searchers is to get their attention—rank highly on the results page and have an eye-catching title and snippet. But after you get their attention, what makes them click your page?

Why Searchers Click Where They Do

Searchers click pages because they expect those pages will satisfy a need. So navigational searchers expect to land at the right site, information searchers expect to find their answer, and transactional searchers to take action—or at least get one step closer.

No matter what they do, one thing to keep in mind is that they do it fast. Most searchers choose the first promising link they see, and they do it in less than 5 seconds. They look at only the top two or three links, and they are most likely to click the first link. Searchers also seem to favor organic results over paid, clicking them 70% of the time, although some studies show that transactional searchers click much more often on paid search ads.

But why does a searcher click one result rather than another? No matter what type of keyword—navigational, informational, or transactional—studies show that searchers tend to click a result that contains the exact words of their keywords in its title and snippet, and they also scan for other related words that were not part of their keyword. In addition, for informational and transactional keywords, searchers click when they see trusted information sources and brand names (and reviews and comparison information). For transactional searchers, showing a low price (along with promises of discounts or other offers) enhances clickthrough rate, especially when the searcher can buy online.

After you begin getting good search rankings for your pages, you will want to continue to learn about what motivates searchers to click on your page in the search results, but you also need to understand what stops them.

When Searchers Don't Click Results

Although search engines can often seem magical in the way they find the right page for a keyword, the truth is that many searchers do *not* click a result on the first page of search results. A recent study by SlingShot SEO showed that only about half of searchers click on an organic search result. Even if 25% more click on paid ads (a high estimate), a significant portion are not clicking on a search result. What are they doing instead?

Are they usually moving to page two of the search results? No. Most searchers enter a new keyword when the first page results are unappealing. In fact, many searchers plan to start with a broad keyword, making it more specific as they go.

Increasingly, searchers are failing to click because the search engines have answered their question right on the search results page! Try searches such as *cleveland weather* or *convert 20 dollars to euros* and you see how **direct answer** technology works. As the years go by, more and more searches get answers without the searcher clicking on anything. A stock ticker symbol shows the current stock price. A famous person's name shows a mini-Wikipedia entry, as shown in Exhibit 2-8. That can't make Wikipedia happy, because some of the clicks they once got are no more.

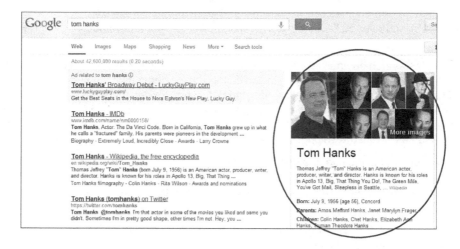

Exhibit 2-8   Direct answers reduce clicks. Google does an end run around Wikipedia.

Each search engine provides this kind of direct answer capability, where searchers don't need to click through to a search marketer's page; the search engine gives the answer itself. Sometimes the search engine favors content from one of its own properties or one from its partners. Google loves to show Google News or YouTube videos. Bing Travel allows searchers to check flight prices and availability right on the search results page.

Searchers always want to save a step in the process, so they like these direct answers; expect to see more of them. But as search engines begin to provide product listings and other responses as direct answers, it may threaten some search marketers who don't have a deal with the search engines. If searchers begin to expect to see direct answers to their keywords, then search marketers want to be seen in the direct results.

Enhancing Your Search Result's "Curb Appeal"

Realtors have long provided tips to home sellers on enhancing "curb appeal"—that certain something that makes a house enticing to a potential buyer. Search marketers must think similarly, especially because searchers spend on average fewer than eight seconds looking at each search result page. If you consistently enhance your titles and snippets, your content will have the curb appeal you need to drive heavy clickthrough rates.

The most-examined part of a search results page is the snippet, the two- to three-line page excerpt that search engines use to show where the search terms were found on that page. Searchers spend over 50% of their time looking at the snippet before deciding to click that link.

Typically, the search engines take the first full sentence of page text that contains the search terms. It moves down the page pulling in additional clauses containing the search terms until it reaches the maximum character limit. If a page does not contain the search terms within a sentence (or at all), the search engine might even take the content found in the description tag. If you understand how this snippet is created, you can adjust your content so that the search engine will use the snippet you want, rather than something cobbled together.

Above the snippet is the title, the underlined (usually blue) text taken from the title tag. The title normally garners a little more than 30% of the searcher's scanning time. Exhibit 2-7 shows that the searcher's eyes stopped on every bold occurrence of the search terms.

Smart search marketers spruce up their pages to increase their appeal to searchers, so that their high rankings for search result in a high clickthrough rate, too. Chapter 8 shows you more tips on increasing curb appeal.

The Searcher's Follow-Through

Just getting people to click your link on the search results page is not enough. Your website has a purpose, whether it is persuading a customer to purchase more of your product, coaxing a prospect to provide his email address, or convincing someone to exercise. No matter what you do in search marketing, the job is not done unless the searcher not only finds your site, but also follows through.

Visitors landing on your site from search engines exhibit specific behavior when they arrive; searchers typically decide within seconds whether to click further. Searchers tend to click further when your page contains the following:

- The searcher's exact search terms in the page heading or another prominent location
- Videos, pictures, or other eye-catching content

- Wide selection of products or information (for informational searchers)
- Price, features, and value (for transactional searchers)

But what stops them from completing their task? Like it or not, people are much less patient with websites that do not work their way than they are with offline businesses.

Consider what you would do if you drove to the store, spent a few minutes putting items in your cart, and went to the register and saw a rather long line—maybe you will be waiting for 5 or 10 minutes to check out. Most of us would grin and bear it. We might be annoyed, but we would wait semi-patiently and check out. If it happened often enough, though, we might start avoiding that store.

Now think about an equivalent experience on the web. You spend a few minutes placing several items in your cart, and then you get to the checkout and it is slow. Each time you click it takes 10 to 15 seconds to respond. Then it takes 30 seconds on the next screen. What would you do?

Many of you would abandon that site and go somewhere else, even though it means starting all over (and though you would wait 10 minutes in a brick-and-mortar store to do the same thing). Why? Because it is so quick to go to another web store, that is why. You know that you will only spend a few minutes doing it, and you will recover all your lost time, whereas it might take considerably longer to retrace your steps in a physical store.

Successful websites construct the optimal path for their visitor to follow to complete any task, and the only way to do that is to understand your visitor's behavior. Throughout this chapter, we have discussed how searchers get to your site, but now we need to consider how they follow through after they have arrived. To understand your web visitor's behavior, you need to develop a **behavior model**. We show you one technique for developing behavior models for the Buyer's Journey.

Customer Behavior and the Buyer's Journey

You work with behavior models every day, but perhaps you do not think of them in those terms. If you own a retail store, it is understood that customers enter the store, look around at the merchandise, pick a few things out, and take them to the register to pay. That is a behavior model. Your web visitors use a model, too, and you need to take that into account when you try to measure the success of your search campaign.

Just like the retail store, your website is designed to drive to a **conversion**, such as purchasing a product. Moreover, both the retail site and your website have secondary goals, such as allowing returns or repairs of products, which you can also count as successful web conversions.

We should account for the main user goals in our behavior model, which we call the **Buyer's Journey**. In Chapter 4, "Unlock the Business Value of Search," we help you define your own Buyer's Journey to model visitor behavior on your website. But for now, let's look at just one example, as shown in Exhibit 2-9.

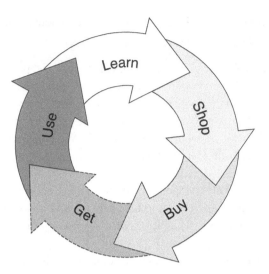

Exhibit 2-9   A behavior model for personal computer sales. Visitors satisfy their information needs before buying, "get" the computer offline, and return for technical support.

As we look at our example of the Buyer's Journey, we can see that visitors might start out with a problem (primary demand) and must *Learn* about what kinds of solutions exist. When informed, they can choose a type of solution and *Shop* for a particular product (selective demand). If they are persuaded that they have found the right product and the right deal, they can *Buy* the product, and then wait to *Get* it before they *Use* it. Let's look at each step in more detail.

Your visitor starts by *learning* how to solve her problem, and can be said to be in the *Learn* step. The information on your site was carefully written to discuss her problem and to gradually lead her to explore your products, which can solve her problem.

At the moment she begins examining pricing or comparing features of your product, she is *shopping*. Visitors in the *Shop* step need different information than those in the *Learn* activity; learners are trying to figure out what kind of product can help them, whereas shoppers are gathering information leading to the purchase of a specific product.

After your shopper chooses a specific product, she is *buying*. In the *Buy* step, she lands on a particular product page, examining the information carefully to decide whether to place the item in her cart. The *Buy* activity includes all the steps of placing an item in her cart, checking out, and actually completing the purchase.

After buying the product, the visitor waits to *get* the purchase, which typically takes several days. During the *Get* step, she might check online order status to see when the item is shipped and might use tracking numbers from overnight shipping vendors to ascertain the delivery date of her order.

After she has received her purchase, she begins to *use* it. Depending on the product, there might be many specific steps in the *Use* activity, ranging from assembly, to installation, to asking "how to" questions, to solving a problem. If the customer is happy with the product, she might decide to return to your site to purchase something else from you.

Search Marketing and the Buyer's Journey

There are lots of ways to use the Buyer's Journey in your business, but we can start by examining how these visitor behaviors affect the search keywords they enter and how you can design your pages to capture those searchers for your site. Let's look at four of the most important steps in the Buyer's Journey and see where search fits in.

The Learn Stage

Many visitors start out needing to learn more about what you sell before they consider a purchase, and they often use informational search keywords to do so. To ensure visitors find your site when they enter the informational keywords, write articles with objective information comparing multiple solutions to the problem. The articles should lead visitors to conclude that your product is the best solution in most cases. Make sure that you help them understand the product category and show them a few choices (retailer) or show them why yours is best (manufacturer).

The Shop Stage

Not all visitors start at the *Learn* step. Some know what kind of product they want to buy, but need to shop for the particular brand or model. They are still entering informational keywords, but they are more specific now than in the *Learn* step. Learners search for *computer*, whereas shoppers look for *laptop computer*.

As you design your site, you must ensure that you have product category pages, not just model pages. For example, create a page that lists of all of your DVD players with an explanation of how they work. That way, you capture search traffic for shoppers entering the *dvd players* keyword, not just buyers using keywords that name particular brands or models. Use the 3-second rule from direct marketing: Can the customer tell what you are selling in 3 seconds? If not, simplify your copy.

The Buy Stage

The most valuable searchers to capture for your site are the ones who are ready to buy. Even if they did not visit your site to learn or shop, if you can capture them here, you can make the sale.

When searchers want to buy your product, they enter specific transactional keywords, such as *sony dvd player* or *dell inspiron 1545 battery*. Your content is probably already using the right words for these keywords to ensure being found, but you must also add messaging that answers any lingering questions to encourage the visitor to put the product in a cart and check out. Digital marketing strategist Dr. Augustine Fou refers to this as a "missing-link analysis." What is missing from your marketing that is stopping the conversion?

You might be looking at these keyword examples and asking, "Okay, but suppose that I am not working for Sony or Dell? How can I capture those searchers with my content?" You probably can't; you need to yield to the companies who actually sell those brands. This underlines the necessity of winning searches in the earlier stages. If you haven't persuaded searchers to name your brand in their keywords by the time they get to the *Buy* stage, you probably aren't getting the sale.

The Use Stage

For some products, especially technology products, the majority of website visitors need help while trying to use the product. A few years ago, customers needing help were more likely to come directly to your site to solve their problem, but more and more they now head to Google to search for their answer.

CASE STUDY: USING THE BUYER'S JOURNEY IN YOUR SEARCH STRATEGY

You might look at the Buyer's Journey and say to yourself, "If only things really went this smoothly!" and you are correct; all visitors do not sail through the steps as easily as it appears in the diagram. Real life is rarely as neat and clean as shown here, but a simple model helps you analyze what is really going on. Let's look at a realistic example of how the Buyer's Journey might work with your search marketing strategy.

Suppose that you are the marketing manager for Intuit's TurboTax, the software so many Americans use to file their federal income taxes. Some prospective customers are clearly looking for a solution to the annual problem of filing their taxes, and might enter the keyword *income tax return*. These searchers are in the learn activity. Now you can imagine the search engine providing several different types of answers to that keyword:

- **How-to information:** Advice from the government or other well-respected sources on how to fill out tax forms, usually in layman's terms.

- **Tax services:** Descriptions of accounting firms and tax-preparation firms, such as H&R Block, that will fill out your tax return for a fee.

- **Tax software:** Explanations and video demonstrations of computer programs that complete a tax return using a personal computer.

- **Comparisons:** Articles that contrast doing it yourself, using accounting and tax-preparation firms, and using tax software to determine the best way to complete tax returns.

You want these searchers to find your site for several reasons:

- If you can solve their problems, they will value your company more highly, which might lead to future business. It might seem illogical, but studies show that customers report higher satisfaction with companies that promptly correct problems than they report for companies that do not cause any problems in the first place!

- People who solve their own problems on your website will not contact you by phone. You save the phone costs and the costs of your personnel interacting with your customers.

- If you can get customers to find *your* content for their problems, rather than your competitor's, you might generate revenue from a service call, or from upgrading a warranty, or by selling an add-on product, or by convincing them to scrap what they have and to buy a new one that works better.

Appreciate the power of Buyer's Journey for your marketing. What other marketing allows you to prepare messages based on where the customer is within the *Buying* cycle? Think of how

As the TurboTax marketing manager, you have undoubtedly placed pages on your site and created social media that explain the workings of computer tax software. Even better, you could create content that compares the advantages of tax preparation software versus having it prepared by professionals (or doing it by hand). Both types of content will help you get high rankings in search engines for the keyword *income tax return*.

But some searchers will be further along in the *Buying* process. They might be searching for *computer tax software* because they have already decided how to solve their problem and are shopping for exactly the right solution. This particular kind of informational keyword is looking for the product category, and is typical of those in the *Shop* activity. The content you created on tax software to satisfy informational searchers will also serve you well here. In addition, content devoted to features of TurboTax might also rank well.

Other searchers know exactly what they are looking for. They are in the *Buy* activity. In this case, they want to buy a copy of TurboTax. For these keywords, you, the marketing manager, must create pages that clearly show how to buy the product and perhaps display some special offers that might help people decide now. Because the customer has already decided on your product, your search marketing here is focused on selling directly from your site rather than having a retailer or other distributor make the sale.

Other searchers need help with your product. They are in the *Use* activity, which is a common reason to visit a software manufacturer's website. Technical support issues prompt keywords such as *turbotax printing error*. And do not forget Intuit's favorite *Use* keyword: *turbo tax upgrade* (which for U.S. tax software comes along every March). That is the kind of keyword that can close the loop in the Buyer's Journey and return the customer to the *Learn* activity.

much more persuasive your marketing can be when you let searchers tell you what kind of information they are looking for, and you immediately supply it.

How to Work the Searcher

Very few of us are interested in learning more about our customers just to be knowledgeable. We pursue these insights so that we can use them to our advantage. If knowledge is power, then knowledge of our customer gives us powerful weapons of persuasion that produce bottom-line results our competitors cannot match. So, now that we've learned about how searchers work, we now want to work the searcher.

But it isn't that easy.

Without doing a lot of thinking about what searchers are looking for, and what kind of content will satisfy them, you are likely to make big mistakes, with some of the biggest ones revolving around the keyword you choose to target in your search marketing program. As we explore in Chapter 6, your keywords are your primary market segments in search marketing and the ones you choose to go after can mean the difference between success and failure.

You will hear a lot of theories about the right keywords to choose, so you will need to make up your own mind. You will often hear variations on one of these two approaches:

- **The "hot" keyword approach:** You have to target very popular search terms if you want to drive substantial traffic to your site.

- **The "cold" keyword approach:** You need to target less-popular keywords that have little competition if you want to get a high ranking.

But the world just is not that simple. Either one of these approaches can be right in your situation, or they might both be wrong. The key is that you understand your situation and develop a philosophy that matches your content.

Goldilocks has a lot to teach us about keyword planning. When she tasted the porridge, she avoided the bowl that was too hot, and the one that was too cold, and settled on the one that was "just right." So it is with your choice of keywords. The keywords you select cannot be too hot or too cold for your website; they need to be "just right." So let's look at the Goldilocks approach to choosing keywords.

Don't Pick Keywords That Are "Too Hot"

Popular keywords are very seductive. We cannot help but have visions of instant success, with searchers streaming onto our website overnight. But, as is usually the case in life, it is not as easy as it seems. Let's look at why some words can be too hot for you.

Overheated Subjects

Be honest. Is your organization a household name? Do people naturally associate your products with its generic name? For example, anyone interested in a lawn mower would naturally think of

Snapper. They might also think of other companies, such as John Deere or Toro. Is that the kind of website you have? Your company is very identified with a product?

If so, you can think *big*. You *should* target the word *lawn mower*, if you work for Snapper. You make every kind of lawn mower there is: electric mowers, gasoline mowers, riding mowers, mowers that mulch, and probably some that do the fandango. You make every flavor of lawn mower known to man, so why not go after that big broad keyword?

But what if you don't work for Snapper? What if you work for a small lawn mower manufacturer? Yes, you have many good, loyal customers. And lots of folks think your lawn mowers are even better than Snapper lawn mowers. And they are cheaper, to boot. It is tempting to target that keyword *lawn mower* too, isn't it? No need to check how popular that word is; you know it has a zillion searches every day. If you only get some of those searchers, that's okay. You want to fish where the fish are, right?

Well, no. The keyword *lawn mower* is too hot for you, and you *will* get burned. You see, you do not make *every* kind of lawn mower. You make only *riding* lawn mowers. Uh, *hybrid* riding lawn mowers, as a matter of fact. You are the leader in the emerging hybrid engine lawn mower market. You save gas, you go green as you manicure the cutting green, and make people feel all warm and fuzzy every time they plug in your battery to recharge.

But of all the people searching for the keyword *lawn mower*, only a few are looking for hybrid riding lawn mowers. *Those* are your potential customers—no one else. Now, that does not mean that the only keyword that you should buy is *hybrid riding lawn mowers*. It probably makes sense to buy *hybrid lawn mower* and *hybrid riding mower* and others, too. But if you purchase paid placement for *lawn mower,* you probably are looking at a bad outcome:

- **You get very few clicks:** This is what will happen if your paid placement ad for the keyword *lawn mower* is titled *"Breakthrough Hybrid Riding Mower."* Most people searching with the keyword *lawn mower* are not looking for a hybrid riding mower, so they will not click. If your clickthrough rate is low enough, eventually the paid placement service will drop your ad completely. So, you will rack up next to no sales on your paid placement campaign.

- **You get many clicks, but low conversion:** This is your probable outcome if your *lawn mower* ad says, *"Low-priced mowers with free delivery."* Now, you might have low-priced mowers and you might offer free delivery, but you only sell hybrid riding lawn mowers, so many of the folks will click your ad, see you do not have what they want, and abandon your site. After you are charged for the click, of course. Charged handsomely, in fact, because that keyword *lawn mower* is very expensive (*because* it gets a zillion searches a day). So, you will rapidly run through your paid placement budget, racking up next to no sales.

But, you might ask, "Suppose I do not use paid placement? I can go after organic search." Think again. There are millions of pages with the keyword *lawn mower* on them, so why should Google show yours on page one? There are many other companies that sell a wider range of lawn mowers and are more well known and well respected. However, you might have a great chance at getting a high ranking for *hybrid mower* or *hybrid riding mower*, or especially *hybrid riding lawn mower*.

And think about it. If you do optimize your page for those more attainable phrases, the keyword *lawn mower* will be all over the page anyway. So if by some chance you do have a shot at ranking well for *lawn mower*, you will. But it is more realistic to pick terms that are just right for your website, rather than too hot, because it will cost you just as much to perform organic optimization for the wrong keyword as for the right one. You just will not drive any qualified traffic with the wrong one. Just as with paid placement, most people searching for *lawn mower* are not looking for you, anyway. So what is the point of ranking well for *lawn mower* when it will not get you many conversions?

Before you go overboard in the other direction, however, there are times when a very broad keyword *is* "just right" for you. Consider whether Apple Computer should target the keyword *computer*. At first blush, you might reject *computer* as being too broad a term. After all, most people looking for a computer want a computer that runs the Windows operating system, and many want servers, which Apple is not well known for. But do people that have specific ideas about what they want (such as a Windows server) actually search for the word *computer*? Probably not. It might be that the novices who know they want to buy "a computer" are exactly the kind of people who might buy an Apple.

The most important thing to learn is not to be seduced by the high volumes for the most popular keywords. Go after the keywords that are the closest match for your site, even if they are not the most popular ones. If it turns out that those popular keywords are "just right" for your site, by all means target them. But don't overreach. Don't go after words that are too hot for you, because you will not get the conversions you want anyway.

Overheated Meanings

There is no best-selling book titled *Lincoln: The Man, the Car, the Tunnel*, because even though a Lincoln Continental and the Hudson River crossing share the name of America's sixteenth president, they do not have much else in common. All of which is a roundabout way of saying that words with multiple meanings are another cause of "too hot" keywords. In addition, slightly different words sometimes have very different meanings.

Overheated meanings occur in a number of common situations:

- **Multiple audiences:** The keyword *security* means one thing to an antivirus software maker and something else to a home burglar alarm installer. As with the *lawn mower* example, sometimes you can add qualifying words (*computer security* or *home security*) to bring down the temperature and make a keyword "just right." At other times, you might decide to just avoid that keyword entirely.

- **Related meanings:** If you sell auto insurance, the difference in your conversion rate between searchers for *car* and *car insurance* is substantial. Stay away from a broad term when a more specific one will do. Yes, some people buying cars are in the market for car insurance, too, but you are panning an awful lot of water for a few gold nuggets.

- **Multiple intents:** Although it is true that the word *hotel* and the word *lodging* mean the same thing, a hotel operator will find much higher conversion rates for the word *hotel* itself. Searchers for *lodging* are often looking for alternatives to hotels, such as bed-and-breakfast inns, which is why they used the less-common word. Jobseekers look for the word *job*, whereas employers search for help with *recruitment*—both might search for *recruiters* (which might be too hot a word).

- **Singular/plural meaning changes:** Search engines typically look for both the singular and plural forms of a word, but that can sometimes cause overheating. The word *sale* has a different meaning than *sales*—*appliance sale* might be searched for by a consumer, whereas a job-seeking salesman might want *appliance sales*—and that difference can overheat the keyword. *Cosmetic* and *cosmetics* are two more words that seem seductively similar in meaning, but in fact are not. Think carefully about every keyword you target to see whether changing from singular to plural changes the meaning.

- **Acronyms:** It is quite common for the same acronym to mean several things, causing the keyword to be overheated. Does *CD* mean a disc or a certificate of deposit? Does *SCM* stand for supply chain management or software configuration management or source control management? Actually, it stands for all three, which is why it is hard to get qualified traffic when your content matches just one meaning of the word.

Most search marketers follow "the more, the merrier" theory. If *women's fashion boots* is a good keyword, *boots* will be even better! There are so many more people searching for *boots* that it is sure to drive a lot more traffic. The problem is that if you sell only women's fashion boots, that extra traffic will not produce many more conversions. Instead of looking for hotter and hotter keywords, look for "just right" keywords.

Don't Pick Keywords That Are "Too Cold"

Often, after being burned by a flaming keyword or two, people go in the opposite direction, afraid to go after any keyword that has too much competition. Even some search marketing consultants would rather go after "cold" keywords so that they can show you how quickly they get high rankings in search. Goldilocks will tell you that this is not the right way either.

Sometimes cold keywords—ones with few or no searchers looking for them—are chosen by accident. An Italian tour operator targets *milano tours*, but misses all the American tourists who use the anglicized spelling *milan*. Or the shortest word forms of keywords are chosen, such as *manage your finances* instead of *personal financial management*; search engines usually find the shorter forms when you target the longer forms (but not always vice versa).

One particularly troublesome cause of accidental cold keywords is translating campaigns into other languages. If you take a search marketing campaign you have run in your native language (say, English) and merely translate those keywords to French, for example, you are likely to have chosen numerous cold keywords. Just as searcher intent differs in English for many terms with similar meanings, you might have chosen an accurate, but unpopular, French translation for your English keyword. At times, this approach yields even worse results. The same Spanish word in two different Latin American countries could be perfectly normal in one and an obscenity in another! Take the time to pick "just right" keywords for your site in every local market.

Another accidental chill can occur when you assume that different audiences for the same product search the same way. Tor Crockatt of Microsoft loves to show examples of how searchers performing similar tasks do different things. Tor describes a major electronics manufacturer whose Scandinavian customers did research online but whose German customers did little research online (although they did buy the product online). If the manufacturer had assumed that buying habits were the same in Germany as in Scandinavia, many cold keywords would have been targeted around the learn stage of the Buyer's Journey. Similarly, IBM has found that consumers tend to *shop*, whereas business people tend to *procure* or *purchase*, even when they are buying the same product. If you expect that every market segment will approach searching for your site the same way, you are likely to land in some cold spots.

Some choices of cold keywords are actually done on purpose, however, by intelligent people who really should know better. Some software tools that purport to help you target search keywords produce a mathematical representation of the popularity of a keyword (the number of searches containing it) compared to its popularity in usage (the number of web pages it is found on). As a tool, there is nothing wrong with this. In fact, it can be quite useful in helping you avoid "too hot" keywords that are not right for your site. But it can be abused.

Some might use this kind of analysis to dissuade you from going after any keyword with even a modicum of competition. That's misguided. Although it is true that the more pages a word appears on, the more difficult it is to get a top ten search result, the simple fact is that *someone's* content is ranking #1 for that word. How did they do it? Whatever they did is what you have to do just a bit better if you want to rank #1.

Just as it was silly for our hybrid riding lawn mower manufacturer to want to rank #1 for the hot *lawn mower* keyword, it is equally silly to shy away from the keyword *hybrid riding lawn mower* just because other pages might contain those words. If you have found a set of keywords that perfectly describe your content, it's time to fight for that ranking, not slink away to some backwater set of keywords that no one is looking for (just so you can say you have a #1 ranking). Remember, it costs just as much to optimize an organic page for a cold keyword as for a "just right" one, so spend your efforts on the ones that will pay off.

Before we move on to "just right" keywords, you should know that paid placement differs from organic search when it comes to cold keywords. In the case of paid placement programs, there might be little downside to targeting cold keywords. Even if very few searchers enter the keywords each month, if you are getting conversions at low per-click rates, there is no reason to stop (unless it is costing you too much time to manage). In general, however, stick to the "just right" words; they will have the best payoff.

Pick Keywords That Are "Just Right"

So why do "just right" keywords work? It is not that hard to understand, really. Search engines actually do a very good job of finding the right pages for each keyword, and people do a good job of clicking the right pages from what they see. What that means is that if you target keywords that are truly relevant to your content, and you follow through on the techniques in the rest of this book, you will likely improve your search traffic with highly qualified visitors. In short, sticking to keywords that truly reflect your site will make it easier for you to attract search rankings and will pay off in more conversions than if you do anything else.

Conversely, if you find that you are seeing the symptoms of targeting "too hot" keywords (low paid clickthrough, dropping organic search referrals, or low conversion rates), you have a choice. You can move back to "just right" keywords, or you can change your website. If you want to compete for the *lawn mower* keyword, what content can you put up to attract all lawn mower buyers? Affiliate links for products you do not sell? Comparison information that shows why every lawn mower buyer should buy yours? It is not easy, but there are times when you can expand your content so that it really is a good match for a broad keyword.

For those of you who are less ambitious (and more realistic), however, there is good news. The days of searchers entering overly broad keywords in large numbers are coming to an end. Although there are still cases where a single search word is very descriptive of what the searcher wants (*ipad*), there are many more situations in which only multiple words will truly pinpoint the information desired, and searchers are growing in sophistication. A recent study showed that over 60% of searches contain two or more words, with 30% using three words or more. What this means is that more and more searchers are entering long keyword phrases that much more accurately pinpoint the pages they want. More searchers are using "just right" keywords, so you can feel comfortable targeting them.

But, for search marketers, your idea of what makes a keyword "just right" goes beyond what searchers want; you need to know which keywords convert searchers to buyers, so that those keywords are "just right" for you, too. You can use a tool available at our website (SEMincBook.com/keyword-conversion-calculator) or use Back Azimuth Consulting's Keyword Management tool to help identify your "just right" keywords.

Summary

Understanding the "need behind the keyword" can provide a significant advantage to search marketers. You use this knowledge to deliver the best possible content to searchers at the very time they need it.

This chapter covered the various types of searchers and how they approach their keywords. You learned how they view search engine results and how they decide which result to click, all of which is summarized in Exhibit 2-10. You also learned how web visitors follow a behavior model that describes what they do on your site—and whether they complete that action.

Searcher Type	Keyword	What Searchers Want	Why Pages Rank Highly	Why Searchers Click
Navigational	amazon	Amazon home page	Keywords in title and URL	Keywords in title and snippet
Informational	low carb diet from several sites and brands	Deep information with keywords	Text-rich pages	As above, with trusted sources
Transactional	atkins diet	Buy page from bookseller	Keywords in title and text	As above, with a great offer

Exhibit 2-10   Understanding searchers. Different types of searchers use different keywords to do the same thing. In this case, each searcher wants a book on weight loss.

Now that you understand what's going on inside the mind of the searcher, it's time to peek inside the search engines themselves. Chapter 3, "How Search Works," examines what a search engine actually does. As you learn how search engines work, you will be better prepared to take advantage of the huge search marketing opportunity.

How Search Works

So far, we've covered the basics of search marketing and taken a tour into the mind of the searcher. But by now, you might be wondering, isn't there a lot of technical details we need to know about search?

Well, yes. But we've got the whole book to give you all the gory details. For now, we want to give you just what you need to get moving in the right direction. You can think of this as the "Bert and Ernie" version of the explanation. And it comes in two parts:

- **How search engines work:** Yes, here is your first foray into the moving parts when you type words into that search box. What is happening in that split second between search keyword and search results? And why does it work that way? We'll sprinkle in a few tips here and there so you'll know why you care about all of these details, but we'll hold most of the advice for the next section.

- **How to work the search engines:** This is what you really need to know, because who wants to learn all this stuff just to be smarter? What you want to know is, "What do I do about it?" We'll help you understand what your philosophy should be about approaching search marketing, based on how those search engines work.

So, what are you waiting for? Time's a-wasting. Let's pull open the hood on those search engines and see what's inside.

How Search Engines Work

You type a few words into Google, and you get a screen full of highly relevant results in seconds. But how did it happen? How does a search engine find the right content? You have learned that search engines return both organic and paid results, but how do search engines decide what to show on those results screens? In this chapter, we examine exactly how a search engine works, showing both what happens at the time a searcher enters words to be searched and what happened beforehand to prepare the search engine for that search. We spend most of our time on the more complicated organic search, but we explain how paid results are chosen, too.

The first thing you need to know about search engines is how much work they have done long before you search for something. Although it looks like Google is scanning each and every web page and social media on the interwebz at the moment you search for something, it is not really that magical. It turns out a lot of preparation led up to that "magical" moment when the words are searched—organic search experts call that preparation indexing. Indexing is the process that creates an organic search index, a special database that holds a list of all the words on all the pages on the web. Paid search ads are similarly held in an ad database, a collection of all of the advertisements that paid search marketers have written for the search engines to display. Each search engine has its own search index and its own ad database; they don't share.

Later in this chapter, we explain how the organic indexing process work (and the simpler process of collecting paid search ads). For now, just be aware that a lot of the magic of search occurs long before anyone enters anything to search.

Without yet knowing how the search index and ad database works, you can still learn how the search engine uses them when search keywords are entered. Google and other search engines do four major things, as shown in Exhibit 3-1:

- **Analyze the search keyword:** Search engines must analyze the words the searcher typed in to determine what the searcher is looking for.
- **Choose matches to the keyword:** Search engines identify the content that is most likely "the right stuff" for the search keyword.
- **Rank the matches:** Most searches return many matches, so search engines must sort the matches so that the best ones are at the top.
- **Display the search results:** After the best matches are chosen, search engines display them on the screen for the searcher to see.

Analyzing the Search Keyword

The search keyword is the technical name for what searchers type into a search engine to get search results. When someone enters *glaucoma treatments* into Google (or any other search engine), that is the search keyword. Experts usually describe each word in the search keyword as a **search term**. (In this example, the words *glaucoma* and *treatments* are each search terms.) The search engine goes through several basic steps to find the pages that match, starting with analyzing the keyword.

As soon as the searcher types his keyword and presses the Enter key, the search engine goes to work analyzing the keyword—examining each word (search term) in the keyword and deciding how to find the best content that matches. Search engines do not all analyze keywords the same way, but most of them share some basic analysis techniques. That is what we look at in this section.

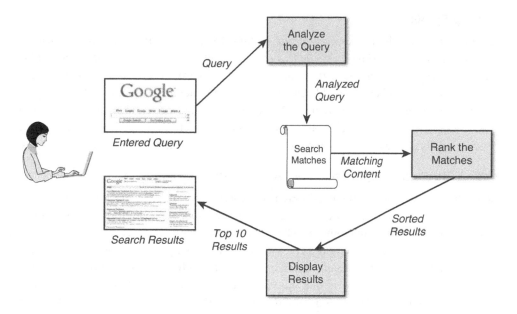

Exhibit 3-1 How search engines work. Every search engine analyzes search keywords, locates the matching content, ranks the matches, and displays them as search results—both paid and organic results.

Finding Word Variants

In English and other Western languages, the same word can be written in different cases (*Glaucoma Treatments* rather than *glaucoma treatments*). Most search engines pay no attention to case, which is usually what the searcher wants, because a word that starts a sentence (for example) is just as good a match as one that does not. Occasionally, searchers might want a keyword for *the White House* to match only occurrences in the proper case (and not match a sentence such as "He lives in the white house on Fourth Street"), but search engines generally find better matches by ignoring case.

Moreover, simply matching the exact words in the search keyword does not always locate what searchers are looking for. For Western languages, most words have multiple forms—singular and plural nouns, verb conjugations—that mean basically the same thing. Many of these words look similar to each other: *house* and *houses* mean essentially the same concept in a sentence, and they look basically alike. But others that are equally related, such as *mouse* and *mice*, look a bit different. Verbs such as *is* and *were* look completely different but mean about the same thing. Most search engines know that these **word variants** should be searched for whenever one is used in a keyword, so a search for *mouse* looks for *mice*, too.

Correcting Spelling

We have all seen search engines correct our spelling for us, sometimes just going ahead and changing our entry into a correctly spelled word, but sometimes asking us some variant of "Did you mean...?" and prompting us with a correctly spelled word. Although a wonderful feature for searchers, search marketers should beware of clever product names that look like misspelled words; they might get corrected to real words, making it harder for searchers to find your product. And if customers cannot spell your product names correctly, the spelling-correction algorithms will not always help, so choosing names people can spell easily will work in your favor.

Detecting Phrases, Antiphrases, and Stop Words

A **phrase** means something slightly different in search parlance than in its normal use. You might know that most web search engines allow searchers to enclose multiple words in double quotation marks when they should be searched together, as though they are a single word. These enclosed words are what search engines call a phrase. Phrase searches look for the words exactly as they are in the keyword, in the same order, and prove useful for finding specific information.

What you might not know is that modern search engines analyze keywords to look for phrases even when the searcher does not use quotation marks. Search engines can identify words that occur frequently together and give preference to pages that use the words together.

Similarly, many searchers enter extraneous words that really are not what they are looking for, as in this keyword: *What is the treatment for glaucoma?* You can imagine that *What is the* does not help find the proper pages and might even throw the search engine off by finding pages that contain *what*, *is*, and *the*. These search terms are called **antiphrases** and are ignored (or at least treated as less important) in keywords by most search engines.

This is important to search marketers because you might have a brand name (such as *Where's Waldo?*) that looks more like a searcher's question rather than the actual keyword. Search engines use other techniques to recognize popular examples such as *Where's Waldo*, but if your brand name is not well known, the search engines might not handle it well. If you can avoid cutesy names that will confuse search engines, you will be better off.

Google is trying to improve the approach to antiphrases by making its keyword analysis more conversational. Some believe that this approach is important for mobile searching—where searchers are more likely to be speaking their search requests into a phone than to be pecking them out on tiny on-screen keyboards. Google actually tries to understand what the searcher is looking for across multiple searches, such as: *Which pizzerias have whole-wheat pizzas?* followed by *Which one is the closest?* and *What is its address?* In these searches, other search engines might have ignored the word *its* or treated *one* and *closest* as literal words to look for in the content. Google has moved beyond ignoring antiphrases to attempting to understand them, but other search engines haven't followed suit as of this writing. Nevertheless, Google might still misinterpret your cutesy brand name if it contains antiphrases—even with this interesting new conversational approach.

Finally, some words are just more important than others. Extremely common words (such as *a* or *the*) are usually called **stop words** because in the old days search engines would not ever look for them. Modern search engines know to pay attention to stop words at times, such as when you are searching for the rock group *The Who*. As a search marketer, if you can avoid using stop words as critically important words in your brands and your trademarked names, that will make your names more easily searched.

If you work for clothing retailer The Limited, however, you probably do not have the luxury of changing the name! Unfortunately, you might find it is harder to get high search rankings because some search engines insist on looking simply for *limited* even when searchers enter *the limited*. Now, The Limited is a well-known company, so when searchers enter *the limited*, they will still probably find the right page. If your small business is called The Company, however, you might not be so lucky.

Examining Word Order

Some search engines consider word order when they search, so the results differ depending on whether the search is for *Little Joe* versus *Joe Little*. These engines try to find pages in which the words occur in the same order as they do in the keyword.

Again, this is a boon for searchers, but not always for search marketers. If your product has the catchy name of Enterprise Management Storage System, do not be surprised if some customers remember it as Enterprise Storage Management System or Storage Management Enterprise System. To the extent that your names are memorable in the correct order, that will aid searchability.

Processing Search Operators

A few savvy searchers know how to use the plus and minus operators in their keywords, such as *big brother –tv* to find the Big Brother charitable organization rather than the TV show of the same name. Similarly, searchers can demand that a term be included in the results, as in *+the white house* to avoid sentences that talk about a white house (and ignore *the* as a stop word).

As search engines get smarter, it is less and less important for searchers to use these operators, but search marketers need to know them. If you have a choice, you want to avoid using brand and trademarked names that require these operators to produce good results.

Identifying Searcher Intent

Perhaps the most interesting form of analysis that search engines perform on keywords pertains to searcher intent. As you saw in Chapter 2, "How Searchers Work," different search keywords imply a vast array of possibly relevant content. So, one of the most important decisions that a search engine makes during this keyword analysis phase is exactly what kinds of results is the searcher looking for? In Chapter 1, "How Search Marketing Works," you learned that there are many different kinds of search results that might be appropriate for any particular keyword.

If you have an idea of some keywords that might be important to your search marketing program, try entering them into Google and Bing, taking note of the kinds of search results that appear. Do you see web pages? Blog posts? Videos? Photos? Local maps? Notice that different keywords bring back different mixtures of results. For your content to appear, you need to have the *type* of content that is being returned for your targeted keywords. If Google thinks people want to see videos and images for a particular keyword, spending years optimizing your web page is likely a waste of time.

Choosing Matches to the Keyword

After the keyword has been analyzed, the search engine must decide which results to present. With so many possibilities, how does the search engine find matches so quickly? The secret is in the **filters**, software operations that rapidly remove the content that should not be shown. For example, a searcher's preferred language can be used as a filter, so that search results written in other languages are excluded.

Filters decide which content is in the list or out of the list—if your content meets the filtering criteria, it will be in the list somewhere. Pages that are not included by the filters for a keyword do not appear in the results. We'll first look at filters that apply to *both* organic and paid search, and then follow up with the ones specific to each kind of search. Remember, filtering just decides which content items are *in* the list. Later, we'll talk about how the search engine performs **ranking**, which decides how high in the list each content item is shown.

Common Search Filters

Several important filters can apply to both the organic and paid search results:

- **Language filters:** When a searcher enters a keyword into Google Japan, only content written in Japanese will be shown in the search results. In some countries, such as Japan and China, the vast majority of searchers want their results limited to their native languages; in other places, however, such as Sweden, searches can be conducted in Swedish or English, as shown in Exhibit 3-2. For paid search, language filtering is simple, because you, the search marketer, tell the search engine the language of your ad. For organic search, the search engine must detect the language of the content. Language identification is simple for some kinds of content—for YouTube, the person who uploads the video specifies the language. For other kinds of content, including web pages, search engines analyze the text to identify the language—usually getting it right. To be absolutely sure the search engines identify the content with the correct language, Google and Bing allow you to specify your content's language in their Webmaster Tools interfaces. For more on language identification, see our site (SEMincBook.com/language-detection).

- **Country filters:** Often, searchers do not want to limit results to a language—they want all results within a particular country. This is particularly true of transactional searchers in the *Buy* stage of the Buyer's Journey. They want to buy from a vendor in their country that uses their currency and will not charge a king's ransom to ship the item. Limiting by language does not do that. German pages exist in Germany, Austria, and Switzerland; French content in France and Canada; Spanish pages in Latin America as well as Spain—you get the idea—and English content all over the place. So, most search engines apply filters by country or by region. Most local searches have a default filter, or allow selection between two or three filters on the search page, specifying a particular country, region, or language. Specifying the country for your paid search ad does the trick once again, but organic search is tougher. Search engines use the country domain to place most sites in their proper country (.de for Germany, for example). But many multinational sites are hosted globally under a .com domain, so you can again use Webmaster Tools for each search engine to alert them as to the proper countries for your content. You can get more details at our site (SEMincBook.com/country-detection).

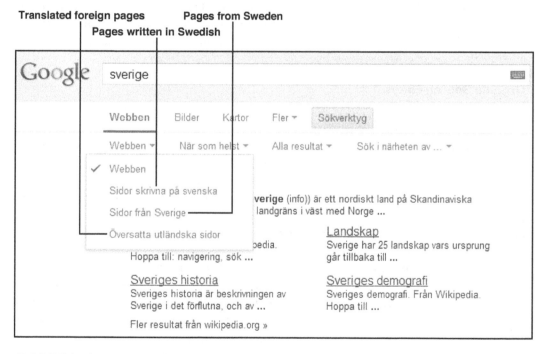

Exhibit 3-2 Language and country filtering in Google. Searchers can choose to limit results to their local language or their country.

- **Adult content filters:** The so-called adult content filter suppresses pornographic or otherwise sensitive material from the results. The issue for search marketers, as you might expect, is how accurate the filter is. In the past, news reports have trumpeted breast cancer sites (for example) suppressed by such filters, but modern search engines generally do a good job on these filters because of their strong text-analysis capabilities. Most search engines, by default, filter out just the most egregious scatological and sexual content, while leaving in explicit scientific and informational content. A strict setting can be chosen by searchers as their preference; if so, setting the preference just once then employs the strict filter forever. Search marketers whose site might contain sensitive material might want to monitor their page rankings so that they are not unfairly filtered, and might want to police word usage on their sites to avoid being filtered. Pay special attention to message boards on your site frequented by your visitors—if your visitors use inappropriate language in their posts, your site might be snagged by this filter. Paid search ads are regularly reviewed and approved by the search engines, and at the same time classified as to whether they should be filtered for adult content. You can get more details at our site (SEMincBook.com/adult-content).

 If your search marketing program operates in multiple languages, multiple countries, or might contain sensitive content, you might want to follow the links above to get more details on how these filters work. For most search marketers, you can move ahead to understand filters that are specific to organic and paid search results.

Organic Search Filters

An organic search engine uses its search index to locate the matching pages. Basically, the keyword analysis we discussed earlier determines which words to look up—not just the words that were typed as the keyword, but any word variants (*mouse* and *mice*)—and which words to ignore (stop words and antiphrases). Following this analysis, the search engine goes to work looking up each word in the keyword to see which pages contain the word.

The search index can be thought of as an alphabetic list of every word that occurs on every page of the web (as shown in Exhibit 3-3). The index contains a list of every web page and social media item that contains each word. So, when you look up the word *glaucoma*, you get a list of every piece of content that contains that word.

That is the simplest case. It is more complicated when searchers enter more complex keywords. If the searcher were looking for *glaucoma treatment*, the engine would look up every piece of content that contains *each* word, giving it a list of content items that contains the word *glaucoma* and a list that contains the word *treatment*. Most search engines, faced with this decision, decide to show just the items that contain both words. So they look through the two lists and find which items are listed on both.

Some engines have more sophisticated rules about what they show for multiple-word keywords. Consider a keyword such as *glaucoma eye treatment*. Because the word *eye* is so much more common than the other words, some search engines might show some pages that contain the words *glaucoma* and *treatment* even if they do not happen to contain the word *eye*.

For each word entered by a searcher, the search engine finds that word in the keyword table and looks up the documents that it is found within.

Keyword Table

Keyword	Document Numbers Containing Keyword
glaucodot	43278, 652389, 722227, 7234532, 8231234...
glaucoma	*1345*, 46891, 233343, 1827365, 9273524...
glaucomotous	2343, 261562, 2563516, 2635265, 4536524...

Document Table

Document Number	URL	Title	Description
1344	www.reliableauto.com/about	Reliable Auto – The one to trust for your next pre-owned car	For more than 50 years, Reliable Auto has been the leading car dealer in the central valley...
1345	www.glaucoma.org	Glaucoma Research Foundation	The Glaucoma Research Foundation is a national non-profit organization dedicated to conquering...
1346	www.cameras.com/us/sale.html	50% Off All 5 Mega Pixel Cameras	Our "Don't Settle For Less" sales event is your best reason yet to upgrade to five mega pixel quality...

Exhibit 3-3 How content items are retrieved from the index. Organic search engines check an index for the list of content that contains each word within the search keyword.

When you start adding word variants (*eye* and *eyes*, or *treatment* and *treatments*), you can see that there might be many lists of content items that the search engine must look through quickly to determine the final list to display.

Paid Search Filters

Paid search results are not retrieved from a search index, the way organic matches are, but the search engine does consult a database that stores all the ads that advertisers have submitted. Each advertiser selects the keywords that should match its listing, and submits a bid amount. That amount is the maximum fee charged to the advertiser each time the ad is clicked by a searcher.

The search engine uses the keyword analysis to decide which keywords should be searched for (just as with organic search) and looks up those keywords in the database. Each listing associated with the keyword terms is retrieved from the database.

Although the process sounds similar to organic search, in practice it is far simpler. The advertisers typically control exactly which keywords should match their ads, so far less analysis is required to find synonyms, for example. Moreover, rather than sifting through billions of pages, there are far fewer advertisements to pick from. In short, paid search results are chosen much the same way that organic results are—the keyword is analyzed, and the results that match the words in the keyword are selected. For paid search, however, there is typically a lot less work for the search engine to do.

The most important filters exclusive to paid search are called **match types**. Most paid search engines offer three basic match types, along with some extensions that we'll discuss in Chapter 6, "Choose Your Target Market Segments":

- **Exact match:** This is the easiest match type to understand—your ad might be shown only when the exact keyword you specify is searched for, or it contains only very close variants. So, if your streaming video site shows an ad for the movie *A Star Is Born* using the movie's title as the exact match keyword, only when searchers type those exact words in order will your ad be shown. Your ad might also be shown for *Stars Are Born* or keywords that contain misspellings of your words or other close variants, such as singular/plural, verb tenses, or misspellings.

- **Phrase match:** Less restrictive than exact match, your ad might be shown when the exact words within your keyword in order are entered, but extra words can be entered, also. So, if someone enters *A Star Is Born Today*, your ad for *A Star Is Born* would be shown.

- **Broad match:** The loosest match type. Your ad might be shown when the words within your keyword are shown in any order, any variations and with extra words. So, if someone enters *Born Was a Star Yesterday*, your ad will be shown.

You've now finished your grand tour of search filters. Next, you'll learn what is behind a search engine's ranking algorithm.

Ranking the Matches

Merely displaying the list of all the content items that contain the search terms in the keyword is not much help when there are thousands or millions of search results. And with search marketing, that is almost always the case. So, one of the most important parts of a search engine is its **ranking algorithm**—the part of the search engine that decides which pages show up at the top of the results list.

A ranking algorithm is the mathematical formula a search engine uses to score content against the keyword to see which content items are the closest matches. But what goes into that formula? How can your content get consistently high scores for your targeted keywords? That depends on whether the algorithm is ranking content for organic search or ads for paid search. And it depends on the search engine's analysis of searcher intent, as we discussed earlier. To keep things simple, we'll constantly refer to *the* ranking algorithm, as if each search engine had just one. The truth is that search engines have dozens, if not hundreds, of ranking algorithms, and that a big part keyword analysis is figuring out which types of content to show and which ranking algorithms to use.

But let's keep it simple. **Ranking** is just another word for **sorting,** the act of collating results into a certain order. Product search engines typically use simple ranking algorithms that the searcher can choose. When the searcher is looking for a product to buy, the Product search engine might start by ordering the results by price (lowest to highest), but the searcher can decide to sort the list by other columns, such as availability (in stock, within one week, and so on), or any other features of the product.

Organic search engines require a much more sophisticated approach to ranking than product search engines. For some kinds of information, such as news stories, ranking results by the date of the information (newest first) might make sense, but most organic search results are ranked by relevance, the degree to which the pages match the subject of the keyword.

More and more, organic search engines differentiate themselves on how their **relevance ranking** algorithms work, but every search engine uses certain standard techniques. We look at several factors that go into ranking algorithms, but one of the most interesting parts of designing a search engine is the interplay between those factors. Each factor is an ingredient in the ranking soup, and some engines use more of one ingredient than another—one reason why different search engines show different results for the same keyword. Some place more value on one ranking factor than others do.

Because your goal as a search marketer is to get your pages to the top of the list, it is crucial that you understand why search engines put some pages at the top and others far down the list, where few searchers will ever see them. As we discuss these ranking factors, we constantly talk about tendencies, such as, "All else being equal, pages with more of the terms will rank higher than pages with fewer of the terms." But ranking algorithms are deliciously complicated and all else rarely equal. Suffice it to say that if you pay attention to each of the factors as you design your site, you will have the best chance at high rankings.

If your content is included by the filters for a particular keyword, the ranking algorithm takes over, looking at every web page, social media item, paid search ad, or any other content item containing that keyword. The algorithm decides how your content stacks up against the others for that keyword. There are no right or wrong answers from the search engine—the engine tries to find the highest-quality content matching the keyword. The ranking algorithm contains many factors, components that are scored for each piece of content. If your content scores the most points, according to the ranking algorithm's factors, it will get the #1 slot in the results. As you learn about ranking algorithms, keep in mind that the highest rankings mean nothing if your pages are excluded by the filters listed previously; strike out on a filter and your page is out of the results list no matter how closely it matches the keyword.

Both paid and organic search use ranking algorithms, but they don't share very much in common, so we'll look at them separately. The organic ranking algorithm is by far the most complicated, so we tackle that first.

For each keyword, search engines sort the search results by relevance to decide which content is shown at the top of the list. The better your content, and the closer it matches your keyword, the higher it will rank in the results. Because a ranking algorithm is such a closely guarded secret, no one knows exactly what factors each search engine uses, but we know there are hundreds. Clearly, not all factors are equally important, so we concentrate on the more important factors here. In addition, those factors are constantly changing, so you can learn the latest at our companion website (SEMincBook.com/ranking-factors).

Ranking factors come in two main varieties:

- **Content factors:** Content factors are a surrogate for the quality of the content. Organic search ranking algorithms rely heavily on components that have nothing to do with the keyword entered, such as the strength of links to web pages, social media activity, and many more. These factors boost content in the rankings for searches on any word that occurs in the text of that content.

- **Keyword factors:** As you might expect, the particular keyword the searcher enters weighs heavily. The number of occurrences of the words in the keyword, where they are found on a web page (title, body, and so on), and many other elements are weighed by the search engines when ranking results.

We'll tackle content factors first.

Ranking Organic Search Matches Based on Quality

Content factors are used by organic search engines to determine the quality of the content. Human beings can read or view content and immediately develop an opinion as to its intrinsic quality, but search engines have mere algorithms to rely on. Content factors are the quality detectors in the ranking algorithm.

Content factors can take into account anything the search engine knows about the content itself, the pages that link to a page, the number of views of a video, and many other components. What this means is that the content factor of any particular page or social media item is exactly the same for every keyword. A web page with strong content factors starts out with a high score for every word that is on that page. A video starts with a high score for every word in its associated text.

Every search engine uses content factors as a critical component in its ranking algorithm—Google's PageRank is the most famous example. When a searcher enters a broad keyword, such as the word *camera*, the search engine needs a way to decide which few pages or other content items, among the millions that contain the word *camera*, are the ones to rank at the top of the list.

The items with the most occurrences of *camera* are probably not what searchers want; they want the most definitive content. Only content factors can make that determination.

It might seem to you that locating keywords would suffice for good relevance ranking, but more is needed. These keyword-based techniques comprised state-of-the-art ranking algorithms before the web, but the sheer number of pages on the web has overwhelmed their effectiveness. Luckily, the web also made possible a new factor, called **link popularity** (sometimes called **link analysis**), which dramatically improves ranking when used in conjunction with these older techniques. Link popularity is the most important content factor for web pages, so we will cover it at length, but we'll touch on other content factors before we're through.

Link popularity is a fancy name for a simple concept: web pages that other pages link to are better pages than web pages that no one links to. It makes sense, doesn't it? The best pages on the web are linked to by lots of other pages, and bad pages are not. Now there are certainly perfectly good pages that are new that no one has discovered yet, but the more links there are to a page, the more it tends to be a high-quality page with up-to-date and valuable information. If it weren't, people would stop linking.

For this reason, link popularity has emerged as a major factor in results ranking, sometimes outweighing the other two factors previously discussed. So, other things being equal, pages with more links to them tend to rank higher than other pages. It is easiest to see why this is a good idea by looking at an example.

Consider a search for the word *glaucoma*—a one-word search keyword. It seems simple enough, but just imagine how difficult a task this is for the search engine. A million pages contain the word *glaucoma*. Why should we expect that the pages that have the most glaucoma occurrences or that contain *glaucoma* in the title are the best ones? There must be tens of thousands of pages with *glaucoma* in the title anyway. How does any search engine pick the top ten from such a long list?

Link popularity is the answer. The best pages for glaucoma are the ones that are the most respected sources of information. And the best surrogate a search engine can find for respect is how well each site is linked to the rest of the web. Now, this being a book about search engines, we can't leave it that simple, but that is the basic idea.

For a few reasons, the actual algorithms that search engines use are more complex than a simple count of the number of links. One reason is that all links are not equal. If you think about this, you will agree it is true. If you knew that one site about glaucoma was linked to by the American Medical Association's website, and another glaucoma site was linked to by someone's personal web page, which one would you trust more? Undoubtedly, it would be the AMA link. But how can a search engine tell the difference between those links?

It's simple, really. Every website on the Internet is given a calculation of its **authority**, or its intrinsic value, based on the links that come to it. So, as you might expect, the AMA site has high authority, because it has thousands of links coming in, and many of those links are themselves from highly respected sites. And each high-authority site, such as the AMA, conveys some of that authority to each site it links to. So sites that are linked to by high-authority sites have a little bit of that authority rub off, which they can then pass along to the sites *they* link to. It is complex to calculate, but every search engine uses this type of calculation to help rank its search results.

Google's algorithm, known as **PageRank**, is the most well known. Google calculates the PageRank of every page on the web as a number between one and ten. To continue with the previous example, if the AMA page that links to a glaucoma site has a PageRank of six, and the personal home page has a PageRank of one, the AMA page confers great authority to its link, whereas the other conveys almost none. Now if that personal home page turns out to be that of a well-known glaucoma researcher and other sites begin to link to that page, its PageRank might rise to three and thus confer more status on pages to which it links.

But links alone are not specific enough to yield good search rankings. A site might receive many inbound links from well-respected sites, but those links might be on different subjects from what is being searched for. Suppose the AMA linked to the glaucoma site because an AMA board member is on the board of the glaucoma organization, and the link was to that board member's biography? What at first seemed like a credible endorsement of glaucoma information now seems like quite a bit less than that.

To be sure about the relevance of the link to the searcher's keyword, search engines use **anchor text**, the words that appear as the name of the link on the page. Therefore, a link from the AMA site to the glaucoma site that is actually named *glaucoma* is much more pertinent than one that contains the name of the AMA board member. That is why the search engine uses the names of the links as part of the link popularity analysis, giving much higher consideration to links that contain search terms in the link names.

Link popularity is only one of the content factors, albeit the most important for web pages. Let's look at the other important content factors in a search ranking algorithm:

- **Social media activity:** While link popularity does a good job identifying high-quality web pages, other content requires a different approach. Videos, for example, are best ranked by the number of views. In addition, search engines have turned to social media activity as a content ranking factor even for web pages. Some unscrupulous search marketers have been faking links just to impress the search engines, so Google and friends are cross-checking their link popularity scores with social media activity, betting that quality content will score high in both.

- **Human ratings:** While both link popularity and social media activity use human activity to alert search engines to quality content, search engines actually ask people directly whether the search results are any good. Google and Bing (as well as Yandex and Baidu) have each handpicked a large panel of searchers who rate the quality of the search results—highly rated content gets bumped up in the rankings.

- **Freshness:** If your page has not changed in a long time, its rank might be reduced because search engines suspect its information is out-of-date. So if you are trying to rank for *digital camera reviews*, don't expect your year-old review to be there. But don't change the biography of your company's founder who has been dead for 30 years; change only what needs changing.

- **Page style:** Pages that are grammatically correct allow the search engine to better score relevance. Pages that are organized like a newspaper article (important words at the top, somewhat repeated throughout, and reinforced at the end) are sometimes said to have an advantage. In many cases, folks who use unethical spam techniques are flagged by these factors because their content is written in a stilted way to repeat keywords *ad nauseum*.

- **Site organization:** One of the best ways to strengthen your content factors is good web design. Work with information architects to make the site simple to navigate with a well-thought-out linking structure. Use meaningful words in your URLs, but do not take the spam route by stuffing in three or four keywords between hyphens. Use as simple a page layout and design as possible.

As mentioned previously, although it is easy for us to think about these factors as relevant to just one page on your site, search engines are more sophisticated than that. They look at links to your whole site, not just one page. They check for profanity on your whole site, even if most pages are "clean." If most of your pages are updated when needed, do not obsess about changing your "History of the Company" page every 2 months.

As you read the list, you might notice that you do not have a lot of control over some of these factors, and it is true, in general, that content factors are harder to influence than keyword factors. But you are not helpless. We'll explain what you can do to improve your content factors in Chapter 9, "Prove Your Content's Quality."

Content factors are constant across every keyword. A page with high-scoring content factors takes that score with it for every keyword. And although content factors are important, there must be something going on that is keyword related, or else the same content items would be at the top of the search results for every keyword. There *is* something going on: the keyword factors.

Ranking Organic Search Matches Based on Keywords

Keyword ranking factors help search engines decide which content is most closely related to the actual keywords the searcher enters. This section will help you understand how the presence of keywords in your content is used by search engines to rank organic search results. Because your content contains words, every piece of content emphasizes some keywords. Keyword factors affect the rankings for content for the precise keyword that the searcher has entered in a particular search.

Before talking about keyword factors for ranking, there is one filter that we did not address back in the filtering section, because it makes more sense to discuss it now. A very powerful filter is used on every keyword—at least one (and typically all) of the words in the keyword are expected to be found in your content. If none of the words are on your page, that content is filtered out of the search results list, no matter how wonderful its content factors are.

In general, your page or social media content must *contain* the keyword to rank highly for that keyword. (There are some growing exceptions around image recognition to keep an eye on.) When your page gets past that filter (and the other filters we discussed earlier), it is in the results list and ranking takes over. Each page in that list comes with its predetermined page score, such as Google's PageRank, the score associated with that page based on its cumulative content factors. Pages with high content factors get a head start in the scoring. But then the keyword factors take over to decide the winner.

The most important keyword factor is known as **keyword prominence**. Besides knowing that a page contains the words in a search keyword, isn't it important to know *where* they appear on the page? You better believe it. All other things being equal, pages where keyword terms appear in important places, such as the page title, tend to rank higher than pages where the terms are buried at the page bottom. Pages that feature keyword words in titles and initial paragraphs are said to have high keyword prominence for that keyword, because the keyword appears in more prominent places than on other pages.

Why do search engines emphasize keyword prominence? Because search engines are, at heart, pattern-matching machines. They are tuned to recognize various patterns associated with pages that strongly match keywords—pages with a pattern of keyword matches in prominent places are stronger matches than others.

So how does the search engine evaluate the prominence of terms it finds in various parts of the page? Here are the major categories, which are also depicted in Exhibit 3-4:

- **Title:** This is the most important part of the web page to a search engine. The title is what displays in the search results page, and it is also shown in the window title for the browser. You can think of a web page's title as similar to the title of a magazine article, which usually strongly indicates what the entire article is about. A web page isn't the only content with a title—videos and images have titles, blog posts have headlines—and the title is the most important part of every kind of content.

- **Headings and emphasized text:** Some search engines give more weight to terms found in bold headings, and to italicized or colored text, assuming that these are more important occurrences of the terms. Headings are most similar to bold section headings inside a magazine article that break up the running text and indicate what the paragraphs below are about.

- **Body text:** Body text includes all the words that appear on the page, but body text that appears closer to the top of the page is considered more important than text found in the middle or at the bottom of the page. Pictures on the page also contain alternate text that search engines use to "learn" what each picture is about.

- **Description:** Web pages and blogs generally contain a summary that search engines still show under the title in the search results. Most search engines, however, no longer show the description nor give it any more weight than body text.

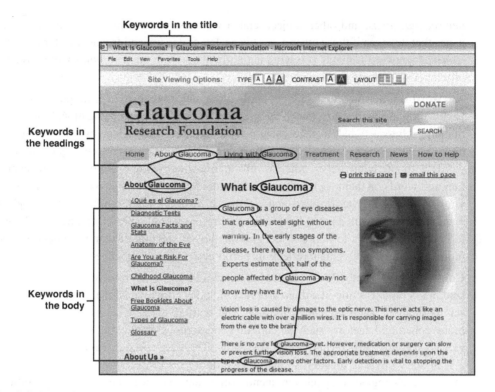

Exhibit 3-4 Keyword prominence within a page. Search engines treat matching words differently based on where those words are found on a page.

You can find much more detail on how to craft your pages to be more attractive to search engines through clever term placement in Chapter 8, "Optimize Your Content."

Some keyword factors can apply to any keyword, whereas others kick in for only multiple-word keywords. Here are some universal keyword factors:

- **Content theme:** Search engines once ranked content based on simpler algorithms using **keyword density** (sometimes called **keyword weight**) and keyword frequency. Density values content whose text has a higher ratio of the search keywords to the rest of the words, while frequency gives credit for the sheer number of keywords found. (Note that text consisting of just one word—the keyword—has 100% density, but ain't that good of a match, so its frequency correctly lowers that page's rank.) In recent years, however, search engines have become more attuned to content themes, the idea that a really good match for a keyword will also have many other words on the page related to that keyword. So, if someone searches for *digital cameras*, a page with high density and frequency of that keyword, but which is missing words such as *megapixel, shot, frames* *per second*, *focus*, and other subject-related words would not rank as highly as other pages that do, even if those other pages have a lower density and frequency of the *digital cameras* keyword itself. If you write naturally about your subject, you should have no problem using plenty of theme words.

- **Keyword intent:** As search engines apply more and more analytical firepower to your pages, they are working to match the searcher's intent (such as navigational, informational, and transactional) to pages that satisfy that intent. Although no two search engines treat searcher intent identically, search engines generally respond to navigational keywords with site home pages, whereas informational keywords yield pages with several hundred words on them. Certain keywords contain clues about the type of documents to return—a search for *maytag jetclean dishwasher manual* might return the PDF product manual or a page with a list of links to the PDFs, for example. Search engines are always looking at new ways to improve recognition and satisfaction of searcher intent, so the more accurately your content reflects its purpose, the better your edge.

- **Contextual relevancy:** We've talked before about how search results are now personalized, and context is how it's done. Context includes components that are permanent or semipermanent, such as gender, job role, and marital status. Context can also include more ephemeral factors, such as current geographic location, the subjects of pages viewed recently, and recent search keywords. The major search engines try to guess a searcher's physical location so that keywords for *hardware store* will see ones near them. Search engine companies frequently offer many services that require registration, so they can collect more permanent information about the searcher. Google does this with Gmail and Google Docs.

You can see that every keyword undergoes complex analysis, but keywords containing more than one word are evaluated in an even more complicated way, because of the interplay *between* the words. Take a look at some factors that apply only to multiple-word keywords:

- **Term rarity:** When keywords contain more than one word (search term), the search engine wants to know which words are the most important across the web, because that helps the search engine find the best pages. Consider the keyword *hotels in london* from the search engine's point of view. A search engine knows the frequency of every term's occurrence across the web. The term *in* occurs on most English pages and is therefore not a "good discriminator"; it does not help the search engine pick the best pages for the keyword because pages containing the word *in* are just about as likely to be good answers as pages that do not. Rarer is the term *hotels*, but it is not as rare as *London*. For each term, the engine calculates its inverse document frequency—a logarithmic formula that produces very high values for rare words and very low values for common words. The search engine then takes each of the three terms and executes a formula for each page in the search results known as TF*IDF: normalized Term Frequency (what we have called keyword density) multiplied by Inverse Document Frequency. This complicated math tells the search engines which pages have the highest keyword densities for the rarest terms in the keyword.

- **Term proximity:** The best matches contain all the terms in the keyword right next to each other in the same order they were listed in the keyword. So, pages containing *hotels in London* might be the best. But the search engines apply more judgment than that. Because the term *in* is so common, for this keyword pages containing *london hotels* might be just as good as those with *hotels in london*. Other keywords that contain no common words might emphasize word order more. In all cases, having all the words close to each other is a good thing—certainly better than a page that has numerous occurrences of *London* and *hotel* separated by several words or sentences.

Remember that search experts spend their whole careers crafting and polishing these formulas, so no short explanation will give you a complete understanding—and you do not need one. You do need to understand the basics of what search engines are looking for, however, and now you do.

Although we have dealt with content factors and keyword factors separately, to make them simpler to explain, on every keyword the search engine mixes them together to derive the best ranking for the results list—and different keywords emphasize one set over the other. For example, imagine a keyword such as *digital camera*. There are millions of occurrences of those words, and keyword density does not help much in determining the best pages. So content factors become critically important in deciding the top ten. But for the keyword *maytag jetclean dishwasher manual*, relatively few pages contain all of those words, especially in proximity to each other, so keyword factors probably drive the top results more than content factors. Obviously any page that excels in both, for a particular keyword, could be the #1 result. But every search engine differs, and they handle different types of keywords in different ways; that's one reason they have different results for the same keyword.

Search engines are fiendishly complicated, so in truth these algorithms are even more intricate than described here, but this is enough for you to understand the basics.

Ranking Paid Search Matches

Paid search matches use much simpler ranking algorithms than organic search, but they still require a bit of explanation.

The oldest way of ranking paid matches is the simplest: The highest bidder wins. Overture, the paid search company that invented the paid search genre introduced the **high-bidder auction**. Each advertiser bids the amount of money it will pay when a searcher clicks its advertisement, and the search engine displays the highest bidder's ad first among the paid results. Bids can change minute to minute, but the search engine always shows the current high bidder at the top of the list. A few paid search engines around the world still use high-bidder auctions, but the top engines have a different approach.

Google, never one to shy away from innovation, pioneered the first real paid search ranking algorithm when its AdWords program began using the combination of the bid and the clickthrough rate (the percentage of searchers who click on the result after it has been displayed) to choose the #1 result. Now, nearly all paid search engines use clickthrough rate as part of their ranking algorithm, and some use many more factors. Let's look at why.

Think for a minute about how search engines stay in business. No matter how many keywords searchers enter, search engines don't make any money unless searchers click the ads. So, it stands to reason that search engines want those ads to bring them as much money as possible. Google was the first to figure out that giving the top slots to the high bidders didn't maximize income to Google.

If an advertiser bids $100 a click for a certain keyword, but no one clicks that pricey ad, Google doesn't make any money. Google maximizes its profits when it gives priority to the ads that have the highest clickthrough rate and a high cost per click but not necessarily the highest cost per click.

So, that was the first paid search ranking algorithm, and the almost all of other paid search engines soon followed.

But there is another reason that clickthrough rate is important to Google's income. If clickthrough rate is such an important part of the ranking algorithm, then more relevant ads are more likely to be shown on the first page of search results. Over a long period of time, showing more relevant results should result in more searchers being enticed to click on paid search results. Given how many searchers adamantly proclaim that they "never" click the ads, making the ads more relevant seems like a no-brainer.

Over the years, Google and Bing have added more factors to their paid search ranking algorithms, although it is still nowhere as complex as their organic search ranking algorithms. Because the factors are much more complex than a simple clickthrough rate, both search engines describe the confluence of all of the ranking factors (except for your bid) as your Ad's **Quality Score**. Search engines constantly tinker with the ranking factors, just as with organic search, but some of the factors that comprise Quality Score include the following:

- **Different types of clickthrough rates:** So far, we've treated the clickthrough rate on your ad as a single ranking factor, but search engines usually consider multiple clickthrough rates as separate ranking factors. For example, one factor might be the clickthrough rate of all your ads for that keyword. Another might be the clickthrough rate of all ads to your display URL. Yet another could be the clickthrough rate of all the ads in your account. Search engines can weigh each of these factors differently, rather than treating "clickthrough rate" as one factor.

- **Different types of content quality:** Search engines frequently examine the quality of your *ad* by looking at the relevance of your ad copy to the keyword entered. They also usually consider the quality of your *landing page* by examining its relevance and its page loading speed.

- **Different contexts:** Search engines often weigh the history of your ad on different devices or with searchers from different geographies.

You might be wondering how you know what your Quality Scores might be across your paid search campaigns. We cover that in Chapter 9.

Displaying Search Results

After the search engine knows which content matches, and what rank order to show them in, it's time to display them on the search results page. Displaying the results is a lot simpler than some other parts of the process, but there are a few important things to pay attention to.

Each search engine has a slightly different layout for its search results, but they are very similar to each other, with each showing a mixture of organic and paid results. Most search engines distinguish organic and paid results through visual treatments and their locations on the page.

Organic search results look similar no matter which search engine you use. They all use the title of the page followed by a snippet—a summary of the text from that page that contains the search terms. The search terms usually display in bold, drawing the searcher's eye to them. You should understand that everything displayed in the search results is drawn from what the search engine previously stored in its index. The search engine never examines the actual page while it is displaying search results, which is why the results page can sometimes contain outdated information, or even display pages that no longer exist (which are discovered when searchers click them). The information displayed on the results page was correct when the spider last crawled the page, but the page might have changed (or even been removed) since. As you saw earlier, many kinds of search results might look different from web page results, with videos and images previewing an image of what searchers can expect by clicking them.

Paid results have also taken on a more uniform appearance across search engines over time, because ads that look like organic results (a title and a short text description with no picture) seem to get higher clickthrough than glitzier-looking graphics.

Now that you understand how the results are displayed, it's time to understand how the actual search results are shown. When the searcher clicks a particular search result (organic or paid), the chosen content is displayed, but not by the search engine. The search results screen merely links to the website page (or other content) that was listed in the organic search index or the paid search database, just like other hypertext links to that page from anywhere else. If everything has gone well, the information the searcher is looking for is on that clicked page. If not, the searcher can click the web browser's back button to see the results page again.

Now that you understand how both organic and paid results are found, ranked, and displayed, you need to learn how those organic search matches found their way into the index.

Finding Content for the Organic Index

Sounds easy, right? Searchers enter keywords, and then the search engine looks up the search terms in its organic index, ranks the best matches first, and then displays the results. But how did all those pages get into the index in the first place? That is what Exhibit 3-5 shows, and the rest of this chapter explains. This information is critical to you, the search marketer, because if your pages are not in the index, no searcher can ever find them.

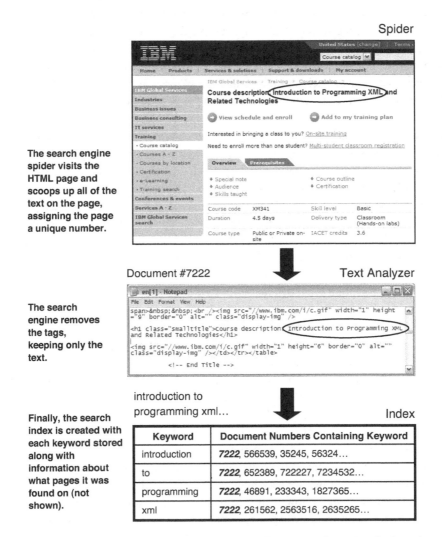

The search engine spider visits the HTML page and scoops up all of the text on the page, assigning the page a unique number.

The search engine removes the tags, keeping only the text.

Finally, the search index is created with each keyword stored along with information about what pages it was found on (not shown).

Keyword	Document Numbers Containing Keyword
introduction	*7222*, 566539, 35245, 56324…
to	*7222*, 652389, 722227, 7234532…
programming	*7222*, 46891, 233343, 1827365…
xml	*7222*, 261562, 2563516, 2635265…

Exhibit 3-5   How organic search engines index pages. Every search engine finds web pages, analyzes their content, and builds a search index.

To build up the inventory of pages in the search index, search engines use a special kind of program known as a **spider** (sometimes called a **crawler**). Spiders start by examining web pages in a **seed list**, because the spider needs to start somewhere. But after the spider gets started, it discovers sites on its own by following links.

Following Links

The spider looks at web pages and follows the links to other content—the same way you do in your web browser. When the spider examines the page, it sees the Hypertext Markup Language (HTML) code that indicates a link to another page (see Exhibit 3-6)—the same HTML code that your browser formats to show you the page.

The spider scoops up the HTML for each page, noting links to other pages so it can come back to collect the HTML of those pages later. You can imagine that, given enough time, a spider can eventually find every page on the web (or at least every page that is linked to another page). This process of getting a page, finding all the links on that page, and then getting those pages in turn, is called **crawling** the web. Later in this chapter, we explain what the spider does with the HTML it collects from all of those pages that it crawls.

Your organization's website is undoubtedly known to the search engine spiders, and you certainly have some pages listed in their search indexes. But you might not have as many of your pages listed as you think, and any page that is not in the index can *never* be found by the search engine. So, it is important to have as many pages in the index as possible. Chapter 7, "Get Your Content Listed," shows you how to find out how many pages are indexed from your organization's site and some simple ways to get more of them indexed.

Remembering Links

Following links is important because it is the best way for a spider to comprehensively crawl the web. But it is important for another reason, too. Spiders must carefully catalog every link they find—checking which pages link to your page and checking the words displayed that describe the link (the anchor text). Earlier in this chapter, we discussed how search engines rank search results; they do so with this information. Exhibit 3-7 shows how spiders collect the link information that is so important to ranking the results.

Keeping Up with Changes

As you can imagine, web crawling is not the most efficient way to keep up with changes to those billions of web pages and even more social media content. New content can be added, old content removed, and existing content changed at any time—the spider will not immediately know that anything has changed. It can be days before the spider returns to see what happened. That is why a searcher sometimes gets a "page not found" message when clicking a search result. The spider found that page during its last crawl, but it has since been removed or given a new address.

<a href="/antiques/index.html">Antiques</a>

<a href="/PV/index.html">Photography & Video</a>

The spider inspects the markup for each link (the <a> tag) to see what page is being pointed to.

The spider then requests this new page to index it and to follow its links to yet more pages.

Exhibit 3-6 How spiders follow links. Every spider sees the same HTML code that your browser sees and can follow links to other pages.

The anchor text for this link is "Destination Maps"

```
        <td class="secNavBoxContent" valign="top" width="50%">
<a href="/travel/plan/destination_maps/index.jsp">Destination Maps</a></td>
        <td class="secNavBoxContent" valign="top" width="50%">

<a href="http://delta-air.deltavacations.com" target="_blank">Delta vacations</a></td></tr><tr>
        <td class="secNavBoxContent" valign="top" width="50%">
<a href="/travel/plan/aircraft_types/index.jsp">Aircraft Types & Layout</a></td>
```

Exhibit 3-7 How spiders collect link information. Spiders pay attention to which pages link to every other page and what words they use on each link.

This can be an especially vexing situation for some business websites. Your site might have fast-changing content, such as product catalogs that list what you have available each day. If you have new products introduced often, or a volatile supply environment, your pages on your site might not be a close match to the pages the spider has put in the search index. Chapter 7 walks you through ways to ensure the search index is as up-to-date as possible.

The best spiders keep their indexes "fresh" by varying their rates of revisiting sites. Spiders return more frequently to sites that change more quickly. If a spider comes to two pages on the same day and then returns to both 1 week later, if one of them has changed and one has not, the spider can decide to revisit the changed page in 2 days, but wait 2 weeks to return to the unchanged page. Over time, this technique can greatly vary the return rate for the spider, raising the freshness of the index by revisiting volatile pages most frequently. Spiders also revisit sites that have the highest-quality pages more often than other sites. Google, for example, tends to revisit pages with higher PageRank more frequently (perhaps once per week) than other pages.

Analyzing the Content

Now that you see how spiders find pages on the web, it's time to see what search engines do with all those pages. The first thing that you will find is that not every document in the search index is an HTML-coded web page.

Converting Different Types of Documents

Up until now, we have assumed that all web pages are made of HTML, but many are not. Modern search engines can analyze Adobe Acrobat (PDF) files and many other kinds of documents.

When search engines come across a non-HTML document, they convert these documents to a standard format that they use to store all the other documents. For simplicity's sake, we examine the rest of the text analysis work as if all the documents are coded in HTML, but you know now that it is a bit more complicated than that.

Deciding Which Words Are Important

If you take a look at the average web page, you will see a lot more than just the text that appears on the screen. If you view the HTML source, in fact, most of what you see is **markup**, or HTML tags. Because you do not want the names of these tags found when you search, you might imagine that search engines throw them away, but they do not. They use the markup to help them analyze the text.

When you look at a web page on your screen using your browser, some words stand out more than others. Some words are in color or bold type; others are set in a larger size; some are set apart as headings. Also, because most web pages are written in "newspaper style," the most important information tends to come near the top of the page.

As discussed previously in this chapter, search engines realize that emphasized words and words near the beginning of the page are more important than the rest of the words on that same page. This is the step of the index-building process in which search engines decide which placements of words make them more important than others. In Chapter 8, you learn how to use this information to your advantage as you create and edit your own content.

Spotting Words You Don't Normally See

Some of the most important tags are ones that you do not usually see. Because search engines see the actual HTML code, they can learn things about the page that you would never notice unless you viewed the HTML source yourself. These tags that contain information about the page are often called **metatags**.

The most important metatag is the **\<title\>** tag, but the \<title\> tag might not do what you expect. The words at the top of the web page—the ones that your eye tells you make up the title—are probably generated by a heading tag or by an image. The actual HTML \<title\> tag shows up in the title bar of the browser window, as shown in Exhibit 3-8. (The words coded in the \<title\> tag also appear as the name of the page when you bookmark it or save it as a favorite.)

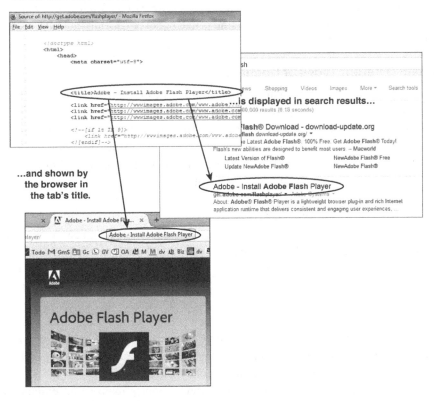

Exhibit 3-8   How titles are used. You can see titles in several places if you look hard, but the search results page is where it matters the most.

Even though you often do not notice the title, search engines know that this tag provides a lot of information about your page. The theory is that the title contains the words that best describe the page. Search engines pay special attention to the words you use in your `<title>` tag, as mentioned in the ranking discussion earlier in this chapter. Moreover, search engines display the title when they show your page in the search results. Searchers use the title as a big factor in deciding whether to click through to your page.

Another important metatag stores the **description** of the page. As with the title, search engines expect that the words in your description summarize your page, and some search engines give words found in your description special importance. Unlike the title, searchers rarely see the description. In the past, many search engines displayed your page's description right under its title in the results list, but few do that today. Therefore, the description tag is less important than it once was. Chapter 8 covers metatags in detail.

What Search Engines Don't See

But as smart as search engines sometimes seem to be, it is striking how much they miss. The most striking misses are the pictures. Search engines read and understand text of any kind, and as you have read, they even deduce information beyond what is encoded in the text.

But, in general, pictures have no meaning to search engines. Although a person can look at a picture and immediately recognize that it is a zebra, a search engine cannot make any sense of the pattern in that image file. Some search engines, such as Google, can find zebra images through tricky use of text, such as noticing that the image file is named zebra.gif or that some text associated with the image contains the word *zebra*, as shown in Exhibit 3-9. Google also has some technology that you can check out—called Google Goggles—that does some decent image recognition, but most search engines have nothing close to that.

In fact, one way to think about most search engines is that they use the web the way sight-impaired people do. Blind web users employ software called screen readers that literally read the text on the screen out loud to them, using the computer's speaker. Screen readers can speak any text, but they have nothing to say when confronted with a picture—any picture—even a "picture" of text.

Most search engines share a similar "blindness." This is an important reason not to use images for display text—the large titles that often occur at the top of the page. Even though sighted visitors to the page can easily read the words displayed from the image, search engines cannot. (Another important reason to avoid images containing text is that screen readers cannot read them to sight-impaired web users.)

These examples show how important it is for you to use alternate text that strongly describes all of your images so that search engines (and sight-impaired readers) understand them as well as possible.

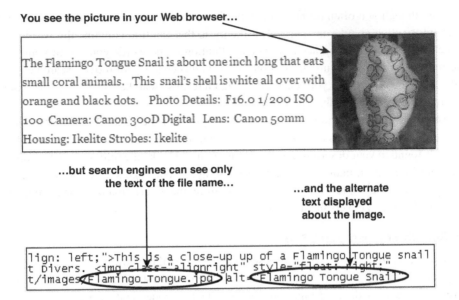

You see the picture in your Web browser...

The Flamingo Tongue Snail is about one inch long that eats small coral animals. This snail's shell is white all over with orange and black dots.   Photo Details: F16.0 1/200 ISO 100 Camera: Canon 300D Digital Lens: Canon 50mm Housing: Ikelite Strobes: Ikelite

...but search engines can see only the text of the file name...

...and the alternate text displayed about the image.

```
lign: left;">This is a close-up up of a Flamingo Tongue snail
t Divers. <img class="alignright" style="float: right;"
t/images/Flamingo_Tongue.jpg alt="Flamingo Tongue Snail"
```

Exhibit 3-9 How search engines "see" pictures. You recognize a picture when you see it, but search engines see only the text associated with the image.

Building the Organic Index

So far, the spider has crawled the pages, and the search engine has analyzed the markup and text on each one. The next step is creating the search index, which is a specially designed database that the search engine uses to quickly find the matching pages in response to any search keyword.

A search engine "remembers" which words are on which pages by storing them in its search index. In its simplest form, a search index contains a record for every word, followed by a list of the pages that contain that word. So, when searching for the word *glaucoma* in Google, the Google search engine looks in its index for the record for glaucoma and retrieves the list of pages.

When a search engine creates its search index, it examines the unique words on each page that the spider finds, and for each word it checks to see whether a record exists in the index. If so, it adds the web page's address (Uniform Record Locator, or URL) to the end of the record. If no record for that word exists, a new record containing that URL is created. The actual URL would take up a lot of space in the index, so the search engine converts each URL to a unique number that it stores in the index. Exhibit 3-3 showed how a simple search index might look.

In addition, the search engine stores the metadata about each page for use in displaying the search results. So, it stores the URL, the title, and any information needed to display the snippets that highlight where the terms were found. That way, when it must display that page as a search result, it has all the information in the index to do so.

How to Work the Search Engines

Okay, so now you know enough about search engines to be dangerous. Unfortunately, the person in the most danger from your newfound knowledge is staring back at you in the mirror each morning. You've learned the basics about how search engines work, but if we stop right here, you are likely to draw many of the worst conclusions about what to do next:

- If search engines look for the keywords on the web pages, then I should fill my pages with the right keywords so that they'll rank first. Wrong. In fact, search engines actually downgrade pages that have *too many* keywords on them, and not enough other words.

- If search engines want pages that have lots of links to them, I'll pay other websites to link to my pages so that they'll rank at the top. Wrong. If the search engines believe you've paid for links, they will ignore your links.

- If search engines use your bid to decide where your ad goes, I'll bid more than everyone else so that the most searchers see my ad. Wrong. You could bid so much that you actually lose money on every sale.

We apologize if now everything seems even more complicated than before, but it's not too bad. We'll walk you through three key ways to think about your search marketing so that you can take the right actions that lead to success:

- **How to write for organic search engines:** If you write first for searchers, you'll be doing most of what you need to appeal to search engines, too.

- **How to bid without overbidding:** You might think you can "wing it" when it comes to your paid search bidding philosophy, but a more data-oriented approach tends to do better.

- **How to approach the question of quality:** Search engines have ways of detecting that your site contains high-quality content—understanding them sends you in the right direction.

So, put on your thinking caps. It's time to learn how to think about search marketing.

Your Organic Search Writing Philosophy

As you continue your education in search marketing, you will discover many articles that answer the basic question, "Just what are search engines looking for?" Each article has slightly different answers. Sometimes the articles contradict each other. Do not be concerned about that.

Search engines are fiercely complex, and they change all the time. In addition, "what search engines are looking for" strikes to the heart of a search engine's trade secrets: its ranking algorithm. So, maybe the article's writer observed a few situations and concluded something that wasn't quite true; the search engines will never publicly divulge the truth. Or maybe what one writer wrote might have been true when it was written, but is not true anymore. Perhaps two writers performed tests with two different search engines, and what is true for one is not true for the other.

Unfortunately, divining how search works through observation is hopelessly subjective. You will read conflicting and erroneous information about what search engines are looking for, so you need to take everything you read with a grain of salt—including what you read here. We do not have any inside information. We have lots of experience, just like most of those other writers, but what we write might not be any more accurate than anyone else's story. And by the time you read this, the search engines might have added a new wrinkle.

But maybe you can take a different approach. What is more important than the details of how any particular search engine works is your philosophy for feeding them tasty spider food. How you think about what search engines want is more important than what they actually want at any particular moment in time. If your philosophy is to outsmart them at every turn, constantly tuning your pages to fit the latest ranking algorithm, that's one philosophy—one we do not recommend. Wouldn't you rather use an approach that does not need to be changed every week, one that people without any special training can learn and stick to?

You picked up this book to learn how your site can appeal to search engines, but now we turn the tables on you. The best philosophy for writing for search is: Write for people first, not for search engines.

We know, we know—that's what you were doing before you picked up this book. In fact, you were writing for people first, last, and only. We are not telling you to go back to that extreme. But neither should you take a pendulum swing in the other direction. Do not write for search engines and forget about people.

We are warning you about this because a far-too-common response of newbie search marketers is to optimize everything for search engines. To go overboard learning about every tiny part of search ranking algorithms and to overanalyze and overtune their sites to appeal to search engines every way they can think of. To "chase the algorithm," by constantly reoptimizing to keep up every time the search engines change. This is a huge mistake.

If you somehow get high rankings in search because you "chase the algorithm," but you have not written with people in mind, you might not get anyone to click through—eventually buy something from you—your real purpose for doing search marketing in the first place. Let's look at an example. To optimize a page for a *digital cameras* search marketing campaign, a fictitious company called Snap Electronics could have produced the prose in Exhibit 3-10.

It makes your brain hurt just reading it, doesn't it? How many sales do you think that kind of writing will produce? Most people reading that drivel would run screaming into the night.

What's more, most search engines aren't fooled by that kind of writing, anyway. So, you don't actually get those high rankings you're looking for. Search engines actually check for words that are related to digital cameras but might not be the keywords people search for—words such as *megapixel* or *focus*.

EASY DIGITAL CAMERAS, THE BEST DIGITAL CAMERAS, SNAPSHOT DIGITAL CAMERAS FROM SNAP ELECTRONICS

Digital cameras are hot and Snap's SnapShot digital cameras are the hottest. SnapShot digital cameras are not just the best digital cameras, but they are easy digital cameras, too. If you want digital cameras that are not just the best digital cameras, but are also easy digital cameras, you need to choose one of Snap's SnapShot digital cameras.

Exhibit 3-10   Overoptimizing your content. When you try to stuff keywords into every phrase, you produce stilted, unreadable copy that persuades no one to buy.

Chasing the algorithm seems simple and we all want something simple. But it simply doesn't work. What's the alternative? Writing for people first. First, write strong, interesting, action-oriented copy. Your words must help your visitor complete her task—that's how you persuade people to buy. Take a look at Exhibit 3-11.

SNAPSHOT DIGITAL CAMERAS—THE BEST DIGITAL CAMERA IS THE EASIEST ONE TO USE

Snap's award-winning SnapShot digital cameras have been named "2013's Best Digital Camera" by Camera Views magazine. Find out why, like all Snap products, SnapShot digital cameras are easy to use and best in class with the features you need:

18 megapixel (18MP) resolution

Snap's patented OneTouch focus—the easiest to use in the industry according to clickpick. com

---

Exhibit 3-11   Writing for people first. You can write for your reader while still taking care to repeat the phrases needed for high search rankings.

Wasn't that better? Granted, we did not squeeze as many keywords into the same 60-word body (or 13-word title) as in the original, but you can read it without your brain imploding, which means that *some* people might actually buy (as opposed to none). And you just might find that you get a better search ranking for the well-written version as for the overoptimized one, because you have attracted far more links to the information-rich, visitor-friendly page.

Besides, chasing the algorithm will drive you nuts. Search engine ranking algorithms can be extremely volatile. Some believe that search engines regularly tweak their formulas as one way to doom search marketers who do chase their algorithms. And how do you know what is in that algorithm anyway? The only people who really know how the algorithms work are the search engine designers themselves—and they aren't telling.

You *should* write with keywords in mind. You should use them early and often, in titles, and throughout the body. Yes. Do all of that. But not to the point of insanity. Not until your words seem like a computer tried to translate them from another language. Or that you were paid by the keyword.

 There are even more reasons to avoid prose so laden with keywords. Search engines are wise to **keyword stuffing**, which can actually cause your page to be penalized in the rankings. And if search engines do not flag all of those pages today, someday they will. They get smarter every year. Beyond search engine smarts, overoptimized pages also leave you vulnerable to being reported by your competitors to the search engines for spamming—violating the rules of the search engines (which can lead to your site being banned from the search index). So, if the search engines do not catch you, your competitors probably will. Don't take the chance. In truth, only a few very smart operators with loads of time on their hands are able to consistently stay ahead of the search police and truly fool the search engines. It is a lot easier to have a different philosophy.

So, pick your own reason for writing for visitors first:

- **You don't have time to chase the algorithm:** If you are one of those people waiting for a book called *The Four Habits of Highly Overworked People*, you know that you are not going to make time for a new full-time job of outguessing the search engines. Even when you guess right, you need to make time to guess again next month. As the years go by, ranking algorithms increasingly reward rich content written in an engaging way, so the higher the quality of your content, the better your site will do as search engines continue to improve. Excellent content is the best way to invest your precious time.

- **You cannot afford the bad publicity from spamming:** If your executives are squeamish about any hint of negative reporting about your company, a story about unethical search practices is not a risk you are likely to take.

- **You are focused on sales, not rankings:** You know that the illusory gains you make from overoptimizing do not bring you customers anyway, so why not work for sales first?

- **It's the right thing to do:** Ethically, you feel better about yourself because you know that when your pages come up, the searchers really do want to see them and you are providing a valuable service to them, rather than wasting their time.

So, play it straight. Be factual. Avoid the overheated hype. Unlike other forms of marketing and advertising, a straightforward approach is often the most convincing on the web—even a "soft sell" can sometimes be best. Now let's look at some specific techniques search engines use to detect whether your content is of high quality; that's what they want to serve to their searchers.

Your Paid Search Bidding Philosophy

Just because it is so easy to start a paid search program doesn't mean that you should not do some thinking first. In fact, because it is so easy to shoot from the hip, it is probable that some of your competitors run their programs that way. So, just a little thinking on your part can pay big dividends.

Look for Value

Gunning for #1. That is the philosophy of the rookie search marketer. But let's take a step back and see whether we can adopt the philosophy of a cagey veteran marketer instead. The savvy marketer is looking for value, so let's examine how you find value in paid search.

So what's wrong with gunning for #1? It seems to make a lot of sense. You are in paid search to drive traffic, and ranking #1 drives the most traffic. Well, if you have an information site, you might be happy with merely generating traffic; perhaps your goal is to sell advertising on your site. For most of you, however, web conversions are your focus. So, does getting a top paid search ranking give you the greatest number of sales? Not always.

The good news is that you can pay considerably less than what it costs to rank #1 for many keywords and still convert at a high rate. However, the bad news is that you will have to redouble your keyword research efforts to find those low-volume keywords. You will also have to work harder at measurements, so that you can see when you are converting and when you are not. We also might conclude that Google's ranking algorithm might give the savvy search marketer an edge, because it places so much value on clickthrough. Perhaps those #8 ranking keywords are converting well in part because they get high clickthrough, and their per-click costs are modest.

Search marketers would do well to purchase deeper keywords to take advantage of the abundance of never-before-seen keywords. Twenty percent of all Google keywords are new each month; those new keywords drive traffic to your website, too. In fact, Back Azimuth Consulting surveyed clients that use broad match, finding that as many as 10% of the keywords that bring traffic to their sites are new each month.

So, the first part of our philosophy is that you are looking for value, regardless of the rankings. Although top rankings generally drive more traffic to your site, you saw that rankings do not always correlate with traffic. And besides, your goal is to drive the most conversions at the lowest price; that is what *value* means. We know that we might need to do a little extra work to find value, but the studies say that the value is there.

Play the Market

Paid search is a marketplace, so you might as well apply what you know about markets as part of your paid search philosophy. All markets are made up of buyers and sellers, and prices fluctuate based on supply and demand. When supply is high relative to demand, prices are cheap. As more and more buyers chase after fewer and fewer goods, however, prices rise, the economists will tell you. So how does that apply to paid search? There aren't any "goods," after all; it's just a spot on a web page, isn't it?

Although economists like to talk about goods, market forces apply to services, too. Think about how passenger seat prices are set for an airline. Tickets bought far in advance are usually discounted because the airline collects the passenger's money long before the flight.

Nonrefundable tickets are cheaper than refundable tickets because the airline locks in a sale. Because early payments and guaranteed sales have value to the airline, the airline lowers the price of the ticket in those circumstances. But what happens as the day of the flight approaches? If there are few remaining seats, the airline raises prices, so that last-minute business fliers pay top dollar because they have no alternative. If many seats remain, however, the airline might deeply discount each ticket hoping to attract impulse vacationers, because every ticket sold, even at a deep discount, is worth more than an empty seat.

Advertising follows market principles, too. Commercials on highly rated prime-time TV shows cost more than those during the Late Late Show. When more people watch the show, advertisers pay more to reach them. For the same reason, high-demand keywords tend to cost more than less-popular ones because search marketers are paying for traffic (and they hope sales).

Paid search bidding is based on auctions, and auction markets follow supply and demand. When the number of buyers is high, the prices at auction markets tend to be high, too, because more buyers are chasing fewer goods (and perhaps because the prices more accurately reflect the value of what is being sold). Auction markets also result in more sales, because items that would go wanting if priced too high are sold at a price that might disappoint the seller, but they are still sold.

Think about how eBay works. Many unique items sold on eBay would have brought a fraction of their price at a garage sale, simply because a higher number of serious collectors are exposed to the item on eBay. However, commonplace items sell for cheap prices because of the high number of sellers who make them available compared to the size of the buyer market for those items.

Economists call this phenomenon *scarcity*: Rare items cost more when many people desire them. And scarce items fetch far higher prices at auction, which is why auction houses are always selling memorabilia or a celebrity's estate. If there is only one of something, and two rich people both want it, the price can go sky high.

Paid search follows the scarcity principle: Only one result ranks #1 for every keyword within a search engine. If two bidders are determined to be #1 for a keyword, prices can sky-rocket in a matter of hours. More often, you'll watch prices gradually rise to the highest sustainable point. As more and more search marketers begin to play the paid search game, prices tend to rise. They aren't making any more #1 positions for the *digital cameras* keyword. There's only one. The more bidders who want it, the higher per-click fees will go.

Economists call this tendency market efficiency: Sellers will, over time, maximize the price based on the value to the buyers. And economic price theory holds that, over time, all benefits of an item will be incorporated into its price as buyers' knowledge becomes "perfect." Well, nothing is perfect in real life, only in economic theory, so inefficiencies exist everywhere in markets, just waiting to be exploited.

Your job: Find them. Think about how the stock market works. If everyone knew exactly what every stock was worth at any given moment in time, there would not be much point to buying and selling. However, one of the reasons that shares of stock are bought and sold is that two people have very different opinions about what the stock is worth. One reason this is so is that, economic theory notwithstanding, some of the "knowledge" that people have is irrational. It makes no sense at all. Search marketing is no different. If you are rational, you will usually outdo emotional types and guessers. It is like the stock market in that you need information to get an edge, but not hot tips. The information you need is right under your nose and you *can* gather it.

Unlike the stock market, paid search is not worth the same amount to every company. Even if every site paid the same 25¢ per click, some companies would make more money on that click than others. If you gather the information available to you, you will know what each keyword's position is worth to you, so you will never overpay.

So how do you know what to pay? How do you know whether that #1 placement for a keyword is worth 93¢? We explain that in Chapter 4, "Unlock the Business Value of Search." If you know the value of every visitor to your site, you can decide what to pay. (It is usually more complicated than that because sophisticated bidders change their bids to be higher when they convert better.) But what should you think when paid search keywords are bid through the roof? How can others afford to pay when you cannot?

Two answers are possible. One is that they are nuts. They are bidding to keep that #1 position, and they lose money on every sale. If that's the case, you probably have a short-term problem; economics has this funny way of correcting problems such as money-losing bidding. Although annoying, you can withstand that situation for as long as it lasts.

But you might, in fact, have a more serious problem. Perhaps they can pay higher prices because they are more efficient than you are. Maybe they can make money at that high rate, but you cannot. Several reasons could account for this:

- **Their costs are lower:** If they can turn a much higher profit per item than your business can, they can afford to bid higher per-click costs and drive their sales up from improved traffic.

- **They turn their inventory faster:** If they can sell twice as many items per month as you do, they tie up their cash in inventory for far shorter periods of time for the same amount of merchandise. (In brick-and-mortar-retail, grocery stores can operate profitably with a much lower profit margin than furniture stores because grocers "turn" their inventory so many times more each year.) Their higher turn rate will lower their costs and allow them to bid higher in paid search.

- **Their clickthrough rate is higher:** If their ad copy (or their brand name) causes higher clickthrough rates, they might drive more traffic for the same ad budget than you do. That means each click costs them less than it costs you.

- **Their conversion rate is higher:** The number of searchers who buy compared to the number visiting is the **conversion rate.** If their website visitors convert at higher rates, they sell more items than you do for the same ad budget. Each click is worth more to them than to you.

- **They know something you don't know:** Maybe you are trying to get the lowest cost per order, and they are going for the highest revenue. Perhaps you are budgeting based on profit margin, and they are budgeting based on lifetime value—what it is worth to acquire a new customer over that customer lifetime, rather than just this transaction. Chapter 4 highlights your metrics choices, and you can decide which one truly captures the value of every search click. The higher that you are able to justify the value, the higher you can profitably bid, so having the most complete model of value puts you in the strongest competitive position.

So, to take advantage of inefficiencies in the market, you must make your business as efficient as possible, so that you will have all of those advantages over your competitors, rather than the other way around. As a search marketer, you will not have much impact on whether your company is the low-cost producer in your field, and you will not have a great deal to do with how fast your inventory turns, but there are a lot of things you can affect, which we discuss in Part III of this book.

Keep in mind that the only way to affect anything is to have the necessary information. As you drive for efficiency, you want to know the conversion rate for every keyword you buy, but you want to know much more. Are conversion rates higher...

...from certain search engines?

...in certain positions?

...with certain copy?

...with certain landing pages?

...at certain times?

If so, you can take advantage, as we explain in Part III. By gathering the most detailed information possible, you will know the right situations to play the market and when to hang back. But ratcheting up your efficiency is only part of the game. You also need to learn about an old business maxim of using other people's money.

Some of the richest people around got there by investing other people's money. If the investment fails, they lose nothing; if it succeeds, however, they will get something out of it. Often, these smart people get a management fee or a cut of the proceeds for their contribution to the success.

Smart search marketers can use other people's money, too. Here are several ways to do that:

- **Raid sales budgets:** One of the best ways to get investment in your paid search campaign is to raid other budgets, and the sales budget is one place to start. If you can show that your paid search program is wildly profitable, but you do not have a high enough budget to fund any more of those oh-so-profitable clicks, maybe your sales team does. If you can show that your return on spending is higher than the payback on their latest incentive program, you might get some of their money.

- **Raid marketing budgets:** If your company spends money on brand marketing, maybe you can take some of it for paid search. You expect that paid search delivers sales, but did you know it can raise brand awareness, too? A Google study shows that the paid search combined with print ads has a 9% higher brand impact on consumers than print ads alone.

- **Raid other product budgets:** Does your product "drag" other sales in its wake? A sale of a computer might include software, services, and financing. Selling a washing machine might include a maintenance agreement. A sale of a stapler might include staples. Think about your product. If there are other things that can be sold along with your product, other people in your business are just as interested in you selling your product as you are. Can you offer these tie-in products on the checkout page? If so, will other product lines help subsidize your paid search costs to help improve their sales?

- **Raid your supplier's budgets:** Do you sell a product that your supplier is as anxious to sell as you are? Steal a page from the offline marketing playbook and suggest cooperative advertising. Still rare in paid search marketing, Intel, among others, is working with its key customers to defray the costs of search marketing. For example, Intel might pay part of Dell's per-click fees for Dell computer products that contain Intel components. You might want to approach your suppliers with a similar idea.

- **Raid your supply chain's budget:** Suppose you are a business-to-business marketer but your paid search keywords are attracting consumer clicks that just go to waste. Perhaps you can team up with one of your resellers to share the clicks (and the costs). If you sell wholesale and they sell retail, put up a landing page for those keywords that siphons searchers to the right site (yours or your retailer's), and you can split the per-click charges for the traffic you get. By doing so, you can share much higher bids for those keywords because none of the clicks are wasted.

Any of these techniques can make your budget go much further than if your philosophy is to go it alone, but you will be forced to share more information with your newfound partners than ever before, so you need to have close relationships for it to work well.

Iterate, Iterate, and Then Iterate Some More

So far, you have learned a lot about how to develop a paid search bidding philosophy, but the most important lesson is humility: You will *never* get it completely right. Your job is to get it a little less wrong every day. Here's a secret: Paid search might not work. At least, it might not work at first. When you start, you might find that your ads get so few clicks that you can't even spend what you budgeted. Or you might find that your ads get loads of clicks, but almost no sales. Expect this. Expect it not to work. Your program might start badly.

But no matter how badly you start out, if you are willing to track your numbers and keep tuning your program, you will eventually succeed. The secret is to start small. You know you are not going to get it right, so why not lose as little as possible while you learn? You learn just as much about horse racing betting at the $2 window as you do at the $100 window; you just have a lot more money left over after the last race.

Know that your success won't turn on how your paid search campaign starts, but in how you improve it every day. To learn how to succeed through experimentation, read Mike's book, *Do It Wrong Quickly: How the Web Changes the Old Marketing Rules* (MikeMoran.com/writing/do-it-wrong-quickly/).

If you can afford to start out with a large budget, the best way to spend it is on as relevant a set of keywords as possible. Never use single-word keywords, and always use negative keywords to reduce irrelevant matches. Choose the keywords that are most relevant to your site and see how they perform. Gather as much data as possible.

After you have collected this early data, see who the winners are. Do you have some keywords that are highly profitable? Spend more on them to see whether higher rankings bring more traffic (and more profits). Do you find keywords that you had not considered? When you use broad match, you can find new keywords that you can move to exact match to reduce your costs with the same conversions.

In Part III, we show you how to improve your clickthrough rates and your conversion rates so that you make more and more of your targets profitable. But that is not the most important lesson. The most important thing to learn is that you must iterate. You will not get it right the first time—don't try. Instead, commit yourself to a constant feedback loop. Then adjust to that feedback for continuous improvement.

Clearly, you have a lot to think about before plunging into your first campaign, but don't feel like you have to figure out everything before you start. One of the biggest advantages of paid search is its incredible adjustability. No matter what you start out doing, you can see what works and what does not in a few days and then do something else. The most important philosophy for paid search bidding is no different than for search marketing as a whole—try something, measure its success, and then try something better. That way, you optimize your campaigns for the biggest return.

Your Content Quality Philosophy

It wasn't long ago that organic search results looked at quality in a very narrow way—based solely on the links to your website. Paid search results didn't look at anything beyond the clickthrough rate on your ad. But times have changed. Now search engines have ever-changing criteria by which they judge the quality of your content—for both organic and paid search.

Links to your site are still a major factor in organic search rankings, even if they are less important than they once were. But what if all search engines got together and decided that links were no longer important at all? Suppose, in a blink, they all changed their ranking algorithms so that link popularity meant nothing to your search rankings. Would that mean that you should not care about getting links to your site? Of course not!

Links are hugely important in and of themselves. The best links are always contextually relevant to the visitor. Those are the links you want; they drive qualified traffic to your site.

And that should be your linking philosophy. It sounds crazy, perhaps, but you should practically forget about search engines. If you chase what you think search engines want when it otherwise makes no sense, it will not make any sense to the search engine either. You want the links that drive the highest number of qualified visitors to your site, so that you can convert them. If you relentlessly pursue that strategy, you will find that the search engines reward you, too.

To prove the point that your best policy is to ignore what search engines think about your links, it is worth exploring the alternative. How have sites fared by chasing the algorithm to build up links? Well, it has been an interesting ride.

We begin our story back in the B.G. times—Before Google—because at that time no search engine ranked sites based on links. Sites linked to other sites purely because their visitors would benefit, so the number of links to a site was a good sign of how good its information was. From its inception, Google, in its wisdom, used the link information to determine which sites were of higher quality (that determination was very important to its ranking algorithm) and was able to rank the better sites at the top of its search results. This technique worked so well that many people began to use Google.

As Google began to attract more and more searchers, and as other search engines began to adopt similar ranking approaches that also relied on links, search marketers began to see how important links were. So they tried to get every site in creation to link to theirs. "Get more and more links!" they told themselves, no matter what the source. Search marketers with multiple unrelated sites heavily linked them all together, all in an effort to impress the search engines. For a short while it worked, but the search engines adjusted.

Search engines began to look at the *quality* of the site being linked from, weighing links from important sites more heavily than from unknown sites. They rated each site on the quality and quantity of links and used that rating to judge the strength of each link's endorsement. As a result, pages with links from only low-quality sites plummeted in the rankings, so the search marketers adjusted.

"Get links from the biggest sites!" the search marketers exclaimed. The **directory** frenzy was on. Find the sites that seem to be the most important and get your site listed. Yahoo! Directory and countless smaller directories were the places to be. However, the search engines noticed that many of these directories were not careful enough about what sites were linked, and many popular sites seemed willing to link to almost anyone, regardless of how relevant the links were. So the search engines adjusted.

Search engines noticed that these links tended to go to the home page of each site, but the interior pages got very few links. The search engines began to place more and more emphasis on the anchor text of each link, looking for more than just the name of the company pointing to its home page. Sites with just home page links stopped getting high rankings for informational and transactional keywords, so the search marketers adjusted.

"*Deep links* are what are important!" they told themselves. Soon, they started the two-way (reciprocal) linking frenzy. "I'll link to your pages if you link to mine," they told each other. Some sites set up dozens of links to each other to get those interior pages connected, causing the search engines to notice that two-way links do not call out quality sites as well as one-way links. So the search engines adjusted.

Suddenly sites loaded with reciprocal links began to fall in the search rankings, as sites with many incoming one-way links began to receive more weight. The search marketers noticed again, and they adjusted.

"We need as many one-way links as possible!" the marketers realized. They started message boards on new sites with links to their URLs. Marketers discovered that posting to blogs was especially easy; you could even write a program to do it for you. Some of these links were legitimate services to visitors, but many were designed only for search engines to find. Those links did not really identify the best sites, just the most aggressive marketers. They even started paying other sites to link to them—the most money from the largest sites. So, the search engines adjusted.

Each search engine began to look more closely at the type of each link, placing more and more emphasis on how important the linking sites seem to be. Search engines also discounted links from pages with dozens or hundreds of links. The sites with thousands of random one-way links from message books stopped ranking #1. Instead, the core sites (from the bow-tie theory) were thought to be more important than other sites, so links from those sites were also deemed more important. Again, search marketers noticed. And they adjusted.

"Buy one-way links!" was the new rallying cry. Because a search engine cannot tell the difference between a one-way link that was freely given from one that was purchased, search marketers went out to buy as many links as they could. They had to pay top dollar to get links from those very best core sites, on pages that did not have many other links on them, but it was worth it. For a while, at least. Until the search engines noticed that little-known sites would suddenly leap up in the rankings when nothing about the site had improved—but they had begun to get a lot of important links. And they noticed that the paid links seemed to always have the same anchor text. So the search engines adjusted.

Search engines started downgrading links between sites that had wide disparity in popularity with no strong relevance between them. (Just why did that popular technology newsletter suddenly start linking to this new gambling site?) Search engines began to downgrade sites that were new or small that take sudden leaps in link popularity, assuming that they have bought their links, especially when those links all seemed to use the same words in them.

"Relevant links are what are important!" they told themselves. And they were right. Relevant sites linked to other relevant sites. They linked to home pages and to deep interior pages. Is that the way the story ends? Only in fairy tales. This story never really ends. It will go on as long as there are search engines and search marketers to adjust to each other.

And our story was a fairy tale, too. The evolution of ranking algorithms and search marketer behavior is much more complex than our little story shows. It did not play out in the neat order we show here, but you get the point. You can decide to play this game of cat and mouse with the search engines, but we recommend that you play a different game instead. Our game takes a lot less energy, and you will not be subjected to bumpy ups and downs in your rankings every time the algorithm zigs when you zag. Instead of fooling the search engines or trying to give them exactly what they are looking for, you ought to create high-quality content.

Veteran search marketers remember a few years back when "link sculpting" was all the rage among SEO folks in the know. Much digital ink was spilled describing how you could carefully craft where internal links led on your website to raise the Google rankings of certain of your pages. It's possible that this trick actually worked at one time, but in reality, Google quickly moved to neuter it. About a year after Google's change made link sculpting a waste of time, Google publicly announced that people should stop doing it because they were sad to see so many people frittering away their efforts on nothing. If you think that this is no big deal, stop to consider what those people could have been doing instead. All that effort could have been going into this little movement that was about to have a big impact on search rankings: social media!

Think about the fact that there are three parties in a search transaction: the searcher, the search engine, and you, the search marketer. You need to constantly ask yourself whether what you are doing is good for all three parties, or just for you. If your tactics are merely self-serving (link-sculpting), you can expect that Google will do whatever is necessary to eliminate your advantage. If what you do is good for everyone (high-quality social media), expect it to eventually be rewarded.

More and more, it is difficult to fool the search engines, anyway. Both Google and Bing use social media activity to double-check the quality that their link analysis indicates for your site. It is quite unusual for a quality site to have lots of great links but almost no social media activity, so the search engines discount that site's quality level. Google, in fact, goes so far as to use human raters to check on quality levels, so we're not sure how you'll fool those human raters. It's starting to look easier to just give up and create high-quality content.

And paid search is becoming just as fixated on quality. In the olden days (2001), whatever advertisers bid the highest for a keyword got their ads placed at the top of the list. But the next year, Google pioneered the first step toward higher-quality paid search results—adding click-through rate to the ranking algorithm. Over the years, paid search ad rankings have started to take into account many other factors, including the presence of keywords in the ad itself and on the landing page. In fact, using the same landing pages for both paid and organic search can give your paid search ads a boost in quality.

So what do you do? Think about searchers more than search engines. Sound familiar? Yeah, it's the same advice we gave you for writing content. It works just as well for content quality. And it makes sense, if you stop to think about it. Links, social media activity, and clicks on your ads are valuable to you, regardless of whether the search engines use them for ranking purposes. All of these activities drive visitors to your site. These extra visitors can buy from you the same way that searchers can. Treat their impact on search as an added bonus and you'll do the right thing—create content that is truly helpful and informative to searchers. If you do, your content should fare well with search engines no matter how the ranking algorithms change over time.

Summary

You need to know a lot more to be a successful search marketer, but you already know more than most people. You know what happens when a searcher enters a keyword into a search engine. You learned how search engines match keywords to the right pages in the search index. And you understand how pages get into those indexes in the first place.

So now you know how search engines work. Most of the rest of this book focuses on what to do when search engines do not work—when they do not show searchers the pages from your website. But you already know how to think about the problem. Search engines are not simple creatures to be understood and manipulated. They are complex, ever-changing systems that will defy your attempts to trick them. Your best bet is to craft your marketing strategies to appeal to searchers, rather than to search engines, by creating high-quality content that meets searchers' needs.

In Part I of this book, you have learned the basics of search marketing: what it is, how it works, and what you can do about it. In Part II of this book, the focus changes to examine your site's goals and how to measure success. No matter what your organization does, your website has a specialized purpose, and search marketing must support that purpose. The next chapter shows how to isolate the exact mission of your site before you embark on any search marketing effort.

PART II

Plan Your Search Marketing Program

Search marketing is unlike other marketing programs because it requires the support of many people within your organization. To gain their support, you need to develop a very clear program whose value can be explained to anyone. Part II is where you learn to do that.

First, in Chapter 4, "Unlock the Business Value of Search," we identify your website's underlying goals and how to measure that site's success, whether it is an eCommerce site that directly drives revenue or it is designed to raise brand awareness or generate leads. We'll also help you learn the basics of measuring your search program's success.

Part II concludes with Chapter 5, "Create Your Search Marketing Program," where you learn how to assemble your proposal for a search marketing program in your organization, gain support for that proposal throughout your company, and get it approved and set up.

At the conclusion of Part II, you will have approval for a search marketing program in your organization and you'll have the resources to carry it out. You'll be ready to start your first campaign and execute your plan in Part III.

CHAPTER 4

Unlock the Business Value of Search

So why are you trying to attract search traffic anyway? Every reader of this book will have a slightly different answer to that question, because each website has a different intrinsic purpose, one that your search marketing efforts must support. In Chapter 2, "How Searchers Work," we examined the motivation of searchers, but in this chapter we are examining your motivations as a search marketer. Your biggest motivator is to achieve the goals of your organization.

This chapter grounds your search marketing program in business value:

- **Identify your website's goals:** Every website needs to drive traffic, but there are many different reasons for doing so. Your site might be selling online, or gathering contact information for offline follow-up, or maybe just generating market awareness. Your organization's site could also be focused on something else entirely, such as changing people's health habits or donating to charity.

- **Measure your website's value:** We'll focus on the value your website provides your organization and teach you how to measure traffic and conversions so that we know how important it is to drive traffic to your site.

- **Measure your search marketing value:** Based on the value of your website's conversions, we'll begin to measure the impact of search marketing in monetary terms.

So, let's dig in and identify your goals for your site.

Identify Your Website's Goals

For some of you, this will be a simple exercise, because you think about the goals of your website every day. But maybe you are like the trout, who when asked, "How's the water?" replied, "What water?" Maybe sometimes you get so mired in the day-to-day details that you have trouble remembering what your overall goals are.

No matter your goals, attracting traffic from search engines requires an understanding of search from the inside. Most of this book contains tips that do not vary much based on your specific goals for your site. However, your precise goals can sometimes be important, because your goals determine how you *measure* your search marketing success, which is the point of this whole chapter.

There might be a few of you engaging in search marketing without a true website; you might be driving people to buy from eBay or your Facebook fan page or from some other social media venue. Just think about *that* destination as your website for the purposes of this exercise. Whatever online location is the place where your customers can complete your web conversion, that's what we're talking about.

Now, you might be wondering why it's so important to know the goals of your website. It all goes back to **direct marketing**, a branch of marketing that focuses on getting a response from a marketing message. Traditionally, direct marketers work with printed catalogs and pitch letters mailed to prospective customers. Only a small percentage (often under 1%) of those prospects actually respond to the mailing by filling out the order card or calling in to order by phone, but that's okay, because it doesn't cost much to print and mail the materials. Similarly, you can apply direct marketing principles to your digital marketing, counting how many of your web visitors respond by completing your website's goal. Just a small percentage of web visitors will complete your website's goal, but that's okay because it costs very little to run a website. Those low costs can make your return on investment very high.

In addition, offline direct marketers test their materials, trying different catalogs and letters that contain different pictures and copy, gradually settling on the version that creates the most response. Digital marketer scan do the same. You can begin to vary your website's content, navigation, product mix, and many other factors to increase the number of visitors that complete that goal. This is the essence of how direct marketing principles can be applied to online marketing, including search marketing.

Your website probably has one or more of the following goals:

- **Web sales:** Ring the digital cash register! Your customer buys your product online.
- **Offline sales:** Ring that *other* cash register! Your customer uses the web to research your product, but buys it in a brick-and-mortar store or through a phone call.
- **Leads:** Find a new customer! Your prospective customer uses the web to research a problem and leaves contact information.
- **Market awareness:** Tell your story! Your customer learns about what you do or engages in an activity (sponsored by your brand).
- **Information and entertainment:** Inform people! Your visitor wants to learn something or have fun killing time.
- **Persuasion:** Change someone's mind! Your organization might be trying to help people with a problem or medical condition, or you might be trying to influence public opinion.

At this point, you need to take our word for the fact that identifying your website's goals will help you unlock its business value. But even before we show that to you, just take a look at how search fits with different goals, as shown in Exhibit 4-1. So, find your website's goal (or goals) in the leftmost column and check the other columns for suggestions on the right priority for each type of keyword in your marketing efforts—and the appropriate search marketing approaches.

Website Goal	Priorities for Keyword Types			Search Marketing Approaches
	Navigational	**Informational**	**Transactional**	
Web sales	Medium	Medium	High	Organic and paid
Offline sales	Medium	Medium	High	Organic and paid
Leads	Medium	High	Low	Organic and paid
Market awareness	High	Low	Low	Emphasis on paid
Information and entertainment	Low	High	Low	Emphasis on organic
Persuasion	Low	High	Low	Organic and paid

Exhibit 4-1 Appropriate search strategies for your site's goals. Your website's goals drive the priority of each type of keyword and the applicability of each search marketing approach.

No matter how many of these goals are *your* website's goals, you want to draw traffic from search engines. Understanding each goal will help you better focus your search efforts and prove their value.

Web Sales

Ringing the digital cash register is an easy goal to understand, and it is easy to measure success. If your site has a shopping cart and sells directly to visitors, web sales is one of its goals. Amazon.com is probably the best-known example of a pure web sales site, but many corporate websites sell something directly to visitors.

Saying that your goal is "web sales," however, is a broad goal. It helps to be more specific about exactly what kind of business you have, because different kinds of businesses need different search marketing strategies.

Online Commerce Versus Pure Online

An **online commerce site** offers items that can be purchased right on the site, but it delivers the items offline. In contrast, a **pure online site** not only sells on the web, but delivers electronically, too; no physical package is sent to the buyer. Your business might be squarely in one of these camps, or it might be a hybrid, where some of your products are delivered online and some are delivered offline. So, although we contrast online commerce businesses with pure online businesses, keep in mind that in real life businesses fall on different points of a continuum, not always at the extremes.

Many successful web businesses are pure online businesses. Charles Schwab sells investments: The buyer makes the purchase online and might receive a mail confirmation, but the asset is owned immediately. Downloaded software, eBooks, and music are other examples of pure online businesses. In contrast, online commerce businesses include everything else actually sold on the web: printed books, packaged software, CDs, clothing, and so many other things. Every day, something new is available for sale on the web, to be shipped to the buyer's address. In many ways, the package delivery industry is the biggest winner in the eCommerce revolution.

But why is this distinction between online and offline delivery important? Because the faster the buyer gets the product, the more impulse purchases are made. And impulse purchases differ from a well-researched purchase in important ways. Those differences go to the heart of your search marketing strategy.

When we examine pure online businesses, we see that they inspire the most impulsive purchases possible. Think about how online trading has rocked the securities industry. Time was, buying or selling stock was a big decision, one not made often. Advice was often sought from a stockbroker, a financial advisor, or even friends and family. Buying or selling an investment usually received careful consideration.

What happened when investments could be bought and sold online? Everything changed. First, there was huge competition over the lowest fees charged for each sale, the simplest customer experience, and the trustworthiness of the electronic broker. But that was only the beginning. Completely new needs began to emerge. Brokers began to compete on the information available: real-time quotes, investment analysis, and portfolio management tools. And then day traders emerged. Day traders are the ultimate impulse purchasers in the electronic brokerage business. And they are highly sought-after customers because the churn in their accounts brings in large fees. They are the high rollers of the brokerage business.

You see the same thing in music today, as brick-and-mortar retailers that first came under attack from web retailers such as CDNow and Amazon have been overtaken by Apple iTunes, the music download store. Digital commerce and digital delivery inexorably result in more impulse purchases at lower prices. Whereas we formerly thought a bit before trooping to the store to buy a $15 CD, now we think nothing of downloading a single song for a dollar or so. You can see the same shift underway for books and can imagine it affecting many other industries as the years go by.

What does this shift to more impulsive purchases mean for search marketing? First off, it means more of your business comes to you from search engines than ever before. If you think about, an impulsive searcher buys more easily than a deliberate one.

Moreover, the rise of impulsiveness changes the search keywords, because impulse purchasers search for different things. For example, a day trader is looking for different brokerage features (with different keywords) than a conservative investor. The same is true for other industries—people buying cloud software have a lot less to research than those that must check software compatibility with their hardware, so they use different keywords. As you saw in Chapter 2, informational and transactional searches differ: Impulse purchases tend to be far more transactional than informational.

As your business moves from *offline* to *online commerce* to *pure online*, you might see similar shifts in searcher behavior that need to drive your search marketing strategy.

Retailers Versus Manufacturers

In offline businesses, manufacturers and retailers usually do not compete with each other. Distribution networks connect manufacturers to retailers directly or through wholesalers, and are so efficient that most manufacturers do not even sell their products directly to end customers. The web has changed that manufacturer-retailer relationship in many industries.

On the web, any manufacturer with a commerce system and a shipping label can deal directly with the end customer, completely bypassing the wholesalers and retailers. At first, people talked about **disintermediation**, a fancy term that basically means that the manufacturer cuts out the middleman. But what happened, as usual, is more complex and nuanced than disintermediation, and has varied by industry.

Many consumer manufacturers have added the ability to sell directly to customers or have expanded the volume sold directly. For example, book publishers that rarely sold books except through intermediaries now sell more direct than ever before. Manufacturers of little-known products that had trouble getting wide distribution have huge advantages in selling direct on the web.

However, Amazon and other online retailers show that, for many businesses, immense value still remains in aggregating the wares of many manufacturers in one place. Many manufacturers well-schooled in drop-shipping large volumes of their products to a warehouse found they are not necessarily proficient at shipping one item to someone's home and dealing with the customer service issues that go along with it. Book publishers, for example, cannot offer the low prices and fast shipment to customers that Amazon does because the publisher's low direct sales volumes prevent investment in the most efficient distribution systems.

Dr. Michael Hammer, the originator of the reengineering concept, offered the example that a central air-conditioning manufacturer *can* sell direct on the web, but there are so many questions before purchase and so many thorny installation problems (as well as post-installation maintenance needs) that it might not make any sense to do so. That manufacturer's website might be better devoted to offline sales through its traditional dealer network. So, manufacturers must think carefully about the value of direct sales to their end customers before pursuing a disintermediation strategy. Many manufacturers are better off pursuing offline sales as their website's primary goal, as we discuss later in this chapter.

Just as manufacturers and retailers have different business strengths, so do their websites, as shown in Exhibit 4-2.

	Manufacturer (e.g., Sony)	Retailer (e.g., Best Buy)
Breadth of products offered	One manufacturer	Many manufacturers
Depth of product information	Deep and detailed	Surface only
Objectivity of product information	Biased to own product	More objective
Frequency of return visits	Moderate	High

Exhibit 4-2   Strengths of manufacturer and retailer websites. The strong points of manufacturer sites differ from those of retailer websites.

Exhibit 4-3 shows two web pages, one from Sony®, a manufacturer of video game players, and one from retailer Best Buy. At Sony.com, you obviously see only Sony PlayStations, whereas BestBuy.com shows game equipment from many manufacturers. Sony's site is likely to have much more detailed information about its products and underlying technology (including how it works and what the benefits are) than any retailer does, but the content is also slanted in favor of Sony, rather than being objective.

Beyond their relative strengths and weaknesses, the very goals of manufacturers and retailers differ, too. Best Buy does not care which game console customers buy as long as they buy from them. Likewise, Sony does not care who customers buy from as long as they buy a Sony PlayStation. These differing goals lead to different web approaches, with Sony emphasizing deep product expertise and branding that leads to a Sony product purchase. Best Buy emphasizes customer experience, one-stop shopping, competitive prices, third-party reviews, and quick shipping.

Obviously, both manufacturers and retailers also care about customers considering their companies for future purchases. Even here there are differences, however. A manufacturer's brand image for product value and quality is a different proposition than a retailer's reputation for low prices and strong service. Manufacturers sometimes differ from retailers in frequency of return visits, too. Some retailers get more frequent return visits than manufacturers, so features that depend on return visits, such as personalization, might be more useful to retailers.

These important differences between retailers and manufacturers also lead to somewhat different search strategies. Both retailers and manufacturers emphasize informational and transactional keywords, but it is usually easier for manufacturers to get high search rankings for keywords that contain their brand names and model numbers. Thus, the keyword *sony playstation* is much easier for Sony to rank #1 for than it is for Best Buy. Best Buy and other retailers might do better than Sony, however, for the keyword *video games*.

Even if your business is not purely a manufacturer or a retailer, some of these principles might still apply. Dealers that act as manufacturer's representatives often sell just one manufacturer's products, so they are basically extensions of the manufacturers, and their websites usually have the same strengths and weaknesses as those of manufacturers. In contrast, dealers that sell competing products from multiple manufacturers might resemble retailers more than manufacturers on the web.

Exhibit 4-3 Comparing manufacturers and retailers. Both sell PlayStations, but each has a different emphasis in making the sale.

Courtesy of Sony Electronics, Inc.

Retailers and manufacturers also differ in terms of the importance of navigational keywords. In general, manufacturers are more searched for than retailers. Many more searchers look for *sony dvd player* than *best buy dvd player* (or even *amazon dvd player*). A well-known retailer such as Best Buy does need to pay attention to being found for navigational keywords, but unbranded informational keywords, such as *dvd player,* are more important.

Manufacturers and retailers that sell online have many characteristics in common, but they also have different strengths that bring value to their customers in the buying process. These varying strengths influence both the design of their websites and their search marketing strategies.

Offline Sales

Ringing that *other* cash register can be trickier to measure than ringing the digital cash register. You might be trying to get people to come into your store or buy over the phone. Perhaps you sell direct on the web, too, but you find that people often ask questions before buying. Or maybe you have no eCommerce capability at all. You might be a forklift manufacturer, a car dealer, or you might sell many other big-ticket items. Your site encourages research and comparison because most of your sales close through more traditional channels. Your company might be a product manufacturer or a manufacturer's representative. If this sounds like your business, your primary goal is offline sales. As discussed before, however, your goals might not be so black-and-white. You might have a mix of products, some of which are conducive to online sales and some that are better served with an offline approach.

For products where you do emphasize offline sales, you need to work hard at your **call to action**, which is sales-speak for the thing you are trying to get someone to do. Where the call to action for web sales might be as simple as a shopping cart icon next to a sales pitch, your offline sales site must move the customer to the sales channel where you will eventually close the deal. Depending on your business, that channel can take different forms, as depicted in Exhibit 4-4.

A toll-free telephone number

Directions to your store

A list of locations of stores that carry your product

A link to a retailing website that sells your product online

Regardless of the methods your company uses to move people from the website to the offline sales channel, the search strategy for offline sales is similar to that for web sales: optimizing your site for a mix of informational and transactional keywords. Likewise, companies with well-known names also need to focus on their ranking for navigational keywords.

Web sales sites and offline sales sites differ most sharply in how they measure success. For web sales, measurement is simple: Your web traffic measurement system tells you how many people came, and your eCommerce system tells you how many people bought. But offline sales are much tougher to measure. Later in this chapter, we help you close the loop on your offline sales measurements.

Best Buy highlights in-store pickup on each individual
item and allows customers to check availability.

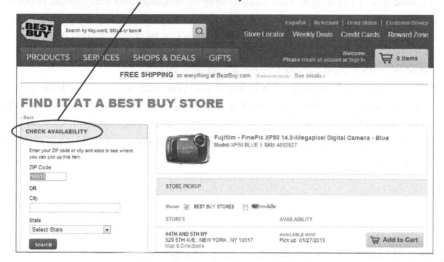

Exhibit 4-4   Calls to action for offline sales. Your offline sales site must move the customer to
the channel that will eventually close the deal.

Leads

Finding a new customer is the goal of many websites. Similar to offline sales, websites looking
for leads attract visitors who eventually buy elsewhere, but those visitors tend to switch channels
far earlier in the sales process. When someone walks into your home improvement store with a
printout of the web page with the snow blower's model number and price, you are making an
offline sale. When someone downloads your article on the difference between snow blowers and
electric snow shovels, he becomes a customer lead. Many corporate sites exist entirely to generate leads, such as consulting firms, construction contractors, or other companies that normally
bid a custom service for each customer.

Regardless of how the sale is closed, the main distinction between a lead and an offline sale
is at what point in the sales process the searcher switches to the offline channel. Searchers who do
online research and immediately switch offline are leads, whereas searchers who know the model
number and the sale price walking into the store are offline sales.

You need a different search marketing strategy to handle searchers who switch earlier in
the process. Using the terminology developed in Chapter 2, businesses seeking leads should
optimize their sites for informational rather than transactional keywords, because leads-oriented
websites are optimized for the early online research part of the sales cycle. If you are selling
above-ground swimming pools, your prospective customers do not know the name or number
of the exact model they want. This might be the only time they ever buy one in their lives. They

cannot enter a transactional search keyword until after they have entered an informational keyword and done a lot of research. You want to snag those customers early in the process and sell them when they are doing their initial research. So, articles favorably comparing above-ground pools to in-ground pools (they are less expensive, they can be disassembled and moved to a new home, they require less maintenance, and so on) will attract customers who are still deciding what kind of pool they want—those informational searchers.

If one of your site's goals is identifying leads, you want to concentrate on techniques for attracting informational searchers, although well-known companies also need to pay attention to navigational keywords. As with offline sales sites, measuring sales can be tricky for sites generating leads. Later in this chapter, you will learn several techniques for judging your lead-passing website's success.

"LEADS R US": ARE YOU AN AFFILIATE MARKETER?

Often leads are handled within the same company, but they can be passed to other companies, too. A special kind of business, called an **affiliate marketer**, exists solely to create leads for other businesses. Affiliates are usually paid based on sales (typically online sales), but their goal is the same as other lead-passing websites: to get a customer interested in a product and close the sale elsewhere.

Although some offline businesses work in similar ways to affiliates, affiliate marketing has really grown up on the Web Pioneered by Amazon, affiliate marketing provides a way for a retailer or manufacturer to attract traffic from other websites (the affiliates) by setting up financial compensation for affiliates to send prospective customers their way. Amazon has since renamed its affiliates *associates*, but the name affiliate has stuck to describe this unique form of web marketing.

An **affiliate program** is created by the **affiliate program sponsor** (the retailer or manufacturer, sometimes called the *merchant)* to enroll companies such as yours as affiliates, providing you with links to place on your website. When your visitor clicks your affiliate link, the visitor is taken to the program sponsor's website, where they might purchase one of the sponsor's products.

Depending on the terms of the affiliate program, that visitor's click might cause you, the affiliate, to get paid for directing the visitor through the affiliate link. Most affiliate programs, however, require more. Most programs pay commissions on online sales made to any visitor you sent. A few pay for leads, such as when the visitor you supplied provides contact information (name, phone number, email address, and so on).

To succeed at affiliate marketing, you typically must build a strong information site, attracting visitors on specialized subjects with your interesting content. The best affiliate marketing sites draw a crowd with their information and sell products related to those

Market Awareness

Telling your story is at least a secondary goal for every organization's website, but many websites exist almost solely to enhance brand image. If your company sells children's cereal, the games you put on your site do not have any direct impact on sales, but they might create loyal little consumers tagging along with their parents in the grocery aisle. Many low-priced consumer goods companies have websites to raise awareness. Entertainment sites for current movies have a like purpose.

If you have a site designed mainly for market awareness, you might emphasize contests, quizzes, games, or other ways of generating interaction with your visitors. But some market awareness sites are changing in subtle ways. Movie sites, for example, often do some web sales (for the soundtrack, for instance), or they link to Moviefone or Fandango to directly sell tickets at the proverbial theater near you. Cereal sites are starting to sell action figures and other toys on top of the free interactive games.

same subjects. If your site presents merely warmed-over product information cribbed from the program sponsor, you might have trouble attracting search traffic, because search engines go to great lengths to lower your rankings for transactional keywords.

If you think about it from the searcher's perspective, it makes sense for search engines to lower affiliate rankings for those keywords. If a searcher is seeking a specific product, the product's manufacturer and well-known retailers for that product are the best matches. An affiliate link to one of those retailers is not a great match, because the searcher has to click through the affiliate link to get to the retail site that could have been directly shown in the search results. In other words, why show the affiliate site when Google can show the program sponsor's site directly?

In fact, some program sponsors prohibit their affiliates from targeting certain keywords, such as those that mention the brand names of the products. Their reasoning is that affiliates add little value to that transaction, so why should the sponsor have to pay an affiliate fee on that transaction for the search version of arbitrage? But other sponsors think about this problem differently. After all, if the affiliates aren't soaking up that ad space, who will? Competitors! Proponents of this way of thinking would rather pay the affiliate fee than lose the sale completely to a competitor.

Regardless of your sponsor's attitude, if you are an affiliate marketer, it usually isn't the basis of long-term success to try to compete with your program's sponsor on transactional search traffic. Instead, opt for the kind of content that your sponsor does not provide, such as impartial product reviews, usage tips, or some other angle that is hard to find. Then target informational keywords with your search marketing strategy. When you get the visitors to your site, enough of them will click through your affiliate links if the products appeal strongly to your audience.

If your site exists mainly for awareness, do not overlook opportunities for web sales of other products, but make sure that your site fulfills the awareness need first. Cereal sites that spend too much time amusing children with games might upset a mom who wants to learn more about the cereal's nutritional content.

Regardless of what your awareness site is trying to do, your search strategy focuses mostly on navigational searches. Cap'n Crunch cereal mostly gets searches (from kids or moms) for *capn crunch* or even *captain crunch*, but not for the specific games or action figures on the site (unless they have an ad campaign for them). Searchers will be typing in the name of the cereal, the name of the movie, or other brand names.

Market awareness sites are also more likely to be "trendy" than sites with other purposes because they are great places to start "buzz" about a product (movies are again a good example). Because it can take a while to get organic search engine results (you must design and optimize your pages and wait for search spiders to find them), market awareness sites often benefit from paid placement techniques, as discussed in Chapter 1, "How Search Marketing Works."

Information and Entertainment

Informing people is a basic goal of any website, but some sites exist for that sole purpose. During the web's "Content is King" phase in the late 1990s, many sites arose offering visitors just another form of media, much like TV or magazines. Some of these sites are adjuncts to offline media, such as CNN's website. These sites exist in part to increase market awareness of the mother ship, as discussed earlier. However, an information and entertainment site can also be an end in itself, existing only to provide information on a particular subject.

Your information and entertainment business might be based on a combination of ad revenue and premium subscriptions, for content that is not available to the general public. Many sites offer free content available to everyone, but "premium products" that offer more exclusive analysis, tools, or deeper content to subscribers. Some interactive game sites, for example, offer free games, but offer multiplayer games by subscription only.

The few well-known information and entertainment sites, such as ESPN, should focus on navigational keywords, but informational keywords are the lifeblood of all information and entertainment sites. ESPN might capture new visitors with its breaking sports news, but makes a profit on premium services, such as ESPN Insider, which offers premium content and analysis. Similarly, game sites might capture traffic for a *multiplayer games* keyword, but they make money only through subscriptions.

Because the keywords for information and entertainment sites are so varied and so topical, paid search often does not pay off. In contrast, organic search optimization techniques can be built in to the process of creating each news story; the search engines learn that these sites change quickly and the spider visits frequently to pick up the new content.

One specific paid search service is of interest to information and content sites. As discussed in Chapter 1, Google AdSense and similar services can place contextual advertisements on your site's pages that relate to the content of each page. Most digital marketers buy contextual ads to bring visitors to their sites, but information and content sites do not—instead, they are the sites where the contextual ads are shown by the search engines. Each time a searcher clicks on a contextual ad, the search engine collects a per-click fee from the advertiser and shares some of it with the information or content site that showed the ad.

Persuasion

Changing someone's mind about an issue or a behavior is the primary goal of an ever-increasing number of websites. These information-oriented sites exist not to make money, but rather to persuade people to do something: give to charity, vote for someone, stop smoking, donate blood, or volunteer to be a Big Brother. All of these causes have websites that try to persuade people to a particular point of view. Increasingly, websites are an integral part of any public relations or political campaign, and are also critical to charitable organizations. If your website falls into this category, you are probably trying to influence public opinion or to help people with a particular problem.

Influencing Public Opinion

The web is fast becoming the tool of choice in influencing opinions. Shallow TV ads are losing credibility with citizens and are increasingly being used to direct people to websites for more information. Just such a website is shown in Exhibit 4-5. These websites are written to persuade people to a point of view, with calls to action that differ somewhat from those of businesses. Obviously, navigational keywords are important to campaigns with TV and other media ad campaigns, but all of these sites emphasize informational keywords, focusing on the best search words (*springfield school budget* or *presidential election*) to attract visitors.

Exhibit 4-5 A persuasion site. Burning public issues more and more are argued by sites on the web.

These influencer sites are not selling a product, but they can function the same way that lead-passing websites do, by moving the visitor to deeper involvement. If you are running a political campaign website, you can offer email newsletters, forms to volunteer as a campaign worker, or the ability to donate money.

Usually, nonprofit organizations try to influence public opinion, but sometimes for-profit businesses do it, too. Verizon might want to dampen public support for workers on strike. WalMart wants public support for building stores in new areas.

However, most opinion influencers are indeed nonprofit organizations. Many are political campaigns, both for candidates for public office and for other ballot initiatives. Bond issues, school budgets, and other ballot questions are more and more being argued by dueling pro and con sites on the web. Other sites mobilize public opinion against government actions, ranging from anti-war sites to those opposed to building that expensive new sports stadium.

No matter what the cause, influencing opinion is a different kind of goal than driving sales. Online sales are a snap to measure, but with public opinion it is quite hard to know how successful you have been. How can you tell that a voter cast a ballot for your candidate? And how can you tell it is because of your website? Usually, you cannot tell, but you can use surrogates that help you measure effectiveness, much the way offline sales and leads can be tied to web activities. Your website can use calls to action (sign our petition, join Citizens for Smith, volunteer to stuff envelopes, sign up for our email newsletter, and so forth) that can be counted to plot your progress.

Public relations campaigns are also different in their duration. Selling a product is usually a long-term effort; you can build your brand over the years. But PR campaigns sometimes last only a few weeks; you must ramp up quickly and might abruptly stop (on election day, for example). Traditional organic search optimization might start up too slowly to get the quick traffic boost you need. In contrast, paid search marketing (as discussed in Chapter 1) can be started at a moment's notice and can be turned off the instant it is no longer needed (such as when your candidate withdraws from the race). The immediacy of paid search (at start and finish) makes it an appealing technique for influencing public opinion when time is of the essence.

Helping People

Charitable organizations have goals that are the hardest to measure of all. How can you tell whether people stop smoking, much less whether they did so because of your website? Just as with the influencer sites previously discussed, calls to action can serve as surrogates for your real goal and help you track something measurable. Evan Balzer, the Vice President of Business Development for Guideposts (the publisher of the inspirational magazine of the same name), says that "helping those in need" is a primary goal of their website (www.guideposts.org), but that they are also beginning to attract volunteers and donors to their organization.

Obviously, raising money and becoming a volunteer are major calls to action, but there are many others. Organizations frequently measure themselves on the basis of information distributed, so the success metrics might be the number of pages viewed, papers downloaded, or free subscriptions ordered. Balzer notes that Guideposts tracks the number of downloads of their inspirational material as a key measure of their success in helping people who come to their site.

Like other persuasion-oriented sites, charities must emphasize informational keywords, because that is what people at their point of need will use. You can see how *stop smoking* and *lung cancer* would be important targets for the American Cancer Society. But such a well-known organization must also consider its ranking for navigational keywords such as *cancer society*.

Unlike quick PR campaigns that benefit from paid search techniques, helping organizations typically have long-term missions wherein slow and steady work in organic search optimization of informational keywords yields great results. Organic approaches are usually less expensive, too, so it fits more easily into constrained charity budgets.

How Do I Juggle Several Goals for My Site?

Your website might have multiple goals—many do. IBM has some products (server accessories and software upgrades) that it sells online to customers, many other products (mainframe servers and business consulting) it sells offline, and some (servers with industry software) that it sells by passing leads to resellers. Like most companies, IBM also wants to create market awareness for its broader brand image campaigns. How does IBM juggle all of these goals?

IBM, like most large businesses, has lots of goals, but each individual area usually has only one or two. For example, IBM's consulting business is aiming for leads while its cloud software business might be aiming for online sales, but these are different parts of the IBM site, so the goals do not conflict. You might also imagine that searchers use different keywords to find each area of IBM's site, so examining the keywords helps you realize both the offering the searcher is interested in as well as the website goal to direct them to. If your site has multiple goals, you can think through which keywords are used to attract them and which products and goals would be appropriate for them.

Every website is created for a purpose, most for more than one. As time passes, however, we sometimes lose sight of why our websites exist. It is critical that you, the search marketer, keep in mind the overarching goals of your website so that you choose the appropriate search marketing strategy. Remember also that no website stands still: Goals can and do change as the years go by. You must regularly examine your goals and choose a search marketing strategy to match.

Next, we examine how to use your site's goals to measure success, setting the stage for measuring your success specifically in search marketing.

Measure Your Website's Success

Search marketing is not an end in itself. The purpose of search marketing is to drive traffic to your site so that your site can reach its goals. Before you can concentrate on search marketing, however, you need to know how to measure your website's success. Only by measuring your site's success can you prove the business case for search marketing.

Beyond the business case, metrics are important to *any* activity that you intend to continuously improve. Management guru Peter Drucker's famous quote, "If you can't measure it, you can't manage it," could easily have been coined for the web, where seemingly *everything* is measurable. Metrics are the lifeblood of any ongoing marketing campaign, including search marketing. In the preceding chapter, we looked at your website's goals. Now we show how you measure success at achieving those goals. This chapter covers the following topics:

- **Counting conversions:** Every time a visitor achieves your website's goal (buying something, entering contact information, donating to your campaign, and so on), you have converted that person from a mere visitor to someone having a new relationship with your organization (a customer, a lead, a donor, and so forth). The first step in measurement is to identify what the right conversions are for your business and to accurately count them.

- **Counting visitors:** Just knowing the number of conversions does not tell you enough. What you really want to know is what percentage of visitors you convert. You can figure that out only by carefully counting visitors, too.

- **Counting dollars:** The most persuasive thing to count is dollars—the extra revenue you earn due to search engine marketing. You can learn to translate into dollars the impact of every visitor who converts, using those dollars as justification for your search marketing efforts.

Even if you are not really a "numbers person," you can learn to quantify what visitors do into extra revenue for you. Let's start with the most critical site metric by counting conversions of your visitors.

Count Your Conversions

It all goes back to the goals you laid out earlier in this chapter. Depending on what your goal is, you measure success in different ways. We will look at each of the goals discussed earlier and determine which visitor outcome you should measure for your business. We call these successful visitor outcomes *conversions*. After we take a close look at what conversions are, we explore which conversions make sense for each kind of business.

Conversion is a sales term that refers to converting prospects into customers, and you might often hear about a business raising its *conversion rate*, the ratio of "lookers" to "buyers." For a web sales business, you can think of the conversion rate as the number of visits to your site divided by the number of orders. Raising the sales conversion rate means that you book more sales with the same number of folks coming into the "store" (your website). Exhibit 4-6 shows how to calculate your website's conversion rate.

September	
Number of orders	4,000
Divided by: Number of web visits	100,000
Conversion rate	4%

Exhibit 4-6 Calculating the sales conversion rate. Dividing the number of orders (buyers) by the number of visits (lookers) yields the conversion rate.

We can use the concept of conversion more broadly than just for sales. There is no reason you cannot apply the same kind of conversion rate calculation to *any* goal for your website. Instead of discussing only sales conversions, you can track **web conversions**, any web activity that can be counted as reaching your site's goal. You might hear sales sites discussing how to **monetize** search—to convert your search results into its business impact in dollars. Counting your conversions is your first step to monetizing *your* website.

Earlier, we showed that every website has a goal for its visitors to achieve, which we are now calling a web conversion. Now, let's measure the effectiveness of each kind of site by *counting* its web conversions. For example, your website's goal might be creating as many leads to an offline channel as possible. Perhaps you have placed a form on your website that enables visitors to provide their contact information, which gets routed to your offline sales force. You can treat each completed contact form as a web conversion, and you can calculate your web conversion rate as shown in Exhibit 4-7.

December	
Number of orders	7,500
Divided by: Number of web visits	100,000
Conversion rate	7.5%

Exhibit 4-7 Calculating the web conversion rate. Dividing the number of leads (completed forms) by the number of visits yields the conversion rate.

Now that you understand the concept of web conversions, we can examine the same list of website goals that we covered earlier and see how you can measure web conversions for each one.

Web Sales

If the goal you chose for your site is web sales, the conversion metric you should count is the number of web orders taken by your site. To analyze what a visitor is doing on his way to becoming one of your conversions, we again turn to the Buyer's Journey methodology introduced in Chapter 2.

We first looked at a visitor behavior model for a web sales site in Chapter 2, and we show it again here as Exhibit 4-8. The Buyer's Journey models how visitors use your site, as each activity leads to the next one. Visitors might set out to *Learn* more about a need or problem they have and what solutions there are. Once informed, they can narrow their choices to a particular kind of solution to S*hop* for a specific product, comparing prices and features, perhaps. After they identify the best product, they are ready to *Buy* the product, and then wait to *Get* it before they can *Use* it.

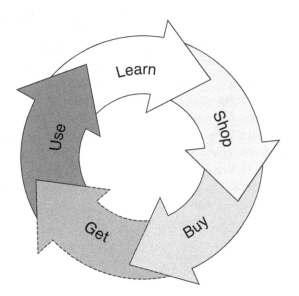

Exhibit 4-8   A behavior model for personal computer sales. Visitors satisfy their information needs before buying, and then return for technical support.

There is nothing terribly hard to understand about any of these steps, and it might exactly fit the kinds of products you sell. For example, a personal computer fits this model quite well. Customers start out not really knowing what to buy. (There are laptops and desktops, and there are even different kinds of desktops that actually sit on your desk or "towers" that go under your desk.) Most people need to learn more about what is out there before they even know what category of computer is right for them, and they can do that right on your website, if you have this kind of information available for them.

After the customer has chosen a particular category, such as a laptop, she needs to decide which one. She must analyze Dell versus ThinkPad versus Apple, and she must also make decisions about operating systems, weight, battery life, screen resolution, memory, disk space, and lots of other features. These are all the tasks that shoppers go through while they shop for a computer, and they are increasingly done on the web. If you are a retailer, you can provide objective information for all the brands you carry, and manufacturers can differentiate their wares against their competitors'.

After she has narrowed down her choices to just a few, she begins thinking about whether to buy. She starts to think about where she can get the lowest price and the fastest shipping for one of the models that she wants. The web is also a great place to do this, if you have designed your site to make it easy to compare prices (including shipping) for different models and if you explain shipping options and any special offers that are available.

After purchasing, she wants an email confirmation. While waiting to get her computer, she can check the status of the order at any time right on the website. If she has chosen express delivery, you can help her track the package through UPS or any other shipper, also right on the web. Because most of the *Get* interaction occurs off-web, we show that step using dotted lines in Exhibit 4-8.

The moment she receives her computer, she can begin to use it. She can install it and get right to work. As she does, she can get answers to her problems on the manufacturer's website. She might sometimes have trouble throughout the life of the computer and come back to get technical support. If the manufacturer has done a good job in support, she might at some point want to upgrade her computer by adding more memory, or she might want to replace her computer with a new model, in which case she begins to learn all over again as she considers a new purchase.

As exciting as it is to count conversions, you can also use your Buyer's Journey to count **microconversions**, moments when your buyer moves from step to step in the journey. If you focus on increasing the percentage of microconversions from *Learn* to *Shop*, you are automatically improving your conversions, too. But it can be much easier to use your microconversion rates to diagnose problem areas in your Buyer's Journey for improvement than merely looking at an overall conversion rate that lumps together several steps. If the conversion rate is low, you might not have a clue where to start to improve it.

This Buyer's Journey for personal computer sales shows why websites must be designed with customers in mind; after all, customers might use the web every step of the way. But *your* business might be different than PCs. You might need different steps in *your* version of the Buyer's Journey. Read on to design your own Buyer's Journey that is just right for your business.

What if you have a pure online business, where you download the software that you sell? Your model might look like Exhibit 4-9, which is similar to the personal computer model, where customers need to *Learn*, *Shop*, and *Buy* (and *Get* support when they *Use* it), but there is no truly distinct *Get* step; instead, the software is downloaded to their computer as part of the *Buy* step. So, no order status is needed because no package is being physically shipped.

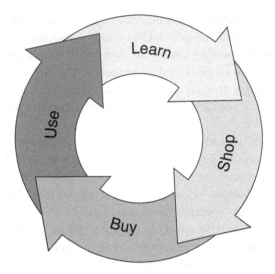

Exhibit 4-9   A behavior model for a software download store. For pure online businesses, there really is no distinct *Get* step.

It is also possible that your model might not require any substantial post-sales support, such as an eBook store. In that case, your model might resemble the one in Exhibit 4-10, where (after the *Buy* step) your customers do not return to your website until they need to consider their next purchase.

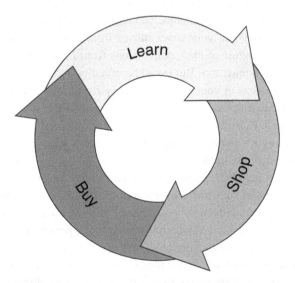

Exhibit 4-10   A behavior model for an eBook store. Products that require no post-sales support might not require an explicit *Use* step.

In Exhibit 4-11, we show how a web bookstore might operate, where you physically ship your product (requiring a get step) but usually have no post-purchase customer interactions until the next buying opportunity.

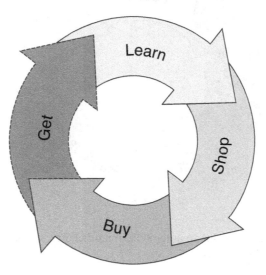

Exhibit 4-11   A behavior model for a bookstore. A *Get* step is required, but no *Use* step because no post-sales support is required.

Regardless of which version of the Buyer's Journey is right for your web sales business, it is simple for you to calculate your success. The same eCommerce system that takes your customer's order can count the number of sales that you make from your site, and your web analytics system can count the number of visitors to your site. You use these two numbers to calculate your conversion rate, as was shown in Exhibit 4-6 earlier. Later in this chapter, we show you how your conversion rate helps measure the impact of your search marketing campaign in dollars.

Offline Sales

If your business focuses on offline sales, you need to take special care in deciding what to count as web conversions. Offline sales businesses have visitor behavior models that closely resemble those of their web sales competitors, except that some steps occurs offline—often through face-to-face interaction or by phone. In Exhibit 4-12, we use the example of an automobile manufacturer, and we depict offline interactions with the customer with dotted lines.

For offline sales, just as for web sales, the customer needs to learn about what kinds of cars are available, because so many choices exist (and they increase each year). People do not buy cars every year, and they typically do a lot of research on the web before making a decision.

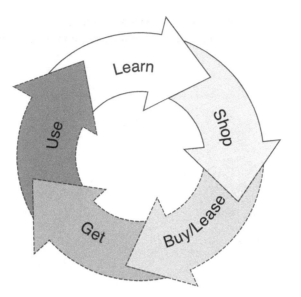

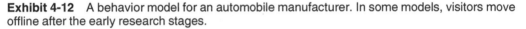

Exhibit 4-12   A behavior model for an automobile manufacturer. In some models, visitors move offline after the early research stages.

Increasingly, people are starting to shop for a new car on the web. If your customers typically walk into a dealer showroom with a web printout of exactly what they want, they have actually completed the *Shop* step on the web. Exhibit 4-13 shows how Ford does it, but most auto manufacturers have similar facilities. If your website does not offer this capability, *your* Buyer's Journey would show the *Shop* step with dotted lines because your goal is to shift your customers to offline channels following the *Learn* step.

Relatively few cars are actually purchased on the web, so the model in Exhibit 4-12 shows the *Buy/Lease* step in dotted lines, emphasizing that it happens offline. It is possible that this step might shift to the web at some point in the future, with customers dropping by the dealer to get their new car, but most customers still haggle and purchase in person today.

Customers still get their cars at the dealer and return to the dealer (or elsewhere) for maintenance while they use their cars, with relatively little interaction with your website, so these steps are shown as offline, too.

Although web sales and offline sales share significant similarities, one crucial difference exists: It is easy to know how many visitors to your website also bought your product on your website, but it is a lot harder to accurately measure offline sales driven by the web. No matter what you do, you will never have perfect measurements, but there are some basic ways to tie offline sales to the web:

Simple steps lead to an offline purchase

In the last step, after the choices are made, shift to get an Internet price, or search inventory of a nearby offline dealer.

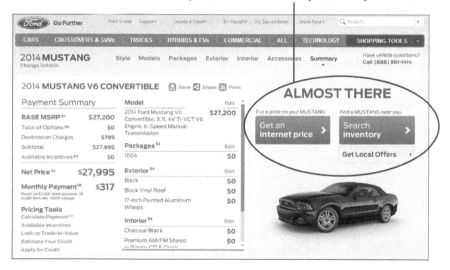

Exhibit 4-13 Shop for a car on the web. Ford's site lets you "build" your Ford and present the result to a dealer for purchase.

- **Provide a special phone number:** If your goal is to shift web visitors to your call center to take the order by phone, you can use some simple tricks to tie the call to your website, such as displaying a phone number that appears only on your website and is not used in TV or print ads or any other materials. That way, anyone who uses that number must have come from your site. A variant on this is to call your regular number but advise them to "Ask for Operator 123" or "Ask for Alice." (Not all of your visitors will do this, however, so you might have them "Ask for Alice to receive a free mouse pad with your computer.")

- **Call them:** You can provide a form on your website that lets web visitors complete their contact information so you can call them. IBM has had success with a Call Me Now button. When the button is clicked, the customer is prompted to supply a phone number, and an IBM telephone salesperson calls the customer within a few minutes.

- **Bring this printout:** As you saw in Exhibit 4-13, Ford encourages customers to select the color and options for their car before coming to the dealer. The dealer can note any customer who brought in that printout for tracking purposes. If your product does not require extensive customization, you could provide an online coupon for a freebie or a discounted price the customer can print and bring to the store.

- **Request for quote:** Ford's website also demonstrates an RFQ capability, where the car the customer "built" can be shown to a local dealer who prices it. The customer needs to fill out contact information to receive the quote, so any sales made to this customer can then be accurately tracked as assisted by the website.

If, as you read this list, you are thinking that these techniques are excellent goals for your web conversion rate, you are catching on! Your web analytics system can count the number of visitors who come to the site, and you can also count how many visitors reach each of these goals. Your web analytics system can count how many folks click a Call Me Now button, or print out a form, or request a quote, but you need to take steps in your call center procedures to ensure that your web callers are accurately logged. No matter what the right technique is for your business, you can calculate your web conversion rate as shown in Exhibit 4-14.

December		
Out of 100,000 Visitors, How Many...	Number of Web Visitors Converted	Web Conversion Rate
Called a special phone number?	10,000	10%
Brought discount coupon to a dealer?	3,000	3%
Requested an online quote?	1,000	1%

Exhibit 4-14   Web conversion for offline sales sites. You can track different web conversion rates for each goal you have for your site.

However, your web conversion rate still needs to be expressed in terms of dollars. That's why it is critical to choose web conversions that can be linked to offline sales, as we have in these examples. Your offline procedures must ensure that call center operators log each call accurately or that dealers report the printouts brought in, for example. By doing so, you ensure accurate sales reporting, because if you track these events in your sales reporting system, you will learn how much of your sales derive from the web, as shown in Exhibit 4-15.

December Average Order: $2000	Web Conversion	Sales Conversions Rate	Offline Orders	Sales Revenue
Special phone number	10,000	1.0%	100	$200,000
Discount coupon	3,000	10.0%	300	$600,000
Online quote	1,000	10.0%	100	$200,000
Totals	14,000	3.6%	500	$1,000,000

Exhibit 4-15 Web conversion for offline sales sites. You can track your monetary results for each goal you have for your site.

If you examine Exhibits 4-14 and 4-15 together, you can begin to see how to measure the impact of your website in terms of sales, even though your site makes no direct sales. By creating a way to tie the offline sales back to the website, you can see that your site was the catalyst for $1 million in sales in December. You can also calculate your *sales* conversion rate (not your web conversion rate) for your web visitors as shown in Exhibit 4-16.

December	
Number of offline orders	500
Divided by: Number of web visits	100,000
Sales conversion rate	0.5%

Exhibit 4-16 Sales conversion rate for offline sales. You can track your offline sales conversion by dividing offline orders by total web visitors.

When you can measure the conversions of your website, you can do a little math to express your goals in purely monetary terms. Exhibit 4-17 shows how to monetize each web conversion so that you know the value to your business.

This table tells you that every time your website persuades someone to call on the phone, it is worth about $20 in revenue, whereas persuading someone to print a discount coupon or to request a quote are worth about $200 each. When you understand this, you can see how improving your website so that more visitors take these actions can directly affect your sales.

December Average Order: $2,000	Web Conversions	Sales Revenue	Sales Revenue per Conversion
Special phone number	10,000	$200,000	$20
Discount coupon	3,000	$600,000	$200
Online quote	1,000	$200,000	$200

Exhibit 4-17   Web conversions in terms of revenue. You can calculate, on average, how much each and every web conversion is worth.

These examples show how, even for an offline sales site, you can tie your web conversions to your true sales. Later in this chapter, you will learn how to build on these calculations to measure the dollar impact of your search marketing efforts.

WHAT IF I CAN'T TRACK OFFLINE SALES BACK TO MY WEBSITE?

Don't worry. If you have no systems in place that enable you to track your offline sales back to your website, all is not lost. After all, it is not that hard for you to set up special phone numbers or offer printable discount coupons. But maybe you cannot get your organization to take even those minimal steps. If you truly cannot track actual sales instigated by the web, the next-best thing is to estimate them. How to go about that estimating depends on your business (as always), but there are a few possibilities:

- **Ask customers when they buy:** If you close most of your sales on the phone, add a question to the call center script to ask customers whether they used your website before calling.

- **Use barcodes:** Add a barcode to your offer and scan their printout when they come into the store. Quick Response (QR) codes and SMS codes can also make that critical connection.

- **Update your warranty cards:** If your product already requires the return of a warranty card, change your questions to ask about use of your website.

- **Add a question to a survey:** Your business might regularly survey your customers. Add one question to the survey to see whether customers used the website before their last purchase.

None of these methods are as scientific as tracking actual sales, but they are better than nothing. After you choose your estimation method, the number that you calculate can be used in the rest of our formulas to estimate sales conversion rates and any other statistic. You can also use estimates to perform trend analysis, checking the ups and downs month to month. If possible, however, you should try to eventually implement systems that accurately track sales by each discrete purchase.

Leads

Websites designed to generate leads can measure their conversions in much the same way as sites that generate offline sales. Let's first examine a typical behavior model for a leads site, in this case a swimming pool dealer, in Exhibit 4-18.

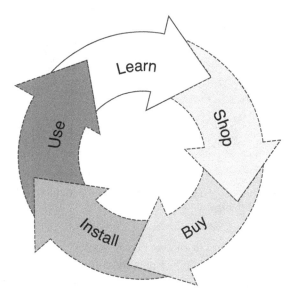

Exhibit 4-18 A behavior model for a swimming pool dealer. Some models shift offline quickly in the sales process.

The first thing that you notice is all those dotted lines! For the typical lead-oriented site, visitors learn on the website, but tend to do everything else offline. Customers looking for a swimming pool want to get information about whether to choose above-ground or in-ground pools on the web. When a customer begins to shop for a specific pool, however, he needs a dealer to come to his house and tell him what it costs to be installed in his backyard. Similarly, the *Buy*, *Install*, and *Use* steps each occur offline, for the most part, although some dealers might have some helpful do-it-yourself pool-maintenance tips on the web.

If your business is not based on product sales, you might need a different model. Consider how a consulting firm might model visitor activities, as shown in Exhibit 4-19. This model differs from product-oriented businesses. In product-oriented businesses, the products are largely offered as is (or can be somewhat customized), whereas a customer requiring consulting services is focused on explaining the problem to suppliers so they can solve it.

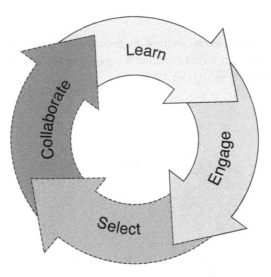

Exhibit 4-19   A behavior model for a consulting firm. Highly customized services require a model focused on agreeing on the service being provided.

Consulting customers need to learn about their problem so that they can understand what kinds of solutions can be provided, but they quickly move to *engage* with a few possible consultants. The *Engage* step typically includes a request for proposal (RFP), in which customers describe their specific situations. The *Engage* step is more often being executed online, as customers describe their problems and provide contact information in web forms. The *Select* step, in which the customer receives written responses to the RFP and selects a consultant to work with, is almost always done offline, as is the engagement itself, during which the consultant and the customer *collaborate* to solve the problem. Successful consulting firms make it a point to use engagements to teach their customers about other problems they can solve, starting the *Learn* step all over again.

After you develop the right version of the Buyer's Journey for your lead-oriented website, you are faced with the question of how to measure its success. Although methods can vary from business to business, it is usually easier to measure leads than offline sales. **Lead management** systems help your business store contact information for each visitor who fills in his contact information, and they help track the progress of that lead all the way through to a sale. So, the easiest way to measure your site is to ensure that your web contact form (the one that all leads fill out) is connected to your lead management system. When it is, your lead management system will track the number of leads submitted from the web, and will show you exactly which sales resulted. You can use this information to calculate the value of each lead, as shown in Exhibit 4-20.

December Average Order: $2,000	Total	Conversion Rate	Sales Revenue per Event
Web visitors	100,000	100%	$20
Web leads	2,000	2%	$1,000
Orders from web leads	1,000	1%	$2,000

Exhibit 4-20 The value of leads. You can calculate the average worth of each lead as well as the web conversion and sales conversion rates.

You can divide total sales (in this case, $2 million) by the number of orders to determine that the average order size is $2,000. Using the same logic, you can divide sales by the number of leads to learn that each lead is worth an average of $1,000. This calculation shows you the value of improving your website to drive more and more leads. Similarly, if you take the same calculation back one more step, you can divide total sales by the number of web visitors to see that each visitor to your website is worth about $20. Later in the chapter, you will learn how to use these calculations to put together your business case for search engine marketing.

Market Awareness

Because their goal of "raising awareness" for a product is so nebulous, it is critical that market awareness sites carefully choose exactly what to count as their web conversion metric. If you design your website to persuade visitors to complete specific web conversions, you can calculate measurements that can show the value of your market awareness website.

Exhibit 4-21 shows a specific example of a market awareness behavioral model for a children's cereal. The website is promoted on the cereal box itself and in TV ads for the cereal, leading kids to *discover* the website. Once there, they engage by reading stories and playing games that reinforce the brand as fun for kids. The goal of the site is to get kids to *enroll* in a club by providing their mailing address. Club members are mailed a monthly newsletter with fun games for the kids, action figures to buy, and cereal discount coupons for their parents. Because most cereal companies sell multiple cereals, the *Enroll* step might also trigger mail solicitations for other kids' cereal clubs, starting the cycle again.

You are probably getting the idea by now. You can track club enrollments as your web conversion and coupon redemption as your sales conversion. After tracking for a while, you might find that club members buy two more boxes of cereal a month than nonmembers, demonstrating the value of the website.

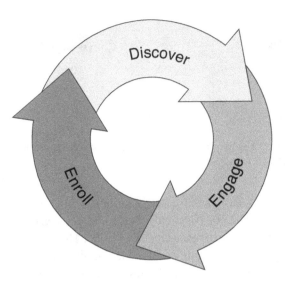

Exhibit 4-21   A behavior model for a children's cereal. The website is used to form deeper relationships with children who influence parents to buy.

Information and Entertainment

Information and entertainment sites frequently derive most of their revenue from advertising, but they often sell premium services, too. For premium service sales, the number of orders is the proper web conversion metric. You can use the Buyer's Journey methodology to model premium services sales, as shown in Exhibit 4-22.

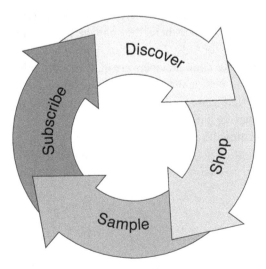

Exhibit 4-22   A behavior model for a subscription information site. Premium services are constantly marketed with free trial periods leading to purchase.

The first step for these sites is taken when visitors *discover* the site, often from a search keyword, and continues as each visitor returns to the site for free content and discovers that premium services are available. On espn.com, for example, "Insiders" can view exclusive content not available to others. These premium stories are shown alongside the free stories, and a sales pitch for Insiders is shown each time a nonmember clicks on them, as shown in Exhibit 4-23.

Most ESPN content is free, but some is for "Insiders" only

When an Insider link is clicked on by someone who is not a member, the premium service is described and a chance for a free trial is offered

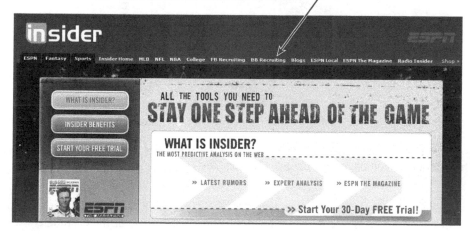

Exhibit 4-23 Premium services on an information site. ESPN shows Insider premium content alongside free content.

The enticement for ESPN Insider places the visitor in the shop phase, as he is continually exposed to the value of premium membership each time he sees a link that is exclusive to Insiders. The next step is to entice the visitor to *sample* the premium service, typically with a 30-day free trial; visitors *subscribe* at the end of that period if they have not explicitly cancelled. Most premium services capture email addresses for the trial period, which they use to periodically contact prospective customers whenever new services become available, beginning the *Discover* step over again.

In this case, the model is similar to online sales in that the web conversion and the sales conversion are exactly the same event, so calculating the revenue value of visitors is relatively simple.

Persuasion

So far we have looked only at businesses, but any website can benefit from behavior modeling. Exhibit 4-24 shows a possible model for a political campaign that you can use to both choose and measure your web conversions. Just as with buyers making a purchase, each voter might go through several steps in response to the candidate.

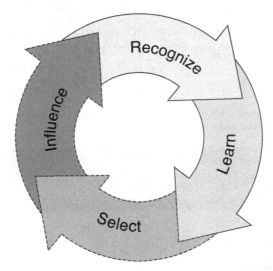

Exhibit 4-24   A behavior model for a political campaign. Each voter's activity can be modeled throughout the campaign right up until Election Day.

The first step is for a voter to *recognize* the candidate's name, which might happen online (searching for a candidate's name) or offline (seeing the name of the candidate's website in a TV ad). At some point, the voter decides to learn more about the candidate's background and positions on the issues, and comes to the website. Voters eventually *select* the candidate they will vote for, but this is an offline conversion that cannot be accurately measured before Election Day. The trick for the website is to set up a web conversion that *can* be measured. That is why the *Influence* step is so important.

If your website can attract people who are willing to influence other people, you can be fairly certain you have their votes locked up. What's more, they might start attracting more supporters. So the best web conversions for your site might be influencer goals:

- **Email a friend:** Provide a function that sends a position paper to someone else with a personal note from your visitor. This goal has the added value of placing the friend's email address in your solicitation database.

- **Volunteer to work for the campaign:** There is never any shortage of work to do, and free labor conserves funding for TV ads and other expenses.

- **Donate to the campaign:** The web is becoming a powerful force in raising political contributions. Each election seems to set a new record in online contributions.

Other web conversions besides influencing others might also correlate to racking up votes at the polls, such as subscribing to email newsletters or downloading position papers. But whether your site is persuading a voter or someone else, you must decide what your web conversions are so that you can measure your information and entertainment site's effectiveness.

Count Your Traffic

We've spent a lot of time discussing how to measure your website's effectiveness at achieving conversions, and each time we do, we talk about visitors to the site. As you have seen, you cannot determine your conversion rate unless you know how many visitors are coming. But how do you count visitors? *That* is what this section explores.

Web analytics experts refer to visitors coming to your websites as **traffic,** and you need to understand the fundamentals of traffic measurement because it is a critical part of tracking your success.

Page Views

The most fundamental metric in web measurements is the **page view**, which is just what it sounds like: a count of how many web pages have been shown to your site's visitors. Web analytics reports always summarize page views for a particular time period, so you can see how many page views occurred in a day, a week, or a month.

By analyzing the trends of page views, you can see whether your views have gone up this month from last month, or from the same month last year. Many businesses can compare this month to last month, but seasonal businesses should compare to the same month the previous year. For example, a toy retailer should contrast January's page views to those of last January rather than comparing January to last month's Christmas-inflated December numbers.

More importantly, the page views of individual pages can be analyzed, so that you can see which particular pages on your site have been viewed the most, and you can analyze the trends for each page over time.

Visits and Visitors

More interesting than analyzing page views is examining just who is viewing those pages. Most web analytics programs can identify a series of pages that have been viewed by the same visitor, by using **cookies**. The web analytics program "drops" a cookie file on each visitor's computer when she enters the site. This file contains a unique identifier not shared by any other computer's cookie. The web analytics program reads the identifier from the cookie file each time a page is viewed and remembers which computer viewed that page.

Identifying visitors allows analytics programs to provide you with better information. Now, instead of merely counting page views, you can count the number of **visits** to your site. Visits, called **sessions** by some analytics facilities, let you see how many people are coming, not just how many pages were viewed by all people. For example, two websites might each show 100 page views, but one site has four visits with 25 page views each, whereas another might have ten visits that average ten views each. If you count just page views, all you know is that 100 pages were viewed. If you count visits, you know that one site got four visits, but they stayed and looked around for a while, whereas the other site got ten visits from people who looked at fewer pages in each visit. This information is critical because you cannot get more conversions from more page views; you get more conversions from more visits.

In addition to identifying visits, you can also track the number of **visitors** (sometimes called **unique visitors**), because you can track whether the *same* visitor has returned to your site multiple times. So, the analytics report could show 100 page views in ten visits by eight different visitors, because a couple of those eight visitors had more than one visit. This is important, too, because for many websites, people tend to visit multiple times before they convert; therefore, knowing the number of *new* versus *returning* visitors can tell you even more than tracking visits alone.

Indeed, many sites calculate their conversion rates using visitors rather than using visits, as we showed you earlier. Sites that do this typically require multiple visits to get a single conversion, such as an automobile manufacturer's site. Sites that could conceivably log a conversion on every visit (Amazon, for example), tend to stick with visits in their conversion formula. It doesn't matter much which one you use, as long as you do it consistently without switching between one and the other.

It is true that web analytics programs accurately count all of these measurements, but it is critical that you use a *single* analytics facility across your entire site. Although small sites would undoubtedly do so, large websites with hundreds of thousands of pages might implement different analytics facilities for different parts of the site. If you are in this situation, collecting accurate measurements across your entire site is impossible.

To see why it is impossible, suppose that you have two analytics systems, one used in the sales part of your site and the other in the support area. In this situation, you cannot just add up the number of visitors in each system to get your total, because each system drops a visitor cookie when it sees a new visitor. Any visitor whose visit crosses both sales and support pages will be double counted. It will seem like two separate visits when it was, in fact, one. If you have more than two systems, the problem is even worse. Double-counting your visits lowers your reported conversion rate and makes your efforts appear less effective than they are, because sales are reported accurately, but the number of visitors who created the sales is artificially high.

If you must live with a situation where multiple analytics facilities are used for the same website, just keep in mind that the visit and visitor numbers will not be accurate when added up for the total site. It is *still* better to use those inaccurate numbers than to ignore them, because you can perform **trend analysis** on even inaccurate numbers because the inaccuracies are relatively constant. For example, if you add up visitor totals across three separate analytics systems, they might not be right, because some of those "visitors" are actually the *same* folks who headed into different parts of your site. Regardless, if you see that you added up 30% more visitors this month than you added up last month, you can probably conclude that *something* good is happening, even though you really cannot be sure that the improvement is actually 30% as opposed to 22% or 45%. It is definitely worth the effort to get to a single analytics system so that your numbers *are* accurate, but do use whatever data you have, no matter how imperfect. Some data is better than no data.

Count Your Money

Earlier in this chapter, we spent a lot of time analyzing the behavior model for visitors to your website and determining the business value of what they do. You can use that analysis to make the case for investing in search engine marketing. If you are running a political campaign, this section does not apply to you because you cannot justify your spending based on higher revenue. For everyone else, however, this is the section that will get your search marketing campaign funded. Businesses invest money because they can count the revenue that comes in after that investment.

The simplest business case for search engine marketing for any business is this: If they can't find it, they can't buy it. But that will not convince too many green-eyeshade types like your chief financial officer. And, like anything else, a search marketing program requires investment.

So, how do you convince accountants to open the checkbook? Start with the Buyer's Journey. Go back to the model you developed earlier in this chapter—the one that best fits your business. No matter what the model, you have chosen what to count as your web conversions. Maybe yours are simple, because you sell direct on the web and you just need to count web orders. Or maybe they are more complicated to track, such as leads or offline sales. But no matter what your conversions are, you can use the formulas presented earlier to place a dollar value on each web conversion. Check out Exhibit 4-25 for a summary.

Website Goal	Formula
Web sales	Total sales ÷ Total orders
Offline sales	Total sales from web ÷ Total web conversions
Leads	Total sales from web ÷ Total leads

Exhibit 4-25   Calculating the value of web conversions. You can calculate the average worth of each web conversion for any website goal.

Exhibit 4-25 can be simplified even further, because the formula listed for offline sales actually works for any goal. No matter what your goal, if you can count the total sales that came from the web and divide that dollar figure by the total number of web conversions, you will find the value of each conversion.

Although that is interesting, and useful for showing the value of your website, it does not yet justify spending money on search marketing. To make that case, we need to take the model one step further. We need to identify the value of each visitor to the site.

The formula for the value of each visitor is also simple: Divide the total sales from the web by the total number of visitors. Exhibit 4-19 provided an example of this calculation, where 100,000 visitors came to the site and each visitor was worth about $20. This calculation is the basis of your search engine marketing business case, because the purpose of search engine marketing is to increase the number of visitors to your site. Exhibit 4-26 shows a simple example of how the calculation could work for the site modeled in Exhibit 4-20. The 10% rise in traffic yields 10,000 new visitors worth $20 each for a $200,000 increase in revenue, for example.

If Traffic Increases By	Revenue Increases By
5%	$100,000
10%	$200,000
15%	$300,000

Exhibit 4-26   Calculating the value of increased traffic. You can calculate the sales impact of additional traffic to your site.

If the flinty-eyed accounting types at your business do not need any more than what is shown in Exhibit 4-26, consider yourself lucky and go get the money to start your search marketing campaign. Most businesses, however, need more than this. They need to know exactly how much you are projecting to increase site traffic, and they want to know what it will cost. These are reasonable questions, but we are not yet able to answer them. That's what we will tackle in the last section of this chapter, when we go beyond existing website measurements to a set of new metrics that help you move your organization where it needs to go. We start by assessing where your site stands today and show you the opportunity that you are missing. We build on the calculations we introduced in this chapter to show what search engine marketing is worth to your own website.

You probably know that "you get what you measure." Now we show you how to track the measurements that prompt the behavior you want. So, say goodbye to generalities. No more theory. Let's put your site under the microscope

Measure Your Search Marketing Success

It might seem backward to talk about how to measure the impact of your search marketing at this point. After all, don't you do that after the campaign? Well, yes and no. Certainly, you cannot measure what happened until after it has happened, but you must focus on measurements up front to justify the initial investment in search marketing. Unless you can project the value, you will never get that investment funded in the first place.

Defining your search metrics from the beginning helps you justify the investment, and it also focuses your activities. Too often, search marketing is treated as an art rather than a science—a set of arcane incantations that when repeated with fervor (and mixed with eye of newt and toe of frog) will somehow magically lead to success. Nothing could be further from the truth.

Although intuition is a normal part of anything you do, it should be the exception rather than the rule. Without measurable results, you cannot tell a skilled practitioner from a quack, or a successful campaign from a flop. When you painstakingly measure everything you do, you can do more of what works and less of what does not. You make these adjustments every day and gradually improve your results. Intuition can still be important, but even then, informed intuition is the best kind.

Enough philosophy! It's time to roll up your sleeves and get to work. Instead of just listing the search metrics and explaining them to you, we walk you through an example. At the same time, we encourage you to choose your own example—your first search marketing campaign—and work through the measurements in your own business.

In this final section, we take several steps to understand search metrics:

- **Target your first campaign:** You can always change your mind later, but you will find that choosing the first target for search marketing now will make it easier to study search metrics. Most people find that learning with their first campaign in mind is highly motivating.

- **Assess your current situation:** The first use for search metrics is figuring out what shape you are in right now. Your assessment provides objective evidence of the importance of your search marketing plan—both the overall plan and each piece of the plan. Every task in your plan will be driven by what you find in your assessment. You will finalize your choice for your first search marketing campaign, and you will take action based on your own situation.

- **Calculate your opportunity:** Another use for search metrics is "what if" analysis that shows you how well you will be doing after you execute your plan. Although no one can promise exactly what your results will be, you can estimate your outcome to show the potential impact on your organization.

There are many more search metrics than we cover in this chapter, so we return to the subject of metrics in Chapter 10, "Make Search Marketing Operational." In this chapter, however, we focus on the basic metrics required for you to show the business case for search marketing. Your first search marketing campaign is the place to start.

Target Your First Search Marketing Campaign

Before you dive into search metrics, you need to first choose a project to measure. To do so, you must decide the area of your site that you want to drive search traffic to. Which product sale? Which marketing program? A signup form? You have to pick something.

You might be saying to yourself, "How should I know where to start search marketing in my business?" Don't worry. It's not as hard as it sounds. And, you can always change your mind. As you read through this chapter, you might realize that you should have started search marketing somewhere else in your organization. If so, just retrace your steps and figure out the new campaign.

To choose your first campaign, go back to the goals of your website from the first part of this chapter. If your site sells online, pick a top-selling product and try to raise sales. If you generate leads for offline sales, choose a hot new product and work on increasing leads. No matter what your site's goals are, you can choose some area of your website and declare, "This is the best place to start." After you choose the target area, you will then discover which search keywords to target in your campaign.

Choose the Target Area of Your Site

What makes a particular area of your website the best place? After all, your first campaign is important. You want it to succeed and to persuade others that it succeeded. To choose your "best place," follow these rules when you make your selection:

- **Pick something high profile:** If you want to get attention with your first campaign, don't pick some sleepy product that no one cares about. If you do, you might execute a great search marketing campaign and still ring up few sales.

- **Make sure the business impact can be measured:** Using the methods outlined in previous chapters, you can measure almost any outcome and place a value on it. But make sure that your organization already has those measurements in place, or that you can put them in place. If your first campaign delivers 50% more leads to the sales force, that is great; but it is not so great if no one knows how much a lead is worth. You have obviously succeeded, but it is hard to decide how much to continue to invest. That is a bad thing.

- **Keep it simple:** Your first campaign should not tackle any of the difficult problems that we cover later in this book; if you know there are big search problems in one area, pick another area. It is also easier if you avoid areas of your site that already have some paid search activity, because your first campaign should usually be in organic search. Having existing paid activity makes your impact harder to measure. Leave the advanced topics for later and take on something manageable now. When you conduct your assessment, you will get a clue as to how hard your problem might be.

- **Make it practical:** If your top-selling product has a team that is always hopelessly busy with their own plans, maybe you should choose your #2 seller. If your #2 product team is located two time zones away, maybe the #3 team that sits in your building would be your best choice. Think about who maintains the content for your targeted area and pick a group that you can work with easily.

So take some time and think it over. Which part of your website offers the best tradeoff between business impact and degree of difficulty? Answer that question and keep that answer in mind as we explore search metrics. As you look deeper into your current situation, you might find that you have chosen a project too difficult for your first one. If so, you will realize it while you read this chapter, and you can always change your mind and circle back.

While you are thinking through your target project, we walk you through a fictional case study of our own. Imagine what you would do for Snap Electronics, a large consumer electronics manufacturer with a well-known brand name and an equally large website (SnapElectronics.com) that does brisk online sales. (Snap is a completely imaginary company not patterned after any existing corporation.)

Snap Electronics has a long history of innovative consumer electronics designs ranging from TVs to DVD players to home theater systems. Snap is well known for its breakthroughs in ease of use; its tag line is "Our products are a snap." As you look at our rules for choosing the right product area to target, Snap's evaluation is shown in Exhibit 4-27.

Product Area	High Profile?	Measurable?	Simple?	Practical?
Televisions	Yes	No	Unknown	Yes
DVD players	Yes	Yes	Unknown	No
Home theater	Yes	No	Unknown	No
VCRs		No	Yes	Unknown
Digital cameras	Yes	Yes	Unknown	Yes

Exhibit 4-27 Snap Electronics product suitability. You assess the suitability of a product area for your first search marketing campaign according to a few simple rules.

As we consider the contenders, we realize that most of Snap's TVs and home theater systems are sold offline, so it is harder to measure the impact of your search marketing campaign for those products. We also remember that the group that handles DVD players is redesigning its entire site for a launch in two months, so they are probably not in the mood to hear from us now. We dismiss VCRs because the technology is fading, so it is not as high profile as the others. But digital cameras might be promising.

Snap was late to the digital camera party, but introduced several innovative models under a new SnapShot brand that (as usual) were markedly easier to use than competing models. Snap blanketed TV and magazines with advertising touting SnapShot's easy design, raising brand awareness. But after the successful launch, marketing costs need to come down this year. Snap cannot continue to spend so much on advertising year after year. Each of these factors make SnapShot digital cameras a strong candidate for Snap's first search marketing campaign.

As we sum up the factors we considered in Exhibit 4-27, we see that the digital camera product area is high profile, we can measure its online sales, and the product team seems practical to work with, but Snap's one concern is simplicity. They know that there are no paid search campaigns underway, so it will be simple to measure the organic search results without the complexity of paid search obscuring what is going on. But it is still hard to judge the difficulty of changing the digital camera content to rank well in search, because we have not yet investigated the site deeply enough. We will have to wait for the assessment to find out how simple this campaign might be.

Focus on the Keywords Searchers Use

Perhaps you are not sure what searchers might enter into search engines when they want to buy a digital camera. Fortunately, there are lots of ways to find out, which we cover in Chapter 6, "Choose Your Target Market Segments." But you do not need that much sophistication yet.

Which keywords do you think are the most popular for finding a digital camera? Kind of obvious that *digital camera* might be one of them, huh? After you have settled on one or more phrases, it's time to find variations. Again, you will learn much more about this process in Chapter 6, but for now, let's just find some keywords to target.

You can use just about any keyword research tool for this exercise, but let's use Google Trends, because it is free. Google changes the way its tool works all the time, but if you point your browser to the right URL (google.com/trends/explore), you'll see something similar to the piece of the screenshot in Exhibit 4-28. You can type in a few words and see what other suggestions Google makes.

It was easy for Snap to think of *digital camera* as the phrase searchers are likely to enter, but your site might be a bit harder than that. You might need to do some brainstorming. Ask other people, look at your web pages, and check out your competitors' pages. Think about what words you use to describe your products to your family. What do industry pundits call this kind of product?

	Related terms ⑦		Top	Rising
Competitor	canon digital camera	100	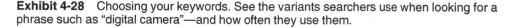	
Competitor	canon	100		
Competitor	canon camera	100		
Competitor	sony camera digital	85		
Competitor	sony camera	80		
Good	best digital camera	60		
Good	digital cameras	55		
Good	cameras	55		
Competitor	nikon digital camera	55		
Good	camera reviews	55		

Exhibit 4-28   Choosing your keywords. See the variants searchers use when looking for a phrase such as "digital camera"—and how often they use them.

It is tempting to settle for the names your company uses for its products—sometimes those *are* the most popular names. (Searchers do use some brand names a lot, such as iPad or Windows.) But most companies are not blessed with a product whose brand name overshadows its generic name. Try to think of the generic (not proper name) phrases people use to find you—do not use the name of your company or your product. Brand names are also good keywords to target, but your goal with this tool is to identify variations on the most common search keyword, so try to think of the most popular way to refer to your product. In Snap's case, the most popular keyword is *digital camera* rather than its brand name, *SnapShot*.

So, after you have amassed your generic keywords and variations, what do you do with this list? Well, it is clear that many folks are searching for *digital camera* all by itself. All of Snap's competitors are trying to rank #1 for the keyword *digital camera*—anyone in their business would want that—but maybe they are overlooking these other keyword combinations.

You might be dreaming about ranking #1 for *digital camera* (and someone does rank #1, so it *is* possible). But it takes quite a bit of work to get that top ranking because so many others want that ranking, too. Although we will not drop the idea of getting a high ranking for an extremely popular keyword such as *digital camera*, we need to look at less-popular keywords, too. These less-popular keywords generate plenty of traffic, but fewer companies target them, making it easier to get a high ranking for them. You will see that these medium-popularity keywords are often the perfect targets, generating just enough traffic to be noticeable but without the intense competition for high rankings that comes with the top keywords.

You also want to focus on the purpose behind each keyword—the searcher's intent, which we explore in Chapter 6. Matching your content as closely as possible to the searcher's intent drives higher conversions. Some of the keywords on this list might be perfect for Snap, whereas others might not, which we will determine by analyzing each one.

So, let's look at the list of Google suggestions shown in Exhibit 4-28. It's disappointing that Snap's competitors are being searched for by name—Canon, Sony, and Nikon—but Snap is not. Searches for Snap's brand names (such as *snap digital camera* and *snapshot digital camera*) are apparently lower on the list. Regardless, brand name phrases are important for Snap, both because Snap should easily rank well for them and because competitors *cannot*. What's more, Snap will likely close sales with a far higher percentage of customers who are searching for their very own brand.

Snap didn't stop at the list of the most popular Google suggestions. They looked deeper, finding some exciting possibilities, such as *best digital camera* and *digital camera reviews* that might be perfect for their products. They also tried variations of keywords—trying *cameras* by itself, *digital* photography, megapixel, and other related words.

When they did, they found lots of other related keywords. Some of these keywords, such as *digital video camera*, are not for the right kind of product. When you make your list of target keywords, you must be ruthless about eliminating any keyword that, while valuable in and of itself, is not part of this particular campaign. Video cameras can have their own campaign.

What's left? After wiping out the competing brands, accessories, and incorrect products, there were only a few left, but these are the most important keywords to look at:

- *digital camera reviews*
- *best digital camera*
- *digital camera comparison*
- *compare digital camera*
- *cheap digital camera*
- *digital camera sale*

For some companies, all of these might be good targets for search marketing. They all bring heavy traffic, and they all seem like keywords that informational and transactional searchers use; those are the ones most qualified to sell to.

But for Snap, two of them do not belong—*digital camera sale* and *cheap digital camera*—because Snap is a premium brand with innovative but pricey designs that they never discount. To keep things simple, we'll also combine singular and plural forms, such as *digital camera review* and *digital camera reviews*, leaving us the list shown in Exhibit 4-29.

Although the keyword *digital camera* is probably searched for more often than many of the others, we're fooling ourselves if we think Snap can swoop right in and get the top ranking for that keyword. Remember that the competition for these **mega-keywords** is fierce, so a top ten ranking is hard to achieve without a lot of work. Moreover, you recall that many of those searchers are seeking information about how to *use* digital cameras, rather than buy them, so those searchers are not as highly qualified as someone searching for *digital camera review*, for example. Each of the keywords in our list gets enough traffic for Snap to target, and it is easier to get good rankings for less-popular keywords that have fewer companies targeting them.

Keyword	Search Volume	Keyword Type
digital camera	High	Product category
snapshot digital camera	Medium	Brand + product category
snap digital camera	Medium	Company + product category
digital camera review	Medium	Product category variation
compare digital camera	Medium	Product category variation
best digital camera	Medium	Product category variation
digital camera comparison	Medium	Product category variation

Exhibit 4-29 Snap Electronics keyword targets. You create your short list of keywords to target—these are the initial keywords for Snap's first campaign.

Take a deep breath. That wasn't too hard, was it? You can do the same thing with the area of your own site that you picked. Brainstorm the right words and come up with seven to ten phrases that will generate more traffic to your site. You will likely find that your top keywords fall into the same types: your brand name and a generic category name, along with a few variations. This is true regardless of whether you are driving traffic to a site for a product or not. For example, The Police Athletic League will want to capture keywords for *police athletic league*, of course, but also wants to generate traffic for *boys clubs* and *children's sports*, too.

Most of the time, your organization has a brand name (what you call it) and a generic name (what most people call it). You will rank higher for your brand name, but usually fewer people will search for it, so you need to target *both* brand names and generic names to maximize your success. Searchers who use generic names can find your site *only* if you focus on the generic names in your search campaigns. Otherwise they will find your competitors.

Perhaps you are already so familiar with your website that you know your first campaign is simple to conduct, but many of us must assess the simplicity of the campaign to be sure. Armed with our target keywords, now we're ready to assess our site on how well it draws search traffic for each of those keywords.

Assess Your Current Situation

No two search marketing situations are the same, which is why you need to assess your situation on its own merits. No matter how little search marketing you have done up to this point, you are probably drawing some amount of organic search traffic. But regardless of how much or how little traffic you are drawing, you cannot tell how well you are doing unless you take a more systematic approach. The first step in your new system is to decide exactly which pages on your site you want the search engines to show when searchers enter a keyword.

Identify Your Search Landing Pages

It's not enough to choose the keywords that relate to your campaign. You need to identify pages on your site that you want those keywords to lead to. When a searcher enters one of those keywords, which page from your site do you want shown in the search results?

COMING IN FOR A LANDING

At first, display advertisers did not understand the importance of landing pages, but they do now. Let's look at an example to illustrate why.

If Snap places a banner ad on a leading photography magazine site that offers "30% off a SnapShot X5," that ad could simply be linked to the SnapShot X5 page as its landing page. When the ad is clicked, visitors would go to the regular SnapShot X5 product details page with "SnapShot X5" at the top of the page. They'd see the detailed list of features and a picture of the X5. At the bottom of the page they'd see a small notice that says "Now 30% off" next to the "Add to cart" button. As we said, Snap could link its banner ad to this page, but if it does, that won't maximize sales.

Why? Because the product details page does not reinforce the offer in the banner ad. It's not the best landing page for that ad. It's a terrible choice of landing page, but it's just not the best.

The best approach is to use a landing page that repeats the offer for this specific banner ad. When visitors click through from the ad, the banner landing page amplifies the offer—it says "30% Off SnapShot X5" in big letters at the top of the page, and it shows a picture of the X5 with its key features. At the bottom of the landing page, it provides buttons that let visitors go to the existing X5 product details page for more information or to add the X5 to their carts.

You'll sell more when you employ landing pages, because you have reinforced what the visitors are trying to do. They clicked the ad because it said "30% off SnapShot X5"; so, when the landing page emphasizes that they are "in the right place" after they click, they are much more likely to continue reading about the offer. If the ad sends them to the product details page instead, they may be disconcerted as to whether they are in the right place and may not be sure they are getting the discount. If it takes time to figure out they are in the right place, many visitors won't take that time and won't take that offer.

What's this got to do with search marketing? Plenty. When searchers click on a search result, they expect that the landing page on your site will reinforce what they were looking for, or they might immediately hit the back button and look for another page that does.

To answer that question, it is useful to understand the concept of a **landing page.** Originating in banner advertising, the landing page is the place on your website visitors will go when they click a particular banner ad. **Search landing pages** are similar to banner landing pages; they are designed to reinforce the searcher's intent. Search landing pages emphasize the keywords the searchers entered to get there, so that visitors to your site from search engines will know they are in the right place and begin to make their way through your site.

One difference between search landing pages and banner landing pages is their longevity. Because banner ads are often tied to time-sensitive promotions and discounts, marketers often design a new landing page for each banner ad because no appropriate page already exists. Marketers throw away these special landing pages at the end of the campaign. Searchers, however, use much the same keywords month after month, so it is less important to design new search landing pages; many sites have perfectly appropriate existing pages that reinforce the searcher's intent.

You must identify good search landing pages for each keyword that you picked—pages that reinforce the keywords they are searching for. In fact, it's not enough for those pages to be merely good—you want them to be the best landing pages possible—better than every other page on the web, so that the search engines will show your page first.

Often, you are choosing a landing page that you don't see showing up in search results at all. (That's why you are reading this book.) Sometimes, one or more pages from your site might be showing up in the search results, but they are not the best landing page from your site. Search marketers often refer to **preferred landing pages** (PLPs) to denote the specific pages from their sites that are the best pages to be shown for particular keywords by the search engines. Let's go back to our example and see how to identify search landing pages for Snap Electronics.

As we look over our list of keywords, we see that several of them might share the same search landing pages. The keywords *digital camera*, *snap digital camera*, and *snapshot digital camera* might all lead to the same place, perhaps the product category page that lists every model of digital camera that Snap sells. You can see this product category page in Exhibit 4-30.

Just as we saw that several keywords above can share the same product category page as their search landing page, the keywords *digital camera comparison* and *compare digital camera* should also share a common landing page (because both are seeking the same information). But Snap's site does not have any page that compares cameras against each other—no pages compare different Snap models nor any page that compares Snap models to competitive models. Snap could try to use the same product category page used above, but that seems unwise because it contains mostly fuzzy marketing speak; these information seekers want detailed specifications and features. Snap must create a new search landing page to handle these comparison searches. (We explain how to optimize those pages in Chapter 8, "Optimize Your Content.")

Our attention now turns to *digital camera review*. Snap has a page titled "News and Awards" that lists several links to digital photography sites with positive reviews and awards for SnapShot cameras. That looks like a good choice for that keyword.

Exhibit 4-30   SnapShot product category page. Informational searchers looking for *digital camera* want to land on an overview page.

That leaves the keyword *best digital camera*. It is hard to know exactly what these searchers are looking for, because what makes something the "best" is subjective. After a little thinking, we decide to target the most expensive SnapShot model in the product line, the SnapShot SLR X900.

Summing up our analysis, we chose existing pages to serve as our search landing pages for most of the keywords, but the two keywords containing the word *comparison* require a single new landing page to be created for them. Exhibit 4-31 shows the complete list.

See Whether Your Existing Landing Pages Are Indexed

Now that you have identified the best pages on your site for searchers to find for each of your targeted keywords, it is time to check whether those pages are indexed by the search engines. Certainly, if they are not indexed, they cannot be returned by the search engines for those or any other keywords.

We decided earlier that the two keywords containing the word *comparison* required that Snap create a new search landing page for them, so inevitably that page is not already indexed. Snap will have to ensure this page gets indexed when it is created. But let's check out Snap's existing pages to see where they stand.

Keyword	Landing Page URL
digital camera	SnapElectronics.com/stores/Cat?cat=6&lang=1&cntry=840
snap digital camera	SnapElectronics.com/stores/Cat?cat=6&lang=1&cntry=840
snapshot digital camera	SnapElectronics.com/stores/Cat?cat=6&lang=1&cntry=840
digital camera review	SnapElectronics.com/cameras/news
best digital camera	SnapElectronics.com/stores/Prd?prd=9&lang=1&cntry=840
digital camera comparison	New search landing page needed
compare digital camera	New search landing page needed

Exhibit 4-31   Snap Electronics landing pages. You must choose an appropriate search landing page for each targeted keyword in your list. Snaps are shown here.

Every search engine has a special inclusion operator you can use to see whether a URL is included in its index. For Google, you search for *info:* in front of the URL (such as *info: www.SnapElectronics.com/cameras/news*), and Google will return the page in its result list if it is indexed, or no results if it is not. Bing and Yandex have a similar capability but use the operator *url:* instead of *info:* in its syntax, while Baidu substitutes *domain:* as its operator.

It takes some time, but you can check each of your URLs in each search engine. Exhibit 4-32 shows the results for Snap. For space reasons, we have eliminated the leading "www. SnapElectronics.com" from the URLs in the table.

Target URL (www.SnapElectronics.com...)	Google	Bing
/Cat?cat=6&lang=1&cntry=840	Yes	No
/cameras/news	Yes	Yes
/Prd?prd=9&lang=1&cntry=840	No	No
New page needed	—	—

Exhibit 4-32   Snap Electronics inclusion check. Each search engine indexes some of the pages from your site (indicated by "Yes"), but not others.

The inclusion check for Snap yields some disconcerting results. We already knew that Snap needed to create one new page and get it included, but now we see that two of Snap's existing pages are also problems: Only the "News and Awards" page is indexed by both major search engines. We do not have any insight into *why* these pages are not indexed; we will have to wait until Chapter 7, "Get Your Content Listed," for that. However, at least we know that there is some work to do. That is a critical part of our assessment. Some sites have difficult (and expensive) technical problems that prevent spiders from indexing their pages. Because there are only four pages that we have identified, the worst-case scenario is that we need to create a few new pages on the site that search spiders can find to replace the existing pages that they are not indexing. In later chapters, you will see that you *never* create special pages for your site for the sole purpose of ranking well in search (that is an unethical spamming technique), but you should replace pages that cannot be crawled with those that can.

Hearkening back to the question of whether the digital camera area of Snap's website is a simple enough choice for our first campaign, it appears to be. Some of the critical pages are indexed already, and we have identified other pages that we might get indexed. If we fail to get them indexed, we could create a few new pages to compensate. Overall, it seems to be a simple proposition, so we finalize the choice for Snap's first marketing campaign; it is the SnapShot digital camera.

Check the Search Rankings for Your Landing Pages

Now that you know which pages are in and out of which search indexes, it is time to see whether those that are included are ranking in the top ten, and if not, where they are.

There are two ways to check search rankings. You probably thought of the first way: entering the keywords by hand and scrolling through the search results until you see your page. You can do it that way, but checking multiple keywords in several search engines can get old fast. So, you might want to try the other way of checking rankings—using an automated tool. Google has started restricting access for rank checking, so rank checking tools are in a state of flux. Check out our site for the latest rank checking tools available (SEMincBook.com/rank-check-tools).

Whether you do it by hand or use a rank-checking tool, the basics are the same. You record the organic search rank (paid does not count) of your site's page for the targeted search keyword. You start counting from the #1 organic result on the first page—that is the top result on page one (which may be underneath paid results in some search engines). For search engines that show ten results on a page, the last result on page one is obviously #10, with the first one on the second page #11, and so on from there.

If you do it by hand, make sure that you aren't logged in to the search engine that you are checking. So, for example, you'd want to sign out of your Google account before checking your Google results, so that there is less chance that they will be personalized. If you don't, Google might mislead you by showing your site as #1 just because you have clicked on it in the past—which wouldn't happen to another searcher. Because you want to know what will happen with the average searcher, you need to log out. Automated tools don't have this problem because they are never logged in to Google.

Of course, the higher the rank, the better. Searchers do not split their clicks evenly among the top ten, so the higher up in the list you are, the more visitors you will get. Exhibit 4-33 shows the results that Snap Electronics found for its targeted keywords.

Keyword	Google	Bing
digital camera	45	—
snap digital camera	3*	4*
snapshot digital camera	3*	1*
digital camera review	—	34
best digital camera	—	47*
digital camera comparison	—	—
compare digital camera	—	—

Exhibit 4-33   Snap Electronics ranking check. Knowing where you rank is the first step to improving your search traffic.

* Page found from SnapElectronics.com site, but not the targeted landing page.

Looking further into the rankings, we see that although the landing page for *digital camera review* was indexed in Google, it was not found in the Top 100. It turns out that for *snap digital camera* and *snapshot digital camera*, the Snap home page was returned. It is not the targeted landing page, but it is better than being missing completely. Similarly, the page that was returned by Bing for *best digital camera* is an interesting one. Titled "The SnapShot Difference," it explains why SnapShot cameras are better than all others—what technology is included and why SnapShots are so easy to use. This page seems better to target than the most-expensive camera's product detail page, which was our original choice.

The bad news, however, is the dismal rankings of most of these pages. Unless searchers explicitly specify Snap's company's name or product's name, they are not going to find SnapElectronics.com with these keywords. We do not yet know *why* Snap's pages are ranking so poorly, but we explore those reasons in later chapters of this book.

Check Your Competitors' Search Rankings

If Snap is not getting the top spot, who is? It's easy to take a look and see. Exhibit 4-34 shows the results for *digital cameras* in Google. You can see that the top of the first page lists retailers and review sites rather than camera manufacturers such as Snap.

One look at the Google results for *digital cameras* tells you that this is a keyword that every manufacturer wants to rank highly for—one of Snap's competitors is already in the top five. Studying the Google results for a few of the targeted keywords can result in a competitor-ranking matrix, as shown in Exhibit 4-35. You can see where each competitor's website ranks for each keyword. For example, the first page from SnapElectronics.com returned by Google for the *digital camera* keyword is result #45, whereas Sony has a page from its site ranked #5.

Exhibit 4-34   Google results for the *digital cameras* keyword. A broad keyword such as *digital cameras* returns many sites besides the camera manufacturers.

Keyword	Snap	Kodak	Canon	Sony	Olympus	Nikon
digital camera	45	8	9	5	11	13
snapshot digital camera	3	—	—	—	—	—
snap digital camera	3	—	—	—	—	—
digital camera reviews	—	—	10	6	22	19
best digital cameras	—	—	—	—	—	—
digital camera comparison	—	—	8	9	58	24

Exhibit 4-35   Snap Electronics competitor-rankings matrix. Major digital camera manufacturers have wide variation in Google rankings for the primary keywords.

Looking beyond the *digital camera* keyword, we find that the other keywords are more hospitable to manufacturers and suggest more qualified buyers. Focusing first on the searchers for Snap's own SnapShot brand (*snapshot digital camera*), we can conclude that they already desire the brand and are far more likely to buy from Snap. We also see that *snapshot digital camera* already has a #3 ranking, so perhaps part of Snap's campaign should focus on moving it up to #1.

When we look at the remaining keywords, we notice that the rankings for the manufacturers look healthy. Despite this, Snap is missing in action for all but its own SnapShot brand name. Clearly, this competitor matrix is showing how Snap's lack of organic search rankings is costing it traffic to its website.

The matrix has another value, too. When it is time to persuade other people in your organization to invest in or work on search marketing, showing your competitors' rankings usually gets the competitive juices flowing. When you appeal to people's competitiveness, they will want to win. Remember, too, every page that you get into the top ten pushes your competition down further; you are helping yourself while denying them exposure at the same time.

See What Traffic You Are Getting

All the rankings in the world don't mean much if searchers don't click through to your site. So although we know there is a strong correlation between high search rankings and high search traffic, we need to track that traffic to accurately measure the business impact of search marketing; tracking rankings is not enough.

So the next step is to check the traffic that Snap is getting for each keyword. As you saw earlier in this chapter, web analytics software can track page views, visits, and visitors, but they can also count which of those visitors came to your site from search engines. Web analytics facilities determine where each visitor comes from by examining the referrer for each page view. The referrer is the actual URL of the web page that the visitor viewed before coming to your page.

Clearly, referrers can be used to see which visitors followed links to your page from other pages within your site or from pages on other sites. But analytics facilities provide special support for **search referrals**—referrals that come from a URL known to be a search engine (such as Google.com). Your analytics software comes with a list of the popular search engine URLs, and you can add any that are missing. This list is used to generate a report showing how many page views were referred from search engines.

But you might want more detail. You might want to know how many referrals your website receives for particular keywords. Both Google and Bing make popular search referral information available in their respective Webmaster Tools sites. For example, Snap might want to know how many visitors reached their website using the *digital camera* keyword by analyzing the Webmaster Tools data (see Exhibit 4-36).

Keyword	Search Referrals
digital camera	1,412
snapshot digital camera	5,278
snap digital camera	4,044
digital camera reviews	0
compare digital cameras	0
best digital cameras	0
digital camera comparison	0
Total Search Referrals	**10,734**

Exhibit 4-36   Snap Electronics visitors from search engines. Webmaster Tools sites can provide referral information for popular targeted keywords.

SHRINKING KEYWORD REFERRAL DATA

Google and Bing now encrypt the organic keywords from searchers, so search marketers can no longer tell which keywords searchers use to find their websites.

The search engines' stance on the privacy of search keywords has dramatically reduced the visitor information that search marketers can collect. Most search marketers find that their most popular search keyword is now shown in your Google Analytics dashboard as "not provided." Check out Exhibit 4-37 to see an example of how Google Analytics displays the hidden keyword referrals. (Other analytics packages might use other terminology to describe the missing data, but the effect is the same.)

Referrals whose keyword are "not provided" indicate that we have traffic from the search engines without revealing which keywords were used, because Google is hiding them. Some browsers have begun to go even further than Google, withholding even more information—*all* search traffic to your site is not even shown as search traffic at all, but rather "direct traffic" (the same as a using a browser bookmark or typing in the page's URL).

The effect has been dramatic.

Almost every website now shows "Not Provided" as its "most popular" search referral keyword. Most sites show the lion's share of their search traffic as "Not Provided"—and that doesn't even count all the traffic mislabeled as direct traffic.

It's not as easy as it was in the good old days, but you still have information to work with. This situation is quite fluid, so head to our site to get the latest (SEMincBook.com/referrals).

For this site, the keyword "not provided" comprises over 65% of all keyword referrals.

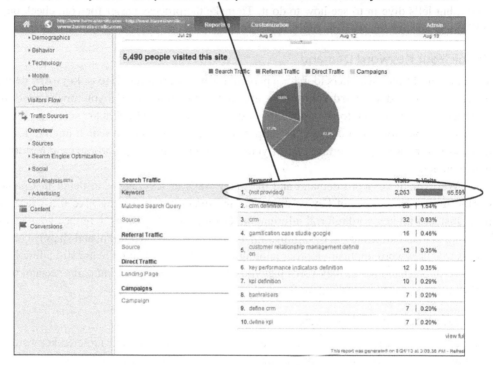

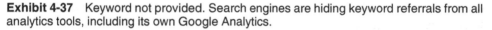

Exhibit 4-37 Keyword not provided. Search engines are hiding keyword referrals from all analytics tools, including its own Google Analytics.

Snap Electronics does not have any paid search campaigns underway for digital cameras, but as you tabulate current search referrals for your own site, be aware of any paid activity. If you are using paid search, you need to assess that, too, because it affects your referral numbers. That's why we advised you that is easier to start with an area of the site that has no current paid search program active: It's simpler to avoid the problem of separating paid from organic traffic for your first assessment.

Assessing your site is a critical step, but knowing where you stand is just the beginning. Let's see where you can go from here.

Calculate Your First Campaign's Opportunity

It's interesting to find out how many searchers are being referred to your site with the keywords you have targeted, but you also need to know how many of those searchers do *not* come to your site. Those are the people you want referred your way; those searchers comprise your search marketing opportunity.

In recent years, it has become more challenging to calculate your search marketing opportunity, but let's dive in to see how to do it. To make the process easier for you, check our site (SEMincBook.com/forecast) to see how each step unfolds one click at a time.

Check Your Keyword Demand

The number of times searchers look for a particular keyword is referred to as **keyword demand**, which is also called **keyword volume**. So, although search referrals tell you how many of those searchers clicked through to your site, keyword demand tells you how many searchers used that keyword in total to search during a given period of time in a specific search engine. Keyword demand will be a very important part of your opportunity modeling and ongoing performance management.

We explain keyword demand and the many ways to leverage it in detail in Chapter 6, exploring several sources of keyword demand information, but we can give it a "once over" here. Just as with keyword referral information, Google has taken steps to reduce your access to keyword demand information, by eliminating its open access keyword tool and sharply curtailing access to its keyword application programming interface (API). But there are still a few ways to estimate the demand for the keywords that you have targeted for your campaign. Again, our site (SEMincBook.com/forecast) can walk you through it.

Discover Your Missed Opportunities

Although it is helpful to see how many searches are performed on your targeted keywords, you must remember that you are already getting some search traffic to your site. How many searchers are you missing? To answer that question, we must develop a **missed-opportunity matrix**.

Because every searcher who uses your targeted keyword is an opportunity to bring a visitor to your site, merely subtracting your search referrals from the total number of searches yields the number of searches where no one came to your site. You can also calculate your share of the search traffic by dividing the number of your referrals by the keyword demand. Now, because Google is restricting both the referral and demand information for organic search, it isn't as simple as it once was. Our site (SEMincBook.com/forecast) can help you with your calculations.

Exhibit 4-38 shows how Snap Electronics calculated their missed opportunities.

Project Your Future Traffic

Now it is time to calculate what you really want to know: How many more search referrals can you reasonably obtain if you execute a strong first search marketing campaign? Although those searchers who failed to come to Snap's site are literally missed opportunities, it is not realistic to expect that any one site could collect all the clicks for any keyword. The question then becomes how to estimate the *reasonable* number of clicks that can be achieved after a successful first search marketing campaign.

Keyword	Search Demand	Search Referrals	Actual Total Missed Traffic	Share of Opportunities
digital camera	2,942,328	1,412	0.05%	2,940,916
snapshot digital camera	10,734	4,044	38%	6,690
snap digital camera	13,735	5,278	38%	8,457
digital camera reviews	157,533	—	0%	157,533
compare digital cameras	22,717	—	0%	22,717
best digital cameras	39,303	—	0%	39,303
digital camera comparison	26,099	—	0%	26,099
Totals	3,212,449	10,734	0.33%	3,201,715

Exhibit 4-38   Snap missed opportunity matrix. Juxtaposing the actual search referrals with the keyword demand shows how many searchers were missed.

Before we begin our analysis of future traffic, you should know that it is impossible to accurately calculate something as nebulous as a "reasonable number of clicks." Anyone who tells you that he can pinpoint the answer is oversimplifying the complexity of searcher behavior. But we can use estimates to help make a business decision on how to invest in search marketing. Although it will not be terribly precise, it will help you make a better decision than using the seat of your pants.

One thing you notice from looking at the exhibit is that the models differ across the three companies. Why would this be? Some of it is just random variance you should expect in any study. But the three firms each have different clients whose search keywords differ from each other. Clickthrough rates are affected by various factors. For example, navigational keywords tend to have much higher clickthrough on the #1 result. Informational and transactional keywords will have clicks spread out more throughout the results page, especially if competition is strong among our high-quality content items.

So, how do you use this information? First, you can see that in every model, ranking higher gets you more clicks, which is no surprise. Second, you can see that the clicks are heavily concentrated in the first three positions.

Your ability to drive clicks is a function of rank, relevance, and brand awareness. The higher that you rank, the more relevant your content is to the searcher, and the more they recognize and trust your brand, the more likely they are to click.

If you are considering mounting both an organic and paid campaign, your eventual clickthrough rate could be considerably higher due to the collaborative impact of having the more search results visible on the results page. When searchers see your brand prominently featured in both organic and paid search results, sometimes the clicks go up substantially. In Chapter 9, "Prove Your Content's Quality," we discuss how to use **co-optimization** tactics to make paid and organic search work more effectively together.

Although you cannot be sure of the number of clicks you can get, you can work under some reasonable assumptions. We can start with the model shown in Exhibit 4-39, which shows some average clickthrough rates collected from three different search optimization companies across a range of clients.

	Back Azimuth	Slingshot SEO	Optify	Average
#1	22.20%	18.20%	36.40%	25.60%
#2	12.96%	10.05%	12.50%	11.84%
#3	10.62%	7.22%	9.50%	9.11%
#4	7.72%	4.81%	7.90%	6.81%
#5	6.56%	3.09%	6.10%	5.25%
#6	1.65%	2.76%	4.10%	2.84%
#7	1.44%	1.88%	3.80%	2.37%
#8	1.41%	1.75%	3.50%	2.22%
#9	0.48%	1.52%	3.00%	1.67%
#10	0.65%	1.04%	2.22%	1.30%

Exhibit 4-39   Organic result clickthrough rates. Three models that show how many clicks to expect based on where your content ranks on the search result page.

Buying cycle phase, audience segment, and searcher intent are all major contributors to increasing your clickthrough rate, according to research from Back Azimuth Consulting—all of which are discussed in Chapter 6. For now, take an educated guess at how much you can improve your search rankings, then you estimate the improvement in your visits to your site by using one of the models (or an average of all three). Later, once you have a better understating of your own rank distribution, you can use your own estimates.

So, by looking at Exhibit 4-39, we can take some educated guesses as to how search ranking can affect the number of clicks to your site. If you rank in the top three, you might get clicks for somewhere around 8% to 35% of the demand for a particular keyword. If your page ranks #4 through #10, perhaps you will get a click for 0.5% to 7% of searches. If your page shows up on the next two result pages (ranked #11 through #30), you will pick up a few clicks—maybe clicks totaling 0.01% of all searches. One one-hundredth of 1% might not sound like much, but it is better than nothing, which is your likely fate beyond position #30. At the other end of the spectrum, some search marketers report getting clickthrough rates of more than 50%, especially when their listing is in the top three of both the organic and the paid placements for the same keyword.

When Snap went through this exercise, they put together the table shown in Exhibit 4-40 to see what kind of traffic potential their targeted keywords have.

Keyword	Monthly Keyword Demand	Estimated Monthly Search Referrals				
		0.25%	1%	5%	10%	25%
digital camera	2,942,328	7,356	29,423	147,116	294,233	735,582
snapshot digital camera	10,734	27	107	537	1,073	2,683
snap digital camera	13,735	34	137	687	1,373	3,434
digital camera reviews	157,533	394	1,575	7,877	15,753	39,383
compare digital cameras	22,717	57	227	1,136	2,272	5,679
best digital cameras	39,303	98	393	1,965	3,930	9,826
digital camera comparison	26,099	65	261	1,305	2,610	6,525
Totals	3,212,449	8,031	32,124	160,622	321,245	803,112

Exhibit 4-40 Snap Electronics traffic potential model. You can use the estimated monthly keyword demand to estimate search referrals at various clickthrough rates.

The next step requires a cold look at what your potential improvement in rank can be for each keyword. Let's haul out yet another table to show the potential improvements from a successful search marketing campaign. Exhibit 4-41 shows a **projected-rankings matrix**, with the current rank for each of Snap's targeted keywords along with a guess at what the new improved rank might be.

Keyword	Current Rankings			Projected Rankings
	Kodak	Canon	Snap	Snap
digital camera	8	9	45	10
snap digital camera	—	—	3	1
snapshot digital camera	—	—	3	1
digital camera reviews	—	10	—	10
best digital cameras	—	—	—	30
compare digital cameras	12	—		10
digital camera comparison	8	17	—	10

Exhibit 4-41 Snap Electronics projected-rankings matrix. Where Snap and its competitors rank in Google today gives clues for where Snap could rank in the future.

When you develop your projected-rankings matrix, you are realistically assessing where your pages can rank—in this case for Google. (A more complete approach, avoided here for brevity, would be to analyze each of the major search engines and all major camera competitors.) Taking the keyword *digital camera*, we can see that because the current top ten results include three camera manufacturers, it is entirely reasonable for Snap to move from "off the charts" to a respectable #10.

When we look at the keyword *best digital cameras*, we see that all the camera manufacturers are missing in action. But there might be some hope here. We note that none of the other manufacturers use that phrase on their pages, possibly because large corporations do not want to appear boastful. Snap does not like to toot its own horn either, but many third-party digital camera reviews actually call the SnapShot the *best digital camera*; Snap can quote these reviews on its site without appearing boastful, and the search engines will find the words on Snap's pages. Armed with this information, it might be reasonable to project that Snap can break through at least to the top 30 for this keyword where the other manufacturers did not.

When you develop your own projected-rankings matrix, you must make similar decisions, keyword by keyword, and you need to be as realistic as possible. You might find that your projections are conservative at times, but that is better than overpromising and underdelivering.

After you have decided what rankings you can achieve, you need to assign your clickthrough rate based on the position you expect to achieve, which our forecasting tool makes easier (SEMincBook.com/forecast). Exhibit 4-42 shows Snap's decisions. Projected "top 30" rankings are valued at a 0.01% clickthrough rate, whereas a #1 ranking for a quasi-navigational keyword such as *snap digital camera* might get 50% clickthrough. They opted to take an average click rate of 0.50% based on the estimates in Exhibit 4-39 for a #10 position, because they decided to be conservative. Multiplying these clickthrough rates by the estimated monthly searches produces the projected visits resulting from the search marketing campaign.

If Snap Electronics planned to place a top paid search bid in Google and Bing for every keyword, they could add as much as 5% to their clickthrough rates to generate a larger number of added referrals. But Snap wanted to take a more conservative approach. Rather than buying each of these keywords across three search engines, Snap decided to buy just *one* keyword in Google as an experiment. They chose the most popular keyword, *digital cameras*. This approach allowed them to gain experience with paid placement without having to make a big commitment of money and management time. Based on the results of the experiment, they will decide how to approach paid placement in the future.

Snap's approach required them to project the added search referrals for paid placement for the *digital cameras* keyword, which was fairly easy. Because Snap opened a paid search account with Google, Snap was able to see the keyword demand for *digital cameras* using the Google AdWords Planner (1,337,422) and could multiply by a 1% clickthrough rate. Some paid search ads yield 5% clickthrough rates or more, but Snap decided to make a conservative projection for their first paid campaign. Multiplying the keyword demand by that 1% clickthrough rate produced an additional 13,374 monthly search referrals from paid placement.

Keyword Phrase	Monthly Keyword Demand	Current Monthly Visits	Current Share	Current Rank	Projected Rank	Projected Share	Projected Search Referrals	Added Search Referrals
digital camera	2,942,328	1,412	0.05%	45	10	0.50%	14,712	13,300
snapshot digital camera	10,734	4,044	38%	3	1	50%	5,367	1,323
snap digital camera	13,735	5,278	38%	3	1	50%	6,868	1,590
digital camera reviews	157,533	—	0.00%	—	10	0.50%	788	788
best digital cameras	22,717	—	0.00%	—	30	0.10%	2	2
compare digital cameras	39,303	—	0.00%	—	10	0.50%	197	197
digital camera comparison	26,099	—	0.00%	—	10	0.50%	130	130

Exhibit 4-42 Snap's organic traffic model. For each keyword, Snap can project the percentage of clickthrough per organic search and project added referrals.

If we add the 17,329 organic search referrals from Exhibit 4-42 to the new paid search referrals, it results in 30,703 new search referrals each month. That kind of number will draw the attention needed to get your search marketing program off the ground. It is hard for anyone running a website to turn down additional traffic, but you can make your case for search marketing even more enticing by projecting not just traffic, but conversions.

Project Your Future Conversions

Regardless of what your website's goals are, you saw earlier in this chapter that you can choose certain visitor events as your conversions. Obviously, if you are selling your product online, it is easy for you to translate your conversions into revenue, but you saw earlier that you can translate most conversions into some kind of business value.

Although search marketing can drive new visitors to your site, you might need to make other changes to your site to increase conversions. Although marketing opportunities certainly exist, they are not particular to *search* marketing because your changes affect every visitor to your site, regardless of how they landed there. To go beyond search marketing, pick up Mike's book *Do It Wrong Quickly: How the Web Changes the Old Marketing Rules*, which is loaded with ways to measure your website's success and to make improvements.

Continuing our fictitious scenario for Snap Electronics, we can project our digital camera search marketing campaign's conversions and its incremental revenue. Snap needs to know a few numbers to do so:

- **Projected added search referrals:** As we calculated earlier, the estimate for the extra traffic to Snap's site due to successful search marketing consists of referrals from both organic and paid search. Snap's total comes to 30,703 more visits.

- **Conversion rate:** What percentage of visits results in sales? If Snap knows the conversion rate for digital cameras (the percentage of visitors to the digital camera pages who buy digital cameras), that would be the best conversion rate to use. But many companies, especially large companies, have trouble isolating individual product metrics. In Snap's case, isolating digital camera conversion rate is not possible, but they do know that their overall conversion rate is 2%. They can use that 2% conversion rate as a conservative estimate, because they expect that the digital camera conversion rate is higher than average.

- **Average transaction price:** What is the typical price paid for a digital camera? Snap should be able to monitor all digital camera sales and divide the total sales by the number of transactions to find out the average transaction price. In some cases, you need to use the average transaction price across all products, rather than the product you are targeting, but Snap happens to know that its average digital camera price is $348.

After you have compiled the necessary numbers, you can put them together to project the incremental revenue from search marketing for digital cameras, as shown in Exhibit 4-43.

	Added Monthly Search Referrals	30,703
Multiply by:	Conversion rate	0.02
	Added monthly sales	614
Multiply by:	Average transaction price	$348
	Added monthly revenue	$213,672
Multiply by:	12 months	12
	Added yearly revenue	$2,564,064

Exhibit 4-43 Projecting Snap's search campaign's revenue. A simple formula converts projected incremental search referrals into projected revenue.

As you calculate the opportunity for your own first campaign, you might be wondering how big the opportunity can be if you go all out with a site-wide search marketing program, consisting of many individual campaigns. In Chapter 5, "Create Your Search Marketing Program," you decide how broad your overall search marketing program should be and you will see how large the profit could be.

Summary

Search marketing is, after all, *marketing*, so you need to be armed with the business impact of your search marketing plans. No matter what your site's goals, you can use search marketing to drive traffic to your site to achieve those goals.

Every website has a goal—a purpose it was designed to fulfill. Most sites are designed to sell, to inform, to persuade, or some combination of all of them. In this chapter, we explored the various behavior models that apply to website visitors, and we showed how to measure what visitors do on your site.

 We looked at several different versions of the Buyer's Journey model, each customized for a different website. We hope that you developed the appropriate model for your website, too. Throughout the rest of this book, we return to the Buyer's Journey concept at various points, identifying those passages with the icon shown here.

In this chapter, you also learned how to choose the right events to count (web conversions), and you now know how to translate those events into revenue dollars. More important, you know how to calculate the revenue value of each visitor who comes to your site, forming the basis of the business case of your search marketing campaign.

You also learned how to project the traffic your campaign will generate and how to translate that traffic into its business impact. You decided on your first search marketing campaign, you assessed where your search results stand today, and projected what it will take to produce the business impact you expect.

In the next chapter, we look past your first campaign and dive into your overall search marketing program. What should your strategy be? What are the tasks required? Who should perform each task? How large should your overall search marketing program be? What will your program cost? How do you put your proposal together and how will you sell it to the higher-ups and your peers? Read on and see how your opportunity can be realized.

CHAPTER 5

Create Your Search Marketing Program

We've covered the basic of search marketing. You understand how it works, who's doing it, and you understand its value. So, now it's time to take action. Now, you need to complete the planning and get started, in three simple steps:

- **Define your search marketing strategy:** Before going further, you have some critical decisions to make so that search marketing can succeed in your organization. Every company needs a different approach, so let's discover yours.

- **Sell your search marketing proposal:** Once you know what will work, you need to sell everyone else. You'll obviously need approval from executives in your company, but you'll need to persuade your colleagues, too.

- **Set up your search marketing program:** With the proposal approved, it's time to roll up your sleeves and get this program off the ground. Paid search requires a lot of work to set up, but you need to know a bit about organic search and local search setup, too.

At the end of this chapter, you will know exactly what your search marketing program will set out to do, you will know how you intend to accomplish it, and you will know approximately what it will cost. You'll have assembled a complete proposal that you have sold to the powers-that-be for approval, and you'll have actually begun the process of setting up your program in search marketing.

With all that to accomplish, there's no time to lose. Let's start with strategy.

Define Your Search Marketing Strategy

Strategy. Do you get a bit suspicious just hearing the word? "Strategy" discussions sometimes seem disconnected from reality—the kind of "where the rubber meets the sky" conversations that are funny in a Dilbert cartoon. But when you hear some consultant show a bunch of pretty charts with no semblance of understanding your business, or the risks being run, or the effort required, it's not funny anymore—it's scary.

When done properly, strategy is critically important before you undertake any task. We try to avoid the pixie dust and give you a set of practical tasks to shape your search marketing program and carry it out. Let's look at the major strategic steps to develop your search marketing program:

- **Choose the scope of your search marketing program:** The most important part of your strategy—the part you must decide first—is: How big are you going to do this? You must choose the breadth of your program across your organization. (A product line? Division? Country? The whole company?) In Chapter 4, "Unlock the Business Value of Search," you chose your first search marketing campaign. Now you will decide how large your entire search marketing program will be—a program consisting of many campaigns.

- **Divide the work:** Some duties need to be centralized in a new search team, whereas the existing web teams should perform others. As you set the strategy for your search marketing program, it is important to understand what these duties are and who the best people are to take them on.

- **Choose your approach:** How are you going to execute your search marketing program? Will you use an internal team alone or will you engage an external firm to assist you? You must understand the reasons to choose one approach or the other.

- **Project your costs:** The final part of your strategy must total up the investment required. In Chapter 4, we identified the opportunity. Now, we assess the cost of reaching the opportunity. We actually total up two different costs. One is the investment you need right away to run your first campaign. The other is the cost of your full search marketing program, projected over several years.

Let's begin by deciding the breadth of the program.

Choose the Scope of Your Search Marketing Program

Any strategy starts with a firm definition of what the project will do. When you set out to succeed in search marketing for your website, your most critical question might be the scope of your program. On what scale are you working? A single business unit? Corporate branding across the enterprise?

Before answering that question, you need to remind yourself of the distinction between your first search marketing campaign and your overall search marketing program. Exhibit 5-1 shows how Snap's overall program consists of many campaigns, starting with the digital cameras campaign we have discussed. Although we show just four here, Snap's program will eventually consist of dozens of campaigns as it gradually covers each product in its product line.

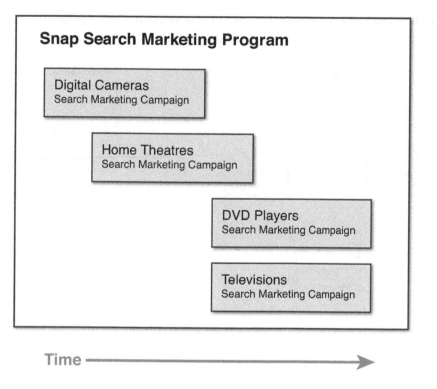

Exhibit 5-1   Search marketing campaigns within the program. Snap's digital cameras campaign is just the first in its overall search marketing program.

You need clear objectives for your search marketing program before you start. Are you looking for a long-term solution or just a quick fix to get a few keywords ranking well? Are you expecting to do just a few campaigns or do you have dozens (or hundreds) of product lines? Without asking yourself these questions up front, you are likely to take the wrong actions.

Occasionally, these questions are moot. If you are reading this book because a particular executive has ordered you to "fix search" (as sometimes happens), you will *know* your program's organizational scope; it covers the executive's organization. In short, if the Snap executive for home entertainment had charged us with improving search traffic, we probably would not have chosen digital cameras as our first campaign! We would choose home entertainment as our program scope, and we would pick one of those products (such as home theatre systems) as our first campaign.

Much of the time, however, *you* will be the one making the recommendation, so you need to take a close look at your situation. To make a smart decision on your search marketing program's scope, you must consider how your web teams are organized. Exhibit 5-2 shows four kinds of organizations; yours might be different yet. Regardless, you need to consider how *your* organization works when choosing the scope of your search marketing program. Your organization certainly has some elements of these four if it is not a direct match.

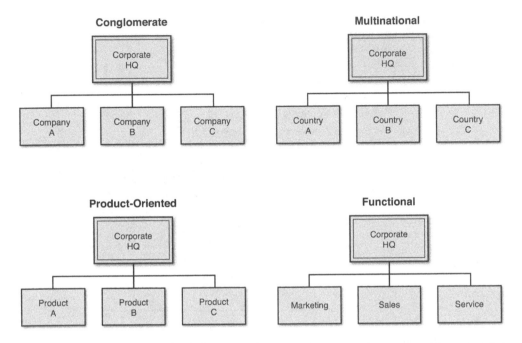

Exhibit 5-2 Analyzing your organization. Most organizations have some underlying principle that they are organized around, so figure out yours.

There is no "right" way to organize, and you might firmly believe that your organization ought to be reorganized. (Take heart, it probably will be soon.) What is important for your success as a search marketer is to understand your *current* organizational style.

Functional Organizations

Functional organizations tend to have a small number of products that are similar to each other and are sold to the same customers; many small-to-medium companies are organized functionally. Your teams have been divided into specialties based on what people do (such as marketing versus sales)—their *functions*.

If your organization has one webmaster group, a single team of programmers, and one marketing department (for example), your web organization is structured more by function than one with groups for every country (or every product, or every audience, and so on). The more your web organization is organized functionally, the easier it is to adopt a site-wide scope for your search marketing program. Use existing functional groups within your organization to carry out many search marketing tasks.

One of the challenges of search marketing in a functional organization is to persuade the functions themselves to collaborate. In the good old days, the marketing department was in charge of delivering brand messages to groups of customers (market segments) and the sales department was in charge of selling the product to each individual customer, and they did not have to work together all that closely. With the advent of the web, you might find these long-standing functional relationships in flux, because no one can agree where web marketing leaves off and web sales begin, for example. They did not need to cooperate closely in the past, but they need to do it now.

Despite these challenges, implementing search marketing in a functional organization is less challenging than in some of the others we touch on later, simply because you do not need to coordinate across many different groups of specialists. All the marketing folks are in one group, for example, so you can train them all in search marketing at one time.

Product-Oriented Organizations

Product-oriented organizations might have centralized a lot of business functions into corporate headquarters, but they leave manufacturing and sales to product groups. Does each product have its own website? Do the websites share the same technology and content infrastructure or different ones? The more that the infrastructure is shared, the more easily you can engage in a site-wide search marketing program.

Do the products have a common set of customers? Do some of the search keywords overlap between your products? Companies whose product units target mostly the same customers and keywords are more likely to benefit from a company-wide search marketing program.

Conversely, if your products appeal to completely different market segments, or each product area has a separately managed website, you might need to treat each product area as its own scoped search marketing program.

Product-oriented organizations (in which each product has its own website and web team) require significant coordination for site-wide search marketing programs to succeed. You might need to bring together a dozen web programming teams to explain how search marketing changes their jobs. You might require agreement from several groups for new standards and procedures.

Apple Computer is a good example of a product-oriented company (whose products share common customers), but because it uses a single overriding brand with a central website, its search marketing might be centralized, too. The more different ways that your web team operates your website, the more coordination you must do.

Alternatively, if your products are sold to different customers who use different search keywords, and your product sites are organizationally separate, you might pull back from centralizing a lot of tasks, and use the same approach discussed later for conglomerates—setting up separate search marketing programs for each product. General Electric does not sell aircraft engines and light bulbs to the same customers, nor does it use the same website for each, so perhaps its search marketing programs should differ for each product line, too.

There's no one right answer. What you decide depends largely on how your company is organized today.

Multinational Organizations

Multinational organizations tend to have strong global brands that are managed centrally, but each country has substantial control over how it is done.

As before, you need to look at the details of how things are done in your organization. Look for parallels to search engine marketing. Are technology investments managed centrally? Advertising? Marketing? Find one or two examples of central management of something similar to search marketing and use them as prototypes for setting the scope of your search marketing program.

IBM is an example of a company that is organized by country. It has centralized a lot of its marketing and advertising, however, so centralizing search marketing is accepted by the corporate culture. Other companies might provide the country organizations with more autonomy than IBM does, so they might need to do more of the search work locally, with separate search marketing programs in each country.

Conglomerates

Conglomerates are *highly* decentralized. Your corporate website (conglomerate.com) might be a small undertaking that exists mainly for investors because all the action happens in the individual companies that make up the conglomerate. Each company makes its own decisions about what to do and how to spend its money with little direction from corporate. Each company has its own website (company.com) that many customers do not even realize is part of the conglomerate, because the brand identity mainly resides with each company.

In some conglomerates, such as Berkshire Hathaway, a centralized search marketing effort makes no sense because their corporate culture is not centralized. They are far better off setting up separate search projects in each individual company, possibly sharing ideas and consulting across the companies.

Now that you have analyzed the type of organization you work in, you are ready to make some decisions about your search marketing program's scope. How broad should the program be in your organization? Should it cover your entire enterprise, just your business unit, only your country, or something else? Choosing your program's scope affects which executive(s) and which web team(s) you need to persuade, a topic we address later in this chapter.

If you work in a small organization, this decision will not take terribly long; in a medium-to-large company, however, it might take some thought. Consider the points we covered as you analyzed your organizational structure. Do you work in a highly decentralized conglomerate or a highly centralized functional organization? In a conglomerate, you might decide to limit your program's scope to one of the semi-independent companies, whereas you might decide to tackle the entire enterprise in a functional organization.

You should also consider your *role* in your organization. If you are the webmaster for the North American website, maybe that is the easiest scope to tackle first. If you are a product manager, maybe the best scope to start with covers just your product. If there is an executive you know you can convince to invest, perhaps his organizational scope is the right one for you. Remember, you can think big for your search marketing program's scope, but still start small with a single campaign. It is common, in medium-to-large companies, for the initial search marketing campaign to be limited to a single product. Think about what is practical for you.

Company size also plays into your program scope decision. The larger the company, the more difficult it is to take on the whole organization at once. Larger websites suffer from many technical and organizational complexities that make the effort more difficult as you make the scope larger. Similarly, the larger the scope you choose for your program, the longer it takes to get approval. You might decide to start small to show some success before requesting an enterprise-wide commitment.

The lesson is for you to think critically about your own situation. No matter what generalizations we write here, your company is not a generality; it is your own specific reality. You might work in a culture that likes to try new things, so maybe you can give paid search a shot. Perhaps your conglomerate has a tradition of working together on marketing, even though everything else is separate, so you can undertake an enterprise-wide search marketing program. If your product-oriented organization centralized its technology group, maybe you can tackle organic search across your whole site. Think carefully about your situation and choose the best program scope for your organization.

The folks at Snap Electronics carefully considered what the best scope would be for their search marketing program. Because Snap is a large company with significant name recognition, it has already attracted many links to its website, giving it a big leg up on organic search. Unfortunately, as you saw in Chapter 4, some of Snap's most important pages are not in the search indexes, and it is not clear how easy that will be to fix. Snap's management is generally open to new ideas, but is a bit suspicious of paid placement because it sounds too much like the dreaded banner ads (which Snap got burned on a couple of years ago). Snap is a highly product-oriented organization, but its marketing is aligned by country.

After taking all of this information into account, Snap chose to focus on the United States, its largest market, across its entire product line. So, Snap's overall scope for its search marketing program covers its U.S. products, and its first campaign will be for digital cameras. Snap decided to concentrate on organic search, targeting Google and Bing. Although concentrating on organic search, Snap chose to experiment with paid search, too, deferring a final scope decision on paid search until the experiment is complete. These basic scope decisions will drive the rest of Snap's strategy.

Divide the Search Marketing Work

Successful search engine marketing requires highly specialized work. If you thumb through the remaining chapters in this book, you will see all sorts of arcane techniques important to your success. You can't rely on everyone learning search marketing on their own, however. You cannot rely on specialists being motivated to do search marketing. (Although it is true that *some* specialists will embrace search marketing without a larger program in place, most will not.) And no amount of evangelism on your part will prove sufficient by itself; you cannot execute an enterprise program based on the sheer force of your personality.

You need to organize. And when you organize, you will split into two groups:

- **The center of excellence:** When you start your search marketing efforts, the central search team is you. In a medium-to-large organization, that is not enough. (In Chapter 10, "Make Search Marketing Operational," you will learn which skills you need and how to staff your search center of excellence.) Although we use the words **central** (and **center**) throughout, central is relative—relative to the program scope that you have chosen. So, if you have chosen a scope of a single country within your multinational company, the center of excellence manages search marketing throughout the country, not throughout the enterprise.

- **The extended search team:** Your organization already has an existing team (maybe many teams) to manage your website today. These specialists decide your website's strategy, write the content, create the pages, design applications, and do many other things. You must take advantage of these existing resources as your extended search team, because search marketing cannot succeed unless they do the right things. You need to understand these specialists and speak their language, because you must convince them to add search marketing tasks to their day-to-day jobs.

You need to carefully plan what work will be done centrally and what will be done by your extended search team. You must make search marketing part of the normal processes that every web specialist performs each day. If you do not, you are fighting a losing battle with a new search crisis every day:

- Last month, they finally fixed the title tag so that customers can find our top-selling product page in search engines, but yesterday they updated the page again and the title is now wrong, as before.

- They just released a new version of the eCommerce application, and no spiders can see the pages anymore. Now we have to wait until the next release to get them back in the search index so that customers can find them.

- They just changed the left navigation bar across the entire site, but now search spiders cannot follow the links, so interior pages are not being crawled for storage in the index. Now we have to get them to change it all over again, which could take months.

What do all these problems have in common? The amorphous "they" in each scenario are the folks on *your* extended search team. But they don't know they are. Or they don't know what they need to do. See, they are probably good at what they do. They probably work hard, and they want to do the right thing. You just need to make "doing the right thing" possible for them.

Exactly how you do that depends on how your organization works today. Methods that work in some organizations might be rejected in others. But here are some ideas on how to prevent these three crises:

- Last month, they finally fixed the title tag so search engines can find our top-selling product page. Last week, the page needed to be updated for an unrelated reason, and the title was inadvertently messed up. The central search team checked the page as part of the normal review process and spotted the problem before it was promoted to production.

- The release plan for the next version of the eCommerce application included a new technique for displaying pages, but in the customary design review it was found that it did not adhere to the searchability standard. The technique was modified to comply before the coding began.

- The team assigned to redesign our website's linking structure came up with three alternative ways to implement their new navigation idea. Because that redesign team included someone from the central search team, they realized that one of their approaches would stop spiders from crawling the site, so they chose one of the other ways.

Sound like a dream? It's not. But it does take planning and hard work to get your organization to function this way. It will not happen by itself. Defining the search marketing tasks, and then dividing them between the central and extended teams, is where you start turning that dream into reality.

List Your Search Marketing Tasks

Before you can divide the work, you need to make a list of exactly which tasks are involved in search engine marketing. Some search marketing tasks apply to organic search, others to paid search. Many are used for both. This list is not intended to be exhaustive—we've got the rest of the book for that—but we want to show the broad categories of tasks that search engine marketing requires:

- **Choosing the search marketing strategy:** Someone needs to set the search marketing strategy. Do we hire a search marketing agency? Do we do everything in-house? A little of each? Are we focusing on organic or paid? Where does the budget come from? How can we prove return on investment? All of these questions must be answered by someone.

- **Targeting search engines:** Which search engines are you trying to get traffic from? Are they the same worldwide or do you need to target different engines in different countries? Someone must decide.

- **Planning keywords:** This is a fancy search marketing name for deducing which keywords your visitors will be searching for. To optimize your content so that your pages have the right words on them, someone needs to decide what those words are. Who does that?

- **Managing bids:** If you are using paid search services, you must bid against your competitors to get a sponsored listing on the search results page. Each time your competitors change their bids, you might want to change yours. Every paid search campaign needs someone to manage it.

- **Optimizing content:** If you are pursuing organic search, a lot of the work revolves around changing the content on the pages—titles, descriptions, and any other words you see—and making sure that the HTML is coded and maintained properly. Each page has someone (if not many "someones") assigned to maintain its content.

- **Developing technology:** Websites are based on technology, even if your site uses only a simple Apache web server to display HTML files. As they grow, many websites start using more technology to display their pages and provide other functions, from eCommerce servers to registration systems to personalization techniques. Each of these technologies can make or break your organic search marketing efforts by making it easy, hard, or even impossible for spiders to crawl your site. Someone needs to make sure that the technology is developed to be search engine friendly. Whose job is that?

- **Defining standards:** Every website has standards for how HTML tags should be used, or what URL patterns are acceptable, or what kinds of software technology might be used. Many existing standards need to be amended, and some new ones need to be created to make organic search marketing work. Someone is in charge of each one.

- **Selecting search marketing tools:** Search engine marketing, like anything else, requires specialized tools to manage your bids, check your page rankings, analyze your pages, identify which sites are linking to yours, and many other functions. Someone must be in charge of identifying the need for a tool, justifying the expenditure, selecting the best one, and making sure that it is installed and operating properly (and that those who need to use it know how). Who is that someone?

- **Reporting metrics:** How many visitors came to your site from search engines this month? What is the trend from last month? Which keywords seem to be the most popular? Which popular keywords do not find your pages in the search engines? Someone must be assigned to track and report these measurements. Who?

Don't worry if you do not deeply understand all of these tasks yet. You don't need to. By the time you finish this book, you *will* understand them (and more). It is also normal for the list to seem overwhelming; we help you tackle one task at a time. Right now you know enough to decide which tasks ought to be performed by your central search team and which ones you need the extended team to do. Later in this book, we help you get each one done properly.

Decide Which Tasks to Centralize

There is no one-size-fits-all organization. You might have to experiment to see what works. You might find that some of the preceding tasks might need to be modified, divided up differently, or even shared between groups. That's okay. Every organization and process is a work in progress anyway. In this section, we give you some rules of thumb that work in many organizations. In the next section, we help you analyze your organization to see whether you want to break any of these rules.

As we look at each task, and decide whether to centralize them or give them to the extended team, keep in mind that *centralize* is a relative term—relative to the scope of your search marketing program, that is. If you have chosen your program scope to cover a division of your company, your central search team operates across the entire division; if your program's scope is your whole company, the central search team works company-wide.

When deciding which tasks to centralize, the most important guideline is to decide whether the task is new for your organization, or whether you already have a team that performs that task (or *should* perform that task). Many search marketing tasks require changing the way someone's existing job is done (such as a copywriter adding keywords to page titles)—those tasks usually belong with your extended search team. Other tasks require deep search marketing expertise or heavy additional workload and are not being done in your company today (such as setting the search marketing strategy)—likely tasks for the central search team. Let's look at each of the major tasks and think through how they might be divided in your organization:

- **Choosing the search marketing strategy:** If this task could be performed well by the extended team, you probably would not need this book. This task requires enough search marketing expertise and enough time that it needs to be centralized in almost all cases.

- **Targeting search engines:** Your center of excellence is probably best equipped to select the worldwide engines to focus on, but picking the right local search engines in each individual country around the world might be best done by the people on your extended team who maintain your website in each country. If you work for a small company with few international sales, just focus on Google and Bing. However, a large multinational company, with sales in dozens of countries, must explicitly target local search engines in each country, in addition to the big worldwide players. With some training, your extended team members in each country might be able to handle that.

- **Planning keywords:** Some organizations can allow the extended team to handle all keyword planning, if the keywords for one business unit do not overlap with the ones desirable to other business units. For many businesses, however, it is essential for the central search team to arbitrate keyword contention between the business units. It would not be good for General Motors to discover its Buick division trying to outbid its Cadillac group for the paid search keyword *luxury sedan*. Both business units would be paying more than necessary. Better for the GM central search team to create a great landing page for *luxury sedan* that shows off both Buicks and Cadillacs, allowing visitors to click either one to learn more. That way, Buick and Cadillac can pool their paid search budgets for that keyword and drive traffic to each of their sites. So, even if you distribute bid management to the extended team, be sure that the center of excellence monitors any overlapping bids across the organization. In addition, some keywords truly apply to the entire organization, and therefore must be handled centrally.

- **Managing bids:** Where this task lands depends mostly on who pays for it. If you are running your paid search campaigns centrally, the central team holds the budget and manages the bids. But if each business unit is managing its own paid search budget, they will undoubtedly want to manage their own bids. In a large organization, it is easier to let each business unit handle its own paid search budget rather than manage it centrally, just because of the amount of work involved in juggling thousands of bids simultaneously.

- **Optimizing content:** This task is rarely one the central search team can do well. The central team will educate and help the existing content teams to do their job with search in mind, but they cannot make the actual changes themselves. Your organization might have a single content team that maintains the entire site, in which case the central search team can work closely with it—maybe even be part of the content team. If, like most businesses, the folks that maintain content are scattered hither and yon across the various parts of your organization, however, the center of excellence must evangelize each team, helping them to understand what processes they must change to optimize their pages on a daily basis.

- **Developing technology:** If you have a central information technology group, it is already purchasing and developing all of your website's technology. You just need to get them to understand how their decisions affect search marketing. Let them tell you how to make it work—whether they need your help when they do their designs, or they need to update code review procedures, or add some automated tests that prove their new technology works with search engines. If your IT group is not centralized, you might need to hire a technical architect for the central search team who can work with each IT group so that they each make the needed process changes. No matter what, your central team cannot take over the technology role, so you need to figure out the best way to persuade this crucial part of your extended team to meet search marketing requirements.

- **Defining standards:** Wherever possible, have the extended team modify your existing standards. For example, you probably already have content tagging standards—make sure those standards include what makes a good title for search marketing purposes. Modifying an existing standard allows you to police compliance using whatever procedure already exists; if your central team creates a new standard, however, you need to set up your own compliance process. For every task, you need to persuade the extended team to do, try to find an existing standard and persuade the standard owner to modify it. The central team should define new standards only when they are clearly needed and have no obvious extended team owner.

- **Selecting tools:** Most search marketing programs use tools for keyword research or bid management, for example. It is usually best for the central team to choose the tools and pay for them out of a central budget and distribute them to the extended team. You need specialized search marketing expertise to make good selections, and your life will be easier if everyone is using the same tools. You will get a volume discount, and you will have only one set of tools requiring training and support.

- **Reporting metrics:** Your website certainly has a group already responsible for web analytics, so you can ask them to add a few reports on referrals from search engines (if they do not have them already). But most web analytics groups will balk at providing reports that are not traffic based, such as summaries of search rankings for important keywords, or a list of all the pages that do not have titles. You will probably have to devote part of your center of excellence for these new reports that fall out of your analytics team's comfort zone, but it cannot hurt to ask.

Regardless of the advice given here, use your own good judgment when deciding what to centralize and what to leave with the extended team. Consider the existing groups in your web organization to be your extended search team and try to get them to do everything appropriate, because search marketing must permeate so many jobs in your organization to be successful. You will find that your existing organization provides the best clues as to which search tasks should be centralized and which ones the extended team must be persuaded and trained to do.

Different Organizations Centralize Different Tasks

There's no recipe for who does what. As you formulate your plans, you need to carefully consider which tasks should be centralized and which tasks should be distributed to the extended team. Some tasks might need to be shared across the two. Exhibit 5-3 lists a subset of these search marketing tasks and summarizes some possibilities of how centralization decisions might differ based on your organization type. Even when each organization has chosen the same scope (in this case, their entire website), the table shows that they might make different decisions about how each search marketing task is executed.

Task	Functional	Product-Oriented	Multinational	Conglomerate
Targeting search engines	Central	Central	Extended	Central
Planning keywords	Central	Extended	Extended	Central
Reporting metrics	Central	Central	Central	Extended
Defining standards	Central	Central	Central	Extended

Exhibit 5-3 Centralizing search marketing tasks. Different types of organizations centralize different tasks even with the same site-wide search marketing scope.

Our friends at Snap Electronics faced the same decisions on dividing tasks between central and extended teams. Snap adopted the approach suggested in Exhibit 5-3 for a product-oriented organization. As its search marketing program's scope eventually expands to encompass countries outside the United States, however, it might adopt the multinational approach, allowing each country team to choose the local search engines to target.

You can see that there are many ways to divide up the search marketing work between a central and an extended search team. There are no surefire answers, but if you carefully consider the type of organization you work in, you can choose a mix of responsibilities that offers the best chance of cultural acceptance, and therefore success.

Choose Your Search Marketing Approach

Now that you have analyzed the search marketing tasks to perform and made some preliminary decisions about who in your organization will perform them, it's time to decide exactly how to get started. Do you have the expertise on your team to do this? Or do you need to hire some outside help?

You might hear people talk about the choice between outsourcing search marketing and "doing it in-house," but that is a false choice. Certain search marketing tasks, such as changing the content or doing proper redirects, are almost never done by outsiders; your extended team does them. You will *always* do some of the work in-house.

The real question is whether you hire an external vendor to help you. Do you conduct your search marketing program with completely internal resources, or do you also hire an outside firm to augment your own personnel? To answer that question, you need to consider several factors:

- **Corporate culture:** If your executive never "throws money away on consultants," you are unlikely to persuade him on this one. So, one reason to avoid an external vendor is that it does not fit your corporate culture. Most companies, however, benefit from the specialized expertise that search marketing vendors bring. Search marketing is exactly the kind of focused specialty where a consultant can be extremely valuable.

- **Budget:** It is sad but true that some organizations do not have the money to hire an external firm, or at least they believe they do not. This can be extremely shortsighted. Some "starter packages" from search marketing firms cost just $5,000 to $10,000 for a quick analysis with a recommendation for a single product line, for example. You might spend that much to do it yourself, and you would be unlikely to do it as well as the outside firm. Your time is not really free, and you might spend a lot more time doing it than an expert would, especially when you consider the specialized tools and experience a professional brings to the task.

- **Expertise:** Do you have the necessary skills to staff a search center of excellence internally? If not, could you afford to hire someone who has those skills? Would you know how to locate such a person? If you have sufficient expertise available in-house, you do not need any external firm to help. Be aware, however, that a good search marketing firm has a breadth of expertise that you could never find in one or two people. You might need help on arcane technical topics—topics such as rewriting URLs to help dynamic pages get indexed. To solve that problem requires deep expertise in search marketing as well as skills in the particular brand of web server software you purchased to run your website.

- **Time:** In Chapter 4, you probably found that search marketing is an extremely valuable opportunity for your business. It follows that every minute you fail to cash in on that opportunity is costing you money. So, one factor to consider is how quickly a vendor can get your program in gear as opposed to you going it alone—and how much that is worth. If you can see results two months faster, would that more than pay for the professional fee?

- **Quality:** Do you believe that you can get the same (or better) results from your completely in-house search marketing program as if you hired an outside vendor to advise you? It is not easy to assess this factor, but it is worth pondering. A search marketing firm has worked with a lot of clients and has undoubtedly seen something before that is similar to your situation. That experience might result in more traffic from your search campaigns.

After assessing these factors in your situation, you might still not be able to decide what to do. If you are undecided, you can interview several search marketing firms to see whether they convince you to hire their firm. They can develop proposals for you to help estimate what your search marketing costs might be—many will do that for a modest fee (or perhaps no fee if you are a large company that could make them a lot of money). Next, we look at how to engage a search marketing firm and select one if you are interested.

Select an External Search Marketing Vendor

As discussed in Chapter 1, "How Search Marketing Works," the search business is big business. Many companies are clamoring to become your search marketing vendor, and more firms enter the industry each year. How do you decide which one is right for you?

Any time you select a vendor to provide services to your company, it makes sense to follow a methodical step-by-step process. Your procurement department can help you with some of these steps, but there are specific tips you need to know. We provide those tips as we walk through each step.

Decide Your Vendor Requirements "Common sense is not so common," goes the old saying. And so it is with selecting vendors. You would think that every company would make a list of what is needed before buying, but many do not. Because we know how sensible you are (hey, you were so smart you bought this book), we are confident that your first step is thinking through your requirements for a search marketing vendor.

Now that you have already made a decision as to which search techniques you would like to use, you should ensure that your vendor has expertise in organic, paid, or both, depending on what you picked. Some vendors do much more of one kind of search marketing. Know what you need.

Decide which search marketing tasks you would like the vendor to perform. Help you with the strategy? Keyword planning? Make your list so that you can check the firm's expertise for each task that you want help with. Your list will drive the questions you ask when you talk to each firm.

Do you have any other requirements? Do you want the firm to be available for in-person meetings (so maybe they should have an office located near you) or is it okay that they do the work remotely? Do they need international experience?

Make a list of every requirement and decide how you will grade each one. For example, if you require that your vendor meet your team frequently in person, you might use specific criteria to grade each company:

- **Strong:** Every member of the vendor team on your account is available in a local office.
- **Moderate:** The key members of your vendor account team are local, but some members are not.
- **Weak:** Few or none of your vendor account team members are nearby.

Think carefully about every requirement you have. Decide up front what you are looking for from a vendor to meet that requirement. Then prioritize your requirements. Which ones are critical—no vendor can be selected unless they qualify—as opposed to those that are of medium importance or just nice to have? After you have chosen your requirements, your scoring criteria, and your priorities, you can look for the search marketing vendors that meet them.

Create Your List of Vendor Candidates   Before you can start listing individual firms, you should first decide whether a particular type of search marketing vendor meets your needs better than others. You can consider three major types of firms:

- **Search consultants:** Called search engine optimization (SEO) or search engine marketing (SEM) consultants, these new firms specialize in search marketing. Some search consultants are smaller firms whose resources could be overwhelmed by a large account, but nowadays some of these agencies are highly stable businesses with significant resources. Like most small companies, they are usually far more flexible in the way they work with your company, which can be critical if you work for a large organization used to doing things its own way. Some search consultants are stronger at organic search than paid search, but most handle both well.
- **Traditional advertising agencies:** Branching out from their traditional advertising business in TV, radio, and print media, well-known agencies have moved to the web. Agencies have tended to be more proficient at banner ads and paid placement than organic search, but they are steadily making strides there, too. These companies have enormous strategy experience and huge resources to throw at almost any problem, but might not

always provide the most personal attention to your account. Many companies already have a relationship with one or more agencies.

- **Interactive or digital marketing agencies:** Consisting of mostly small firms (although usually larger than search consultants), a new type of agency handles all digital marketing needs, including social media, email, banner ads, and search marketing. Some interactive agencies are better at paid search than organic search, but others have strong SEO expertise. Small firms suffer all the expected small company vendor risks, but also provide more personal attention than their larger agency counterparts.

Perhaps one type of company fits your situation better than the others, or maybe you want to interview a couple of firms in each category, so that you can evaluate the full gamut of vendors available. Regardless, you must put together a list of firms to consider.

Recommendations from others, web searches, and trade association lists (such as Search Engine Marketing Professionals Organization) can all help you compile your list. You can visit each firm's website and read comparisons of each firm to come up with your "short list" of vendors to consider. On our website (SEMincBook.com/vendors), we list several industry conferences where you will find vendors selling their wares; it never hurts to meet them and hear a 5-minute sales pitch before going further.

After you have your short list of vendors, you can use your requirements list to put together a matrix to assess each vendor against the others. Snap Electronics put together such a matrix, as shown in Exhibit 5-4. (The vendors shown, like Snap itself, are fictitious operations that are not intended to bear any resemblance to real firms.)

Stolid Advertising Agency Vendor Requirements Priority	Mega Internet Marketing, Inc. Boutique SEO
Organic search experience	High
Paid search experience	Medium
Search strategy	Medium
Keyword planning	High
Technical expertise	High
Business reliability	Medium
Local presence	Low

Exhibit 5-4 Snap Electronics vendor scorecard. Set up a matrix to assess your vendors against each requirement according to the criteria you have decided.

In the interest of space, we are showing a short list of both requirements and vendors for Snap. Yours would likely be considerably longer for both. Right now, there are no ratings for each vendor in that table, but we will fill them in as we meet each one.

Meet the Vendors   Now that you have a scorecard, it's time to start the game. Depending on the size of your company, and the size of the deal the vendor anticipates from you, you might be able to get a free proposal for your search marketing plan. If you have a small organization, you can at least get them to conduct a teleconference with you during which they "strut their stuff" and answer your questions. So what questions should you ask? That's what we will show you here.

The first set of questions should cover the vendor's methodology. After reading this book, you should be able to ask specific questions about each technique that your vendor proposes to use. You need to ensure that your vendor does not use unethical spamming techniques and that your consultant's approach is right for your situation. You should expect a document or presentation that lays out the strategy the firm intends to use.

HOW DO YOU SPOT A SPAMMER?

No smoking gun proves a search marketing vendor practices unethical techniques, but you can use this list to raise enough red flags to eliminate suspicious candidates:

- **Do they guarantee top rankings?** No reputable firms will promise you top results—too many variables are out of their control. Firms that promise top results will usually do *anything* to get them. Spam techniques might have temporary results, but they will probably be caught in the long run, which could result in the search engines banning your site.

- **Do they promise that top rankings require only minimal changes to your site?** You might be dealing with a **link farm** operator. Another way to spot a link farmer is that they want you to include special HTML on your pages. They hide links to their other clients on your pages (and hide links to you on other clients' pages).

- **Do they talk about secret techniques that give them an edge?** If they claim to have inside information about "what Google wants" or they say they know special tactics that will give you an advantage, that's a red flag.

If you get a "yes" answer to any of these questions, you might be dealing with a spammer. One way to flush out a spammer is to check the references provided. Another way to spot a spammer is to act as though that is exactly what you are looking for. Talk up how you have heard that you need to do some really secret stuff to get high rankings and that you need an expert who knows how to do it. A spammer will likely take that bait, but an ethical search marketer will talk you out of it and explain the right way to do it.

Each firm should be able to itemize the steps they will take to diagnose any problems on your site and work with you to correct them. How specific they can be depends on whether they have done only a quick site audit or a full-blown proposal for you.

You need to be realistic in your expectations. If you are a small company looking for a $10,000 contract, you cannot expect any vendor to provide you a 30-page proposal before you have signed a deal with them. In contrast, a large corporation that wants a long-term relationship should expect a free detailed proposal before signing a six-figure agreement.

Some vendors will perform a site audit that clues you in to search marketing challenges before you sign up with them. Even if they do not, you should be able to review a step-by-step pro forma project plan. Maybe your plan will differ a bit, but each vendor should be able to show what they typically do. Unless a vendor has done a site audit, you cannot expect a specific plan for your site, but they should be able to tell you what they do in certain hypothetical situations.

One last methodology question might be important to you. You might care deeply how wedded your vendor is to their own methodology. If you work in a large, inflexible organization, you might require supreme flexibility in your search marketing vendor's methodology. If your vendor insists on only one right way to do its work, you might not be able to carry out the plan.

Beyond methodology questions, there are the normal business questions you would ask of any prospective vendor. Your procurement experts can help you analyze the pricing, contract terms, and the firm's financial viability. Remember that in the fast-moving Internet world a company's financial health can change rapidly, so be sure to check out a firm's records, not its past reputation. Your procurement specialist should also weigh in on whether liability insurance is required.

Perhaps the most important set of questions center on the account team that will be assigned to your company by the vendor. A high-priced dream team might call on you before you sign the deal, but, after you sign, are they going to be your actual account team? Insist on meeting *your* account team beforehand. Those folks will be working with you every day, and their opinions and experience will prove far more important than the rainmakers who close the deal. There's nothing wrong with a junior staff member doing preliminary keyword research or running reports or other preparation work—that saves you a lot of money—but the real brain work must be done by experienced senior search marketers.

Ask the members of your account team how long they have been employed by the firm, and whether they are permanent employees (who get W-2 statements) or are contractors (receiving 1099s). Team members who are longstanding permanent employees provide reassurance that your account team might remain stable, without members jumping to new jobs and leaving you with a rookie to break in. All team members should be covered by nondisclosure agreements for confidential information. If possible, ensure that team members do not also work on search marketing for your competitors.

Question account team members about their specific expertise and search marketing experience. They should be able to name their other accounts and supply references you can contact. Those references should testify to the team's results in previous search campaigns. Insist on talking to former clients, not just current ones. Firms routinely recite long lists of impressive clients, but you should only be impressed by the clients that you verify are satisfied.

As you ask these questions, fill in your scorecard. Exhibit 5-5 shows Snap's scorecard.

Stolid Advertising Agency Vendor Requirements Priority		Mega Internet Marketing, Inc. Boutique SEO		
Organic search experience	High	Weak	Moderate	Strong
Paid search experience	Medium	Strong	Strong	Moderate
Search strategy	Medium	Strong	Strong	Moderate
Keyword planning	High	Moderate	Moderate	Strong
Technical expertise	High	Weak	Moderate	Strong
Business reliability	Medium	Strong	Moderate	Weak
Local presence	Low	Moderate	Weak	Strong

Exhibit 5-5   Final Snap Electronics vendor scorecard. Using the criteria that you set at the beginning of the process, each vendor can be graded against the others.

Snap used its interviews with each vendor to decide its rating on the requirements. Not all of the assessments were clear-cut, and no real leader emerged. The final decision came next.

Make Your Vendor Decision   If you have done a good job recruiting strong candidates to become your search marketing vendor, your final decision will not be easy. You need to return to your original priorities. Which requirements are the most important and how does each vendor stack up on those?

Do You Need a Global Search Marketing Vendor?

Maybe your business has been a global marketer for many years. Or perhaps the web has put global markets within your reach that were impossible before. Regardless, more and more businesses are marketing globally on the web. If you are hiring a search marketing vendor for a program with global scope, you need to ask more questions to find the right match.

Unfortunately, there are no easy answers to some of these questions. You will quickly find that each vendor you interview has a different story about how they execute global programs, so it quickly comes down to what you need. You must ruthlessly prioritize which countries and languages you need coverage for, because a vendor strong in one area might be weak in another. Know which countries and languages are your top priorities—that cannot be compromised—and be willing to accept a little less for other markets.

Snap faced a difficult decision among the three vendors on its short list. To simplify the choice, Snap focused on its highest priorities: organic search experience, keyword planning, and technical expertise. Boutique SEO was rated "strong" on all three counts. Boutique's only weakness was business reliability, due to its small size and short experience. Snap decided to take that risk, negotiating a low-priced deal to compensate for the risk. Boutique, as a hungry small firm, was eager to land the high-profile Snap account as a great reference customer (that will help persuade new customers to sign with them).

Your decision might be just as difficult as Snap's. Before you decide, however, also consider whether you should run your program completely in-house, with no search marketing vendor on your payroll.

Run a Completely In-House Search Marketing Program

It is not easy to go it alone—without hiring an outside vendor—but it can work, if you know what you are doing.

The biggest benefit to doing it in-house is that your program will take an insider's approach rather than an external approach. Your in-house team understands your organization. Your depth of knowledge will allow you to set your priorities based on which campaigns are the easiest to do—that can be good. Sometimes external vendors know a lot about search marketing but not much about your company; they can possibly lead you astray. Of course, if you manage the vendor properly, you will not run this risk.

After you have your target market list, check out the vendor's expertise, country by country:

- **Local presence:** Does the vendor have native speakers residing in the country? Many do not. Does that person work for the vendor? Many have subcontracted relationships with local search marketers—sometimes two or three levels of relationships, which can make things sticky if you run into disagreements.

- **Integration:** How do they enforce the strategy of the overall program in each country? How do they report results across the whole program? Many do not have any way of performing these critical operational tasks.

- **Local references:** Insist on speaking to customer references in each country. Search marketing vendors can have wildly different capabilities from country to country, so make sure you check them out in every top-priority locale on your list.

After you have spoken to each vendor, think carefully about the right tradeoffs. If 80% of your revenue is from the United States, is it worth compromising global markets to get the best vendor for the United States? Could you hire multiple vendors to get stronger coverage across your target markets, or would the coordination headaches be too great? You might not have an easy decision; if you ask the right questions, however, at least you will have fewer nasty surprises.

The hard part of going it alone is in finding the needed expertise in-house. It is rare that you can find search marketing experts inside an organization that, up until now, has not been doing any search marketing. It is possible you can find such skills if your search marketing program is run on a small scale (one division, perhaps) and you want to expand to an enterprise-wide program.

Failing to find the needed expertise, you can develop your search experts from within. You can send folks to classes and conferences, and buy them books (they each need three copies of this one), teaching them what they need to know. This approach can work, but it is slow—usually taking months of startup time before you really get rolling.

Typically, you will be in a hurry, forcing you to hire experts from the outside. The best of both worlds can be to hire an "embedded strategist" who acts as a facilitator to the organization; you try to hire the same kind of person who a search marketing vendor hires.

If you can locate, develop, or hire the search marketing experts that you need, you will likely find that you still do not have the same experience that hiring an outside vendor brings. Vendors work with many different companies and see myriad situations. You are unlikely to replicate that experience in a one- or two-person search team. You will, however, save a lot of money. Internal search experts are typically cheaper than buying the same expertise from outside. With a few key hires and an investment in training, you can staff a strong internal team and create additional loyalty from employees gaining new skills.

And that loyalty might prove vital, because a 100% in-house approach has a key danger of employee attrition. Search marketing skills are hot and getting hotter in today's job market. External search marketing vendors can usually pay a higher salary than you do (because those companies charge more to cover the costs). If you lose your key team members to competitors or to vendors, your search marketing efforts can be severely damaged, at least in the short term. Although members of a vendor account team also might depart, the vendor is more easily able to withstand those changes and replace people with others of high skill. Replacing defectors from *your* in-house team with equally talented people might be considerably more challenging.

In short, it is possible for you to run a successful search marketing program with no outside vendor, but it has its own set of challenges and risks. If you can find, train, or hire the experts you need—and retain them—your search marketing efforts will bear strong results while also costing less than using an external firm. You might find, however, that the slow "ramp up" time to start your program, coupled with the risks of hiring less-skilled resources and unexpected employee defections, might not make the cost savings worth the pain.

Project Your Search Marketing Costs

Deciding your search marketing strategy is critical to formulating your program, especially when it comes to assessing your costs. You cannot win approval for a program when you have no idea how much you need to spend to carry it off.

To paint your cost picture, you need to go back to your strategy decisions. You need to keep your scope in mind: How broad is your program? A search marketing program that handles only a few areas of your site is not nearly as big as one that covers the whole site. Your program scope directly impacts your costs.

You must also know what your approach is to budgeting. Will you budget to build or will you build to budget? That's the shorthand way of asking whether you will add up all your possible costs and ask for that budget (budget to build) or you are being told a budget and can build a program that includes any tactics you can afford under the budget.

The budget to build approach is the most accurate, and we use it here. If, on the other hand, you are handed a budget, you use the same calculations to determine your costs, but you prioritize your most important costs and choose your program's scope based on what you can afford.

Project Your Personnel Costs

Depending on your particular strategy, you might find that personnel costs are the largest expense in your program. Perhaps you will have just a small central search team (maybe it is just you—and a part-time you, at that), but whatever personnel time is expended on search will cost something. You might know exactly how much your organization allots for each person assigned to a project—if you do, use that. Most organizations budget between $75,000 and $150,000 each year for each "head count," so your company probably lands somewhere in that range.

If you can get away with it, it is best to avoid calculating the costs of the extra work your extended search team must do to support search marketing. In some organizations, you might be required to take a shot at this number, but it varies widely based on your situation. You are better off making the case that this is part of their job, and always should have been part of their job. The marketing department does not have to justify why the web team should change copy when they develop a new slogan; it is part of their job. Point out that this is part of developing a good website that meets your business needs, and should be absorbed as part of their current workload. You can show real return for the work you are requesting, which is more than can be said for a lot of the work they do that no one ever questions.

Before you decide to hire an external vendor, you should receive an estimate on what will be charged. You can do small one-time audits for as little as $5,000 if you hire someone with little experience, but a full-blown program in a large enterprise can easily run hundreds of thousands of dollars each year. Whatever you decide, you need to include that cost in your proposal for your program.

Snap Electronics decided to staff a three-person central search team. The team leader is an experienced Snap web marketer (who already knows the U.S. product managers) whose mission is to sell the program internally and to manage the central search team. Snap will hire an organic search expert and a paid search expert from outside the company, because they cannot seem to find those skills internally. Snap's finance department insists that all proposals use a flat rate of $130,000 per person for planning purposes, so the three-person team is budgeted at $390,000 each year.

Boutique SEO, the vendor that Snap chose, initially provided an estimate of $140,000 annually to provide strategy and keyword planning services, but that was more than Snap wanted to pay. Snap wanted to keep the total personnel costs at half a million dollars or less, because investments more than $500,000 required higher-level executives to approve. Snap negotiated with Boutique to train its central search team to perform keyword planning internally, instead of doing the keyword planning at Boutique. This change reduced the annual costs to $110,000. When that $110,000 is added to the $390,000 cost for the central search team, it totals a more palatable $500,000 combined annual investment. Making this change will slow down the rate of rollout of the search marketing program because it will take longer to do the keyword planning across the entire product line, but it was believed that the tradeoff was worth it to get the program approved more easily.

Project Your Organic Search Costs

If your search marketing strategy includes organic search, you must project how much money to budget to carry out your organic optimization efforts. If you remember assessing your organic search situation in Chapter 4, you will recall that you identified which of your site's pages should match your targeted keywords, and whether those pages are stored in search indexes. As you learned, it can be difficult to get some pages included in the search index. (In Chapter 7, "Get Your Content Listed," we explore all the reasons that spiders can be blocked from your site.) Because it is hard to estimate the cost of eliminating these spider problems, we simplify our cost projections by assuming that we will create new pages that are designed to be crawled by the spider to replace the hard-to-crawl pages if we have to.

Even if your pages are already in the search index, you still need to work on them. You need to update the titles and content on your pages to include mentions of your targeted keywords, as discussed in Chapter 8, "Optimize Your Content." You need to make these changes not only so that your pages achieve high rankings in the search results, but also so that your title and snippet invite the searchers to click through to your site. Luckily, most modern websites are dynamically generated using page templates, so optimizing the template can optimize hundreds or thousands of pages, greatly lowering the costs. But the title and content for each page must still be optimized individually.

After you read Chapters 7 and 8, you might be able to project your costs much more closely, but you can use techniques right now to come up with a ballpark estimate. As you saw back in Chapter 1, it usually costs between $100 and $300 to optimize each page template for organic search.

Snap Electronics knew that all of the pages in the product areas of their site were delivered using just five templates in their content management system, one for the product category pages, one for product home pages, one for product features pages, one for product reviews pages, and the last one for the eCommerce catalog page. Snap estimated it would cost $300 apiece to optimize each template, for a total of $1,500.

After you know your per-template cost, you then need to estimate the number of templates you must change. If your site required that you optimize ten page templates for organic search, and optimization costs you $123 a page template on average, you will spend $1,230 for your site.

Returning to our case study for Snap Electronics, you recall that Snap identified five page templates it had to optimize for its digital camera campaign for $1,500. Snap used a vendor to make all changes to its web pages and they knew from experience that it costs $111 on average for each change to a page. To be conservative, they estimated it might take ten tries for each page before they were happy with their organic search results, resulting in $1,110 per page multiplied by five pages per product, yielding a $5,550 cost per product line. That means that Snap's first organic search marketing campaign will cost $7,050.

Because Snap has 70 product lines in the United States (its total scope of its search marketing program), Snap estimates it will cost $388,500 to optimize its content ($5,500 multiplied by 70). When you add the original $1,500 to optimize its page templates, you get $390,000 to optimize Snap's website for organic search. You can see how seemingly small costs can add up quickly in a large company.

Project Your Paid Search Costs

If you decided to pursue paid search as part of your strategy, you need to project the costs before you can get budget approval. But paid search is tricky to project costs for, because of the search engines' clever ranking algorithms; they show your ads based on a combination of your bid rate and your quality score. If you design your ad to get a higher clickthrough rate than your competitor's, you will get a higher ranking for the same bid. However, the same cleverness that can give you that edge wreaks havoc with your attempts to budget for paid search. You cannot predict what your clickthrough rate will be. Moreover, you don't know how your competitors will change their bids in the future; they might even change their bids based on your bid, because the former #2 bidder wants to regain that top spot you grabbed from them.

Because you cannot easily project your ranking in paid search, you also cannot easily project your clickthrough rate, because you know that your rate in part depends on where you are ranked. (Does your brain hurt yet?) What's more, you can only get an average number of clicks based on your average bid, so your projections could be wildly off if you bid higher or lower than average and if your clickthrough rate diverges from the average (higher or lower). And you have to change your bids to optimize your program—in fact, that is what the most successful paid search bidders do. (Now do you have a headache?) But there is even more complexity, unfortunately. If the paid search ranking formula were as simpleminded as multiplying the click rate by the bid, no new ads would ever be shown, because their initial click rate is zero. So, the search engines actually have a default clickthrough rate to put new ads into rotation, waiting for a certain number of impressions before applying the ad's *actual* clickthrough rate to determine its ranking. (Head pounding by now?) It gets even more complicated. The search engines even assess the quality of your landing page as part of the formula; well-designed landing pages that are closely related to your ad copy are favored with better ad placements. (There, now you are finally reaching for the Excedrin.)

So what do you do? Accept that it is an experiment. Put together a budget that you believe will get you started so that you can test your way to something smarter in the future. It's not possible to perfectly project costs, but you can make a good estimate. There are three major costs in paid search:

- **Creative costs:** It costs money to get your information into the search engine. For paid placement, you will develop titles and descriptions for your advertisements for each keyword you buy—that can run anywhere from around $15 to more than $50 per ad if you contract with an agency, but might be cheaper if you have the skills to do it in-house. For product search, you must supply a trusted feed (as discussed in Chapter 7) of your product catalog, whose cost can vary widely depending on the flexibility of your product database and its associated software program.

- **Management costs:** You can contract an external vendor to manage your paid placement bidding (and product search submissions), and they can provide a free estimate for your costs. If you plan to do it yourself, you need to project the amount of time your central search team will expend. In Chapter 7, we explain how bid management works; if you decide to buy a bid management tool, you must add the cost to your budget.

- **Media costs:** Most of your budget will go to the search engines in the form of per-click fees—the results of your paid search bids or the fixed fees for product search. We spend the rest of this section estimating those costs.

Snap Electronics signed up for several ad accounts with different search engines to check out their similar projection tools. They eventually decided to use Bing's projection estimator to figure out their spending. By experimenting with several different bid levels, they saw estimates of how many clicks to their site they could expect for each one.

Snap eventually decided that a $1.40 bid was the one that provided them the best value for the keyword *digital camera* but they knew that they were taking a shot in the dark. They knew that only by starting the campaign and testing what's really happening could they learn how much traffic they will receive at what price. After all, once they get in the game, others will adjust their bids. If Snap outbids those unknown others, they might respond by bidding more. But at least these projection tools give you some idea of the cost and the traffic associated with your paid search program. As your campaign unfolds, you'll learn much more and be able to project ongoing costs better.

Using an estimate of $1.40 per click, Snap can calculate the budget required for a Bing paid search campaign for *digital cameras* by multiplying the bid rate ($1.40) by the monthly keyword volume (around 880,000 according to Bing's estimation tool) by the estimated clickthrough rate (Snap conservatively projected 1%) to yield the estimated monthly paid search cost of $12,320. Multiplying that cost by Snap's 70 product lines yields a cost for the overall search marketing program of over $860,000! Clearly, that is impossibly more than anyone at Snap wants to risk for such an unproven idea, so they decide that they will project a much smaller cost more befitting with the experimental status they have chosen for paid search.

Instead, Snap decided to experiment with just the *digital cameras* keyword for the first year. Multiplying $12,320 by 12 produces the yearly paid search budget for the first campaign of $147,840, which Snap rounded up to $150,000 for its proposal. Unable to be sure how much creative and bid management costs might be involved, Snap decided to double that budget for the overall program to $300,000 a year, but the outcome of the experiment will ultimately tell them whether that is the right figure.

Total It All Up

In Chapter 4, you chose your first search marketing campaign—one that you believed would be high impact and relatively easy to do. Your first campaign lets you start small, show success, and build from there. Recall that your alter egos at Snap chose *digital cameras*. We can itemize the costs of Snap's first campaign in Exhibit 5-6. To keep things simple, we allocate the costs of the entire central search team and of the SEO vendor to our first campaign, but you might want a more complex calculation to spread those costs over multiple campaigns.

	Organic Search	Paid Search	Personnel	Total
Year 1	$7,050	$150,000	$500,000	$657,050
Year 2	$0	$150,000	$500,000	$650,000
Year 3	$0	$150,000	$500,000	$650,000
Year 4	$0	$150,000	$500,000	$650,000
Year 5	$0	$150,000	$500,000	$650,000
Total	$7,050	$750,000	$2,500,000	$3,257,050

Exhibit 5-6   Snap's first campaign costs. Startup costs incurred in Year 1 for organic search drop off in Years 2 through 5.

Snap Electronics made its search marketing program scope decision right along with you, choosing an ambitious U.S. program across all of its products that emphasizes organic search and experiments with paid search. Exhibit 5-7 summarizes Snap's estimated costs for the first five years of its program. The organic search costs are one-time only, but the remaining costs apply each year.

These costs look large, but the benefits look larger, as you will see later in this chapter. We take the work we did in Chapter 4 to analyze the opportunity across the scope of the program that we chose in this chapter. For Snap Electronics, we calculate the revenue opportunity for all U.S. products.

	Organic Search	Paid Search	Personnel	Total
Year 1	$390,000	$300,000	$500,000	$1,190,000
Year 2	$0	$300,000	$500,000	$800,000
Year 3	$0	$300,000	$500,000	$800,000
Year 4	$0	$300,000	$500,000	$800,000
Year 5	$0	$300,000	$500,000	$800,000
Total	$390,000	$1,500,000	$2,500,000	$4,390,000

Exhibit 5-7   Projected costs for Snap's search marketing program. Each expense must be totaled to develop your overall business case.

We're just getting started, however. Next, we go beyond the numbers to close the deal. How do you convince all the members of your existing web team (your extended search team) to change their jobs to include search marketing? And how do you persuade the toughest audience of all—your executives—to part with the cash you need to get started? Now, we show you how to convince your organization to take a chance on a search marketing program.

Sell Your Search Marketing Proposal

It's time to close the deal. Time to get the approvals for your proposal to start a search marketing program. Next to actually managing a search marketing program, the most complicated activity is getting "buy-in" from your extended search team and your executives. How hard that is to do depends on the scope of the search marketing program that you selected earlier in this chapter. The larger your scope, the tougher your approval process will be.

We've got three steps to take:

1. **Assemble your proposal:** You calculated the revenue opportunity for a single campaign in Chapter 4, and the costs for both your first campaign and overall program earlier in this chapter. Now we put them together and craft a proposal that you can use to persuade others in your company. Your proposal will contain business cases that justify the investment in both your first campaign and the program as a whole. Your proposal will also include a step-by-step plan with a time line to implement your first search marketing campaign.

2. **Sell your proposal to the extended search team:** Your organization already has an existing team (maybe many teams) to manage your website today. These special-ists decide the strategy, write the content, create the pages, design applications, and

do many other things. You must take advantage of these existing resources as your extended search team, because search marketing cannot succeed unless they do the right things. You need to understand these specialists and speak their language, because you must convince them to add search marketing tasks to their day-to-day jobs.

3. **Sell your proposal to your executives:** In most places, no money gets released without executive approval. You will learn what executives are looking for in a proposal, so that yours will be approved.

In some organizations, you can sell your proposal to the executives, who then order the extended team to execute, but in most companies that will not work. Many corporate cultures do not allow executives to bless a proposal until there is consensus among all affected. You can assess how your organization works to decide whether to talk to the extended team first, the executives first, or to work them in parallel. Regardless of which you approach first, you need to assemble your proposal so you have something to talk about, so let's do that now.

Assemble Your Search Marketing Proposal

In the preceding chapters, you've laid the groundwork for your proposal, but you need to put it all together. Your proposal contains two business cases—one for your overall search marketing program and one specifically for your first search marketing campaign. This way, you explain why search marketing is important strategically, for many campaigns, but also focus on a tangible, practical first effort. Your proposal must also include a detailed plan of tasks on a time line to execute the first campaign, but we start with the business cases.

Making the Business Case for Your Program

A business case serves two primary purposes. First, it is an unbiased and objective analysis of projected costs required to achieve expected benefits. The second purpose is to convince your decision makers to accept your recommendations. In short, your business case ought to persuade *you* before you use it to persuade others. Too often, business cases get a bad name because they are cobbled together as a pretext for doing something that does not actually have much value. Search marketing has a great deal of value; you do not need a sham business case. You can build a case to convince even the most tight-fisted bean counter.

In Chapter 4, we discussed the revenue opportunity for your first search marketing campaign, and earlier in this chapter we calculated the cost, both for your first campaign and your overall search program. Here, we put them together to show the payback of search marketing—the payback of pursuing search marketing across the full scope of the search marketing program that you chose. We look at the bigger picture, going beyond your first campaign. How can you project the revenue opportunity of your search marketing program across your program's entire scope? We first return to your calculations from Chapter 4 for the revenue opportunity and expand it to the entire program. Then we revisit your costs based on the work you did earlier in this chapter.

Your Search Marketing Program's Revenue Opportunity   If you followed the logic to determine the revenue opportunity for mounting a search marketing campaign, you might be wondering how we can estimate the revenue opportunity for your entire search marketing program. What if you embarked on a search marketing program across all your products? How much incremental revenue could you drive? There is no precise way to answer these questions. No matter what we do, we will be making some assumptions. But we can come up with ballpark figures that give you a glimpse into your search marketing potential.

Returning to our fictitious firm, Snap Electronics, we recall that they chose as their search marketing program scope their entire U.S. product line. To estimate the total search marketing potential for Snap's site, we can extrapolate from our first campaign.

Exhibit 4-42 from Chapter 4 projected the number of additional organic search referrals Snap could achieve with a well-executed search marketing campaign for digital cameras. Because Snap's scope emphasizes organic marketing over its 70 product lines within the United States, we can examine our projections for Snap's first campaign and then apply them across the entire scope. Exhibit 4-42 shows that the referrals to the digital camera area of Snap's site total just 10,734 each month, but are projected to rise to 28,063 referrals, a 161% increase. We can apply this same percentage increase to Snap's overall U.S. search referrals—the referrals associated with any keyword, not just those related to digital cameras—to estimate the traffic increase possible for Snap's entire search marketing program. In Snap's case, its web analytics facility showed 52,634 organic search referrals for its U.S. site last month. Multiplying by 161% yields an opportunity for 137,374 organic search referrals—an increase of 84,740 each month across Snap's whole U.S. site.

But we need to estimate our paid referrals, too. Because paid placement is an experiment, Snap decided to limit its spending to $300,000, just twice the cost of the first campaign for digital cameras, which it conservatively estimated will yield an extra 8,800 visits per month.

To estimate the overall added referrals for our search marketing program, we can total the organic search projection (84,740) and the paid search one (8,800) to produce 93,540 added referrals per month.

As we did with digital cameras, we can calculate the revenue impact of the entire Snap search marketing program for all U.S. products, as shown in Exhibit 5-8. We had used the site-wide conversion rate of 2% in Chapter 7, so that remains the same, but we now use the average transaction price of all U.S. sales on the site, which rises to $493. It is $13 million in incremental revenue a year!

	Added monthly traffic	93,540
Multiply by:	Conversion rate	0.02
	Added monthly sales	1,871
Multiply by:	Average transaction price	$590
	Added monthly revenue	$1,103,890
Multiply by:	12 months	12
	Added yearly revenue	$13,246,680

Exhibit 5-8 Projecting revenue for Snap's search marketing program. We use a familiar formula to project incremental search revenue program-wide.

Although no one can predict the exact numbers with pinpoint accuracy, clearly Snap has a lot to gain from a search marketing program across the U.S. product line. As you work through your organization's opportunity, you might find a similarly exciting prospect in your own backyard.

Your Search Marketing Program's Costs You saw earlier in this chapter that, as tough as it is to project revenue opportunity, it might be even harder to figure out what it all will cost. Nonetheless, we can use the estimates we calculated in the preceding chapter to project our costs over the next several years.

In your situation, you might make different (and more complex) assumptions, but in our Snap case study, we keep it simple. The organic search costs we estimated ($390,000) can be assumed to be incurred in the first year. That is probably an unrealistic expectation, because most companies would make their investment over a period of years, but spending money earlier is the most pessimistic business case, so we do it that way.

The organic search costs are a one-time cost—after the technology and the content are cleaned up, your central search team and your improved standards and processes will keep them clean. But the other costs are annual, and need to be reflected in each year's cost projection. You can review Exhibits 5-6 and 5-7 to refresh your memory for the cost calculations both for the first campaign and the overall search marketing program.

Your Search Marketing Program's Business Case We can construct a business case for the Snap Electronics search marketing program based on the revenue we calculated in Exhibit 5-8. To keep things simple, we round off the revenue number and assume it to be constant over all

5 years. Obviously that is also unrealistic, because you would likely see a gradual rise in revenue from a slow start, but it makes the example simpler to understand. Exhibit 5-9 consolidates our work to show the estimated profit over five years from Snap's search marketing program.

	Revenue	Cost	Profit
Year 1	$13,250,000	$1,190,000	$12,060,000
Year 2	$13,250,000	$800,000	$12,450,000
Year 3	$13,250,000	$800,000	$12,450,000
Year 4	$13,250,000	$800,000	$12,450,000
Year 5	$13,250,000	$800,000	$12,450,000
Total	$66,250,000	$4,390,000	$61,860,000

Exhibit 5-9   Snap's search marketing program business case. In a large company, the payback from search marketing can be sizable across the enterprise.

Even in a company as large as Snap Electronics, $61 million over 5 years is a big deal. So big a deal, in fact, that they reduced their numbers drastically before they showed this business case to their executives. They reasoned that search marketing was a great idea even if they were wildly off in their calculations, so they wanted to be careful not to overpromise the benefits and risk early disappointment.

This book is not devoted to developing business cases, so there are certainly many more sophisticated methods to use. Check with your finance folks to see whether they have a methodology that they like. Whatever method you use, the payback for your search marketing program is likely to be *very* positive. And that is the point of this exercise. Estimate what search marketing can do for your organization, and then make the decision to get started.

Your First Search Marketing Campaign's Business Case

The business case for your overall search marketing program shows why search marketing should be strategic to your organization, but you need to have a more tactical proposal. Few businesses would lay out sizable cash in the first year for a totally unproven idea. Therefore, your proposal also needs to make a strong case for your first search marketing campaign.

In Chapter 4, we calculated Snap's revenue opportunity for its digital camera campaign in Exhibit 4-43, and we carry those revenue projections into our business case in Exhibit 5-10 (along with the costs we estimated in Exhibit 5-6).

	Revenue	Cost	Profit
Year 1	$2,550,000	$655,000	$1,895,000
Year 2	$2,550,000	$650,000	$1,900,000
Year 3	$2,550,000	$650,000	$1,900,000
Year 4	$2,550,000	$650,000	$1,900,000
Year 5	$2,550,000	$650,000	$1,900,000
Total	$12,750,000	$3,255,000	$9,495,000

Exhibit 5-10 Snap's first campaign business case. The digital camera product line does look like a promising initial target for search marketing at Snap.

As with the overall program business case, we round off the overly precise revenue projection we calculated in Chapter 4. The reason you round off is that you want the precision of the estimate to match the precision of the model. Our model is not precise enough to estimate anything down to the dollar, so why show a number that makes the model look more precise than it is? How much would you trust a man who sticks his hand into a cold stream and announces "49.2 degrees"? Being overly precise takes away attention from the real message to your executives: "Search marketing is a big opportunity. Even though our numbers are estimates and might be very far off, you can *still* see the right decision to make."

That wraps up the business case sections, but you need to create a more complete proposal for your search marketing program. As we continue assembling our proposal, we need to explain exactly what we will do to deliver on the business case for the first campaign.

The Plan for Your First Search Marketing Campaign

Which tasks will you undertake? When will they happen? You will not have a persuasive proposal without a plan. You need to show, task by task, who will take the actions required to deliver the value promised in your business case. You also need to show the time line for each action. Every search marketing campaign needs a plan with several phases:

- **Organization phase:** You have completed much of the organizing for your first campaign already, but it can be one of the longer phases of some projects. The primary organizational tasks include choosing the team, deciding the approach (organic, paid, or both), setting the scope of the campaign, and performing preliminary keyword analysis to help set the budget and opportunity. We have worked through each of these steps in Chapters 4 and earlier in this chapter for your first campaign, but you will take these steps for *every* campaign.

- **Auditing phase:** For organic search, you need to audit your technology and content to determine what problems afflict your site. The diagnoses for these problems drive the later phases.

- **Learning phase:** Early in your organization's efforts, it is typical for gaps to exist in search marketing knowledge. As your company grows in experience, more of the problems found in each campaign's audit can be handled without requiring additional learning. But you will find that you've never learned everything. There are always fresh issues and the search industry keeps changing, so you might have a learning phase for most of your campaigns no matter how long you work in search marketing.

- **Implementation phase:** Finally, the wrenches start to turn and the search marketing machine comes to life! Both organic and paid campaigns are tuning content (web pages or ads) and monitoring traffic and conversions. For paid campaigns, bid management is a major task; organic campaigns are constantly improving the quality of content and ensuring spiders can index that content.

Snap Electronics put together the plan shown in Exhibit 5-11 to explain the campaign for its digital camera product line. You can see that each phase of the project takes a month or two to execute—*your* project plan might be shorter or longer, depending on what you want to do, the pace of your organization, and how thoroughly you persuade your extended team and your executives (which we cover later). Each phase in the plan lists the major tasks that must be accomplished, the group that leads each one, and the other people that must assist that task's completion. The central search team leads many tasks, but your extended search team must lead some, too (especially in the implementation phase). You might want to produce a more exhaustive chart that shows all the tasks in each phase, but for brevity we show just the major ones to give you the idea.

This chart is important in explaining your plan. Your executives and your extended team will each want to know exactly what you plan to do. They will want to know what your timeframe is and who will perform each task. When you speak to the extended team, each group will scan this chart looking for its name. The copywriters will see that they are leading a task in the implementation phase, which will make them nervous. It is important that you explain how you will help and why they ultimately need to own the task. When they understand why search marketing is important and that you are deferring to their ownership of the content, they will understand why they must lead the optimizing content task for organic search marketing.

The checkpoint line on Exhibit 5-11 is also important. Your plan must include a checkpoint for evaluating success. Give yourself enough room in the schedule not just to complete the actions, but for them to show results. You should not expect to have everything "done"; you will find it is *never* done. There is always one more tweak to improve the clickthrough rate, and another competitor that leapfrogged you to the #1 spot last week. Implementation never ends, but you must periodically assess your success, both to fuel continuous improvement in your first campaign, and to justify investment in future campaigns in your overall program. So, pick a date on which you will show the results that you promised in your campaign's business case (or at least a strong step toward those results). Chapter 10 shows many ways of continually measuring and improving.

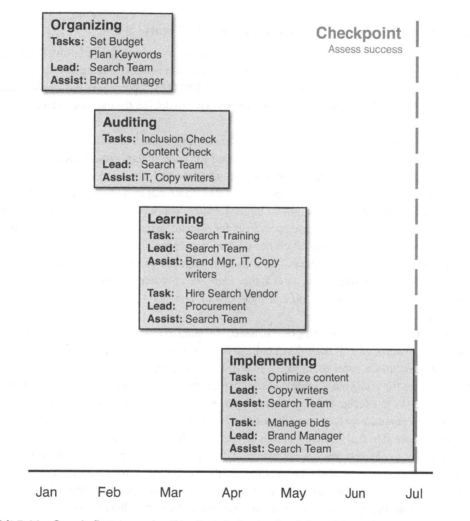

Exhibit 5-11 Snap's first campaign time line. A simple visual that shows what needs to be done can explain the campaign in one glance.

After you have pulled together your campaign's plan, recognize that this is really just a first draft for your plan. To get agreement from others, you will undoubtedly need to make some changes. Now is the time for you to start "shopping your plan around" to the rest of your organization to get the go-ahead to execute it. Remember Dwight Eisenhower's famous quote, "Plans are nothing; planning is everything." You have now done all the planning that you can do by yourself. Your *real* planning starts when you explain your plan to others and hear their suggested changes. As much as you might persuade them to follow your plan, you also need to be flexible about modifying your plan to suit them.

Sell Your Proposal to the Extended Search Team

No matter how much work your central search team does, every search marketing program relies on the extended search team to succeed. The extended team actually manages your website. The extended search team writes the page copy, codes the HTML, programs the applications, and chooses the URLs. The central search team knows what to do, but the extended search team must do it.

Who makes up the extended team? Business people (such as sales reps and marketers), writers who develop copy for your web pages and for your advertisements, technologists (such as webmasters and web developers), and operations personnel who keep your website humming.

In a small company, the extended team is also small, but in a large company the team can be thousands of people. For medium-to-large websites, you will work with a daunting array of specialists. You need some of these specialists for organic search marketing, some for paid, and some for both. Not every organization has each of these specialists, and sometimes the roles go by different names, but every specialty has its own language and its own search marketing blind spots. So read the descriptions as *roles* rather than *jobs*. Someone in your organization is doing these tasks, regardless of what you call that person. Your job (er, role) is to find them and get them to do what you need.

Now that you have your proposal in hand, you need to evangelize the extended team to persuade them to approve it. If they don't believe in your proposal, it will not work well, no matter how many executives order them to execute it. Remember that your proposal has several parts: business cases for both your strategic search marketing program and your first campaign, plus a plan of the tasks to execute for your first campaign. Each part of your proposal is there for a reason, either to persuade people as to the value of search marketing, or to show that it is possible. Use your proposal to fuel your sales pitch to your extended search team.

Start by explaining your ideas using whatever methods seem to work in your organization. If people need you to show up in person with a slide deck in tow, do that. If your company expects regular conference calls to answer questions and check progress toward your goals, do that. If you find that you need to create an intranet website that lists all of the tips for search improvement, go for it. They might like an email newsletter? Try it. There is nothing different about selling this idea from selling any other new concept in your organization. You work there and you probably know how to do it.

CASE STUDY: PERSUADING THE EXTENDED SEARCH TEAM IN A LARGE COMPANY

The web's largest auction site, eBay, is no different from your company when it comes to search marketing. Sure, eBay excels at search marketing today, but it wasn't always that way. Corey Clark, the head of eBay's International Marketing Team, knew that he needed to mobilize the extended search team to turn around eBay's search marketing.

Clark outlined how eBay got it started: "We first brought all of our Internet marketing partners together and focused on the ones that were 'search-specific.'" Clark then embarked on an "internal road show," delivering a PowerPoint presentation month after month, to any department that would listen. The road show yielded valuable feedback from people within eBay who had experience in search marketing campaigns for other companies. "We gathered enthusiastic interest from every business unit that wanted to get [search marketing] working for them," Clark says.

"When it comes to natural optimization of the eBay site, we have a long ways to go," Clark admitted, but eBay shows that a focus on paid search can pay off when you first persuade the extended team. You might be thrilled to achieve the success that eBay has in search marketing, but everyone always has more work to do, as Corey's comment shows.

But first, a warning: Do not expect the extended team to listen. That might be the toughest lesson to learn for the central search team. *You* read this book, *you* are fired up, and you expect everyone else to be as excited about this as you are. Well, they're not.

Search marketing is *your* job. It's not theirs. At least they don't think it is. *That* is what you need to change. You must start by explaining why search engine marketing is important. Show them how your competition is doing this better than you. Explain the technical challenges to the "techies" and the business value to the marketers. Challenge them.

But when you do, remember that someone walks in every day with another new task they should add to their already jam-packed days. They are busy, just as you are. Figure out how to make it fun. Figure out how to make it easy. You *can* persuade them, but you must understand who they are so that you can speak to them in *their* language.

We show you how to do that right now. We look at several kinds of specialists on your extended team and help you reach them. Each one has a special perspective on the world, and you can learn what motivates them. After you win them over, and not before, you will be on your way to search marketing success.

Business People

Money talks. Use the search marketing opportunity information you put together in Chapter 4 to persuade the business people of the importance of search marketing. Whatever drives sales will drive the investment you need to jump-start search marketing.

Who are the "business people"? Most are sales and marketing personnel, all trying to sell your products to customers. We also discuss how to work with your legal department, whose job is to protect the business from unnecessary risk.

The business people are important to convince, because they will make your case to the rest of your organization. Remember, marketing and sales people excel at persuading people. Get them to help you persuade your organization.

If you work at a nonprofit organization, the principle is the same, even if the particulars are different. Your "business people" might not be marketers or sales reps, but they are responsible in some way for the growth of your organization. Your website has some overarching goal that we identified in Chapter 4, and anything that supports that goal will justify the investment that you seek. For a business, it is usually sales, but those of you working in nonprofits can use organizational goals to convince people in similar ways. We use business-oriented roles here, but you can translate "brand manager" to "campaign manager" if your website supports a political campaign.

Now it's time for you to learn how to talk to brand managers, sales people, public relations folks, and lawyers to persuade them to participate on your extended search marketing team.

Brand Managers   **Brand managers** focus on promoting a particular set of products within your company. They have detailed knowledge of their products and are well-skilled in marketing techniques, such as market segmentation, advertising, and message management. Brand managers are responsible for targeting the right people to buy your products and then reaching them with the message that causes them to take action.

In a small company, you might have only one brand (often the name of the company), and you might call this role the **marketing manager**. In contrast, a company the size of Honda has one brand manager for the Civic and another for the Accord. In fact, Honda might need one brand manager for each *model* of Civic and Accord.

Brand managers typically review and approve all marketing activities associated with their product set, and are accustomed to dealing with their traditional marketing channels (face-to-face sales, telemarketing, retail, and others, depending on your business). They are *not* typically well-schooled in web marketing, although that is beginning to change. Even those who do understand web marketing are unlikely to understand *search* marketing.

Your first task with a brand manager is usually one of education. You must convincingly show why search marketing is a good way to spend scarce marketing budgets. Because neither paid nor organic search marketing is ever completely free, it is critical that the brand manager be your biggest supporter. In addition, you will need his help whenever one of the other specialists does not fall into line. When the brand manager says that search marketing is a priority, everyone else will listen.

So, how do you get the brand manager behind the search marketing program? If your brand managers are web savvy, they are already using search personally, and you merely need to show them a few keywords for their products so they can see how little traffic they must be getting; they'll realize that if their content is not being shown on the search results page that searchers are not flocking to their site.

Regardless of how web savvy they are, show them the missed opportunity reports described in Chapter 4 (Exhibit 4-38). Brand managers tend to be swashbuckling risk takers, always on the lookout for the next opportunity to sell more, so they are usually easy to convince.

Sometimes, brand managers will object to search marketing because they do not have any budget to spend on it. In that case, show them that the cost of searchers converting to customers is lower than for other forms of marketing, such as direct mail. That usually persuades them to shift some of the budget from their other marketing activities to search. If there really is no money to spend, start with free organic search techniques and ask the brand manager to help you spread the word to the other teams that must be convinced to change how they do their jobs. Although brand managers will not get into the technical details, they will apply pressure in the right places if you convince them to.

After you have persuaded a brand manager to give search marketing a try, your first campaign is critical. It must show strong results to lead to a second campaign. Brand managers should be heavily involved in choosing the keywords to target for the campaign, but they might need your help. They often have blind spots when it comes to a customer's perception of your product. For example, brand managers tend to expect that customers will enter only brand names (*honda accord*) rather than generic ones (*family sedan*). You need to convince them to work on both kinds of keywords.

Brand managers also must review and approve all paid placement advertising. As they do, educate them so they are thinking about qualifying customers as well as selling to them. They typically do not think about the cost per click; they usually want to get everyone to click because that is their experience from offline and other online media. You need to show them how to optimize the tradeoff between clickthrough rate and sales. Teach them what every good sales rep knows—that it is just as important to dissuade the wrong searchers from clicking (and draining your budget) as it is to persuade the right ones to click. Top sales reps do not waste their time on prospects who will not buy; you should not waste your search marketing budget on them either.

And keep selling the brand managers on search marketing even after you have campaigns in high gear. Take care to regularly report success to the brand managers as search marketing takes off, so that they are not tempted to move to another new and exciting initiative a few months down the road. If they were easy for *you* to convince, the next person coming along with a bright idea might persuade them to dump your project in favor of a new high flyer.

Sales People   In larger companies, there might be specialists who use particular channels to pump up sales directly, or to assist in sales being made by others. Although none of these roles are as critical as the brand manager, there are ways you can get help from them:

- **Direct marketing:** Those responsible for the direct sales from your website can be critically important to search marketing. They are interested in anything that drives higher sales, and they are often the perfect folks to operate paid placement campaigns, with their knowledge of why people click and buy from an ad. They are experts at calls to action and rotating advertisements. In addition, direct marketing folks are frequently the best people to track search success (organic or paid) because they have affiliate programs or other web sales tracking mechanisms in place that can also track search-related sales.

- **Lead generation:** If your business is based on offline sales, your website's major goal might be passing leads. The folks responsible for lead generation from the website will be most interested in promoting search marketing when they see how it yields more leads. You can ask them to capture the search referrers in their lead-generation forms to track those leads back to search. They can also report which keywords seem to bring the highest number of visitors.

- **Partner relations:** If your company sells through distributors, resellers, or other partners, the partner relations team regularly interacts with these other companies. You can teach them how to request links to your website from each partner site. Partner links that go straight to the product pages on your site are the best (rather than a generic link to your home page).

No matter what kind of business you have, there are folks who sell things using the web. Sales people are usually excited about any new idea that can drive sales. Find them and get them to sell search marketing throughout the organization.

Public Relations   **Public relations** people are responsible for the press releases that are important for organic search marketing. When people get wind of the news, they tend to search for the rest of the story. If your press releases are optimized to be found by search engines, and they contain links to deeper information in your site, you can turn information searchers into conversions. If your press releases are truly newsworthy, your PR folks can directly feed your stories to press release wires or online press release sites, causing search engines to highlight your stories as news. (This works especially well with product launches and other announcements.)

But PR people can be helpful in much bigger ways than press releases. PR folks spend all of their time developing relationships with influencers—the media—which can be hugely important for designing messages that resonate in social media, a critical way that search engines know which content is best. We'll talk about that more in Chapter 9, "Prove Your Content's Quality."

This leads us to perhaps the biggest way that PR people can help your search marketing program: Communications professionals have made their careers out of persuading others to pass their messages along. They've always had to get past the gatekeepers—newspaper editors, TV news producers, and many more. Now, Google is just a new gatekeeper. When you explain it that way, they are likely to rise to the challenge.

Your PR people might be able to help your marketers to write copy that people would *choose* to read instead of ads that they shove in front of unwilling readers. Marketers are not accustomed to having any gatekeepers; they have always written ad copy that goes out exactly as they want it. PR folks can help marketers learn to couch their messages inside copy that is more reader-oriented. Search engines are much more likely to show reader-oriented content than typical marketing content.

The PR people are also responsible for your organization's image, so web "negative" or "hate" sites targeted at your organization (yourdomainsucks.com) are their problem. You can explain strategies to your PR department that minimize the impact of these hate sites when searchers are looking for your company:

- **Check search results regularly:** Your PR team should be on the lookout for the emergence of these sites by regularly executing searches using your leading brand names, your company name, and the names of high-profile executives. Hate sites depend on search results to get attention, so spotting them quickly helps you take action sooner.

- **Take legal action when warranted:** If the hate site is misusing your trademarks, or has lifted copyrighted material from your website without permission (such as product images), you can pursue legal remedies.

- **Crowd them out of the search rankings:** Search results never contain more than two listings from any one domain, but you might be able to get a little help from your friends. First, make sure your pages are optimized so that you get your legitimate two listings (#1 and #2 is what you are shooting for). Next, if your company has multiple domains (for subsidiaries, international affiliates, and so on), you can ethically optimize those sites for your company's target keywords. If you have social media venues (a YouTube channel, a Facebook fan page, and so on), optimize them, too. Your vendors, business partners, and other friendly companies might also have pages on their sites that legitimately speak of their relationship with your company—you can assist them to optimize those pages. Never do anything unethical to divert searchers to places that are not relevant, but you should cultivate the help of friendly sites. If your friends provide more relevant results than your enemies, the hate sites will be pushed down in the list so they do not draw as much attention.

PR teams are usually very open to search marketing opportunities when you explain to them what they need to do. They are just as interested in getting positive publicity as you are; so if you show them how search can provide that, they will be on board.

Lawyers   Lawyers are not marketers, but we talk about them among the business people because they often pass judgment on marketing material—the content on each page so critical for organic search as well as paid placement advertisements. In some corporations, the legal department checks every word before it goes live on the website, so that errors are avoided (those "expose us to a lawsuit" kinds of errors).

In some industries, including pharmaceuticals and financial services, protracted legal reviews can significantly affect a search marketing campaign's flexibility. Lawyers are sometimes derisively known as the "business prevention people" for their "go-slow" approach that mitigates all risk, but your organization has made a policy decision about what risks they want to run, and loss of speed is a tradeoff that they are making. Rather than whining about it, it is smarter to factor legal reviews into your time lines under these circumstances. Your competitors might be laboring under similar constraints, anyway.

It is important to educate your legal team on search marketing for several reasons. First, if they understand the importance of quickly changing copy on pages, they might try to accelerate their review cycles. Another reason to train the legal team is to give your paid search program some oversight, particularly as you make decisions about other companies' trademarks. Finally, your legal team is perfectly positioned to negotiate links to your products and services from outside suppliers as part of any deal, improving your search rankings for your site.

When you work with your legal team, you will find them picky about using the best word for search optimization. For example, searchers might be looking for "hair restorer" but your lawyer knows your company cannot legally make that claim about their product. How do you work something out? Sometimes you can try some clever copy, such as in Exhibit 5-12, which uses your search keywords but does not run afoul of legal restrictions.

LOOKING FOR A HAIR RESTORER?

In truth, there is no universal hair restorer. Baldness, a common male problem, can be caused by myriad different conditions, and no two men respond to treatment the same way.

But there is hope. Clinical studies show that FollicFill, a new scalp treatment specially designed for male pattern baldness, delivers remarkable results.

Exhibit 5-12   Evading the law(yer). Not every legal team will go for this, but if your lawyers understand the importance of search marketing, they might.

Most lawyers avoid risks as a matter of course, but when your legal team sees the value of search marketing, they might occasionally take a risk to support it.

Writers

Search marketing depends on having the right words; that is what writers do. We examine three different kinds of writers: copywriters (who develop "sales-y" descriptions of products), content writers (who create objective information about a subject), and translators (who convert content to other languages).

If you do not win over the writers, you will never excel at organic search marketing, because those keywords must be meaningfully placed across your pages. In addition, you need well-written paid placement ads for maximum clickthrough. No one but the writers can perform these tasks, so pay attention to how to persuade them.

Copywriters   Web **copywriters** create marketing copy for a company's products and services. As you might expect, they write action-oriented prose that is sometimes more flowery than you would see in an encyclopedia, for example. That is what they have been taught to do, but search marketing usually requires a different style than a sales brochure.

Searchers are looking for both your product's brand name and its generic name ("Snap-Shot" and "digital camera"), and organic search engines want to see those words prominently and frequently on your page. Copywriters are often unaware of what search engines need, so your first job is to teach them. Similarly, copywriters sometimes overlook the fact that customers search for generic names, not just brand names, and that they are unfamiliar with acronyms and other insider terms. You need to explain to them what search engines and customers need from their writing so that your business converts searchers to customers.

Sometimes copywriters object to changing their style of writing. They have succeeded in their careers writing as they do, and they might be reluctant to change. Some might complain that using the same words throughout their copy is repetitive and poor writing, but you need to overcome their objections. Without search-friendly copy, you will be hard-pressed to attain high rankings in organic search.

Copywriters know that their job is to generate sales, so you can usually persuade them to alter their styles when they see that their pages are not found by search engines—especially if your competitors' pages are. Show them the kinds of search keywords their customers enter and show them which pages show up. Let them see that their precious words are not being read.

Do not listen to their complaints about the "repetitive" style. Challenge them to integrate search requirements as just one more constraint they deal with. Tell them that you know that they are talented writers and that you are confident they can write search-friendly pages that are well written, too. Show them how they need only make a few tweaks to what they already do—that will be enough.

Content Writers   We distinguish **content writers** from copywriters, not because they have a different role to play in search marketing, but because they view themselves differently and you need to speak to them differently. Content writers create the prose for web pages just as copywriters do, but rather than selling products, their pages convey information.

Websites that present news, health, travel, and other information employ content writers. Content writers often have an academic or news reporting background and are skilled at taking a subject and making it simple and interesting. What they do not have is any understanding of what search engines need. *That* is where you come in.

Just as with copywriters, it is imperative that content writers produce pages that contain the keywords that searchers are looking for, along with related words within the same content theme. Like copywriters, they will object to you changing their style—often decrying censorship or lack of editorial integrity. Unlike copywriters, content writers are not trying to sell anything, so you need to talk to them differently.

Luckily, content writers are just as interested in having their words read as any other writer. When you show them that their prospective readers are not finding their treatise on the best restaurants in Des Moines—they are reading that information from a competitive site—*that* will get their attention. You can appeal to their pride as writers and tell them they can make it interesting while taking search marketing into account, just as you did with copywriters.

But you have one other advantage that makes all the difference in the world. Content writers are relentless researchers because they must constantly check their facts before they write. That means that they are searchers themselves. If anyone can put themselves in the shoes of searchers, it is content writers. When you show content writers how hard it is for searchers to find their pages, they will usually come around quickly.

CASE STUDY: PERSUADING WRITERS TO WRITE WITH SEARCH IN MIND

A large content website, with dozens of staff writers, realized that it was receiving far fewer visitors from search engines than it could be, so it embarked on a search marketing initiative. Almost before starting, the writing staff went into full revolt, irate at the idea of "compromising their editorial integrity." What to do?

The first rule in these sensitive situations is to move gingerly. Rather than coming in full of advice, we approached them cautiously, full of questions. In this case, the best way to start was asking the writers how they came up with their story ideas. This led to a freewheeling discussion detailing a number of sources for ideas, including news stories, their personal interests, and the popularity of similar stories. We looked at a current article as an example.

Together, we examined the writer's most important keywords for that article and used a keyword research tool to show other variants of those words that were missing—missing from the article but not missing from searchers' minds. The writers' eyes started to open to the idea that many potential readers were searching for their articles but never finding them.

Translators   You might not think of translators as writers, but they are. And how they translate your content to other languages can make or break your search performance. If you have thoroughly optimized your English content for organic search, but the translators do not use the right French keywords (with the proper prominence and density), your French keyword rankings will be literally lost in the translation.

You must show the translators how their work is critical to good search rankings. Just like other writers, they will object to you cramping their style; if you demonstrate how their current practices are preventing their readers from finding their pages, however, they will come around.

Technologists

Technologists might be the most unapproachable specialists, because their knowledge seems so deep in areas other people do not understand. Sometimes technologists are so specialized that they intimidate each other. But that cannot stop you. Unless you train the technologists in search marketing, your organic search efforts will fall short.

It probably sounds by now that no matter what specialist we discuss, we tell you how important it is to get them on your side. Unfortunately, one of the biggest challenges of search engine marketing is that *everything* is important. Unless you convince each member of your extended team to do the job right, search marketing will not work. Webmasters, web developers, information architects, and style guide developers are next up on your dance card.

That was just the start. Next, we began searching for the keywords missing from the story and looking at the search results. The writer of the article gasped, commenting that the search results showed other publications that contained five other variations of his article that he should write. The mood of the meeting completely changed, as writer after writer tried this technique to get ideas for future stories.

In a single meeting, the writers had become convinced that their readers were just like them. The same way that they searched to find story ideas, their readers were searching to find the information *they* desired. At that point, we showed them how they could meaningfully improve their writing with keywords and ensure they have given them the proper prominence.

Training in search-friendly writing was exactly what the writers needed all along, but only by approaching them with respect and interest in their job were the writers open to learning the lesson.

Webmasters   The most important technology role for organic search marketing belongs to the webmaster. On small sites, this role might belong to a single person, but it is not unusual to have dozens of webmasters on large corporate sites. Webmasters make sure your site does not go down and that it responds quickly when visitors arrive, but they do a lot more, too. They set the domain names and URL names. They decide which servers display each web page. They handle load balancing—and a lot more.

Some webmaster tasks are critical for organic search marketing, so we concentrate on those:

- **Site availability:** When spiders come visiting, your site must be up and respond quickly for your pages to be indexed. If spiders continually find slow or unavailable pages on your site, they will visit infrequently or not at all. Spiders can visit at any time of the day or night, so there is no safe time for your site to be down.

- **URL names:** Webmasters name the domains and subdomains (such as subdomain. domain.com) and they often decide how directories (folders) are named as well (domain. com/directory). Using keywords in your URLs helps your search rankings, so you need the webmaster to focus on that.

- **URL redirects:** One way that webmasters change the URLs on pages is to code something called a **redirect**, which tells a browser (or a spider) that the page has changed to a new URL. There are several kinds of redirects, all of which work for browsers, but only one type works for spiders. Obviously, you want your webmaster to use that one, which we explain in detail in Chapter 7. Webmasters are very practical and might be happy to use the wrong kind of redirect because "it works"; you need to show them that it does not work for search.

- **Directions for the spiders:** The webmasters control a special file, named **robots.txt**, which contains instructions to spiders on how to crawl your site. This file can tell spiders to go away completely, to crawl everything, or something in between. You must ensure that your webmasters allow the spiders to crawl all of the pages that need to be indexed in search engines. We cover robots files in Chapter 7.

With so many critical search marketing tasks, you can see how important it is for webmasters to understand the right way to perform each one. But, as you have probably guessed, some webmasters do not understand even the basics of search marketing. Some webmasters have been known to completely block spiders from their sites, mistakenly believing they are improving site performance by keeping those pesky spiders from wasting the time of our precious web servers!

Because webmasters are technically proficient (and you might not be), it can be intimidating to approach them, but you must do so. If you pay proper deference to their technical abilities, you will probably find that they truly have the best interests of your site in mind. They really do care that your visitors see your pages load quickly and get what they are looking for. When you explain how important search marketing is for your visitors, they will listen. Webmasters usually use search themselves, so showing them how hard it is to find your site will be convincing.

Occasionally, the webmaster team is concerned about how many more visitors will show up at the site if your search marketing is successful. You might need to help them justify more servers to handle the additional load that you expect as you succeed.

After you have them on your side, the webmasters can be your best ally in spreading the word to other technologists. The webmasters work with many people in the course of their job, and they often enforce standards and evangelize best practices to others.

Web Developers   Web programmers develop the HTML and JavaScript code that displays the pages in your visitor's web browser. They are typically at the receiving end of lots of changes from different sources—brand managers who changed the logo for a product, designers who decided that the navigation bar should be royal blue, copywriters who have updated the kind of information they want on the product details pages, and many more. When you approach your web developers with yet more changes, they will roll their overworked eyeballs, thinking, "Here we go again."

But don't be too concerned. If you have done your work convincing the brand managers and sales people of how important search marketing is, the web developers should be easy to persuade. They are knowledgeable about web pages and will immediately understand why you need the changes you do. They are usually avid searchers themselves and will probably find your project interesting.

You need to ensure that they are trained to code HTML and JavaScript the way you need them to, which we cover in Chapter 8. Also in Chapter 8, you will learn how to audit your pages to find specific search problems; the web developers will get the results of these audits to correct those problems.

Training and persuading this group will pay off, because if they design pages to be search friendly from the start, they do not have to correct problems later.

Information Architects   **Information architects** do not really consider themselves technologists, but the average person does. They decide the navigational structure of the site: how information is divided into separate pages, which pages link where, what nomenclature is used on a link to ensure people know what it is, and many other tasks.

Information architects think deeply about what your visitors need and what they will understand, always striving to satisfy their needs in the simplest way. Unfortunately, what is simple for visitors is not always simple for spiders. Many compelling user experiences are based on using JavaScript pull-down navigation. It looks pretty, it is easy to use, but spiders cannot follow it at all, so every page behind that JavaScript code is missed by the spider. Understand, most use of JavaScript is perfectly okay, but JavaScript navigation is a problem. In Chapter 7, we show you alternative ways to design flashy navigation that is spider friendly.

As with every other specialist, your first job is one of education. You need to explain how spiders are stymied by JavaScript navigation, and how that affects our site's visitors terribly. That will get an information architect's attention. You need to explain what the equally useful alternatives are and persuade the architects to choose something more search friendly.

Like the other specialists, information architects have their job to do. They see the world a certain way, and they do their job within that perspective. When you widen their perspective, most adjust and cooperate with you, because down deep they want the best for their site just like you do.

Style Guide Developers   **Style guide developers** create and maintain the rules governing the look and feel of the website, including page layouts, color schemes, information architecture, and many other areas. All websites of any size have a style guide. For small sites, this is a part-time job for one or two people, but larger sites have a full-time person or even a team that maintains the style guide. Each standard in the guide is enforced, often by reviewing projects while they are still under development; only after they pass the standards are they launched on your website.

Style guide developers require website design and information architecture skills, and often know HTML, too. These skills help style developers to understand and suggest changes to the standards, as well as to explain them to the people designing the pages on the site. As you might expect, however, style guide developers usually do not possess search marketing skills. Because the standards in the guide are used throughout the site, rules that inhibit search marketing can have broad implications.

Your job as a search marketer is to make sure the style guide is analyzed with organic search in mind, and to identify the rules that need to be changed. After those changes are made to the style guide, they will be enforced along with the rest of the guide, providing you with an important tool to make your entire site more search-friendly. Don't underestimate the power of the style guide to mold behavior across your organization. Make sure that your style guide motivates the behavior you want.

Unfortunately, it is not always easy to get developers to make the changes to the style guide that search marketing requires. People attracted to a job based in enforcing stringent rules are not always the most flexible people on Earth. And your story about why the standards should be changed to accommodate search might not sound any different to them than all other changes that have been requested. There are ways to reach these folks, however.

The most important mission for style guide developers is to maintain the brand image and the overall consistency of the site. So, your challenge is to explain to them how your site's poor search results negatively affect the brand image. Show them how your competitors' brands are being shown in response to important informational search keywords, whereas your site is notably absent. When explained as a poor branding experience, style guide developers tend to be persuaded. If you cannot persuade them to do anything, enlist the brand managers, webmasters, and other specialists to lobby for your changes, because the style guide developers are accustomed to listening to them. If you do not convince them to make *all* of the needed changes, take what you can get and come back for more another time.

Site Operations

If you thought that after you get your search marketing program going that you are home free, think again. Search marketing is not a one-time thing, and you will fail unless you engage the operational management of your site to put ongoing focus on search. (We know that you are getting sick of hearing about how many different groups you need to work with, but rest assured that we will show you how.)

For search marketing, the two most critical groups within site operations are web analytics and website governance. The analytics team helps track and publicize your success, and the governance folks enforce the standards so painstakingly written into your company's style guide.

Metrics Analysts   **Metrics analysts** are the keepers of the statistics: how many visitors come to the site, customer satisfaction survey results, the number of sales, and many more. You learned in Chapter 4 that we want to track new metrics on the success of search marketing—both organic and paid.

In some web organizations, there is no central metrics role. The webmaster might report traffic metrics. The marketing team might report survey results. The finance department might report sales. Regardless, you need to spread the search marketing word to your organization's metrics analysts, because you need them to help you report search marketing metrics.

Metrics analysts are already experts at collecting some of the critical search marketing metrics, but no one might have ever asked before. They know how to tease search referral statistics out of your company's web analytics tool. They know how to correlate sales with those referrals. They have the quantitative analysis skills to track trends and to tell you when changes are statistically significant.

It's a real coup if you can convince metrics analysts to devote some of their time to search metrics, and even better if you can incorporate a few search metrics into their regular reporting. These weekly or monthly reports tend to be reviewed by many different people working in your web organization, including your executives. That will help you draw attention to the importance of search and to your growing success. Perhaps you could get them to include the compliance reports described in Chapter 10 that show how well each part of your website is adhering to best practices in search marketing.

At times, metrics analysts will object to taking on the extra work associated with search metrics, but if you can show them how important search marketing is to your overall site objectives, they will usually come around. Metrics analysts want to demonstrate their value to your organization. Any time they can trot out a new statistic and open some eyes, it makes them look good. If you can show metrics analysts that the brand managers are looking for these numbers, they will quickly figure out how to absorb the extra workload to report search metrics.

Website Governance Specialists   A **website governance specialist** is a clunky name for someone who enforces your site's standards. What process on your site puts teeth in your style guide? It is not enough for your style guide to be rewritten with organic search in mind—you need to police everyone to comply with those rules. Perhaps there is a single group devoted to compliance with your standards; regardless of how your site does it, however, you need to get your organization to enforce search standards.

As usual with all of these specialists, it is unlikely that governance specialists have more than a middling familiarity with search. They do not typically have every standard committed to memory, so how do they enforce compliance? Typically, they enforce the standards that they know. So your job is to help them understand why search is important and which specific standards are critical for success. If you get these specialists familiar with search marketing, they can help enforce the standards critical to your success.

Sometimes your discussion will not be welcomed, because governance specialists have too much to do as it is. This position is usually underfunded because it is hard to show the business value of the standards police, so when you come around adding more rules to enforce, it can be hard to hear. Your best approach is to make the compliance work as simple as possible—automating everything you can. Chapter 10 shows how your checklists can simplify the governance specialist's job, even explaining how software tools can automatically check compliance with some standards.

Much like the webmasters, your governance team is ideally positioned to spread the word across the organization. They work with every group that puts up a web page, and they typically have the power to order compliance to the rules. The governance team can block a project manager trying to launch a change to the website—that is the ultimate "teachable moment." That project manager will make sure the next project is designed to be search-friendly from the start.

The governance specialists are the people who make the difference between paying lip service to search standards and really "walking the talk." If you persuade the governance folks of search marketing's importance, they will help transform your site one project at a time.

Sell Your Proposal to Executives

To sell your executives on your search marketing proposal, you must think like an executive. To understand what executives are looking for, we explore the questions on their mind, and then show you how to close the deal at the end of your presentation.

In a sense, there is nothing different about search marketing from any other proposal you would sell to an executive. With any proposal, your executive wants to understand what it's about and why we should do it. We have found that almost all executives are interested in the same information to make their decisions. Not every executive asks all of ten of these questions, but you should be prepared to answer them, or, better yet, answer them in your presentation without waiting for them to be asked.

What Is Search Marketing and Why Do I Care?

Typically, your executive will not understand the basics of search marketing. Although you should gloss over the details, a couple of charts that explain Google should convince any executive to hear you out the rest of the way.

Demonstrate that search is a growing area of marketing and that it complements current marketing activities. If you have done surveys of your customers, or you have industry surveys showing that your own customers are using search, that's even better.

How Does This Help Me Achieve My Corporate Goals?

Remember spending all that time in Chapter 4 figuring out what your website's goals are? This is why.

The more closely the benefits of a search marketing program align to the executive's existing goals, the higher the probability that you will get your program approved. With every executive, showing that your organization's goals are being met by your proposal makes the sale easier. However, different executives have somewhat different goals and concerns. Make sure you know who is on the receiving end of your pitch:

- **Chief executive officer or any sales executive:** This can sometimes be your easiest sell. They typically will be convinced by your business case and do not care about the details of the work to be done. A credible business justification coupled with a realistic plan will persuade them to take a chance on your proposal.

- **Technology executive:** This might be your toughest sell. You must show that same compelling business case, but you must also convince this executive that the IT team will not be saddled with an impossible job. It is critical that you demonstrate a grasp of the details, especially its feasibility within your proposed budget. Walk through the plan step by step, explaining exactly what needs to be done. Show how you can make the IT exec a hero by taking on this low-risk project that will raise revenue.

- **Marketing executive:** How warm a reception you get from this executive might vary depending on whether the marketing group is responsible for the content on the site or not. In many organizations, the marketing group manages the copywriters, and this exec will be concerned about what is expected from his team. As with the technology executive, your confidence about what the copywriters need to do will carry the day. When an executive knows his team can do what is required, there is no danger to his reputation, so the benefits of the project carry the day. Marketing executives with no content responsibilities should be very excited about search marketing, but some might be concerned that other favorite marketing programs will be cut to fund search marketing.

- **Chief financial officer:** Numbers, numbers, and more numbers. Show your business case and show how search marketing is cost-effective compared to other marketing programs. CFOs are sometimes risk averse, so showing that other companies are succeeding at search marketing can be very important.

You probably get the idea. Think carefully about the executives you need approval from, and make sure you appeal to their needs and concerns.

Where Do We Stand Today?

Most executives are born problem solvers. As these fix-it types size up your proposal, they will ask themselves, "Exactly how bad is this, compared to all the other pressing problems I know about?" The best way to answer that question is to show them. Show your executives that when your customers search for your products, they don't find your company. Show them over and over. Keyword after keyword. That usually gets their attention.

For some executives, just performing the searches in front of them is compelling, but others want to see more data. You can dig out the ranking check that you did back in Chapter 4 (in Exhibit 4-33). Seeing how poorly your site ranks for a slew of keywords across all the search engines will win over even the most skeptical data wonk.

If your executives use the web, remind them of the way *they* search. Are they checking out result #45? No? Neither are your customers.

What Are Our Competitors Doing?

Executives are, by nature, notoriously competitive. They are supremely motivated to beat the competition, and they do not like to lose. Go back to Chapter 4 and break out your site's competitor-ranking matrix (Exhibit 4-35). If you can show executives they are losing and convince them they can win, you will get strong consideration for your proposal.

You can use your competitors in other ways, if you know how to pitch to your executives. Risk-averse executives will be comforted if one or two of your competitors are actively pursuing search marketing. Alternatively, if none of your competitors are engaged in search marketing yet, you can play that up with a visionary executive as the new way to get an edge.

What Are You Proposing to Do?

This question requires a crisp answer—you need a high-level version of your plan, such as the one shown in Exhibit 5-11. Executives get proposals every day. They have a sniff test for which ones are practical enough to implement and which ones are pipe dreams. It is not enough for you to show a business case.

Executives check a proposal's practicality in several ways:

- **Consensus:** If you have agreement from key members (preferably leaders) of your extended search team that they will do the work, it can go a long way.
- **Speed:** The faster you can deliver, the less time the executive needs to wonder whether it will work.
- **Specificity:** The more detailed your plan is—granular tasks, with people assigned to each one, on a defined schedule—the more credence an executive will place in that plan.

- **Measurability:** Executives tend to trust plans with objective measurements that can be checked after the fact. Snap Electronics presented a detailed grid of all projections so that results could be measured each month. Chapter 10 shows the kinds of operational metrics that can be tracked to show the business impact of search marketing.

If you are presenting to an executive who wants to see the details, make sure you explain the cause and effect of each action with its beneficial result. If you are recommending to the IT executive that all dynamic URLs be rewritten into a spider-friendly format, be ready with the explanation of why that is important. Do not assume that you can show a laundry list of actions without justifying each one. Eliminate any actions that are not absolutely necessary, at least from your first plan. Propose the Volkswagen, not the Mercedes.

What Business Value Do You Expect to Achieve?

This is a broader question than it might seem. Yes, you should present the missed-opportunity matrix you developed in Chapter 4 (Exhibit 4-38). And we do want you to show your business opportunity—the case for your entire scope and the one for your first campaign. But you need to think more broadly than that. Remember the other work that you did in Chapter 4. Explain how the search marketing program directly leads to higher sales or more leads or whatever conversion your executive is interested in. Don't just show the numbers; demonstrate your logic, too.

Keep in mind that anyone can show big numbers, but the executives are judging whether your plan will *deliver* on those numbers. If you have a track record of solid proposals, or you can demonstrate that others have followed this plan to success, or your executives have all read this book (okay, that is unlikely), they will believe that executing your plan will actually produce the promised results.

How Much Does It Cost?

You will, of course, be ready for this question. You have the costs estimated and totaled for a full search marketing program across your entire scope, but you also have today's request: funding for the first campaign.

You need to be prepared for a lot more questions on cost than just the raw numbers. Executives know that estimates are just that—estimates. They want to know why you believe these estimates are correct. They want to assess the risk that the actual costs could be higher.

There are several ways to buttress your estimates. If you are using an external search vendor, you can present the cost estimates from each vendor to show what the range can be. Another approach is to show the details behind the estimates, if your executive can judge that level of detail. You can also appeal to the expertise of your extended search team, who can validate your cost projections for the tasks they must perform.

How Long Will It Take?

This is a difficult question to answer. Make sure that you understand this question. Because you are down in the details, you might think the question refers to when the actions in your plan will be executed. It does not. Your executives want to know when they will see the results.

You need to be careful when you provide your answer, because some factors are hard to predict:

- **Will resources be available?** You cannot assume a "green lights all the way" schedule. Make sure that your extended search team is committed on the schedule that you are planning. Ensure you have contingency built in for unforeseen problems.

- **How frequently do spiders visit your site?** Some sites have spiders visiting every day, but does yours? If you have a small site, or you have lots of spider problems, they might not visit more than once a week, so plan accordingly. If it takes you three tries to get the perfect title on your page, will that take 3 weeks or 3 days? You must take the frequency of spider visits into account in your planning or you will have the wrong time line. We explain how to determine the spiders' frequency in Chapter 7.

- **How much iteration will it take?** Whether you are managing an organic or a paid campaign, you usually do not get everything perfect the first time around. For example, paid placement ads didn't have the best calls to action. The technology project delivered the wrong fix for a spider problem. The brand manager released a set of new models that changed which keywords are the best choices. These examples demonstrate that search marketing depends on taking a shot, checking how close you are to the target, and taking another shot. Do not make promises based on hitting the bull's-eye the first time.

Everyone wants to promise quick results, but it is more important that you show credible results. Coming back to an executive to ask for more time will not position you well for your second search campaign.

When executives ask you how long it will take, they might actually be asking a different question: "When will I see payback?" This question tells the executive how fast the costs of the program are recouped, and is usually expressed in units of time. Fortunately, most search marketing campaigns pay back in a matter of months. In Chapter 4, we analyzed the monthly revenue expected. You can plot your revenue and expenses month by month to be ready for this question.

Why Should I Fund This Project over Current Projects?

Be prepared for this question. There is no "new money" for a search marketing program. Whatever money you want is money that cannot be spent on something else. You must demonstrate that your search marketing program will generate better results than whatever it replaces, which is not that easy. Your business case must carry the day here. If it honestly isn't a better way to use that budget, expect to get a "no."

What Are the Risks?

All projects have risks and a search marketing campaign is no exception. You can line up all the usual suspects—cost overruns, schedule delays, and overbooked resources—but search marketing has its own special risks.

The biggest risk concerns organic search. No matter what anyone tells you, high organic search rankings cannot be guaranteed, no matter what you do. Consider that there is only a single #1 spot for each keyword. If ten companies perform that perfect search marketing campaign, only one of them can be #1. If your keywords are highly competitive, it might be very difficult for you to get the rankings (and therefore the traffic) that you want.

Similarly, ultra-competitive bidding in paid placement is also a risk. When you investigate your chosen paid keywords, you might assume that paying a few cents more than the current bid maximum will land you #1, but others might raise their bids in response. You could find yourself in a bidding war that is unaffordable for you. You might have the unpalatable choice of losing traffic or blowing your budget. Despite these possible risks, search marketing is rarely a high-risk proposition.

Okay. So if you *are* armed to answer all of your executive's questions, you need to be prepared to do something else as well: Get your proposal accepted. You must enter every executive meeting knowing exactly what requests you want to make of that executive that day. Do not explain your whole proposal "as an FYI." Know what you want and ask for it.

Here are the typical things you should request:

- **Approve this project:** We figured you remembered this one. But be specific. Make sure you have the money and you are authorized to spend it. Sometimes (in large companies especially), "approvals" take weeks before you can actually spend any money.

- **Order the extended search team to cooperate:** You want your "letter from the king" to use with any recalcitrant extended search team members. Although most people will listen to your search evangelism and go along with the plan, a few can be painful to persuade—maybe impossible. At that point, you want your executive to stand behind your plan and use his power to get the objectors into line.

- **Review the metrics with us every month:** At first, there will not be much to see, but as your program reaches its full scope, and you introduce the operational metrics explained in Chapter 10, you will have a wealth of data to analyze. You will want executives to review the metrics so that they can take action to correct problems. You will find that situations will arise, such as ill-considered technology changes or poor content coding, where executives can focus resources and attention to get them corrected.

Your thorough proposal will convince almost any executive. Make sure that you are prepared for success—that you know precisely what you need from that executive to maximize your success.

Set Up Your Search Marketing Program

Once you complete this chapter, you'll be ready to get moving, but there is one step left before you can get into gear: You need to set up your search marketing program. If all you want to pursue is organic search, you're already done; no setup is needed. But if you want to embark on paid search or local search, you've got some work to do. That's what we lay out in the final section of this chapter.

Organize Paid Search

You already know that paid search differs from organic search in that you must make explicit choices about how many different search engines you want to work with. Deciding which search engines you want to buy search ads with is your first step, followed by setting up your accounts, and finally, choosing your bid management software.

Decide Your Paid Search Engines

As you have contemplated your search marketing program, you have probably made some decisions on which paid search programs make the most sense for your business. If you sell the kinds of products offered in product search engines, you might want to sign up and give it a try. If you know from your organic search experience what keywords your visitors are likely to search for, you have all the information you need to test paid search ads for your business.

It might be tempting to sign up with every vendor out there. Don't. The work that goes into managing a paid search campaign is larger than you think. To be successful, you must focus on your content, your per-click charges, your clickthrough rates, your conversions, and your profitability. You need to do that for every campaign with every vendor, because each one is different. Don't become overwhelmed with work before you even know how it's done. Start small.

If you decide to start with just one vendor, you will probably want to use a paid search ad vendor rather than a product search engine because setup is usually simpler. Google and Bing are the two biggest paid search engines, so pick one of them. Choosing a single vendor also simplifies your decision on bid management and reporting tools; you can avoid investigating and paying for a third-party tool until your program gets bigger later. (We walk you through all of your bid management choices shortly.)

If you decide to experiment with product search, Google Product Listing Ads (PLAs), activated through Google Shopping campaigns, might be an option, but there are other choices, too. Check out our website for an up-to-date list of the leaders (SEMincBook.com/shopping-search-engines).

Snap Electronics wanted to test both paid search ads and product search for its digital camera product line, but because it wanted to simplify the management and setup, it went with the market leader for both—Google.

Set Up Your Accounts

Setting up your account can often be one of the simpler steps, but it is very important. As with the other steps, you can always go back and change your setup later, but getting it right up front can save you some time; changing the structure of a large account is a labor-intensive process.

If you are working with an external search marketing consultant or agency, you can ask the vendor to perform all sorts of search marketing tasks. If you did so, as Snap Electronics did, you can leave the setup work to them. They help you develop and manage the program from start to finish. Their experienced staff has the tracking tools and the relationships with the paid placement vendors to drive the maximum return from your paid search investment.

But many companies, especially smaller ones, handle the setup themselves. Most paid search engines require a small setup fee to create your account, but you can decide to spend only small amounts or even zero in any particular month, so don't feel pressured that you are making a large commitment.

For any paid search account, you provide a credit card number and decide how much money to place into your account, and you are on your way. When a searcher clicks your ad for a keyword, the amount you bid for that click is deducted from your account. You can have the account automatically replenish from your credit card, you can have a set amount taken from your credit card each month, or you can be notified when your account dips below a certain point (so that you can manually add more funds).

As you set up your account, you are asked to specify the geographic locations for where your ads should run. The default country is usually the United States, but you can specify any other country where ads are shown. Think carefully before you decide what to do—if you do not do business in all of these countries, you do not want your ads running there. Similarly, if you do not intend to translate your ads and landing pages to local languages (to tie into your country website), you will not drive many conversions.

You can further select location down to city and zip code if you want to refine your targeting using the geographic targeting capabilities discussed earlier in the chapter. We discuss this technique more in Chapter 6, "Choose Your Target Market Segments."

Setting up product search accounts is similar in nature—the hard part comes when you need to load up your actual catalog of products, which we cover in Chapter 7.

Select Your Bid Management Tool

Now that you have set up your paid search accounts, it is time to choose the software you will use to manage your campaigns, which is called a **bid management tool**. Bid management tools automatically adjust your paid search bids and aggregate click and conversion data. A good bid management tool can spell the difference between a successful campaign and a failure.

A few bid management tools are distributed as software you install on your own computer, but most are offered as services from websites. Which specific tool you choose depends on which paid search engines you have selected.

If you are using only product search engines, you do no bidding and need no tool to manage bidding. If you are using just one paid search engine (just Google, or just Bing, for example), you can use the tool they each provide for free with your paid search fees. (If you use the paid search vendor's free tool, it will monitor only the bids placed with that vendor.) Also, if your budget is less than $10,000 per month, it might not make sense to pay the fees for a high-end bid management tool.

But if you use more than one paid search engine or you have a large paid search budget, you will probably want to use a third-party bid management tool that can monitor bids across search engines and provide enhanced tracking and adjustment of bids. If you choose a third-party vendor, you must be sure to pick one that is authorized by the paid placement vendors you are working with. Double-check before you buy.

TIMING IS EVERYTHING: ARE YOUR CONVERSIONS ON A SCHEDULE?

In your relentless drive to become more efficient in the paid placement marketplace, your business might benefit from analyzing the timing of your conversions. Some businesses have obvious timing characteristics—the toy industry sells a huge portion of its inventory before Christmas, for example. But such seasonal shifts do not always matter in search marketing unless conversion rates change, too.

Here's why. If all that happens during the Christmas shopping season is that more searchers are looking for toys, but they click through and buy at the same rate, your per-click bids should be the same all year round. If conversion rates are higher at Christmas, however, those clicks are worth more than the rest of the year. If you have analyzed your business and found that Christmas shoppers convert at a higher rate, you can raise your bids (and lower them the rest of the year) to increase your sales with the same search marketing budget. If your competitors bid the same year-round, they might be bidding a bit too low at Christmas and a bit too high at other times.

Your analysis might uncover patterns much more granular than seasonal swings. Suppose that Snap Electronics found that their digital camera conversion rate is much higher on weekends than on weekdays. Perhaps their customers are more likely to spend the time to research the model they want and make a purchase decision in the comfort of their home when they have some free time, rather than while they are busy at work. If true, the clicks Snap gets on the weekends are more valuable than those on weekdays, and thus worth higher bids. Snap could drive more revenue by raising their bids on weekends to reflect the true value of those clicks, and lowering them on weekdays. That way, they will land higher in the rankings at the times their customers are most likely to convert.

If you are working with a search marketing vendor, they might handle the tracking and reporting for you, so you might not need to choose a tool yourself. Some search marketers prefer to be more hands-on, however, even when delegating the paid search campaigns to a vendor. If you want to use the tool to see how your campaigns are doing, you might want to provide guidance to your search marketing vendor about the features you want.

Even if you did not decide to work with an external search marketing vendor for your overall program, you might find that you would like to work with one to handle your paid search program to reduce the work for you. Our companion site has a list of Paid Search Agencies (SEMincBook.com/paid-search-agencies) that are especially noteworthy, although there are many other good choices.

For those on smaller budgets, or those who would prefer to manage their campaigns themselves, bid management tools that do not require a full-service relationship with a search marketing vendor are available. However, bid management tools are no one-size-fits-all proposition.

But why stop there? **Dayparting** is a technique that enables you to set your bids based on time of day. What if Snap analyzed its conversions and found that, during weekdays, conversions dipped under 1% during working hours (except for a three-hour window for U.S. lunchtimes) and peaked at 3.5% just after 8 p.m. U.S. eastern time? Wouldn't it make sense to tune the bids by time of day to reflect the value of the clicks? Bid management tools that support dayparting do just that, automatically adjusting your bids through the day based on rules you provide. You might even find times you should "go dark" by shutting off your bids completely.

You should notice that even during periods of low conversion, if your conversion rate is high, it might still be very profitable. Snap might find that early morning hours, although delivering low sales compared to other times of day, have a high conversion rate. Although conversions are not very high, clicks are also low, so the low fees with high conversions make it a very profitable time period.

It is typical for conversion rates to fluctuate for every business, but you want to know, "Is there a pattern?" Without a repeating pattern, timing techniques do not work. After all, you need to know what will happen, not what has happened.

All this analysis can be a lot of work, but it pays off. Many times, the pattern crosses your whole product line; as the market gets more efficient, however, you might need to analyze product by product or even keyword by keyword to keep finding the edge you need. If you keep looking, however, you will find it.

What you need depends on your circumstances. Here is a checklist of questions you should answer before researching the right bid management tool for your program:

- **How much time are we willing to invest in this project?** Full-service vendors do all the work for you, high-end tools automate most of the work, and inexpensive tools leave a lot of manual work for you.

- **How many keywords will I need to manage?** Most bid management tools are priced based on the number of keywords that must be monitored. The more keywords, the higher the price.

- **How high is my paid search budget?** As you might expect, the lower-end tools often lack the functions needed for large paid search budgets—$100,000 a month or more. Better tools can handle high volumes of click and conversion data while providing strong analysis functions. Don't skimp on your tool when it can mean so much more in revenue and savings.

- **How detailed must my reporting be?** If you want to calculate your statistics by keyword, by engine, by time of day, and by other very detailed breakdowns, choose a tool with the strongest reporting capabilities. If you are serious about search marketing, and have a large budget, you will need the detailed reporting to give yourself the information that keeps your efficiency high. We discuss reporting on paid search in Chapter 10.

Our website has a list of popular bid management tools to help you decide on the right one for you (SEMincBook.com/bid-management-tools).

Bid management tools can sometimes help you automate the complexity of searches from different devices. You might find that searches from mobile devices convert far less frequently than searches from computers, but those searches might be "top of funnel" searches that are important for later sales that happen from computers. Analyze the data but be sure that you aren't focused only on conversions to the detriment of your overall campaign.

Any bid management tool can raise your efficiency while reducing your workload, but they cannot eliminate human monitoring. For example, they might lower your bid to the minimum amount if it gets few conversions, but they will not drop the keyword completely, which might be the best thing to do with a real loser. Regardless, the higher your paid placement budget, and the more competitive your keywords, the more you will need a strong bid management tool.

Well, there you have it. You have learned all the tasks necessary to set up your paid search program. Next, we'll look at how you do the same thing for organic search. Don't worry. It's simpler.

Organize Organic Search

Many people don't even think about setting up an organic search program as a real step in the process. We're guilty too, having not even included such a step in the first two editions of this book. After all, you can just start optimizing for organic search, so why not just "do it"? We now believe that is a mistake, especially for a larger program.

We've seen how skipping a setup step for organic step leads to problems. While it might be perfectly fine to have separate teams work on paid and organic search, they should share a strategy and should regularly check in together. We think that it makes sense to share landing pages and to do keyword planning together. We've seen large companies that don't even have a central list of organic keywords. By treating your organic search program as something you must explicitly create, you're more likely to take these additional steps.

We don't want to overly complicate organic search, however. To really be ready for organic search, you need to take one critical step. You must set up your Webmaster Tools accounts in Google (google.com/webmasters), Bing (bing.com/toolbox/webmaster), and any other search engine you use that offers such a capability.

The setup process for both Bing and Google are quite similar—and rather simple—but you need to think through some questions in advance in order to get through the process as smoothly as possible.

The first question is actually deceptively simple—which email address will you associate with your Webmaster Tools account? You might not give this much thought—just use the webmaster's email address, right? Well, no. What happens if the webmaster leaves your company for another job? It's far better to create an account under a name such as Search-Snap@gmail. com or search@snapelectronics.com. Another mistake to avoid is letting your agency create your account; that makes it much harder when you inevitably switch agencies.

Next, you need to be sure of who should have access to your Webmaster Tools accounts. Don't worry if you aren't sure how many people can be entrusted; you can change access at any time. But make sure that you have at least two people with access at all times.

The biggest question revolves around validating your account. Both Bing and Google require that you prove that you are actually the owner of the website represented by the account. This validation step actually is for your own protection. Without it, your competitor could set up an account for your website and be given access to all sorts of data you'd rather they not have. If you have a large site, not only do you need to validate your primary domain (yourcompany.com) but you will also need to validate each subdomain (subdomain.yourcompany.com).

For this final setup question, you'll want to consult with your IT team. Any of these methods will work to validate your site, but your team might find some of them easier to pull off than others:

- **Metatag verification:** When you choose this approach, the search engine generates an arcane string that you must place in the HTML header of the home page of your site. This is an easy method for sites that use flat HTML pages, but most content management systems can use this approach also. Exhibit 5-13 shows examples of metatags generated by both Google and Bing.

- **File verification:** With this option, the search engine provides a file for you to place in the root directory of your web server. For some sites, this can be easier than updating your home page's markup, but you must ensure that this file is never deleted from your server during a routine cleanup.

- **DNS verification:** This might be the most difficult way to validate your account, but it can validate all of your subdomains in one shot. The catch is that a TXT line must be added to your DNS record, which sometimes conflicts with security techniques.

- **Google Analytics sync:** This last approach works only for Google Webmaster Tools— and only if your company uses Google Analytics, but it is easy to do. This option validates immediately, while the first three require you to click a Validate button in your Webmaster Tools account to complete the process.

```
<meta name="google-site-verification"
      content="8Q8ltnw3FhWY82tZqgFaOpdJGg8p-0" />
<meta name="msvalidate.01"
      content="F4986012ABC20E0430AC2543BF172D3F" />
```

Exhibit 5-13   Metatag validation for Webmaster Tools. Both Google and Bing allow you to add one line to your home page HTML to claim your account.

Once you validate your account, you'll get access to a treasure trove of data that we'll refer to throughout the rest of this book.

Organize Local Search

Local search is one of the biggest changes in search marketing in the last few years. Local search has always been important for businesses that attract foot traffic to their locations, but the increasing number of searches from mobile devices have made local results more important than ever.

Local search spans both organic and paid search; both kinds of results are possible within local search. You've already completed one step in your *paid* local search setup earlier in this chapter when you chose a default country for your paid search program. In Chapter 6, we'll complete the paid local search setup when we set geographic targeting for each paid search ad, keyword by keyword.

This remainder of this section focuses on the setup steps for *organic* local search. You can think about both Bing and Google as having a local directory of businesses, just like the Yellow Pages—your setup involves updating that directory by **claiming your listing** and maintaining its accuracy. That's what we'll explain here.

But many small businesses have not taken the steps to claim their own directory listings. Even stranger, many *large* companies don't realize how important local search is—they have neglected their setup also.

Make sure that your locations are claimed—and that your sales and channel partners have claimed their locations also. Any business location that you want your customers to visit should be claimed. But you might not be convinced that you should bother with the work of claiming your listing. You might have already searched for your business and you found it—the name, address, and phone number are all listed correctly. So, no work needed, right? Wrong.

All of these location directories use publicly available information from the Yellow Pages (for example) as a head start in creating their directory listings, so your location might already be listed. But if you don't *claim* your listing, someone else might be able to. It's not easy for someone to claim the listing improperly, but it has happened. That unscrupulous claimant can modify your listing with incorrect information or even delete it completely.

What's more, the kind of basic information shown before claiming your listing is missing important information that you want added—critical information such as hours of operation. By claiming your listing, you can add all those juicy details that help more searchers find you and that persuade more of them to come knocking on your door.

The first step in claiming your entry is to collect all of the information needed to validate your location information. If you run the local barber shop, this won't be very taxing, but if you are a large bank with thousands of branches, it might take a bit more work. Here is the kind of information that you need for *each* location:

- **Business name:** Use exactly the same name as what appears on your sign, in the phone book—anywhere you promote yourself.
- **Address:** This is the address of your physical location—not a PO Box or mailbox store.
- **Phone number:** Where should customers call? Will there be an answering machine or an operator who takes a message 24 hours a day? You might also want mobile phone numbers and fax numbers listed, depending on your business.
- **Email address:** Make sure that this is an address that is monitored and that it doesn't disappear if someone leaves the company.
- **Website:** Use the URL that corresponds to the home page for this location.
- **Hours of operation:** You'd be surprised how many national chains have little information about when their local operators open and close, but you can imagine that this is one of the most sought-after pieces of information by local searchers.

Some specific kinds of businesses might want to be prepared with more information that describes parking or which credit cards are accepted or many others. (When you sign up with Google and Bing, you'll see what information they allow.) We're providing information for these two location powerhouses, but you might also want to register for other location directories. We maintain an up-to-date list on our website (SEMincBook.com/local-search-venues). But even if you want to ignore that long list of location directories, you need to sign up for Bing and Google.

You start by creating local merchant accounts with Google and Bing—both call their sites "Places for Business." So you can sign up at Google Places for Business (google.com/business/placesforbusiness) and then head over to do the same thing at Bing Places for Business (bingplaces.com).

Small businesses simply fill out the forms to enter their information but large companies can also bulk upload a file that contains the information for hundreds or thousands of locations at once. For example, Crispin Sheridan, the Senior Director of Global Search at SAP, submitted nearly 1,000 sales office addresses to Google to ensure that if someone searched for SAP in any city where they had an office, that local contact information would be reflected in Google. If you take this approach, however, make sure that you aren't submitting location information for warehouses and other locations that you would never want a customer to visit.

Beyond this basic information, two fields constitute the most important part of your location information:

- **Category:** You can think of this as your type of business or industry, but it gets very specific. And you want to be as specific as possible. Just as you want those "just right" keywords that perfectly describe what you sell, you want that ideal category that will attract searchers who will actually frequent your establishment. Never accept a default category offered unless it is an exact match to what you do. Don't accept the category Asian Restaurant if you are really a Sushi Restaurant—be *that* specific. Even though you might serve some Asian food beyond sushi, you will make people looking for sushi happier than people looking for Asian food, so go with the category that truly fits.

- **Description:** Your description is the place to show off what your business is about. For now, you can just fill this field with any existing description you might have, but we'll return to this field in Chapter 8 to optimize the description with the keywords and calls to action that give us better findability—and raise our conversion rates.

After you create your merchant accounts for both Google and Bing, you will be mailed a post card to your physical locations containing a code for you to provide to verify that you indeed control that business at that physical address. Once the code is entered, you are validated.

It sounds easy to respond to that post card, but will the person who handles the mail know what it is? Or how important it is? Will every operator of your three dozen locations know what to do? It's critically important that every person at each location who handles the mail be waiting for that postcard so that you can handle it properly. If you fail to complete this last validation step, you'll need to get the search engine to send out a new postcard and do it again. This might not be a pain if you have only one location, but it can be a real time waster if you've got 100 locations.

That completes the setup step for local search, but there will be much more we do later in the book for local search. In Chapter 6, you'll learn how geographic targeting can show your ads and product listings to people in exactly the right locations. And in Chapter 8, you'll learn how to use special encoding on your web pages so that the search engines provide detailed location information when they display pages from your website.

Summary

We have covered a lot of ground in this chapter. You chose the scope of your search marketing program, decided what strategy to adopt, and estimated the costs involved. All of these points were critical to the next step: convincing the rest of your organization to approve your program.

And nothing is easy about creating a search marketing program in any organization. Your organization has dozens, maybe even thousands, of folks who all need to do things the right way, but they are ignorant (and possibly apathetic) about what to do, and they are so busy that even asking them to listen to you might take some persuasion.

But, in this chapter, you learned how it is done. You assembled your proposal, because that is the basic selling point for any audience. You are familiar with the critical daily tasks. You now know how to decide which tasks should be performed by a central team, and which must be done by the rest of your web team, your extended search team. You have met each kind of specialist on that extended team, and you are armed with approaches to persuade them to do their part in improving search marketing for your site. We also helped you to persuade the toughest audience of all—your executives. You know what questions they will ask, and you know what requests you have for them.

Then we went ahead and actually set up your program. You learned how to set up your paid search accounts and select your bid management tool, and why both of those tasks are so important. We also tackled local search, which for some of you is the most important search marketing work that you will ever do.

By now, if you've been following along and working on your own program, you should have an approved proposal for a search marketing program—and have your initial setup complete.

We are just getting started, however. In Part III, we go beyond the planning to the execution: What specific tasks must you undertake to make your search marketing plan a success?

PART III

Execute Your Search Marketing Program

Search marketing is at the convergence of business and technology. To successfully execute a search marketing program, you'll need to tame the technology while sticking with sound business procedures across your team. That's what Part III is all about.

We begin in Chapter 6, "Choose Your Target Market Segments," with your target market: searchers. What words are they using to find what they want? Which ones should you be targeting in your search marketing campaigns? Your marketers must understand how to identify what searchers are looking for.

Chapter 7, "Get Your Content Listed," focuses on getting your content listed in search engines. For organic search, your technologists must ensure that your site design makes it easy to index; otherwise, the search engines won't find you. Paid search is simpler; placing your ad gets you listed, but there is more to it than that.

Once you know your target keywords, it's time to optimize your content in Chapter 8, "Optimize Your Content." Your writers and your technology team must work together so that each ad and each page is designed and written to please a searcher. That way, your pages will rank highly and drive web conversions.

Chapter 9, "Prove Your Content's Quality," addresses the challenge of quality for both paid and organic search. Organic search quality depends on drawing links to your site, getting social approval, and more. Paid search lives and dies with the Quality Score that can raise your rankings and save you money.

Chapter 10, "Make Search Marketing Operational," helps you design your operating procedures to manage your search marketing performance each day. We'll explain the best practices for developing your search team, monitoring your success, and diagnosing the inevitable problems that crop up.

By the end of Part III, you'll know how to turn your search marketing program into a well-oiled marketing machine—a successful mix of business and technology. Your program won't always work flawlessly, but you'll be able to identify your challenges and take action to correct each one. Day by day, you'll make the right decisions to improve your search marketing effectiveness.

CHAPTER 6

Choose Your Target Market Segments

Get out your crystal ball! That's one way to guess what searchers are looking for. If your crystal ball is as cloudy as ours, however, you might want to use a few other methods, too. That's what you will learn in this chapter.

You need to get your pages to be highly ranked in the organic search results to generate traffic to your site. Or you need to invest in paid search techniques for your site's pages to show up on that search results page. No matter whether you are focusing on organic or paid search or both, you need to know which keywords searchers are using. If you do not know which words searchers are entering, you cannot purchase the right keywords (for paid search), nor can you make sure those words are prominently featured on your pages (for organic search).

In this chapter, we show you that choosing the right keywords for your search marketing campaign does not have to be guesswork. We explain the basics of keyword planning—the method by which you deduce your keywords. This chapter covers the following topics:

- **Understand the value of targeting:** You will see how keyword planning improves brand awareness for your organization and how it helps you improve web conversions— the ones you chose back in Chapter 4, "Unlock the Business Value of Search," for your website.

- **Choose your primary targets:** We dive into the targeting process itself, showing you how to begin the process of identifying the right keywords for any campaign.

- **Deepen your targeting:** Once you have your initial keyword list, you must examine ways to further specialize your targets to identify the right audiences for your business.

- **Organize your targets:** Having a long list isn't enough without prioritizing and organizing that list so that you can maximize your impact.

At the end of this chapter, you will be able to choose the best keyword targets for every search marketing campaign you undertake. Let's start by getting an appreciation for why keyword planning is so important.

If that seems like a lot of work, well, it is (only slightly harder than finding a needle in a haystack). But it is work you need to do. Proper keyword targeting will actually save you enormous amounts of work later—all the wasted time of managing paid search campaigns and optimizing your organic content for all the wrong keywords. We also introduce you to some tools and techniques that reduce the work as much as possible.

Understand the Value of Targeting

You might be tempted to skip the whole process of keyword targeting. Perhaps you think you already know what searchers are looking for. If you do, that's great. Unless you have done a comprehensive keyword analysis in the past, however, you likely don't know which words searchers enter. Oh sure, you know *some* of them. But what about the ones you do *not* know? Every valuable keyword you miss is an opportunity for your competitors.

And what about the keywords that you are sure *lots* of searchers are using? Time and again, we have seen smart people focus scarce resources to target a keyword and find very little traffic as a result. Often, the words that *you* search with are not the same as what your *customers* use. You are an expert, and they are not.

So, the basic value of keyword targeting is to make sure that your search marketing resources are focused on *all* the valuable keywords (so that you haven't missed any) and not targeting words of *low value* (which costs you unnecessary money and time).

But the value of keyword targeting goes deeper than that. As you saw in Chapter 2, "How Searchers Work," searchers exhibit very specific behavior when they look for information. Keyword targeting enables you to present searchers with the right content at the right time—your content, that is. As with all of search marketing, keyword planning derives its value from the basic goals of your site that you developed in Chapter 4. There are two basic reasons to engage in search marketing: building brand awareness and increasing web conversions. Let's look at each one before we take on the keyword planning process itself.

Building Brand Awareness

Whether you like it or not, many people have never heard of your company. These people might be customers, if only they knew they should be buying from you. It is well accepted in other forms of marketing that raising awareness is the first step in landing a new customer, and many forms of advertising are devoted to nothing but brand awareness.

When someone sees your TV commercial about that new car, you hope that viewer might be in the market for a car at that moment and head down to the dealer to buy, but relatively few people are in that situation at any one time. The vast majority of people watching that ad have no interest in buying a car. But someday they will. Advertisers know that the messages in their constant commercials—the name of their company, the model of their car, and how exciting/ practical/sexy/inexpensive/luxurious the car is—will stick in viewers' minds, who might remember the message later when they are in the market for a car. Marketers call this **brand awareness**.

Raising awareness of your brand identity is a basic part of any marketing effort, but it is just starting to be recognized as a legitimate goal for search marketing. You might or might not have a goal of building brand identity through your own search marketing efforts. If you do, keyword targeting is essential to that goal. At the end of this chapter, when we prioritize the most important keyword candidates for your organization to target, you will take into account any brand awareness goals as you do so.

Remember, searchers might not know you offer a particular product or service. Unless they see it listed in the results, they may not consider your product as an option. Searchers researching a product or service for the first time might not be aware of any specific brand or company. They are just gathering information. They might not even have any intention to buy anything yet, because they are just looking into a problem and do not know they need anything to solve it. But if you are not listed in the search results, you are not a "big brand" in the searcher's mind. If you *are* listed there, you must be. Such is the branding power of search.

These searchers (who are in the *Learn* phase of the Buyer's Journey discussed in Chapter 2) might or might not ever become your customers, but your product has a far better chance of being considered. Marketers call the group of companies that shoppers might purchase from their **consideration set**. To be in the consideration set, you need to have high brand awareness.

So how does search improve brand awareness? The simplest way is to ensure that you are targeting broad keywords that capture prospective customers while they are still learning—*before* they have made any brand decisions. But there are other ways, too.

In your paid search ad copy, always use a well-known brand name, if you have one. And if you don't, you might find that constantly using your brand names will begin to build some level of awareness. Searchers are much more likely to click results with brand names they know. So, paid search ads for Snap Electronics should always have *Snap* in the ad, or *SnapShot* for its digital camera ads. Because that name is well known, searchers will choose it over a generic ad for *digital cameras*. When you purchase unbranded keywords, such as *digital cameras*, and you put your brand name in the ad, you are building brand awareness.

Another way to build brand awareness through search is with tie-ins to traditional advertising campaigns. As mentioned previously, most traditional advertising has some brand awareness goals, such as the TV commercial for cars. But where do people go after they see the commercial? Where do they go when they see your print ad in the airline magazine? They probably do not troop down to the dealership for a brochure. More and more, their next step is to go to the web.

Perhaps you think that they remember the name of your company, and they type in the URL of your website. Or they remember the URL you printed at the bottom of the ad? Well, maybe they do. However, it is more likely that they perform a search, for several reasons:

- They remember your company name, but they do not know what your website address is.
- They do not actually remember the name of your company; they just remember the name of the car.
- They did not catch anything from the ad except your slogan, but they were interested in that car.

If you do a good job generating attention with your print and on-air advertising, then you prompt people to seek out your website, which they will often do by searching. If you are introducing a new product or a new concept about your product, you might find people wanting more information when no one was interested before. So, if you are raising interest offline, you must follow through online.

Search marketers are often caught unprepared when a new offline (print or on-air) campaign begins. A keyword that was not important in the past is suddenly hot, but you have no search campaign in place to capture the traffic. Perhaps your company is introducing a new catch phrase. Maybe your product designers are adding a hot new feature to a product. Any of these events can draw attention and prompt searchers to start using new words—the words you use in your offline campaign. Stay in touch with your offline counterparts so that you are ready for sudden success from unexpected places.

Sometimes a keyword that seems unpopular simply might not be popular *yet*. You should continue to target an unpopular keyword when you know your organization is committed to building its level of awareness. Terry Cox, Global Search Manager at Disney, refers to this phenomenon as *keyword timing*, noting that each keyword has its own life cycle, where it rises from out of nowhere, might become very popular (sometimes quickly, sometimes slowly), and eventually fades into oblivion.

It's not just big companies that can build awareness around a keyword. Whenever you send out a press release or hold a gala event, it's news. Make sure your search marketing program has a campaign cooking to catch the happy result of your publicity.

Increasing Web Conversions

As you saw in Chapter 4, the simplest justification for search marketing for most businesses is "If they can't find you, they can't buy from you." And, as you also saw, online purchases are only *one* kind of web conversion. You decided all of the important conversions for your website, and you will use search marketing to drive them.

How does keyword planning help you do that? The first benefit of keyword planning is driving qualified traffic to your site. Note the word "qualified." As we have already learned, the value of search marketing is that the searcher has initiated the interaction—they have told us exactly what they are interested in. The better you can interpret searchers' interests and present them with highly relevant content, the greater your conversion rates will be. That is where keyword targeting comes in; it helps you interpret what searchers actually want, so that you can target just those searchers in the right phase of the Buyer's Journey who you have a higher opportunity to convert.

So, although keyword planning can help you drive more traffic to your site, even better is that it shows you how to drive more qualified traffic to your site. Later, when we assign priorities to different keywords, we look at how to use your Buyer's Journey to decide your searchers' place in the buying cycle, thus increasing your web conversions by selecting the proper keywords.

As you learned in Chapter 2, we reviewed the Goldilocks approach to keywords—avoiding those that were too hot and those that were too cold to find the perfect mix of words that best represents your business. This next section takes you through the process of narrowing down the best set of words for your business needs.

Choose Your Primary Targets

Let's start by making a list and checking it twice. Every website has a wealth of information to consult for keyword planning, even though you might not be aware of it.

We go through each source of data you can check, but the very first place to start is inside your own head, and inside the heads of your teammates. Bring together the folks most familiar with the subject of the search marketing campaign at hand—experts in the content of the product, service, or whatever the campaign is centered on. You will start your keyword targeting with a brainstorming session.

SEARCH WITHOUT SEARCHING

We might excuse you for thinking that the title of this sidebar is a bit loopy, but Google Now is providing search results to what it *thinks* you need, without you even asking. Launched on mobile phones, but starting to appear on tablets and desktops soon, Google Now anticipates what's needed and presents the "results" automatically.

How does it accomplish such magic? Google is constantly mining sources of information, such as location, calendar entries, email, search history, and social network sharing—all from its Google network of properties. From this information, it might present your predicted commute time to work each morning, the score from your favorite sport team, and the stock price the company that you seem to keep checking.

Google Now is rudimentary today, but the idea of search without searching is here to stay. People have talked for years about how shopping will become more automatic: Google sees you searching for a new tablet without buying and later tells you it went on sale. You place a meeting with a client in a distant city on your calendar, and Google Now starts showing you hotel rates and plane fares. Maybe Google Now will someday suggest gifts for your daughter's birthday. All without being asked.

This will raise the stakes for search marketers to know their targets. If you think local search is competitive now, wait for the next level, when search engines understand searchers' intentions before they utter them. When every local business is vying for their attention. And when every national brand believes that getting a spot on their cell phone screens is the most prime real estate ever.

At that point, you'll need to be on top of your search game. Because it's the search engines that will be running this show.

Brainstorm with Your Team

You have probably participated in brainstorming sessions before; this one is no different. Approach it in the standard way. Get together the people who are knowledgeable about your search marketing campaign's focus, be it a product, service, or something else.

Go into the brainstorming session prepared with all of the ancillary information you can gather. For example, you should have lists of all the products and services that you offer. If you have other marketing collateral, such as white papers, case studies, brochures, or other material, make lists of the words that you use to describe your offerings' features and benefits—as well as the problems they solve.

Make sure all participants get to add their two cents and do not censor any ideas; you will remove erroneous choices and prioritize the most important keywords later. Let each one add words to your master list of keyword candidates. We prompt you along the way with techniques that lend structure to your brainstorming session, to make it easier for you to develop a more comprehensive list.

The easiest way to start your brainstorming is for everyone to stop and answer the simple question, "What do we do?" As you answer that question, make a list of all the words that describe your product, service, or other subject of this campaign. Focus first on nouns. Let's see what one Snap Electronics team member listed for its digital camera campaign: *camera*, *digital camera*, *SnapShot*, *Snap digital camera*, *X5*, *X6*, *X7*, *SLR X800*, and *SLR X900*. Each team put together a slightly different list that had more than 30 unique names on it by the end of the exercise.

The next step is to organize your nouns into categories, as shown in Exhibit 6-1. Sometimes putting each name in its proper column helps to identify ones that are missing.

Category	Segment	Brand Group	Products/Models
Camera	Digital camera	Snap SnapShot	X5, X6, X7, SLR X800, SLR X900
PC	Notebook	ThinkPad	X1, X1 Carbon, X1 Carbon Touch, X230, X230t
Car	Luxury sedan	Lexus	IS, ES, GS, LS
Chair	Desk chair	Herman Miller Aeron chair	Graphite Frame, Titanium Frame

Exhibit 6-1   Keyword noun brainstorming. Organizing each noun by its type can reveal omissions in your list.

If your names use acronyms, remember that some searchers will look for the full name of the product or service. Snap tried to keep that tip in mind, but also realized that few searchers know what *SLR* stands for, so the acronym in that case was sufficient.

After you have a fairly complete set of nouns, break out the adjectives. Think in terms of qualifying words that hone in on more details, such as qualities, characteristics, or attributes. Some of the noun phrases identified in Exhibit 6-1 can be viewed this way—*digital camera* or *luxury sedan*—but now it's time to list a lot more adjectives. Exhibit 6-2 shows how Snap Electronics carried out this exercise. Listing several different categories of adjectives can help you flesh out the adjectives you need. Don't be concerned about which category your adjectives fall in, or whether you list one more than once. When you are done, it will not matter how they are categorized. The point of the exercise is to identify as many of those multiword phrases that describe your subject as possible. The categories just help you think of more adjectives.

Comparisons	Qualifiers	Functions	Attributes	Actions
best digital camera easy digital cameras	cheap digital camera discount digital camera smallest digital camera fastest digital camera lightweight digital camera	image stabilizer interchangeable lens camera	12 megapixel camera slr format camera	buy digital camera download camera software compare 12 megapixel camera

Exhibit 6-2 Keyword adjective brainstorming. Develop several categories of adjectives that describe your product, and have everyone fill in the blanks.

As you complete the matrix, think about which adjectives truly fit your product. For example, Snap makes high-end digital cameras, so they ultimately decided to shy away from the adjective *cheap*, even though someone wrote it down during brainstorming. While it is common in offline advertising to use "opposite" keywords to "turn" buyers of cheap products into purchasers of high-end products, that approach rarely works in search marketing.

By this time, you should have a solid list of keyword nouns and a longer list of phrases with adjectives to qualify those nouns. Before getting too self-satisfied, however, you should know that most folks have missed a number of very important keywords at this point in the process. It's time to think about the road not traveled.

It is natural for you to think narrowly about your product or service because you are an expert on that subject. Your list of candidate keywords contains all the words that you and your team would use to search, but it is probably missing a bunch of keywords your *customers* use. Broaden your list further by asking yourselves some questions:

- What do your customers need? What problems are they trying to solve? What words do they use to describe their needs and problems? For example, in a B2B situation, they might want to know about **high inventory carrying costs** and this is an opportunity to explain how your supply chain management solutions can help them.

- What content do we have on our site that would satisfy someone's search? What words would you search for to find that content?

- How would you describe your product to a novice? What if your product never existed before? What phrases could you use to help them make the connection?

"HEY! THAT'S MY TRADEMARK!" WHAT TO DO WHEN SOMEONE BIDS ON YOURS

When people think about trademarks and search, they always think about their competitors first. What would you do if your competitor bid on your trademark? Fortunately, it does not happen all that often. If it does, you have some rights (as we explain later). The more interesting cases, however, are not your competitors; they are your partners.

The most common instance of other companies bidding on your trademark stems from your own distribution channels. Your affiliates bid for the names of your products that they sell. So do your retailers and resellers. And you are probably okay with that. Sure it's a little annoying that your distributors might outbid you and have a higher rank for your product. Yes, it's not the greatest when a searcher buys from the more expensive affiliate channel than direct from you. (It is more expensive because you have to pay the affiliate for the sale.) But after all, that is just good marketing, and that is why you have distributors—so they can sell your product.

Unfortunately, it is not always such a positive story. Sometimes your partners can be your worst enemy in paid search. Suppose we told you that your affiliates were sending searchers for your trademark to a landing page that showed not just your product, but also several cut-price knockoffs from your competition? Or refurbished versions of your product? Now how do you feel? Your affiliates might be taking searchers predisposed to buying your product and parading them in front of other companies' products, too. To them, it is just a way to pump up their sales; they do not particularly care whose product they sell. But to you, it is a variation on the old bait-and-switch scam.

As long as your partners feature your products on the page, it is unlikely that you can win a suit against them for trademark infringement. However, you have a few other remedies

- What words do industry magazines and industry analysts use to describe your products? Is there a product category name that they use?

You might call your computer a notebook, but do others call it a laptop? Do novices search for *digital photos* or *digital images* or *electronic camera*? If you do not know, write it down anyway. If your team is having trouble with this part of the exercise, bring in some folks from your target market and ask them the same questions. What words would they use?

If you take the time, you will identify many of your target keywords from brainstorming. You will never get all of them, but you have many other data sources to consult to complete your list of keyword candidates. Let's look at the first such source next, the keywords that your existing site visitors use.

available to you. First, they are your partners. You can set ground rules for how they sell your product. You can insist in the affiliate agreement that affiliates put no other products on their landing pages except your (new) offerings. Some marketers are banning affiliates from bidding on trademarked names at all, ensuring that you get the traffic for your trademark keywords.

In many situations, you can also take your case to the search engines. Search engines do not all have the same policies—even the same search engine might have different policies in different countries—but most search engines allow your competitors to purchase ads for your trademarked keywords while simultaneously prohibiting the use of trademarked names in the ad copy itself.

Trademark owners must initiate any actions to protect their trademarks, which they may do regardless of whether they have any advertising relationship with the search engines. Despite these policies, trademark handling is controversial and is increasingly being played out in court. As with so many things in search marketing, use the resources section on the companion site (SEMincBook.com/trademark) to stay abreast of this fast-changing topic.

Even with these protections, you must remember that some conflicts over trademarks are inherent in the trademark law itself. Trademarks are issued within particular industries, so do not be surprised if several companies have trademarked the exact same product name, albeit in different contexts. So if you work for Delta Airlines and you are annoyed about sharing your trademark with dozens of companies that have offerings that contain *delta*, such as *delta faucets* or *delta dental*, you'll just have to get over it. It's their trademark, too.

Check Your Current Search Referrals

Some of your best keywords are right under your nose—they are keywords customers are already using to find your site. Chapter 4 introduced the concept of search referrals, showing how your web analytics facility can tell you the search keywords that visitors use to find your site.

You'll recall from Chapter 4 that many referrals have been hidden by Google as "not provided," but you can find more information by logging in to your Bing and Google Webmaster Tools accounts to see information for a limited number of keywords, including average rank, clicks, and the number of impressions for your content in the search results. Although these tools typically provide information on merely your most popular keywords, sometimes you'll see information for less-popular, so-called *long tail* keywords also.

Search referrals are a gold mine for developing your candidate list for keywords because they are phrases that searchers are already using to reach your site, so you know they relate to your products. Don't look only at the keywords that get lots of traffic; you are already succeeding with those. Notice keywords that you get *little* traffic for, too. Those low-volume keywords might actually be popular searches, but your site just does not rank very high in the results, so it attracts little traffic for those words. They might turn out to be your biggest opportunities for improvement.

As you use your list of referrals to add more keywords to your master list, you might notice that many of the referred keywords have very low volume. You might even notice some of the keywords already on your master list have few searchers coming to your site using those keywords. Seeing this, you might be tempted to remove a keyword already on the list just because you do not see many (or any) referrals for that keyword. It's natural to think that way, but it's wrong. One of your goals is to find those keywords that your site is drawing little or no traffic for today; those keywords might have great potential for the future.

Next up, you'll tap another source of valuable keyword data: your website search facility.

Consult Your Site Search Facility

If your website has its own search engine—one that returns the pages of your site for searchers—you can study the list of keywords those searchers enter to see what words you are missing. Check out the more popular keywords most closely—no need to look at every keyword that was searched for just once in the last month. Website search can be a goldmine for identifying new keywords for your list because website searchers enter words that they believe you have content for on your site. Your customers are telling you what words they use to find your content, so they can be great words to add to your keyword list.

Remember that the context for the site searcher is different from someone searching in Bing or Google, precisely because site search results are limited to content that appears on your website. For example, when Snap Electronics examined their site search keyword log, they found that there were almost no searches for *snap digital camera* because the searchers knew they did not have to include the word *snap* in their keyword. They are already at Snap's site, so they searched merely for *digital camera*.

Depending on your business, you might find that there are many keywords from visitors in the use phase of the Buyer's Journey who are seeking technical support, for example. Snap found keywords for downloading some digital camera utilities they offer, but realized that only existing customers were interested, so they are not great choices to target for their search marketing campaign. Later, we'll look at deeper ways to identify the right targets, including using your Buyer's Journey, but right now we will check out some software that helps you solidify your keyword list.

Use Keyword Research Tools

You've brainstormed, you've reviewed multiple data sources, and you've compiled quite a list. By now, you should have many possible keyword targets, but do you have them all or know how searchers enter any of them? Bring on the keyword research tools!

Keyword research tools reveal which keywords on your list are heavily used by searchers and which ones are rarely used as well as those actively used by your competitors. Research tools can also expand your list by showing variations of your keywords using various stemming methods. These tools examine countless keywords used by searchers to reveal the patterns of what searchers are looking for.

Keep in mind, however, that keyword tools are just that—tools. They arc not magical, and they do not substitute for the step you just completed to gather your own keyword list based on your in-depth knowledge of your product. It is so easy to use these tools that you will be tempted to skip the gathering step, but overreliance on keyword tools is one of the ways that search marketers miss some very valuable keywords and target keywords that do not match their product very well. In addition, it is seductive to fall in love with one tool and use it exclusively. Don't! Instead, share the love with a wide range of tools. Each one has different strengths and weaknesses, so researching with multiple tools results in better information for your decisions.

The biggest danger in using keyword research tools lies in chasing popularity rather than the correct fit. It's tempting to see the big keyword demand numbers for popular keywords and imagine that your content will be #1 for those mega-keywords, but it is more realistic to target the keywords that are great fits for your company's strengths. Snap Electronics might love the high keyword demand for *cheap digital camera* and *discount digital camera*, but they don't have those products as part of their high-end product line. Better to focus on less popular keywords that are strong fits for their content.

In the first two editions of this book we had an exhaustive list of keyword tools, but keyword tools are changing more rapidly than ever, so we now keep that information up to date on our companion website (SEMincBook.com/keyword-research-tools).

You might have been wondering all along whether you can learn anything from keeping an eye on your competitors and their search marketing campaigns. That's next.

Check Out Your Competition

Take the time to look at the web pages for your top competitors for the subject of your campaign. For example, if your campaign revolves around one of your products, examine your competitors' web pages for competing products.

Look at the words they use. Obviously, competitors have their own brand names and model numbers, but look deeper. Which words do they use to describe their products? Which words are found in their titles? Crack open their HTML and look at which words they use in their title and description tags. Check out their site navigation and their "Products A–Z" pages—which words do they use to describe the product's category? Add promising new keywords to your list.

If you were wondering whether there are some magical tools that can detect which keywords your competitors are buying in paid search and which keywords your competitors' content is shown for in organic search—there are. Competitive keyword research tools analyze the keyword data available from numerous sources to show you keywords that your competitors are focusing on—often they can even show you the ads they are currently running. Just as we have advised with previous keyword techniques, use these competitive research tools to suggest new keywords that you might not have previously considered for your own keyword list. Again, you can turn to our website to see an up-to-date list of competitive keyword tools (SEMincBook.com/competitive-keyword-tools). Many require monthly subscriptions but you can often check them out with free trials.

Keep in mind, however, that just because your competitor uses a keyword, that does not make it a good idea for you. Your competitor might not have performed any keyword analysis to see whether it is a popular keyword. And what makes a keyword a good fit for your competitor doesn't necessarily make it a good fit for you, so don't blindly follow what competitors do. Your product's differentiation might be completely different. For example, remember that Snap Electronics avoids the keyword *cheap digital camera* because their cameras are rather expensive. Just because a competitor might target that word doesn't mean that it is a good idea for Snap.

If you have a page that legitimately mentions a competitor—such as a feature comparison page—that is perfectly okay. However, steer clear of any tricks using your competitors' brand names or other trademarks, such as dumping your competitors' trademarks into a description tag on your page. Searchers entering your competitors' names are not looking for your products. If you try to hijack those brand-loyal searchers with tricky pages that mention your competitors' brand names, you will annoy those searchers and risk a lawsuit for trademark infringement or unfair competition.

You've been through Keyword Targeting 101, but there is more to it than the basics, so next we look at several techniques for ever-deeper keyword targeting.

Deepen Your Targeting

It's not necessary that you pursue deeper targeting, but our experience is that the steps we out-line here are often the difference between and an average and a great search marketing program. You have identified a good group of keywords thus far, but you can specialize your list to more closely target your best search audiences—and to ensure completeness that adds critical traffic to your search program's results.

Use Your Buyer's Journey

Now we want to build on our work in Exhibit 6-2, expanding our keyword list using your Buyer's Journey. We'll use Snap Electronics as an example, dusting off their *Learn/Shop/Buy/Receive/ Use* model for digital cameras that we explored in Chapter 2. We can take every keyword on Snap's list and assign it to a particular phase of the Buyer's Journey. As we do, we quickly realize that any keywords that Snap put into the mix for the *Receive* or *Use* stages are unlikely to bring any conversions. (Some *Use* keywords might help you sell accessories or supplies, but those key-words are part of another campaign.)

So Snap is left with the keywords associated with the *Learn*, *Shop*, and *Buy* phases, which are shown in abridged form in Exhibit 6-3. (You should categorize every keyword according to your Buyer's Journey, but we are shortening the example.) To accurately categorize each key-word, you need to think about what each stage in the Buyer's Journey means. So, a searcher who knows nothing about digital cameras is in the *Learn* phase, and is likely to use search keywords, such as *digital cameras* or *buy digital camera*. A searcher who knows more would enter key-words based on features of digital cameras (*Shop* phase), such as *12 megapixel digital camera*, whereas searchers who know precisely what they want to buy (*Buy* phase) might enter the exact model number to shop for the lowest price.

Learn	Shop	Buy
digital cameras	*8 megapixel camera*	*buy snapshot x5*
digital camera reviews	*lightweight camera*	*buy snapshot x6*
best digital camera	*easy digital camera*	*snapshot x7 sale*
digital camera options	*snap digital camera*	*snapshot slr x800*
compare digital cameras	*snapshot camera deals*	*snapshot slr x900*

Exhibit 6-3   Snap keywords and the Buyer's Journey. Snap categorized each of its prioritized keywords according to its customers' *Buying* cycle.

Snap already culled the list to remove any search keywords, such as *cheap digital camera*, that are not close matches for their site's content. Our next step is to identify the relevant words from the *Buying* cycle for your business. To make your job easier, we have compiled a variety of lists of Buyer's Journey phrases at our companion site (SEMincBook.com/buy-cycle-modifiers) for different industries and cycles. We also offer a tool that enables you to merge your keyword list with relevant words from the *Buying* cycle. You probably already include obvious words, such as *buy* or *purchase*, but what about *coupon code* or *trade up*?

B2B companies have different Buyer's Journeys, usually focusing on lead generation rather than online sales. In addition, B2B companies often have a different set of words that should be added to their primary keywords, such as *data sheets* or *spec sheets*. Often, B2B searchers are looking for very specific bits of information such as dimensions, heat displacement, or even whether the product is at its end of life. The more of these key information needs you handle in your keyword targets, the more prospects you will convert to customers.

Decide a Match Type for Each Paid Search Keyword

For each keyword in your paid search program, you need to specify how the keywords you choose ought to match the words that the searchers use. At first this might seem odd to you. After all, search engines decide which organic pages match searcher keywords all by themselves, so why do they need your help for paid search?

Paid search differs markedly from organic search in that search engines look less at the landing pages to decide which ones are the best matches. Instead, they spend more energy examining the bids for the keywords, the ad copy, and each ad's click rate. That's why they need your help. Besides, you want to help them, because the right assistance will increase your conversions and lower your costs.

The way search engines get your help is through **bid match types**—the labels that tell the search engines which rules to apply to decide whether a particular ad matches the searcher's keyword. We'll look at every match type to help you decide which one is the right one to try with each keyword in your paid search program. Google and Bing offer all the match types discussed here; if you are using another paid search engine, check how it works.

The most inclusive match type, the one that matches the most searcher keywords, is called **broad match**. Here is how broad match works. If Snap Electronics bids on the keyword *digital camera* using broad match, any searcher keyword that contains both of those words can trigger Snap's ad, including a keyword such as *camera for digital photography*. In addition, related searches or synonyms might also trigger a broad match if the search engine thinks the keywords are closely enough related, such as *dslr camera*. The broad match type provides the most matches for your keyword, increasing your impressions and your referrals (as well as your fees).

Broad match is the default for Google and Bing—the one you get if you do not select anything when you enter a keyword. In addition, Google's broad match also matches synonyms, close variations, and misspellings. Be very careful with broad match. Not only can it can run up a lot of costs in a hurry, but it might also be matching keywords that you have no hope of converting with. When you are searching, pay attention to the "weird" ads that seem to show up sometimes; they are probably generated with a broad match keyword.

More restrictive than broad match is **phrase match**, which matches any keyword that contains the keyword in order with only close word variants. The close word variants rule means that Snap's keyword purchase for *digital camera* allows matching for *reviews for digital cameras* and *camera for digital photography*. With phrase match, the keywords *digital camera accessories* and *digital camera sale* both match *digital camera*, but your ad would not be shown for *digital slr camera* (because *slr* breaks up the order of the *digital camera* keyword).

The most restrictive match type, **exact match**, finds only the exact words as typed, so if Snap purchases *digital camera* with exact match, no other keywords will match, except very close variants, such as *digital cameras* or misspellings such as *digtal camra*. Using this match type drives fewer referrals, but might give you higher clickthrough rates (and thus better rankings) and higher conversion rates.

But you might want finer-grained control. Because broad match can take in so much ground and exact match is so restrictive, the search engines provide ways to identify individual words within the keyword that must be present or must be absent.

The newest aspect of paid search matching is the **broad match modifier** that ensures that no synonyms or related search words match for that particular word. To designate a word with the broad match modifier, precede it with a plus sign (+) with no space, like so: *+snapshot digital camera reviews*. The reason to use the broad match modifier is that Snap wants to match synonyms for some of the words (it should match *snapshot digital camera reviews*) but does not want the same treatment for its brand name (it should not match *photograph digital camera reviews*).

Another way to control matching is with **negative keywords**, which enable you to specify words that, if found in a searcher's keyword, would prevent your ad from being shown. You should already have a fairly extensive list from our keyword gathering and segmenting exercises earlier in this chapter. Snap Electronics, for example, should have the word *cheap* on its negative keyword list, because their brand does not offer any inexpensive cameras. Don't allow your ads to be shown to searchers who clearly won't buy from you.

But negative keywords should be used for more than just the wrong brand image; you need to eliminate searches for the wrong products. If Snap wants to use a broad match type for *digital camera* but found they were getting too many clicks that do not convert for *digital video camera*, they could add a negative match for the keyword *video* to eliminate those keywords while retaining more inclusive matching for all other keywords. Similarly, many occurrences of *digital camera* might be the phrase *digital camera accessories*. Do you want to negate accessories because you want a lower bid for that phrase and a higher bid for *digital camera*? Or because your clickthrough rate will go up (raising your ranking)? Do your homework on what searchers enter and use negative keywords to target your keywords as tightly as possible.

Broad match (or broad match modifier) works best for very specific keywords, such as product numbers or unique product names (*snapshot slr* or *onetouch autofocus*), where nearly any keyword containing those words has a reasonable chance of being relevant to the searcher—and converting. More common words can be good candidates for broad match if their meanings always match your scope (*snap electronics*) or if their meanings are unambiguous (*honda* or *ipod* or *cancun vacation*). Longer phrases can also be good candidates if you want to capture all variations—*snapshot digital camera* matches *buy a snapshot digital camera* and *snapshot accessories for digital cameras.*

But broad match does not work in all situations. Phrase or exact match is far better when your keywords have ambiguous meanings—they can mean more than one thing. Single words and acronyms are especially susceptible:

- **ivory** (soap or some jewelry?)
- **mp3** (a download or a player?)
- **china** (the country or a dinner setting?)
- **ford** (a car or a person's name?)

For these ambiguous terms, you must use longer keywords (*ford taurus* or *mp3 player*) or add negative keywords to reduce ambiguity (Ford Motor can use *ford -gerald*).

But broad match isn't just for handling ambiguity. Sometimes you know exactly what the searcher means, but they don't want what you are selling. If a searcher types *leather jeans*, your broad match for the keyword *jeans* will match even if you sell only denim jeans. That will cost you money and lead to no conversions. But maybe you never thought of that possibility when you put your campaign together. How can you figure out these problems and correct them?

One of the best strategies for match types is to start most keywords with broad match with any obvious negative keywords that you know. Then, you use your referral metrics to gradually identify which keyword variations have the highest conversions. When you do identify them, you can buy those highly converting keywords using phrase or exact match (possibly with higher bids because they are worth more) and eliminate the original broad match keywords. Another alternative is to add negative keywords to your broad match keywords to eliminate the low-conversion variations and to add broad match modifiers to enforce restrictions on the keywords that need them. So, in this case, you might have started with broad match for jeans, but when your analytics shows you many searchers coming to your site with the keyword *leather jeans*, that is your signal to add the negative keyword *leather.*

Regardless of which strategy you employ for match types, keep an eye on the search engines for changes to their match types—you never know when they will upend the *status quo*. Our resources page on our companion site will help keep you informed (SEMincBook.com/match-types).

Localize Your Targets

Digital marketing has always been a great way to expand your reach beyond your local area, but in recent years, search marketing has allowed truly local businesses to reach their close-by clientele. If you have a small-town dental practice or coffee shop, local search can be exactly what you need. What's more, even large companies with national brands need local search so that individual branches and stores can have each location found by their nearby customers. So whether you own a local McDonald's or an independent hamburger joint, you care about localized search results—and it all starts with your keyword targets.

Even if you are a national brand, you still want to think carefully about localizing your keywords. After all, even though October is the peak season for snow blowers in the United States, it doesn't make sense to run those ads in Florida.

For most of these local search opportunities, the geographic target is fairly small, but it varies from business to business. For example, you probably wouldn't be looking for a Starbuck's more than a few blocks away, but you might be willing to travel 15 miles or more for the right medical specialist.

The most obvious kind of local keywords include the geographic words within the keywords (*detroit cosmetic dentist* or *orange county furniture*). Many searchers will use such keywords and you need to identify those that pertain to your business; many of them have already come up as you have walked through this process, but you should focus on completeness. If your local furniture store is located in Anaheim, California, you obviously want to target *anaheim furniture* and *orange county furniture* and the names of other local communities that you draw your regular customers from. Perhaps you even want to target *southern california furniture* if you draw from a wider area. You need to identify all of the different ways that searchers might specify your store's location. These keywords become good targets for both organic and paid search.

You can also look for additional ways that people might seek your location—ones that you might not be thinking about. The simplest approach uses Google's Autocomplete, as shown in Exhibit 6-4. Simply start typing a location name and one of your products and see what is suggested. The suggestions are shown in order of the highest keyword demand first. Now, you might not be surprised that *new york city cameras* and *new york city camera store* were good keywords, but maybe you might have missed *new york city camera shops*. A lot of marketers might have overlooked *new york city camera rentals*, especially if they are the national brand manager and don't realize how many tourists rent cameras when visiting New York. Could this be a new opportunity for Snap Electronics to rent their high-end cameras in a few local markets jammed with tourists?

Exhibit 6-4   Location-based keyword suggestions. Google Autocomplete shows the most popular ways searchers finish any keyword that you start typing.

In recent years, however, local search has moved beyond the need for searchers to actually type their location. Exhibit 6-5 shows how the simple keyword *dentist* produces both organic and paid search results that are localized to the geographic area around the searcher at the time of the search. The searcher did not need to provide any location words as part of the search keyword. (Google Trends provides a simple way for you to see where searchers tend to be located when they use specific keywords.)

When the searcher looks for dentist, Google shows results near the searcher's physical location—in this case, Bergen County in northern New Jersey.

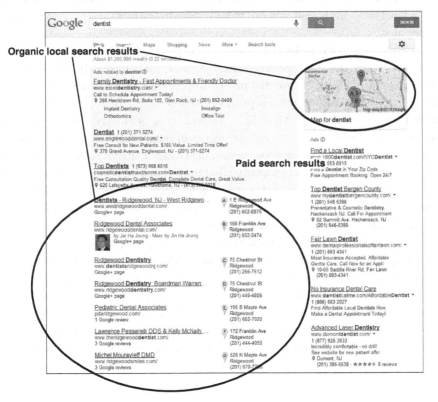

Exhibit 6-5 Local search results. A simple keyword triggers a complex set of location-targeted results for both paid and organic search.

Search engines are guessing that the keyword *dentist* carries searcher intent for local results, rather than, say, the Wikipedia entry to explain what dentists are. Because search engines are beginning to do this for so many searches, searcher behavior has actually begun to change so that fewer searchers are using location words—they assume that Google will show them the local result when they want one. So, when they once entered *los angeles thai restaurant*, now they save a few keystrokes and merely type *thai restaurant*.

Search engines use several techniques to identify the searcher's location. Searchers using computers or other devices attached to wireless or wired networks can be located through a technique called **reverse IP lookup** or **reverse DNS lookup**. They compare the IP address of the searcher's computer against a table that notes that address's geographic location. Cell phones can be located, even while in motion, by *triangulating* the cell phone towers whose signals can reach the phone, or with similar techniques based on WiFi hotspots. The searcher's location calculated by these techniques is usually accurate, but not always.

When accurate, searchers located within (perhaps) 25 miles of that furniture store will see the local search results when they look for *furniture* but others outside that range might see different stores in their results. The organic search engine shows the stores listed in its local directories (such as Google+ Local or Bing Local, for example) that are near the searcher's current location.

For paid search, you chose a country or a set of countries as your target for all your keywords when you set up your account. Even companies that don't care about local search at least want to select one or more countries, because they don't want paid search ads to appear in a country where they do not do business. They also don't want ads to appear in countries that speak different languages from the one used in the ad copy.

But businesses designed to attract local customers need to localize their paid search campaigns even more. If your business depends on attracting customers to your location, such as a bank branch or a restaurant, you want to restrict your paid search ads to be shown only to searchers within your local geographic area. All the major search engines enable you to target the geographic locations of the searchers who should see your ad, keyword by keyword. The major search engines all support geographic targeting by city, state, ZIP codes, and even a specific radius around your location.

You might be surprised to see how some companies use that radius targeting. You might have heard of **showrooming**, where shoppers standing in physical retail stores are shopping online with their phones to purchase the item they are holding in their hands. They wanted to see it before they bought it, but they wanted that low price. Macy's is one retailer that is combatting showrooming by using paid search ads for key products that are limited to a tight radius around their store locations. They can even place a sign next to the product that offers more savings with a coupon—and provide a geotargeted ad within the store's radius for *macys coupon* that delivers the coupon to the searcher's phone. Not only do these approaches increase the odds that Macy's gets the sale, but the couponing process can also capture consumer contact information for future promotions. But how does Macy's know that its ad is being shown on only mobile devices? Both Bing and Google allow targeting by device type, as Exhibit 6-6 shows.

Sometimes the best way to use a location is by exclusion. Imagine you run a tourist attraction that wants to ensure that its offers are *not* seen by locals; you can offer discounts for advance purchases that are shown only to searchers outside your local area. So, if you run a Napa Valley wine tasting tour that allows discounts for 2-week advance bookings, you can run your ad nationally but exclude the San Francisco Bay area. Anyone in the Bay Area 2 weeks before the tour is either a local or a tourist who will be home 2 weeks later.

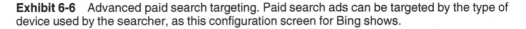

Exhibit 6-6   Advanced paid search targeting. Paid search ads can be targeted by the type of device used by the searcher, as this configuration screen for Bing shows.

Another kind of local targeting uses a type of location rather than a precise location. American Express wants to target international travelers, but how can they do it? One way is to run paid search ads that are shown only in international airports using Google's Airport Targeting. But you can be even more precise than that. Snap Electronics sells their premium cameras at duty free shops in several airports. They can run Google Product Listing Ads for *30 megapixel camera* at only those airports where the shops stock their cameras.

But this idea works better if you can target by device. Snap will probably raise their conversion rate by running their ads only on tablets and mobile phones that tourists are using rather than the computers used by businessmen who are merely researching a camera and not interested in buying one now in the airport. Luckily, all search engines enable you to target ads by specific device. The increased use of tablets gives advertisers reasons to use this new kind of targeting.

If you run multiple locations, you can adjust your ads based on what sells at each location. For example, Home Depot can run specialty product listings in areas that purchase them; *air conditioner* can show small sleeve units that fit in tiny apartment windows for New York City searchers. In suburban areas, they might emphasize whole-house air-conditioning units for the same keyword. Location by location, you can optimize your ads to show the most demanded and profitable products.

Organize Your Targets

Even small companies often have hundreds of keywords in their search marketing program, but large companies can have hundreds of thousands. To properly manage your keywords, you must prioritize and structure your keyword list so that you know which keywords ought to get the lion's share of your attention—and so you can measure the performance of groups of keywords to improve performance.

Understand the Need to Prioritize

The keyword research tools helped round out your list by unearthing variations that you might not have thought of. They also brought you important information you can use to prioritize your list—the popularity of the keywords (keyword demand).

Remember, you do not want to blindly target the keywords that are the most popular. You want keywords that are "just right" for your site. You use the popularity numbers for keywords to ensure that you are not choosing keywords that are too cold. Other than that, try to identify the keywords that are the closest matches for your site's content. This next step is critical to your overall success. Both organic and paid search rely on how well you prioritize your words.

There are natural limits when planning for organic keywords—you cannot put landing pages in place for an unlimited number of organic keywords without ruining your site. With paid search, you can target as many words as you want. But should you? Probably not.

Just as organic search has a natural limit, paid search does, too. You will eventually get to the point that more keywords do not bring you more conversions—they are not worth their costs. They might not be worth the per-click costs, or perhaps it just costs too many people to manage them. So although most businesses find that they can target more paid search keywords than they target for organic search, they need to prioritize even those paid ones.

If you are just starting out, it makes sense to concentrate on the keywords that might bring the highest returns. Definitely start out with transactional keywords, especially those with your own brand names in them. Add informational keywords that you believe will convert. (If you have done a good job tracking your conversions for organic keywords, you have an excellent head start.)

One of the biggest mistakes for paid search rookies is to chase keyword demand. Just because a keyword gets high demand does not mean it will convert for you. Remember the lesson of "too hot" keywords. As challenging as those overheated words are for organic, with paid search you are paying for every one of those nonconverting clicks.

Paid search also has some advantages for search marketers who want to increase brand awareness. You can buy keywords that hit your target market for brand awareness and design relevant landing pages. For example, if you have a famous spokesperson, buy her name. Now, we know that searchers are not actually looking for your company, but if you put up a "fan-zine" site about her that happens to have a bunch of ads about your product, you might be pleased with the brand awareness you can raise at a very low cost. For example, Adidas could buy the names of the tennis players who wear their shoes. If you sponsor a golf tournament, buy golf words before the start of the tournament—you not only get brand awareness, you also get viewers for the event.

The website for Absolut Vodka has a page featuring one of it collaborating artists, Wood-kid, who appears in their commercials, online videos, and social media campaigns. Absolut also received permission from his recording label to purchase keywords using his name so that they can connect with his fans (see Exhibit 6-7).

Exhibit 6-7   Buying brand awareness. Absolut Vodka's website contains information on a celebrity spokesperson whose name draws many search clicks.

TEST HOW SEARCH ENGINES HANDLE NON-ENGLISH KEYWORDS

Global search marketers need to perform some tests before making final decisions on key-word priorities because search engines do not always do the best job of finding all key-words in languages other than English. It's easy to get the impression that there is one Google around the world, but the truth is that every country and every language has a differ-ent search index and different ways of parsing keywords. Without testing, you are making assumptions that might be false.

Search engines sometimes process text incorrectly when there are no blanks in between words, as is the case for many Arabic and Asiatic languages. Search engines sometimes split the text in the wrong places, changing the meaning of the words. Search engines have an especially hard time segmenting Japanese words. Japanese uses four different ways to write its words, and can even combine these formats.

Western languages, except for German, do not suffer from these errors because each word is separated by a space. German employs many compound words, so sometimes search engines fail to find matching words if they do not "decompound" correctly.

Remember that your search for keywords will pay off handsomely. Your friendly search engine rep will happily give you a starter list of words to buy for your industry, but don't you think your competitors get the same list? Those words are bound to be somewhat overpriced because they are the only ones being bought by any of your competitors that are too lazy to do the hard research work. This is where your iteration philosophy comes in. Continually expand your keywords to find new ones that convert at an acceptable rate. Find that keyword your competitors have not discovered yet.

Choose Your Keyword Tiers

It's time to take everything we have learned and decide on your prioritization system for your keywords. Most companies use a tiered system where higher tiers contain the most important keywords.

As you comb through the list, set a priority for each keyword:

- **Negative keywords:** The keyword is a word or phrase that you do *not* want to be associated with your company or products. Perhaps you haven't thought about this list as a "priority" but it is critical to identify the words that you must keep away from your campaigns. These negative keywords can be assigned to a product, phrase or the company as a whole. In paid search your ads will not appear when they are used. By treating them as part of your prioritization process, you will ensure that your whole team has reviewed the list and are on board.

You might wonder why Google seems to dominate many country markets but not Russia or China. Well, Yandex does a far superior job of parsing Russian keywords than Google. With Russian conjugations, the exact same word can look very different, so search engines need a lot of special processing to handle Russian keywords well. Similarly, Baidu leads in China in part due to superior keyword parsing; it has even run TV ads in China making fun of Google's mistakes.

Search marketers must test every keyword in these languages to ensure that it is correctly processed and the right pages are found. Perform searches in every major search engine in each country in question. Make sure good results are being returned. Sometimes you will find that the word that you wanted to use is not handled as well as another one. In that case, you might want to target a different keyword and optimize your organic content around that word.

- **Low priority:** The keyword is a close match to your site and has enough searches to be worth a paid search bid, but not worthy of organic search optimization efforts. Most companies call these low-priority keywords Tier 3 or Tier 4 keywords—or just leave them unclassified and out of your search marketing program.

- **Medium priority:** The keyword is a close match to your site and is somewhat popular with acceptable conversion rates. Many companies divide these keywords into Tier 2 or Tier 3, but you can put them into a single bucket if that works for you.

- **Top priority:** These are the keywords that are the essence of what you offer as a company. The keyword is a close match to your site's content and is very popular or moderately popular or has high conversion rates. Companies commonly call these Tier 1 keywords.

- **Always on:** A number of advanced search marketers have adopted this classification to represent a set of words that are critical to always have representation in the search results. These words are often a subset of your Tier 1 keywords because they are your most important "mission-critical" set of words.

For example, Absolut Vodka requires that their always on keywords rank in the top three positions of organic search results. If a keyword does not rank or drops from that top three position, the business unit is required to make up the exposure using paid search. Because this kind of attention is both time and budget intensive, it's impossible to treat more than a tiny subset of your Tier 1 keywords as always on.

In case you haven't gotten the message yet, you should not be targeting any keywords that are *not* close matches to your site. You just waste your time as well as the searcher's time. Focus on only those keywords that you believe your site is truly a good response for—keywords for which the search engine honestly should send people to your site. Those are the only keywords that will get you strong clickthrough rates and high conversion rates.

Your upper-tier keywords are candidates for both organic search and paid search campaigns. Your lowest keyword tier is not useful for active efforts in organic search because there is a natural limit to the number of keywords that you can target organically. That being said, you still may rank and receive a few visits for some of those keyword variations. As you will see in Chapter 8, "Optimize Your Content," when you optimize pages for organic search, you can usually only target three to four keywords per page. So, you will find that you eventually run out of pages that you can plausibly link together for the search engines to index for organic search. With organic, your landing pages must be linked together cohesively to coax the spider to index them, so there is a natural limit as to the number of keywords you can target organically before your site begins to look maddeningly repetitive, with multiple pages that say the same thing with slightly different words.

For paid search, the number of pages is not an issue, so you can freely target your low-priority words for paid search (as long as you believe it is worth the time to manage the extra words in your campaign). You can develop a separate search landing page for every paid search keyword, and those landing pages do not need to be cohesively linked into your site. Each page can have just one or two links from the landing page to other parts of your site—no other pages on your site need to link to each landing page—and searchers using other keywords won't ever see all those extra landing pages.

To make your priority decisions for each keyword, you need to take into account popularity, of course, but you also need to remember your goals for your campaign. If your search marketing campaign is designed to build brand awareness, you need to decide which keywords are "must win" because your company must be shown for those words. You might even decide to target a few "too hot" keywords if you believe that the branding awareness you will build compensates for the lower conversion rates. Basically, your branding awareness keywords are marketing decisions—for which keywords do your branding goals demand your content to be seen?

Prioritize Keywords by Your Buyer's Journey

If your search marketing campaign is designed to increase web conversions, as most are, your decisions are a bit more complicated. You need to prioritize based on which keywords bring the highest conversion. For organic search, it costs the same amount to optimize a page for any keyword, so your priorities are based purely on which keywords will drive the most conversions. For paid, your decision making is more complex, because the per-click cost of each keyword must be taken into account, too. The problem with prioritizing by conversion potential, however, is that you have no idea which keywords will have the highest conversions before the campaign starts.

As you will see in Chapter 10, "Make Search Marketing Operational," you will be able to track conversion metrics over time so that you can gradually place more emphasis on keywords that convert and deemphasize those that do not. It is seductive to look at high conversion rates, but it is more profitable to go after a higher number of gross conversions. (Would you rather convert 10 out of 20 or 30 out of 100?) Regardless of what you will do after the campaign is underway, your problem now is to figure out which keywords to target to begin your campaign.

Keywords from the Buy Stage

Because you start out with no idea what kinds of conversion rates are associated with each keyword, you cannot accurately prioritize based on that, but you can take guesses. You can guess, for example, that Snap will achieve higher conversion rates for the keywords that mention its own brand and model names—those from the *Buy* stage. And because Snap already has product pages for each individual camera model, it will not be hard to optimize each page for its keyword. Those product pages already contain the "features and benefits" information that buyers need to confirm their decision and complete the purchase. All of this adds up to keywords that closely match Snap's site, and (we believe) will have high conversion rates. Go back and review the modifiers we showed you for the *Buy* stage and you might have a group of very important keywords—Tier 1.

A very common element in *Buy* stage keywords is *coupon code*. When you are checking out an online shopping cart, that "coupon code" box stares at you, begging you to search for a code to fill in to cut your price. When a searcher is considering a purchase at the popular sporting goods retailer REI, many decide to search for *rei coupon code*, or a variant, as shown in Exhibit 6-8. REI can help close the deal by providing a page that lists their current coupon codes. But even if there are no valid coupon codes at the moment, REI could have a page that says, "Sorry, no coupon codes are active right now—would you like to sign up to be informed the next time we have a sale?"

▲ Keyword	Competition	Global Monthly Searches ⑦
coupon code for rei ▾	Low	12,100
coupon code rei ▾	Low	12,100
coupon codes for rei ▾	Low	12,100
coupon codes rei ▾	Low	12,100
online coupon for rei ▾	Low	2,900
online coupon rei ▾	Low	2,900
online rei coupon ▾	Low	2,900
rei coupon code 20 ▾	Low	480
rei coupon code 2011 ▾	Low	480
rei coupon code free shipping ▾	Low	73
rei coupon online ▾	Low	2,900
rei free shipping coupon code ▾	Low	73
rei online coupon code ▾	Low	390
rei online coupon codes ▾	Low	880
rei outlet coupon code ▾	Low	260
rei outlet coupon codes ▾	Low	260

Exhibit 6-8   Capturing coupon clippers. REI can check the number of people searching for coupons with different keyword variants to capture more sales.

But what about the *Learn* and *Shop* stage keywords? Well, you quickly see that some of the *Shop* stage keywords contain the brand names *snap* or *snapshot* in the search keyword, too. Once again, they should carry very high conversion rates for Snap. And they also seem like "must have" keywords from a branding standpoint because Snap is aiming for brand awareness as well as conversions. Make those top priority, too—maybe even always on.

Keywords from the Shop Stage

So far, you have picked out the keywords that seem to have high conversion rates, but you have not looked at the rest of the list. It's time to focus again on how close a match these keywords are to Snap's site. For the *Shop* stage list, the keyword *easy digital camera* is a direct hit for Snap's product line, but *12 megapixel camera* and *lightweight camera* (although accurate) are not quite as distinctive. (Other camera manufacturers can validly make those claims.) When we examine keyword demand data from our keyword research tools, we see that *12 megapixel camera* is a somewhat popular keyword, whereas *lightweight camera* is less so. On that basis, we will make *easy digital camera* a top-priority keyword, assign *12 megapixel camera* a medium priority, and make *lightweight camera* a low-priority keyword to consider only for paid search.

In real life, your list would be far longer than this, but this is the kind of decision process that you will go through. You will target very close matches almost regardless of popularity because they will have high conversion rates. In fact, if they are less popular, it is easier to rank well for each keyword (although you must make sure you do not focus organic search optimization efforts on "too cold" keywords). For keywords that are related to your site, but not direct hits, you will make judgments based on popularity and anticipated conversion rate.

Keywords from the Learn Stage

When you examine the *Learn* stage search keywords, one jumps out as a great target: *digital camera reviews*. You know that Snap has gotten wonderful reviews, so putting up a few pages that boast about those reviews (with links to the magazine sites that contain the actual review articles) is excellent spider food for that keyword. Snap's competitors do not always get the same rave reviews that Snap does, so this keyword is a direct hit for Snap's digital cameras. Make that one a top priority. Because some of the reviews literally say that Snap makes the "best digital camera," that keyword should be at least a medium priority, too.

But what about the others? Broad search keywords such as *digital cameras* and *point and shoot cameras* do not seem to promise a very high conversion rate, but they are in high demand since that is often the first search in the purchase process. Because you do not know what the conversion rate might be, it is worthwhile to try out a few keywords that are very popular to see how much traffic you can draw and test the conversion rate. You do not want to spend precious resources on a large number of them at first, but you should not completely ignore them, either. These words are often the words that get those unaware of your brand to add you to the consideration set. For example, Snap decided to make *digital camera* a top priority precisely because it is extremely popular. Snap considered it critical to get into the searcher's consideration set at the earliest point.

The keyword *compare digital cameras* might be a medium priority because Snap has enough different models that it can put together a few pages that compare them against each other. In addition, Snap might be able to use the pages that target *digital camera reviews* to subtly compare Snap to its competition.

You can probably tell from this process that keyword prioritization is as much an art as a science. Your initial prioritization at the start of your campaign will almost never turn out to be the best one. It is important to mix in some words that you are not sure about to gather information, rather than to play it safe and choose only words you expect will drive high conversion rates. Conversely, you should not go all out with many dubious choices because this will expend more resources that could be put to better use elsewhere. Target the words that seem to promise high conversion, but also go after some keywords in every stage of the Buyer's Journey to learn which ones convert for you better than others.

Now that you know how to prioritize your keywords, we turn to the second part of organization: how you structure your keywords so that you can manage them profitably.

Structure Your Paid Search Keywords

Even if you are a habitually sloppy type, you need to think about how to structure your paid search keywords. How you group your keywords will simplify the management of your paid search program, align ads to keywords, and enable you to measure performance you could never track any other way. Throughout the book, we've also advocated that you co-optimize paid and organic search together. So if you want to organize your organic search keywords the same way as paid, that is not a bad idea.

All search engines provide ways of organizing your keywords into logical groups of ads. Luckily, their approaches are very similar. Each search engine has the concept of an **account**, as we explained when you set up your account in Chapter 5, "Create Your Search Marketing Program." Even small accounts are too large to be manageable without logical subdivision, however, so each search engine gives you ways to slice and dice your keyword lists.

The first step of organizing keywords into **ad groups** is to decide the basis on which to split them. Different search marketers group their keywords different ways:

- **Division of audience:** You might have some keywords directed at business customers and others at consumers that will have different products and messages, so these could be segmented into different ad groups.

- **Division of market:** You will want to separate keywords by the country or location market, to account for different offers, price and languages.

- **Division of bidding:** If you are employing different bidding strategies or tactics with different groups of keywords, you must organize them into separate ad groups.

- **Division of product line:** Snap will place the *digital camera* keywords into a different set of ad groups than the *home theater* keywords.

- **Division of reporting:** Because you can roll up your measurements by ad group, you might want to isolate keywords from each other if you are testing something. For example, you might separate *Learn* stage keywords from *Shop* stage keywords so that you can test the difference in conversion rates. A good conversion rate for a *Learn* stage keyword might be unacceptable for a *Shop* stage keyword.

- **Division of message:** It can often make sense for all the keywords in an ad group to share the same advertising message. So all the Snap keywords for a certain product might have the same (or very similar) ad and the same landing page, whereas those for other products would not.

You can see there are many reasons to group keywords, but luckily many of them overlap. For example, you can group keywords for each individual product within a country that share the same message, with reporting divided on that same basis.

You should use ad groups to contain individual keywords and ads associated with them. You can also collect multiple ad groups into **campaigns**. Campaigns give you a higher-level organization that can make reporting much simpler. If you placed each related product within a country into an ad group, you could decide to do your reporting by country (by creating a campaign with all of the ad groups for that country) or by product (using a campaign that collected all of that product's ad groups). This way, you can use very specific ad groups to manage your keywords, but use campaigns to aggregate ad groups for reporting purposes. Although these constructs are designed for paid search keyword management, you should realize that grouping organic keywords for reporting purposes is a good idea, too.

You'll make your life easier by grouping keywords that share the same messages, or two to four versions of the same message. You will want to place synonyms, for example, in the same ad group because they might share the same ads and landing pages.

However you decide to divide your keywords, take advantage of what search engines offer you; it will simplify your reporting and your management.

Optimize Your Keyword Models

Organizing your keywords is an important step, as we just learned, but we've touched on only the simplest structuring techniques. Advanced search markets build **keyword models** that help them exhaustively cover the entire landscape of the content needs of their customers.

Most search marketers who resort to keyword modeling have tens of thousands—sometimes millions—of keywords, so you can imagine that it can be a complex topic. But you can see that the simple high-level keyword model in Exhibit 6-9 could be very useful in helping a pet supply manufacturer ensure that they don't forget an important keyword for cats that they already thought of for dogs. As you go through the list, you might find that you have added a keyword that doesn't make sense (e.g., *dognip*), but it is better to overgeneralize a keyword that you can later delete than to fail to list one that searchers are actually using.

Exhibit 6-9 A simple keyword model. A pet food manufacturer uses keyword modeling to ensure that the keyword list is exhaustive.

While ensuring completeness is one motivation of the keyword modeler, many search marketers find that the biggest value in keyword modeling is in the way it helps you segment a large list of keywords. As with any type of market segmentation, the purpose is to identify segments that are more valuable than others—segments that attract more loyal customers, or higher-spending customers, or easier-to-convert customers, as just a few examples. When you analyze your segments, you can find groups of keywords that you should spend more time and money on and others that should be forgotten.

Segmenting keywords is immensely valuable for several reasons:

- **Segmentation yields organization:** No one can manage a million individual keywords, so any reasonable grouping is better than nothing. You can even use multiple organizations that you slice and dice different ways to see how different segments perform.

- **Segmentation yields insight:** Some groupings will be silly, but some will be unexpectedly brilliant, by clustering together items that someone else might not have thought to connect. By allowing keywords to appear in multiple groupings, we can allow many different ways to cut the data.

- **Segmentation yields differentiation:** By analyzing unexpected groupings based on performance and other metadata, the company's differentiation from competitors might be understood in new ways. If you sell more canned organic dog food than other kinds of dog food, that fact tells you how customers think of your brand.

Let's look at a few techniques that you can use to optimize your keyword models.

Segment Your Keywords by Categories

Depending on your business, there might be lots of worthwhile ways to segment your keywords, so let's look at a couple of typical categories.

One very commonly used category is the *audience* of the searcher. For some kinds of companies, knowing *who* is searching makes a big difference in the number of conversions they get. Some searchers just buy more than others. In other cases, you will want to know the role or audience of the searcher so that you know what kinds of content to show the searcher.

Let's look at an example from the pharmaceutical industry in Exhibit 6-10. If you contrast the words in the left column with those on the right, you might notice that many of them mean something very similar. But the ones on the right are much more likely to be used by healthcare practitioners, whereas the ones on the left are more likely used by patients.

This audience segmentation technique can apply to B2B companies, too. IBM can sometimes identify keyword audiences by just examining the keywords—the same way that the pharmaceutical company did. Senior IT audiences focus on strategy, while lower-level IT managers tend to focus on uptime and implementing technology. Therefore, any keyword containing the word *strategy* was assigned to senior executive roles, while keywords with the words *implementation*, *monitoring*, or *performance* were assigned to the IT manager segment.

depression	antidepressant
depression treatment	partial dopamine agonist
bi-polar disorder	aripiprazole adjunctive use depression
bi-polar medication	abilify drug interactions
abilify	abilify contraindications
use abilify with another antidepressant	abilify caremark formulary
caremark abilify coverage	aripiprazole
generic abilify	

Exhibit 6-10   Keywords that reveal audience. A pharmaceutical company can look at the words used to guess the type of searcher they are attracting.

As just one example, IBM focused its cloud computing strategy campaign on CEOs and wrote all of its content for them. They assumed that CEOs cared about cloud strategies and that they comprised the most important audience to reach. But how could they be sure that their assumptions were correct?

IBM didn't take any chances. Because they were using LivePerson to chat with visitors who came to their site, they were able to ask those visitors their job titles—to verify the content was attracting the audiences expected. Exhibit 6-11 shows the surprising result. While one-third of visitors would not volunteer their titles, a miniscule fraction of 1% of the visitors stated they were CEOs. When they saw that the majority of the visitors were IT managers and consultants, they adjusted the content to these audiences—seeing an exponential increase in leads. If you don't use similar technology for your visitors, you could just as easily check the job titles collected from your leads to see whether your audience assumptions are holding up.

Job Title	Visitors	Percent
Unknown	12,223	33%
Consultant	9,763	26%
IT Manager	8,456	23%
CIO	3,986	11%
CTO	984	3%
VP Technology	882	2%
IT Services	663	2%
Owner	321	1%
CEO	12	0.03%
Total	37,290	100%

Exhibit 6-11   Keyword audiences. Just because they looked for *cloud computing strategy* topics didn't mean that they were CEOs.

Another often-used keyword category is the *timing* of the search. For most companies, any time a person searches is a good time to be included in the search results. But this may not be the case for all keywords, so you need to ask yourself whether any of your keywords are time sensitive. For organic search, you have no control over when your content is shown in response to a search, but you have control over the timing of your paid search ads.

As we discussed in Chapter 5, dayparting is a technique that allows you to adjust your bids or your ad content based on the time of day, day of the week, or other timing factors. Perhaps you'd want to add a Google AdWords Ad Extension to show your phone number in your ad during the hours that your call center is open. Or your restaurant can run a discount for a dinner special in the late afternoon and turn it off later. By using timing as a part of your keyword modeling, you can test these and countless other ideas to see which improve conversion rate and profitability.

Use Searcher Interests for Content Development

John Battelle has famously referred to search engines as the "database of intentions" by which he means that we can detect what our customers are interested in by the keywords they use. Global Strategies pioneered the process of "consumer intent modeling," segmenting keywords into logical clusters identifying the interests and intent of searchers.

For an example, a designer shapewear site analyzed keyword data to understand which features and functions searchers for *shapewear* wanted. They immediately found a number of missed opportunities. The keywords data showed people wanted to use their shaping leggings for yoga and running so that they looked trim while exercising. The product team had not identified the sporting vertical as a target market. The content team simply created new pages for shaping yoga and running leggings and they became top sellers immediately.

Further mining revealed that nearly 75% of the keyword volume contained a part of the body that the searcher wanted to shape. Simply creating pages and ads focused on keywords using the combination of a body part and a clothing type enabled them to capture these previously missed opportunities. Further analysis found searchers appending occasions to the type of shaping garment. The site brand team had previously described their item as a *tummy shaper* rather than as a *wedding tummy shaper* or *bridal shapewear*, which allowed them to add critical conversions.

This shapewear company also had shied away from keywords containing the words *plus size*, fearing potentially offending their shoppers. But keyword research indicated that women wanted to find *plus size tummy shapers*. Drilling into the keyword data can be a gold mine of opportunity if you take the time to understand what searchers need. Mining search keywords can be your most inexpensive and effective form of market research.

Use Social Data to Improve Keywords

Many companies have begun monitoring social media data in recent years, but few have mined social data to optimize keyword modeling. While most companies have focused on mainstream uses of social media listening, such as crisis management and customer service, the biggest value to your keyword modeling doesn't involve counting the number of tweets, likes, or followers.

Companies such as Converseon help clients sift through social media data to identify keywords that might not have been found through other forms of keyword research. Monitoring social media for emerging keywords can often spot trending new ideas. In addition, the use of **sentiment analysis** to identify negative feelings can help find problems that can be a perfect subject for content marketing approaches. High volume negative subjects can be the very problems that searchers are trying to solve. If your products solve them, these can be your best targets.

For example, an online travel site used social media monitoring to identify destinations of interest for long weekends. Their analysis found that searchers were making comments and asking questions about destinations for holiday trips a full 45 days before they planned to market trips for those weekends. In response, they freshened up their paid search ads and their organic search snippets to mention the holidays and the popular destinations—and their conversions increased.

Social media listening can also reveal when customer confusion is derailing a new product. For example, when Absolut Vodka launched their new Hibiscus Flavored Vodka product, social media monitoring detected that people were unsure of how hibiscus tastes. Unlike raspberry or vanilla, searchers did not know what kinds of cocktail recipes hibiscus would work with. Absolut quickly began promoting appropriate cocktail recipe ideas through social media, which inspired artisan mixologists to create many new drink ideas. Absolut posted these recipes on their product page to capture searchers with keywords such as *what to mix with absolut hibiscus* or *what does absolut hibiscus taste like*. If you are not monitoring social media reaction to new products, you might be missing some of your most important keywords.

For Snap Electrics, the photo sharing site Flickr is a goldmine of data for them to understand the photo habits of users. In addition to mining keywords from metatags, they can total the number of photos by each model of camera to stay on top of popularity trends within their prime target market—the most prolific photographers.

Don't overlook this key source of information. Just as co-optimizing your keywords lists between paid and organic search can improve the completeness of both sets, your social media listening team is monitoring dozens if not hundreds of keywords that can help you optimize your keyword models.

Summary

Choosing and classifying your target keywords is the real beginning of any organic or paid search marketing campaign. After you have chosen the product or other focus of your campaign, you must carefully decide which keywords to target before you can start the real work of search marketing.

In this chapter, you learned the value of careful keyword targeting, along with a philosophy that helps you make decisions every step of the way. Rather than blindly reaching for the most popular keywords, or gravitating to unpopular keywords because they are "easy" to get high rankings for, you saw how "just right" keywords closely target your site, almost regardless of popularity.

We walked through the entire keyword planning process step by step, discovering how to gather a list of keyword candidates, how to research each candidate to uncover hidden variations and determine its popularity with searchers, and how to prioritize the keyword list so that the most valuable ones get the most attention in the campaign. You also learned how to organize your list and to optimize your keyword modeling.

In the next chapter, we focus on ensuring that your content is listed. Now that you know which keywords drive your customers, it's time to ensure that your content is listed in organic search and that you have paid search ads running for those keywords. Knowing what people are looking for is just the first step. Now let's start getting your content in front of them.

CHAPTER 7

Get Your Content Listed

"You've got to be in it to win it," the lottery commercials blare, but they do have a point. Winners did have to buy a ticket, or they would never have won. To win the search lottery, search marketers need to buy tickets, too; you need your content listed with the search engines. The more content you have listed, the more chances you have to win the search lottery. And take heart, because you have much better odds at winning the search lottery than the Powerball lottery.

To win, however, you need to know the rules of the game—and to play by them. That's what we do in this chapter. But it isn't just one game; there are actually several different games:

- **Website content:** Organic search is the most complex game with lots of rules. We spend most of this chapter helping you get your website content listed in each search engine's organic search index.

- **Social content:** You have lots of important content outside of your website. Most is easily indexed, but you need to pay attention to a few rules here, too.

- **Local content:** If you have physical locations that you want customers to find, understanding how to get your locations listed might be your most important search activity.

- **Products:** If you have a product catalog that you want to be shown in Product Search results, you need to know how to get it loaded up.

Not all of these games might make sense for your company to play, but we will explain them all if you need them.

Get Your Pages Listed in Organic Search Indexes

In the organic search lottery, you must learn the rules that **spiders** play by, so that your site plays by them, too. After you understand what spiders cannot or will not do, you can make sure that your site does not run afoul of the rules. Because when you break these spider rules, your page will not be indexed. And if your page is not in the index, it cannot be found by searchers.

It might sound simple, but getting web pages indexed by search engines can be challenging for corporate websites. Corporate websites are often designed without spider rules in mind, so their pages are frequently left out of search indexes. As you start your organic search marketing efforts, getting your pages indexed is the first step to take, because it can take some time for your team to correct the design problems you find on your site. You need to discover whether your pages are indexed, to diagnose indexing problems when they are not, and to correct them.

In this section, you will learn to

- **Assess how many of your pages are indexed:** A few sites have no pages indexed at all, but you want to know how many yours has.

- **Increase the number of pages indexed:** That's the most important job here. What problems are preventing your site from having all of its pages indexed, and what can be done to correct them?

Remember, for organic search, pages that are missing from the index can never be found by searchers. This section helps you include as many of your pages as possible in each search index.

Assess How Many Pages Are Indexed

Maybe we scared you when we said that some sites have no pages indexed. Not many sites have this problem, but a few do. More likely, you have pages already stored in the search indexes for each major search engine, but wouldn't you like to know how many? That's what we tackle here.

How Many Pages on Your Site Are Indexed?

The number of your site's pages that you want indexed is *all* of them—all of the *public* pages, anyway. Many of your pages might be *private*—unavailable to the general public because they are secured behind passwords—but that's fine, because you do not want private pages indexed for the whole world to see anyway. No, the real problem is when public pages that you want to be searched are missing from the index.

Later in this chapter, we look at why some of your public pages are missing from search indexes, but first, we simply check how many pages you already have indexed.

Determine How Many Pages You Have   Although this might sound exceedingly odd to those of you with smaller sites, it is not always easy to know how many pages are in a website. Especially for large decentralized sites, it might require a lot of thought to even estimate the total number of pages in your website. If you can easily estimate the number of pages on your site, feel free to skip ahead to the next section to check how many pages you have indexed.

As you begin the task of counting your web pages, keep in mind that you should be counting "publicly available" pages only. That means no private (secured) pages—pages locked behind passwords—ought to be part of your calculation, because you do not want those pages on public display in a search engine. So, if you have special pages that show your customers their invoices or their order status, it makes sense that you have them password-protected so that each customer sees only his own information. Don't count these pages in your site total, because you do not want them in the search indexes anyway.

It's wonderful if you know precisely the total number of pages on your site, but it is not required to be so accurate. If you do not know the exact number, there are several ways to make a reasonable estimate:

- **Ask your webmaster:** Your webmaster might not know either, but he has probably been asked this question before and at least he has thought about the answer. Question your webmaster's logic in guessing the total so that you can evaluate its credibility.

- **Check your XML sitemaps:** As you'll see later in the chapter, Extensible Markup Language (XML) sitemaps are a great way to get more pages indexed on your site. But they are also a way to get at least a rudimentary idea of how many pages you have.

- **Check your website search engine:** If you have a search engine that allows visitors to search only your site, check to see how many of your website's pages are in your website search index. Be aware that if your website search engine's index is updated through crawling, your site search index will be missing many of the same pages that Google and other Internet search engines are missing. (If you instead have a content management system pushing its content into the website search index, it is likely to include all the pages.)

- **Add up the counts from your content sources:** Most web pages are really document pages; they have a document somewhere in your content management system or your eCommerce catalog. For example, AbsolutDrinks.com has a catalog page for each product, and they know they have 3,239 drinks in their database, so they expect to have at least that many pages indexed. Granted, you might not be able to count all of your pages accurately using this method, but it helps you make a more accurate estimate than taking a stab in the dark.

- **Check your web analytics:** Most web analytics programs (such as Google Analytics) can provide a list of all the pages that received at least one visit in the last year, for example. Although this might not be a comprehensive list of all pages, we suspect that pages that haven't been visited in a year aren't all that important anyway, so it gives a good enough count.

- **Use a special spider:** You can unleash a special spider on your site, such as the free Xenu (home.snafu.de/tilman/xenulink.html) or Screaming Frog (screamingfrog.co.uk/seo-spider/). Unfortunately, as with a website search engine, many of the same barriers that block Internet search spiders will block these special spiders, too. The good news is that special spiders can show you where they were blocked, so that you can take the corrective actions we show later in this chapter.

After you have estimated how many pages are on your site, you are ready to check how many pages you have indexed in the major search engines.

Check How Many Pages Are Indexed   Search engines understand that you want to know how many pages of your site are indexed, and they have made it easy to do. Every search engine has a special search operator designed to show you how many pages it has stored in its index for a particular site.

To check how many pages you currently have included, enter *site:yourdomain.com* into the keyword box in Google or Bing. That special site: operator will display a rough estimate of the number of pages indexed on the *yourdomain* website, as shown in Exhibit 7-1.

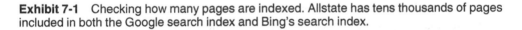

Most search engines accept what's called the *site*: *command* or *site*: operator along with your domain to show you how many pages are in their search index from your site.

Notice that there is a different number of pages in Bing's search index than in Google's.

Exhibit 7-1   Checking how many pages are indexed. Allstate has tens thousands of pages included in both the Google search index and Bing's search index.

If you've signed up for Google and Bing Webmaster Tools, you can get more accurate count of your pages indexed in those search engines by signing into your respective accounts. Both Google and Bing give you a good sense of how many pages they have and some of the errors they have detected. Because this comes from the search engines themselves, it's often the best source of information.

Don't expect the same number of pages to be indexed in all search engines. Each search engine has its own spider and they each work differently and they come to your site at different times. You will almost always see a different number of pages indexed in different search engines for the same site.

Calculate Your Inclusion Ratio   You probably already guessed how to calculate your **inclusion ratio** (the percentage of your site's pages residing in a search index). Just take the number of pages found in a search index (Bing, for example) and divide that by the total number of pages you have estimated to be on your site. For example, if Bing reports that you have 10,000 pages indexed, and your content management system has 15,000 documents in it, your Bing inclusion ratio is $10,000 \div 15,000 = 0.67$, or 67% (see Exhibit 7-2).

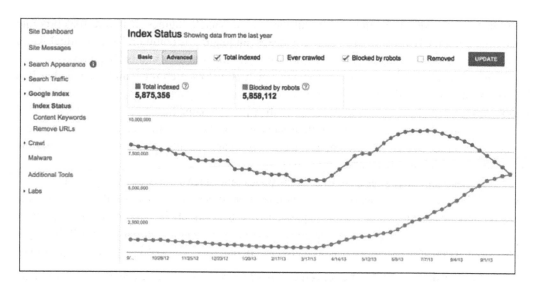

Exhibit 7-2   Using Google Webmaster Tools to check indexed pages. Both Bing and Google offer ways for webmasters to see how many pages are indexed, and why some pages might go missing.

So what is the right metric to shoot for? It is minimally acceptable for you to have about 50% of your publicly available pages in the search indexes, but you don't have to settle for that. You can get nearly 100% included, if you work at it.

On rare occasions, you might find a website whose inclusion ratio exceeds 100%. No, the search engine is not handing out special bonus pages. Instead, you may have a serious problem on your site. The search index might contain duplicate pages, possibly because you have many dynamic URLs (which are explained later in the chapter). The search index might include error pages that are not returning the proper error codes. In some scenarios, such as poorly imple-mented faceted navigation, the spider can get stuck indexing thousands of useless pages until it gives up—probably without indexing some of the important pages on your site. Even more seri-ous, your site's private content (information that should be protected from public view) might be in the search index through a security error. Or, you might have underestimated the total pages on your site, which would be the happiest cause of a runaway inclusion ratio.

If you have nearly 100% of your site's pages indexed in all search engines, that's great, but most websites have far less than 100% indexed; some have less than 5%. Next, you will learn how to increase your inclusion ratio, perhaps to 100%.

What If Your Site Is Not Indexed at All?

Let's take a look at an unusual but critical situation: What if your site has *no* pages in the search indexes? If your business has been around for a while and has a website, your site is overwhelmingly likely to be indexed by all the leading search engines. It is rare for corporate sites to be completely missing from search indexes, although it is common for individual pages from the site to be missing. (We show you how to figure *that* out later in this chapter.)

One way to tell whether your site is indexed at all is to search for it and see whether it is found. (Yeah, we figured you thought of that one.) If your company has a common name (AAA Plumbing), you might want to search for more than just the name (*aaa plumbing syracuse*). It's common for site owners to panic when their sites are not shown by the search engine for these navigational keywords for their company names. It's easy to jump to the conclusion that the entire site is not indexed, but that is rarely the case.

Nearly all corporate sites have their home pages (and at least a few other pages) in the leading search indexes, but if somehow you do not, read on. It is unlikely but possible that your site is completely missing in action—it *has* happened, even to relatively large companies. Or perhaps your search marketing program's scope does not cover your whole company, but *all* the pages within your scope are missing from search engines. In that case, you need to ask a few questions:

- **Is your site banned by the search engines?** Search engines have specific rules for being included in their index. Sites that violate these rules might find all of their pages removed from the search index.

- **Is the spider visiting your site?** Your pages cannot be indexed if the spider never comes. Later, we tell you how to check.

- **Are other sites linking to yours?** Spiders find your site by following links from other sites, so you must verify that your site is linked into the larger web.

If you can find at least a few pages of your site when you perform searches in the major search engines, you can skip ahead to the next section to determine how many pages you have indexed. If your site is not found at all, however, you must explore these questions to solve the mystery of the missing site.

Verify Your Site Is Not Banned or Penalized   The most difficult situation occurs when one or more search engines have *banned* or *penalized* your site. If your site is well represented in some search engines, but completely missing in others, your site might be banned. Sites are banned when search engines conclude that those sites are trying to "fool" the search engine to rank that site's pages more highly than they deserve.

Search engines do not ban sites on a whim—they do so only when your site has persistently violated their rules. As you might expect, some search marketers are unscrupulous, trying to take unfair advantage with tricks that provide an edge. Your company might have unwittingly become involved with an unethical search marketing consultant who uses **spam** techniques that try to fool the search engine, or you might have unwittingly violated a search engine's guidelines. (You can look at Google's guidelines at google.com/webmasters/guidelines.html; other search engines have similar rules.)

If your violation of the rules is not severe enough for a search engine to ban your site, you still might suffer from **penalization**—when the search engine starts dropping large numbers of your pages from its index or begins to lower your search rankings. You should investigate further if you see the following:

- You receive notification of an automated or manual action.
- Your site's search engine referrals have dropped drastically in a short period of time.
- The number of your site's pages included in the search index rapidly decreases.
- Your home page can be found only by a direct search on the URL—informational keywords containing words on your home page do not seem to find it.

If you suspect a problem, you first need to diagnose the cause. As you can see in Exhibit 7-3, both Bing and Google post problems they find with your website in your Webmaster Tools accounts and will email you notifications. Even if you don't receive an email, you should log in periodically to check.

Crawl Error Alert for .... .com: 503 (Service Unavailable)   ×

    Site: http:................. .com/
    Date: 9/23/2013
    Priority: High

Dear Webmaster,

We encountered a large number of requests that returned the following status: **503 (Service Unavailable)**.

We saw **4762 errors** of this type, which accounts for **6 percent** of all requests we made during the last 24 hours.

Explanation/Recommended Action:
Your server reported that it was not able to handle our requests. This could have been a temporary issue, but you check your logs and scripts for performance-related issues.
To see which pages were affected check Crawl Information. Note that we were able to send this message before uploading the full crawl data to your Webmaster Account so there may be a delay. Learn more.

Thanks,
The Bing Webmaster Team

Manual Actions

Site-wide matches None

▾Partial matches Some manual actions apply to specific pages, sections, or links

Reason	Affects
Unnatural links to your site—impacts links Google has detected a pattern of unnatural artificial, deceptive, or manipulative links pointing to pages on this site. Some links may be outside of the webmaster's control, so for this incident we are taking targeted action on the unnatural links instead of on the site's ranking as a whole. Learn more.	**Some incoming links. Examples:** http://bank-of-america-mortgageygaqgpphif.blogspot.com /2008/04/making-money-easily.html

Exhibit 7-3 Notifications from Webmaster Tools. Both Bing and Google offer ways for webmasters to see whether their organic search rankings have been affected by penalties.

Other search engines might not be so forthcoming, so you need to figure out what the problem could be. In the next section, we discuss a spam technique called **cloaking**. We cover **doorway pages** and other stupid content tricks in Chapter 8, "Optimize Your Content," and **link**

farms in Chapter 9, "Prove Your Content's Quality." These are the most common spam techniques. If your site has been banned or penalized for using these techniques, you can clean up your site and request reinstatement, which is usually granted (although reinstatement sometimes requires an extended period of explanation and begging).

Make Sure the Spider Is Visiting   If the spiders are not coming to your site, your pages cannot be indexed and your site will not be found by organic searchers. Your webmaster can help you check your web servers' **log files** to see which search spiders have been visiting your site. (Most web servers are configured to log search spider visits, but some servers might need to be adjusted by your webmaster to capture this important information.) The log file indicates the name of the **user agent** that accessed the page noted, which indicates the software, such as a web browser, that was used to see the page.

Because the great majority of the visits to your website are in fact from web browsers, your site's log listing will show the user agent names from each web browser, such as Chrome or Firefox. But a small number of log entries might indicate that the spiders are crawling. Googlebot, as you might surmise, is Google's user agent, but our website has a complete list (SEMincBook.com/user-agents).

By examining your log, you can tell which spiders are crawling your site, and how frequently they do so. Spammers use these user agent names for more nefarious purposes, however. Variously known as **cloaking** or **IP delivery**, they use a high-tech version of the old "bait-and-switch" scam. Here's how it works. The spammer sets up a URL served by a program dynamically and waits for someone to request it. When the request is received, the user agent name and its IP address are checked. If a browser is making the request (with Mozilla in the name, for example), the program returns the page that human visitors should see. If it is a search engine's spider, however, the program sends back a page full of keywords designed to attain a high search ranking. There are situations where you can legitimately use IP delivery techniques, but using this technique to fool a search engine about what visitors see on the page is clearly spam, and the search engines will deal with it harshly. Unless you know that what you are doing is acceptable, cloaking is a dangerous game that can get your site banned. Cloaking can bring quick rankings, but when competitors see what you are doing, they will complain to the search engines and shut you down.

Each search engine spider has its own frequency for returning to your website. Spiders return to a typical website at least once a month, but popular corporate websites might be revisited weekly, or even daily. In general, spiders crawl sites based on their importance, with more important sites and more important pages being crawled more frequently. By analyzing how frequently spiders crawl your pages, and which pages they check the most, you will know how quickly content changes on your site will be reflected in search indexes.

Although it is rare to find a site that the spiders do not visit at all, it can happen for a few reasons:

- **Your site is not linked:** If you have a brand new site that is not linked to by any other site in the spider's path, you will not get any spider visits. If the search engine spider does not know your site exists, it obviously cannot visit.

- **Links to your site are not effective:** Some links cannot be followed by spiders, for many reasons that we get into later in this chapter. Or the links to your site are from sites that themselves are not crawled by spiders, perhaps because they are also new, or possibly because they are banned for using unethical techniques.

- **The spider has given up:** Perhaps the spider was visiting your site at one time, but your site was blocked so that the spider could not index any pages in the search index. After a few months of fruitless visits, spiders sometimes permanently stop visiting.

If your site truly is not being visited by spiders, the remedy depends on which of the above reasons is the cause. If your site is not linked or links to your site are not effective, the best way to get the spider to visit is to make sure other well-respected sites link to yours (explained in more detail later). If the spider has given up, first remove the spider trap (also explained later), and then you should manually submit your site to the search engines, as explained below.

Search engines vastly prefer to find new sites by following links because analyzing link patterns is one of the ways engines judge relevance; if your site is linked and spiders are not visiting, however, you should manually submit your home page's URL. (If you create a new site but are too impatient to wait until someone links to you, you can also submit, but waiting to be found from a link will help your pages rank higher.)

Search engines typically allow you to submit your content with an "Add URL" page. (At Google it's at google.com/addurl, and at Bing it's at bing.com/toolbox/submit-site-url.) But if you have access to Google and Bing Webmaster Tools, you might rather use their "Fetch as" function. Tests have shown that fetching as the search engine gives instant feedback on the spider's ability to reach and index the page. In addition to this feedback, we find that the search results are updated typically within four hours of your request. This is a great way to make quick changes to your search result snippets, for example. Unfortunately, this magical function is capped at a limited number of requests each month so that it is not abused.

Remember, if your site is missing from multiple search indexes, you need to submit to each search engine. Typically, pages submitted are included in the search index within a few weeks; you can check your log files to see whether the spider is visiting.

Submitting to local or country-specific search engines is no different from worldwide search engines. The spiders can detect the language of the site and will add it into the appropriate-language version of the index, which we cover in detail in Chapter 8.

WHAT *NOT* TO DO IF YOUR SITE IS MISSING FROM INDEXES

Before you get excited about submitting all your web pages to the search engines, a word of caution is in order. Some will advise you to submit your site early and often, and to submit many pages from your site. *Don't.* It is a lot more complicated than that.

Submitting your site should be a last resort because you have tried everything else without success—you cannot get anyone to link to your site, or your site has been blocked so long that the spider has given up. If you are forced to submit, submit only your home page. The spider should be able to find the rest of your pages from your home page. (If that isn't true, and the other pages on your site need attention, we'll explain how to submit an XML sitemap later in the chapter.) Often, people submit their sites over and over without ever checking to see whether the spider is blocked from their site. Before submitting, follow the advice in this chapter first. If you do, you will probably see that you do not need to submit after all.

 Even worse than manually submitting your site is automatic submission. You might have received unsolicited emails offering to submit your site to thousands of search engines for $19.95. The email might include some compelling statistics about millions of visitors this service will generate. Avoid "automated submissions" entirely. If you are lucky, these services just set you back $20 and do no harm. But some search engines consider these automated submissions to be spam, and many actually have measures in place to block such submissions. At best, these submissions are ignored, but at worst your site could be penalized or banned for excessive submissions.

Get Sites to Link to You   As we have emphasized, the best way to get indexed is through a link from another site (one that is already indexed itself). If you have a well-established site, you have probably already attracted many links, but a new site obviously does not have any.

The best kind of link is one from a high-profile site, but almost any link has some value. By creating high-quality content on a subject, you will eventually attract links from other sites. Chapter 9 explains how to attract more links to your site, an important subject whether your site is new or well known.

Increase the Number of Indexed Pages

After you have determined that your site has at least one page in each search engine's index, and you have calculated how many pages you have indexed, you are certain to be greedy for more. The number of pages you can have indexed is limited only by the number of pages on your site. Many sites have millions of pages included, whereas some prominent websites have only their home page indexed.

You can take several steps to raise the inclusion ratio of your site, including the following:

- **Eliminate spider traps:** Your website might actually prevent the spiders from indexing your pages. You will learn what the traps are and how you can spring the spider from each one.

- **Reduce ignored content:** Spiders have certain rules they live by, and if your content breaks the rules, you lose. Find out what those rules are and how to reduce the amount of content spiders ignore on your site.

- **Create spider paths:** You can coax spiders to index more of your site by creating sitemaps and other navigation that simplifies the link structure for all of your site's pages.

Many complain about the inability of spiders to index certain content. Although we are the first to agree that spiders can improve their crawling techniques, there are good reasons why spiders stay away from some of this content. You have a choice as to whether you wring your hands and complain about the spiders or set to work pleasing them so your pages are indexed. You can guess which path will be more successful.

If your site is suffering from a low inclusion ratio, you can take several steps, but eliminating spider traps is the most promising place to start.

Eliminate Spider Traps

As we have said before, spiders cannot index all pages. But we have yet to say what causes problems with the spiders. That's where we're going now.

Spiders are actually rather delicate creatures, and they can be thrown off by a wide variety of problems that we call **spider traps**. Spider traps are barriers that prevent spiders from crawling a site, usually stemming from technical approaches to displaying web pages that work fine for browsers, but do not work for spiders. By eliminating these techniques from your site, you allow spiders to index more of your pages.

Unfortunately, many spider traps are the product of highly advanced technical approaches and highly creative user-experience designs—which were frightfully expensive to develop. No one wants to hear, after all the money was spent, that your site has been shut out of search. Yet that is the bad news that you might need to convey.

Luckily, spiders become more sophisticated every year. Designs that trapped spiders a few years ago are now okay. But you need to keep up with spider advances to employ some cutting-edge techniques.

So here they come! Here are the most widespread spider traps.

Carefully Set Robots Directives   Pretend that you are the webmaster of your site, and you just learned that a software probe has entered your website and appears to be examining every page on the site. And it seems to come back over and over again. Sounds like a security problem, doesn't it? Even if you could assure yourself that nothing nefarious is afoot, it is wasting the time of your servers.

Sometimes, that is how webmasters view search spiders: a menace that needs to be controlled. And the robots.txt file is the way to control spiders.

It is a remarkably innocuous-looking file, a simple text file that is placed in the root directory of a web server. Your robots.txt file tells the spider what files it is allowed to look at on that server. It is technically possible for the spider to look at any file it wants, but there is a gentleman's agreement that spiders will be polite and abide by the instructions to avoid the disallowed files.

A robots.txt file contains only two operative statements:

- **user-agent:** The user agent statement defines which spiders the next disallow statement applies to. If you code an asterisk for the user agent, you are referring to all spiders, but you can also specify the name of a particular spider.

- **disallow:** The disallow statement specifies which files the spider is not permitted to crawl. You can specify a precise filename or any part of a name or directory name; the spider will treat that as a matching expression and disallow any file that matches that part of the name. So, specifying *e* eliminates all files starting with *e* from the crawl, as well as all files in any directory that begins with *e*. Specifying / disallows all files.

Exhibit 7-4 shows a robots.txt file with explanations of what each line means. Note especially that the files listed are case sensitive. In the case of Microsoft Internet Information Services (IIS) servers, especially, that means you might need to list your directives for whatever case your server uses, such as *disallow: /cart*, and *disallow: /Cart* (and possibly other variations).

```
robots.txt - Notepad
File  Edit  Format  View  Help

User-agent:   *
Disallow:     /cgi-bin          Block all spiders from
Disallow:     /java             examining the cgi-bin and
                                java directories.

                                Stop "roguespider"
User-agent:   roguespider       from crawling any file
Disallow:     /
```

Exhibit 7-4   Coding robots.txt files. Robots.txt files direct the spider on how to crawl your website, or direct them to avoid your site completely.

Webmasters have a legitimate reason to keep spiders out of certain directories on their servers: server performance. Most web servers have programs stored in the cgi-bin directory, so it is a good idea to have your robots.txt file say "disallow: /cgi-bin/" to save the server from having to send the spider all those program files the spider does not need to see anyway. The trouble comes when an unsuspecting webmaster does not understand the implications of disallowing other files, or all files.

Although many webmasters use the robots.txt file to deliberately exclude spiders, accidental exclusion is all too common. Imagine a case where this file was used on a beta site to hide it from spiders before the site was launched. Unfortunately, the exclusionary robots.txt file might be left in place after launch, causing the entire website to disappear from all search indexes. Sometimes search engines don't remove the pages from the search index, but they do remove descriptions and other information that help the pages rank highly and get clicked on, so it is still a serious situation.

If coding this robots.txt file seems dangerous to you, given the impact of an error, you are paying attention. To help you avoid these damaging errors, many free tools exist that can help you test your robots.txt files. You can find a list of them at our website (SEMincBook.com/robots-checkers).

In addition to robots.txt that controls spiders across your entire site, there is a way to instruct spiders on every page—the **robots metatag**. In the `<head>` section of the HTML of your page, a series of metatags are typically found in the form `<meta name="type">` (where the `"type"` is the kind of metatag). One such metatag type is the robots tag (`<meta name="robots">`), which can control whether the page should be indexed and whether links from the page should be followed.

Exhibit 7-5 shows the variations available in the robots metatag for restricting indexing (placing the content in the index) and `"link following"` (using pages linked from this page as the next page to crawl). If the robots metatag is missing, the page is treated as if `"index, follow"` was specified.

Instructs spiders to index the page, but not follow any links on the page:

```
<meta name="robots" content="index,nofollow">
```

Instructs spiders not to index the page, but to follow all links to other pages:

```
<meta name="robots" content="noindex,follow">
```

Exhibit 7-5 Coding robots tags. Robots tags on your web page direct the spider on whether to index the page, follow links from it, or do neither.

Although you would normally want your pages to be coded without robots metatags (or with robots metatags specified as `"index, follow"`), there are legitimate reasons to use a robots tag to suppress spiders. There's no need to index software programs, for example.

Another reason to use a "noindex" robots tag is to prevent an error for the visitor. Your commerce facility might require a certain route through pages to work properly—you cannot land on the site at the shopping cart page, for example. Because there is no reason to have the shopping cart page indexed, you can code "noindex,nofollow" on that page to prevent searchers from falling into your cart.

When many pages from your site are indexed, but a few that should be indexed are not, this robots tag is sometimes the culprit. Unfortunately, it is common for this tag to be defined incorrectly in templates used to create many pages on your site. Or misguided web developers employ the tags incorrectly. This was the case at Snap Electronics.

If you recall from Chapter 5, "Create Your Search Marketing Program," Snap's search landing page for the keyword *best digital camera* was not in any of the indexes. Examining the pages showed that a number of Snap pages had restrictive robots tags. The product directory page was using the <meta name="robots" content="index,nofollow"> version of the tag. This caused the spider not to follow any of the directory page's links to the actual product pages. Moreover, even if this problem had not existed, each of the actual product pages had the <meta name="robots" content="noindex,nofollow"> version of the tag. The web developers indicated it was done so that the commerce system would not be overloaded by search engine spiders. After educating the developers about search marketing, the tags were removed and the pages were indexed.

You might be wondering how the rbots.txt file and the robots metatags might work together on your site. Let's look at an example. If the robots.txt file disallows a particular page, it does not matter what the robots metatag on that page says because the spider will not look at the page at all. If the page is allowed by the robots.txt instructions, however, the robots metatag is consulted by the spider as it looks at the page.

Robots directives are not the only way to control how the spider controls your site. Later in this chapter, we explain ways to change the way the spiders operate on your site, but first we want to finish explaining the various spider traps that can bedevil your site.

Eliminate Pop-Up Windows   Most web users dislike **pop-up windows**—those annoying little ads that get in your face when you are trying to do something else. Pop-up ads are so universally reviled that most browsers include pop-up blockers that are turned on by default. A few sites still use pop-ups, however, believing that drawing attention to the window is more important than what web users want.

Some websites use pop-up windows for more than ads. So, if user hatred is not enough to cure you of pop-up windows, maybe this is: Spiders cannot see them. If your site uses pop-ups to display related content, that content will not get indexed. Even worse, if your site uses pop-ups to show menus of links to other pages, the spider cannot follow those links, and those pages cannot be reached by the spider.

If your site uses pop-ups to display complementary content, the only way to get that content indexed is to stop using pop-up windows. You must add that content to the page that it complements, or you must create a standard web page with a normal link to it. If you are having trouble convincing your extended search team to dump pop-ups, remind them that the rise of pop-up blockers means that many of your visitors are not seeing the content in the pop-up windows.

If you are using pop-up windows for navigation menus, you can correct this spider trap in the same way, by adding the links to each page that requires them and removing the pop-up, but you have another choice, too. You can decide to leave your existing pop-up navigation in place, but provide alternative paths to your pages that the spiders can follow. We cover these so-called spider paths later in the chapter.

Don't Rely on Pull-Down Navigation   As with pop-up windows, spiders are sometimes trapped by pull-down navigation shown with JavaScript coding. And spiders are stymied by these JavaScript pull-downs for the same reason as with pop-ups: They cannot simulate clicking the links. As you might expect, the same solutions prescribed for pop-up navigation will work here as well: You can redo the links with full path URL's, use normal HTML, or you can provide alternative paths that allow the spider to reach those pages. Exhibit 7-6 shows how plain old HTML with a well-done style sheet can achieve the same visual effect.

Clever use of HTML and style sheets can provide the same pull-down visual effect as JavaScript, without blocking search spiders.

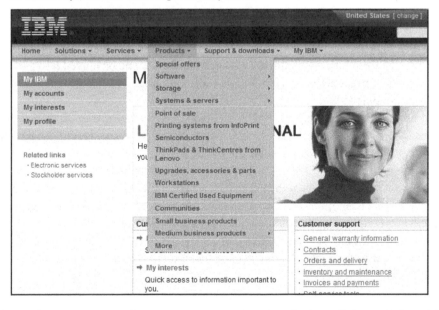

Exhibit 7-6   Pull-down navigation can prevent crawling. JavaScript pull-down windows block spiders, but you can achieve the same effect with HTML.

In addition to those solutions, there is one more way to remove the JavaScript spider trap: through the use of the `<noscript>` tag. People familiar with HTML know that some older browsers and mobile devices do not support JavaScript, and that a few web users disable JavaScript on their browsers. These browsers that are not running JavaScript cannot execute the JavaScript code found on web pages, which can cause big problems. If your pull-down navigation requires JavaScript, non-JavaScript browsers cannot display any navigation to their users.

Enter the `<noscript>` tag. Page designers can add this tag to provide alternative code for any browser that does not support JavaScript—or for any user who has disabled JavaScript. Spiders will not execute JavaScript, so they process the `<noscript>` code instead. If you must use JavaScript navigation, you can place standard HTML link code in your `<noscript>` section. However, for search spiders to follow the links, they must contain the full path names (starting with http) for each linked page. To further ensure the spiders can find these pages, list these pages in your sitemap.

Remember that this advice applies only to JavaScript *navigation*. Other uses of JavaScript can create pleasing user experiences without upsetting the spider in any way.

Simplify Dynamic URLs   So-called **dynamic web pages** are those whose HTML code is not stored permanently in files on your web server. Instead, for a dynamic page, a program creates the HTML "on-the-fly"—whenever a visitor requests to view that page—and the browser displays that HTML just as if it had been stored in a file.

In the earliest days of the web, every web page was created by someone opening a file and entering his HTML code into the file. The name of the file and the directory it was saved within became its URL. So, if you created a file called sale.html and placed it in a top-level directory called "offers" on your web server, your URL would be yourdomain.com/offers/sale.html (and that URL remained the same until you changed the file's name or moved it to a new directory). These kinds of pages are now referred to as **static web pages**, to distinguish them from the dynamic pages possible today.

It did not take long to bump into the limitations of static pages; they contained the exact same information every time they were viewed. Soon, clever programmers came up with ways for a web server to run a program to dynamically create the page's HTML and return it to the visitor's web browser. That way, there never needs to be a file containing the HTML. The program can generate the HTML the moment the page is requested for viewing. At first, only a few pages were generated dynamically, but the rise of content management systems—even free ones such as WordPress and Drupal—have transformed the web into mostly dynamic pages.

Dynamic web pages often have URLs that look different; they contain special characters that would not occur in the name of a directory or file. Exhibit 7-7 dissects a dynamic URL and shows what each part of it means.

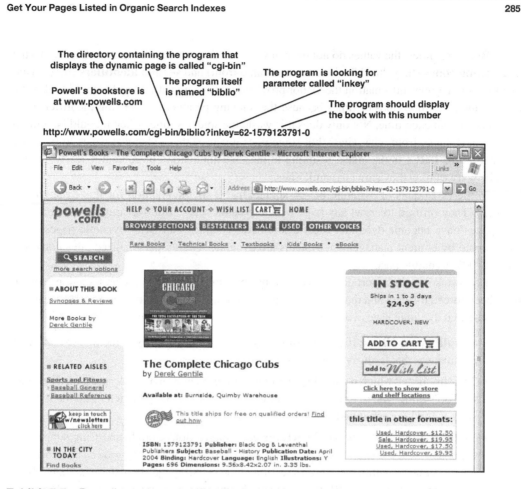

Exhibit 7-7 Decoding a dynamic URL. Each part of a dynamic URL has a specific meaning that governs which content appears on the dynamic page.

The **parameters** in each dynamic URL (the words that follow question mark [?] and any ampersands [&]) are what might cause complications for spiders. Because just about any **value** (the words that follow the equals sign character [=]) can be passed to the variable, search spiders have no way of knowing how many different variations of a page can be shown. Sometimes, different values passed to each parameter indicate a legitimate difference in the pages, such as in Exhibit 7-7—each book has a different number. At other times, content management systems repeat parameters or sort them in random order, which makes a single page look like multiple ones.

But other times, the values do not have anything to do with what content is displayed, such as **tracking codes** (they "track" where visitors came from) and **session identifiers** (they ensure that pages remember information the visitor provided through a visit). A spider could look at the exact same page thousands of times because the tracking parameter or session identifier in the URL is different each time. Not only does this waste the spider's time (when it could be looking at truly new pages from other sites), but sometimes it causes these identical pages to be stored under multiple URLs in the index, resulting in massive duplication of content. Clearly, spiders must be wary of how they crawl dynamic sites.

In the early days of dynamic pages, spiders had a simple solution for this dynamic site problem: They refused to crawl any page with a dynamic URL. But over time, more and more web pages have become dynamic. Most eCommerce catalogs consist of dynamic pages. Most sites served by content management systems are dynamic. Highly personalized sites consist of almost 100% dynamic pages.

Because so much important web content has become dynamic, the search engines spiders have been forced to adapt and they can crawl at least some kinds of dynamic pages. How can you make sure that dynamic pages you want in the index actually get into the index?

- **Simplify your URLs:** If you can shorten your dynamic URLs by reducing the number of parameters, that is always a good step to take.

- **Tell the spider which dynamic parameters to ignore:** Both Google and Bing Webmaster Tools allow you to tell their spiders which dynamic URL parameters can be ignored, such as tracking codes and session identifiers.

- **Tell the spider the "correct" URL for each page:** Both Google and Bing support the canonical tag (`<link rel="canonical" href="http://yoursite.com/">`), which is placed within the `<head>` section of the HTML page. The canonical tag tells the search spider the exact URL that the page should be stored under, no matter what actual URL caused the spider to retrieve the page. Dynamic pages might be generated under different URLs, but if the matching pages share the same canonical URL, they won't fool spiders.

- **Link to the "correct" URL from category lists or sitemaps:** Because some dynamic pages can use almost any value for its parameters, there is no way for the search spider to know every valid product number for your product catalog. You must ensure that there are direct links to every valid dynamic page on your site.

There is one more way to tame dynamic URLs, called the **URL rewrite** technique, which allows your dynamic URL to resemble a static URL. For example, the URL in Exhibit 7-7 might be rewritten as powells.com/book/62-1579123791-0 so that the page appears static. This is a completely ethical technique that search spiders appreciate, with the added benefit of showing more readable URLs for your human visitors.

Each server platform and content management system has its own method of rewriting URLs. The most widely used web server, Apache, uses "mod_rewrite," which is very powerful. (Just so you know, when technical people call a tool "powerful," it means that you can do anything you want with it, if you could only figure out how.) Using mod_rewrite to change URLs is not dissimilar to performing woodcarving with a chain saw. You can do it, but you can also hurt yourself along the way. The mod_rewrite module allows an unlimited number of rules to be defined, requiring great attention to detail to ensure proper results, as explained at Apache's website (httpd.apache.org/docs/current/mod/mod_rewrite.html).

If you use open source content management systems, such as WordPress or Drupal, they can produce search-friendly URLs with the right setup. Come to our site (SEMincBook.com/search-friendly-URLs) to see how to coax your favorite technology to rewrite URLs.

Snap Electronics used IBM's WebSphere Commerce Server, which has a similar capability it calls "URL Mapping." Snap used WebSphere's URL Mapping technique to convert its dynamic URLs for its eCommerce catalog to appear to be static URLs. This allowed many of its product pages to be crawled that were missing from search indexes previously.

Many experts still consider URL rewrite techniques the best way to handle dynamic URLs, but because so many have botched their attempts to rewrite URLs, Google now advises that marketers use the techniques we listed above rather than using URL rewrite techniques. Some cynical observers point out that Google has reason to discourage the use of this technique, because Google's spider often handles dynamic URLs better than competing spiders. If Google can handle your dynamic URLs while other spiders can't, then it is in Google's interest to discourage you from rewriting them. Because not all spiders are as adept at handling dynamic URLs as the Googlebot, we continue to recommend URL rewrite techniques as a good way to get your pages indexed in all search engines. Not only do search-friendly URLs open your pages to all search spiders, but they allow you to use your keywords in the URL, which can help your rankings, as discussed in Chapter 8.

Eliminate Dependencies for Displaying Pages   Websites are marvels of technology, but sometimes they are a bit too marvelous. Your web developers might create such exciting pages that they require visitors' web browsers to support the latest and greatest technology. Or have their privacy settings set a bit low. Or to reveal information. In short, your website might require visitors to take certain actions or to enable certain browser capabilities in order to operate. And although that is merely annoying for your visitors, it can be deadly for search spiders, because they might not be up to the task of viewing your website.

If you are as old as we are, you might remember the Pac-Man video game, in which a hungry yellow dot roamed the screen eating other dots, but changed course every time it hit a wall or another impediment. Search spiders are similar. They will hungrily eat your spider food pages until they hit an impediment; then they will turn tail and go in a different direction. Let's look at some of the most popular technical dependencies:

- **Requiring cookies: Cookies** are information stored on the visitor's computer that web pages can use to remember things about the visitor. For example, if your site says "Welcome Jane" at the top of the page every time she returns to your site, the name **Jane** is probably stored in a cookie on Jane's computer. When Jane views your page, her browser reads the cookie and displays her name in the right spot. Normally this works just fine, but what if your web page requires that Jane's browser use cookies for this function, or else it displays an error page? First, some of your site visitors turn off cookies (for privacy reasons) and would not be able to view your site. But search spiders cannot accept cookies either, so they are also blocked from your pages. The bottom line is that your site can use cookies all it wants, but it should not *require* them to view a page. If your site's design absolutely depends on all visitors accepting cookies (such as to pass a required session identifier), this is a legitimate reason to use the IP delivery technique we discussed earlier in this chapter. By detecting a spider's user agent name and IP address, your program could allow spiders to look at the page without accepting the cookie, while still forcing cookies on all web browsers. Make sure that your developers are careful to deliver the same page content to the spider as to the visitor, so you are not accused of spamming.

- **Requiring software downloads:** If your site requires certain technology to view it, such as Flash, Silverlight, Java, or something else, your visitors must download the software before entering your site. In addition to being somewhat inconvenient for your visitors, it usually blocks spiders. Spiders are not web browsers, so they cannot interact with your site to download the required software. Your entire site might be blocked from indexing if you have this spider trap on your home page.

- **Requiring information:** Sites are often designed to be personalized in some way, which can be very good for visitors, but sometimes the designers go too far. Sites that require visitors to answer questions before viewing your pages are annoying to your visitors, and (you are getting the idea now) unusable by spiders, because all the spiders see is the HTML form that requests the input, and they cannot enter any words to get your site to show the actual pages. If visitors must enter their email address before they download a case study or their country and language before seeing your product catalog, you are asking for something that spiders cannot do. So the spiders cannot enter the required information to see the case study or the product catalog, and they will mosey on down to your competitor's site. Similarly, if your pages require an ID and password to "sign in" before you show them, the spider is unable to do so. The simplest way to think about this issue is that if your site prompts the visitor to do anything more than click a standard hypertext link, the spider will be at a loss and move on.

- **Requiring JavaScript:** By far the most common dependency for web pages is on JavaScript. JavaScript is a very useful programming language that allows your web pages to be more interactive, responding to the visitor's cursor, for example, and JavaScript also allow your web pages to use cookies, as discussed earlier. Used properly, JavaScript causes no problems for spiders, but often it is misused. In the next section, we discuss the pitfalls of JavaScript usage, but for now, just understand that your page should not *require* JavaScript in order to be displayed. Spiders get smarter every year, and some spiders can interpret some JavaScript code, but you can't count on spiders to understand it. If your page tests for JavaScript before it allows itself to be displayed, it will not display itself to spiders, and none of its links to other pages can be followed. These days, many web designers favor AJAX (Asynchronous JavaScript And XML) techniques, but make sure that you are not hiding your content by requiring JavaScript for it to be shown. Later in this chapter, you will learn how to design AJAX pages that can be fully indexed by some search spiders.

To see these problems for yourself, turn off graphics, cookies, and JavaScript in your browser—the Firefox Web Developer add-on (addons.mozilla.org/en-US/firefox/addon/web-developer/is great for this—or use the text-only Lynx browser (lynx.browser.org). You will see which pages force the use of certain technologies, and you will get a good look at what a spider actually sees. Any time you need to do anything more complicated than clicking a link to continue, the spider is probably blocked.

You might not realize it, but every time the spiders get smarter about indexing pages, they might start indexing pages that you never imagined they would see. Because spiders are beginning to index JavaScript and Flash content, pages that you never expected to see in the search index might now be included. Although usually this is good for your site, sometimes spiders get caught in JavaScript or Flash forms that cause them to spend inordinate time accomplishing nothing. All that useless spider time extracts a performance toll on your servers without benefiting your marketing at all.

In addition, some spiders have "budgets" for how much time they spend on any particular website. The more time they spend caught in useless crawling of forms, the less time spent indexing the truly important content on your site. Before you know it, the time budget runs out and the spider moves on to the next site, leaving some of your important pages out of the index. You can use robots directives to steer the spiders away from content you don't want indexed, saving crawl budget time for indexing more of the good stuff.

Use Redirects Properly   The inventor of the web, Tim Berners-Lee, once observed that "URLs do not change, people change them." The best advice to search marketers is never to change your URLs, but at some point you will probably find it necessary to change the URL for one of your pages. Perhaps your webmaster might want to host that page on a different server, which requires the URL to change. At other times the content of a page changes so that the old URL does not make sense anymore, such as when you change the brand name of your product and the old name is still in the URL.

Whenever a URL is changed, you will want your webmaster to put in place something called a **redirect**—an instruction to web browsers to display a different URL from the one the browser requested. Redirects allow old URLs to be "redirected" to the current URL, so that your visitors do not get a "page not found" message (known as an HTTP 404 error) when they use the old URL.

A visitor might be using an old URL for any number of reasons, but here are the most common ones:

- **Bookmarks:** If a visitor bookmarked your old URL, that bookmark will yield a 404 error the first time the visitor tries to use it after you change that URL.

- **Links:** Other pages on the web (on your site and other sites) link to that old URL. All of those links will become broken if you change the URL with no redirect in place.

- **Search results:** As you can imagine, search spiders found your page using the old URL and indexed the page using that URL. When searchers find your page, they are clicking the old URL that is stored in the search index, so they will get a 404 if no redirect is in place.

Now that you understand that URLs will often change for your pages, and that redirects are required so that visitors can continue to find those pages, you need to know a little bit about spiders and redirects.

Spiders, as you have learned, are finicky little creatures, and they are particular about how your webmaster performs page redirects. When a page has been permanently moved from one URL to another, the only kind of redirect to use is called a **server-side redirect**. (You might hear it called a "301" redirect, from the HTTP status code returned to the spider.) A 301 status code tells the spider that the page has permanently changed to a new URL, which causes the spider to do two vitally important things:

- **Crawl the page at the new URL:** The spider will use the new URL provided in the 301 redirect instruction to go to that new location and crawl the page just as you want it to. It will index all the content on the page, and it will index it using the new URL, so all searches that bring up that page will lead searchers to the new URL, not the old one.

- **Transfer the value of all links to the old page:** You have learned how important it is to have links to your page—the search engine ranks your page much higher when other pages (especially other *important* pages) link to your page. When the spider sees a 301 redirect, it updates all the linking information in its index; your page retains under its new URL all the link value that it had under its old URL.

Unfortunately, not all webmasters use server-side redirects. There are several methods of redirecting pages, two of which are especially damaging to your search marketing efforts:

- **JavaScript redirects:** One way of executing a redirect embeds the new URL in JavaScript code. So, your web developer moves the page's real HTML to the new URL and codes a very simple page for the old URL that includes JavaScript code sending the browser to the new URL (such as `<script language="JavaScript" type="text/javascript">window.location="http://www.yourdomain.com/newURL"</script>`).

- **Meta refresh redirects**. A meta tag in the `<head>` section of your HTML can also redirect a page—it is commonly called a "meta refresh" redirect (such as `<meta http-equiv="Refresh" content="5; URL= http://www.yourdomain.com/newURL" />`). This tag flashes a screen (in this case for 5 seconds) before displaying the new URL.

Search spiders normally cannot follow JavaScript, and in any case, both of these techniques are commonly used by search spammers so they can get the search spider to index the content on the old URL page while taking visitors to the new URL page (which might have entirely different content). These kinds of redirects will not take the spider to your new URL, and they will not get your new URL indexed, which is what you want. Make sure that your webmaster uses 301 redirects for all page redirection, and make sure that your web developers are not using JavaScript and "meta refresh" redirects.

How your webmaster implements a 301 redirect depends on what kind of web server displays the URL. For the most common web server, Apache, the webmaster might add a line to the .htaccess file, like so:

```
Redirect 301 /OldDirectory/OldName.html
http://www.YourDomain.com/NewDirectory/NewName.html
```

You would obviously substitute your real directory and filenames. Understand, however, that some Apache servers are configured to ignore .htaccess files, and other kinds of web servers have different means of setting up permanent redirects, so what your webmaster does might vary. The point is that your webmaster probably knows how to implement server-side redirects, and search spiders know how to follow them.

Server-side redirects are also used for temporary URL changes using an HTTP 302 status code. A 302 temporary redirect can be followed by the spider just as easily as a 301. Webmasters have various reasons for implementing 302s, but the important one to search marketers concerns the so-called vanity URL. Sometimes it is nice to have a URL that is easy to remember, such as yourdomain.com/product that shows the home page for one of your products. You tell everyone linking to your product page to use that vanity URL. But behind the scenes, your webmaster can move that page to a different server whenever needed for load balancing and other reasons. By using a 302 redirect, the spider uses your vanity URL in the search index but indexes the content on the page it redirects to. Because it is a *temporary* redirect, the value of any links to that URL are not passed by the redirect, the way they are with permanent redirects.

Before implementing any 301 or 302 redirect, your webmaster should take care not to add "hops" to the URL—in other words, not adding a redirect on top of a previous redirect. For example, if the vanity URL has been temporarily directed (302) to the current URL and now needs to be directed to a new URL, the existing 302 redirect should generally be changed to the new URL. If, instead, the webmaster implements a permanent (301) redirect from the current URL to the new URL, you now have two "hops" from your vanity URL to the real page. Not only does this slow performance for your visitors, but spiders are known to abandon pages with too many hops (possibly as few as five). Visit our site (SEMincBook.com/redirect-checkers) to test your redirects.

Make sure that your webmaster is intimately familiar with search-safe methods of redirection, and confirm that the proper procedures are explained in your site standards so that all redirects are performed with care. Make sure that redirects are regularly reviewed and purged when no longer needed so that the path to your page is as direct as possible.

Ensure Your Web Servers Respond   If it sounds basic, well, it is; however, it is a problem on all too many websites. When the spider comes to call, your web server must be *up*. If your server is down, the spider receives no response from your website. At best, the spider moves along to a new server and leaves your pages in its search index (without seeing any page changes you have made, of course). At worst, the spider might conclude (after a few such incidents over several crawls) that your site no longer exists, and then deletes all of your site's pages from the search index.

Don't let this happen to you. Your webmaster obviously wants to keep your website available to serve your visitors anyway, but sometimes hardware problems and other crises cause long and frequent outages for a period of time, possibly causing your pages to be deleted from one or more search indexes. Your webmaster can use the error code 503 (service unavailable) to alert the search engines that your site still exists and that you are working to restore its availability.

A less-severe but related problem is slow page loading. Although your site is technically "up," the pages might be displayed so slowly that the spider soon abandons the site. Few spiders will wait 10 seconds for a page. Spiders are in a hurry, so if good performance for your visitors is not enough of a motivation, speed up your site for the spider's sake. Even if spiders do wait patiently for your slow-loading site, Google has publicly stated that they rank faster sites higher, which we will explain more in Chapter 8. Check out our site for links to tools that check for site outages and help diagnose site speed problems (SEMincBook.com/performance-tools).

If your site really can't respond fast enough (perhaps due to a temporary problem), you can use Google and Bing Webmaster Tools to control how the spiders work. If your site's servers are spending too much time responding to spiders, when you need them to respond to customers, you can slow down the rate of the crawls. Some webmasters do so during seasonal or event traffic peaks.

Reduce Ignored Content

After you have eliminated your spider traps so that spiders can crawl your pages, the next issue you might encounter is that they ignore some of your content. Spiders have refined tastes, and if your content is not the kind of food they like, they will move on to the next page or the next site. Let's see what you should do to make your spider food as tasty as possible.

Slim Down Your Pages   Like most of us, spiders do not want to do any unnecessary work. If your HTML pages routinely consist of thousands and thousands of lines, spiders are less likely to index them all, or will index them less frequently. For the same time they spend crawling your bloated site, they could crawl two others.

In fact, every spider will stop crawling a page when it gets to a certain size. Some spiders seem to stop at about 100,000 characters, but every spider has a limit programmed into it. If you have very large pages, they might not be getting crawled or not crawled completely.

Once in a while, someone decides to put all 264 pages of the SnapShot DLR200 User's Guide on one web page. Obviously, the 264-page manual belongs on dozens of separate web pages with navigation from the table of contents. Breaking up a large page also helps improve keyword density by making the primary keywords stand out more in the sea of words. Not only is this better for search engines, your visitors will be happier, too.

The most frequent cause of fat pages, however, is embedded JavaScript code. No matter what the cause, there is no technical reason to have pages this large, and you should insist they be fixed. It is even easier to fix JavaScript bloat than large text pages; all you need to do is to move the JavaScript from your web page to an external file. The code works just as well, but the spider does not have to crawl through it.

Validate Your HTML   When you surf your website with your browser, you rarely see an error message. The web pages load properly, and they look okay to you. It is understandable for you to think that the HTML that presents each page on your site has no errors. But you would be wrong.

Here is why. Web browsers are designed to make visitors' lives easier by overlooking HTML problems on your pages. Browsers are very tolerant of flaws in the HTML code, striving to always present the page as best as possible, even though there might be many coding errors. Unfortunately, spiders are not so tolerant. Spiders are sticklers for correct HTML code.

And most websites are rife with coding errors. Web developers are under pressure to make changes quickly, and the moment it looks correct in the browser, they declare victory and move on to the next task. Very few developers take the time to test that the code is valid.

You must get your developers to validate their HTML code. They must understand that coding errors provide the wrong information to the search spider. Consider something as seemingly minor as misspelling the `<title>` tag as `<tilte>` in your HTML. Browsers will not display your title in the title bar at the top of the window, but because the rest of the page looks fine, your developers and your visitors probably will not notice the error. The title tag, however, is an extremely important tag for the search engine. After all, a missing title makes it much harder (sometimes impossible) for that page to be found by searchers. Validating the code catches this kind of error before it hurts your search marketing.

Sometimes the errors are more subtle than a broken `<title>` tag. Comments in your HTML code might not be ended properly, causing the spider to ignore real page text that you meant to be indexed because it takes that text as part of the malformed comment. In addition, browsers sometimes correctly display pages with slight markup errors, such as missing tags to end tables, but sometimes search spiders might lose some of your text. So, the page might look okay, but not all of your words got indexed, so searchers cannot find your page when they use those words. Occasionally, HTML links—especially those using relative addresses where the full URL of the link is not spelled out—work fine in a browser but trip up the spider.

It is easy for your developers to validate their code. They can use the Firefox Web Developer add-on or go to validator.w3.org to enter the URL of any page they want to test. There are several flavors of valid HTML, from the strictest compliance with the standards to looser compliance that uses some older tags. As long as your page states what flavor it adheres to in the `<doctype>` tag, it will be validated correctly, and search spiders can read any flavor of valid HTML code. Make sure that your everyday development process requires that each page's HTML be validated before promotion to your production website.

Avoid Frames and Flash   If your site's design has not been updated in a while, you might still have pages that use **frames** or depend on Adobe Flash. Neither are good choices for content you want indexed in search engines.

Frames are an old technique of HTML coding that can display multiple sources of content in separate scrollable windows in the same HTML page. Frames have many usability problems for visitors, and have been replaced with better ways of integrating content on the same page— using content management systems and dynamic pages. But some sites still have pages coded with frames. If you are among the unlucky to have frame-based pages on your site, the best thing to do is to replace them. Your visitors will have a better experience, and you will improve search marketing, too, because spiders have a devil of a time interpreting frame-based pages. Typically spiders ignore everything in the "frameset" and look for an HTML tag called `<noframes>` that was designed for (ancient) browsers that do not support frames. There are techniques that people use to try to load the pertinent content for search into the `<noframes>` tag, but it is a lot of work to create and maintain. Our advice is to ditch frames completely. Creating a new frame-free page will end up being a lot less work in the long run and will improve the usability of your site, too.

Adobe Flash brought a far richer user experience to the web than drab old HTML, allowing animation and other interactive features that spice up visual tours and demonstrations. Flash has been losing popularity in recent years because it is not natively supported on Apple iOS systems, such as iPhones and iPads, but it is the inability of spiders to index most Flash content that causes us to advise you to avoid its use. Google and Adobe have worked together to greatly improve indexing of Flash content, but Flash is still not indexed very well. With each passing year, both Adobe and the search engines make progress on indexing Flash, so that some Flash can now be indexed by some search engines, but the best advice remains to use Flash sparingly. Reserve your use of Flash for content that you are happy not to be indexed—that 3D interactive view of your product or the walking tour of your museum's latest exhibit. You can also use Flash for application development, such as your online ordering system—something that you would not want indexed anyway. If you must use Flash for content that you do want indexed, take care to use what Adobe calls SWFObject2, which is far easier for search engines to index, because it serves up HTML of the text for spiders and other non-Flash browsers. (Just make sure you serve up exactly the same text as you do in the Flash experience, because it might otherwise be construed as cloaking.) You should also make sure that you are using the SWFAddress library so that links can be resolved by search engines.

Ensure AJAX Pages are Spider-Friendly   AJAX pages can be great for search visitors, using JavaScript to be more interactive and to load faster than straight HTML pages. For example, AJAX pages can allow tabbed pages to load just the contents of the tab that is visible instead of slowly loading the content of all the tabs when the first tab is shown.

The problem, however, is that the *J* in AJAX stands for JavaScript, and search spiders don't always process JavaScript correctly, leaving much of your content out of the search index. Baidu, for example, at this writing, advises that you provide a separate spider-friendly HTML page for each AJAX page. But most search engines (including Google, Bing, and Yandex) can process AJAX pages using what's known as the #! (hash-bang) method.

This method requires that you add the exclamation point (bang) after the hash mark in your AJAX URL (so domain.com/page#tab-one becomes domain.com/page#!tab-one) and provide an HTML version of the page under a different URL (in this case, domain.com/page?_escaped_fragment_=tab-one). The benefit of this approach is that it can work in every browser—even outdated ones—and in most search engines. The disadvantage is that it produces odd-looking URLs and can easily be implemented incorrectly by the average web developer.

A new, simpler method has emerged that uses HTML5. And that's the bad news, at least at first, because not all browsers support HTML5. But as time goes by, more and more visitors will have HTML5-capable browsers, and this new method is more fool-proof for developers.

HTML5 allows AJAX developers to provide an HTML version of the page to spiders, with the AJAX version reserved for browsers, but use the pushState function to change the URL that is shown in the status bar so that the URL appears to be the same for both pages. (In our example, domain.com/page?tab=one could be the URL for both the AJAX and HTML versions.)

Be sure to choose one of these implementations to index any AJAX pages on your site. While spiders get better at indexing JavaScript each year, you want to be *sure* your content is indexed properly.

Help Spiders Index Unusual Page Structures   Spiders are optimized for the typical case—a web page is a self-contained "article" of content on one subject. Spiders struggle with the two ends of the extreme—a single page that scrolls forever or a single article that is broken up into multiple pages. Spiders need some help to properly index content in these situations. Let's look at paginated content first.

You will often see articles divided up into multiple pages, with users expected to click Next or Page 2 at the bottom of the first page to keep reading. Media companies, such as newspapers and magazines, sell advertising on their pages so they want to break up longer stories so that more ads are served. If you have a "View All" page that shows the whole story in one page, your best bet for spiders is to code individual pages with a canonical tag that tells the spider that the "View All" page is preferred (`<link rel="canonical" href="view-all.html"`).

But media companies trying to sell advertising won't want to reduce their ads, so there is also a way for spiders to correctly index the multipage articles without resorting to a "View All" page. Let's look at an example where your story spans three physical web pages:

- domain.com/story?page=1
- domain.com/story?page=2
- domain.com/story?page=3

Spiders, left to their own devices, might show any of these pages in the search results, but it isn't a great user experience to find an article but be taken to Page 3 just because that is where the keywords were found. To alert the search engine that the pages are linked as one article, add some markup to your pages:

- **Page 1:** `<link rel="next" href="http://domain.com/story?page=2" />`
- **Page 2:** `<link rel="prev" href="http://domain.com/story?page=1" />`
  `<link rel="next" href="http://domain.com/story?page=3" />`
- **Page 3:** `<link rel="prev" href="http://domain.com/story?page=2" />`

This information gives Google the option of showing the first page of the article when it finds keywords on any of the pages, which is often what searchers want.

Maybe you can guess how spiders want help with modern-looking infinite scroll pages (such as you see on Pinterest) where users can keep scrolling to see new content added for as long as they are interested. Break them up into multipage articles using the `rel=next` and `rel=prev` markup! If you do, make sure that are not duplicating items on any pages. If Page 1 contains items 1 through 10, make sure that Page 2 doesn't repeat any of those items, but rather shows the next 10 unique items, 11 through 20.

A special case of multiple-page content occurs when faceted browsing (sometimes called multifaceted search) techniques are used, such as in a shopping site where visitors can filter the list of all cameras to just those with over 8-megapixel resolution and prices under $300. As you might expect, if a spider gets loose inside your faceted browsing experience, it's likely to index thousands of pages that all contain the same lists of products, just diced up in different ways.

The simplest solution here is to block all of these pages from indexing (with robots.txt or robots tags) *if* your product and product category pages can all be indexed through other means.

But if some of your faceted search pages are actually key navigational points in your information architecture, or there is no other navigation that reaches your individual product pages, then you need a better approach.

The first thing to do is to identify the simplest path that will index all of the pages without duplicates. For example, if you have thousands of products but they all fall into 15 categories, consider making only those category pages available to the spiders, blocking the rest with robot directives. That way, you'll get all the content indexed but without wasting the spider's time (leaving that time available to index other pages on your site). Of course, if your faceted category pages are themselves paginated (Page 2, Page 3, ...), then use the tips above for handling multi-page experiences.

Websites contain more tricky ways of presenting content than ever before, so make sure that your modern information architecture gives the spiders the clues they need to index it properly.

Create Spider Paths

Now that you have learned all about removing spider traps, let's look at the opposite approach, too. Sometimes it is too difficult, costly, or expensive to remove a spider trap. In those cases, your only option is to provide an alternative way for the spider to traverse your site, so it can go around your trap. That's where **spider paths** come in.

Spider paths are just easy-to-follow routes through your site, such as sitemaps, category maps, country maps, or even text links at the bottom of the key pages. Quite simply, spider paths are any means that allow the spider to get to all the pages on your site. The ultimate spider path is a well thought-out and easy to navigate website. If your website has no spider traps, you might already have a wonderful set of spider paths. With today's ever-more-complex sites full of spider-blocking technology, however, you might need to make accommodations for spiders trapped by your regular navigation.

Design Your Site Navigation   In the old days, a common page in your site was your user sitemap; you probably had it linked from your footer on every blessed page on your site. This was a great idea for search spiders because they could find every page on your site easily from that one sitemap page. But as your site got larger, you soon realized how difficult it was to maintain a sitemap, and you probably don't have one anymore.

What do you do instead? You need site navigation that is exceedingly comprehensive and clear. If it is easy for your visitors, it will likely be easy for search spiders (as long as you avoid the spider traps mentioned earlier). Your directory structure on your site must make it easier for spiders to get access to your site's pages, but they also serve as very powerful clues to the search engine as to the thematic content of the site. The words you use as the anchor text for links in your navigation and the words in your folder names can sometimes carry a lot of weight. Work closely with your information architects to develop your site navigation, and you will reap large search dividends.

Your top-level site navigation should link to your category hub pages; from each category hub page, your visitor can link deeper into the site to see all other pages. This approach can work even for sites with 10,000 pages or more. Very large websites (100,000 pages or more) often have multiple top-level hub pages. IBM's website (IBM.com) uses this approach, with its hub pages for "Industries & solutions," "Services," "Products," and "Support & downloads," as you can see in Exhibit 7-8. These pages are shown in a navigation bar at the top of every page on the site, including the home page, making it very easy for spiders. Each page lists a number of categories relevant to the page. The "Products" page lists all of IBM's product categories, for example, with the other hub pages similarly serving as catalogs of links for their subjects. Taken together, these pages form clear navigation that spiders feast on, returning daily to see whether any important links have been added to IBM's site.

Industries & solutions, Services, Products, and Support & downloads are shown at the top of each page, including the ibm.com home page.

Exhibit 7-8   A system of sitemap pages for a large website. IBM has several hub pages that are visited regularly by the search engines.

As you have seen, different websites have different versions of site navigation that might list product categories, services, or anything else that appears on your website. You can always categorize your pages in an organized manner and display them as a kind of hub page. One important kind is a **country map**.

Many medium-to-large organizations have operations in multiple countries, often requiring them to show similar products and other content in each country using different languages, monetary currencies, and legal terms. These organizations frequently organize their corporate web domain as a series of country sites. Depending on how the country sites are linked to the main domain, spiders might easily find them all or might be completely stopped.

That is why you need to use country maps. Country maps, like sitemaps, are search-friendly pages that link all your country sites to your overall corporate domain. As we've emphasized, your country map must link to each country site using a standard HTML link—not a JavaScript pull-down or any other spider-trapping navigation technique.

Regardless of what kind of website you have, spider paths are an invaluable way to get more pages from your site indexed by providing the spiders with easy access to every page on your site. Next up, we look at one last way of getting more of your pages in the organic search index: telling the spiders what pages to index.

Use Search Engine Sitemaps   The sitemaps protocol (sitemaps.org), pioneered by Google but now supported by all the major search engines, is a free way to get more of your pages included in search indexes.

The sitemaps protocol (commonly called sitemaps) makes no promise that your pages will be included or how often they will be refreshed. Regardless, some sites have succeeded in using sitemaps to add hundreds of thousands of pages to each search engine's indexes. The sitemap protocol also enables you to tell spiders when pages were modified and which pages change most frequently, so the spider may come back to check those pages more often.

You have your choice of several ways to create sitemaps, which we cover later in this chapter, but for now the most important thing to understand is that sitemaps are low risk. Using sitemaps does not replace any search engine's regular crawl of your site, so you really can't lose. Sitemaps give the spiders more information that might help you get more pages included in search indexes, and it might get them refreshed faster, but it won't take away any pages you already have indexed. Oh, and did we mention that it's free?

Although most search marketers use sitemaps only to feed the main search index for each search engine, you should know that the special indexes for search engines can sometimes be fed by sitemaps also. Google introduced each of these special sitemap formats, but other search engines are beginning to support them, too:

- **News:** If you have content that should show up under Google News, you will want a special sitemap that is updated regularly with your news stories. Press releases are a great example of this kind of information.
- **Image:** To provide Google with more information for its image search, you can use image extensions that augment your images with a caption and license information for each image, and more.

- **Video:** If you have video content, set up a video sitemap that adds, in addition to the regular sitemap data, a title and description of the video, video format and player requirements, and a link to the landing page.

- **Mobile:** If your website has been optimized to look good on mobile devices, such as cell phones, let a mobile sitemap alert the search engines to load up the special mobile search index. It's best to use responsive design so that you have one website that is displayed on any size device, but having a separate mobile site can work, also.

Now that you know some of the various flavors of sitemaps, it is time to learn how to use them.

Use of the sitemaps protocol is free, but requires more technical acumen to set up than paid single URL submission programs. The work consists of three steps: creating your sitemap, alerting the search engines about your sitemap, and updating it when needed. Alerting the search engines and updating your sitemap don't take a genius, but creating your first sitemap can be a little tricky.

First off, you have several choices about how to create your sitemap, some of which require more technical expertise than others. The simplest version of a sitemap is just a text file that contains a list of URLs, one per line, but you can get a lot fancier than that. The XML version of the sitemaps protocol can tell the spider when pages have been updated and which pages are the most important to crawl frequently. You can hand encode a file that uses that protocol, but most site owners will find it smarter to automate the process, whether by writing a custom program or by using a sitemap generator.

The best ways to generate XML sitemaps are as follows:

- **Your web server:** Some web servers have built-in capabilities to generate sitemaps. If you are not using one of them, read on.

- **Your content management system:** If your site uses a Content Management System (CMS), you might be in luck. Many moderns CMSs have integrated the sitemap creation/update process into their publishing process and need only be configured to start working. Check with your IT folks or your CMS vendor to see whether yours has this capability.

- **A separate tool:** There are plenty of sitemap generator tools out there, ranging from free tools for small sites to industrial-strength tools for enterprises.

Depending on your situation, you might have several different options. Check out our website to get a current list (SEMincBook.com/sitemap-generators).

When you finish creating your sitemap, you must place it on your web server in the root directory (or the highest directory that you want crawled). If you use sitemaps for country sites, you will want to place each country sitemap in the highest directory containing country pages, which is the root directory for some websites (such as yourcompany.de) but could be a subdirectory for other country sites (yourcompany.com/de). In this latter case, you must follow the instructions to set your Geographic Target in Google Webmaster Tools.

Once your sitemap is uploaded to the right location on your web server, you must alert the search engines to look for it. The easiest way to do that is to update your robots.txt file to include a line specifying the location of the sitemap (Sitemap: www.yourcompany.com/sitemap.xml). But if your site has been ignored by spiders, you will want to alert each search engine individually by using a special webmaster account:

- Google Webmaster Tools (google.com/webmasters/tools/)
- Bing (bing.com/webmaster)

Then you wait for the spider and hope for the best. Remember that sitemaps won't remove all spider traps. If your pages require JavaScript or are excluded by a robots.txt file, your sitemap won't override these problems. But if you struggle with long dynamic page URLs or pages hidden behind registration forms or many other problems, a sitemap might be the only way to get your page indexed. And although they do require someone with technical skills to set them up, once they are running they require little expertise.

Now that you have learned all the ways to help get your pages indexed, it is time to list the content beyond your website, starting with social media content. That is what we discuss next.

Get Social Content Listed in Organic Search Indexes

As you've seen, some search result pages contain more social media content than website pages, so how do you make sure that your social content is in the organic index, too? Just as with website pages, you'll be happy to find that most of the time your content gets indexed without you needing to do anything special. But different kinds of social media can benefit from specialized techniques that we cover here.

Get Your Blog Indexed

When you create a blog post, you'd like for it to be indexed right away. Luckily, blogs provide a simple mechanism that makes that happen, called a **web feed**. Web feeds, such as Really Simple Syndication (RSS) and Atom, are generated by your blogging platform, such as WordPress, and they are sent to the search engine to be indexed upon publication of every new post.

For the purposes of search marketing, it doesn't really matter which kind of web feed you use. The most popular blogging platforms, such as WordPress, Movable Type, and Blogger (blogger.com), can generate each type of feed anyway. What is important is what web feeds can do for you.

All mainstream search engines index web feeds, and because blog information is so time sensitive, they index them quickly. To make sure that your feeds show up right away, simply ping the search engines every time you post so that the updated URL is sent to the search engine. You can instruct your blogging software to ping each one, typically through "update services" or you can send one ping to a free service such as Ping-o-Matic (pingomatic.com), which can ping dozens of search engines and blog aggregators for you. As soon as the search engine receives the ping, it dispatches its search spider to scoop up the new page.

Spammers have started co-opting ping mechanisms to quickly index low-quality pages that they want to quickly get into the search index. Pinging doesn't help improve search rankings, but might grab attention for fast-moving topics.

Earlier in this chapter, you learned the importance of validating your web pages' HTML coding. You can do the same thing for your web feeds, using sites such as Feed Validator (feedvalidator.org) and the W3 Feed Validation Service (validator.w3.org/feed/).

Some might prefer to use XML sitemaps rather than web feeds to index their blogs, especially if their blog is hosted on the same domain as their website, rather than on its own domain. Most blog platforms have plug-ins that update sitemaps with new posts as they are published. Yoast's SEO plug-in is an example of a popular plug-in for WordPress that maintains sitemaps as well as helps you optimize your blog content in other ways, which we discuss in Chapter 8.

Get Your Videos Indexed

With each passing year, videos become more and more visible in the search results. Increasingly, video is the content type of choice for mobile devices, and it is often the best kind of content to show for "how to" searches, regardless of device. But your video won't be shown in the search results if it isn't in the index.

If you host your videos on YouTube, or some other public video venue, you probably have nothing to worry about. All of those videos are indexed as long as you ensure the videos are *public*. You can mark your videos to be private, which keeps them out of the search index. You can host the videos on these public sites while still embedding them in web pages on your own website.

Don't stop with YouTube! Use OneLoad (oneload.com) to submit your clips to over a dozen sites simultaneously (and to track their viewership). OneLoad offers a free option as well as multiple paid options based on the type and size of your videos.

What about videos that you physically host on your own website? Some search sites crawl videos along with all other web content, so placing all your videos in the same directory (as close to the root directory as possible) can help those spiders find everything you've got. If you are constantly adding videos, consider setting up a web feed for videos (just as you did for blog posts), and then ping the search engines each time you add a new video. As we discussed earlier in the chapter, you can also use a video sitemap (sitemap.org) to get the same treatment for your videos that you get for your web pages.

Getting Your Images Indexed

Making sure that your images are listed in search indexes isn't much different from what you do for videos. If you post your images on public sites, such as Flickr, your image will likely be indexed as long as it is public. And if you host images on your own website, they will likely be indexed without much work on your part, although you can use image sitemaps to increase your odds.

One new way to get the most out of your images is through Pinterest, the popular "pin board" of images that can be shared with others. For many creative sites such as recipe or art sites, Pinterest is often one of the top five referrers of traffic. The two main ways of getting your content into Pinterest is to upload the images or "pin" the image through a pin function in your browser toolbar.

The best way to maximize Pinterest is to utilize your keyword research to create descriptive categories for the pins and actively pin new content to those categories—thus getting those new pictures indexed. Once you have content, start engaging with others in Pinterest to increase awareness and build relationships. Don't go crazy posting every picture of your products; use Pinterest creatively to get images listed that will most likely be shared.

Snap Electronics uses Pinterest to showcase images from their staff and from their pool of beta test photographers. These images span many interest areas that attract users from all photography skill levels.

Getting Your Social Network Content Indexed

Perhaps the most talked-about content in all of social media is from social networking sites, such as Twitter, Facebook, LinkedIn, and Google+. Unfortunately, because this content is owned and controlled by each social network, how it is indexed changes quite rapidly. Google once indexed all of Twitter, but when Google+ came out as a competitor to Twitter, Twitter cut off access to Google Search, although Google still is able to access some Twitter content. Bing has a deal with Facebook to mine what your friends are saying, while Google has little access to Facebook, because most Facebook content is private (as is LinkedIn). You can imagine that Google Search includes lots of Google+ conversations, but other search engines might not have access to any data that is not public.

So, it's difficult to make sweeping statements about what any particular search engine will show from social networking sites. Because it changes so often, we have provided up-to-date information on our website (SEMincBook.com/social-media).

The simplest advice is probably the best: Your content (social and otherwise) needs promotion in social networks. You are probably using social networks already, and the more that you use, the more people might be exposed to your content. The same is true of search engines.

For larger companies, your social networking presence is often featured prominently on search results pages when searchers look for your brand name. Different search engines might highlight different social venues, but keeping your Facebook Fan Page or your Google+ Company Page up to date can make a big difference for you. If you think of the search results page as a shelf in a store, you'd want your content to take up as much shelf space as possible. So, if searchers for your brand find your website home page as well as several social media venues at the top of the search results, you are likely to get a click to one of your properties. In addition, your social content crowds out less-flattering information posted by your competitors and detractors from the top search results.

Search marketers should focus on publicly available social networking content; search engines do not index private content, such as a Facebook conversation between two friends. Public content, such as Facebook Fan Pages, Google+ Business Pages, LinkedIn Company Pages, and all of Twitter is often indexed. You don't need to do anything to get the content indexed besides to create it.

Get Your Merchandise Listed in Product Search Databases

If your business sells the kind of product online that is offered by product search engines, you might find it very profitable to be listed. Product search has changed a lot over the years. Variously called shopping search or comparison search, just a few years ago most shoppers went to product search sites, such as NexTag, Shopzilla, Become.com, and others. While those sites still attract traffic, they are not riding high the way they once were. Most product search traffic now comes from the mainstream search engines, especially Google.

But Google isn't the only reason that the Shopzillas of the world are on the decline. They have been hit with a double whammy: The search engines are taking their traffic for themselves with mainstream searchers, and brand-name retailers are attracting shoppers directly to their site. If you are more likely to choose between Amazon and Google when you are shopping than to head to a shopping search site, you are not alone. It isn't just Amazon—some shoppers head for WalMart, eBay, or even Wayfair, but the idea is the same. Increasingly, people go direct to a mass retailer or they use a mainstream search engine, rather than heading to special product search engines.

As a marketer, you have the option of getting your products listed in Amazon or eBay, but that isn't part of search marketing. In this book, we'll help you get listed in the product search engines, including those from Google and Bing. Each search engine has slightly different ways of getting your products listed, but they usually required a **product feed** of some type—a file that lists all of your products in a structured format.

Google Shopping has morphed from a free "trusted feed" service of all of your product data to a service directly integrated into their AdWords program that shows products in context of the search results. This new program has been renamed Google Product Listing Ads, which are offered on a per-click basis. The Google program requires merchants to participate both in the Google Merchant Center Program and AdWords. Bing is beta testing a similar program that allows an advertiser to blend product specific information directly into the ads to make them more enticing to click.

Feeding Your Data to Product Search Engines

No matter which program you go with, they all require a feed of your product information. These feeds have very specific information that you must include as well as keeping them updated with price and inventory. Your programmers must create a file containing the content you want included and send that to the search engine. Different search engines accept different formats, ranging from CSV (comma-separated variable) files to Microsoft Excel spreadsheets to custom XML. Just about every search engine accepts XML format, which is the cheapest to maintain in the long run. (XML is a markup language similar to HTML that allows tags to be defined to describe any kind of data you have, making it very popular as a format for data feeds.)

Which data you must put in your feed depends on the search engine you are sending it to, because each engine has different data requirements. Product search engines typically expect the price, availability, and features of your products, in addition to the product's name and description. Most data feeds include some or all of these items:

- **Page URL:** The actual URL for the landing page on your site for this search result. It can be a static or a dynamic URL, but it must be working—no "page not found" messages; otherwise, the product search engine will delete the page from its index.

- **Tracking URL:** The URL that the searcher should go to when clicking this result. It can be the same as the page URL, but sometimes your web analytics software needs a different URL to help measure clicks from search to your page—one that contains a **tracking code** to help your analytics system attribute your visits to the right source of traffic.

- **Product name:** All variants of your product's name that a searcher might use as a keyword, including acronyms and its full name. Pay special attention to what searchers might type in to find your product name and include them here.

- **Product description:** A lengthy description of your product that should include meaningful occurrences of the keywords you expect searchers to enter. (See Chapter 8 for more information on how to optimize your content for search.) Every search engine is different, but most allow 250 words for your product description.

- **Model number:** The number you expect most searchers to enter to find this product. If a retailer and a manufacturer have different numbers for the same product, you can sometimes include both, depending on the particular product search engine that you are submitting the feed to.

- **Manufacturer:** The complete name of the manufacturer of the product, with any short names or acronyms that searchers might use.

- **Product category:** The type of product, according to a valid list of products maintained by the search engine. Each search engine has somewhat different product lines that they support, with different names. Snap found that some called their products "home electronics" and others "consumer electronics." You need to use the exact name for your product's category that each search engine uses.

- **Price:** A critical piece of information for product search engine feeds, which typically require tax and shipping costs, too. Be sure that your prices are accurate each time you submit your feed, because price is one of the main ways that product searchers find your product.

Different product search engines use different feed formats, so make sure that you check the fine print of the feed instructions for the engine you are supplying.

Making the Most of Product Feeds

Feeds are a bit complex to set up, as you have seen, so you want to make sure you get the most out of them and that you avoid any pitfalls along the way. Here are some tips to make your feed program a success:

- **Avoid off-limits subjects:** Most search engines have off-limits subjects that they refuse to be associated with. Because of local laws in various countries, some search engines reject "adult" (pornographic) content, sites with controversial themes, gambling sites, and pharmacy and drug information. All content submitted undergoes initial and ongoing quality reviews. If pages are rejected, some search engines do not refund your fees.

- **Take advantage of "on-the-fly" optimization:** The better your source data and the better your feed-creation program, the better your feed can be. One advantage of **trusted feeds** over crawling is on-the-fly optimization—having your feed-creation program add additional relevant words to the feed that were not in your original source, such as keywords to your titles and descriptions. For example, Snap Electronics discovered that all of its product pages contain the words *Snap* and *SnapShot*, and the model number, and a picture, but they actually do not all contain the words *digital camera*. Snap made sure that the program that produces its trusted feed optimized its data on-the-fly, by adding the generic product keywords *digital camera* to the titles and descriptions of the trusted feed. That way the search engine has that information even though Snap forgot to optimize the original page to contain *digital camera*. You can test variations in the generated text (brand name first, brand name last, and so on) to see which version seems to provide the best results.

- **Optimize for both fielded data and keywords:** Product search engines use a mixture of keywords and fielded data to display your product. While searchers will start by entering keywords (such as *digital camera*), they will also drill down using facet values ("under $300" or "over 8.0 megapixels"), so it's important that your product catalog data contain the write copy and the right specs.

- **Do not add keywords unrelated to your content:** Although optimizing on-the-fly can be a real advantage for you, it can be very dangerous for the search engines, because it leaves them wide open to anyone unethically adding keywords that do not really describe the data, just so they can get high search rankings for those keywords. Regardless of whether you use a simple URL submission program or the more complex trusted feed, search engines are very strict about what content they accept. Many unethical search marketing techniques (known as spam) try to fool the search engines to find your pages when they really should not match, and every search engine takes measures to avoid being fooled. Product search engines are sensitive to errors in your trusted feed (such as sending "in stock" in the feed when the product is temporarily unavailable). If your pages use some of these tricks, expect search engines to begin rejecting your submissions. But there's a better reason to avoid this practice: You are sacrificing sales for rankings. Adding extraneous words or falsely claiming "in stock" neither sells your products nor makes your customers happy.

- **Make your feed-creation program flexible:** Even if you start using trusted feeds for just a single search engine, be prepared to expand to work with others in the future. Each engine uses a slightly different format, so make sure your programmer is prepared to change the program to create feeds for other search engines when they are needed.

- **Stay on top of daily operations:** In addition to the work of creating the program, you must ensure that your operations personnel run the program to send the data whenever it changes, or else the search engine will not have the most up-to-date information for your site. Don't do all the expensive upfront work and then fall down by not operating reliably.

These are just general guidelines. Each search engine has specific guidelines that you must follow for your products to be listed. Pay close attention to these guidelines as they change; violations can cause the search engine to drop items from your feed or even ignore your entire feed.

Feeds for product search engines can require some work up-front, but they can pay off handsomely when executed properly. If your site would benefit from sales from product search engines, trusted feeds could be the extra lottery ticket it makes sense to buy.

Summary

This chapter covered a great deal. If you started out having no idea how to get your content stored by search engines, you can't say that any more.

You learned how to check to be sure your website is indexed by the organic search engines, and what to do in the unfortunate situation that it's not. You now know how many pages you have in each index and approximately what percentage is indexed (your inclusion ratio). But you also know how to get nearly all of your content indexed.

You learned how to recognize spider traps and eliminate them. You now know what content spiders ignore. You can now create spider paths through your site so that spiders can find every public page. You now know how to control the search spiders so that they do your bidding for you.

You also learned how to ensure that social media content is indexed, along with local content. And how to get your products listed in paid search.

In short, you've learned how to "kick-start" your search efforts, because it all starts with getting your content listed. However, you still have more to learn. In the next chapter, you will learn how to optimize your content so that it is found, it attracts clicks, and entices conversions—for both organic and paid search.

CHAPTER 8

Optimize Your Content

Two-time American presidential candidate Adlai Stevenson once said, "Words calculated to catch everyone may catch no one." Such is the dilemma of optimizing your content. You know that search engines are looking for specific word patterns to decide if your content—landing pages, ads, social media, and so on—should be shown at the top of the results list, but you also know that your content must appeal to the searchers themselves. How do you avoid "catching no one"? We show you the way.

And, although optimizing content is mainly a task for search marketers pursuing organic search rankings, paid search marketers should pay attention, too. Increasingly, paid search landing pages are subjected to quality algorithms to ensure that the page is relevant to the keyword purchased. We note where our tips are for just organic, or for paid, too.

If your head is spinning because you are trying to remember exactly what search engines are looking for at the same time you are trying to write for your visitors first, take a deep breath. You can do this, and do it well, if you are willing to take it one step at a time. Each step in the search content-optimization process builds from the previous ones, as shown in Exhibit 8-1.

You can see from the process that some of the steps are iterative—for example, you continue to change content and check rankings until you get the search results you need. That way, you can take as many tries at them as necessary. Sometimes you get what you need right away, but other times it takes months. Let's look at an overview of each step:

- **Choose a search landing page for a set of keywords:** Start by looking at your keyword list from Chapter 6, "Choose Your Target Market Segments." Pick a strong search landing page from your existing website for one or more of your targeted keywords from your list.

- **Analyze your metrics:** See how your page is performing. For each keyword that you are targeting for your landing page, find out how far down the search results list your landing page is. Find out how many search referrals you get to that page and how many of those visitors complete a web conversion.

- **Improve your content:** If your search marketing is not performing the way you would like (a strong possibility as you start your program), you can analyze your organic search results and paid search ads and check out your landing pages to find areas of improvement for rankings, referrals, and conversions.

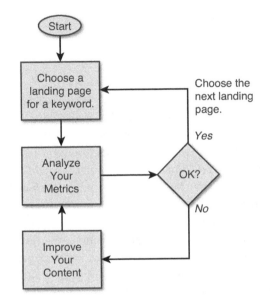

Exhibit 8-1   The process for optimizing content for search. Search ads and landing pages can be continuously improved to get high search rankings and web conversions.

Faithfully following each step will get you where you want to go. So don't feel overwhelmed by all there is to do. Just take the first step by choosing a search landing page to start working on.

Choose Your Search Landing Pages

The place to start optimizing your content is exactly where we left off in Chapter 6 with your list of targeted keywords. For each keyword, you need to identify the page on your site that is the best **search landing page**—the perfect place on your site for a searcher's keyword. Because most of your search keywords will be devoted to increasing traffic on your website, we'll talk about landing pages on your site, but understand that any content that you want to be found for a keyword: A YouTube video, a post on Tumblr, your fan page on Facebook—they can all be considered landing pages, whether on your actual website or not.

It is not necessary for every keyword to have a *unique* landing page; some landing pages can be used for more than one keyword. It *is* important for the keywords to be closely related, however, if they share a landing page. Harkening back to our fictitious company, Snap Electronics, you can imagine that some of their keywords for the *digital camera* campaign might share landing pages. The product category hub page for SnapShot Digital Cameras—the home page for Snap's entire digital camera product line—might be a good search landing page for keywords such as *digital cameras*, *snap digital camera*, *snap camera*, *snapshot*, *snapshot camera*, and *snapshot digital camera*. Even though they are each somewhat different keywords, a searcher wants to see the main digital cameras page on Snap's site in response to any of these keywords.

We will repeat part of that sentence again, because it is *so* important: A *searcher* wants to see the main page on Snap's site for any of these keywords. A *searcher*. You choose your landing page based on what the *searcher* wants to see, not necessarily what *you* want the searcher to see. It is very tempting for folks who have grown up in other forms of marketing to think "message first," as in, "What message do I want to deliver to this person?" Search marketing does not work this way. You *must* consider what information the searcher wants to receive as the primary point of the page. Only when you satisfy the searcher's need can you think about how to "spin" your message around that need.

How Not to Choose a Search Landing Page

Too often, dyed-in-the-wool marketing folks approach landing page selection the same way they do target marketing for print ads. They believe they should be able to select any message they want for the target audience. So you will ask, "What organic search landing page should come up when searchers look for *digital cameras*?" And the marketers reply, "Our 30-day holiday offer for a SnapShot SLR X900 and a free copy of Adobe Photo Elements!" This is probably a bad idea, for a few reasons:

- **That page won't rank highly in organic search:** The pages that rank well for the keyword *digital cameras* are ones that contain basic information about them. Remember, a broad keyword such as *digital cameras* might find a million web pages that contain those words, so the ones that rank highest have many links to them using the words *digital cameras*. Snap's 30-day offer page won't garner that kind of attention. However, the SnapShot digital cameras hub page might, so it is the better choice for a landing page.

- **That page skips several steps in the Buyer's Journey:** You need to match the type of keyword with the type of information on the landing page. An informational keyword (such as *digital cameras*) needs to produce an informational page, not a transactional page that is screaming at searchers to "Buy Today!" Your landing page must be the *perfect* page for the searcher's keyword; otherwise, searchers will not click through (or will abandon your site immediately if they do click through). Visitors will be perturbed by your reaching for their wallets when they were just trying to figure out whether they even want a digital camera. So, in the unlikely event you could get a high ranking for your 30-day offer page, you will not get many conversions from people searching for "digital cameras."

- **That page will soon disappear:** Search marketing is not like other forms of marketing that constantly creates new campaigns that soon disappear without a trace. Search marketing campaigns are more perennial because they are based on searchers' keywords—which tend to remain relatively static. It's true that searcher behavior *sometimes* changes quickly (usually in response to seasonal changes or current events), but more often it changes very slowly. Searchers for "digital cameras" are going to be around during the holiday season, but they will be there in January, too. Will this page? No. So if by some chance Snap *did* get high rankings, and people did convert, all the hard search marketing work is worthless the minute the offer expires. As soon as the 30 days are up, the offer page disappears from the site, and the search engines soon find other pages to put in its place—probably pages from other sites.

For all of these reasons, you need to take a more permanent approach to search landing pages. The closer you design your landing page to the searchers' intent, the easier it will be to put the words they are looking for in context on the page. (It would be odd to mention *digital cameras* six or seven times on the 30-day offer page, but it is quite reasonable on the SnapShot hub page.) Further, the closer your landing page is to the searchers' intent, the more likely it will draw those all-important links from other websites for that subject. And if it matches the searchers' intent, searchers are much more likely to click through to your page. It makes sense to choose permanent pages on your site for keywords that are permanently being searched for.

Does such slavish attention to searcher intent mean that Snap cannot show them the 30-day offer? Not at all. Snap can add a link to the 30-day offer page from the search landing page for *digital cameras* by placing a merchandising spot on the right side of the page (and many other pages, too). After searchers have satisfied their original intent, a merchandising spot with a nice picture of the SLR X900 and an Adobe logo might generate interest in the offer.

Landing Pages for Multiple Keywords

You can choose the same search landing page for multiple keywords, but it is important that they be closely related. You saw earlier that several related keywords might all target Snap's digital camera hub page.

Often, it is necessary for your keywords to share words to make a single landing page effective. The search keywords *digital camera comparison* and *compare digital cameras* can easily share the same page because they are merely variants of the same words. One way to examine how closely your keywords are related is to assess the number of concepts they share. Exhibit 8-2 shows some examples. There are no hard-and-fast rules on how to separate your keywords into concepts. The idea is to think about how closely keywords do relate to each other before choosing the same landing page for them.

Phrase	Concepts
digital cameras	1 (digital cameras)
discount digital cameras	2 (discount) + (digital cameras)
digital camera reviews	2 (digital camera) + (review)
snap digital camera	2 (snap) + (digital camera)
snap digital camera accessories	3 (snap) + (digital camera) + (camera accessories)

Exhibit 8-2 Keyword concepts. You can analyze your keywords to compare how many different ideas are embedded in each one.

Now, it is certainly possible that a single landing page might draw traffic from many different keywords, but that doesn't mean that you can optimize a page to be the best page about each of those keywords. If you think that dozens of competitive keywords will routinely land on the same page, you are fooling yourself.

Different keywords imply different intents on the part of the searcher; they require different search landing pages. If you try to optimize your page for unrelated keywords, you will find that your words calculated to catch everyone will catch no one. Optimizing two unrelated keywords will dilute the density of each one, lowering the page's organic ranking for each keyword. Although your paid search rankings won't necessarily drop from writing about too many keywords, your conversion rate probably will. Better to bite the bullet and choose a different landing page for each one.

In short, if you truly believe that two keywords are so closely related that searchers will want to see the same page, optimize your page for both keywords. Otherwise, go with multiple landing pages. Remember, you can't write a single page about five different things. When you think it is about five things, it is actually about nothing.

When You Can't Find the Right Landing Page

What if you can't think of a good landing page for one of your keyword targets? When Snap Electronics looked at its targeted keywords in Chapter 4, "Unlock the Business Value of Search," the related search keywords *digital camera comparison* and *compare digital cameras* had no strong landing page already on Snap's site. You might be in a similar predicament, or perhaps you know of so many pages on your site that you cannot decide on the best landing page.

Either way, you can get help from search to try to find the best search landing pages. If your site's pages are all indexed by your site search engine, you can search for your keyword and check each page that comes up. Similarly, if you have followed the advice in Chapter 7, "Get Your Content Listed," to get your pages indexed, you can get help from the search engines.

Use the `site:` operator in your keyword the same way you did in Chapter 7 when you were checking how many pages you have indexed. Just add your keyword to the `site:` operator, as Exhibit 8-3 demonstrates with the search keyword *liability insurance* for the Hartford Insurance company. The keyword *liability insurance site:* www.thehartford.com finds all pages containing *liability insurance* within the primary domain of The Hartford Insurance company (revealing 817 matches in Google). You can look at each result to select the best landing page for your keyword.

Exhibit 8-3   Finding possible search landing pages. Using the `site:` operator reveals the pages on your site that contain your targeted keyword.

If you have several possible pages that all seem plausible to you as landing pages, it is fine for you to optimize each one for the same keywords. It is more work than focusing on one page, but it pays off in the long run because a site with multiple pages linked together that are all optimized for the same keyword will receive higher rankings for its pages. Search engines do not

SEARCH LANDING PAGES VERSUS DOORWAY PAGES: WHAT'S THE DIFFERENCE?

Search landing pages are pages you have designed for searchers to enter your site from a search engine. And so are **doorway pages**. But that is where the similarity ends.

A doorway page is a spam technique designed to fool the search engine into providing a high ranking for a page that has no other purpose except organic search rankings. A doorway page is heavily optimized (usually by using other spam methods) to capture searchers and is usually kept hidden from other visitors to the site. Frequently, doorway pages get high rankings from a combination of content optimization and large numbers of links (using a spam technique called a **link farm**, which we expose in Chapter 9, "Prove Your Content's Quality"). A doorway page is a search landing page gone wrong—it serves no purpose on the site except search rankings and is not linked to by the other pages of the site—it has links from the doorway page into the site. So, it is a door that only opens *in*. Doorway pages go by other names, such as **gateway pages** or **entry pages**, but the name is not important. If the page is designed merely for the consumption of search engines, it is spam.

look at just one page; they look at your whole site. In this chapter, we focus on choosing one page to keep things simple, but the more pages you optimize, the better your search rankings will be.

If you have exhausted these methods and still cannot find an acceptable page, it might be time to create a new page. You will not draw any organic search referrals for that keyword if you have no content on your site that matches—and your conversions for a keyword for paid or organic search are likely to be low when you don't have a good landing page.

Analyze Your Metrics

Now that you have chosen a search landing page for a small set of keywords, your next move is to check the performance of your page, according to all the measurements you can amass. Depending on your site's sophistication in search metrics, which will grow over time, you might have a sizable amount of page performance data available for your analysis:

- **Organic search rankings:** Check the organic search ranking of your search landing page for each keyword that you are targeting—in multiple search engines. In Chapter 4, we showed how to project your rankings. Are you achieving the ranking that you expected? If not, you need to make some changes.

- **Search referrals:** If your rankings are good, you should see a high number of visits to the page referred by search engines for your targeted keyword. In Chapter 4, you projected the expected referrals based on good search rankings. Are you achieving what you projected? If not, changes are required.

Search landing pages are different. They are legitimate pages on the site that are linked from many other pages on the site. Although optimized for search rankings, they are designed for visitors first and search engines second.

Some search landing pages—specifically those pages used only for paid search—are actually designed to be closer to doorway pages. You recall from Chapter 6 that some of our low-priority keywords were used for paid search only—this is the reason. You can create paid search landing pages that are not part of the mainline site navigation and have links merely leading into the site. The difference between these pages and doorway pages is they are not being used for organic search at all. (You should use a robots tag or robots.txt file to block them from organic search.) Because you are not fooling the organic engines with these pages, they are not spam.

So, be sure to heavily link organic search landing pages into your site's main navigation paths. You can create somewhat more hidden pages for use as paid search landing pages, but be sure that they are never crawled by spiders; you don't want to be inadvertently guilty of spamming.

- **Web conversions:** Remember, the point of search marketing is not top rankings or even high referrals, but increased web conversions. If your page is getting high rankings and referrals, but visitors do not convert, your landing page and other pages on your site need to be changed.

If you were only to track one metric for all of your pages, web conversions would be the one because it correlates to your overall goal for search marketing. Until conversions increase, you have not succeeded. But it's helpful to track the others, too, because they can help you figure out what's wrong and what to do about it.

If you think about it, if search rankings are low, referrals and conversions will be, too. Similarly, if rankings are okay, but referrals remain low, conversions will continue to be low, too. However, you will take different actions in these two situations, because the ways to improve search rankings are not always the same as the ways to improve low referrals when you have high rankings. Moreover, the actions designed to raise low conversions differ from what you do to raise disappointing referrals. So all three measurements help you diagnose what is wrong with your pages.

And if these three measurements do not sound like numbers you calculate once and then forget about, well, you're right. You will be tracking these metrics for all of your landing pages forever; because page performance can change at any time, you need to constantly maintain your page to continue to succeed.

If you do not know how to gather these measurements, don't worry about that yet. We cover them each in depth in Chapter 10, "Make Search Marketing Operational," when we explain the various measurements you will want to stay on top of. For now, just understand that each time you optimize a page you will check several different measurements before declaring success. Later in this chapter, you will learn how to change your page to improve these metrics, because you will be making changes to your pages until they meet your metrics projections.

Check Your Organic Search Rankings

Let's take a quick look at organic search rankings. We continue with the insurance example. Although there are 817 pages from The Hartford in the Google index containing the keyword *liability insurance*, Google will show no more than one or two of them (if any) in the top ten, and only a few others throughout the rest of the results. Google (and other search engines) limit the results for any one site because searchers want to see a variety of sites in response to their search.

Does that mean that The Hartford should not try to optimize all 817 pages? Not at all. The more pages are optimized, the more it helps all of their rankings. And many of those 817 pages might be perfect landing pages for other keywords related to liability insurance, such as *product liability insurance* or *professional liability insurance*. When pages are optimized for these deeper keywords, they enhance rankings *for liability insurance*, too, because the words *liability insurance* are contained within each of the deeper keywords.

At our companion website, we list several tools that automatically perform rank checking (SEMincBook.com/rank-check-tools), but for this exercise it's fine to do the checking manually, by entering the keyword and working your way through the results list looking for your company's pages. It turns out that even though there were 817 pages indexed in Google with that keyword, only 3 of them rank in the top 1,000, with the highest at #51.

Check your rankings for every keyword you are targeting for your search landing page, and it's best to check in multiple search engines. It is probable that your first ranking check for your search landing page will not show high rankings any more than The Hartford's check did. After you make changes to your page (we explain what kinds of changes later in the chapter), you wait for the search spider to come around again (which can take days, weeks, or sometimes months), and then you recheck your rankings. You continue this "lather, rinse, and repeat" cycle until you attain the rankings you need to meet the search marketing projections you made in Chapter 4.

In this brave new world of personalized search, you might be wondering how you check your organic search rankings. If each searcher can potentially get a different set of search results, the concept of ranking #1 becomes meaningless. You might think that logging out of Google and Bing would help, and it does, but some personalization is done by location (which search engines can do without you being logged in). Google Webmaster Tools can show the average ranking for your most popular keywords, which isn't everything you want to know, but it is better than nothing. You can refer to our companion website for a list of tools that check the organic search ranking of your content (SEMincBook.com/rank-check-tools).

Measure Your Search Referrals

After you have optimized your page for high rankings, you need to check your search referrals. As soon as the search spider has crawled your updated page and it attains a new organic search ranking, you should see organic referrals change. If you pony up for a paid search ad that points to that page, your paid search referrals ought to increase also. Your web analytics facility can show you referrals for your search landing page, so you can do a before-and-after comparison to determine whether you are getting the projected clickthroughs on your page.

If your page has the high organic rankings you hoped for and your paid search ad is being shown prominently, but your referrals are not what you expected, you need to look at how to make your page and your ad more appealing for searchers to click. Later in this chapter, we show you ways to do that. As before, after you make changes to your page, you wait for the spiders to return and then check your organic referrals again. Sometimes you will find that changes you made to improve clickthrough damaged your search rankings, so you will need to try again. For example, you might have removed an important keyword to add a call to action. You'll have no such issues with changing your paid search ad. Keep tweaking it for clickability, and watch the referrals change immediately.

Calculate Your Search Conversions

Eventually, you will achieve the rankings and referrals that you are shooting for—in paid and organic search—but you are not done until you start getting the conversions that you projected. In Chapter 10, you will learn several ways to track your conversions from search, but let's focus on just the process now. In Chapter 4, you projected the number of conversions you expected to result from your search marketing campaign. Now is the time to see whether you are achieving those goals.

Your web analytics facility (Google Analytics, for example) can measure your conversions as long as you have followed the instructions for your particular facility. For example, Google Analytics allows you to place a snippet of JavaScript on your conversion page to track shopping cart sales.

No matter how many conversions you calculate, however, you always want more. To improve the number of conversions stemming from search, you first need to use your web analytics facility to investigate where most of your visitors abandon your site; it's somewhere between the search landing page and the conversion page. To correct the problem and boost conversions, you might need to make changes to the search landing page itself, or you might have work to do on other pages on your site. You will carefully make changes to your landing page so as not to disturb your rankings and referrals. The good news is that you need not wait for the spiders to see the effects of conversion changes: As soon as you change the pages, you can measure whether the changes improved your web conversions.

None of these problems might seem like search marketing problems to you, but making money is the point of search marketing. And there is one cause of low conversions that is clearly within the scope of search marketing. One reason your conversions might be low, even when you have high rankings and string visitor traffic, might be that you have targeted the wrong keywords. You might have created excellent content that the search engines display in response to your targeted keywords, and searchers might happily click on that content, but perhaps those searchers are not the right market segment to actually purchase your product. You might need to focus on other keywords with higher conversion rates because they attract your potential customers.

Next, you see what to do about low conversions (and low rankings and referrals, too). If your landing page does not deliver the metrics you projected, what can you do to improve the situation? You have to work on your content.

Improve Your Content

We take an expansive view of "content": It's anything you can create as a search marketer. So, landing pages are definitely content. But, what about blog posts? Yes. Videos? Yes. Paid search ads? Yep. Your location data in Google Local for Business? Uh huh. It's all content—and you need to improve all of your content to have the maximum impact on your search marketing program.

We've talked already about the three main metrics that require improvement in search marketing: rankings, referrals, and conversions. Content is the key to improving all three metrics, but we'll look at two separate ideas. The first is what your search results actually look like on the search results page and the second is how other changes to your content affect your conversions.

Improve Your Search Results

You remember from Exhibit 1-2 in Chapter 1, "How Search Marketing Works," that different keywords produce different kinds of search results. Your first step in improving your search results is to identify what type of content the search engines show for your targeted keywords. If your keywords are returning videos, or locations, or blog posts, then it does you no good to spend all of your efforts optimizing your web pages. Likewise, spend less time on paid search ads if your targeted keyword is returning mainly product listing ads.

How Do You Optimize Mobile Apps?

Depending on your content, you might need to research techniques for places you don't usually think of as search engines. App Store Optimization (ASO) is an emerging set of techniques that helps you get high rankings for searches for your mobile app in app stores from Apple, Google, and others.

Many of the same techniques you use in SEO apply here, but you might find a few surprises:

- **Optimize your title:** No surprise here. The name of your app is among the most important pieces of information. Many apps have clever, unique names, but you might consider one rich with keywords if you have no way of promoting your name. The search benefits you get might outweigh the cute branding bounce.

- **Use keywords:** Apple lets you add a few keywords to describe your app—take full advantage.

- **Craft your description:** Your description not only helps your rankings but is the text that searchers read when deciding to download. Make it count.

- **Focus on your user ratings:** Quality counts. The higher your user ratings, the higher your app will rank. Support your users, solve their problems, and be likable. Your search rankings might depend on it.

- **Pick an appealing icon:** Bright color, professional design, that "convey-the-meaning" in one glance look. They all lead to higher clickthrough rates.

- **Show screenshots:** Make sure that your app page contains "at-a-glance" screenshots that show the searcher how it works. Nothing works better to cause the searcher to actually download than if they "get" how this app will help them.

- **Pick the right content rating:** Unless you really have restricted content, make sure your content rating is the broadest—for the general user—so that you aren't blocked for certain users.

- **Don't ignore paid search:** If you have the budget, you can use paid search ads to advertise your app for download.

Remember that search marketing is always evolving. Whenever a new form of content appears, try to use your existing skills to figure out how to apply them.

But before you start checking your search results, you must also sign out of your Google or Microsoft accounts. You don't want to check your own personalized search results instead of the generic results that anonymous searchers get.

That works fine for most kinds of search results, but how can you know what kinds of local search results searchers are seeing? Google offers a way to simulate a local search, as shown in Exhibit 8-4. You can search for one of your targeted keywords—which will show results based on your current location—but you can change your location to any one you like, such as New York City, as shown in the exhibit.

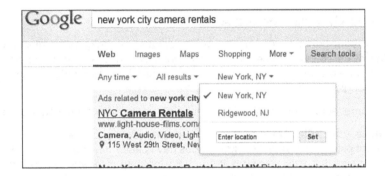

Exhibit 8-4   Simulating local search results. Google provides a way for you to see what the local search results look like as if you were in another location.

We'll dive into how to improve several different kinds of search results, but one thing for you to think about, as you look at the whole search results page, is the impression that entire set of results makes on the searcher. It's tempting to always think in terms of individual organic results, search ads, and the like, but the searcher experiences them as a group.

Often, search marketers have the opportunity to influence two or even more of the results on a page, and they should think about controlling as much of the "shelf space" for their targeted keywords as they can. Research from Google shows that 81% of paid ads do not have a corresponding organic listing from that paid search advertiser. This is a key reason many advertisers use paid search: not having a top listing in organic. Some might say that if you can get the top listing in organic, there is no need to buy a paid search ad for that same keyword. But we also know that appearing in multiple places on the page might impress searchers that your company is "the one." Using metrics to find the optimal balance of paid and organic search results is what we refer to as **co-optimization**. We go into more detail in Chapter 9 on how to maximize your collaborative performance.

We'll focus on improving organic and paid search results separately, because the techniques used are so different. We'll start with organic.

Improve Your Organic Search Results

As you saw earlier, organic search results can take in a lot of ground—everything from web pages to social media to local search. But they have something in common: Most have a title and a snippet that you can optimize so that you are putting your best foot forward for your content. So, we'll start there.

Perfect Your Title   Your titles are the most important elements of any content for organic search. Whether it is the title tag of a web page, the headline of your blog post, or the title field of your YouTube video, it's the same to the search engine. Your content's most important calling card with the search engine is its title.

Your title serves two purposes: to help search engines know what your content is about, and to attract the searcher's click on your search results to see your content.

As we discussed in Chapter 3, "How Search Works," many factors contribute to high organic search rankings. We are covering the keyword factors in this chapter, and we'll walk through the content factors in Chapter 9. We'll be showing some examples in this chapter to give you an idea of how optimizing your content around keywords can help your rankings. These examples are overly simplistic, but do show you the concepts. For less-popular keywords—long-tail keywords—these on-page optimization techniques make much more of a difference than for very competitive keywords, such as *digital cameras*, but they matter somewhat for every keyword.

Your title tag is your best means of improving both search rankings and search referrals. Unfortunately, you typically need to trade one off against the other. If you load up your title with keywords to produce high rankings, its unreadable nature will hinder clickthrough.

This very tension between rankings and referrals causes search engines to give the title such weight for search rankings. Other metadata, such as the **keywords metatag**, are now largely or completely ignored by search engines, precisely because they were used only to achieve rankings; they do not appear on the page. Those tags could be optimized for search rankings, but there was no counterbalance to keep the content accurate—a wide-open invitation for spam. Because titles are shown to searchers, you as the search marketer must design your title to appeal to both search engines and to searchers, so it is less susceptible to spamming.

Snap's referrals and conversions for its SnapShot digital camera hub page are very low because it is ranked #45 for the keyword *digital camera*. So, you'd be excused if you thought that raiding that ranking was the only thing to be working on now. But it's worth considering whether there are any changes needed to optimize *referrals* now. The title tag is crucial in driving referrals because it is the first thing searchers see about your page on the search results screen. As you learned in Chapter 4, of the time searchers spend reviewing the search results page, 30% of that time is spent looking at titles. In contrast, the title has no impact on conversion because visitors do see your web page's title after they land on your page.

"Snap Electronics digital cameras for you" is not a terribly compelling title. Perhaps the Snap Electronics brand name would cause some searchers to click, but the SnapShot brand is completely missing. And for those unfamiliar with the brand, there is absolutely no reason to click. We have some ideas later in this chapter to improve this title to boost both rankings and referrals.

Although Snap's title did not look great, it seems easy to fix. After all, how hard is it to rewrite a title? Exhibit 8-5 shows some of the possibilities for the SnapShot hub page we have been analyzing. Part of the tension between ranking effectiveness and referral effectiveness concerns the length of the title. There is no limit on the amount of text that can be used with a title tag, but search engines do not use all of it. It is not known how many characters in a title the search engines use for ranking purposes, but they clearly truncate the title displayed on the search results page at around 55 to 70 characters, usually at a word boundary, but it varies between search engines. Search engines show that a title has been truncated by adding an ellipsis (...) at the truncation point. Some experts advise creating a title somewhat longer than the truncation point to squeeze in an additional keyword, while tuning the title to be readable and compelling when truncated. Others believe that shorter titles of around 40 characters compel the highest referrals and that truncated titles turn off visitors.

Snap knows that it has a well-known brand name and that many of its highest-converting keywords contain its company name (Snap) and its brand name (SnapShot). Your business might not have that kind of name recognition, so you might be better advised to lead with the generic product name (digital cameras). Tailor your titles to what searchers are looking for and you *will* improve your rankings.

So what creates high-ranking effectiveness? You already know the answer. Keywords—the words they are searching for. But you also need to include thematically related words that will catch the searcher's eye while scanning results. If you want to optimize for multiple keywords (especially several multiple-word keywords), however, you run out of space very quickly unless they are *very* closely related. So, Snap can optimize their digital cameras hub page for *digital cameras*, and *Snapshot digital cameras*, and *Snap digital cameras*, but probably not *digital camera comparison*.

What to leave out of a title is just as important as what to put in. Obviously, words that are neither keywords nor strong calls to action must go. Delete *home page*. In fact, *page* by itself is also useless. Wipe out *welcome, online, menu*. You get the idea. These flabby words do not drive rankings or clickthrough. Every "waste" word you remove leaves more room for words that matter and improves your keyword density.

Combine keywords wherever possible. When Snap writes *SnapShot Digital Cameras*, a double dip takes effect: The page is optimized for the keyword *snapshot digital cameras* but for the *digital cameras* keyword, too. Repeat keywords if you can get away with it. It hurts readability if overdone, but if you can do it naturally, go for it.

Title	Ranking Effectiveness	Referral Effectiveness
SnapShot home page	Just one keyword	No call to action
Snap digital cameras for you	Better, but not enough	Still no call to action
Save on Snap digital cameras	Still weak	Good call to action
Snap Electronics—SnapShot Digital Cameras	Keywords improved	No call to action
Snap Electronics—SnapShot Digital Cameras—Save on digital cameras	Strong on keywords	Good call to action
SnapShot Digital Cameras from Snap Electronics—Save on digital cameras	Strong keywords with improved prominence	Good call to action
SnapShot Digital Cameras—the best digital camera from Snap... Electronics	Very strong keywords (including singular and plural forms) with strong prominence	Good call to action that Save on reinforces brand image, but company name truncated onscreen
SnapShot Digital Cameras from Electronics—Save on the best ...digital camera	Very strong keywords with very strong prominence	Good call to action Snap with brand image reinforcement, with repeated keyword truncated onscreen
Snap Digital Cameras—Save on digital camera	Very strong keywords with very strong prominence and density	Good call to action SnapShot with no truncation

Ellipsis (...) indicates estimated truncation point onscreen.

Exhibit 8-5 Digital camera landing page title alternatives. There are many bad choices for titles, but many good ones, too.

To improve referral effectiveness, cram as many trigger words into the title as you can, making sure it is readable. Happily, for many situations, the keywords and the trigger words are the same. *Snap Electronics* and *SnapShot* are the kinds of well-known brand names that spur clicks. Other trigger words include local place names, low prices, prized features, and time-sensitive offers. But do *not* get the searcher off track; you need to reinforce the searcher's keyword first and foremost. If you can reinforce the searcher's keyword and still have room to add brand image keywords or a strong call to action, do so.

Sometimes the title is not enough to cause a searcher to click. Fortunately, the searcher will see your snippet, too. You need to influence what text shows up there.

Influence Your Snippet   You've seen the "pitch" on the outside of an envelope of a direct marketing piece. A strong pitch causes more people to open the envelope and read the content inside. A snippet is the pitch on the outside of your search marketing "envelope." Your snippet is shown below your page's title on the search results page and can make the difference between a searcher clicking your page or passing you by.

Snippets, the short blurb of text underneath the page title on the search results page, are excerpts of text from your page that aid a searcher to decide whether to click through or not. If your snippets provide searchers with an appealing synopsis of your page, you will raise your referrals for that page. Some studies have shown that searchers spend more time looking at snippets than any other part of the search results page, which makes sense, because the titles usually

HOW DO YOU OPTIMIZE BLOG POSTS?

Blogs are natural-born organic search enhancers, because they provide steady, fresh, high-interest content using the language your customers use. Don't overlook the fine points of blog search optimization. If you're going to invest the time to write one, you might as well optimize it.

Providing content in your blog is not enough. You need to make sure that you are optimizing your content with the right keywords in your titles and your body copy—even in the name and description of the blog itself. That helps you get search traffic for each blog post.

But how do you do that?

You start by understanding the three main formats for web feeds, RSS Version 1, RSS Version 2, and Atom. Your blog software likely can produce all three kinds of feeds. Often, a feed in RSS Version 1 format is created in a file named index.rdf, one in RSS Version 2 is created in rss.xml, and an Atom feed in atom.xml, although you can name your feed files anything you want. Inside these files are tags, similar to HTML tags, containing information about your blog and the most recent blog posts in that blog.

The two versions of RSS each use the `<channel>` tag to identify the blog itself and the `<item>` tag to delineate each individual post. Atom's format is similar, using the `<feed>` tag for the blog and the `<entry>` tag for each post. All three formats allow titles for the blog and the posts, and all three use the `<title>` tag for this purpose.

Just as with web pages, the `<title>` tag is the most important one for organic search. Everything you've learned about HTML titles is pertinent to feed titles, too. In fact, because blogs typically contain no heading tags, there's even more pressure to make the most of your title. Ensure that your feed titles use targeted keywords early and often, but also that they appeal to searchers, not just search engines, without being overly cute or cryptic. It's include the keywords the searcher is looking for while the snippets often have more room for a call to action. The snippets are the real differentiation that helps searchers decide whether to click.

Because you cannot predict every possible variation of search keyword that searchers will use to find your page, there is no way to control what displays in every case. However, you might find it to your advantage to massage your writing to influence snippets for the targeted keywords. To do that, you need to understand a little bit about how search engines choose their snippets.

Each search engine uses different rules for composing its snippets, but it is always good to place the first occurrences of your major keywords together. So, Snap should not allow the first occurrence of *digital cameras* to appear without its brand name. Make sure that your brand name (such as *SnapShot digital cameras*) is the first occurrence, so that searchers for *digital cameras* will see your brand name in the title and in the snippet. Some tools enable you to preview your snippet. Check out which ones at our website (SEMincBook.com/content-analyzers).

of no use to get a #1 result that no one clicks on, nor to have a catchy title that contains no targeted keywords.

You should also pay attention to using keywords in the body of each blog post, just as you do in the body of a web page. The first paragraph of a blog post is the most important part of the body, not just because keywords found near the beginning of the post are treated as more important, but because that paragraph is often shown with the blog post's title to induce clicks. Including an image in that first paragraph often adds a touch that raises click rates.

Link to older blog posts when relevant, and use keywords that show the search engines what that post is about. Internal links are not as valuable as those you get from outside your site, but every hint about what subject your site is about helps establish your credibility on the subject. Search engines are thought to favor sites having strong themes for search queries that match those themes.

For the content that you create, continue using your target keywords in titles and elsewhere, just as you always have for old-fashioned web pages. For nontext content, such as photos and videos, titles and descriptions are especially important. Submit your content to as many aggregators as you have time for, not just YouTube and Flickr, for example. Claim your blog in Technorati (and in other blog search engines and directories). And place social bookmarking buttons on your pages for Digg, del.icio.us, and other sites, so your readers can bookmark your content for other social bookmarking users to see. Similarly, share buttons for Twitter, Facebook, and other social networks encourage your readers to alert others about your posts.

Although designing your content with interesting titles, descriptions, and file names is time-worn advice, it still works. Applying this technique to blog posts and videos is a great way to start.

This is a completely legitimate technique because you are providing an accurate synopsis of what is on the page. The search engines are happy for you to take the care to consider what the snippet will say for popular keywords, although they might change their snippet algorithms at any time. Remember, there is no reason to induce clickthrough for searchers who will not ultimately convert, so you want your snippets to be a factual representation of your page.

When Snap looked at the Google and Bing snippets for the *digital cameras* keyword, they were almost identical, as shown in Exhibit 8-6. This snippet has no strong call to action and no mention of the Snap or SnapShot brand names, making it less likely that a searcher would click through to this page. Snap decided it would try to optimize its snippets later in the process.

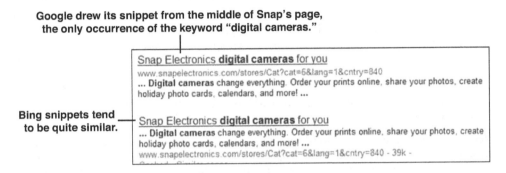

Exhibit 8-6   Digital camera landing pages snippets. Check your snippets in each search engine as your first step in improving them.

Sometimes search engines take the snippet from somewhere that you won't see on the page at all: the **description metatag**. Like all metatags, the description is found in the header of the HTML file and is not normally displayed anywhere. Metatags are designed to provide information about the page—in this case, a short text description of what the page is about. In the early days of search, the description tag's contents were shown as the snippet on the search results page. Because that text was never shown to visitors, search engines soon found description tags littered with keywords from spammers just trying to get better search rankings and clickthroughs. So, search engines responded by using the description tag less and less for ranking or for displaying the snippet, but they sometimes still use it, so it makes sense for you to write something good—up to the approximately 170 characters that search engines might show.

Snap Electronics rewrote their landing page to influence their snippets for *digital cameras*. The original copy was loaded with model names and features but did not mention digital cameras prominently. The first line of text in the body was changed to say, "SnapShot Digital Cameras feature a wide range of models ranging from the award-winning X5 to the top-of-the-line SLR X900...." This opening was considered a good compromise between what the marketing department wanted and what was required for a call to action.

The marketing department asked for its copy to be used for the description, but it was changed a bit to ensure it delivered a strong snippet. The new description begins "SnapShot

Digital Cameras, named 'Best Digital Camera' by Camera Views magazine, features world-famous ease of use based on the OneTouch...."

By tweaking its body text and description, Snap raised its odds of placing action-oriented text into its snippet that reinforced the brand image Snap wants to convey. For your high-priority keywords, similar attention might raise your search referrals.

In recent years, search engines have enhanced these garden variety snippets to become **rich snippets**, which show structured data as part of some search results, including results for people, events, and product reviews. Rich snippets are constructed for pages that contain a set of special HTML tags that define the meaning of the content—sometimes called **microdata** or **microformats**. Events, for example, are defined with names, locations, start times, and ticket prices. Several formats are available—we review them and provide advice as to the best approach on our site (SEMincBook.com/rich-snippets). You can learn more as new types are announced at Schema.org.

Some kinds of content, such as videos and events, benefit dramatically from the use of schemas because search engines don't do a great job of recognizing these kinds of contents without the schema information. That's a big reason schemas were invented in the first place. Exhibit 8-7 shows off a range of Google snippets that can each be influenced by the way you encode the data on your page and by how it is reviewed in social media.

This is an Example of a Title Tag that is Seventy Characters in Length
www.yourdomain.com
Aug 29, 2013 – Here is an example of what a snippet looks like in Google. If your snippet (including the date) exceeds 156 characters, it is truncated ...

SES **Conference** & Expo | Education for Today's Experienced ...
sesconference.com/ ▾
SES **Conference** & Expo is the leading global event series for **search** and social marketing, with a focus on tactics and best practices. ... SES **San Francisco** 2013 ... Greg Jarboe +1'd this

East **Sushi** - **Trenton, NJ** - Yelp
www.yelp.com › Restaurants › Japanese ▾
★★★★☆ Rating: 4 - 23 reviews - Price range: $$
23 Reviews of East **Sushi** "This is a great place, I am very drawn to their Wonton Soup and Excellent Fresh food. The food is ... **Trenton**, NJ 08628. (609) 771- ...

Webinars – **Biznology**
www.**biznology**.com/webinars/ ▾
by Mike Moran - in 568 Google+ circles
September 24 at 11 am ET with Rob Petersen and Mike Moran .... Every other month, we present a new 30-minute **Biznology** Webinar, bringing you the latest on ...
You've visited this page 3 times. Last visit: 5/15/13

Exhibit 8-7 So many kinds of snippets. Snippets might have just text, can include publish dates, bold keywords, reviews, and other kinds of data.

Snap Electronics decided to take advantage of the product data for all of its cameras, encoding the product name, its picture, description, and price to be displayed in the rich snippet. Once done, this data was displayed as part of the snippet right on the result page for all Snap cameras.

INFLUENCE THE LINKS SEARCH ENGINES SHOW IN YOUR TOP SEARCH RESULT

If you are lucky enough to have the #1 result for a keyword, you might have noticed that both Google and Bing sometimes provide extra links to deeper pages within your site as part of your search result, as shown in Exhibit 8-8. Google refers to these extra links as **sitelinks**, Bing calls them **deep links**, but the names are less important than their value to you.

Search Marketing Expo – **SMX Stockholm, Sweden**
smxstockholm.se/ ▾
Welcome to a conference where both marketers and SEO-gurus can grow and learn from each other and global experts.
You've visited this page 3 times. Last visit: 8/18/13

Register	Day 1
Register now for Search Marketing Expo - SMX Stockholm 2012 ...	Keynote: FROM STORYTELLING TO MICROTARGETING: HOW ...
Speakers	Day 1 2012
Razvan is the proud Founder & Chief Architect of ...	Agenda overview 2012 · Day 1 2012 · Day 2 2012 · Speakers ...
Agenda	Call for Speakers
The Agenda Overview of the Search Marketing Expo - SMX ...	Call for Speakers, Search Marketing Expo - SMX ...

More results from smxstockholm.se »

Exhibit 8-8   Links deep within your site. If you get the #1 search result, Google and Bing might show several pages within your site, not just one.

You know that #1 search results already drive many more clicks than other search results, so how would you like to have seven search results, all at the top of that search results page? You can show off deep pages on your site that the searchers can use to immediately find what they are looking for.

While you cannot select which links appear, you can use Google and Bing Webmaster Tools to block pages you feel are inappropriate, which gives you some influence over which links *do* appear. You should regularly review your deeper links and change your titles to improve clickthrough if needed.

Improve Your Paid Search Results

Just as we focused on organic search results, we care just as much about how our paid search results look. It is not enough to set up your paid search program and bid on the right keywords. Just as a direct-mail piece needs the right words to get you to open the envelope, you need to get searchers to click your listings. Effective copywriting is crucial for driving clickthrough rates for your paid search ad listing, but not for product search (which has no copy). We look at both, starting with paid search copywriting.

Craft Your Ad Copy   Nineteenth-century American humorist Henry Wheeler Shaw once said, "Money will buy you a pretty good dog, but it won't buy the wag of his tail." And so it is with paid search, where your per-click fees can buy impressions for your ad, but only your copy will get the clicks you need from searchers.

For organic search, you saw that it can be difficult to craft pages that contain the search keywords (so that both the search engines and the searchers find what they are looking for). With paid search, you will have no such difficulty—you can lead searchers to whatever pages you want with your paid ads. Well, almost.

Paid search engines do have editorial guidelines designed to protect their business. Each search engine has somewhat different rules, but they are very similar:

- **Don't circumvent the click:** Search engines get paid only when searchers click, so they are understandably displeased with ads that show phone numbers or email addresses that allow the searcher to buy from you without clicking.

- **Don't hype it up:** Excessive capitalization and showy punctuation (especially exclamation marks and question marks) are frequently rejected. Use of impossible-to-prove superlatives (best, most, greatest, cheapest, and so on) are also a quick ticket to a blocked ad.

- **Don't hide your identity:** Be clear about who you are. If you are an affiliate, for example, don't try to pass yourself off as the manufacturer.

Google and Bing publish extensive tips about how to follow their guidelines and how to make your ads as successful as possible. There are three critical parts to paid search ads, as illustrated in Exhibit 8-9:

- **Title:** The first line of the ad must catch the searcher's eye or you will get very low clickthrough.

- **Description:** Your benefits and call to action go here. If you hooked them with the title, this is where you get them to click.

- **Display URL:** Not the URL that searchers will click through to, it is a shortened version that usually is just the domain of the company (yourcompany.com) so that searchers know where they are going when they click.

Exhibit 8-9 Anatomy of a paid search ad: All paid search ads have the same three components, as this diagram demonstrates.

When you sit down to write your copy, you'll notice how little room you have. Both Google and Bing ads limit your descriptions to just 70 characters. Make it punchy and edit your ad until all extraneous words are removed. Here's some more advice to guide you in creating good titles and descriptions for your paid search ads:

- **Use the keywords:** Searchers are fixated on finding the words they just typed. They scan the search results page looking for them—ads with keywords attract nearly 50% more clicks. Sometimes, the keyword itself is so long that it does not fit in the title (and it would badly clutter up the description), such as *snapshot SLR x900 digital camera reviews*. In that case, strategically shorten the keyword, perhaps to *snapshot x900 reviews*. If you use the most important words in the searcher's keyword, your click rate should be strong. Remember, however, that most (if not all) of the ads will contain the searcher's keyword, so you need to do more than that.

- **Sell factual benefits:** Why should searchers click your ad? What do your customers want? Do you have a lower price? Free shipping? Quick delivery? Are you a reliable supplier? Do you have a key benefit for the product itself? Can you quantify that benefit? Try to say something factual that your competitors cannot. If you are the manufacturer, make sure you explain you are not an affiliate; that might improve your click rate. Small businesses using local search need to emphasize their location—use the name of the locality (*Central New Jersey*) and also use imagery words, such as *good neighbor*, that a national brand cannot always get away with. Fact-based ads get more clicks than "sales-y" ones. Use full sentences to increase the fact-based effect, rather than breathless phrases that reek of hype. Unless you offer a compelling factual benefit to searchers, they will not click through to become customers.

- **Attract attention:** Although the editorial guidelines restrict your use of capitalization, exclamation points, and hyped-up copy, try to use the strongest words you can within those limits. You cannot use *greatest* but you can use *great*. Test your copy with different words that attract attention. *Save and discount* are always attention-getters, but if you can find exciting words to describe your benefits while remaining factual (and not breathless), that approach is very successful. And include your well-known brand names; recognizable brands cause searcher clicks, so highlight yours.

- **Call the searcher to action:** Make it abundantly clear what you want the searcher to do. Not "click here," but rather, use words that speak to the searcher's task. If you are selling something, use "buy." "Download this case study." "Get a free quote instantly." If you appeal to the searcher's intent (remember Chapter 2, "How Searchers Work"), you will attract the searcher's click.

- **Create urgency:** Your call to action must be clear and must impel the searcher to click now. "Order today to receive before Christmas." "Only 50 remaining." "All orders placed in May receive this free gift." "Discounted 30% through Saturday." You get the idea.

TOO MUCH OF A GOOD THING? HOW TO QUALIFY SEARCHERS BEFORE THEY CLICK

We have emphasized all the ways you can increase the clickthrough rate on your ad, but sometimes you have a different problem: You get the clicks, but not the conversions you expected. Sometimes that is a problem with your landing page, or other pages on your site, but it can also be a sign that your ad is not properly qualifying your searchers.

Just as important as getting the right people to click is dissuading the wrong people from clicking. Write your ads so they attract the searchers who will actually convert. If you attract unqualified visitors, you will drain your budget with low conversion rates. Snap Electronics found that their ad for the *digital cameras* keyword needed to emphasize Snap's exclusiveness and its quality. These words sufficiently positioned the camera away from bargain hunters who clicked and then blanched at the price. By dissuading those unqualified searchers, Snap lowered its per-click fees and raised its conversion rate.

Qualifying customers is important, but it has its risks, too. If the clickthrough rate for your ad drops too low, it will rarely be shown (because the ranking algorithms consider both click rate and bid).

Sometimes the best way to qualify your customers is to change the way you buy keywords. If the click rates for Snap Electronics dropped too low, they could change their keyword strategy so that they purchased keywords that fit their product image. Instead of trying to target *digital camera*, Snap could add negative keywords (such as *cheap*, *discount*, or *bargain*, to eliminate the wrong searchers). Or Snap could go after more specific keywords, such as *best digital camera* or *8 megapixel camera*. Making your keywords more specific lowers your per-click fees and raises your conversion rates without lowering your clickthrough rates.

After you have decided on wording, it's time to actually place your ad. It can save you time to use the same copy for an entire ad group; that is why you collected them together in the first place. Most search engines allow you to edit the individual ads for each keyword within the ad group, also. (Later, we'll show you a way to dynamically insert text into ads to change them for each keyword.)

Search engines usually enable you to add information for local searches to complement your paid ads. For example, Bing offers **Location Extensions** for their ads, which allow advertisers to display their business address and phone number in the text ad. Bing states that the addition of Location Extensions has increased click rates from 8% to 16%. This is even more beneficial on a mobile device because the phone number can be clicked so the searcher can immediately call the advertiser.

We have focused on titles and descriptions, but the last part of a paid search ad, the display URL, is also important. Display URLs tell the searcher where their click leads them. If you have a well-known brand or website, make sure that the display URL plays it up.

Manage Your Paid Search Ads   We have continually counseled you to go after as many keywords as you can profitably afford, and we have told you to place keywords in every ad, and to test variations against each other. How can you reduce the labor for all this work?

Let's start with inserting keywords into hundreds or thousands of ads. You have probably set up ad groups for keywords that are similar in meaning. That's great, because those keywords can share the same ads, reducing your copywriting work. But it causes a new problem, because you want the keyword the searcher entered to appear in each ad. If you have used the same copy for each ad, how do the keywords get inserted?

The search engines allow you to use placeholders in your ad copy that they will substitute with the actual keywords the searcher entered, allowing you to use the same ad for many keywords while still showing those keywords in the ad. Google refers to this capability as **Keyword Insertion**; it is called **Dynamic Text Substitution** by Bing.

When you define your titles or descriptions, you can use curly braces to indicate the place where you want the keyword inserted into your copy. Snap Electronics has two dozen models that they placed in a single ad group so they could share the same copy for their ad across all models. But they wanted the model name in the title, so they coded their title as "Buy {keyword: SnapShot Cameras} direct"—which inserts the searcher's keyword dynamically. For example, if the searcher entered *snapshot slr*, the title of the ad would read "Buy snapshot slr direct." By controlling the match type of the ad group, Snap ensured that only phrases with *SnapShot* were part of this ad group. Sometimes, however, the keyword entered by the searchers is too long to fit in the title, such as *snap snapshot slr x900*. In that case, the default text after the "Keyword:" in the braces would be inserted instead, creating a title of "Buy SnapShot Cameras direct." You can even control the capitalization of the words if you know what you are doing.

The dynamic capabilities of Google and Bing to insert keywords into your title or your description enable you to raise your click rate without much extra work. If you are using a paid search engine that does not offer any comparable tool, they usually accept ad content submitted using spreadsheets, so you can use macros in your favorite spreadsheet to insert your own keywords into standard ad copy. You will have to code your macro to count the number of characters to ensure you do not exceed the length restrictions for the engine you are feeding (substituting default text in that case). It is not as elegant as dynamic text insertion capabilities, but can be equally effective. Whatever it takes, make sure that you get the searcher's keywords into every ad possible. It dramatically raises your clickthrough rate.

You can also raise your click rate by testing multiple versions of ad copy for the same keyword to see which one draws more conversions. As you might expect, this can be labor-intensive, too. **A/B testing** (where you test version A against version B) or **multivariate testing** (where you test many possibilities simultaneously) can be automated by many bid management tools. Google Content Experiments is a free tool that allows you to automatically test content combinations to select the best one. Mike's book, *Do It Wrong Quickly: How the Web Changes the Old Marketing Rules*, delves more deeply into multivariate testing.

Regardless of how you manage your ad copy, finding ways to raise your clickthrough rates with the least possible effort is a winning strategy. You can also work on your product search listings to attract more clicks, as you will see next.

Improve Product Search Listings   Even though Google Product Listing Ads don't look the same way as a regular text paid search ad, you can still use the same principles to improve your clickthrough rates. While you aren't dealing with textual descriptions for your call to action, your ad serves as your call to action just the same. Your price, your reviews, and the appeal of your photo all contribute to the clicks your product listing ad attracts.

If you sell products that are shown in product listings, they can work much better than text search ads. Research from Marin Software found that Google Product Listing Ads receive 21% higher clicks than regular paid search ads.

Understanding the searcher's intent allows you to effectively match the right product with the right searcher. In Exhibit 8-10 we see an example of the ads for a keyword for Adobe Photoshop. Note the variety of products and pricing. Some merchants are showing Photoshop Elements, the entry-level version. WalMart shows Photoshop Lightroom, which caters to digital photographers. Others are showing Photoshop Extended Student Licenses, which are cheaper than the typical license. Only through testing can you determine which of these products is the best match for the searcher's intent.

Next up, we shift from optimizing the search results to optimizing the actual landing pages.

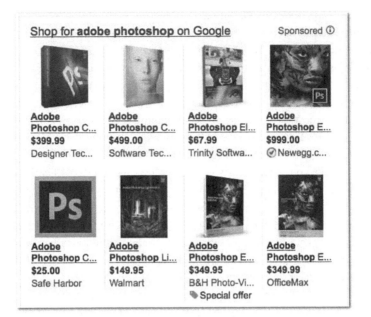

Exhibit 8-10   Google Product Listing Ads. Retailers vie over who can sell Adobe Photoshop software to the searcher.

Improve Your Landing Pages

Your first check of your search landing page's metrics will typically be depressing. It is rare for a page that has not been optimized to rank well in organic search, and rarer still for referrals and conversions to be what you want. After all, that's why you embarked on search marketing in the first place. It's time to audit your page to diagnose problems and see what might be improved. Landing pages used only for paid search could suffer from problems in their quality (which affects their ad's ranking) and all content can have conversion problems.

Remember, that we use the term *search landing page* to refer to any content that the searcher sees after clicking on a search result; it doesn't have to be a web page. YouTube videos, blog posts, your Facebook fan page—any of these can be search landing pages and might need improvement.

Some search marketing programs—especially the larger ones—have implemented separate landing pages for paid and organic search, even for the same keywords. In the early days of search, this made some sense because the organic search pages required a great deal of optimization of its text, whereas paid search landing pages required no attention at all.

In recent years, the focus for both paid and organic search landing pages has shifted to quality—high-quality organic search pages are becoming more similar to high-quality paid search landing pages—so it is becoming more common for companies to merge their landing pages into a single page across paid and organic. The changes that you make to improve organic search rankings will help paid search quality. Focusing on improving conversions for paid search will raise conversion rates for organic searchers, also. We'll look at these questions more in Chapter 9.

Because you need to focus on improving your landing pages for organic search rankings, you need to analyze and improve the text. You will eventually develop your own eye for auditing landing pages, but in the beginning you can benefit from using **content analyzers.** As you do, just keep in mind that content analyzer tools are just that: *tools*. They are designed to *inform* your judgment, not *replace* it. Content analyzers typically offer advice only for search ranking problems, not referral or conversion problems, so you need to consider the advice carefully. It is no victory to improve your rankings while decreasing referrals or conversions. So, don't blindly follow what any tool has to say; it is no search marketing oracle. Use your judgment about whether the advice fits your style and whether it will help you improve conversions as well as rankings. These tools can prove very helpful, but none provide *perfect* advice for all search engines in all situations—that's impossible—so don't check your brain at the door.

Content analyzers offer a more subtle benefit: helping you persuade recalcitrant members of your extended search team to make the required changes to aid organic search rankings. For some reason, many people are more easily persuaded when they see a report from a program than if you tell them the same thing. You should do whatever it takes to get writers to change their words (to optimize the content for higher organic search rankings). If it means running a content analyzer and walking them through the results, go for it. Exhibit 8-11 shows a sample report from Web CEO (webceo.com), a popular site analyzer. We list several helpful content analyzers at our website (SEMincBook.com/content-analyzers) that you can use to help audit your search landing pages.

B. Main on-the-page factors influencing your ranking				
1. <HEAD> area: ⑦				
<TITLE> tag ⑦	···	···	···	···
Number of Titles	2	1	1	1
First tag in the <HEAD> tag	Yes	Yes	Yes	Yes
Characters in Title	60	44	33	50
Words in Title	5	6	5	8
⑩ Stop words in Title ⑦	Yes	No	No	Yes
⑩ Keyword frequency in Title ⑦	0	1	1	1
Keyword prominence in Title ⑦	-	100.0%	100.0%	100.0%
Keyword weight in Title ⑦	0.0%	50.0%	60.0%	37.5%

Exhibit 8-11 A content analyzer's report. WebCEO shows statistics to help you understand where your keywords are used and where they might be missing.

Each tool has different features and might use different names for the content analysis techniques employed. The most full-featured versions allow analysis of your entire site, as discussed in Chapter 10. Keep in mind that your goal is not to optimize your content by mindlessly repeating your keywords just to get a high score in the analyzer. But the analyzer can be helpful as a quick way to get a read on where your optimization places you among the top search results.

Other types of analysis can be useful. You might imagine that search engines do not want to show the same content over and over again in the organic search results, so they suppress all but one version of content using a technique called **duplicate content suppression.** So, even if it was not unethical (and usually illegal) to copy content without permission, it is likely that Google will show the originating page, not yours. If you have multiple duplicate pages within your own website, a page similarity checker can provide a score of how much two pages resemble each other. You can get a list of such analyzers at our companion website (SEMincBook.com/duplicate-content-checkers).

Snap Electronics chose their *digital cameras* hub page as the right landing page for the *digital camera* search keyword, so they decided to perform a content analysis on their page (which ranked #45 in Google) against the top-ranked pages in the Google results. If you think about it, examining what the top-ranked pages have going for them is a simple way to see where you are coming up short.

None of Snap's competitors, such as Canon or Kodak, are listed on the first page of results for *digital camera*, so it might be an uphill battle for any camera manufacturer to crack the top ten. Regardless, Snap can probably learn a lot by seeing what kinds of pages are at the top of the list.

Evaluate Your Body Text

The body of the HTML page is the viewable text on the screen. We just analyzed how the body text is excerpted to form the snippet that drives referrals, but the body text is also important for high rankings and conversion.

Snap's analytics system reveals the conversions for the site as a whole, but it does not allow Snap to check search conversions for a single landing page. (In Chapter 10, we offer some ideas on how to do that.) Snap has been pleased with the overall conversion rate for digital cameras on the site, so they will concentrate on improving those low search rankings (#45 in Google and missing from the top 100 in the other major engines).

For a keyword as popular as *digital cameras*, with so many pages vying to be #1, it stands to reason that the body of each of the high-ranking pages is heavily optimized, not just the title.

When viewed with a browser, Snap's page showed the words *digital cameras* in a heading at the top of the page. That title helped visitors orient themselves, reassuring them they are in the right place—and led to increased conversions. But examining the page's HTML revealed this text was generated by an image with no alternate text specified. To the spider, that title was invisible. The image file needed to be changed to a heading tag, thereby adding a prominent occurrence of a keyword—prominent because it is at the top of the page.

Similarly, the word *cameras* at the top of the screen was generated by an image map—the spider cannot see that one either. As hard as it is to believe, there really was only one occurrence of *digital cameras* on the page, so the page needs to be rewritten. Again, don't just load up on keywords to please the analyzer, but clearly you should be using your important keywords more than once, and other related theme words, such as *megapixel* or *resolution*. There is no need for this to be an artificial exercise. If you write high-quality content that answers the questions searchers have, you will naturally use these words.

Because Snap wanted to use that same page as its landing page for other search keywords as well (such as *snap digital camera* and *snapshot digital camera*), the same content analyzer was used to check the page for the other keywords. The results were similar, showing that scant attention has been paid to this hub page.

As Snap looked at other pages in the *digital cameras* area of the site, it was clear that they all needed the same kind of makeover as the hub page. None of them had strong titles, nor was their body copy optimized. In Chapter 9, we explore how Snap can beef up its content factors to demonstrate the quality of the page, but now let's look at how to optimize page content to boost search rankings, referrals, and conversions.

Here's what you have been waiting for—advice on improving your search landing page to meet your search marketing goals.

Before tackling each element on your page, let's keep in mind the process we are following. Each time we change the page, we wait for it to be re-crawled by the spider and we check the performance metrics again. Is it ranking highly now? Producing sufficient referrals? Conversions? We continue to iterate change after change to the page until we drive the page performance we projected in Chapter 4 when we first conceived the campaign. Smart search marketers go so far as to log every change to their key pages so that they can see which update made an impact on the performance metrics. You can't always tell which changes are working; but if you have a large site, it can be helpful to see what seemed to work in some parts of the site so that you can apply the same thinking to the rest of your site.

Let's look at which changes you should consider for your search landing pages, starting with the most critical part of any page: its title.

Fix Your Body Text

Before you became a search marketing expert, you might not have realized that there was any more to a web page besides what you saw in your browser. All of the text and the images the browser displays on the screen are contained in the *body* of the web page, signified by the `<body>` tag in your web page's HTML.

Except for whatever is excerpted for your snippet, the body has no effect on search referrals, but it is very important for organic search rankings and the most important part of your landing page for web conversions (for paid and organic search). In addition, paid search vendors are increasingly inspecting paid search landing pages to make sure that the page is relevant to the keywords purchased for that page, so paying attention to your keyword usage and to your usage of thematically related words still makes sense, even for paid search.

STUPID CONTENT TRICKS: HOW TO GET YOUR SITE BANNED IN FIVE EASY STEPS

Tricking the search engines to rank your pages higher than they ought to is called **spamdexing**, or simply **spam**. Throughout this book, we have warned you about a host of spam techniques, because spamming can get your site banned from search engines—a nasty wrench thrown into your search marketing plans.

There are many different ways of tricking search engines, people being the clever creatures they are, but we cover only the content spamming techniques here. Our goal is not to teach you how to perform these techniques. Rather, you should know enough to spot them to prevent your site from running afoul of the rules and suffering the consequences. Or enough to discover them on a competitor's site so that you can justifiably turn them in.

- **Doorway pages:** Any page that is designed solely to achieve high search rankings, but otherwise has no value to visitors to your site, is a doorway page. Search landing pages are not doorway pages.

- **Keyword stuffing:** Also known as **keyword loading**, this technique is really just an overuse of sound content-optimization practices. It's good to use your target keywords on your search landing pages, and use them often, but when you start throwing them in just to attract the search engines your pages can be flagged. Dumping out-of-context keywords into the alternate text for images, or into `<noscript>` or `<noframes>` tags, is a variation of this same unethical technique.

- **Hidden text:** HTML offers many opportunities to place text in front of the spider that the visitor will never see. Displaying text in incredibly small sizes, or with the same font color as the background color are hoary spam techniques. Newer approaches include using style sheets to write keywords on the page that are then overlaid by graphics or other page elements. In short, any time you can see text in the HTML source of a page that does not show up when you view the page in your browser, it is probably spam. The only exception is valid HTML comments, which the browsers and spiders both ignore.

- **Duplicate sites:** Spammers duplicate their content in slightly different form under several different domain names and then have each of the sites link to each other (to increase their content ranking factors). Maybe these sites can grab six slots in the top ten results.

And the really bad news about all of these techniques is that sometimes they do work. Search engines do get fooled—usually by people more industrious and harder working than us. Most of the time, however, spam techniques are like stock tips. When you hear the tip, it is probably too late. The stock price has already gone up, and the search engines are already implementing countermeasures.

For paid search, you can place your keywords just about anywhere, but not all words in the body are treated equally for organic ranking purposes. Here are the different places that you might place keywords and other thematically related words:

- **Headings:** Within the body, keywords found within headings are thought to be given higher weight than elsewhere. Because visitors treat headings as more important than other text, the search engines probably do, too. Although all headings carry more clout than surrounding text, an `<h1>` tag is more powerful than lesser headings. Keywords found in heading tags are among the most prominent search words on the page.

- **Opening text:** Keywords that occur at the top of the page have more impact than text that occurs later. Because most pages summarize their central concepts in the first few words, search engines give these words more authority when determining relevance. Putting headings and opening text together creates the most prominent body placement of a keyword—inside a heading tag within the opening text.

- **Emphasized text:** Bold and italicized keywords stand out to a visitor, so search engines give them somewhat more consideration, too.

- **Everything else:** Keywords found anywhere on the page have some value, but not as much as if they were in placements listed earlier. This content includes paragraph tags and many others, but none are treated as more important than the others.

Remember that your goal is not to litter your page with keywords; it is to convert your searchers to customers. So, write naturally. Search engines have become more sophisticated over the years, so they are not only looking for the keyword that the searcher enters (*digital camera*) but other related words (*megapixel* or *image* or *shutter* or *SLR*—you get the idea). If you write high-quality content that truly delivers the information searchers are looking for, you will probably use these kinds of words without even thinking.

Although different body elements count more than others, good writing is not assembled piecemeal—dropping a bold word here and a heading there. If you write naturally, you are likely to use the right number of keywords without making it sound like a keyword-stuffed mess. Some writers like to read their copy out loud so that they can listen to it as well as see it. They say that if it sounds stupid, it is.

Poorly optimized body copy can sometimes lean to the other extreme. Sometimes the targeted keyword is not mentioned even once in the body copy. Here are some tips for crafting your body text for top organic search rankings and high conversions for both paid and organic search:

- **Keep it short:** Search engines will index as many as 100,000 characters on your page, but it is virtually impossible to maintain strong keyword density over a very long page. The best pages are usually less than 1,000 words long. Short pages aid conversion, too. Web visitors do not read your pages the way they read a book. They scan for what they are looking for. Long pages are much harder to scan.

- **Write with variety:** Using variations of your keywords in your copy helps both rankings and conversions. Because searchers do not use the exact same keywords each time they search, peppering your text with both singular and plural forms, varying verb tenses, and using different word orders help your page be found no matter what searchers type. Moreover, writing with variety overcomes tendencies toward the stultifying, repetitive prose that marks amateurish search optimization. Because your writing is easier to read, you will attract more links to your site and higher conversions.

- **Think location:** Search engines are increasingly taking searchers' locations into account. If you are a local business, make sure that all the variations of your place names are woven into your content so that search engines know where you are located. Search engines increasingly attempt to match local searchers with local organizations. And local searchers are looking for those location words before they convert.

- **Think local:** For global marketers, translating pages to local languages can endanger your search marketing. Don't settle for a correct translation. You must do your keyword research over again for each country and language and get the "just right" keywords. The difference between a correct word and the best keyword could cost you a lot of conversions. And insist on translators paying attention to the same organic search optimization and other writing techniques listed here.

- **Think like a newspaper reporter:** Start out with the most important information up front. Continue to emphasize important concepts throughout, and wind up with a strong conclusion. Not only does that help organic search rankings, but it greatly aids conversion for busy customers.

- **Think like a direct marketer:** How do direct marketers get you to open the envelope? To read the copy? To respond? You must think of your content as your direct marketing copy. Study how direct marketers use language to hook you and offer strong calls to action with a sense of urgency. Don't settle for "click here" links. And don't forget to analyze all the pages between your landing page and your conversion page. Visitors can abandon your site as easily as they dump a direct-mail piece that misses the mark. Raise your conversions with compelling and action-oriented direct marketing copy throughout your site.

- **Avoid tricks:** Do not go overboard as a direct marketer. Avoid the dark side full of tricks and hype; they work even less well on the web than they do in direct marketing. Stay accurate and factual. Eschew overblown hype-laden prose and, of course, stay away from stupid content tricks that spam the search engines.

The challenge of writing good copy with these tips in mind underscores how difficult it is to optimize a page for organic search for multiple keywords. You can't put all of your keywords in the title, and they cannot all be the first words on the page. Even worse, the more subjects you write about, the harder it is to talk enough about any of them. Rather than constantly referring to *SnapShot digital cameras*, you might use *SnapShot* and *digital cameras* separately sometimes. As we learned in Chapter 3, search engines look for multiple-word keyword elements in proximity to each other, so it is not necessary for you to use the entire set of words together every time.

In addition to well-written copy, you want your page to be well designed. Throughout this book, we have cautioned you on misuse of JavaScript, and to a lesser extent, style sheets. Used wisely, however, both JavaScript and style sheets improve your site's appearance and usability. But don't embed large scripts or style sheets within your web pages. It is okay for a few lines to be embedded here or there, but anything longer should be "offloaded" (as the techies say) to an external file that is called by the page. You saw in Chapter 7 how bloated pages impede crawling. It is also true that these elements can push the real content further down into the file, moving your keywords farther down from the top of the page.

Technical folks like to speak about "clean" code—HTML that is so well structured and organized that it is easy to understand and maintain. That clean code is good for your extended team as they maintain the page, but it's a pleasure for spiders, too. And the easiest way to maintain clean code is with a Cascading Style Sheets (CSS for short).

Pages that use CSS files can be remarkably smaller than other pages because all the formatting instructions are in the CSS file, not on the page. It is common for half of a traditional HTML file to be formatting instructions, with the other half the text to display. The fewer formatting instructions, the easier it is for the spider, and the more of your pages can be crawled in less time. That speedier performance helps you get more pages indexed for organic search, but it also helps your organic and paid search rankings. Moreover, faster loading pages increase conversion rates.

CSS files also enable you to use more modern page-layout techniques rather than tables or (please, no!) frames. Tables are fine for information laid out in rows and columns, but too many web pages are designed as one big table with the left navigation as a long column, for example. Although this produces the desired result onscreen, the tortured markup is very difficult to correctly maintain and for spiders to interpret. Sites coded without tables sometimes rank higher. CSS files enable you to use <div> tags and other techniques to place your text anywhere on the page, so you can put your most important content nearer the top of the page where the spider wants to see it.

As with all tools, you must be careful how you use style sheets. It is possible for you to define your own set of tags with names of your choosing, but make sure you keep the basic ones intact. Heading (<h1> through <h6>) tags, especially, should be used with their traditional names so that spiders know to treat that text with increased importance. You can define any appearance for these tags that you want, so being limited in the use of the name will not crimp your style.

Clearly, the body element of your web page drives both your organic search rankings and web conversions. We have seen many tips to improve the writing and the coding of your body text—it might seem a bit complicated to you. Don't worry. It gets easier from here as we look at some simple rules for improving your paid search landing page.

For paid search, a few editorial guidelines are insisted on by paid search engines:

- **Include the keywords:** Although you need not optimize your page the way organic landing pages require, the editorial department of every paid search engine will inspect your landing page to make sure it is relevant to the keyword purchased. Do make it obvious that your searcher has landed in the right place for the keyword entered.

- **Stay on topic:** If you buy the keyword *racing cars* to try to sell automobile batteries, the paid search engines will not approve your ad. Only pages relevant to the keyword topic will be accepted.

- **Reinforce your offer:** In addition to mentioning the keyword, you must ensure that anything you have called out in the copy is prominently shown on the landing page.

- **Drop pop-ups:** Visitors hate pop-up or pop-under advertising, so paid search engines do not allow them. We recommend you dump them from your whole site, but you must at least eliminate them from your landing pages.

- **Enable the "back" button:** Some pages disable the browser's "back" button, so that the visitor cannot easily return to the search page. If you want to annoy your visitors, it is hard to top this practice, and paid search engines will not let you get away with it.

For both paid and organic search landing pages, you must make it simple for visitors to convert. If you reinforce what searchers are looking for (their search keywords) and why they clicked your pages (your ad copy or your organic title and snippet), you will likely get a good conversion rate. Remember that you might have several pages between your landing page and your conversion page, so make sure that the entire path is designed with conversion in mind. For product search, the path is usually much shorter—your product search landing page is typically the "buy" page for that product on your site.

Whether using paid search or product search, your landing pages (and your entire conversion path) require careful design and, above all, testing. Just as you test everything else about your digital marketing, test your landing pages, too. Test the amount of copy on the page, the size of the product images, the kind of language used, the links to background information, and more.

That's it for optimizing the text on your landing pages. Now we move on to images, videos, and the other elements of your page that are *not* text.

Handle Nontext Elements Properly

As you know, spiders cannot understand images or video. So these parts of the page don't matter, right? Wrong. Carefully craft your nontext page elements to make them most appealing to the search engines. Let's start with images.

HOW DO YOU OPTIMIZE PODCASTS?

For Google and the mainstream search engines, searching for podcasts is much like searching for images. Google can find a searcher's keywords on the web page that describes a podcast, but can't find podcasts that contain those same words in the spoken audio. That means that a searcher will find your podcast from words in the title or the description that you place on your landing page, but not from any words that were said inside the podcast audio file.

Some search engines look for keywords within the metadata that you can encode inside the actual podcast file, using an audio editor such as Audacity (audacity.sourceforge.net). The ID3 standard (www.id3.org) for metatags was designed for music files, but it's the most popular tagging format for podcasts, too. You can use the title and album tags to store the name of your series and the name of your episode, the artist tag to store the name of your podcast's host, and the year tag for... well, you can probably figure that one out. ID3 also offers a free-form comment field to store a transcript or a URL for more information.

You might suspect that trying to find 15- to 20-minute podcasts using only the words in their titles and descriptions leaves a lot to be desired. You're best served by adding a full text transcript of your podcast to that title and description, but for many people, that's more work than they have time to do.

Optimize Your Images   You've got images on your website and in social media and both need to be optimized for search. First up. Let's look at some dangers of the images on your own website:

- **Overemphasis on images**. There is no harm in having many images on your landing page, so long as they are not crowding out your text. If your page becomes so image-laden that there is precious little text left, you can cause a few problems. First, if you have fewer than two dozen words, the search engine might not correctly identify the language of your page, putting it at risk of being erroneously excluded from keywords using language filters. That same lack of text can make it quite challenging to provide enough keyword occurrences to attain high rankings, and you might also hurt your page's conversion rate if the images are not as persuasive as some well-written text would be.

- **Text hidden in images:** Often, page headings are bold and big—and invisible to the spider—because they are coded as images rather than as heading (`<h1>` through `<h6>`) tags. Heading tags are prominent placements of your keywords—don't hide the keywords from the spider.

- **Poor alt text**. Too often, descriptive text for images is either hurriedly constructed or missing completely. The HTML `<img>` tag is designed to help visually impaired visitors (and those who use text-only browsers) determine what the images contain, by allowing you to specify some alternative (alt) text. This text is shown (or spoken if you are visually impaired) when visitors mouse over an image. In addition, spiders will index this text, so make sure it is an accurate description of the picture. Use keywords in the alt text if appropriate, but don't "stuff" keywords unrelated to the picture—that's spam.

It's great to optimize the images on your website, but you'll improve your results even more when you submit your images to photo-sharing sites, such as Yahoo!'s Flickr (flickr.com). All you have to do is to upload your image, and give it a title and a description. It's that easy, and it's free.

Obviously, you'll want to ensure that your title and description contain the appropriate keywords to improve your picture's findability. Use an `<h1>` tag for your title if the site allows it. Some photo-sharing sites permit a link back to your website, which also can improve your website's search results. Just as with images posted to your own site, you should use keyword-rich filenames.

Some of the most important things you need to do should happen after you post your image:

- **Image names:** The single best thing you can do to your images is to name these something relevant. Don't use alphanumeric names; instead, try to explain what the image is.

- **Tag your photo:** Flickr and many of the other photo-sharing sites allow you to provide keywords as labels for your pictures.

- **Share your photo within the site:** Mark you photo as "public" so that anyone can see it. Most sites offer groups that you can share you photo with.

- **Publicize your photo outside the site:** If your photo is noteworthy, submit it to social bookmarking sites, email people who would be interested, and link to it from your blog or another web page.

Images are becoming more important with each passing year. Don't settle for optimizing your text when you can get traffic from your pictures, too.

Optimize Your Videos   Videos provide the richest way to send a message to your customers, and they might cost less than you expect. We saw how the low costs of podcasts can be targeted at far smaller audiences than radio commercials or mailed CDs. Like podcasts, online video is especially important to marketers targeting younger audiences.

Web video is much cheaper than buying a TV ad or shipping around DVDs. The cost of distributing your video is essentially free, which makes more videos affordable than ever before.

Despite the low cost of web videos, you can't expect to reach people as easily as you would with a TV commercial. With TV, you merely choose the show that matches your target market, plunk down your cash, and your commercial runs. On the web, customers usually find your video through search, so search marketing is crucial to getting your message seen.

Just as with image and podcast files, optimizing videos depends on the words you use—the keywords you place in the filename itself, and in the title and description text that surrounds your video on the page. Also, be sure to place your videos on separate pages, rather than lumping several on the same page. There's more that you can do with videos, however, to set yours apart from the rest.

Videos can be encoded with metadata keywords within the "properties" of the video file itself, by tools such as Autodesk Cleaner (autodesk.com). Video search engines often rely on this information when deciding which videos to show in the search results (and in what order).

You should also consider creating closed captions for your voiceovers—that gives the search engines even more text to work with. Obviously, you can do that by hand, but it takes a lot of time and money to caption every video, so you might consider automated captioning tools, such as CaptionTube (captiontube.appspot.com/).

It's not enough to optimize your videos for search, however. Just as getting a #1 ranking for a web page does not get that page clicked; your video must be watched, not just found. Ensure that videos posted, especially to social networking sites, are marked public rather than private. Some video-sharing sites allow you some control over the image selected as its thumbnail image—the picture shown before the video is played. Selecting an attractive thumbnail causes more people to watch.

Painstaking attention to nontext page elements, such as images and video, can improve your search rankings. If ignored or handled sloppily, nontext elements can undermine your best efforts on your text. So make proper coding of nontext elements one of your priorities.

Optimize Dynamic Content

We've served up a bevy of tips on optimizing your content—everything from working over your titles to coding alternate text for your images. All of those tips are important, and they apply to every web page. If you are working on a static landing page—one that is stored in an HTML file on your server—you can skip this section. However, you have a few more things to learn if you need to optimize a dynamic page.

You recall that dynamic pages are generated on-the-fly by a software program whenever a visitor (or a spider) requests the URL. You know that dynamic sites can pose a number of problems for spiders, as discussed in Chapter 7. Now let's look at how dynamic sites generate their pages and how you can ensure they are optimized for search marketing.

Dynamic pages are created by software programs that use two different kinds of information:

- **Templates:** For each type of dynamic page, the software program fills in a shell with dynamic content (content that can be different every time the program displays the page). Exhibit 8-12 shows a dynamic page with the content in the template overlaid in gray. The content in the template is the same on every page that uses that template. In this case, all books sold by Pearson have a page driven by a template, and the template causes them to have a common look and feel.

- **Database information:** The dynamic content that makes each page different is drawn from some kind of database. It could be a content management system or an eCommerce catalog or any kind of database at all. Pearson maintains a database that has a record for each book that it publishes, and the software that generates the page fills in the title, the author, the ISBN number, the price, the excerpt, and other information on the page.

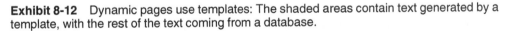

Exhibit 8-12   Dynamic pages use templates: The shaded areas contain text generated by a template, with the rest of the text coming from a database.

The figure can show you how the template looks on the screen, but more is going on behind the scenes than that. The template actually contains all the HTML coding that formats the page. The database contains only the information to be filled into the template.

By now, you might be thinking, "That's all very interesting, but what does it mean to me?" Search marketers need to understand this split between template and content to optimize dynamic pages because the template is controlled by different people than the content is.

Your web developers usually control the template. In some cases, it is a separate file that is easily updated—most content management systems work that way. At other times, the HTML is stored inside the software program itself, which means that the programmers must modify the software to change the HTML.

The content, in contrast, is managed by the operations people who maintain the database. Sometimes these folks are writers, because the content contains long prose fields that require the same care in writing as static HTML pages. For some kinds of pages, however, the content is a long list of features and specifications reminiscent of a printed catalog—if the content requires no writing ability. It might be maintained by data entry operators who key in the data and make sure that it is correct.

So, every piece of text on the screen comes from either the template or the database. And every HTML tag comes from the template. That's important to understand when you want changes made to the dynamic page.

All the tips in this chapter apply as much to dynamic pages as to static pages. Dynamic pages have titles, and you want them to drive rankings and referrals. Dynamic pages have descriptions. They have body text. To the spider, the HTML of a dynamic page looks the same as for a static page. Both kinds of pages are ranked against each other in the same ways.

If there is no static HTML file, however, how do you optimize a dynamic page? There is no single answer to that question; every situation differs slightly. Here are a few scenarios that will give you the idea of what you will be up against:

- **There are no title tags on my pages:** That's obviously not a good thing for organic search marketing. Without titles, your pages are unlikely to be highly ranked in the organic search results and will get low clickthrough. It turns out that the developer left the title tag out of the template for the product catalog. One template change later, your catalog pages have titles.

- **Yeah, but all the titles are the same:** Okay, that's still not great. It turns out that the developer just plugged some boilerplate text into the template, when it should have been taken from the database. Now the developer has changed the program so that the titles are being generated from the product name field in the database.

- **Um, but the titles are wrong:** Yeah, about that—the data entry folks said that the product name field has never been checked all that carefully because it was never used for anything before. Now that they know how important it is, they can fix the data in the next couple of weeks so that the names are right.

- **Okay, but I noticed the descriptions have the same text on every page:** Well, that is a problem. We do not have a field in the database for description text for every product. We can add the field, but it will take a couple of months to change the database design and the template, and then wait for the operations team to write descriptions for every product in the catalog.

All right, it is not always as frustrating as that, but changing a dynamic page usually takes more persuasive powers and more time than getting a static page changed. That's the bad news. The good news is that when you persuade your extended team to change one dynamic page, they usually change them all. With static pages, when you have changed one, you have changed, uh, one. So it is harder to change one dynamic page than one static page, but it is easier to change them all.

Dynamic content has other benefits, too. It is perfect for product listing ads. If you want to participate in product search engines, having your content stored in databases makes it far simpler to do. Optimizing your data in a product search engine is the key to attracting clicks from searchers. To attract clicks on product search engines, you must concentrate on three major factors:

- **Metadata:** As discussed in Chapter 7, preparing your trusted feed properly ensures that your product listings will be found. (Some product search engines will also crawl your site or allow you to enter your listings.) If your product list does not contain complete and correct metadata, your products will not be shown for some searches when they should be.

- **Price:** As you might expect, having a low price attracts clicks regardless of whether the search engine ranks by price.

- **Merchant rating:** With some product search engines, listings with the higher merchant ratings tend to be ranked higher than others. As with low prices, higher merchant ratings persuade more clicks than lower ones. Not all product search engines work this way, however. Google calls them **seller ratings** and does not use it in rankings at all, merely displaying them if the advertiser desires, which can lead to a higher clickthrough rate.

So, pay attention to your product data to ensure that your listing is found, and pay attention to the ranking factors to be placed at the top of the list. When first starting out in product search, you might need to discount your price to attract shoppers until you boost your merchant rating.

Another advantage of dynamic content is quality control. Static pages are usually created with HTML editing tools that cannot check the content of the page, except to validate the HTML. Because dynamic page content is drawn from databases, you can ensure that the database update process checks the content itself. For example, if your company's model numbers always start with two letters followed by five numbers, your update process can check for that when data is entered.

Let's explore a scenario for optimizing dynamic content. The page that Snap Electronics wants to optimize for its *digital cameras* keyword *is* a dynamic page. That means that no one can change its title directly, because no static page contains that title tag. That title tag is generated, along with the rest of the page, by a program that uses a template in conjunction with content stored in a database—in this case, Snap's eCommerce catalog database.

An inspection of the template shows how the current "Snap Electronics digital cameras for you" title is generated. The template record that generates the title (`text: "<title>Snap Electronics" field: PRODCAT text: "for you</title>"`) produces the title tag followed by the company name, grabs the product category field from the catalog database (*digital cameras* for this page), and finally adds the *for you* text and the title end tag.

The marketing team at Snap prefers the new title to be "Snap Digital Cameras – Save on a SnapShot digital camera," but it might take some thinking to pull it off. The web developers proposed a new template record (`text: "<title>Snap" field: PRODCAT text: "- Save on" field: PRODCAT text: "</title>"`), which would produce a title of "Snap digital cameras – Save on digital cameras" (not exactly what the marketing folks had in mind).

The marketing folks asked the developers why they could not add the word *SnapShot* to the template, to come closer to the original idea, but the developers explained that the template is used for all product catalog hub pages, and they cannot use the SnapShot brand name on pages for VCRs and TVs. (They have their own brand names.) As it was, every product catalog hub page would now have the "save on" call to action in its title, but the marketing folks thought that was okay. The impasse was averted when the developers agreed to change the product category name to *SnapShot digital cameras* in the database. By adding the word *electronics* to the template record, the title now reads "Snap Electronics SnapShot digital cameras – Save on SnapShot digital cameras" (not exactly what marketing wanted, but acceptable for now). The developers agreed that they could eventually add a title field to the database allowing the data entry folks to enter any title they wanted for each product in the catalog, but that will take a couple of months to pull off.

Dynamic content is the most efficient way to power large sites with many similar pages. With the right attention to detail, you can optimize your dynamic site for search as easily as a static site.

Summary

Content is king, at least in the land of search engines. The quality and relevance of your content is the biggest factor in succeeding in search marketing. *That* is why optimizing your content is so important. We looked at optimizing your landing pages themselves, but also improving the search results for both organic and paid search. And we talked about how to measure those results in terms of rank, clicks, and conversions.

In this chapter, you learned what search engines are looking for and how you approach writing for them. This chapter covered the steps in a content-optimization process that stresses iteration—working the process over and over until you succeed. No one will optimize a page properly on the first try. Failure is normal. What matters is how many times you will take another crack at it until your pages finally deliver the search marketing value you expected.

We deferred the discussion of one of the major ways search engines rank content for both organic and paid search: content quality. In the next chapter, we investigate the importance of quality in deciding where your content appears and how persuasive it is to make a sale.

CHAPTER 9

Prove Your Content's Quality

Suppose that you open an email that has a link in it to a news story on the web. You click it, and read the headline of the story: "Senator Possibly Implicated in Voter Fraud." You read the story, assessing its credibility. Would the story be credible if it were from the website of CNN? The Washington Post? *The Drudge Report? The* National Enquirer? *Some blogger you have never heard of? You are likely to consider the source in assigning credence to that report because not all sources have the same reputation in your mind. Now understand, some people might have a higher opinion of some sources of information than you do, and regardless of anyone's opinion, even the source held in the lowest regard can be correct on a particular story and the most-respected can be wrong.*

Despite occasional surprises, reputation *is* an effective shortcut for evaluating the quality of information presented to us. Search engines use a similar shortcut. Search engines judge the reputation of every website so that they can present the highest-quality content—the content with the best reputation. The signals of your content quality are among the most important factors in search ranking algorithms for both paid and organic search. Keep in mind that the importance of individual ranking factors changes frequently. You can keep up with those changes at our companion website (SEMincBook.com/ranking-factors).

We've spoken about the need for high-quality content throughout the book, but in this chapter we explain how the search engines *decide* your content's quality—for both organic and paid search. Here's what we cover in this chapter:

- **Organic search quality factors:** Organic search uses the most complex set of signals for content quality and we walk you through all of them.

- **Paid search quality factors:** Paid search has undergone the biggest change in quality factors over its history, so you need to know what the search engines look for.

- **Increasing your content quality:** It's tempting to attack the question of quality as "whatever Google wants, I will give them," but that's the wrong approach. Find out the real secret to improving the quality of your content for search engines.

Search engines reserve the most elaborate mechanisms for judging content quality for organic search results, so we cover them first. In fact, the ranking factors that organic search engines use to judge quality are so varied and complex, that most of this chapter is devoted to them.

Organic Search Quality Factors

Organic search engines have a few ways of judging the quality of content, discussed as content ranking factors in Chapter 3, "How Search Works." Here are the most important ranking factors used to judge organic search quality:

- **Links:** The original organic search quality factor was link analysis, and it is still very important, even though other factors have been added over the years.
- **Social media activity:** If your content is good, it should be popular in social media, at least when it is new.
- **Human raters:** Search engines don't settle for checking your links and your social activity. They actually convene online panels of searchers who assess the search results and privately report their findings to the search engines alone.

You need to get things started with social and maybe some link building, but it should be like a snowball rolling downhill; you just use those tactics to get it started. If your social and link building feels like rolling a snowball uphill, then it is spammy and you are doing it wrong. Also, seeing which content picks up links and social shares is one way to determine which content is your best content. When you are artificially inflating everything, you are obscuring which content is actually working organically.

We'll start our walk through organic search quality factors by looking at how the links between web pages were the first and still most important way that search engines deduce the quality of your content for organic search.

Links as Quality Factors

The web is built on links and, in many ways, organic search results are, too.

If you think about it, links are actually votes for quality by those who link to your content. One simple way to understand why this is true is to consider the motivation of the author of a web page to link to a page on another website. Any such link is actually an invitation to the visitor to leave the author's site. The author will do that only if the information linked to is both related to the page's subject and of very high quality—a service to the visitors to the page. Those are exactly the kinds of pages Google is trying to identify.

If your website is well known, you might already have attracted many links. Perhaps you think that you have no need to improve the links coming to your site. But even some large companies, such as WebMD, the well-known medical information site, attract fewer links than they could. WebMD had more than 12,000 links at one time, but nearly all of them to its home page, with few links to the disease information pages that drive referrals from informational keywords. WebMD ranked #1 for keywords for *webmd*, but not for *allergies*.

In this chapter, you learn all about the relationship between links and organic search:

- **The importance of links:** Every link to your page is a "vote" for its quality and authority on a given subject. Organic search engines tally the votes when they decide which pages possess the highest quality for their search results.

- **How *not* to build links to your site:** You'll hear lots of advice for shortcuts to get links to your site, but be advised: Not only won't these techniques work, they might even hurt your site's organic search ranking.

- **The right way to build links to your site:** Now that you know search engines value links, you'll want more of them. When the links come, your site will benefit both from improved search rankings and from more visitors following the links.

Before learning about how to attract more links to your site, let's examine why links are so important to search engines.

The Importance of Links

"Content is king," the experts all tell you. But content is not the real change ushered in by the web. The web content itself is not remarkably different from what you can read in books or magazines. What *does* differ is the ease with which surfers can move from one piece of content to the next. That's the power of links. Links changed the way people consume content; they can now navigate easily across different sources that once required meandering amid library stacks—after schlepping to the library in the first place.

Just as links transformed readers' content consumption, links changed the game for search engines, too. With the advent of Google in 1998, search engines began to use links to judge the quality of every page on the web.

Google's use of link analysis to judge the quality of content was a seminal event in search marketing history. Until then, search engines almost exclusively used the words on the web page to decide which pages matched the search keyword. Very soon, search results were overrun by unscrupulous spammers who loaded up their pages with keywords just to rank higher in the organic results. Google's emphasis on content quality—as judged by link analysis—was the first shot fired in the ever-continuing war between search engines and spammers. Link analysis was the first quality technique that caused search engines to truly show searchers what they were really looking for, and it is still the most important signal of quality today.

The idea behind link analysis is not a new one. Scientific papers have long relied on **citations**—references to previous papers that attest to the correctness of a basic concept. Scientists vie for the honor of having the most citations to their papers, because when later papers cite a scientist's original work, it provides a rough estimation of that original paper's value. Similarly, new patents regularly refer to "prior art" in old patents, so they can build their ideas on top of the solid ground of previous ideas. These precursors to web links served the same purpose; they created a kind of "information economy" in which the best ideas are discovered because the most experts refer to them.

Many observers will tell you that the reason the web changed our world is due to the huge amounts of content now available. And that is true. But it is this information economy, not the content itself, that is the most striking and innovative feature of the web.

Content can be created easily by anyone, but the information economy allows us to detect the best content because higher-quality information attracts more links than mediocre or poor content. When thousands or millions of pages are voluntarily linked to an article, it is a strong recommendation for its quality. You can think of the authors of each of those linking pages *recommending* that article, much the same way you might recommend a good plumber or a capable auto mechanic. When you recommend a person, you are providing someone access into your network of trusted associates. When your page links to another page, you are providing access to your network of trusted information. It is that trust, built up by the recommendations of thousands or millions of people, that allows search engines to conclude that the article in question is valuable, trustworthy information. In this way, we could say that it is not *what* your page knows, but *who* it knows. Links to your page cause it to be treated with respect regardless of its actual content.

However, it is not that simple, of course. Just as that plumber must have knowledge (what he knows) to continue to attract recommendations from whom he knows, so does your page require strong information to attract links. But the links themselves are what we are interested in here. In Chapter 8, "Optimize Your Content," we looked at how search engines assess your content, but now let's see how they value links to and from your page.

How Websites Link   Links between web pages use an HTML tag, just like all other content, as shown in Exhibit 9-1. The figure shows an **internal** link—a link from one page to another within the same domain (website). Of more interest to search engines are **external** links, which connect one website to another, because those links indicate more impartial recommendations. Websites use these endorsements to determine which sites have the most linked-to pages—the pages with the most **inbound** links. Inbound links act as a surrogate for the quality and trustworthiness of the content, which search engines cannot discern from merely looking at the words on the page.

Way back in 2000, AltaVista, Compaq, and IBM advanced the **bow-tie theory**—that the web is actually composed of four kinds of pages, each with its own peculiar linking patterns:

- **Core pages:** Comprising 30% of the web, these pages are the most linked-to and linked-from on the web. The most popular websites tend to have many pages in this group.
- **Origination pages**. Approximately 24% of all pages have numerous links *into* the core but relatively few *from* the core. These pages might be new or not terribly high quality, so they have not attracted the links back to them that would mark them as part of the core.

Every link you see on a page in your browser...

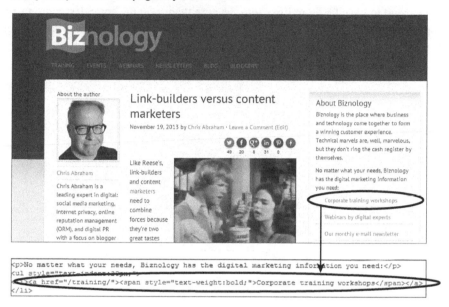

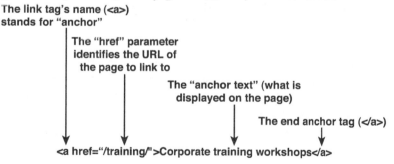

...is generated by a link tag in the page's HTML in a prescribed format:

The link tag's name (<a>) stands for "anchor"

The "href" parameter identifies the URL of the page to link to

The "anchor text" (what is displayed on the page)

The end anchor tag (</a>)

<a href="/training/">Corporate training workshops</a>

Exhibit 9-1 How links are coded in HTML. Web page links use the HTML anchor tag to show the (usually) underlined text on the screen for that link.

- **Destination pages:** Another 24% of the web consists of pages that are commonly linked *from* the core, but do not themselves link back *into* the core. These pages are usually high-quality pages, but they might be corporate websites that tend to link internally more than externally.

- **Disconnected pages**. The remaining pages (22%) are not directly connected to the core. They might have links to or from origination and destination sites, or they might be linked only to other disconnected pages.

As you look at Exhibit 9-2, understand that the pages are categorized comparatively. Origination pages tend to have far more links *into* the core than *from* the core; destination pages have just the opposite tendency. Getting one directory listing for an origination page does not change it to a core page, but getting a number of inbound links from core pages would.

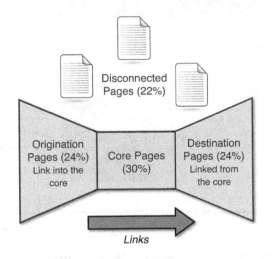

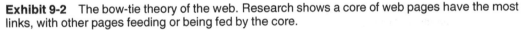

Exhibit 9-2   The bow-tie theory of the web. Research shows a core of web pages have the most links, with other pages feeding or being fed by the core.

For the search marketer, the importance of the bow-tie theory is that core and destination pages have the highest link popularity. Those are the best pages to get links *from*. As you can imagine, destination pages tend not to link to many other external pages, leaving just the core pages as the best targets to get links from. Garnering links from origination pages and disconnected pages will not bring you as many visitors and will not carry the same weight with search engines.

How Link Popularity Works   We introduced link popularity in Chapter 3, where you learned that it's the most critical content ranking factor. Search engines evaluate a page's link popularity in four basic ways:

- **Link quantity:** In general, pages receiving more links to them rank higher than pages receiving fewer links; but all links are not created equal, as discussed next.

- **Link quality:** Everyone has an opinion, but some are worth more than others. Opinions expressed by those creating links are no different. A link to a page is an endorsement of that page, but endorsements have more value from well-respected and authoritative sources than from others. Search engines determine authority by examining the link popularity of the site linked *from*. So, if a high-authority site (one that itself has many other high-authority sites linking to it) links to your page, it is conferring some of its authority on your page. Search engines attribute the highest value to pages with many links from high-quality sites. But it is even more complicated than that. Search engines mathematically split the authority conveyed to each linked page based on the number of links—a high-authority page with 10 links conveys more authority to each linked page than an equally high-authority page containing 50 links conveys. The theory is that there is only so much authority to go around, so the more links there are, the less of a recommendation each linked page is getting.

- **Anchor text:** The text that the visitor clicks to follow the link is very important to search engines because it provides the **context** of the recommendation. Consider two different links to the personal website of Pat Lee, one that uses the name *Pat Lee* in the anchor text and another that uses the anchor text *tax expert Pat Lee*. Both clearly indicate that searches for "Pat Lee" might want to consider this page, but only the second conveys an endorsement of Pat Lee as a tax expert. Anchor text is an important keyword ranking factor in the search engine algorithms; keywords tend to return the linked pages that have variants of the words within the keyword in anchor text. For example, if our fictitious firm Snap Electronics began to attract many links to one of its pages with the anchor text *SnapShot digital cameras*, searches that contain those words would rank Snap's page higher than before. But be careful. Search engines pay attention to anchor text because it is an unbiased recommendation of a page as being about a certain subject. If you, the search marketer, begin to **orchestrate** links from all over the web with the *same* anchor text (your highest-priority keyword, perhaps), that perfect pattern will look suspicious to the search engines—precisely because it is *too* perfect. Truly unbiased recommendations are not orchestrated and they don't look perfect; they have natural anchor text patterns that include their share of "click here" and other less-advantageous words. The lack of these oddities is a signal to the search engines that you've stacked the deck by orchestrating the links. In that case, the search engines won't give you the same boost for your content that more natural-looking link patterns justify.

- **Link relevancy:** Links from contextually relevant sites are also an important keyword ranking factor. When we say "contextually relevant," we mean that the information is on a certain theme (or topic or subject). It is not enough for the anchor text to use similar words, because words can have multiple meanings on unrelated subjects. Beyond the anchor text, search engines look at the words around the anchor text, words on the entire page and even the entire site being linked from. Why? Because sites that are relevant to the topic of the keyword provide more relevant links than others. Continuing the Snap example, links from digital camera review sites, from camera retailers, and from Snap affiliates are more contextually relevant than those from a teen fashion magazine. Random links from popular sites do not convey the same authority as links from sites that are popular *and* thematically related.

If these factors seem hard to calculate, you are getting the idea. Search engines attribute value to pages with many high-quality links to those pages. Search engines attribute high keyword ranking factors to pages with inbound links that are both from contextually relevant sites *and* contain the keywords in their anchor text. Those factors are mixed together, along with many other factors discussed in Chapter 8, to determine which pages rank first for a particular keyword. It is rather amazing that search engines can consider so many complicated factors in the second between the searcher's keyword and the results page, but they do.

So how do search engines calculate the value of links to a page? As you might expect, each uses different detailed techniques, but they have some basics in common, built around the theory of **hub** and **authority** pages:

- **Hub pages:** Web pages that link to several or many other pages on a similar subject. We have spoken of the hub page for Snap's digital cameras. It is the page with links to the rest of the pages on Snap's site on that subject. But other pages are hubs, too. If you create a page on your site that links to the best pages on the web on a particular subject, that makes your page a hub for that subject. One of the most well-known examples of a hub page is a directory page, which is simply a list of linked resources. The reason that directory links can be valuable to search engines is that the subject (or topic or theme) of the directory is a powerful clue as to the subject of the pages it links to.

- **Authority pages:** Web pages that are linked *to* by many other pages on a particular subject. Authority pages are the ones that search engines usually ascribe the highest quality to. And it makes sense. Pages that are most closely related to the searcher's keywords are probably authority pages.

We have expressed the concepts in terms of pages, but some search engines view hubs and authorities as clusters of pages within a site or even as sites themselves. Those engines would give more value to authorities that came from sites that had several pages that were also authorities on the same subject, for example.

Search engines try to rank authority pages higher, but the search engines use hub pages to do a better job of identifying authority pages. Because words can have multiple meanings (*windows*, for example), search engines that look only at anchor text might display pages about the wrong subject, even though those pages contain the words searched for. Hub pages can help search engines zero in on the particular meaning for a word. If an authority page is also linked by hub pages on a particular subject, search engines develop more confidence that the page is also on the right subject. Pella Windows will receive different hub links than Microsoft Windows, for example.

As discussed in Chapter 8, the more pages contain a particular keyword, the more important content factors become in the search result ranking. It makes sense, if you think about it. If your search marketing campaign is targeting a search keyword that very few sites use (such as a new brand name for your product line), optimizing your content and getting your pages indexed might be enough for high rankings. On the other hand, if you are trying to break through for *digital cameras*—a very popular keyword found on millions of pages—you must concentrate on factors in addition to content optimization.

Measure and Build Your Links   As with everything else in search marketing, we want to measure what we do whenever we can. To measure success at attracting links to your site, you perform a **link audit**. Which sites are linking to you? Your link audit analyzes every link to your landing page, or even to your whole site.

The simplest metric for a link audit is the sheer number of other pages that link to your page—what we have called the inbound links. There is no shortage of ways to check inbound links, which are also known by search experts as **back links**. One way to measure the quality of your content is the same way that search engines do—by the number and quality of the links it has attracted. Many tools do a good job of link measurement. You can check them out at our website (SEMincBook.com/link-tools).

Over the years, many search marketers have used link measurement tools to identify great sources of links and then solicit links from those sites—this tactic is called a **link-building campaign**. Link-building campaigns are one way to provide what the search engines are looking for: quality links to your site.

But you might be wondering how the search engines feel about link building. Well, they don't like it much. Google, in fact, has publicly discussed ranking algorithm changes that are designed to identify "unnatural link patterns" so that they can devalue those links when deciding content quality.

Some search marketers have been informed, through Google Webmaster Tools, that Google has identified many links to their site that appear to be the result of link campaigns or other artificial ways of building links. This has resulted in the almost comic activity of webmasters soliciting sites to *remove* the very links that they worked so hard to get just a few years ago.

So, if wholesale soliciting of links isn't really the way to go anymore, why should you measure links at all? The best reason is to give you a sense of the quality level of your content—which is the same way that search engines judge content quality. In addition, some of your competitors might be pretending to use unethical link building techniques on your behalf just so the search engines can catch you, so we'll talk about how measuring your links can protect you, also.

But all link solicitation isn't bad, even if the search engines don't like it. If you have great content, but you don't have a big name or wide exposure, you need to draw attention to your content, just as you share your content in social media, or you employ traditional public relations approaches. One valid way to publicize your content is to solicit links. It stands to reason that you'd focus on sites that are more popular, so that your content gets more exposure, and measuring links can help you identify your success.

So, how do you start measuring your site's links? In the old days, we'd simply search in Google or Bing for the operator "link:yourdomain.com" to see a list of links to yourdomain.com as search results. But spammers began to use this link operator to see how well they were doing in fooling the search engines, so both Google and Bing now show only a subset of links in this way.

Both search engines now require that you sign in to your Google Webmaster Tools account to see a more comprehensive set of links to your site. Note that we said *more* comprehensive. Both engines admit that they don't show all the links that they know about.

Webmaster Tools sites are just the beginning. Remember that we keep track of all the latest tools in link measurement at our companion website (SEMincBook.com/link-tools). Here are some of the questions you might want to ask about a link-building tool:

- Does it count the number of links a site has?
- Can I compare my links with other sites, such as competitor sites?
- Can it measure how many links a specific page has?
- Does it assess the quality of each link?
- Can I view the anchor text for each link?
- Can it identify detrimental links and "bad neighborhoods" to get links from?
- Can I upload my own data into the database for scoring?
- Can I export link data from the tool?

Also at our book's companion site is a sample scorecard that you can customize for use in your own link-building efforts (SEMincBook:com/link-building-scorecard): In the not-too-recent past, link building was in its Wild West phase, with companies spending upward of

How Important Is a Linking Site's Value?

In Chapter 3, we introduced content ranking factors, a search engine's way of evaluating quality. The most well-known compilation of content factors is Google's PageRank, which is often used as a shorthand way of referring to page factor scores for any search engine. When you get a link from another site, how important is that site's PageRank?

Before we answer that, you should know that you can find any page's PageRank if you use the Google toolbar. Rolling your mouse over the green PageRank bar will reveal a number between zero (extremely low quality) and ten (the meaning of life) that shows Google's perceived importance of that page. The toolbar shows the page's PageRank on the PageRank scale, so it will display "10/10" for a page with the highest possible PageRank score. Understand, however, that the PageRank score shown in the toolbar is just an approximation and might not be the up-to-date value Google uses in ranking. Google has also been withdrawing support from browsers for its toolbar, so at some point Google might not be showing it at all.

If you can find your site's PageRank, know that it is not calculated on the normal linear scale, but rather an exponential scale. That's a fancy math term that means that PageRank 4 is not one better than PageRank 3; it is six or seven times better. So the difference between a

$30,000 a month for agencies to solicit links from anywhere and everywhere. We don't recommend this kind of indiscriminate link building, but we do believe that, like any worthwhile content marketing techniques, you need to have an organized way of promoting your content through public relations, social media, and, yes, link. A link-building scorecard is the best way to organize your activities.

The main value of a link-building scorecard is to direct your activities toward higher-quality links. The basic idea is that it is better to obtain ten great links than 1,000 low-quality (or even mediocre) links. So, rather than paying someone to amass as many links as possible, your scorecard can prioritize obtaining links that are more valuable to you, using some of the following factors:

- **Contextual relevance:** How closely related to your page's topic is the topic of the linking page? Google won't give much credit to your page on insurance policies if the link is from a recipe site.

- **Number of visitors:** Websites such as Alexa or Quantcast often can estimate the number of monthly visitors that come to the linking site. Obviously, sites that have many visitors would provide more traffic to your site than those with only a few (but remember the need for contextual relevance, above). You need *qualified* visitors that might be your kind of customers.

PageRank 5 page and a PageRank 8 page is much larger than you might think. When you measure your links to your site, some tools attempt to show Google PageRank for each link, while others use other approximations of page quality (such as MozRank from Moz.com or Authority and Citation from MajesticSEO). Regardless of whether you use PageRank, MozRank, or some other method of checking the quality of links, the question remains as to how important the quality is of the site that links to you.

You might imagine that you want links from the pages with the highest PageRank scores, but it is more complicated than that. Remember that the authority conveyed is relative to the number of links on the page. The fewer the links, the more authority is passed on each link. So, it is often more valuable to be the only link on a PageRank 5 page than one of hundreds on a PageRank 7 page.

Don't fall into the PageRank seduction trap. It is most important for your pages to be linked from sites that will drive heavy, highly qualified traffic to your site, regardless of their PageRank values. So, use PageRank as a tool to help validate your own judgment of the quality of a potential link source, but do not blindly follow PageRank or any other scoring system when you make your list and check it twice.

- **Search rank for the keyword:** A page that ranks well for your primary keyword could be considered very high quality. And remember, qualified visitors will click that link and come to your site even if the search engines don't give you any credit for it.

- **Link placement:** Where will the link be added? To the body or to a list of links or to a blogroll? Obviously, the more prominent the link, the more visitors are likely to follow it.

- **Link destination:** Which page on your site is being linked to? Links to interior pages on your site are generally much more valuable than links to your home page.

- **No follow:** Links coded "nofollow" will not be counted by search engines. Search engines expect paid links to be nofollowed, but *every* nofollowed link has value only for the traffic it generates. Nofollowed links don't affect your search rankings.

One warning: Using this kind of scorecard will help you prioritize the efforts to build quality links on your behalf, but it might annoy many of the companies that sell link-building services. If they are in the business of massive indiscriminate link building, they will bristle at your scorecard because it makes them do a lot more work than they are accustomed to. After all, it's harder and more time-consuming to get a few great links than a ton of lousy ones.

One way to think about successful (and ethical) link building is this: If you will be happy with the link just based on the traffic it drives to your site, it's a great link. If you are trying to obtain a link merely for its search boosting value, it probably isn't such a great link to get.

How *Not* to Build Links to Your Site

It's simple enough to understand that great content will attract links. And you know that you need to employ techniques to draw attention to your content. But some of you might be wondering if there is an easier way to attract links, because creating really great content is, well, hard. But inquiring minds want to know, "Is there a shortcut?"

Um, no.

It's not that people won't tell you about their "secrets." Sometimes it seems that everyone has a trick. We're just here to tell you that they don't work. The real trick is to create content that your customers and prospects want to spend their precious time with. Content that answers their questions. Helps them. Informs them.

But you might think that you have figured out how to fool the search engines. You have an idea for how to get links to your site—the easy way—and Google will be none the wiser. So, in this section we lay out all the tricks that people try that don't usually work. It will save you a lot of time.

 Many people attempt to fool the search engines, but they are getting harder and harder to fool. Employ these tricks at your own peril:

- **Blog comment spamming:** Many **blogs** are very popular and well written, and search engines treat them with the same importance as a well-crafted web page, so links from these blogs are important to search marketers. Readers can subscribe to blogs to read the latest post and usually post comments themselves—which is where the trouble is. Blog spammers post unrelated messages containing links to URLs that the spammer wants to boost in the search rankings. Many bloggers now block readers from posting comments.

- **Link farms:** Tricky search marketers set up dozens or hundreds of sites that can be crawled by search engines, just so they can put in thousands of links to sites they want to boost in search rankings. "Free-for-all" sites allow anyone to post a link on any topic, and are similarly not recommended. Later in this chapter, we explain how to steer clear of links designed just to fool the search engines.

- **Hidden links:** Just as we discussed hidden text in Chapter 8, you can hide links using the same techniques. Hiding links allows your links to be seen by spiders but not by people, so you can load up lots of links on high-ranking pages to other pages that you are trying to boost.

- **Injection links:** A variation of hidden links, nefarious companies can hijack out-of-date blog software, adding machine-generated links to the content of your unsuspecting website. Regularly update your website for the latest security patches and monitor content to keep it fresh.

But maybe you weren't really trying to be sneaky. Maybe you just want to go get some links in a very straightforward way. Since 1998, when Google first started valuing links in organic search results, search marketers have engaged in link-building campaigns, and maybe you have, too. While there is nothing unethical about soliciting links to your site, search engines have begun to devalue those links because they appear to be unnatural—which they are.

So, if you have been orchestrating links to your site, tread carefully, because the search engines are more and more able to detect which links are the products of link-building campaigns. That means that there is a lot of advice that you might hear that is too clever by half:

- **Buy paid search ads:** Google and Bing love when you do this, and they do create links to your site, but the search engines don't count these links for organic search ranking purposes.

- **Link within your site to other pages:** You're undoubtedly already doing this, because that is how site navigation works. You might be wondering if you should be changing the way you link to improve your organic search results. In general, links within your site don't make much difference, because you control the source and target of the link. Internal links are not unbiased votes, so search engines don't give these links much weight. Use internal links to help your readers find more content on your site and that will help search engines understand your content better, too.

- **Link between several sites that you control:** This is not unethical, but if you are doing it only to boost your search rankings, it might not make sense. Search engines have multiple ways of detecting these links including shared IP addresses, analytics codes, and domain registrations so that they value them less than other kinds of links.

- **Obtain site-wide links from other sites:** When another site links to you by placing a link to your site on every page of theirs (often by adding your link to the page footer), the search engines sometimes take notice—and not in a good way. Although a legitimate site-wide link is perfectly ethical, sometimes paid links have been arranged this way, so search engines have sometimes lowered the value of these links.

- **Trade links with other sites:** If you link to a site, you can ask for a link back. Sure, but it probably doesn't help either one of you. Search engines understand that so-called **reciprocal links** might not be entirely natural votes for quality content, so they discount their importance. Once again, this is not against the search engines' terms of service, but just because it is allowed does not means that it is a good use of your time.

- **Solicit links from as many sites as possible:** This was once the biggest part of building links to your site, but no more. Search engines have been analyzing link patterns more deeply than ever before, and these solicited links often fail the "sniff test." If links start popping up out of nowhere, and they have mostly the same anchor text, they seem unnatural to the search engines. It could be the result of soliciting links, or it could be the result of paid link campaigns—which do violate the terms of service of search engines. As stated earlier, targeted link-building with related sites is a perfectly reasonable form of public relations, but wholesale campaigns are not recommended.

Many people try to purchase links from popular sites so that it appears to Google that an important site has linked to their site. Unfortunately, it doesn't work as well as it once did. It's definitely possible to buy links and get away with it, but the search engines have gotten smarter and smarter about detecting "unnatural" link patterns—whether they are from soliciting links for free or from paying for them.

Those unnatural link patterns occur because they are being orchestrated by us, the search marketers. Whether we *ask* for or *pay* for links, it looks the same to the search engine analyzing this activity. Instead of random patterns of anchor text across the links, the search engines will see the same few word combinations coming up—the words that you asked for.

Even if you try to make the patterns *look* random, they won't look *truly* random. And computers are really good at recognizing patterns that are not truly random. Google and Bing can detect the difference between orchestrated links and truly random link patterns resulting from quality content. It reminds us of how auditors catch crooked accountants—their "random" faked numeric entries hardly ever end in the digits 0 and 5, even though about 20% of the entries should—because 0 and 5 are two out of the ten possible ending digits. People tend to fake their entries using the other digits to make them *seem* random, but they really aren't. If you think you are being clever by varying your orchestrated anchor text, the search engines can probably still see through your ruse.

You might have good reasons to solicit or pay for links that have nothing to do with organic search rankings. It's perfectly legitimate to orchestrate links to your site for the sole purpose of increasing traffic from visitors clicking on those links to come to your site. The search engines request that when you pay for links that the linking site code the nofollow attribute for each paid link.

But how do you know whether the search engines suspect that your links are orchestrated? Google actually posts warnings in Google Webmaster Tools that look like the one in Exhibit 9-3. If you see such a warning, should you be worried? Not necessarily. Google is trying to be more transparent in its dealings with webmasters, so it is showing such warnings for sites that have some suspicious links, even if those links haven't caused any drops in your site's search rankings. If the warning truly is important, you'll notice a significant drop in traffic to your site at around the same time.

New and important

⚠ **Google Webmaster Tools notice of detected unnatural links to http://www.** [redacted]

Exhibit 9-3   Detecting orchestrated links. If you use Google Webmaster Tools, you might see a warning like this one.

What's Negative SEO?

Once people discovered that some types of link patterns can actually hurt your organic search rankings, it wasn't long before the unscrupulous among us decided to turn that power against their competitors. So-called **negative SEO** (sometimes called **Google bowling**) refers to an insidious technique where your competitors use spam techniques seemingly on your behalf to knock down your site.

Ethically challenged search marketers are once again bringing a black eye to the industry by intentionally using spam techniques to get their competitors penalized. This is a new kind of search marketing problem. While no one can get access to your site to create spammy content or cloaking violations, link spam techniques can be faked so that your competitors cause Google to catch you and penalize you. Those pesky "unnatural links" that you want to avoid in your own link-building campaigns can be turned against you by competitors.

If this happens to you, you do have options. Both Google and Bing now allow you to **disavow a link**, so you can undo negative SEO, although it is usually a great deal of work. If you need to do this, check out the instructions on our companion site (SEMincBook.com/disavow-links). Still, a few years ago, there was nothing that could be done, so at least this can be viewed as progress.

If you are suffering from reduced traffic from orchestrated links, you can try contacting the linking sites to get the links removed. (For paid links, you can just stop paying.) If that fails, you can **disavow links** by telling the search engines not to count certain links to your pages. The work is painstaking and should be undertaken only by an expert, but it's at least a road to the redemption for your site's quality rating. Of course, if you have a huge site with millions of links and a small percentage are bad, it probably isn't worth working on. But if your site is bedeviled with low-quality links, it's the only game in town.

The Right Way to Build Links to Your Site

By now, you might be wondering whether any methods of building links are valuable. Will you be able to build links to your site? Will the search engines value those links? Can you do it all without turning it into a new full-time job? These are all good questions that we'll try to answer now.

Building links is a slow process. If you commit yourself to keep at it, however, you will eventually succeed when competitors with less stick-to-itiveness falter along the way. Attracting quality links to your site is not easy, but you can do it if you use some of the techniques outlined here:

- **Make your site a link magnet:** The best way to get links is to create a site so excellent that it draws links without them being requested. You can take specific actions to make your site attractive to linkers. We show them to you.

- **Promote your content:** The public relations profession is alive and well. You need to be sure that your PR and social media efforts include promoting your content. We show you how to get attention to your content that results in links.

- **Use your existing network:** Reaching out to others is one of the key tools in your arsenal. If you work your network, you'll undoubtedly see some of those efforts result in links—even if you never ask for links.

- **Build your network:** Some of you might not have much of a network. Or you realize that it never hurts to have a bigger network. Stay tuned for how to engage with others so that they help you.

- **Judiciously use directories:** Directories are an old tactic that was once a critical part of any link-building program. Directory links can still be important if approached wisely.

- **Identify sources of new links:** When you do attempt to build links, you need to find appropriate sites that truly will be motivated to link to you—and will benefit you.

- **Recover lost link power:** Sometimes, changes to your sites result in links being lost. At other times, your URL structures lower the power of links by spreading links across multiple URLs when those links could all be pointed at a single focused URL. We show you how to detect and correct both of these problems.

Let's start with how to spruce up your site so that it attracts the most links possible.

Make Your Site a Link Magnet Some might call it "linkability," whereas others might dub your site "link-worthy." Regardless of the name, you need to make your site a "link magnet": Your site must *attract* links from other sites.

So how do you attract those links? Page by page. You know which pages on your site might attract links; those are your **link landing pages**. Just as a search landing page can attract search engines, you can design your link landing pages to attract links. Each link landing page must provide a strong reason to be linked to:

- **Valuable information:** Many link landing pages provide important information. The information could be an article, a set of FAQs, a blog, a newsletter, a case study, a white paper, a webinar, a game, a survey, a quiz, an eBook, or something else. Sometimes reference information, such as how-to, a tutorial, or even a glossary of terms can garner a large number of links. What makes your information a "must-have" for them?

- **An authoritative source of information:** Your landing page need not have original information. It can be anything from the right place to find links to the most trustworthy pages on the web about a subject. In scientific research, "survey papers" examine all the other papers about a subject and critique them. Your landing page could list links to the important documents on a topic, along with your review of each document; you would be creating a small web directory on a particular subject. Which sites could use your page as background for their visitors?

- **A desirable tool:** You can attract many links with a software tool that provides value to the visitor. If you can develop a simple (or not-so-simple) program that does something useful related to your business, you *will* attract links to it. In this book, we have shown you numerous free tools to help with your search marketing, but you can develop a tool on just about anything people need help with. A life insurer can provide a calculator to determine how much coverage is needed. A charity can show how much of a contribution is tax deductible. A travel site can suggest vacation ideas based on interests. If your tool helps people, you will get your links. To get the most links, your tool needs to be both helpful and unique—give people something useful that they cannot get anywhere else and see how many links you get.

No matter what type of landing page you set out to create, you need to think through the experience that visitors will have when they get there, just as you did for search landing pages. The landing experience is important for visitors. Without a good experience, your visitors will not follow through to your web conversion. However, it is also critical to attract the links in the first place. Who will link to your site if they see that the experience is not a good one for *their* visitors? You must design the right landing experience both to attract the link *and* to get conversions after it is in place. So, how do you design your link landing pages?

- **Reinforce the topic:** To attract links, you must know what the subject of your page is. Why should people link to you? Why should visitors follow the link? You should have a strong idea of what you want the anchor text to be on the link; use that same text as a prominent heading on the page and in the title tag. Remember that the visitor to that page could have been anywhere on the web before reaching you, so smooth the visitor's transition to your site by showing that the link topic followed is exactly what your page is about. Avoid cutesy marketing names. Be 100% sure that the heading of your page is exactly what you expect visitors to call your topic.

- **Stick to the topic:** After you have attracted a number of links, do *not* change the subject of the page. We know that it makes perfect sense to you to put your DVR product on your withdrawn VCR page, because it seems like they would attract the same customers, but the links to that page will be all wrong. Those links will flee, and you will attract fewer links to the rest of your site because linkers believe you will pull another switcheroo. Better to leave the old VCR page up, saying that you withdrew the product but that you have a new product that they might be interested in if they click to a new page. Unfortunately, there are no shortcuts to building strong links to your site.

- **Deliver excellent content:** Your page must be well written and high quality in every way. If you have a well-known brand name, use it. The people whose links you must attract have many choices of pages to link to. Yours must be the *best*; otherwise, you will draw far fewer links. The better your page is, and the more it completely fulfills the visitor's need, the more links you will attract. The single most important tip to attracting links is to make your landing page one that sites *must* link to; otherwise, their visitors have missed out on a gem. Create that gem, and the links will follow.

- **Use the right granularity for your content:** Sometimes you put too much or too little on a single page, and it reduces the links you receive. For example, a page full of biographies might attract fewer links than individual bio pages because some people only want a single biography rather than the page full of them.

- **Use link-friendly URLs:** Make your URLs short—and easy to spell and remember. Use "URL rewrite" techniques (covered in Chapter 7, "Get Your Content Listed") to transform dynamic URLs. You must make your URLs look like they are never going to change; the shorter and more readable they are, the more fundamental they appear to your site. Link landing pages should look like they have always been there and will never disappear. Unfortunately, some websites have the opposite problem with URLs because they use the same URL for multiple documents (usually through frames or tricky programming). This shared URL technique is death for link campaigns because there is no way to link to the exact page desired.

- **Take down the roadblocks:** If you think that people will link to pages that immediately pop up in a registration page or a "choose your country" page, you are wrong. You will drive away many more links than you attract because no one wants to send their reader to that kind of annoying experience. We know that the marketing department wants to collect the email address of everyone who downloads the white paper, but forcing entry before viewing will drastically reduce the number of sites willing to link to you. Take down these annoying roadblocks for all link landing pages.

- **Keep good company:** If you have links to other sites on your link landing page (or pages surrounding the landing page), make sure they link to very high-quality sites. Potential linkers often examine a site carefully before they link to it; they look at much more than the landing page. Don't let questionable links on your site damage your linkability.

If, while reading the list of landing page tips, you asked yourself, "Why shouldn't I do these things for *every* page on my site?" you are getting the idea. If you think of every page on your site as a potential link landing page, you will drive many more links to your site than if you reserve the star treatment for a small subset of pages. But many sites would find this a daunting task; they have too many pages that would require correction, just as performing organic search optimization on every page might be too expensive for many sites.

Snap Electronics believed that they could not afford to treat *every* page as a link landing page, so they decided to treat each of their *search* landing pages as link landing pages. As they upgraded their pages for organic search optimization, they tweaked their content to attract links, too. Snap also created new content to attract links, ranging from a white paper explaining their OneTouch auto-focus technology to employee blogs with new ways to use SnapShot cameras.

If your company cannot make every page a link landing page, start out by identifying the pages that are the most closely related to your targeted keywords for your search marketing campaigns. Don't limit your list to the main navigation pages of your site—frequently that white paper on a new technology will draw a lot more links than the page for the product that uses that technology. Make sure you dress up your site's interior pages as link landing pages for the same reason. You want them found by search engines. The deeper into your site that you pull the visitor, the closer they are to a conversion.

Now that you have spruced up your sites for linkability, it's time to start promoting your content.

Promote Your Content Great content should not be kept secret. Great content is important, but it attracts links only when potential linkers discover that content. Promoting your content is a key step that not only attracts links, but also attracts traffic directly to your site.

If you have a public relations team, they can be your key asset in promoting your content. Digital public relations techniques can play a huge role in search marketing. Yes, your PR team can put out a press release when you debut an exciting new piece of content, but there's more to promotion than that. Here are just a few ways you can promote your content:

- **Share in social media:** Okay, you probably thought of this one. Obviously, every time you create a new content item, you need to tweet it, share it on Facebook—promote it using whatever social media resources make sense for your business. When you do, search engines might pick up your promotion as a link, but what's more important is that other people will have a chance to link to and promote your content.

- **Provide subscriptions for your content:** Whether folks follow your Twitter handle, subscribe to your blog, sign up for your email newsletter, or opt in to any other kind of alerting mechanism, you are pinging your most interested audience on a regular basis. Some of them will link to you.

- **Distribute your content:** Instead of posting all of your content *on* your website, you can post videos on YouTube, you can guest post on someone else's blog, you can post articles to industry magazine websites—you get the idea. Why would you do that? Because every time you do that, you are potentially replacing an internal link *within* your site with an external link **to** your site—maybe even more than one link. You can get a link to your home page, to the bio of the author, and maybe other links depending on the content item that you contribute. You can even adopt this strategy with software tools—let others offer your tool with a link back to your site in a "Powered by" link.

Promotion is not the only activity that can use your PR folks. Next up, we look at how to get influencers to spread your message.

Use Your Existing Network   Public relations work has always been about getting others to pass along your message. You can do the same thing to attract links. We've already talked about directly promoting your content, but how can you get the influential people in your industry to know and care about what you're doing?

The most overlooked source of links stems from your existing business relationships. Most companies, especially large companies, have an extensive set of partners that they do business with. Resellers, dealers, affiliates, retailers, suppliers—it does not matter what you call them. These partners often provide the easiest and most valuable links you can attract—what we call **relational links**.

Relational links are valuable because they are from neutral parties—any of these companies can freely decide to link to your site or not. If their relationship with your company ends, the link will, too. These companies are independent from yours. *That* is what makes a link from them such a valuable endorsement.

So start making your list. What companies will want to provide links to your site? Do you manufacture a product they sell? Are you a reference customer for a supplier? Do you have a deal to sell another company's product? Will your customers provide testimonials on their websites? Stop and think. What relationships exist between your company and others?

Depending on the nature of your company's relationships, you might be in a commanding position. If your suppliers want your reference, you can insist on a link. You can require that all affiliates include links. Examine all of your relationships and see whether you are in position to request links (preferably one-way links) that they are very likely to agree to.

Even if your company already has plenty of links from your partners, you might still have work to do. Large companies often have an abundance of links to their home page, but not enough links to interior pages. Snap found its digital camera accessories suppliers already had links to the

Snap site, but the links were all to Snap's home page, using *Snap Electronics* as the anchor text. Snap went back to each company and requested a link to the digital cameras product category hub page, with some variation of *SnapShot digital cameras* as the anchor text. Snap's experience is the norm for big companies. Their big link totals are mostly links to their home page using the company name as the anchor text (as you saw earlier for Nikon). To nudge your search rankings for informational and transactional keywords, you need links to your interior pages for your individual product lines, such as digital cameras.

An opportunity often missed in large companies is sponsorships. Whenever corporate largesse funds a nonprofit or industry activity, it is customary for the funded website to thank your company and provide a link back to your site. If your company sponsors research at a local university, or endows a chair, get links to your site. Perhaps your company sponsors an external organization, or one of its programs or events. Because you probably do not need any more links to your home page with your company name, ask instead for a link to an interior page of your site that is focused on the event topic. IBM's Globalization team, for example, sponsors the Localization Industry Standards Association (LISA) conference, which dutifully placed a sponsor link on its site to IBM's home page. A quick email from IBM got the sponsor link pointed to the IBM Globalization home page—a much more relevant link for that page. This link generated more qualified visitors following the link as well as improved search rankings. Your site might have similar opportunities.

Don't overlook trade associations. Your company might be a member of one or more of these industry organizations. Each trade association has its own website, and most have a member list page, as well as other pages on the site that might link to member websites. Make sure that your organization is listed in the member directory of each trade association you belong to—and that the web directory entry links to your site. Investigate whether there are other opportunities for your company to provide news or information for posting on the site (along with a handy link back to your site, too). These links are especially helpful in establishing your company's credentials in searches for the name of your industry and other industry terms.

Keep in mind that the easiest way to get in trouble with search engines is with that dreaded "unnatural links" pattern. The truth is that these relational links from your existing network *are* orchestrated; it is just that it's expected that friends will help each other. But it's still wise for you to make these links as natural-looking as possible, so no matter what your business relationship is with any of these other organizations, let them decide where they are linking and what words they will use. You'll be tempted to make "suggestions" to them, but the more input they get, the more likely that you are creating unnatural link patterns.

Build Your Network   What if you don't have much of a network? Or you know that you need to grow your network? It's never been easier to do so. In fact, there are so many ways to grow your network nowadays that deciding which tactics to focus on might be one of your largest problems. As you read through these suggestions, think about which ideas you have the experience, talent, or temperament to tackle.

Before you look at any of these ideas, however, you need to be able to identify the right influencers to recruit into your network. Your experience in your industry will make some of these people no-brainers to identify, but those easy choices might seem unreachable—out of your league. For example, if you are an author, you'd probably like to have Oprah to recommend your book, but so would every other author, so you might have to shoot lower than that.

But that doesn't mean that you can't try to connect with people more famous than you in your field. If you aren't sure whom to target, use social media listening tools (SEMincBook. com/social-listening-tools) to identify influencers—you can cross-check their Klout scores (klout.com) as a rough gauge of which subjects they are influential about.

After you've identified some target influencers, there are lots of ways of meeting them—in person or online:

- **Use interviews:** If you have some notoriety, you can usually find people that want to interview you. Those interviews will include links back to your site when they are posted. But you can use interviews, too. Offer to interview people that have bigger followings than you do.

- **Comment on blogs:** Target the blogs of influencers and post intelligent comments. Sometimes you'll get trackback links from the comment itself, but even if you don't, you are bringing yourself to the attention of people who can help you.

- **Answer questions:** Post on forums, message boards, LinkedIn, Quora, and other sites. When you answer questions, you show off your expertise and you never know when other influencers are watching what you say.

- **Write about influencers:** Even if you can't get the attention of influencers in any other way, writing about them is likely to get them to notice you. Every influencer has a vanity Google Alert on their own name. So if you can mention an influencer's blog post or speech, or review their latest book, that can be the hook you need to get some attention of your own.

- **Interact in social media:** When you start conversations with influencers, they will often respond, especially when you do it on Twitter or other public and semi-public venues.

- **Get out and meet people:** Go to meetups, attend conferences, join groups, and find any way you can to be part of the interactions that your target influencers already take part in.

How do these techniques attract links? Some people refer to it as **ego baiting**. When you interview an influencer, publish a guest post, or even just write about them, they will likely promote the content themselves. And when you answer questions, interact in social media, or comment on posts, influencers get to know who you are and how you think and will be more amenable to a subsequent contact.

Make sure that you have the right attitude as you pursue these influencers. You can use any of these approaches as a phony, trying to manipulate people to your ends. Or you can use these tactics in a genuine way; you can actually care about the people that you are engaging and you can be legitimately trying to help them even as you hope that they will help you, too.

If you are doing everything out of completely selfish motives, people will see through that. If you realize that building your network is a long road, and that your authenticity is a big part of a successful brand, you'll attract the influencer relationships that you need—and you will hold on to them for the long term.

You also need to pursue influencers in moderation. If you start bothering people or seem like a stalker, people will notice and that will not help you. Try to help others first, and they will help you, too.

Judiciously Use Directories It wasn't long ago that the highest-quality links you could get to your site came from **directories**. Although directory links no longer have the importance that they once did, some directory links can still be valuable if you are judicious in your choices.

Most sites can benefit from placement in specialty directories (sometimes known as **niche directories** or **vertical directories**) that cover only a single subject area. No matter what your organization does, there are sure to be several specialty directories for your industry, location, and other purposes, such as a directory of blogs or podcasts. Links from these directories can be very powerful evidence to the search engines as to what your site is about, which can translate into boosts for certain keywords. For local businesses, links from the Better Business Bureau and the local Chamber of Commerce can be especially valuable.

Some of these specialty directories allow links without payment. Called **free-for-all directories**, they typically provide only low-quality links. Because these directories charge no money, they usually generate revenue only from ads that don't pay terribly well. These types of directories do not usually have any editorial staff to vet links, allowing anyone who signs up to get a link. These links are easy to get, but they have almost no value. Sometimes, so many spammers have used these sites that they are essentially link farms, actually damaging your site's link quality factor. Other directories are similar to the search engines' own local directories. They cost nothing to be listed, and they are often seeded from public sources with some information. The best of these directories can be quite valuable. Check out Exhibit 9-4 to see an example of how two of these directories can rank highly for an important keyword. Just as with local search directories, you'll want to claim your listing and make sure your information is accurate—especially the link to your website.

Many specialty directories do require payment—they are typically of higher quality than free-for-alls. We've told you that search engines do their best to devalue paid links, but directory links can be a crucial exception. If the directory charges participants a fee that enables them to hire an editorial staff to rigorously check the quality of the sites linked to by the directory that can create a winning situation for everyone. The directory is a listing of high-quality sites that its users appreciate, the sites listed get traffic from the directory's users, and search engines value the directory links because of the care that went into creating and checking them.

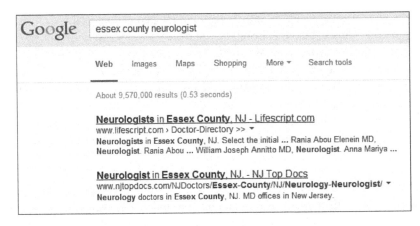

Exhibit 9-4   Valuable directories. You can see from this search results page that these directories are highly regarded by Google.

The problem with many specialty directories is that they are motivated to list as many businesses as possible—because each business pays them to list their link. That can lead to a lax editorial policy where the main qualification for being listed in the directory is that the check clears. As you can imagine, these kinds of directories don't add much value to your organic search rankings.

 So how can you tell which of these sites are legitimate and which ones are link farms— mere shams to try to fool search engines? Unfortunately, it is not always easy, even for experts, but you can use a few clues to spot a spammer:

- **Poor or no search position:** You already saw the best way to find high-quality directories. Search for some of your most important keywords and see if any directories come up. You definitely want to be listed in those places. If you just can't get a directory to come up in the search results no matter what you search for, cross it off your list.

- **More form than function:** The directory appears to have many links to sites that lack value, especially if those links look like advertisements. Large collections of links labeled "sponsored links" that are paid placement or contextual advertising spots are a red flag.

- **Unknown brands:** Although many companies are listed in your industry's category, you do not recognize any of the company names.

- **Non sequiturs:** Your directory has links that seem irrelevant to its topic, or it seems to have no central theme at all. Links to pharmaceutical, banking, or eCommerce services all sit side by side with no rhyme or reason.

- **Dead ends:** The links lead to error pages or sites that are clearly out of date.

- **The more the merrier:** Each directory category has far more links (hundreds) than any visitor could ever use. When you click the links and look at the sites, many seem to have long hyphenated URLs, and the sites resemble each other.

Even if you find a legitimate directory, check out the nature of the link it provides. Many directories use fancy redirect techniques to let them count the number of visitors they send your way, but search spiders will not follow the link. So, you might get visitors from that link, but it will not add to your link quality factor with search engines. If a link will get you qualified traffic, that is the most important thing, but you should realize that these redirection tactics will not help your search quality at all.

Directories are only part of the story for solicited links, however. Industry or trade magazines and blogs possess the journalistic integrity that makes them highly respected links. Make sure that when your executives are interviewed or your product is reviewed that you work with the reporter to add a link to your product or service into the story when it is relevant. The reporter will be interested if the pages you suggest have short URLs and provide a legitimate service for readers seeking more information. You will get more visitors to your site and higher search rankings from the online versions of the articles. Remember that your company can write articles for many of these publications, too. It will not take long for you to develop a wish list of potential partners to approach.

Identify New Sources of Links If too many of your pages are "link free" (or at least free of quality inbound links), what do you do now? Apparently what your website has been doing up to now has not been attracting the links you need. Your first step on the road to improvement is to review the advice we gave earlier: Make your site a link magnet. Sites with few quality links are typically violating some of this important advice.

It is not always that simple, however. Perhaps your site truly has high-quality content, and it should be attracting more links than it does. Maybe your site just is not as well known as you would like it to be. Or it could be that people take your site for granted and do not bother to link to it. Or maybe you just do not have the patience to wait for folks to discover how great your site is. You want to jump-start the link-building process. What do you do?

We should warn you that link-building campaigns are not easy. You have to find sites that would be great sources of links. You need to give them a reason to link to you. And you need to keep track of what you are doing so you stay organized with your requests and measure your improvement. It's hard work, but we show you how it's done.

Let's start with motivation. To get a site to link to you, you need to give them a reason. Why should they link to you? How does that link help their visitors? Do you offer a complementary product or service? Information their visitors need? A useful tool? Do you have an existing business relationship? Are you going to offer their customers a discount? Will you pay them for the link? Link back to them?

Similarly, for each link, you need a reason. Why do you want this site to link to you? Does it draw high traffic? Is it qualified traffic for your web conversions? Does it have high-quality content? Is that content relevant to your site's subject and its industry?

We do not advocate large-scale link requests, but sometimes potential link partners might not be aware of new content, so you need to contact them yourself. In the rest of this section, we offer some specific advice on how to negotiate links to your site from the sources that you've identified. But first, you need to consider a basic question: Why should this site link to you? What's in it for them? You have asked yourself this just about every step of the way in this process, but now you need to provide a personal answer—one just for the site you are requesting from.

To get any of these links we strongly suggest you pick up the phone and call the sites you think you should have a link from. While it is easy to just send an email, if you have to talk to them, you have to "sell the value" of your content and earn a link. Here are some tips for preparing for the call—and the follow-up email that will get you the link you desire:

- **Find a person:** Most sites will have phone or even social media contact details for the person who owns the site or wrote the content page that you believe a link should be added to.

- **Prove you visited the recipient's site:** Be ready to tell them what page and where on that page you want the link—and include it in your follow-up email. By reviewing the site and identifying specific page(s) you will show them you took the time to review the site and believe in the mutual value.

- **Sell:** Explain why this link is good for visitors to your partner's site. This is the most critical part of the discussion. You need a very simple but compelling reason for an endorsement to your site. You may get their voice mail so you need to be crisp and straight to the point with your recommendation.

- **Identify the page to link to:** Be specific about the exact, existing URL on your site you want the link to. Make sure that your URL looks permanent so that the webmaster does not think it will disappear soon. Make sure that it starts with "http://" and that it is short. (An incomplete URL or a URL that wraps to the next line in the email makes it much harder for the recipient to click it to go to the page.) As discussed in Chapter 7, use "URL rewrite" techniques to shorten your URLs if necessary. It sounds silly, but the ability for a busy webmaster to click your URL from the email can mean the difference between getting a link and having your message deleted.

- **Ask for a response:** As with any sales pitch, close with a call to action. If you can inject some urgency into the request, that's even better: "I will keep this link to your site on my page for the next 2 weeks while you consider my request." Or "My summer blowout sale on digital cameras starts on June 6, just in time for vacation travelers, so you will want to have your link in place by then."

It will be hard for you to hear, but everything that we have discussed so far is actually the easy part. What's harder is keeping track of all of your link requests. Which ones were sent? Which ones did you get responses to? When should you follow up? Did you say thank you to the people who responded? Did you take down the links from sites that turned down your two-way link offer? Are the sites that agreed to two-way links last year still linking to you?

Welcome to the world of link management. We cover some of these issues and how to manage link removal requests when we get to Chapter 10, "Make Search Marketing Operational."

Recover Lost Link Power An often-overlooked form of link building concerns techniques that make the most of the links that you already have.

The first technique we examine is to recover links that have been lost by your site—links to pages that have moved or been deleted, or links that never worked because the linkers entered the URL incorrectly.

You begin the process of restoring these broken links by identifying them. You can use Google Webmaster Tools to find the list of "not found" pages on your site. You'll get the list of all the links to old URLs that you've changed, and you'll get the list of most of the typos—but not all of them. Some typos might actually have the errors in the domain name. The only way to capture those is if you've purchased that incorrectly spelled domain name and check Webmaster Tools for *that* site. Regardless, you should at least be able to capture a good portion of the broken links.

Once you've got the list, it's time to redirect those links, the same way you learned about in Chapter 7. For every URL called by a broken link, you need to use a 301 redirect to send it to the right URL. If you aren't sure exactly which URL is the right one, you can examine the linking page and usually figure it out from context. Once you have the redirects in place, the search spiders will restore the value of the links the next time it crawls the linking sites.

Now let's move to the second important technique that helps you maximize the power of your existing links. If you know a little bit about how web servers work, you know that the exact same page can sometimes be accessed under multiple web addresses, or URLs. For example, your site's home page comes up when you type *yoursite.com* and also when you type *yoursite.com/index.html*—which you might think does not make any difference, but it does.

You see, although using any of the various URLs might bring up the same page, the spider might not realize that each of these URLs refer to the same physical page. The spider might store the same content under multiple URLs and, what's worse, other sites might link to your site using any of those various names. When that happens, the search engines do not realize how important your page is, because they have catalogued the links under multiple URLs, rather than consolidating them under one URL.

So, using our example, half the links might be stored with *yoursite.com/index.html* while the rest are stored under *yoursite.com*—fracturing the power across two URLs instead of one. The search engines will realize that both pages have the same content and will only show one of them in the search results, but will think that page has only half the links it really has, thus lowering its search ranking.

For years, smart webmasters have been using 301 redirects, so that the links are consolidated under a single URL. For example, they might redirect *yoursite.com/index.html* to *yoursite.com* to collect all the links under one page URL. That solves the problem of fractured links by combining all the links into one page.

Unfortunately, not everyone knows how to create 301 redirects, and not everyone even has access to their web server to code redirects. Many small businesses hosting sites on shared servers do not control their ability to redirect pages. Those companies were out of luck until search engines introduced a new way to consolidate URLs, called the **canonical tag**.

Many search marketers are also using the canonical tag to correct other URL problems, such as session IDs and other tracking codes that web analytics systems use to track visitors. The canonical tag allows the spiders to store the page under a single URL, even though each visitor might see the page with a different tracking code, and every link might have used a different version of the URL. In addition, some web servers treat URLs that differ by case as going to the same page—the canonical URL can tell the search engines what is going on. The good news is that all the major search engines support the canonical tag, so there is no reason for your link power to be split among multiple URLs that are actually pointing at the same page.

One decision that all websites need to make is whether to choose their canonical domain to be www.domain.com or merely domain.com. The best way to make that decision is based on which form most of your existing links have. You can use a free tool to do so (virante.org/seo-tools/www-vs-non-www-redirect).

Whether you are reclaiming lost links or merely consolidating the power of the links you have, these two techniques can boost your organic search results in short order.

And that wraps up our coverage of links as a quality factor for organic search rankings. Remember that links are valuable far beyond search marketing. High-quality links to your site from all the "right" places (in the popular core of the web) can drive many qualified visitors to your site through those links. In fact, we believe that attracting links to your site should be based on the qualified traffic those links will bring, not based on any calculated effect you are expecting in your search rankings. If you attract the links that bring the right visitors, the search engines will follow.

Social Media as Quality Factors

We have already covered many ways to use social media to attract links. But now we want to talk about how *search engines* use social media; they look at activity in social media as another factor to deduce content quality. So, although you can think of linking to content from social media as an activity, it is only *one* kind of activity. Many other types of social media behavior can provide clues to content quality also.

You might be wondering why search engines need to look at social activity. It is certainly much more difficult to track social activity than for search engine spiders to count links as they crawl the web. Social activity has become an important quality factor because spammers became so successful at faking links. As link farms and other linking tricks became more and more prevalent, Google and its brethren began searching for another way to test quality, and decided on social media.

As search engines now rely more on social media cues to determine content quality, just as they've traditionally used links, it ups the ante on what search marketers must do. You need to do more than post your content to your website. You might need to tag it with keywords, ping search engines with an RSS feed, and let some influential bookmarkers know your story is out there in hopes that they'll Digg it. Publicizing your content through social media is as important as getting it indexed, if for no other reason than anyone linking to your content likely discovered it through social media.

Viral marketing creates search challenges, too. You want your content to be passed on so that more customers see it, but you also want to ensure that the search engines recognize that yours is the original. Search engines will find multiple copies of your content, so marking the content with your brand (spoken on audio, or watermarked in videos and images) makes it more likely that other sites will link to your original copy than to a copy found elsewhere.

Think of each quality factor as an independent measure of the quality of a site. A truly high-quality site would be expected to have many links to its pages as well as plenty of social media activity around its content. On the other hand, a spammy site might have many links to it (from link tricks) but would *not* have much social media activity, because real people won't be talking about this site. So, a search engine uses social media activity as a check against link quality. It devalues sites whose social media quality factors don't support their link quality factors.

How Social Quality Factors Work

While the search engines usually do not reveal which social media activity "counts" for your content quality, we can make some educated guesses from what we observe:

- **Shares and favorites:** It stands to reason that search engines will value content that has more shares in social media—and content that has been "favorited" on Twitter or "liked" on Facebook. Due to a variety of reasons, the search engines tend to have a limited view of this activity, but over time you can expect them to make every effort to give full value for this kind of social activity across as many social venues as possible.

- **Author rank:** As noted earlier, those shares and likes have value. You should connect your Google+ account to other social networks. Doing so gives Google insights into who you're connected with, which will determine how influential you are.

- **Video views:** If you search within YouTube, you'll find videos whose titles and descriptions match your search keywords, but they are ranked based on social activity. *Which* social activity, you ask? Views. The videos with the most views tend to be ranked first.

- **Ratings and reviews:** A good review in Yelp for your restaurant might help your site rank higher in search (and a bad review might downgrade its quality). Social reviews can have a big impact on some kinds of search results, especially with the perception of your search result, which affects the clickthrough rate.

- **Bookmarks:** No, not the ones in your browser—we're talking about social bookmarking, such as Delicious (formerly del.icio.us). You can think of these as links, but they are also shared and "favorited," so search engines probably pay attention.

The influence of the connected network is the biggest value of social media optimization. It starts with great content that is shared by your network with other networks of people. The better the content, the more it is shared. That social sharing activity sends a very strong signal to the search engines, who then reward your content with higher rankings—especially to those *following* you. There have been numerous examples of a site receiving hundreds of new links to a study, new product or some interesting fact as a result of a single tweet or Facebook posting relevant to the community.

We believe this rank improvement is a direct result of the increased links and citations due to improved visibility online from a relevant audience. The most powerful indirect impact of social media is its ability to generate new inbound links by improving brand awareness and overall online visibility.

Shares and Favorites   Different social media venues have different kinds of sharing and favoriting activity, but the idea is the same. It stands to reason that search engines will credit your content with a higher perception of quality if social media users share and "favorite" your content. And the more the merrier: If 20 people retweet that tweet containing the link to your site and if 20 more people "like" your similar share in Facebook, that boosts your content's perceived quality even more. But it doesn't always happen that way.

Different search engines have different visibility to this data. Bing, for example has exclusive access to Facebook. Google alone sees what is done in Google+. Because Twitter is public, all search engines can use tweet patterns to identify influencers—and see what content they share. Sometimes search engines can see more than you think. Google+, for instance, can be connected to other social accounts, so that extends visibility. In general, search engines want to give credit for sharing in social media, and they do it when they can. Watch this space; we're likely to see more aggressive use of this data in the future.

Video Views   The number of views of a video is the major factor denoting video quality. Not long ago, search engines (including YouTube, the second-most popular search engine behind Google itself), used search keywords to filter videos and views to rank them. In recent years, spammers have begun faking views, the same way that fraudsters click on paid search ads on their own properties. Search engines have begun implementing techniques to identify roboviews, where videos are clicked by automated programs merely to play ads and raise the perceived quality of the video.

Enhancing Your Content's Social Media "Curb Appeal"

In Chapter 2, "How Searchers Work," we introduced the idea that search results have "curb appeal,"—that certain something that realtors identify that makes a house enticing to a potential buyer. We related that concept to the appeal that a search result must have to entice the searcher to click on your content.

Well, you need curb appeal for your content in social media, too. Think about how much content flows by each day in Twitter and Facebook streams—and every other kind of social media network. What makes a social media user click on some items and ignore the rest? Curb appeal.

Social media content with catchy titles, compelling teasers, and cute pictures get a lot more attention than the same old boring stuff. But how do you enhance your content's social media appeal? It's easier than you think.

You can add HTML metatags to clue the social networks into the best way to display your content. Different social networks have different metatags, but by far the most important is Facebook's scheme, which they call the Open Graph protocol. Obviously, Facebook uses its own metatags, but several other social networks seem to use them, too, if they don't find their own. Facebook's tags allow you to specify a title, image, and other content to be used in the social media stream. Twitter has its own tags to produce its "summary card," which also provides a title, image, and other data, just like Facebook's Open Graph.

If you create your pages by hand, it's a pain to have to reenter your content multiple times in different tags, but many content management systems can generate these tags automatically—only asking a few questions for very specific differences between the formats. You will need to take care that your image sizes are correct for each platform to really increase your appeal.

Why do search marketers care about social media curb appeal?

The more people that click on your social media content, the more likely that your content attracts links. And the more likely that your content is shared more widely in social media—and the beat goes on. Your content's social media curb appeal is a key factor in improving links and improving social media quality factors.

While it is against the search engines' terms of service to "game" the system by faking views, it is perfectly ethical to raise your view in legitimate ways, such as embedding the YouTube version of your video on your website. Those views will count the same way that views on YouTube's site count.

You are always perfectly free to call attention to your video from other social media venues. A recent survey from Yahoo! found that eight out of ten videos are found from social mentions. Just remember that search engines have visibility into some venues and not others, so you won't get credit from all search engines for each activity. For example, videos uploaded directly to Facebook can't be counted by Google, but Bing might see them, due to Microsoft's deal with Facebook.

In the end, you shouldn't manipulate view counts just to try to influence your search quality. Remember that actually getting people to view your videos is the point, anyway.

HOW ITUNES RANKS PODCASTS BY QUALITY

You might not think of iTunes as a search engine, but it is, in fact, a specialty search engine—the most important one for marketers distributing podcasts. Search engines that locate podcasts, such as iTunes, must use social activity to determine which podcasts are of the highest quality.

Some of the factors that seem to matter include the following:

- **Listeners:** As with YouTube videos, you might imagine that podcasts that have more listeners will be ranked more highly in search than podcasts with few.

- **Subscribers:** If you have a series of podcast episodes, you will attract subscribers who are alerted each time a new episode is posted. Loyal listenership is likely valued more highly than casual listening for search ranking purposes.

- **Reviews:** Each podcast can be reviewed by listeners. Podcasts with higher ratings are likely ranked higher in search.

Some speculate that there are other factors that matter also, such as the podcast's age (older is supposedly better), length (5- to 10-minute podcasts seem to rank highly), and sound quality, but it's possible that these factors are not considered separately from the social activity. It could be that 5- to 10-minute podcasts with good sound quality yield more subscribers and comments—and that the top-rated ones need some longevity to get there— so it might actually be the social activity alone that is making the difference.

Regardless, your goal is the same for podcasts as for any other form of content—to produce high-quality content that causes your audience to take action.

Ratings and Reviews   One place where ratings and reviews obviously matter is with local search. If your search marketing goals include having your locations show up on the maps and lists in local search results, we've already talked about how you must keep the search engines' local directories up to date in Chapter 7. Know that, just as with other measures of quality, your perceived quality in local search depends more on how *others* see you than how *you* portray yourself.

The strength of your reviews is an important quality factor for local search results. Other social activity and link quality matter significantly to your placement, also, but reviews are uniquely important to local search results. Understand that ranking factors change often. You can keep up with which factors matter most in local search rankings at our companion website (SEMincBook.com/ranking-factors).

But reviews are not just an important factor in rankings for local search—good reviews are a critical element of clickthrough. Local results are frequently shown with reviews highlighted, sometimes showing average ratings as well, as shown in Exhibit 9-5. You can imagine that searchers are more likely to click on the businesses with the best reviews.

Midas Garfield Hts
www.midas.com
3 Google reviews
(A) 12700 Rockside Rd
Garfield Hts
(216) 587-0149

Rad Air Complete **Car** Care and **Tire** Centers
www.radair.com
4.1 ★★★★☆ 9 Google reviews
(B) 5266 Turney Rd
Garfield Heights
(216) 663-0663

NTB - National **Tire** & Battery
www.ntb.com
2.8 ★★★☆☆ 10 Google reviews
(C) 6100 Brecksville Rd
Independence
(800) 639-8473

Safelite AutoGlass® Valley View
www.safelite.com
4 Google reviews
(D) 6050 Towpath Dr
Valley View
(800) 800-2727

Turney Town Shell Auto Care
www.turneytownshellinc.com
Google+ page
(E) 5095 Turney Rd
Cleveland
(216) 475-9835

A&H Auto Salvage
www.ahautoparts.com
2 Google reviews
(F) 13100 Broadway Ave
Garfield Heights
(216) 587-4940

Haynes Firestone **Tires**
haynesfirestone.com
Google+ page
(G) 13404 Miles Ave
Cleveland
(216) 561-5600

Exhibit 9-5 Local reviews. Both Google and Bing show the reviews associated with local businesses, as shown in this example from Google.

The first way to get good reviews is something you've probably thought of: Run a business that people really like. Just as the best way to attract links is to create high-quality content, the best way to attract positive reviews is to provide great products and service. Don't just nod your head and say, "We do that." You need to really think carefully about whether your products and services really are better than your competitors' in a noteworthy way. If they aren't, that is the place to start, because none of the ideas we list below will work well if customers don't genuinely appreciate what you do.

Even if you have a great business, customers frequently need a push to go to the trouble to leave a review. Your most loyal customers might be perfectly willing to help you out, but might not know how to leave a review—or might not know how important they are to you.

So how do you encourage customers to review your business?

- **Add review links to your website:** This might seem to be the most obvious advice, but many local businesses haven't done it.

- **Post a sign in your store:** Highlight the main venue that you want reviews on, such as Yelp or Google Places for Business. And point out the sign and ask loyal customers face to face.

- **Email your customers:** Let them know you need reviews and provide links to the review sites that you need them on. Add links to your pages in Google Places, as well as Yelp or TripAdvisor if those sites apply to your business.

It's important that you encourage customers to provide reviews because, despite your best efforts, you'll also encounter the occasional bad review. Some review sites, such as Yelp and Google Places for Business, allow the business owner to respond to bad reviews, which is always a good idea. Respond matter-of-factly and calmly and always apologize to the customer and try to set things right. That kind of response shows others that you care.

Ratings are also critical for your standing in product search, but we'll hold off on discussing that until later in the chapter when we cover paid search quality factors.

Bookmarks   **Social bookmarking** sites such as Digg and Delicious have been around for a few years, but you can consider social media's newest darling, Pinterest, as a social bookmarking site, also. Some people believe that the term *social bookmarking* is outdated and are starting to call this activity **digital curation**. Regardless of the terminology, these sites allow people to identify content they believe is of high quality, so search engines pay attention to these factors for organic search ranking.

Most social bookmarking sites use words to characterize the content's subject; sometimes these words are called **tags**. Search engines love tags because they can be treated the same way as anchor text for links. They tell the search engine what subject the bookmarked content is about.

Tags can help search engines improve their results in several ways:

- **Improved recall:** Social bookmarking tags provide ways for search engines to identify matching content in new ways. If someone bookmarks a page with a tag, searchers who use that tag word as a search keyword have a new way of finding that correct result. Similarly, image, audio, and video sites all allow files to be tagged as they are uploaded to sharing sites. Tagging can help search engines recall pages that they'd have otherwise missed.

- **Improved ranking:** Tags can also be used to rank search results more accurately; you can think of each social bookmark as a "vote" for the value of that page on that subject. Philosophically, this approach is no different from ranking heavily linked pages higher. Even today, some bookmarking services implement their tags as crawlable links. In addition, search engines employ usage information in ranking, too; Ask.com looks at the number of subscribers as a barometer of blog quality. The number of downloads or plays of multimedia content could serve a similar purpose.

- **Improved quality:** Activity on social media sites can provide keen insights as to which content is "better" than other content the search engine sees as similar. Google already values sites linked by high-quality sites, so why shouldn't sites with many social bookmarks be accorded the same treatment? The old Ask Jeeves butler once served up answers to real questions delivered by human beings; is Yahoo! Answers so different?

Using social bookmarks, content ratings, or other criteria in filtering or ranking search results is new, but it works for the same reasons that valuing links has succeeded. All these techniques depend on human behavior to ferret out the truly valuable content from the chaff.

Now that you've reviewed all the ways that social media can provide quality factors to search engines, it might be tempting to artificially inflate your activity. That's what we discuss next.

How *Not* to Foster Social Media Activity

You probably aren't surprised by now that spammers have tried to manipulate social media activity to improve their site's organic search rankings. Any time search engines start looking at a quality factor, you can bet that some people will try to fool the search engines through fakery—and social media activity is no exception.

Think about it. If you have been using link spam techniques to float your organic search rankings for years, what can you do when search engines start looking at social media activity? Those same spammers scurried around creating fake personas for Twitter, Facebook, and other social networks. They friended each other and began having fake conversations with each other. And, no surprise here, they started sharing links to content, pressing "like" buttons on content, and watching YouTube videos. All brought to you by either automated programs acting like people or actual people getting paid pennies a pop in developing countries.

But search fakery in social media isn't even the only kind. Some social media agencies buy Twitter followers just to pump up statistics to their clients. Not only do the fake personas amp up the numbers of the community, but they can also retweet and reshare content to artificially boost those numbers, too. While no one knows for sure, it is likely that 5% of the followers for your Twitter accounts are fake. Some accounts might have much higher percentages if your search agency or social agency has been trying to game the system.

Some technology has appeared that purports to identify fake Twitter followers, so you should expect that Google and Bing are attempting to do the same thing to ensure that their social quality factors are not polluted. If you decide to go the route of fooling the search engines with social spamming techniques, know that you are playing a dangerous game—one that we do not recommend.

Most unethical social media activity falls short of traditional spam, but you should still avoid it. You can ask your employees to haunt the message boards and pretend to be customers raving about how good your products are. You can pay people to provide good reviews. You can pay social network members to back your products while pretending to be just plain folks. Some of these techniques might even work—for a while. But beware the backlash when you're discovered.

Could you get away with less than this? Won't some of your customers let you slide if you pay a blogger without telling them? Or fail to disclose affiliate links? Yes. *Some* of your customers will just chalk it up to human nature, but others will have long memories. You alone can decide between a fleeting advantage and the permanent damage to your reputation.

But ask yourself some questions. Are you doing anything that you wouldn't want your customer to find out about? Or wouldn't want posted in a blog entry? A "yes" answer to these questions might be a red flag waiting to become a black mark. Obviously, every company has trade secrets, such as customer lists, financial records, and the recipe for your secret sauce, but if you have secrets that would embarrass you if revealed, you should treat these questions as a wake-up call to reassess your practices.

The web is the greatest investigative journalism force in history, and you don't want to be its next target. And the rise of social media ensures that any discovered transgression will be widely circulated. So, if you're almost certain to get caught and publicly vilified, why take the risk? That kind of attention will get you links to your site, but maybe not the kinds of links that you want. Don't become the #1 result for the keyword *unethical company*.

Now, there is a fine line between encouragement and payment—and where the line is drawn is a moving target. Just about everyone would say it is okay for you to encourage customers to post reviews, but providing discount coupons for positive reviews seems like paying people. Understand that the reviews that will have the most impact are the ones that are voluntary. You might think that Google will never be able to tell the difference, but that is what people said about paid links a few years ago. Already, technology has been publicly disclosed to discern between faked reviews and real ones, so don't count on paid reviews being undetectable.

The bottom line is that encouraging your customers to voluntarily provide feedback in ratings and reviews is a good thing. Manipulating them to provide positive reviews probably won't end well for your search marketing.

Human Ratings as Quality Factors

Okay. So the search engines look at link activity as a signal of content quality. And, because spammers fake link activity, they now look at social media to detect spammy sites. And, because spammers now fake even social media activity, Google has famously modified its ranking algorithm with updates, code-named Penguin, that specifically target spamming techniques. But is there a quality factor that even the cleverest spammers can't fake?

Yes, there is. And Google and Bing both use it. Both search engines pay panels of human raters to privately alert the search engines as to which sites are higher or lower in quality. Short of identifying these secret raters and bribing them to rate their spam sites highly (the search marketing equivalent of rigging the jury), spammers don't have any way to fake this quality factor. And as we'll see later, even bribery won't beat this system.

Google has been public about its introduction of a human rating system, which it regularly updates with the newest website ratings. Microsoft has been much more circumspect about its human ratings system, but it has publicly admitted that it uses one, too. Training manuals used by the human raters from both Microsoft and Google have been periodically posted online, so it gives us some insight as to how each system works.

Understand that this rating system is *not* the same as the ratings and reviews we discussed earlier. Those are *public* ratings systems. Anyone can provide a review and everyone can read that review after it is posted. In contrast, Google and Bing use their own *private* systems where they hire people to provide the ratings—and those ratings are disclosed to Google or Bing alone.

How the Human Rating System Works

Both Google's and Microsoft's rating systems are surprisingly similar. They each recruit workers that work remotely (usually from their homes), and they supply the workers with a list of keywords that they should check the results for. Rather than focusing on what the search results page looks like, they ask the raters to click through and rate the actual search landing page for each keyword—and some of the other pages on the site. Bing conducts its ratings in the United States. Google has a larger program that operates in many countries and in dozens of languages.

In the training manuals that have come to light, both companies emphasize searcher intent—the thought process of the searcher for each individual keyword. Each rater must consider which types of content the searcher is actually seeking as part of the evaluation. Bing, in particular, separates searcher intent into the three classic types of searches we discussed in Chapter 2: transactional, navigational, and informational searches. Google requests raters to use even greater care in the assessment of quality for critical searcher keywords in the area of high-cost purchases, health, or financial decisions.

While keeping searcher intent in mind, the human raters are asked to answer a series of questions about each search result. The questions are different for Google raters than for Bing raters. They are not merely about whether the content is high quality, but focus on very specific issues that cut to the importance of quality content, such as, "Would you trust this site with your credit card?" or "Would you trust this medical advice for your child?"

The names of the categories differ across Bing and Google, but the upshot of the raters' answers result in each search result's landing page being categorized in one of several ways:

- **Pornography:** Both search engines provide a "safe search" filter, so identifying X-rated content that is showing up for the wrong keywords is critically important. This kind of page should be shown only for keywords for which the searcher intent is to see adult content.

- **Inaccessible:** If the page doesn't load (or loads so slowly that few searchers would wait for it), it is marked as such. You can imagine that these pages disappear from the top search results rapidly.

- **Irrelevant:** This kind of page should not appear anywhere in the search results for the keyword.

- **Somewhat relevant:** This kind of page might satisfy some searchers, but it might be considered off-topic for some.

- **Relevant:** This page is a reasonable result, given the searcher intent, because it is a quality page.

- **Highly relevant:** This kind of page ought to be appearing high in the search results because it is high-quality content that highly satisfies the searcher intent.

- **The answer:** This kind of page is required to be at the top of the search results to satisfy the searcher. For example, if someone searches for the keyword *marriott*, the official page home page for Marriott.com would be "the answer."

Keep in mind that these specific categories are not terribly important to a search marketer. They are different across Bing and Google, and the search engines might retool them at any moment. We present them here only because it helps you to understand how such a system might work. It really isn't rocket science to design a human rating system that can be implemented with relatively low-skilled workers.

How Human Ratings Are Scaled

Some of you might be wondering, "Well, we know that Google and Microsoft have more money than God, but can they really pay enough people to check every blessed landing page for every blessed keyword?" In a word, no.

Trillions of keywords are searched for each year, many of them using keywords that are used only a few times (so-called *long-tail* keywords). Google and Bing have only a few thousand human raters to spread across all those keywords. What's more, an ideal system would have multiple raters cross-checking each other for each keyword, so that the ratings would be less biased by individual subjectivity. Clearly, only a small subset of keywords is being rated.

So, if only a small number of keywords are being looked at by human raters, how can this quality factor be applied to all searches? Enter "machine learning," a software technique that is increasingly used in this era of Big Data. Machine learning techniques are a form of artificial intelligence that uses training data to make predictions about a larger set of data.

Let's explore how it works. The search engines started by having the human raters examine a small set of pages, perhaps 10,000. Then they randomly split the results for those two pages into two groups of 5,000. One group is the "gold standard," and the other group is the training data.

They then engage in "feature analysis," in which they unleash algorithms trying to detect patterns in the data. For example, they might find that more of the pornographic pages contain little text with heavy use of video and images. Or perhaps they will find that low-quality pages tend to contain many more advertisements than high-quality pages. Or they might detect that high-quality pages tend to contain unique runs of text found on no other pages, whereas low-quality pages tend to contain text passages that appear elsewhere on the web. These are mere examples. You can expect that many possibilities will be considered and most discarded, such as the text length of the page, the use of bulleted lists, the grade level of the text, and many more. After many experiments to determine which features are associated with specific quality categories, a testable algorithm is developed.

At that point, the algorithm is tested against the gold standard data to see whether the algorithm correctly predicts the right answer. Remember, we have the human ratings for the gold standard data, so we can tell how well the algorithm works. Looking at where the algorithm makes errors leads to improvements. After many such improvements, the algorithm starts to works well enough to identify the patterns associated with varying levels of quality. At that point, the algorithm can then be used on the rest of the data that no gold standard exists for. And that's how human ratings can scale: Human raters pass judgment on just a few pages, and the pattern-detection algorithm applies what it learns to every page. The algorithm will never do as good a job as the people do, but it does it much cheaper and faster than people do.

But what about the spammers? Couldn't they infiltrate the human rater network and bribe the raters to give their spam sites a "thumbs up"? Besides the practical problem of identifying a significant portion of the human raters, the spammers face a bigger issue. Only a few spammy sites will actually be rated—probably not their sites. So, the only way to game this factor is to make your spam site look like a high-quality site—in which case, maybe it *is* a high-quality site and Google is happy to give it a high rating.

So, if this factor can work so well, why not use human ratings alone? Why are links and social activity still needed? Because human ratings are far less granular than are link factors and social media factors. For example, a few ratings by people won't separate the best site from the second-best site, but it is a sure way to separate a great site from a lousy site. That makes human ratings a perfect check on your other quality factors, even if it isn't the greatest signal on its own.

The Practical Effect of Human Ratings

Now you understand how the search engines arrange for human beings to rate pages, and you also know how they can apply those ratings to the entire web—even to pages that have never been rated. But you might be curious about the *effects* of applying human ratings.

We've already described how spammers are not excited about human ratings, because their tricky pages won't get high ratings. But other kinds of pages are affected, too—basically any page that the raters believe is low quality is downgraded in the ratings. What kinds of pages are typically downgraded?

- "Scraped" pages assembled from snippets from other pages
- Pages loaded with ads
- Older content (when the searcher intent demands fresh content)
- Vertical search sites

It's unlikely that any of your pages have these problems, but that doesn't mean that they will get the top rating: Think about the keywords you are targeting and ask yourself, "Is your content really deserving of the first page of search results?" If an impartial rater would not choose it, you have work to do.

What kind of content gets a boost from human ratings? In general, the sites that saw the biggest boost after the introduction of human rating systems were sites that were heavy in fresh, authoritative content—sites such as CNN, ESPN, CNET, and other kind of professionally authored sites. That makes sense, but shouldn't cause you to despair. Your content doesn't need to compete with CNN for most of your keywords; it just has to be better than the competing sites. Take a hard look at the current search results and ask yourself how you can create content that searchers need more than that of your competition.

Paid Search Quality Factors

Before Google got into paid search, all paid search engines used a simple high-bidder auction to rank search results, but Google's innovation was to multiply the advertiser's bid by the ad's clickthrough rate, which resulted in higher-quality ads rising to the top of the paid search results.

Google's use of clickthrough rate was just the beginning of quality as a factor in paid search results. Over the years, more and more factors have been added, especially ones that focus on the quality of the landing page. Exhibit 9-6 shows why quality is so important. All of these ads miss the mark. If just one advertiser were to provide one good ad and landing page on fence removal, it would likely reach #1 rapidly, even if it had a lower bid. All of these multipurpose ads are shown for *fence installation* and *fence repair*, and that dilutes their quality for *fence removal*.

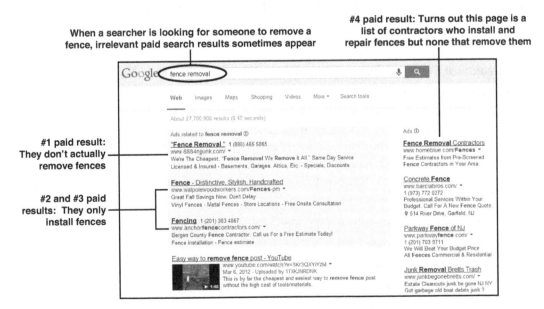

Exhibit 9-6   Multipurpose ads. When advertisers use the same ads for several different search keywords, their ads can be shown for keywords that don't match the ads very well.

In the United States, Microsoft handles about one-third of all search volume across Bing Search and its partner Yahoo! Search, but fewer advertisers tend to place their ads on Bing, with many settling for Google alone. Although it is true that Bing ads tend to have lower than for Google AdWords ads, they also tend to have higher clickthrough rates and lower average costs per click. So, it pays to understand how Bing approaches quality also.

Using Your Quality Score

Bing and Google each call their method of scoring quality, er, a **Quality Score**, and they both allow you to see your Quality Score within your account. Improving your Quality Score can reduce both your cost per click and cost per action, making your campaigns more cost-effective.

Both Bing and Google assign Quality Scores, but they employ them differently. Google uses its Quality Score to directly calculate your rank in the paid search results, whereas Bing reserves its Quality Score merely to provide feedback to you, the advertiser, as to how competitive your ad is. Although Bing does not use its Quality Score in deciding ad rankings, it is still the best way for you to understand how rankings are affected by quality, so you might as well listen to the feedback to improve your ad positions.

Google uses your Quality Score as a huge influence over your **ad position**, the rank of your ad on search result page. (Google refers to its paid search ranking algorithm as **AdRank**.) The higher your Google Quality Score, the easier it will be for your ad to show up on the first page of search results. Conversely, very low Quality Scores might cause your ad not to be shown at all—on any page of the results. Your Google AdWords Quality Score also influences your actual cost per click charges. The higher your Quality Score, the lower your charges tend to be.

Bing's Quality Score is similar to Google's in that they both examine similar criteria. Each engine looks at some form of the following factors and combines them into a single score from 1 to 10. The higher the Quality Score, the more relevant all of the following factors are—and the more efficient your campaigns will be:

- **Clickthrough rate:** Search engines' multiple clickthrough rates—the rate of your keyword and ad combination, the rate of all of your ads with that **display URL**, and even the rate of all the campaigns from your account. Sometimes, search engines also look at the clickthrough rate for your ad on the type of device the searcher is using.

- **Ad relevance:** If your ad contains the keyword and similar words, your ad will be considered relevant.

- **Landing page quality:** If your landing page contains the keyword and thematically related words (just as for organic search), the search engines will consider it to be relevant.

So, given how crucial quality score can be to your ad's position and to your actual costs, you might be developing a keen interest in how to improve these factors for your own campaigns so that you can boost your Quality Score. Luckily, we've already shown you how to do it.

In Chapter 6, "Choose Your Target Market Segments," you learned how to identify the intent of the searcher for your critically important keywords. By carefully testing your ads to satisfy the searcher's intent, you raise both the ad relevance and the clickthrough rate.

So, at this point, you've created an ad that attracts clicks. That makes the search engines money, but doesn't make you any—yet. Improving your landing page quality leads to conversions—and we've covered that subject in Chapter 8. If your landing page has a high bounce rate (the percentage of time that searchers abandon without going deeper into your site), you aren't selling anything—and Google will lower the Quality Score of your ad. It stands to reason that a bad landing experience is a bad searcher experience, the same way a low-quality ad is. Check back in Chapter 8 on optimizing landing pages. Often it is the case that tips from organic search landing pages help with paid search landing page quality.

In addition, new paid search ranking factors crop up all the time, with the Quality Score factors being among the most volatile. Check our companion website (SEMincBook.com/paid-ranking-factors) to stay up to date.

Understanding Product Search Quality

A special kind of paid search ad is the product ad or other product listing, so you need to understand how quality counts for them, too. Recent research indicates that as many as one-third of all Google searcher clicks for retail advertisers are on **Product Listing Ads** (PLAs).

PLAs are designed to show the pictures and prices of the products in response to Google searches, as shown in Exhibit 9-7. Accordingly, PLAs use product targets to determine which items appear for product-related search queries. These product targets are created using the product attributes set within your AdWords account and your Google Merchant Center. Unlike traditional keyword ads, bids are assigned to individual products or groups of products. Bing has a similar capability with a similar name, **Product Ads**.

Search engines don't disclose much about the secret sauce of their product search ranking algorithms. It is believed that, as with other paid search ads, the use of keywords and related words in your product description boosts your perceived quality.

In addition, high ratings in recent reviews can increase the quality of your product listing ad. In addition, some believe that the quality of your landing page matters. Not only must your destination page for your PLAs be a product page, but a page where the searcher can actually purchase the product. The name of the product and price must match what is submitted in the feed to reinforce to the searchers that they are on the right page.

Just as with organic search, paid search ranking factors change regularly, so keep up to date with the information at our companion website (SEMincBook.com/ranking-factors).

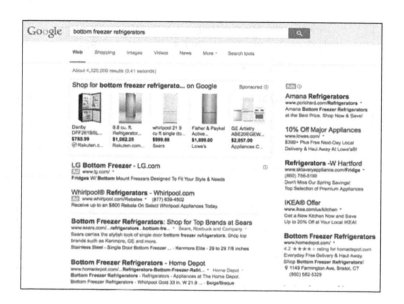

Exhibit 9-7   Product Listing Ads. Sometimes the PLAs get the most prominent positions on the entire search results page.

Improve Quality with Co-Optimization

Many search marketers, especially the larger ones, have separated their organic and paid search programs to such an extent that they don't even share the same landing pages. This separation can make things easier in the short run—the organic search team and the paid search team can operate independently and quickly—but it is often better in the long run to **co-optimize** the organic and search campaigns.

Examining your organic search performance can provide clues to improving your paid search performance—and vice versa. Often, as mentioned earlier, organic search tips can improve your paid search Quality Score. But your most important insights might come from contrasting paid and organic landing page data. When you find something working in one area, you can try to apply those lessons to the other.

For example, you should regularly check your landing pages to see which ones produce the highest conversions. Because paid search ads and landing pages are under our complete control, you can do extensive paid search testing in a short period of time to determine the messages that result in the highest conversation rates. You can apply these insights to our organic search snippet and landing page. Finding these opportunities is the secret. Exhibit 9-8 shows the low revenue associated with several top-ranking organic keywords, whereas paid search landing pages for those same keywords are producing high revenues.

PPC Rev.* ⬍	Organic Conv. ⬍	Organic Rev.* ⬍
$146,811.42	0	$0.00
$156,733.78	24	$1,658.36
$75,813.37	0	$0.00
$69,850.23	12	$829.18
$50,155.88	0	$0.00
$41,735.81	0	$0.00
$38,752.87	0	$0.00
$37,629.80	0	$0.00
$33,492.70	7	$807.81
$22,181.53	0	$0.00

Exhibit 9-8   Improve organic from paid. Review top-converting paid search keywords and landing pages for organic search improvements.

Just as you found opportunities to improve organic search by reviewing paid search performance, you should reverse the process to find paid search opportunities from your organic pages. In the old days, your analytics system could show the number of organic landing page views that were referred from search with your keywords so that you could easily see the conversion rate by keyword. Now that search engines are "not providing" keywords data to analytics systems, it is a bit harder to do, but you can still use the landing page visits and conversions as a proxy, even though you won't know exactly how many of those page views came from search.

In Exhibit 9-9, you can see conversion rates and revenue associated with multiple organic keywords that have exponentially higher revenue than those same keywords in paid search. Imagine if you could improve your paid search revenues to even one-third of your organic revenues in this situation. It is just these kinds of keywords that you can draw lessons from for your paid search campaign:

- Does your paid search ad or landing page fail to match the searcher's intent?
- Does your ad lead to an erroneous or outdated page?
- Does your organic search result's title and snippet attract more clicks than your ad's copy?

CTR ⬍	PPC Rev.* ⬍	Organic Conv. Rate ⬍	Organic Rev.* ▼
3.94%	$9,005.78	4.06%	$729,100.00
51.22%	$34.44	4.28%	$348,368.00
4.48%	$1,409.55	3.62%	$340,463.00
0.70%	$42.12	1.78%	$202,094.00
0.00%	$0.00	6.64%	$87,864.60
0.00%	$0.00	3.59%	$85,149.70
0.75%	$231.52	3.20%	$75,564.30
2.36%	$58.85	2.11%	$64,907.90
0.12%	$33.08	1.83%	$37,033.40
0.00%	$0.00	1.49%	$26,738.40

Exhibit 9-9 Improve paid from organic. Review top converting organic search keywords and landing pages for paid search improvements.

These are just a few of the things you might learn from a simple inspection of the search user experience for organic and paid results for your keywords. You might even find that you should throw away your paid search landing pages and point your ads to the organic landing pages. In this case, your Quality Score might go up, and your conversions probably will too.

Every large campaign (and most smaller ones) has many of these situations—with results juxtaposed between organic and paid. Ferret them out and use what you discover to raise your revenue.

Summary

Content quality becomes more important to search marketing each year. The most searched-for keywords have the most pages vying to be shown at the top of the results, so your content's quality is often the key component in its search ranking.

Organic search relies on several measures of content quality, including link popularity, social media activity, and human ratings. Each of these factors are calculated individually, but they are also used to cross-check each other so that no search spam gets through.

Content quality has always been a key part of organic search rankings, but now is increasingly important for paid search, too. Both Google and Bing help you understand your Quality Score so that you can improve your campaigns to get better results for a lower investment.

But don't stop there. Take the extra step of co-optimizing your paid and organic search campaigns so that lessons from one can be applied to the other.

In Chapter 10, we bring together everything you have learned so far and help you to turn your search marketing program into a continuous system of improvement.

CHAPTER 10

Make Search Marketing Operational

Some people are very good at starting something new—including starting a search marketing program—but tire quickly of the day-to-day work that turns a good start into a long-term success. Happily, for those who like ongoing maintenance work, search marketing is not a one-time event; it is a new way to work. Making your search marketing program a smooth, ongoing operation is the only way you will succeed.

Over the years, search marketing has become increasingly complex, requiring integration with many other parts of your organization. For larger companies, this might be the most important chapter in the book, helping you to scale your efforts and keep them running smoothly and efficiently.

So, if process diagrams make you glaze over, and you don't have the patience to go over the numbers one more time to figure out what's going wrong, make sure that you add people to your team that have the stick-to-itiveness you lack. We walk through that whole process for you here:

- **Understand the challenges:** Before we can describe what your team should do, you need to understand *why* it is so hard. Search marketing programs, especially the larger ones, face challenging problems that must be understood to be handled.

- **Set up your search center of excellence:** You need to know who to hire and how to train them, because the quality of your central search team can make or break your search marketing program.

- **Monitor your search metrics:** Anything of importance to an organization gets measured, and search marketing is no exception. Find out what statistics to track and how to use metrics to drive organizational change.

- **Monitor your search health:** Beyond checking metrics, a world-class search marketing program has regular checkup processes that serve as early warning systems for problems.

Let's start by understanding the big problems that can bedevil even a strong search marketing program.

Why Is Operating a Search Program So Hard?

Let's take a moment to understand why search marketing can be complex and requires a level of organization and adaptation that is unprecedented. Search marketing spans multiple areas of the business and transcends markets, brands, and products; and unlike most marketing efforts, the bigger you are, the harder it is. We know that in marketing, size has inherent advantages. The bigger the budget, the more advertising you can buy, the more free media coverage you can coax, the better a public relations person you can hire, and on and on. But search marketing is different.

Companies with well-known brand names assume it is easy for their website to rank highly in search results, but well-known brands actually have lots of competition for search rankings. This competition comes from both from their competitors and from their allies. (Many resellers rank highly for well-known brands.) Amazon may rank well when a searcher searches for *sony dvd player*—possibly even higher than Sony's website.

It is actually easier in some ways for small websites to succeed in search marketing than large ones. For instance, fewer people need to know what to do, and the whole website is managed one way by one team. As soon as your site is large enough that you hear some telltale conversations about separating your team or even your site into multiple parts, then search marketing has just gotten tougher:

- **We need multiple teams of specialists:** "The copywriters and the HTML coders really should be in different departments...."
- **We need multiple product sites:** "Each product line should really run its own separate website...."
- **We need multiple audiences:** "We should really have different user experiences for consumers than for our business customers...."
- **We need multiple countries:** "It is really easier for everyone if the Canadian and the U.S. sites are separate...."
- **We need multiple technologies:** "We decided to keep using the Apache server for the marketing information, but we are putting all of the commerce functions into WebSphere...."

Make no mistake—those preceding conversations are actually the sweet sound of success! Your website has grown too large to be run in the old simple way. Good for you that your site is growing and needs to be managed differently, but it makes search marketing much more difficult, for many reasons. Let's look at each of these situations and see what can go wrong for search marketing.

Multiple Specialist Teams

As soon as your web team grows to more than about a dozen employees, people will start thinking about splitting the group into multiple teams and eventually several departments. No matter how you split things up, you will start to see communication problems that did not exist before.

If you divide the group by specialties, maybe the webmasters, JavaScript programmers, and system administrators go into the web technology group; and HTML coders, copywriters, and graphics artists form a web creative group. That works well for most tasks, because, for example, each copywriter can work closely with the other copywriters to set standards and ensure that the writing is consistent across the site.

Unfortunately, search marketing gets more difficult precisely because it cannot be handled solely as a specialty. Your specialists must understand what they are personally required to do to make your search marketing a success. Your JavaScript programmers must place their code in files separate from the HTML files. Your copywriters must use the right words in their copy. Your webmasters must choose the right naming convention for your pages' URLs (uniform resource locators—the web page addresses that start with www).

The key point you need to understand is that search marketing is a team effort and that medium-to-large websites have multiple teams that must work together for your search marketing to succeed. Oh, and one more thing: None of these specialists will be focused on search marketing; that's your biggest challenge.

Multiple Product Sites

Your organization might be so highly decentralized that your customers do not even think of your separate products as coming from the same company. How many of you know that Procter & Gamble makes Crest toothpaste, as well as the Era, Gain, and Tide laundry detergents? And how many even care? P&G's customers do not need to know what company makes these products. They know the brand names, and that is enough. And if they need to learn more about the new whitening ingredient in Crest, they are much more likely to go to Crest.com than PG.com. So, Procter & Gamble created separate websites for each major brand, as shown in Exhibit 10-1.

And each website might get its own team. There might be a Crest webmaster, an Era webmaster, a Gain webmaster, and a Tide webmaster, with the other specialists divided by product, too. Multiple product sites foster excellent communication among the specialists assigned to each product, but can create a situation in which there may be almost no communication across products.

For most web tasks, this might not be problematic, but for search marketing, it can be. The Tide, Era, and Gain sites should each be found when searchers look for *laundry detergent*—but the respective teams might be fighting over those searchers rather than working together.

To lead search marketing across P&G, you must coax these disparate product groups to sometimes collaborate instead of always competing. Perhaps they should team up to create the ultimate *laundry detergent* page that showcases each of their products. This is harder to pull off than it sounds because collaboration might violate the competitive corporate culture. This could be especially useful for paid search; they might be able to combine keyword bids to go to this common landing page instead of trying to outbid each other for product landing pages.

Exhibit 10-1   Multiple product sites. Three Procter & Gamble laundry detergent home pages look like they are from completely separate companies.

Alternatively, the three detergent marketers might pool their search knowledge so they each rank in the top ten. Moreover, this technique squeezes some competitors off the front page (because P&G has three listings out of ten). P&G marketers might warm to this approach because it is similar to how they stock supermarket shelves with multiple products to control the shelf space.

None of these separate web teams need to collaborate for other web tasks; for search marketing, however, they do. That's your problem.

Multiple Audiences

Perhaps your company is highly customer-centric, conducting all sales and marketing based on audiences, or market segments. So, you have a website for large business customers, another for small-to-medium customers, and a third for consumers, even though they buy many of the same products. Of course, each of these sites can be run by separate teams that might not need to work together with the other sites' teams.

Separate, audience-focused websites can be an effective way to communicate with your customers, because you can tune your marketing message to each audience's unique needs. Large businesses might want more customized service, whereas smaller firms might be willing to take a one-size-fits-all solution to their problem. These differing needs can be addressed with somewhat different offerings that are described differently on your website.

IBM sells the same computer software and servers to several different audiences, but large customers might have negotiated special pricing based on volume and special configurations, whereas small customers are more interested in ease of installation and service. So, the same underlying technology might be sold à la carte to large businesses but as a packaged "solution" to small businesses. To follow through on this strategy, IBM offers large customers discounted pricing in one part of its site, and markets solutions to smaller businesses elsewhere, as shown in Exhibit 10-2.

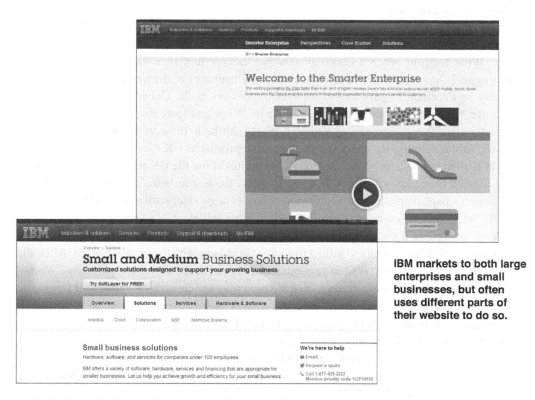

IBM markets to both large enterprises and small businesses, but often uses different parts of their website to do so.

Exhibit 10-2 Multiple audience sites. IBM uses different marketing messages for different audiences, with a different area of its website for each.

And dividing this website based on customer size usually works well—until you consider search marketing. (Are you starting to see a pattern here?) Unfortunately, when a prospective IBM customer searches for "web commerce" in Google, there is no way to know whether the searcher has a small website that needs a turnkey solution or is from a large company wanting to purchase and run its own commerce software on its server. Neither the large company group nor the small company solution group is focused on search marketing, and so—say it with me now—"you will have to do that."

Multiple Countries

Another common way to divide up a website is by country, and like all the other ways discussed so far, it makes a lot of sense. (That's why companies do it!) Your company probably does not sell the same exact products in every country, so it makes sense that each country might have its own website for customers in that country to visit. Each country might have different languages, currency, cultural norms, and laws. It is easy to understand why websites are so frequently divided this way.

But this clever organizational idea, once again, hurts search marketing efforts. Some searchers use country-specific search engines, but many use global search engines, such as Google. What happens when a Canadian searcher enters "four-slice toaster" into the global search engine? Google might be able to determine the language of the keyword as English, but there may be excellent English-language pages on toasters in the United Kingdom, Australia, Canada, the United States, and many other countries. Your company might also have excellent matches for all of those countries; each toaster page is similar to those in the other countries, but is specific to the country. (It shows the toaster that conforms to UK electrical standards and is priced in British pounds, for instance.) Google might just show the UK pages, even though it is not the one the Canadian searcher wants, and suppress the rest as being "similar pages." If the wrong country page displays, your visitor cannot buy your product easily; he might be asked to pay in British pounds when he has Canadian dollars in his wallet.

You can see that if your corporate website is divided by country, you might find web teams responsible for different countries battling to capture searchers with the same keyword. After all, they want their pages to "win" (and so your other country pages are the ones suppressed). Worse, you might have well-known brand names that are used in many countries regardless of language. How do you know which country those searchers want? Exhibit 10-3 shows how Sodexo handles this problem on its home page, but your company could face this problem for hundreds of brand names that cannot all be listed on your home page.

Once again, there may be no incentive within your company for different country teams to collaborate on search marketing; they are not required to work together on most other things. All together now: "It's your job."

The home page has a link to drive navigation to Sodexo country sites.

Hovering over the link provides a list of countries
that can take you where you want to go.

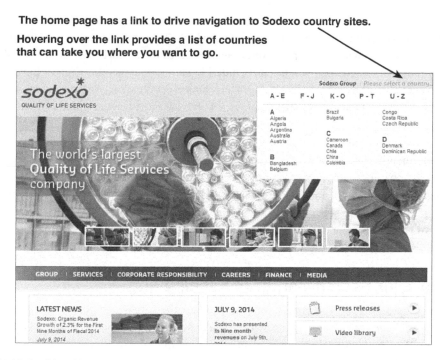

Exhibit 10-3   Handling country sites. Sodexo provides country selection on its home page to get searchers and other visitors to the right place.

Multiple Technologies

Until now, this discussion has focused on the problems of multiple web teams driven by the choices your company has made about how to organize. However, another problem grows as websites grow: multiple technologies that need to work together for organic search effectiveness. And a website can employ a dizzying array of technology:

- **Content management systems** help authors create and store the content for each page.
- **Web servers** display pages on the visitor's screen.
- **Application servers** run programs for the visitor to perform tasks on your site (such as viewing an appliance's service records).
- **Commerce servers** display your merchandise and enable visitors to purchase.
- **Portals** display content based on the visitors' interests (such as showing items for sale that are related to items already purchased).

Each of these components (and more) needs to be carefully configured to support your search marketing efforts. This configuration is complicated when your website has been pieced together across a large organization, however, because your site probably uses different components in each part of the site. So, your multiple product sites (or audience sites or country sites) might each have its own team using different technologies to run each site. In the initial rush to get every part of your company on the web, a divide-and-conquer strategy might have ruled the day, with each division doing its own thing. Unfortunately, you are paying for that now, because every combination of technology that displays a web page must be configured properly to make search marketing work.

The more technology combinations you have, the harder it is to get them all working for search. Frequently, you need to coordinate multiple changes to fix one problem because, for example, the content management system and the portal are both contributing causes. And (by now you are waiting for it), none of these technical specialists will think search marketing is part of their job. It is your job to get them to fix each problem.

If you find that your website suffers from the technology menagerie or any of the other problems listed here, don't despair. We show you how to solve each one.

Set Up Your Search Center of Excellence

If process diagrams make you glaze over, and you lack the patience to go over the numbers one more time to figure out what is going wrong, make sure you work with people who do. Those missing skills will be critical to add to your **search center of excellence** (CoE)—your central team that works across the entire organization.

Your CoE drives your success in search marketing. The central team will prevent the search crises you live with today by collaborating with the extended search team to maintain proper page tagging, avoid technology "downgrades," head off ill-fated navigational designs, as well as dozens more.

Here are the big steps to establishing your central team:

- **Staff the team:** You need to know who to hire, because the quality of your CoE can make or break your search marketing program.

- **Develop the skills:** No matter how much you pride yourself on hiring the right people, the industry changes so fast that you will constantly be training your team.

- **Establish search marketing best practices:** In Chapter 9, "Prove Your Content's Quality," we talked about all the folks on your extended search team who you need to influence. Here we show you how to change the organizational rules to get the behavior you want.

Are you ready to make it real? The startup tasks are almost behind you. It's time to see what makes a search marketing program succeed over the long haul: its operational excellence.

Staff the Team

How large should the search CoE be? As small as possible. Even if you convinced everyone that the search opportunity is huge, it is always better to start small and prove the concept. It is much easier to expand a success than to get cash infusions for something that started too big and did not show value right away. So, be conservative and grow slowly. Even a huge website can start with two or three dedicated people, and small sites can start with you doing it part time. In fact, JupiterResearch found that most search marketers handle five other jobs in addition to their search role.

Remember, too, that the main purpose of your central search team is to help your extended search team. Your extended team must do the heavy lifting, with the central team setting strategy, performing training, answering questions, tracking metrics, and coordinating the overall program. So, staff your central team with the few subject matter experts needed to assist the larger extended search team.

When staffing your team, you need to think carefully about the skills you are looking for. Because a generic list of search marketing skills can be quite long, consider only those skills actually needed in your situation. You must also recognize that you will never find all those skills in one person, so prioritize a few of the most important skills and find the best person you can. Here are some skills you might need on your central team:

- **Web content skills:** This array of skills ranges from copywriting to landing page optimization techniques to HTML coding. Because the central team will be working with the extended team on all of these tasks, the more familiarity the team has with those skills, the better.

- **Content management skills:** If your company uses a content management system, it is critical for the CoE to be knowledgeable in the setup and usage of that CMS. Many of the changes needed to optimize organic search will require knowledge of how your CMS uses web page templates and business rules.

- **Paid search:** If you are planning a paid search program, the central team needs expertise in each search engine's paid services, either because the central team runs the paid program or because they provide advice to the extended team.

- **Keyword research:** The central team can aid the extended team by teaching them the basics of keyword planning, so the extended team can help choose the right search keywords to target.

- **Search marketing tools:** Because the central team chooses the tools and trains the extended team in their use, it is very helpful for team members to know those tools well.

- **Global skills:** If your organization operates in multiple countries, having central team members who speak several languages and know the right local search engines to target in each country can prove invaluable.

- **Web analytics:** The central team must teach the extended team how to analyze metrics to prove return on investment. The central team often must define and track metrics for page rankings and other search-specific reports.

As important as these technical skills are, other skills are also needed for the CoE to lead the extended team:

- **Familiarity with your website's purpose, content, and technology:** Although easy to overlook, consider how much knowledge of your website is required to step in and be productive.

- **Knowledge of the company's products and customers:** Similarly, it is much easier to perform keyword research and to optimize pages when someone on the central search team knows the subject areas and audiences of the content.

- **Working relationships with the extended team:** As with any human endeavor, it takes time to build relationships, so bringing in someone who already has those personal connections will cut startup time.

- **Consulting experience:** All the technical expertise in the world is wasted if the central team does not communicate it to the extended team. A team member trained to listen to problems and solve them might have more impact than an uncommunicative expert. If you cannot hire experienced consultants, teachers are almost as good. Folks with teaching experience excel at explaining complex subject matter, but consultants might be better listeners when specific problems arise for your extended team.

Although it is tempting to hire only folks who have deep technical expertise, it might be useful to hire one central team member from the extended team who possesses these nontechnical skills, because that person might already have the requisite familiarity with the website and the company, and might also possess some important relationships.

Keep in mind that it is the rare central search team that grows large enough to hire people with all of these varied skills. Aim to create the mix of skills that are most valuable for your organization's team.

Develop the Team's Skills

Because you cannot hire enough people to have expertise in every area of search marketing, it is critical to develop the skills of the people you do hire. There is no shortage of ways to grow your team's skills:

- **Just do it:** There really is no substitute for trying to do something new. Even if you hire world-class experts, search marketing is changing all the time, so a good team will always have to experiment. Find people who learn by doing.

- **Read about it:** We highly recommend that you stay informed about the constant changes in search marketing, and you should buy a copy of this book for every member of your team and for your 100 closest friends. (Okay, the publisher made us put that in.) The rise of search marketing has spawned excellent free and low-cost sources of information, including numerous high-quality websites and email newsletters.

- **Take a class:** Although not every search marketing technique is covered in formal classes, your team can learn HTML and web technology skills this way. The web has transformed training classes from time-consuming in-person experiences to quick online training that is ready when you are.

- **Attend a conference:** Some of the best search marketing information comes your way at conferences such as Search Engine Strategies and PubCon. Send your central team and get them the quickest education possible.

- **Cross-train:** If you are able to staff a two- or three-person team, make sure they teach each other what they know. Not only does this help you over rough spots when team members move on to other positions, it also makes your team better rounded and better able to handle issues raised by the extended team.

- **Rotate extended team members:** A real win-win that can stretch your resources is a rotation program. Identify promising extended team members and offer them free training for a few months serving as a temporary member of the central team. Not only do you get someone else to help do the work, you also expand your relationships with the extended team and your team benefits from *their* expertise.

On our companion website (SEMincBook.com/resources), we show you a list of websites, conferences, and other resources that will keep your team busy for a long time. There is no shortage of information about search marketing, so you need to use your judgment about the best use of your time.

As with any team, constantly developing skills has many other benefits. Team members who learn new skills are more likely to remain in their jobs, and you benefit from employees who are better trained for those jobs. In addition, extended team members rotating back from central team assignments become your best allies among the troops. As important as it is to hire well, it is also important to develop the team you hire.

Establish Search Marketing Best Practices

After you staff and train your central search team, you need to put them to work assisting your extended search team. The central team must constantly evangelize, educate, and consult with the extended team, helping them implement each search technique. But that's not enough. The central team must work with the extended team to embed search best practices into the existing standards and processes of your organization.

Why is this important? Because search engine marketing is not a one-time thing. This is not the Year 2000 project, in which everyone gears up to do something once and then goes back to normal when it is over. Search marketing must be worked at every day. You must convince dozens, hundreds, perhaps thousands of people to undertake new tasks, sometimes changing the way they have done their job for years. Those kinds of behavior changes do not come about because you gave them a presentation once. They come about because every process in the organization is gently (and sometimes not so gently) nudging them to do what is needed.

The most important guideline is to go with the flow. Look at how work already flows in your organization and try to add tasks where they belong. Here are some examples:

- Every web page being changed goes through a quality assurance (QA) checkpoint before being promoted to production. Maybe you can get the QA team to enforce your new search standard at this checkpoint for each page?

- All technology projects have their designs reviewed by an architecture board before beginning development. Could you assign one of your team members to the board to ensure that designs are search friendly?

- A content standard already exists that requires a title tag be present on every web page. Can you get the standard updated so that all titles must be a certain length? And that they are unique, rather than the same title appearing on multiple pages? And that description tags must be present too?

- All new web projects are starting to use a content management system. Can you update the publishing workflow so that all pages undergo both HTML validation and keyword analysis (for prominence and inclusion) before they are promoted to production?

You get the idea. Take whatever processes already exist in your organization and tweak them to include what you need. It is much easier to change an existing process than to get agreement to start a new one—a new one can often arouse the corporate immune system (the one that rejects foreign ideas). Although your organization will undoubtedly have unique processes that you must think through, you should consider two key best practices: changing your standards and centralizing keyword management. Let's look at standards first.

Change the Standards and Enforce Them

Embedding search marketing best practices into existing standards and processes helps the extended team in several ways. First, it ensures that search marketing techniques get their attention, if only because their project is stopped to correct a problem. Second, it also helps extended team members justify the extra work to their managers. If there are no teeth in the standards, managers under the gun to cut budgets or meet impossible deadlines will cut the search work, even if the extended team members want to do it. By making search work part of what is required, it cannot be eliminated even when the pressure is on (which it always seems to be).

Now understand, merely enhancing existing standards and processes might not be enough—you might need to create new standards and develop new procedures to enforce compliance—but existing standards are the place to start. It is always easier to change an existing standard than to create a new one, and existing standards already have a compliance process in place. When you create a new law, you might be stuck hiring a new police force, too. It is difficult and expensive and should be a last resort.

We have covered all of these issues in other parts of the book, but here is a consolidated list of items that make sense for almost every organization to cover in their standards:

- **Content standards:** Ban frames, pop-up windows, "meta refresh" tags, JavaScript navigation, and the various other evils we preached against in Chapter 7, "Get Your Content Listed." Demand correct robots metatags as well as validation of all HTML. Consign style sheets and JavaScript coding to external files, and do not allow pages to exceed 100K. Relegate Flash and other non-HTML formats to content that you do not need included in search indexes. Don't require typed entry of information in order to display any page that you want indexed. Also remember the lessons of Chapter 8, "Optimize Your Content," by insisting on unique and well-written title and description tags and keyword-rich content.

- **Technical standards:** Require robots.txt files to be coded correctly and checked frequently. Insist on 301 redirects when pages are moved to new URLs. Minimize the number of parameters in dynamic URLs. Make sure that your pages display properly for spiders by making optional cookies, JavaScript, or any other technical requirement that spiders lack. Order all servers to be available 99.5% of the time or more, and demand that all web pages load within 10 seconds.

Don't forget to apply your standards to everyone doing work on your websites. If your company regularly uses contractors and agencies, consult your procurement department on the best way to add compliance language into vendor agreements to ensure all standards are followed and that deviations must be corrected at the vendor's expense when discovered.

Use existing standards where possible to capitalize on existing compliance processes, but invent your own if needed. One place where you will undoubtedly need to invent your own process is our next topic: keyword management.

Centralize Keyword Management

After you have some experience with search marketing, you will find that some keywords that are very important to you are also very important to others. You will probably find there are a few keywords that are *highly* competitive. Maybe you have someone constantly bidding you up in paid placement, for example. That's not an easy situation, but it's intolerable when that other person is inside your own company.

Yes, large companies often find the right hand bidding against the left hand. Maybe Buick is bidding against Cadillac within General Motors for the keyword *luxury sedan*. Or Tide is fighting with Cheer and Gain at Procter & Gamble over *laundry detergent*. At other times, your company is struggling over customer sets—would a large consulting company have multiple groups battling over *small business marketing*? Sometimes the contested keywords are more subtle. How many departments fight over *linux* or *windows*? Different groups have servers that run Linux or software the runs on Linux or services to help you migrate to Linux—you get the picture. But it is not a pretty picture. It is upsetting enough when your competitors drain your paid search budgets with "crazy" bidding, but how galling is it when it is your own company?

That is why you need to consider centralizing all keyword planning. You recall from our discussion in Chapter 6, "Choose Your Target Market Segments," that *centralize* is a relative term, depending on your organization. When you decided the scope for your central search team, you wrestled with this question—the decision you made then will work now, too. Within that scope, centralizing all keyword planning is usually a good idea.

When you centralize keyword planning, you immediately get rid of runaway paid placement bidding against yourself. You also give yourself a chance to optimize organic search. If you have separate domains within your company (buick.com and cadillac.com), you might be able to get two listings for *each* of them in the top ten organic listings. (That's 40% of the organic results on the first page.) Although you might find some benefits in centralization for organic search keywords, you will accrue the bulk of your benefits by eliminating intramural bidding wars in paid search.

So how do you go about centralizing keyword planning? If you do not yet have any battles over keywords in your company, establish the practice before any damage is done. If the battles have already started, however, how do you wrest control? You start with evangelism: Tell everyone about the problem and show them, when possible, in monetary terms. Calculate what it is costing the company in wasted paid placement fees. Use your metrics to show how much those wasted fees could have returned had they been invested well. Then offer to save that money by handling the coordination across the business units within your central search team. If the coordination work is extensive, you might need to take a cut of the savings to pay for additional resources for your team.

When you wrest control of the mission, you need to organize your approach to coordinate the job. Depending on how much coordination is required, one of these ways will make the most sense in your situation:

- **Manual:** This is the simplest method and the easiest way to start. Simply appoint someone on the central search team as the focal point for all business units to work with on all keyword planning. Some organizations require that this person get the passwords for all existing paid search accounts so that all paid search activity goes through one place.

- **Automated:** If you have a large paid search budget, the manual labor of coordinating all that activity might cost too much. In that case, create a central database for all paid search requests. Anyone who has the budget to run a paid search campaign can submit a list of keywords to your central keyword tool. It does not matter whether your tool is a web program, a database application, or any other shared resource—whatever is easiest for you to implement. What does matter is how the tool works. It should check the list of keywords submitted against all existing keywords to find any conflicts. If no one else in your company is using your keywords, you proceed with your campaign. If a conflict exists, the tool can resolve the conflict, as described later in this chapter.

- **Hybrid:** Perhaps you do not have enough money to fully automate the process. Then just automate the most painful part of the process. Maybe you can post the keyword list that is currently in use so that anyone proposing a new campaign can check the list before the campaign starts. You can often develop an automated process one piece at a time.

Now that you know how to identify a conflict, what exactly do you do when you find one? Your organization probably already has a style it uses for conflict resolution, so take advantage of the existing culture. If disputes between organizations are typically resolved by a high-level executive, you can bring the list of disputed keywords there each week for a decision. If your culture calls for the two parties to work out the dispute themselves, provide the contact information so that they can talk to each other. If your company likes to have impartial boards of experts, go that route. Sometimes you can get the warring parties to agree to objective criteria for resolution, as shown in Exhibit 10-4.

Brand A

Criteria	Answer	Score
Relevant Landing Page	Y	1
Relevant Ad Copy	Y	1
Tracking Metrics in Place	N	0
Current Offline Campaign	N	0
P&L Requirement	N	0
	Total	2

Brand B

Criteria	Answer	Score
Relevant Landing Page	Y	1
Relevant Ad Copy	Y	1
Tracking Metrics in Place	Y	1
Current Offline Campaign	Y	1
P&L Requirement	Y	1
	Total	5

Exhibit 10-4 Keyword ownership scorecard. Scorecards are a key part of your governance that causes the right focus across the organization.

Your goal is to develop a simple approach to settle which business unit gets primary control of the keyword's landing page:

* The group with the most profitable product gets it.
* The group that had it first gets it.
* The group with an active campaign gets it.
* The controlling group rotates week to week.

You can probably think of other ideas, too. But most organizations find that the best way to solve this problem is to develop a new landing page that features the offerings of both warring groups. If you think about it, the reason that each group wants the same keyword is that their customers would likely use it to find either group's product. If that is true, why not let the customer decide?

Think back to the Linux example. If five different groups within your company all have something to say to customers searching for "Linux," why not put the messages of all five on a single landing page? Each group can have to a link to its old search landing page from the new landing page. So if your company sells five kinds of software that all run on Linux, show them all on a single landing page.

This approach helps in several ways. Obviously, it ends the bidding war and provides a seemingly fair solution to the five parties involved. (Yes, they will each argue about which group gets more prominent placement on the new landing page, but you can develop several versions of the page that rotate, if necessary.) But it also makes your company's message far stronger than before. Many more searchers will find your ad copy and your page to be compelling, and some might actually be interested in *more* than one of your offerings, whereas in the past they would only have seen one.

No matter how you resolve the conflicts, make sure that your advertising agency or search marketing consultant (if you have one) is aware that your central search team arbitrates all conflicts. You can also work directly with the paid placement engines themselves so that they know what your policy is. If you are a large enough customer account, the engines will be happy to let you know when they see internal bidding wars and will counsel the combatants to contact you for resolution. If necessary, you can go so far as to require that any new campaign must have your approval before the engines can place any ads.

Intel provides an excellent case study for how well central keyword planning can work. In the early days of paid search marketing at Intel, 19% of all keywords were being bid by more than one Intel search marketer, sometimes by as many as nine at once! You can imagine that this was costing Intel a lot of money as well as making it harder for searchers to find the breadth of Intel's offerings. Intel's Martin Laetsch spent the next year centralizing all keyword planning, resulting in a doubling of clickthrough rates and a 50% reduction in per-click fees. Your company might be able to produce a similar success story with centralized keyword planning.

Monitor Your Search Metrics

Anything of importance to an organization gets measured, and search marketing is no exception. If you regularly track your key measurements, they will prompt you to do everything else required to succeed at search marketing. Your measurements help you identify problems when they occur, causing you to take corrective action. But metrics have other value, too.

Strategic use of disappointing metrics can motivate your extended search team to do what you want them to, and can motivate your executives to approve more campaigns to correct the problems. Sharing successful metrics can prove the value of search marketing to accomplish the same purposes. So, whether the measurements are good news or bad news, you can use them to make your overall point: that we need to improve our search marketing.

Whether your new central search team tracks all your metrics for you or you can talk your existing web analytics team into doing them, the tasks to perform are the same:

- **Assess your site's content:** Every page within the scope of your search marketing program must be checked regularly for compliance with your content standards and for inclusion in search indexes. Organic search landing pages for each keyword in your campaigns must be checked even more closely.

- **Check your search rankings:** Periodically monitor the ranking of each keyword in your search marketing program to see whether it is improving or degrading.

- **Monitor your search referrals:** The number of visitors coming to your site from search engines must be routinely checked.

- **Calculate search conversions:** Ongoing reporting of successful web conversions from search referrals proves the value of search marketing and sometimes identifies conversion problems outside of search marketing.

- **Review your measurements with others:** None of these metrics are useful in and of themselves. Before we close this chapter, we explain how to use these statistics and how to drive the organizational behavior you want.

Search metrics help you to identify and diagnose problems as well as to prove success. We begin by putting your content under the microscope.

Assess Your Site's Content

For organic search, your site's content spells the difference between success and failure, as you learned in Chapter 8. Even though you have done the hard work of optimizing your web pages, you must check your content often to ensure it remains effective.

For paid search, you have a lot less to do. You are advised to check your paid search landing pages to make sure that their URLs have not changed. For both paid and organic search, your landing page copy affects conversion rates, but no easy way exists to check *that*.

Measuring the search friendliness of your content helps you identify problems and correct them—problems in content tagging, keyword prominence and density, links to or from your pages, and inclusion in the search indexes. You might decide that it is too much work, and that you would like to just react to problems as they occur. We advise against that approach; you will never maximize your conversions by just fixing what is wrong. Regular content monitoring will avoid problems and will improve content that is already successful. If you are ready to take a proactive approach, let's tackle the metrics for content tagging.

Content Tagging Measurements

Content tagging metrics report a wide variety of problems in the coding of your HTML pages. Coding problems have various effects on your organic search marketing results, many of them serious. Let's look at the content standards that a content reporting tool can regularly police, along with the damage that can occur when problems are ignored:

- **Malformed HTML:** Your pages might contain errors in HTML coding that affect the spiders' ability to interpret the page properly—and miss some of your content.

- **Poor titles and descriptions:** Some of your pages might be missing `<title>` and `<meta name="description">` tags, or they might contain problematic content. Each page should have a unique title and a unique description—one that does not appear on any other page—so that search engines find the right page for each search keyword.

- **Incorrect redirects:** Your pages might use "meta refresh" redirects—none of them are followed by search spiders. Your URLs might also be redirected through multiple "hops" to get to the final page destination, which spiders will not always follow. These errors reduce the number of pages that spiders can index.

- **Bloated pages:** Your pages might be excessively lengthy (possibly because they contain JavaScript or style sheets embedded on the page). Spiders have time budgets that cause them to leave your site and go to another when your pages are too large.

- **Incorrect analytics tags:** Many measurement errors can be traced to pages that are missing tags for your analytics system—or just have the wrong tags.

A **content reporter** or a more-specialized program can detect all of these problems and more. At least monthly, you should evaluate each page on your site that falls within your search marketing program's scope, checking each page for compliance with your content standards. Your content reporter should analyze each page automatically and generate two reports:

- An **content error log** that lists each page individually by URL, showing what problems were found

- A **content scorecard** that aggregates the statistics by business area

In Snap's case, each business area sells a separate product line, but in your case business areas could be divisions, countries, or something else—your business areas should correspond to your organization's structure. Snap kept its scorecard simple, as shown in Exhibit 10-5, with just five items to check. Later in this chapter, we explain what you do with these statistics.

Business Area	Have Titles	Have Unique Titles	Have Unique Descriptions	Avoid Illegal Redirects	Avoid Exceeding 100K
Digital cameras	81%	73%	26%	100%	97%
Home theater	100%	97%	74%	85%	100%
Televisions	56%	31%	11%	100%	100%

Exhibit 10-5 Snap Electronics content scorecard. For each content standard, Snap's scorecard shows the percentage of all pages that comply.

Depending on your budget, you can license one of the enterprise SEO tools, which range from a quick desktop checker to a large-scale web governance tool. At the high end, Active Standards (activestandards.com) offers a specialized spider that crawls even the largest sites and can identify many areas for improvement in search and in other areas of web governance. It even allows you to customize its checking rules to produce scorecards customized for your situation. For those on a budget, Screaming Frog (www.screamingfrog.co.uk) crawls your site and reports on your content for a small yearly fee. If you have *no* budget at all, Xenu (home.snafu.de/tilman/xenulink.html) can do some basic site checking and (most important?) it's free.

Keyword Relevance Measurements

In Chapter 6, you decided which pages would serve as organic search landing pages for each keyword in your campaign. You need to regularly inspect those pages even more carefully than the rest of the pages in the scope of your search marketing program. You worked hard on those pages when you started each campaign. Don't let them fall into disrepair.

You recall that a critical part of optimizing each landing page is improving keyword prominence and density—making sure that the keywords that page is designed to attract are present in titles and other prominent places, and sprinkled throughout the page. Your keywords should be found early and often.

It is worthwhile to regularly spot-check your search landing pages, using an auditing program as we did in Chapter 8. If you have only a few campaigns totaling several dozen landing pages, you should scrutinize every page once a month. If you have hundreds or thousands of landing pages—too many to check each one monthly—you might need to sample some of them each month. Regardless, regular checks of your landing pages will provide early warning for problems; you will be alerted before you see marked drop-offs in rankings or search referrals. Obviously, if you *do* see a drop off in organic search rankings or referrals for a particular landing page, you need to look at that page immediately. And you *will* see fluctuations in rankings, possibly because your competitors have improved their pages or their offerings. You might see changes because the search engines change their ranking algorithms. Following an ongoing process of checking your organic search landing pages will allow you to maintain and improve your content.

Some auditing programs, such as WebCEO (webceo.com) and Microsoft's IIS SEO Tool (microsoft.com/web/seo) can automatically crawl a set of pages on your site and generate reports, taking some of the drudgery away, but you will still need to stare down each report to see how you are doing. There are a number of enterprise tools such as BrightEdge and Conductor that are now available to companies that can be deployed to handle optimization of large sites. On our companion site (SEMincBook.com/enterprise-tools), we describe these tools so that you can see how they are used.

Link Measurements

Links to and from your pages are critical to your search marketing efforts. The earlier you can detect problems with your links, the less impact they will have on your search marketing success.

Let's look briefly at links *within* your site. Each page on your site should be checked at least monthly for broken links. Most content management tools, such as Adobe CQ, have integrated monitoring to detect broken links, but you can also use a specialized tool, such as Screaming Frog and the aptly named Broken Link Checker from Internet Marketing Ninjas. Broken links break the chain of pages that lead to conversion, for both organic and paid search, and must be diagnosed and repaired.

For organic search marketing, you must also be concerned about broken links *to* your site. In Chapter 9, you learned about how important links to your pages are for proving the quality of your organic search content. Whenever you change URLs on your site, you run the risk of breaking those all-important inbound links. You must regularly review Bing and Google Webmaster Tools to detect any page errors they might have found. Both engines helpfully sort the results based on the relevance and the importance of each page in error. Monitoring these tools weekly, or at least monthly, will help ensure you are identifying the most valuable pages that are broken.

In Chapter 9, you also learned how to redirect your old URL names to your new ones. You learned that the search engines transfer the value of inbound links to your new name when you do that correctly. But no one knows for how long search engines do that. Just as the post office eventually stops forwarding snail mail to a new address, eventually search engines must tire of treating links to your old URL as if they were to your new one.

For all of these reasons, regularly check your inbound links. When your URLs change, ensure that the proper redirects are in place, but also contact the important sources of inbound links and let them know they should change the URL in their link. Because you want to focus on the most important links first, you can prioritize them based on relevance and trust, using some of the tools profiled in Chapter 9. As an alternative, you can prioritize based on the referrals you get from each one, which your web analytics facility can tell you. Whatever way you do it, you want each of those old links changed.

Even if you do not change your URLs, you still want to check inbound links to your organic search landing pages once per month—search experts often refer to these links as **back links**. If you are actively working on link-building campaigns, you should see progress every month. You also want to note any pages for which links are decreasing; they might be candidates for link-building campaigns. But you can track more than the sheer number of links to your site. You can analyze the links to your search landing pages compared to those to direct competitors for that same keyword.

You can decide to measure the efficiency of your link-building campaigns, too. For solicited links, how many requests actually result in links to your site? How can you improve the percentage? You might look at better targeting, improving your email copy, or improving your site to see whether you can attract more links in your link-building campaigns.

Links are important for conversions and for organic search rankings, so check your link measurements at least once each month to ward off problems.

As we learned in Chapter 9, this regular monitoring also allows you to detect any *negative SEO* activities from those who would attack your site's credibility with irrelevant links. Exhibit 10-6 shows a spreadsheet with a list of links exported from Google Webmaster Tools, with an additional column added to manually keep track of links the company believes are suspicious.

Links	First discovered	Bad
http://www.seospecialist.co.uk/google-search-trends-in-u-s-october-2013/	5/15/2014	B
http://76.12.162.199/blog.html?page=10	5/14/2014	B
http://saratonin.co/?paged=5	5/12/2014	B
http://illzwong.blogspot.com/2014_05_01_archive.html	5/12/2014	B
http://www.veetveet.com/page/2/	5/11/2014	B
http://www.pic2fly.com/Dulce+De+Leche+Evaporated+Milk.html	5/10/2014	B
http://www.oaimm.com/oaimm@gg/alexa/?domain=harveysbc.com	5/10/2014	B
http://www.askives.com/is-kahlua-a-coffee-liqueur.html	5/10/2014	B
http://reporting1blog.wordpress.com/page/169/	5/9/2014	B
http://search.m.biz/Kahlua.html	5/6/2014	B
http://popular.jp0.ru/l6135.html	5/5/2014	B
http://just-like.net/page/news/white%20russian%20drink%20mix%20kahlua	5/5/2014	B
http://similsites.com/website-info/kahlua.com?l=tr	5/4/2014	B
http://feedingbigsexy.tumblr.com/page/27	5/4/2014	B
http://www.2684.cn/zool/Alexa/Index.asp?domain=kahlua.com	5/3/2014	B
http://legacy.frdic.com/dict/Kahlua	5/2/2014	B

Exhibit 10-6   Bad link detection. Google Webmaster Tools enables you to export the list of links it has flagged so that you can plan your corrective actions.

Our friends at Snap Electronics were suspicious of some of the links to the website of their competitor, Black Hat. Snap decided to look more deeply into the Black Hat links by visiting some of the sites. A large number turned out to be blogs, but the blogs did not seem to talking about digital cameras. Blogs discussing completely unrelated subjects suddenly had a post linking to Black Hat's site, usually amid a list of many links to other unrelated sites. None of these links were terribly valuable, but apparently the sheer number of links (more than 9,000) was having a strong effect on Google. Some of these links were from sites that have been abandoned and have been hijacked and full of malware. Google will often show the image, as shown in Exhibit 10-7.

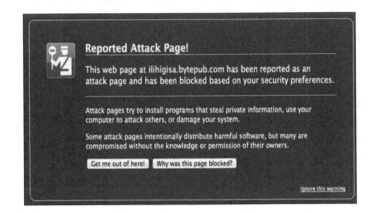

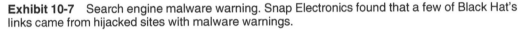

Exhibit 10-7   Search engine malware warning. Snap Electronics found that a few of Black Hat's links came from hijacked sites with malware warnings.

If you ever see such links to your own website, you should add those links to a Google disavow request according to the process outlined in Chapter 9. Google does not guarantee that these will be removed, but does review them.

Snap became convinced that Black Hat was using unethical spam techniques to fool Google and decided to report this activity to Google as a violation of its terms of service. Each search engine and directory provides a means to report violations, as shown in our companion website (SEMincBook.com/spam_contacts).

Search engines receive many spam reports each day and they take each one seriously, acting quickly to penalize or ban true violators. If, like Snap Electronics, you ever need to report someone for spam techniques, include the following items in your report:

- Your search keyword and the URLs that were found that you believe are inappropriate.

- The spam technique you believe is being used and your evidence for that belief.

- Why you believe this technique is detrimental to searchers finding the best results. (It is not enough for you to want your competitor penalized unless you can explain why it hurts searchers.)

As you have seen, examining your competitors' sites can be very instructive. You can see which sites link to them and what anchor text they use. You might even catch one of them playing a few tricks.

Ad Performance Measurements

Hey, you have a paid campaign up and running and your bid management tool is set up, so now you can just wait for the money to roll in, right? Well, not exactly. If you recall, your strategy is to iterate, so it's time to check out how you are doing and then make changes to improve. Bid management tools are very helpful, but they cannot substitute for your good judgment.

You must monitor new campaigns closely, because you are learning a lot. Over time, each campaign requires less monitoring, although nothing stays static forever.

You or your paid search agency needs to monitor your campaigns according to your objectives. If you are tracking profit, see whether it is meeting your projections. If all you can measure is your clickthrough rate, well, at least check that. And watch your bid rates for paid search. If competitive bids are rising and your position is falling, it's time for deeper analysis. Measure as granularly as you can. Track your paid search results by keyword within search engine within time of day, if possible. Examine your product search conversions by product within search engine. Notice which targets are performing and which are not, according to the metrics you have chosen.

When your paid search ads or your product search listings are not being clicked, take action:

- **Test new copy:** Your best way to attract clicks is with copy that demands searchers pay attention. If your paid search ad or your product search listing seems to solve their problem, they will be compelled to click.

- **Test higher bids:** It is possible that accepting a higher cost per action might result in higher paid search rankings. That increased exposure can sometimes dramatically raise click rates, providing stronger overall profits even though the profit per unit is lower.

- **Look for ways they do perform:** Do they get an acceptable click rate at a certain time of day? Day of the week? Time of year? On a particular search engine? With a particular match type? With free shipping? For a discounted price? For searchers from a certain location? If you can find conditions of good performance, you can limit your purchases to those conditions.

- **Try new keywords:** Can you add negative keywords to restrict when your paid search ads are shown? Can you add new words to your keyword to achieve the same effect? Your keyword might be too broad or just plain wrong for your target market. Expand your horizons to get lower per-click fees and possibly higher conversion rates.

What if you are getting clicks, but not enough conversions? Again, look at when those paid search keywords or product search ads do perform well. If you catch them performing under certain conditions, dayparting and other restrictions on your keywords might be appropriate. Limiting your product catalog or restricting it to certain product search engines might make sense. As above, you might also want to experiment with new keywords—especially more specific keywords that might better target your audience. If those measures do not work, try some other ideas:

- **Reduce your bids:** Perhaps your conversion rate would be acceptable if the bid costs were lower. You can try reducing your bids to find out if the loss of sales results in a better return on (a smaller) investment.

- **Check your landing pages:** Did the URL change? Or did the ad copy change and the landing page does not reflect the ad copy as well as it used to? Is your offer competitive with your competitors? You might be able to use your web analytics system to see whether visitors are abandoning your site on the landing page or abandoning deeper within your site.

- **Check the rest of your conversion path:** Are other related keywords slipping as well? Have any changes been made to the site in the conversion path? Again, your analytics facility might reveal where visitors stop their conversion process.

Oh, and one more thing. You should do everything listed above when your targets are performing, too. That is how you follow your strategy of being more efficient. It is far more likely that you will double your conversions by improving your already strong targets than by buttressing your weak ones. And getting more impact out of your winners is not any harder than fixing your losers. In fact, it is often easier. If you make your winners truly efficient, you will do well to spend more money on them and drop the targets that are borderline performers.

Snap Electronics had a lot to learn when they began purchasing paid search keywords. You recall that back in Chapter 4, "Unlock the Business Value of Search," Snap wanted to purchase the keyword *digital camera*, but they found themselves priced out of the market. Reluctantly, they decided to experiment with the keyword *digital camera reviews* instead.

Based on their allowable of $50, Snap needed to average a conversion rate of about 2% to justify a bid of around $1, but we saw that the top bid was only 35¢. Snap started by trying to top the current #1 bidder, knowing they would need to approach a 1% conversion rate if the price went up.

Well, the price did go up, because the previous high bidder topped 70¢, jockeying back and forth with Snap as the average per-click fees for Snap's campaign hovered in the low 70s. But within a few days, Snap saw that its clickthrough rate was way too low—less than 1%—so the conversions were minuscule, far less than the required 1.5% conversion rate expected. Snap was forced to temporarily abandon this keyword to diagnose the problem.

Clearly the first problem was the low click rate. Snap took a close look at its ad copy (shown as Ad A in Exhibit 10-8) and decided changes were needed. Snap quickly revised the ad copy to Ad B to try to boost its click rate. The results were dramatic, as clickthrough jumped to 5%, but the conversion rate was still below 1%, far less than the desired 1.5%. Clearly, unqualified searchers were now clicking and then abandoning, so Snap set out to change the copy again, to what is shown as Ad C, in an attempt to attract only those with a propensity to buy. It worked. Although click rate went down, conversion rate went up, but not quite to the magical 1.5% they needed.

What now? At this point, they examined their metrics, and found that many of their clicks were for keywords such as *cheap digital camera reviews, bargain digital camera reviews,* and *discount digital camera reviews*. They also found that some of the keywords contained the names of competitors (*nikon digital camera reviews*) that drew few clicks and next to no conversions. *Digital video cameras* was a keyword that brought many clicks from hurried searchers, but near-zero conversions. By ferreting out a list of additional words that correlated with a lower conversion rate, Snap was able to add negative keywords and increase their conversion rate to more than 1.7%. Not satisfied yet, they began to look at dayparting to see whether their conversion rates have any pattern to them. And the beat goes on.

Ad Unit	Ad Copy	Clickthrough Rate	Conversion Rate
A	Digital Camera Reviews Confused about what to buy? Find the best camera for you.	0.93%	0.21%
B	Digital Camera Reviews Don't know what to buy? Find your next camera and save 30%.	5.11%	0.87%
C	SnapShot Digital Camera Reviews Research Snapshot cameras and save 30% on yours.	3.41%	1.22%

Exhibit 10-8   Snap's shifting ad copy. Paid search campaigns require great tinkering at first, especially with the words in your paid search ad.

Check Your Search Rankings

After verifying your content is search friendly and that it is stored in the major search indexes, now you are ready to check your search rankings. Just because your pages ranked well when you did the initial campaign work does not mean that those high rankings will last forever. Regular measurement of search rankings is a key operational function.

Every campaign in your search marketing program has a list of targeted keywords—the list you learned to choose in Chapter 6. To measure the success of each campaign, you need to check the search rankings for each keyword in that campaign at least once a month. (Most search marketers check their highest-priority terms weekly.)

As with inclusion, you do not need to check your rankings in every search engine around—just the ones that drive the bulk of your traffic. Most search marketers check Bing and Google; some check others, too. (Global marketers might need to check many local search engines in the countries they do business in.)

You know by now that high search rankings are important, because the higher your ranking for a keyword, the more clickthroughs you are likely to get. A #1 result sometimes has a 70% clickthrough rate, whereas results that fall below #10 can draw clicks less than 1% of the time.

Is Click Fraud Eating Away at Your Paid Search Budget?

Click fraud is the elephant in the living room that the paid search industry does not like to talk about. Although it's diminished from the early days of paid search, click fraud remains very real, and you need to understand the issue and keep abreast of the latest news to protect your search marketing budget. Click fraud, in essence, drains your search marketing budget with clicks that are not intended to ever convert—clicks designed just to collect your per-click fee. Let's examine how click fraud occurs.

Whenever your paid search or product search listing is clicked, you must pay your click fee, but you get nothing for that fee unless the visitor buys something from you. So, someone who wants to drain your budget could repeatedly click your listing without buying anything. But who would take the trouble to do that?

Competitors and hucksters, that's who. Your competitors might want to exhaust your paid search budget while their listings remain (to scoop up the customers you are missing out on). Hucksters are even more motivated; they can pocket a cut of your fees by accepting the paid search ads on their site and then fabricating the clicks. No one believes that Google or any of the other paid search vendors are instigating fraudulent clicks on their ads, but many suspect that their syndicators are. Any site that accepts paid search (especially contextual ads) could just start randomly clicking those ads to ring the cash register.

Your competitors might be engaging in "drive-by" click fraud—rogue employees clicking away at your listings from an overstimulated sense of competition (and a lack of ethics). The real problem stems from professional hucksters using this deviant technique to siphon your cash for themselves. Some use automated programs that click listings in random ways while disguising their locations, whereas others go so far as to hire networks of workers, sometimes in third world countries, who click away all day.

The paid search engines have massive anti-fraud squads to crack down on problem clicks, automatically providing rebates (known as "make goods") for fraudulent clicks they uncover after the fact. But some fraud still goes completely undetected.

How can you protect yourself? Experts will tell you to monitor your reports for strange activity patterns, which you should; but if a significant portion of your clicks are fraudulent, that advice does not help much. Sure, you can spot a listing that suddenly gets a threefold increase in clicks in a day, but the folks perpetrating this fraud are craftier than that. Some tool vendors and web analytics vendors have attacked this problem, which you can read about on our companion site (SEMincBook.com/click-fraud). Also keep in mind that larger paid search vendors tend to have the strongest fraud detection programs, so the small engines probably carry higher risk.

Know that the higher your cost per click, the more likely you will be targeted by fraudsters. For instance, keywords with more than $5 fees are much more likely for hanky panky than lower ones.

As long as click fraud remains at its current level, it is merely an unpleasant cost of doing business, not unlike insurance fraud or shoplifting. It drives up everyone's prices, but if your paid search campaign is making money for your business, click fraud is no reason to shy away.

Measuring search rankings on a regular basis is important, to both show success and to identify problems when they occur. Publicizing high rankings within your organization helps convince people that search marketing can work, and motivates marketers whose campaigns have not yet succeeded. People like hearing about search rankings, possibly because everyone can understand what it means to go from #19 to #8, and maybe because it is thrilling to pass your competitors. As your search campaigns are executed, you should see steady improvements in the keywords targeted for those campaigns.

Conversely, regular monitoring can uncover a sudden drop in rankings, enabling your team to take quick action to correct what is wrong before losing any more search referrals. Although you would eventually spot a ranking problem in your other metrics (as referrals and conversions drop), you can see the rankings drop sooner. Detecting a problem faster allows you to fix the problem faster so that your campaign gets back on track before costing you any more precious conversions than necessary.

The problem with checking your search rankings, however, is that it is time-consuming for you (and time-consuming for the search engines themselves, which we discuss in a minute). Search marketing campaigns, once started, do not stop. As long as you still have a need to attract visitors, the campaign continues. By the time you have cranked up several campaigns, you have developed a long list of keywords for which to track rankings.

Consider our fictitious company, Snap Electronics, which built on early success to have four search marketing campaigns running after just a few months. Each campaign averaged 25 keywords, totaling 100 keywords in all. Because Snap targeted Google and Bing, it required 200 manual searches (two search engines multiplied by 100 keywords) to check their search rankings. And, for each of these keywords, someone had to manually check the results, sometimes paging forward to multiple search results screens, to find what the highest ranking was for a page from Snap's website. This took days to do each time.

Fortunately, a number of tools are available to automatically check organic search rankings. In addition to these tools, Bing and Google Webmaster Tools will give you the "average rank" for a number of keywords, as shown in Exhibit 10-9. Every tool supports English, but if you are a global marketer, you should check that the tool you choose supports all the languages of your campaigns. On the companion site (SEMincBook.com/rank-check-tools/), we look at the various tools for the desktop, online, and enterprise-level needs.

You should know that automatic rank checking is considered a violation of the terms and services of the search engines, because it consumes precious server resources for searches run by software programs—not by people who might click through on an ad to make the search engines some money. So, not only don't the search engines make money from rank checking, it also costs them money to host the extra servers to run all of those extra searches. Google has been the most outspoken about this issue and has actually banned websites and IP addresses that check many of their keyword rankings frequently—daily or even multiple times a day. Besides blocking your IP address, you might notice Google demanding you enter a captcha string before you can perform a search. Some companies that have created automated rank checking tools have had their access to Google APIs or other products revoked. The safest way to check your rankings is with Google and Bing Webmaster Tools, as noted earlier.

Query	Impressions	Clicks ▲	CTR	Avg. position
☆ back azimuth	336	5	1%	5.0
☆ azimuth consulting	140	3	2%	4.3
☆ keyword management	368	2	1%	6.2
☆ bill hunt	191	2	1%	11
☆ keyword management software	58	2	3%	2.8
☆ backazimuth	35	2	6%	2.1
☆ preferred landing page	24	2	8%	1.5
☆ back azimuth consulting	2	2	100%	1.0

(Table toolbar: Download this table · Download chart data · Basic · With change · Show 25 rows · 1-25 of 121)

Exhibit 10-9 Average rank positions. Google Average Position within Google Webmaster Tools shows the average of all rankings for a keyword during a period of time.

As time-consuming as it is to check organic search rankings, it's even trickier to analyze your paid search ad positions. Because clickthrough rate is part of the algorithm, every time you search for a keyword and display your own ad to check its rank, it is likely that you aren't clicking on that ad. That makes sense because you know that if you click on your ad, your account will be charged the click fee by the search engine. Unfortunately, failing to click has an impact, too. It lowers your clickthrough rate, thus lowering your ad position.

Moreover, when Google sees regular searches for the same keyword where certain ads are never clicked from the same range of IP addresses, it starts hiding that ad whenever that keyword is searched. So, if your (clueless) boss thinks he is being clever by checking up on your paid search campaign, he might be costing you money and getting erroneous results. Fortunately, both Google and Bing offer tools in your paid search account to tell you the average position of your ads, so use them.

One twist on search rank checking is competitor rankings. Sometimes you can motivate the extended search team to take the actions you need by showing where competitors rank, so it can be a useful metric to track regularly. There is no need to check competitor rankings on all of your keywords. (Most of your high-priority keywords do not apply to your competitors because they contain your brand name.) When Snap Electronics decided to look at competitor rankings, only *digital cameras* and *easy digital camera* were selected because those keywords were critical to Snap's branding goals. Snap decided that tracking competitor metrics for the other keywords was not worth the effort. If you decide to track competitor rankings, restrict the keywords you select to your critical branding or conversion battles.

Whether or not you track competitors' rankings, you should create a rankings scorecard for every keyword (or at least the high-priority ones). Your search rankings scorecard might average the rankings for each keyword across all of your targeted search engines. So Snap Electronics would average its rankings for *digital cameras* across all five targeted search engines, as shown in Exhibit 10-10. Whenever a Snap page was not found in the top 100 results for a particular keyword, it was assigned a rank of 100.

Keyword Phrase	Bing	Google	Average
digital camera	56	62	59
snap digital camera	1	2	2
snapshot digital camera	1	1	1
digital camera review	39	26	33
best digital camera	17	13	15
digital camera comparison	100	100	100
compare digital camera	84	71	78
Campaign average	52	39	46

Exhibit 10-10 Snap search keyword ranking scorecard. Some keywords return your pages at the same rank in different search engines, but others do not.

If you would like to be more scientific about it, you could use a weighted average that gives Bing and Google more emphasis based on their share of searches, but you might prefer to use a simple formula that is easier to calculate. You can check out the rankings for each keyword, for each campaign, even for your overall search marketing program, tracking your progress over time. Later in this chapter, we show you another use for this scorecard.

Search rankings are an important measurement because high rankings lead to more traffic to your site, in the form of search referrals. Next we measure those referrals directly.

Monitor Search Referrals

Search rankings are important, but high rankings are useless unless they lead to higher **search referrals**, a metric introduced in Chapter 4. As you recall, search referrals are the visitors who come to your site from a search engine. We count overall search referrals—the number of visitors who come from search to any page within your search marketing program's scope—but we also slice and dice referrals to learn more. We examine the significance of referrals from each search engine, and you will learn to zoom in on your individual search campaigns to check referrals by keyword. And (say it with us now), we do it regularly. Checking referrals as a campaign first unfolds is exciting, but you need to continue to check them long after your enthusiasm has waned.

The search engines and browsers, in the name of privacy, have recently thrown us a curveball by hiding most of the keyword search referral data. Google, Bing, and Yahoo! remove referral information by using secure search techniques. You can use Bing and Google Webmaster Tools to restore some of the removed data, but not all. This is an fast-changing area, so keep abreast of developments with our companion website (SEMincBook.com/referrals)

Overall Search Referrals

The first way we track search referrals is across the scope of your entire search marketing program, from both organic and paid search.

Almost any web analytics facility can report on search referrals, but you might need to customize your reports so that they fit your search marketing program. For example, Snap Electronics chose just its U.S. website as the scope for its search marketing program, so it wanted to look at just the search referrals to its U.S. site, ignoring those to the other country websites at SnapElectronics.com—those referrals will become important when Snap increases the scope of its program. Snap customized the referral reporting to examine its U.S. site only. Exhibit 10-11 shows Snap's results for the first 3 months of its search marketing program.

	Baseline	May	June	July	Total
U.S. search referrals	12,112	19,457	71,890	90,030	248,650
Divided by U.S. referrals	326,543	317,986	289,786	327,045	1,261,360
Search share of referrals	3.71%	6.12%	24.81%	27.53%	19.71%
Search referral increase		61%	494%	643%	

Exhibit 10-11   Snap's search marketing program search referrals. Snap tracks all search referrals across the scope of its search marketing program, its U.S. site.

As the table shows, search referrals increased markedly over the period, as the digital cameras campaign (and later others) made a dramatic difference. You will notice that search referrals did increase each month, but that a decrease in referrals for the entire site hid the extent of the improvement. That is why we also calculate the search share, the percentage of search referrals compared to the total referrals. This measure reveals that search marketing was still improving even during a downturn in overall traffic to the site.

If your site has seasonal ups and downs, you probably already have ways of interpreting your statistics to compensate. Some organizations use rolling averages, others use "year-over-year" comparisons, whereas your company might do something else entirely. Whatever method you use to smooth out seasonality should work just as well for search referrals as it does for everything else.

Search Referrals by Search Engine

Although most organic search marketing work is not directed at any particular search engine, sometimes your efforts work better in one engine than in another. Segmenting search referrals by search engine can show you how your success differs in each engine. Moreover, for paid placement, your efforts are highly targeted to specific paid search vendors working with specific engines, so analyzing each engine separately is required.

Examining referrals by search engine will help you track progress as your campaigns take shape, but it will also aid in identifying problem areas that might affect one search engine more than the others, or one search engine *before* the others. A sudden drop in traffic from a single search engine might be caused by a decrease in rankings or fewer pages included in the index.

As before, most web analytics facilities can separate referrals by search engine, but they might need some tweaking on your part to accurately categorize certain referrals as being from the correct search engine. For example, Google contextual search referrals are usually shown as coming from googlesyndication.com no matter what site they were actually from. Know that sometimes you will get clicks with no referrer at all; just remember that counting most of the traffic is better than nothing. Exhibit 10-12 shows how Snap Electronics measured search referrals by each of the five search engines targeted by its search marketing program.

	Baseline	May	June	July	Total
Organic Search Referrals					
Google	5,623	7,647	10,556	15,840	59,369
Bing	2,365	2,126	3,542	3,970	16,097
Yahoo!	1,972	6,853	6,986	11,786	44,529
Other organic traffic	836	689	1,508	1,041	4,181
U.S. organic search referrals	**10,796**	**17,315**	**22,592**	**32,637**	**124,176**
Paid referrals	—	—	18,668	33,967	52,635
Google AdWords					
Bing ads	—	2,617	28,587	20,227	51,431
U.S. paid search referrals	**—**	**2,617**	**47,509**	**55,492**	**105,683**
Total U.S. search referrals	12,112	19,457	71,890	90,030	238,996
Total site visits	326,543	317,986	289,786	327,045	1,261,360
Search share of referrals	3.31%	6.27%	24.10%	26.55%	18.09%
Search referral increase		**84.62%**	**546.97%**	**704.29%**	

Exhibit 10-12 Snap's referrals by search engine. Snap tracks all search referrals across the scope of its search marketing program, its U.S. site.

Beyond your need to track referrals to make decisions about your campaigns, you also need to track paid referrals to audit your per-click fees. But don't expect your referral reports to match the bills from paid search vendors, for several reasons:

- **Counting methods vary:** It is amazing how many different methods exist for counting referrals. The chances that your counts will match your vendor's counts are minuscule.

- **Time zones might differ:** If your web servers are in different time zones from the vendors' servers, you will see different counts each day because the hours will put some clicks into different days on your report compared to the vendors' ledger.

- **Vendors remove fraudulent clicks:** When a search engine suspects a click is fraudulent, it will be removed from your bill, but that click will still be counted by your analytics system as a referral.

- **Vendors eliminate repeat clicks:** Sometime visitors inadvertently click your ad multiple times, especially when network speeds or other factors slow performance, but vendors delete fees for those clicks from your report.

Given all of these discrepancies, you might wonder why you should bother auditing your bills at all, but it is important. You should expect your referral reports to show as much as 10% variance from vendor ledgers. However, you should look for trends. If counts have varied by 3% to 4% for months, but this week they are 7% off, you should investigate.

Search Referrals by Keyword

High search rankings typically create high search referrals, but occasionally a top search result does *not* garner heavy clickthrough by searchers. You will detect those situations by carefully tracking your search referrals by keyword for every search marketing campaign. Each month, you can calculate your referrals for each keyword, both for organic and paid search. Exhibit 10-13 shows a sample report from Snap Electronics for July.

As the months go by, you can examine the referral trends to see how your keyword referrals are trending. Snap Electronics used the simple form shown in Exhibit 10-14 to track its monthly search referrals.

Both Google and Bing decided, for the sake of privacy, to migrate to secure search, hiding keyword referral data from web analytics systems. Some analytics programs now show those search keywords as "not provided," accounting for around 85% of search traffic at this writing. For sites with large volumes of traffic, the data is still extremely valuable, even if you are getting data for only 15% of the visits. For smaller sites, unfortunately so much of your keyword data will be hidden that it is much harder to discover insights than in the past.

The only alternative is to capture keyword traffic data from Bing and Google Webmaster tools, as we did in Exhibit 10-9. Unfortunately, the webmaster sites show data for only a small subset of keywords. One workaround to this is to create multiple accounts for each of the subdomains of your site, but the search engines might at some point restrict this access, also.

Keyword Phrase	Baseline	Organic Search				Paid Search			
		Referrals	GG	YH	Bing	Impressions	Clicks	Click Rate	Added Visits
digital camera	1,412	7,356	15	22	28	2,886,532	48,336	1.67%	50,636
snapshot digital camera	4,044	6,027	1	2	2	11,821	421	3.56%	1,404
snap digital camera	5,278	7,290	1	1	2	12,936	362	2.80%	2,374
digital camera reviews	—	394	20	31	31	160,227	5,464	3.41%	5,858
compare digital cameras	—	88	22	45	68	22,888	92	0.40%	180
best digital cameras	—	590	4	22	22	40,136	96	0.24%	686
digital camera comparison	—	152	16	18	6	26,539	451	1.70%	603
Totals	10,734	21,796	11	20	23	3,161,079	55,222	1.75%	61,740

Exhibit 10-13 Snap's referrals by keyword for July. For its digital camera campaign, Snap tracked the detailed data for each keyword for both organic and paid search.

Keyword Phrase	Baseline	May	June	July	Total
digital camera	1,412	5,231	32,687	55,692	95,022
snapshot digital camera	4,044	5,799	4,931	6,448	21,222
snap digital camera	5,278	6,325	6,874	7,652	26,129
digital camera reviews	—	163	3,652	5,858	9,673
compare digital cameras	—	66	210	180	456
best digital cameras	—	219	690	686	1,595
digital camera comparison	—	145	466	603	1,214
Total	10,734	17,948	49,510	77,118	155,310

Exhibit 10-14 Snap's search referrals by keyword. For its digital camera campaign, Snap tracked the referrals for each keyword targeted in that campaign.

Because the search engines limit data to just the most popular keywords, it pays for you to import data each week and save it for future reference to get the widest coverage of keywords possible. To avoid this manual drudgery, Back Azimuth has expanded the functionality of their keyword modeling tools to import data each week from multiple subaccounts in Google Webmaster. More information and a discount code is available on the companion site (SEMincBook.com/keyword-modeler).

Tracking referrals is important, but you must keep your focus on the real prize: conversions.

Calculate Search Conversions

None of the measurements we have discussed will make more of a splash than counting conversions. We have emphasized all along that search marketing is only useful insofar as it furthers your website's basic goals—coaxing more searchers to visit and more visitors to **convert**. You have chosen what events on your website constitute conversions. Regardless of what they are, the value of search engine marketing is to produce more visitor conversions. Now you need to count them, and count them regularly. Strong early results count for a lot less if they are allowed to atrophy from inattention.

Why would your conversions change over time? Because everything that causes conversions changes over time:

- **The competitive mix:** The other players jockeying for position for each keyword change over time. Perhaps a new company introduces a hot product, and its product page is crawled by the organic search engine. Or maybe an existing competitor cuts back its paid search budget and disappears from view. (In paid placement, especially, competitors can appear and vanish quite rapidly.) Whenever a player enters or exits the organic or paid competition for a keyword, it affects the rankings of every other player. Each time your rankings change, it affects your clickthrough rate (and can thereby raise or lower your conversions).

- **Paid placement bids:** Your bids and your competitors' bids can change multiple times each day, which changes your rankings, which (ankle bone connected to the shin bone) changes your conversions.

- **Ad and page copy:** Page copy directly affects rankings in organic search, and both page copy and paid placement ad copy affect conversion rates. Whenever you or your competitors change your ad or page copy, everyone's conversions can be affected. For example, if your competitor provides a more compelling offer, your click rate (and therefore your conversions) might go down. If you improve the wording on your landing page copy, your conversions might go up.

You might be wondering exactly what an acceptable conversion rate would be. You might be tempted to research averages for your industry, but that is the right answer for you only if you are an *average* business in your industry—average in every way. You know that across your product line, you have wide swings in conversion rates that are all rolled up into one homogenous average across your business. Some products convert at 4% and others are under 1%, perhaps. Moreover, conversion rates for branded keywords tend to be far higher than for unbranded ones. So what does it tell you that your average conversion rate is 2%? Not much.

Similarly, getting an average conversion rate across your whole industry is even less helpful. The only way to assess your success is to compare your present against your past. You should see that you are improving over time—not across the board perhaps, but overall. You should see that the conversions for each product tend to go up over time.

Now that you are convinced that you need to track conversions, we have bad news. Your web analytics facilities might or might not enable you to accurately track the behavior of visitors who began their visits through a search referral. You should consult your local metrics expert to see how your system works, because there might be ways to get your existing measurement system to track conversions for you. Here are the kinds of devices that are most often used to track search conversions:

- **URL tracking parameters:** Web analytics systems can usually record parameters passed in your landing page URL identifying a visitor who is on a certain path through your site—a search referral path, in this case. The URL itself can be changed, such as adding refer=Yahoo&ad=67 to the end of your existing URL, to tell you which ad in Yahoo! generated the referral. The analytics system might be able to tell you how many visitors who complete your conversion event followed this path.

- **Programmed tracking parameters:** Some analytics systems can handle tracking parameters passed programmatically. One tracking method requires you to add JavaScript code to each page in your conversion path—each page passes the tracking codes along in a daisy chain—but if your visitor goes to an unmarked page, you lose the tracking for that sale. Alternatively, as discussed in Chapter 6, you can use a tiny picture (called a single-pixel image) to track your visitors. However, if the picture is displayed from your vendor's server, your security folks might not allow you to use it.

- **Affiliate codes:** If your company maintains an affiliate marketing program, it already has an elaborate system for tracking referrals so that the affiliates get paid the proper commission. You might be able to get affiliate codes assigned for each search engine (or even each keyword for each search engine) and let the affiliate tracking system do the rest.

- **Cookies:** You can use some JavaScript for a few strategically placed pages to measure your search conversions. Here's how it works. On each search landing page, call an external JavaScript that checks the referrer URL (the page the visitor was on before reaching the landing page). When that page is from a search engine, it means that your visitor clicked a search result to navigate to your landing page. Your script can drop a cookie containing the name of the search engine and the keyword used. You then call a similar script on your conversion page to read the cookie. Whatever system you use to log the conversion can also note that this visitor was referred from a search engine (and log the keyword used). Later, when you add up the conversions, you will be able to count search referral conversions separately from all other conversions, and you will know the keywords used each time. Note that some paid search engines will happily offer to drop the cookie for you, but that can cause security problems which most IT groups will not allow.

• **Microsites:** If all else fails, you can set up a completely separate site just for your search referrals. It's a lot of work, but if it is the only way to track your search conversions, it might be worth it for you. It is very easy to set up a microsite for paid search, but some do it for organic search as well, especially when their main site is full of spider traps. Exhibit 10-15 shows the microsite for Absolut's handcrafted vodka, called Elyx, which they use to count their search conversions.

Exhibit 10-15   A microsite. If you cannot fix the reporting capabilities of your current website, a drastic approach starts a new website just for your campaign.

If you can use one of these methods to calculate your web conversions of searchers, you can show how many referrals you are getting, the number of conversions (and the conversion rate), and the value in business terms of those conversions, just the way we did in Chapter 7. And you can track search conversions at any level of detail: a keyword, a group of keywords, an entire search marketing campaign, or even your overall search marketing program. (With paid placement, you can set up your categories or ad groups to simplify reporting.) So, if you can track that last month your site received 1,000 extra visitors from search for a particular campaign's keywords, and 2% (20) of them bought your $500 product, you generated $10,000 in extra revenue from that search marketing campaign. Exhibit 10-16 shows the revenue scorecard for Snap Electronics.

	Baseline	May	June	July	Total
Search referrals	12,112	19,457	71,890	90,030	238,996
Conversions	101	413	1,510	2,044	4,067
Conversion rate	0.83%	2.12%	2.10%	2.27%	1.70%
Incremental revenue	$50,500	$206,500	$755,000	$1,022,000	$2,033,500
Cost of SEM	$0	$20,000	$37,500	$37,500	$95,000
Cost per search referral	$0	$1.03	$0.52	$0.42	$0.40
Cost per action	$0	$48.43	$24.83	$18.35	$23.36

Exhibit 10-16　Calculating Snap's incremental revenue from search. Incremental revenue can be tracked by subtracting your baseline from your total to show the value of search marketing.

When you can pinpoint the value that precisely, you can learn a lot. Suppose you find that 1% of visitors who come to the site by other means convert, whereas searchers convert at a 2% rate? That might justify a shift in marketing resources to search. If you find the search conversion rate lower, perhaps you need to examine whether there are ways of raising conversions, or whether there might be other keywords that convert at a higher rate. Remember that it is crucial that you analyze your conversion metrics at this detailed level to make good decisions. Looking at averages across your whole program is fine for a snapshot of progress but does not help you decide which organic search landing page to tweak or which paid placement keyword should be dropped.

Some companies, especially large companies, have complex infrastructure issues that make tracking search conversions difficult or impossible. If you find yourself in this position, it's not the end of the world. You can still estimate your business impact using the same method used in Chapter 7 to forecast your campaign's impact. Merely take the number of incremental visitors being referred from search for your campaign's keywords and multiply by your site's conversion rate. Using the example above, if we assume those same 1,000 extra visitors converted at a rate of 1% (the site-wide rate), we would estimate that 10 of them purchased the $500 product for $5,000 in incremental revenue from your campaign. It is not exact, but it is far better to estimate the value than to be silent about it.

If you can accurately tie web conversions to the search referrals, you can track your conversions as granularly as your referrals. You can examine the revenue driven by each keyword in a campaign, as well as check conversion rates across your program for search referrals from individual search engines. This kind of analysis can help you gradually improve your campaigns, as you learn what works and what does not.

Review Your Measurements with Others

Well, we sure calculated a big pile of statistics in this chapter. Let's see what you can do with them.

As noted throughout, there are two main reasons to compile these statistics: to prove the value of search marketing and to identify problems that require action. When these metrics show your success, we suspect you will know what to do. Have a party, review the numbers with executives, and bring them up every time you want to do more. You will get the attention you need when things go well—congratulations.

But few people know what else they can do with these measurements: compel changes in behavior. That is what we talk about here. You can follow a simple step-by-step process to change organizational behavior:

- **Change the rules:** Earlier in this chapter, we went over the standards you need to change in your organization. Your first step in changing behavior is to set up the rules in your favor and develop a policing system to enforce compliance as much as possible.

- **Set benchmarks:** Develop a set of statistical thresholds for acceptability that are attainable within a defined period of time. For example, if you start out knowing that only 70% of your pages even have titles on them, set a benchmark that 85% contain titles within one year. (For a small website, that would be very easy, but for a large website, that goal might be just right.) State that all business areas with 85% of their pages with titles are "green," whereas those with over 75% are "yellow," but all others are "red." Do this for every important statistic.

- **Review business area scorecards:** Every month, you calculate your scorecards for each business area—a content scorecard, a rankings scorecard, a referrals scorecard, and a conversion scorecard. Use just the scorecards you need to compel the behavior you want. If your site is loaded with content problems, start there. If you cannot get product managers to focus on search, start with rankings or referrals, perhaps. Show your scorecards to the executives responsible for the state of the metrics on the scorecards. (Exhibit 10-17 gives a complete list of metrics and with whom they should be reviewed.) And post all scorecards throughout your organization. Avoid the temptation review scorecards only when they are bad; it will be much harder to get the appointment to do that. Instead, review the scorecards *regularly*, good or bad.

	Scope	Frequency	Audience	When Things Go Wrong
Content Metrics Content Tagging	All pages	Monthly	Writers	Gain commitments to bring pages into compliance with standards.
Keyword prominence and density	Search landing pages	Monthly	Writers	Persuade to add keywords to the right places on each landing page.
Broken links	All pages	Monthly	Writers	Gain commitment to fix broken links.
Back links	Search landing pages	Monthly	Product managers	Persuade to solicit strong links to pages.
Inclusion in search indexes	All pages	Weekly	Writers and technologists	Diagnose root causes and gain commitment for corrective action.
Ranking Metrics Keyword rankings	All keywords targeted in any campaign	Monthly	Product managers	Diagnose root causes and gain commitment for corrective action.
Competitor rankings	Selected keywords	Monthly	Product managers	Diagnose root causes and gain commitment for corrective action.
Search Referrals Total search referrals	Site	Weekly	Product managers	Isolate the areas of the site that have dropped.
Search referrals by search engine	Top search engines	Weekly	Product managers	Isolate problems with specific search engines.
Search referrals by keyword phrase	Selected keywords	Monthly	Product managers	Determine why individual keywords are not performing.
Web Conversions Search conversions	All keywords and all campaigns	Monthly	Product managers	Diagnose root causes (usually changes to the site) and gain commitment for corrective action.
Conversion rate	All keywords and all campaigns	Monthly	Product managers	Diagnose root causes (usually changes to the site) and gain commitment for corrective action.

Exhibit 10-17 Search marketing metrics. Tracking metrics on a regular basis proves your successes and pinpoints problems so they can be corrected.

- **Demand action plans to deliver improvement:** This will not be as hard as it sounds if you post your scorecards within your company. It is the rare executive who will sit still watching his area show up red month after month while other areas are green or at least yellow. If you arrive each month to display the latest scorecard with helpful suggestions as to how to turn it around, eventually most executives will tire of the embarrassment and order their folks to "go along with the program"—your search marketing program, that is.

For some of these metrics, you need to see where you stand to decide what a good benchmark should be. If your site is riddled with "meta refresh" redirects on 15% of your pages, for example, you might choose a goal for 90% refresh-free pages earning a yellow score, with 95% earning green. However, if 95% of your pages are already clean, you might want to shoot for 97% and 99%.

For search rankings, you might decide that any keyword that averages a ranking below #30 should be scored red, and that anything that drops out of the top ten is yellow, because that is simple and everyone understands it. If you want to be more precise, you could have higher benchmarks for keywords containing your brand name (such as *snap digital camera*) because it is so much easier to attain high rankings for them.

For organizations that focus on organic search, benchmarking content and rankings might be enough. You can use those metrics to drive the actions you want to improve content tagging, page inclusion, and any other behavior needed. If you have problems driving web conversions on your site, or you have significant paid placement activity, you will want to focus on referrals and conversions, too. You can develop your own benchmarks for those metrics and assess each business area against them.

One study showed the average website gets about 13% of all referrals from search engines. So, for every 100 visits to your site, 13% of them are searchers clicking a search result; the rest are following links, using bookmarks, and directly entering the URL. Remember, 13% is the *average*. Well-known websites might have many more visitors who remember the URL or have bookmarked the site from a previous visit. Don't fall into the Lake Wobegon trap of needing all sites to be "above average"; instead, take the baseline for your site and try to keep improving.

If you can track conversions, you have the best information of all. You can use conversion data to address pages that attract high search referrals but fail to convert. Perhaps those pages are at fault, or perhaps other pages between the search landing pages and the conversion page are the problem. Regardless, you know there is something wrong, and you can work on all of those pages and track improvement. Moreover, tracking conversions allows you to test which keywords convert at the highest rates. It is those keywords that should consume your organic optimization resources and command your highest paid placement bids. Management by conversions focuses your resources at the points of greatest returns.

This step-by-step approach using scorecards can prove quite successful when you stick to it, gaining attention for your search marketing program and forcing organizations to pay attention to the actions required. And year after year, it is the gift that keeps on giving, because every time your business areas reach the green benchmarks, you can raise them higher. Each year, your content gets a little cleaner and your rankings a little higher, because these metrics become part of everyone's job.

You can do even more with these metrics, however. In Chapter 4, we made a number of predictions to convince senior management and the bean counters that we would spend the money well. The metrics we have demonstrated should reveal whether your projections are coming true. Creating a simple matrix to share with key executives will keep them happy that they have invested wisely.

Monitor Your Search Health

So, far, we've given you advice on the difficulty of operating a search program, the need to effectively staff your team, and your need to monitor your results metrics to ensure your search program is delivering value to your business. But other kinds of diagnostics can stand regular monitoring, too, the same way you get your car serviced regularly. And once in a while, the "check engine" light comes on, and you need to know what to do then.

Where the car analogy breaks down is that search engines change a lot faster than cars do. So, what worked last year might not work today. Even if you think that everything is under control, it is only by going the extra mile with the ideas below that you can be sure. Large programs should make these checks weekly; smaller programs can get away with monthly.

Your Organic Page Inclusion

The majority of your performance problems will start from the lack of content being indexed by the engines. As you learned in Chapter 7, your pages can be missing from search indexes at any time and for any number of reasons. When you first began your search marketing program, you undoubtedly found a host of problems on your site, and you set to work correcting them. Regularly measuring your progress on getting your pages indexed is what we discuss here.

You probably recall the **inclusion ratio** metric that we introduced in Chapter 7, which shows the percentage of your website's pages that are included in search indexes. Check your inclusion ratio at least weekly to track your progress in eliminating spider traps and enabling spider paths. A regular check of the Webmaster Tools sites can also reveal problems that have cropped up before you have suffered long periods of harm to your search marketing program.

Springing the spider free from the traps that bedevil your website can sometimes take months. At times, you eliminate one spider trap just to find that there is another one in the same spot. By checking your inclusion ratio, you can track how correcting each trap (and opening each new path) allows the spider to include more and more pages in its index.

There is no need to exhaustively track inclusion in every search index. Many search marketers check just Bing and Google, but you can check as many as you believe is necessary to monitor your search marketing program. (If you do not recall how to check the number of pages included in search indexes, Chapter 7 can jog your memory.)

In Chapter 7, we discussed how tough it is for some search marketers to estimate the number of pages on their sites. If this is an issue for your site, you can still easily monitor your inclusion ratio. All you need to do is choose a single, easy-to-calculate number that you can derive each week—the total number of documents in your three content management systems, for example. Although this total probably does not accurately estimate the number of web pages on your site, it will correctly reveal trends and problems if you calculate it the same way each time.

Here's how it works. Each week, as you add up the documents across your three content management systems, the number of documents will fluctuate, as content is added or deleted. If a new product line is announced, for example, you might find 209 new documents across your three content management systems, although just 193 new pages were published to your site. If your site is crawled weekly, you should expect to see a couple hundred new pages reflected in the search indexes the following week. If they are not, it makes sense to inspect that new site for spider traps or missing spider paths. Note that it is not important whether the number of documents truly correlates to the number of pages on the site for this method to work. As long as you measure consistently, you will spot problems and trends from week to week.

Remember, too, that in Chapter 7 we explained how to set up XML sitemaps to increase inclusion. After you've done that, you can check each search engine's webmaster tools to tell you their index counts from those sitemap submissions. None of these inclusion checking mechanisms are 100% accurate, but they are all close enough that you'll see a problem if it occurs.

CASE STUDY: DETECTING AN INCLUSION CRISIS

Typically, IBM's website (ibm.com) has more than eight million pages in Google's search index—until the day the weekly indexing check revealed just 5,000 pages. No one needed to run any fancy inclusion ratio calculation to know something had gone horribly wrong.

Because no major architectural or navigational changes had been made to the site, it was unlikely that all of the spider paths had been removed. Such a precipitous drop in indexed pages points to a new spider trap, so a specialized spider was unleashed to see what was wrong.

It did not take long to determine the problem. When the spider crawled ibm.com's home page, it stopped dead in its tracks, returning an error. A review of the page revealed that a new JavaScript had been added to the home page requiring anyone who wanted to enter the site to have JavaScript enabled. If you did not have it enabled, you were blocked from entering the site; instead, you were shown an error message explaining that JavaScript was required.

Site-Wide Organic Search Problems

It's normal for your search results to fluctuate. Searchers keep changing what they are looking for. Competitors are always upgrading their search program. And the search engines change their algorithms every day and they change them for every keyword and for every searcher. In some ways, it's a wonder that there aren't more ups and downs than there are. So, when you suspect that your entire site has just been hit hard by a change, the first thing to do is to take a deep breath and ask yourself a few questions:

- Did search rankings decline for the whole site or just for specific keywords?
- Did traffic decline to the whole site or just to specific pages?
- Did conversions decline for the whole site or just for specific keywords?

When you see a problem truly affects your entire website, that's what we mean by a site-wide problem. Problems that might be serious but not affecting your complete site can be handled by returning to earlier sections of this book and checking the exact keywords or pages that are affected. Fortunately, both Google and Bing will often tell you when your account is being penalized, both in your Webmaster Tools account and with emailed alerts, whether that penalty is for just a page or two or for your entire site. In Google Webmaster Tools, you can check Manual Actions to see what's wrong. Exhibit 10-18 shows the happy result when your site is not subject to any Google penalties.

If, unfortunately, you do find yourself with a manual penalty, the instructions in Webmaster Tools will let you know what you should do. Usually, penalties are the results of spam issues on your site. One of the most common is when the search engines believe that the links to your site do not form a natural pattern. You might need to examine all of your links and get some of

The misguided web developer who put this in place was trying to help visitors to ibm.com, because some pages on the site did require JavaScript (mostly pages in the ordering process of the eCommerce site). But search spiders now could not index any page on the site past the home page, so only a few thousand pages were left in the index (only because they were linked directly from other sites).

Evidently, the script had been live for about a month, and after numerous failed crawls, Google dropped most of the ibm.com pages from its index. (Yahoo! followed suit a few days later before the script was corrected.) After this script was removed from the pages, the spiders were again able to freely crawl the site, resulting in the return of the pages to the indexes.

Had IBM failed to conduct weekly inclusion checks, search referrals might have dried up for a week or more before anyone noticed the problem.

them removed, or disavow them. See our companion site for more information on disavowing links (SEMincBook.com/disavow-links). You might also see a penalty for links occurring on every page of a website, as shown in Exhibit 10-19.

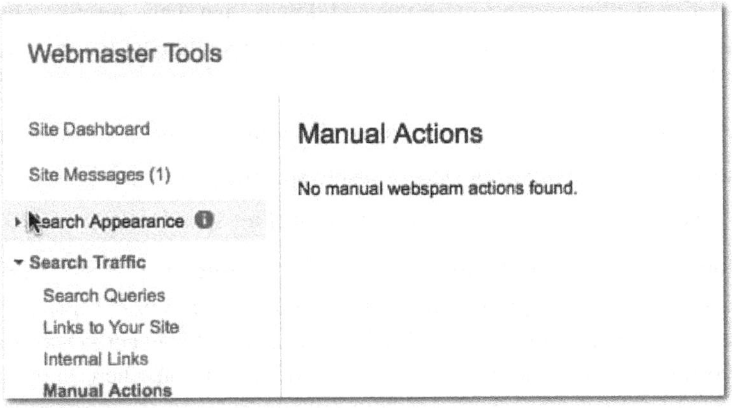

Webmaster Tools

Site Dashboard

Site Messages (1)

▸ Search Appearance ⓘ

▾ **Search Traffic**

  Search Queries

  Links to Your Site

  Internal Links

  Manual Actions

Manual Actions

No manual webspam actions found.

Exhibit 10-18   All is well. Google Webmaster Tools lets you know when no penalties are being applied to your site.

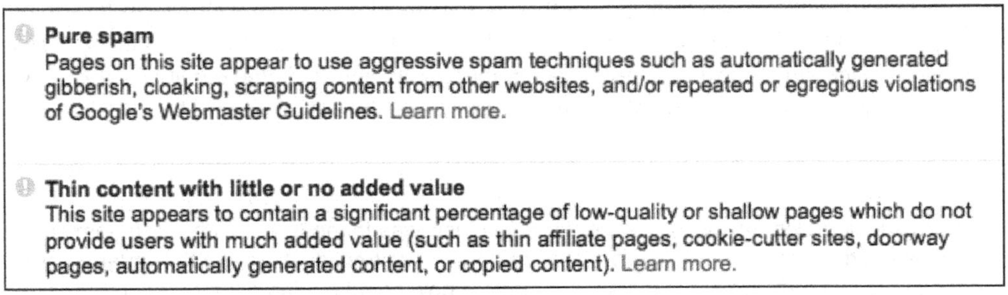

ⓘ **Pure spam**
Pages on this site appear to use aggressive spam techniques such as automatically generated gibberish, cloaking, scraping content from other websites, and/or repeated or egregious violations of Google's Webmaster Guidelines. Learn more.

ⓘ **Thin content with little or no added value**
This site appears to contain a significant percentage of low-quality or shallow pages which do not provide users with much added value (such as thin affiliate pages, cookie-cutter sites, doorway pages, automatically generated content, or copied content). Learn more.

Exhibit 10-19   Site-wide links problems. You will be informed when the search engines detect an abuse of footer links on your website.

After you've corrected your site-wide penalty, you need to let the search engines know that you've done so, through something called a **reconsideration request**. Some experts advise you to be as specific as possible about what was wrong and how you have taken corrective steps, including supporting documentation. They believe that the more details you provide (even to the point of naming offending agencies that steered you wrong), the faster your request will be positively acted upon. It's frustrating, but not uncommon, for you to have to submit several reconsideration requests before one is granted.

But what if you know you have a site-wide problem, but there are no penalties listed in your webmaster tools account? Now it is time to put on your detective hat, to see what site-wide changes you and your team have made to your site.

Often, a blanket change to a content management system (CMS) page template or a Cascading Style Sheets (CSS) file can have unintended consequences, so try to unearth the recent change history to understand what might be happening. As an example, a Fortune 50 company once updated their CMS page templates to remove the `<h1>` (top-level heading) tags and to standardize their `<title>` tags to begin with the name of the company, department, country, and product name rather than the author's keyword-filled title text. In just a few days, the company lost close to 40% of its organic search traffic (worth $50 million). Why? Because those changes to the title tags removed the very keywords that were driving the high search rankings that led to all that traffic. It took their agency a few weeks, but they finally traced the traffic drop back to that ill-considered template change. Two weeks after correcting the template, traffic was back to its former levels. It's obviously best for your search CoE to be in the loop for such template and CSS changes to prevent these problems, but monitoring search health allows them to diagnose what was wrong and correct it.

You'll sometimes see that your organic rankings are unchanged but that your clickthrough rates (and therefore traffic to your site) have dropped. Sometimes this stems from a change that affects your snippets, the text drawn from your page that is shown underneath the page title in search results. Obviously, individual page changes can affect the snippets for each page, but to have a site-wide problem, you need to look for a more pervasive cause. One possibility is a mass change applied to your content in the CMS that affects the copy on the page. But the more likely culprit is a change to the way your meta `<description>` tag is generated.

Paid search programs need monitoring, too. That's what we look at next.

Your Paid Search Program

Paid search programs tend to be aggressively managed, so it is not as likely that you'll miss big problems the way you can with organic search, but there are a few ideas to monitor your paid search health than might be overlooked.

One area that grows in importance each day is your Quality Scores. You learned in Chapter 9 how important your perceived quality is to your paid search rankings and your ultimate cost per click. Reviewing your Quality Scores on a regular basis is a critical way of ensuring your campaign is running efficiently and effectively. Because that can be a tedious job, some tools are beginning to emerge, such as TenScores (tenscores.com) that take some of the drudgery away.

Another area that requires frequent attention revolves around your negative keywords. By checking your search referrals on a regular basis, you can eyeball any new terms that begin to pop up to ensure that you are getting relevant traffic to your site. Often, a keyword that seems just fine can suddenly begin being used for another purpose and you can jump in and stop the bleeding. The most famous example of this is when celebrity Paris Hilton first hit the news. If you were in charge of Hilton Hotels in France, you might have wanted to block that one. Not only did the change in the usage of that keyword drain Hilton's account when people clicked it, it also raised their bid prices when people didn't click it. So, the only way to respond during the popularity surge was by using a negative keyword or removing it from the Hilton account, at least temporarily.

Summary

We have spent most of this book describing why search marketing is valuable to any website and helping you create a program to deliver that value. However, we don't want you to create a "where the rubber meets the sky" plan that looks good when projected on the conference room wall but has no basis in reality.

Your plan is worthless if it is not properly executed. In this chapter, you rounded out your search marketing education with the day-to-day best practices led by your central search team. You learned how to hire your central team, how to foster best practices in your organization, and how to track metrics on an ongoing basis to measure progress and identify trouble.

Above all, you discovered that search marketing is not a one-time event, but an iterative activity that must be improved every day. Armed with that knowledge, you are ready to bring search marketing success to your organization.

But no matter how much you have learned, you can always learn more. No matter how many tips we have crammed into this book, you should know that there is so much that we have left out. We have given you plenty to get started and maybe even explained concepts that some experts do not know, but search marketing is constructed from a whole range of details. There is always another way of designing your website that causes a crawling problem—and the work-around you need to know to fix it. Some smart person will always be figuring out a new bidding strategy for paid search—maybe one that is perfect for the situation you are in. Just about everything we have explained can be done some other way, and maybe that way would be better for you than the way we have shown. If you still believe that you know everything about search marketing, just wait a minute—something will change. Even search marketing experts need to constantly learn what's new in this ever-changing field.

If you are keeping up with the changes happening in search marketing, you will know about what is coming before it hits, and you will have time to think about what you will do differently. Do you want to be prepared, or caught flat-footed? There are new developments in search marketing every day. You need to keep up with what's going on to make sure that you will not be caught napping by your competitors.

As you put down this book, you might be wondering how you keep up with all of this. We've already thought of that. Our companion site, to which we have referred throughout, has a section full of more resources (SEMincBook.com/resources). As you gain experience, you also have to continue to gain knowledge.

Search marketing is a fast-changing industry; that's part of what makes it exciting, fun, and a good opportunity for your business. Stay attuned to the constant changes, and always use your judgment on how you should respond. In the end, your judgment will serve you better than any methodologies extracted from this book. We hope that, beyond any specific methods, we've taught you how to think about search marketing and that you'll think your way to the top. Good luck!

The Companion Website

Throughout the book, we've pointed you to our companion website at SEMincBook.com for more information than we could fit in the book. Not only have we provided extra information on the site, but we also keep that information up-to-date in the fast-changing world of search.

To make it easy for you, we've consolidated the list of each URL on that site that we have referred to in the book, in case you ever want a quick scan for a particular item. We'll be adding more pages after this book goes to print, but here goes:

Chapter	URL
1	SEMincBook.com/country-search-engines
1	SEMincBook.com/ppc-vendors
2	SEMincBook.com/keyword-conversion-calculator
3	SEMincBook.com/language-detection
3	SEMincBook.com/country-detection
3	SEMincBook.com/adult-content
4	SEMincBook.com/rank-check-tools
4	SEMincBook.com/referrals
4	SEMincBook.com/forecast
5	SEMincBook.com/vendors
5	SEMincBook.com/shopping-search-engines
5	SEMincBook.com/paid-search-agencies/
5	SEMincBook.com/bid-management-tools
5	SEMincBook.com/local-search-venues
6	SEMincBook.com/trademark
6	SEMincBook.com/keyword-research-tools
6	SEMincBook.com/competitive-keyword-tools

Chapter	URL
6	SEMincBook.com/buy-cycle-modifiers
6	SEMincBook.com/match-types
7	SEMincBook.com/user-agents
7	SEMincBook.com/robots-checkers
7	SEMincBook.com/search-friendly-URLs
7	SEMincBook.com/redirect-checkers
7	SEMincBook.com/performance-tools
7	SEMincBook.com/sitemap-generators
7	SEMincBook.com/social-media
8	SEMincBook.com/content-analyzers
8	SEMincBook.com/rich-snippets
8	SEMincBook.com/content-analyzers
8	SEMincBook.com/duplicate-content-checkers
9	SEMincBook.com/ranking-factors
9	SEMincBook.com/link-tools
9	SEMincBook.com/link-building-scorecard
9	SEMincBook.com/disavow-links
9	SEMincBook.com/social-listening-tools
9	SEMincBook.com/ranking-factors
9	SEMincBook.com/paid-ranking-factors
10	SEMincBook.com/ resources
10	SEMincBook.com/enterprise-tools
10	SEMincBook.com/spam_contacts
10	SEMincBook.com/click-fraud
10	SEMincBook.com/rank-check-tools/
10	SEMincBook.com/kwmt
10	SEMincBook.com/disavow-links

Give us feedback on the site if you spot any errors or there is anything you'd like to see covered that is missing.

Glossary

301 redirect Also known as a *permanent redirect*, an instruction to web browsers to display a different URL from the one the browser requested, used when a page has undergone a lasting change in its URL. A permanent redirect is a type of server-side redirect that is handled properly by search engine spiders.

302 redirect Also known as a *temporary redirect*, an instruction to web browsers to display a different URL from the one the browser requested, used when a page has undergone a short-term change in its URL. A temporary redirect is a type of server-side redirect that is handled properly by search engine spiders.

account The overall structure of a paid search program that itself contains *campaigns*.

action The searcher behavior that ultimately results in a web conversion, usually the purchase of your product. Typically used in "calls to action" to describe copy written to induce a conversion, and in "cost per action" to describe the fee for each successful conversion.

ad database The file used by a paid search engine that contains all the advertisements that can be shown in response to a searcher's keyword.

ad group   A part of a paid search *campaign* that contains advertisements associated with searcher's keywords.

ad position   A way that some people refer to your paid search ad's ranking. If your ad is listed at the top, it is in ad position #1.

advertising agency   A company that helps clients to plan and purchase promotional announcements. *Interactive* agencies handle email, banner ads, search, and other electronic promotions. *Traditional* ad agencies cover TV, radio, and print media, but might cover interactive media, too.

affiliate marketer   Someone who controls a website that directs its visitors to another website (the *program sponsor*, or *merchant*) in return for commissions paid for sales made to those visitors.

affiliate marketing   A technique of marketing and selling products in which a website (the affiliate marketer) directs web visitors to another site (the *program sponsor*, or *merchant*) and is compensated with a commission for visitor's purchases.

affiliate program   A marketing structure set up by a *merchant* to entice *affiliates* to promote the merchant's products in return for a commission for each product sold to a visitor sent to the merchant by the affiliate.

affiliate program sponsor   Also known as a *merchant*, the company that launches the *affiliate program*, recruits the *affiliates*, and pays the commissions for sales.

allowable   The highest cost per action that you will pay for a particular product. Your allowable is used with your conversion rate to calculate the maximum per-click fee that you should pay.

alt text   The descriptive text for an image coded in the HTML image tag. The alt attribute on the image tag helps visitors with visual impairments to determine what the images contain, by providing alternative (alt) text.

anchor text   The words that are shown on a page for a hypertext link, usually shown as underlined text in a different color from the surrounding text. Search engines use anchor text to infer the subject matter of the page being linked to.

antiphrase   A search term within a search keyword that is ignored by some search engines when it looks for matching pages. In the keyword *what is england's capital*, search engines might ignore antiphrase *what is* and search only for *england's capital* (which will find better results than also looking for *what* and *is* on the matching pages). Some search engines no longer ignore antiphrases, to take a more conversational approach so that they locate pages with the right answer of London.

application server   The system software that executes the programs that run a website. Application servers, also known as *web application servers*, are typically used to display dynamic pages.

atom   A form of *web feed*, similar to *RSS*, which delivers subscribed information from an information provider (such as a marketer) to a feed reader.

audience   A web term analogous to *market segment* in offline marketing that describes a particular group that a website's message is targeted to. Audiences are broader than market segments because they reach beyond customers. Typical website audiences include stock analysts, the media, and distribution channels, as well as each of their customer market segments.

authority   The perceived expertise level of a website, as measured by its network of inbound hypertext links. Search engines typically place great importance on sites that have many inbound links from other well-linked sites, and place those sites at the top of search results for queries on subjects that match the site's subjects.

authority page   A web page that has many links to it on a certain subject.

A/B testing   A technique to determine the better of two marketing tactics, such as two web pages, which pits the first page (A) against the second page (B) to see which one results on more clicks, conversions, or some other marketing result. Repeated testing reveals the better option, which can then be made the permanent version of that page.

back links   Also known as *inbound links*, the hypertext links from a page *to* your page. Inbound links to your page from outside your site are highly valued by search engines performing link analysis when they rank search results by relevance.

banner ad   A promotional message, typically presented as a large colorful rectangle in a prominent part of the page, analogous to an advertisement in a newspaper or a magazine. Clicking a banner ad takes the visitor to the website of the sponsor of the ad.

behavior model   An abstract embodiment of the activities of a group of people performing a task that is used to measure and analyze what they are doing. This analysis can suggest improvements to the process being followed for the task.

bid   The price paid to a paid search engine for each referral to secure a ranking in paid search results. In its simplest form, paid search results show a link to the highest bidder's page at the top of the list, and that bidder pays the bid price to the paid search engine each time a visitor clicks the bidder's link.

bid gap   A significant difference between two bids in adjacent positions in a high-bidder paid placement auction. For example, when the bidder currently ranked #3 has a maximum bid of 50¢, and the #4 bid is 40¢, the bid gap is 10¢.

bid jamming   An aggressive, high-bidder, paid-placement auction bidding technique that raises your competitor's costs, which might drain his budget a bit faster. A bid jammer bids 1¢ less than the maximum bid of the next-highest position, forcing the other bidder to his maximum bid.

For example, when the bidder currently ranked #3 has a maximum bid of 50¢, and the #4 bid is 40¢, the #3 bidder is paying just 41¢ per click. A bid jammer might bid 49¢ to ensure the #3 bidder pays his maximum cost (50¢) for each click.

bid limit   The highest amount that a paid placement bidder is willing to pay for a keyword term.

bid management   The technique used by websites to track and control the prices they pay to paid search engines to have their pages listed. Bid management is crucial for large paid search campaigns comprising multiple search keywords over several paid search engines, usually performed with software tools that automate bids based on constraints chosen by the website search marketers.

bid match type   The way that paid search advertisers decide how their keywords correspond to searchers' keywords. Paid search engines offer varying match types, providing control over how closely the keywords must match the queries before displaying the ad.

blended search   A method of displaying search results that shows multiple content types on a search results page, such as news stories, videos, images, blog entries, and other content that goes beyond traditional web pages. Google Universal Search is probably the best known blended search interface.

blog   Short for *web log*, an online personal journal, a kind of a periodic column on the web. Some blogs are reminiscent of a private diary, but others resemble magazine columns focused on a particular subject of interest.

blogosphere   The collective opinion of the totality of all blog posts and all comments in response.

body text   Normal text written in paragraphs and lists on a web page that have no special significance, as opposed to titles and headings, which connote more importance. Search engines look for keywords in body text, but accord them less relevance than emphasized occurrences, such as in titles.

bookmark   Also known as a *favorite*, the browser function that enables surfers to store the URLs of web pages so they can return at a later time.

Boolean operator   One of the AND, OR, and NOT operators used in search queries to indicate how multiple words should be interpreted by the search engine. For example, the keyword *digital* AND *camera* should find documents containing both terms (only), whereas *digital* OR *camera* should find any document that contains one or both terms.

bow-tie theory   A model of web linking patterns that categorizes each page as core pages (strongly linked from and to), destination pages (strongly linked from the core), origination pages (strongly linked to the core), and disconnected pages (not linked from or to the core).

brand awareness   The recognition by a potential customer of the name of a company, product, or service, and recognition of the qualities associated with it.

brand manager   The marketing specialist responsible for promoting a particular set of products within your company. Brand managers are responsible for targeting the right people to buy your products and then reaching them with the message that causes them to take action.

brick-and-mortar retailer   The web-savvy name for a traditional physical store, to contrast it from a web retailer.

broad match   A paid search *match type* that specifies that an ad should match the searcher's keyword for the most possible variations, including synonyms, misspellings, and other variations.

broad match modifier   A technique that allows a paid search marketer to indicate that a particular word within a broad match keyword phrase be matched more restrictively. Words designated with the broad match modifier (+) will not match synonyms or other related words the way unmodified words do.

browser   The program that a website visitor uses to view and navigate the website, such as Google Chrome.

budget cap   The maximum amount you are willing to spend in a paid search campaign within a defined period of time, ranging from 1 day to 1 month. When you "cap" your spending, you are protected from sudden shifts that could be disastrous to your budget, because your ad or product is no longer shown by the search engine once you reach your cap; no more per-click fees will be charged.

buyer behavior   The actions that potential customers take while considering a purchase.

Buyer's Journey   A behavior model that describes what visitors do when they come to your website and that helps you count your successes as web conversions.

call to action   The sales term for the message that causes the prospective customer to do something that closes a sale or gets them closer to a sale. Web pages that ask you to "add to cart" or "sign up for an email newsletter" contain calls to action.

campaign   1. A marketing term for a marketing effort of relatively short duration with specific goals for success. A search marketing campaign might last a few months, during which specific keywords might be targeted for paid search, with success measured by the number of sales made from visitors referred by the paid search engines. 2. A major part of a paid search *account* that itself can contain *ad groups*.

canonical tag   An HTML tag placed in the `<head>` section of your web page that tells the search spider the exact URL that the page should be stored under, no matter what actual URL caused the spider to retrieve the page. Dynamic pages might be generated under different URLs, but if the matching pages share the same canonical URL, they won't fool spiders into thinking they are separate pages when they are indeed the same page.

Cascading Style Sheets (CSS)   A set of formatting instructions for each tag in an HTML file that can be customized so that the same tagged file can be formatted in different ways with different style sheets.

case   The capitalization of letters in Western languages—UPPERcase as opposed to lowercase.

categorization   A technique in text analytics to discern document metadata that the author did not correctly provide, such as subject (life insurance), document type (prospectus), and other data.

Center of Excellence (CoE)   The group responsible for coordinating search marketing work across the entire organization, directing the extended search team to execute the search marketing plan.

CGI   Common Gateway Interface, the original technique by which a web server runs a program to dynamically create the page's HTML and to return it to the visitor's web browser.

character encoding   The key by which a computer determines which patterns stand for which characters in a computer file. Different national languages contain different characters and require different character encoding schemes.

citation   A technique used by scientific papers to refer to a previous paper on which the work is being based. Scientists use these citations as a way to keep score, believing the "best" papers have the most citations. Google's founders borrowed this concept in deciding that the pages with the most links to them might be the "best" pages.

click   The action that web users take with their mouse to navigate to a new page. Web metrics programs capture all visitor clicks for measurement and analysis.

click fraud   The unethical act of clicking a paid search listing with no intention of converting, but rather to simply cause the per-click fee to be charged.

clickthrough   The web metrics term for visitors clicking a link and navigating to a new page. In search marketing, clickthrough rates of paid search results is a very important metric, because it can show search marketers the effectiveness of ad copy in attracting traffic.

clickthrough rate   The web metrics term for the ratio of visitors seeing a link versus clicking that link and navigating to a new page. In search marketing, clickthrough rates of paid search results is a very important metric because it can show search marketers the effectiveness of ad copy in attracting traffic.

cloaking An aggressive form of *IP delivery*, a technique by which a spammer, for the same URL, designs a program to return one page for human visitors and a different version of the page for a search engine's spider—one full of keywords designed to attain a high search ranking. The term *cloaking* originated from the way site owners blocked visitors from viewing their HTML code to reveal their search optimization secrets.

co-optimization A strategy through which the search marketer uses a single landing page for a keyword for both organic and paid search.

commerce server The system software that displays products for sale, and securely takes orders from customers. Commerce servers often display dynamic pages, a fact that presents challenges for search marketing success.

Common Gateway Interface (CGI) The original technique by which a web server runs a program to dynamically create the page's HTML and to return it to the visitor's web browser.

conglomerate A highly decentralized form of corporate organization typically consisting of quasi-independent companies loosely organized into a single corporation.

consideration set The sales term for the list of suppliers evaluated by a potential purchaser. Companies not "in the consideration set" cannot make the sale to that purchaser.

consumer-generated content Also known as *user-generated content*, any information created by the customers themselves, rather than by the marketer. Amazon reviews, blog comments, and many other customer contributions comprise consumer-generated content.

content A web term for the words and pictures shown on a web page. Search marketing often depends on optimizing content so that search engines can more easily find a page for a relevant keyword.

content analyzer A software tool that examines your web page and offers advice to modify the page's tagging and text to improve search ranking.

content audit A technique by which an organic search landing page is checked to diagnose problems to improve rankings, referrals, and conversions.

content error log A report generated by a *content reporter* that lists each page individually by URL, showing which problems were found—often problems preventing the search spider from correctly indexing your page.

content management system (CMS) The system software that manages the process of creation, update, approval, and publishing of web pages to a website. Search marketing success often depends on proper standards for the operation of the content management system.

content marketing   A technique in which marketers use high-quality information to answer questions of potential customers, designing that information to be found in search and shared in social media.

content pipeline   A series of programs that process your site's pages, perhaps adding metadata, such as language or document type, to all pages to make them easier to find in your site search engine.

content ranking factor   Any characteristic of an organic search match that is unrelated to the terms in the search keyword. Content ranking factors can take into account anything the search engine knows about the page itself—which pages link to that page, the site that contains the page, and many other components. These factors are used in the organic search ranking algorithm to sort the best results to the top of the list. Because it does not vary by the keyword, any particular page's content factor score is exactly the same for every keyword—a page with strong content factors starts out with a high score for every word that is on that page.

content reporter   A program that can should be run regularly to detect deviations on your website from your content standards, generating a *content error log* that lists each problem page individually by URL and a *content scorecard* that aggregates the statistics by business area to track improvement based on error reduction over time.

content scorecard   A report generated by a *content* reporter program that aggregates the statistics by business area of all problems detected when your web pages deviate from your content standards. The scorecard can be used to track the improvement of each business area's content quality over time.

content theme   The subject or topic of a web page or other piece of information, used by search engines to determine the quality of the information as well as the search keywords that match that information.

content writer   The web specialist of the extended search team responsible for crafting the words that appear on a web page designed to convey information, as opposed to selling products.

contextual advertising   A paid merchandising spot displayed on the same page as an article about a related subject. Google AdSense is the leading contextual ad program.

conversion   The sales term for closing a sale: *converting* a prospect to a customer. The traditional definition can be expanded to include *web conversions*—any measurable, successful outcome of a web visit—such as registering an account or donating to a cause.

conversion rate   The ratio of website visitors to web orders—how many people came to the site versus how many actually purchased.

cookie   A method browsers use to store information that web pages need to remember. For example, a page can store your visitors' names in cookies so that their names can be displayed on your home page each time they return.

cooperative advertising   A technique by which multiple companies pool their resources on a campaign that benefits them. In paid search, a company selling a product might split the per-click fees with the supplier of a critical component of that product.

copy   The words that appear on a web page. Search marketing often depends on *optimizing* the copy so that search engines can more easily find the page in response to relevant search queries.

copywriter   The web specialist of the extended search team responsible for crafting the words that appear on a web page designed to sell products, as opposed to conveying information.

core page   According to the bow-tie theory of web pages, one of the most linked-to and linked-from pages on the web. The most popular websites tend to have many core pages.

cost per action (CPA)   A method of calculating fees whereby money is owed only when the searcher converts—typically by purchasing your product. In practice, CPA pricing is often used only for fixed-placement or shopping searches, not bid-based advertising.

cost per click (CPC)   Also known as *pay-per-click* (PPC), *search engine advertising*, or *paid search*, the technique by which a search engine devotes advertising space on its search results page to display links to the advertiser's website based on the quality of the ad and the bid for each click. CPC contrasts with organic search, for which no payment is made to the search engine for delivering traffic.

cost per thousand (CPM)   A method of calculating fees whereby money is owed for each impression of an advertisement—each time it's displayed. Usually referred to as CPM (cost per thousand—M is the Roman numeral for one thousand), it is usually used for fixed-placement or display advertising, not bid-based advertising.

country map   A page consisting of spider-friendly links to the main page of every country site within your overall web domain.

crawler   Also known as a *spider*, the part of a search engine that locates and indexes every page on the web that is a possible answer to a searcher's keyword. Successful search engine marketing depends on crawlers finding almost all the pages on a website.

crawling   The technique used by a search *spider* to discover new and changed pages and other content across the web, extracting the information from that content to update its *search index*.

creative   The copy written for a paid placement advertisement.

CSS   Cascading Style Sheets, a set of formatting instructions for each tag in an HTML file that can be customized so that the same tagged file can be formatted in different ways with different style sheets.

dayparting   A paid placement bidding technique that allows you to set your bids based on time of day, so that your bids are higher at the times of highest conversion.

deep link   A "hotspot" on a web page that, when clicked on, takes the visitor into an interior page within a website—a page that is far from the top of the hierarchy in the information architecture. A deep link connects to a page that might take several clicks for someone to reach if starting from the home page.

description metatag   The HTML element that contains a synopsis of the page. Search engines sometimes match search queries to page descriptions, so improving the description can be a good way to begin to optimize your page.

destination page   According to the *bow-tie theory* of web pages, a page linked from the core but does not itself link back into the core. Destination pages are typically high-quality pages, but they might be part of corporate websites that tend to link internally more than externally.

developer   A specialist who develops software. A *web developer* develops programs or HTML to display web pages in your visitor's web browser.

digital curation   The process whereby people identify content they believe is of high quality to be displayed on a website, shared through social media, or otherwise given more publicity.

direct answer   A technique whereby a search engine attempts to show the information the searcher is looking for right on the search results page, without requiring that the searcher click on a search results to reach another web page. Some examples of the kinds of searches that often result in direct answers are those for weather reports, stock prices, airline flights, and subjects found in encyclopedias.

direct marketing   A technique whereby the distinction between marketing and sales is blurred. The marketing tactics are themselves designed to evoke a response on the part of the prospect such that they can move closer to an actual purchase.

directory   A list of hundreds or thousands of subjects (such as fly fishing or needlepoint) along with links to websites about those subjects. Yahoo! Directory is the most famous example, but most directories are lightly used in comparison to text search technology.

directory listing   One of many hypertext links about a particular subject. Site owners submit a page to request that it be listed in the directory, and say that they have a "directory listing" when their submission is accepted. Yahoo! Directory and Open Directory are the most famous examples of web directories.

disavow a link   An action that a website owner can take to alert the search engines that it is being linked to by a party with low-quality content. Sites disavow links to eliminate spam penalties associated with these links and is the only way to combat *negative SEO*.

disconnected page   According to the *bow-tie theory* of web pages, a page not directly connected to the core. Disconnected pages might have links to or from origination and destination pages, or they might be linked only to other disconnected pages.

disintermediation   A web-savvy term for "cutting out the middleman." Disintermediation was much discussed during the Internet boom, but has not been as sweeping as the hype would lead you to believe.

domain name   The spoken language label for an Internet website that can be used for web surfing or email. The domain name (dell.com) follows the "at" sign (@) in an email address (michael@dell.com) and the www. in a web URL (www.dell.com).

doorway page   Also known as a *gateway page* or an *entry page*, a spam technique by which a page is designed solely to achieve high search rankings, with no value to visitors to your site. Unlike search landing pages, a doorway page is usually kept as hidden as possible from visitors who navigate through the site.

duplicate content suppression   A technique used by search engines to ensure that the search results show different content in the search results, rather than similar content that has been copied to multiple pages.

dynamic page   Web page whose HTML is generated by a software program at the moment the page is displayed. Dynamic pages are necessary when a page contains content that must change based on the visitor, such as an order status screen. A software program must retrieve the order status for the visitor from a database and build the HTML that shows the correct information on the screen. Dynamic pages often pose difficulties for search marketing that *static pages* do not.

Dynamic Text Substitution   Bing's name for a technique that allows a paid search advertiser to use placeholders in your ad copy that they will substitute with the actual keywords the searcher entered, allowing you to use the same ad for many keywords while still showing those keywords in the ad. Google offers the same capability, calling it *Keyword Insertion*.

dynamic web page   Web page whose HTML is generated by a software program at the moment the page is displayed. Dynamic pages are necessary when a page contains content that must change based on the visitor, such as an order status screen. A software program must retrieve the order status for the visitor from a database and build the HTML that shows the correct information on the screen. Dynamic pages often pose difficulties for search marketing that *static pages* do not.

entity extraction   A technique in text analytics that identifies the type of noun in a sentence, such as person names, company names, and place names, for example.

entry page   Also known as a *gateway page* or a *doorway page*, a spam technique by which a page is designed solely to achieve high search rankings, with no value to visitors to your site. Unlike search landing pages, an entry page is usually kept as hidden as possible from visitors who navigate through the site.

exact match   A paid search *match type* that specifies that an ad should match the searcher's keyword only when those exact words are present, with no extra words.

extended search team   The collective group responsible for executing the search marketing plan coordinated by the Search Center of Excellence. The extended search team is a name for the various web teams that already maintain the website, connoting their critical role in search marketing success.

eXtensible Markup Language (XML)   A standard for a markup language, similar to HTML, that allows tags to be defined to describe any kind of data you have, making it very popular as a format for data feeds.

external link   A hypertext connection from one website to another, allowing visitors to move to the new site. Search engines treat these links as endorsements of the receiving site by the sending site.

eye-tracking analytics   A technique in which test subjects' eye movements are studied as they look at a computer screen to determine which content on the screen they view and for how long.

faceted browsing   Also known as *faceted search* or *multifaceted search*, a search technique that allows searchers to restrict the search results by responding to choices offered by the search engine. Faceted browsing allows searchers to continually narrow down their results by choosing another constraint on their search.

faceted search   Also known as *faceted browsing* or *multifaceted search*, a search technique that allows searchers to restrict the search results by responding to choices offered by the search engine. Faceted search allows searchers to continually narrow down their results by choosing another constraint on their search.

filter   A constraint on a search that sets the scope of results, such as a country or language. Pages that are not included by the filters for a search keyword do not appear in the results.

fixed placement   A once-popular technique by which a search marketer negotiates the appearance of an advertisement in a particular place on a page for a given search keyword, usually paying for impressions (the number of times the ad is shown), rather than for clicks.

Flash   A technology invented by Macromedia, now owned by Adobe, that brings a far richer user experience to the web than drab old HTML, allowing animation and other interactive features that spice up visual tours and demonstrations.

folksonomy   Also known as *social bookmarking* or *social tagging*, readers can categorize and vote for your content to alert other prospective readers of its quality, newsworthiness, or importance.

follower   A subscriber who follows the short text updates on a microblogging service, such as Twitter.

forum   Also known as a *message board* or a *news group*, a technique for multiple web visitors to ask questions and share opinions on a particular subject. Typically, broad subjects are broken up into smaller conversations, known as *threads*, for each specific question or comment.

frames   An old technique of HTML coding that can display multiple sources of content in separate scrollable windows in the same HTML page. Frames have many usability problems for visitors, and have been replaced with better ways of integrating content on the same page—using content management systems and dynamic pages.

freshness   The search name for how quickly pages that change have those changes reflected in the search. Search engines that reflect changes rapidly have a higher freshness than those that do not.

friendly URL   A high-bidder, paid-placement auction bidding technique that marketers employ to stay out of costly bidding wars by always bidding lower than the maximum bid of the identified bidder—the one with the "friendly URL" that a marketer does not want to compete with.

functional organization   A highly centralized form of corporate organization typical of small-to-medium businesses with a small number of similar products that are sold to the same customers. The organization is divided by *function*, such as marketing or sales.

gap surfing   A high bidder paid placement auction bidding technique in which you scan the list of paid placement results, looking for significant differences between bids. You then adjust your bid to be just higher than the lower bid in the gap. If the #1 result is bidding 70¢, the #2 result is bidding 50¢, and the #3 result is bidding 40¢, the largest gap is between the first two results, so a gap surfer would bid 51¢ to claim the #2 ranking.

gateway page   Also known as a *doorway page* or an *entry page*, a spam technique by which a page is designed solely to achieve high search rankings, with no value to visitors to your site. Unlike search landing pages, a gateway page is usually kept as hidden as possible from visitors who navigate through the site.

geographic targeting   A technique that search engines use to display paid search results from a particular geographic area. Search engines typically use the searcher's IP address to determine the correct location and then show the listings that their advertisers have requested be shown.

Google bowling   Also known as *negative SEO*, an unethical practice in which competitors pretend to be operating on your behalf and violate the search engines' terms of service, bringing spam violation penalties on your site. For example, spammers might create obvious link farms and point them to your website so that the search engines penalize your site, thereby raising the ranking of the spammer's site that was below yours.

governance specialist   The specialist of the extended search team responsible for enforcing your company's operational standards. A *web governance specialist* enforces your website's operational standards.

guest book   An outdated website technique that allows visitors to post their contact information and comments about that site.

hate site   Also known as a *negative site*, a website whose primary purpose is to discredit another organization or website. These sites often use the name of another site with the word *sucks* appended to the domain name, such as yourdomainsucks.com.

heading tag   The HTML element that contains an emphasized section name that breaks up the body text. Search engines treat matches found in the heading tags as more important than those in body text, so improving headings seems like a good way to begin to optimize your page.

hidden links   A spam technique in which hypertext links are designed to be seen by spiders but not by human visitors. Spammers load up lots of links from high-ranking pages to other pages they are trying to boost.

hidden text   A spam technique in which text on a page is designed to be seen by spiders but not by human visitors. Text can be hidden by displaying text in tiny sizes or in the same color as the background, or by placing keywords in areas overlaid by graphics and other page elements. Spammers load up the page with keywords to gain higher search rankings.

high bidder auction   The original technique for ranking paid placement bids in which the search marketer offering the top price for a keyword click gets the #1 ranking ad for that keyword.

home page   The page on a website that is displayed when the domain name (such as sony.com) is entered into the browser.

horizontal search engine   As contrasted with a *vertical search engine*, a search engine designed to return broad results of any type of content, such as Google or Bing.

HTML   Hypertext Markup Language, the markup tagging system used to denote the semantic element of all content. For example, all paragraphs are marked with a paragraph tag, and all headings are identified with heading tags. web browsers interpret each tag to determine how to format the text on the screen when displaying that page.

hub page   A web page that links to many other pages about a certain subject.

hybrid auction   The modern technique for ranking paid placement bids in which the #1 ranking ad is determined by a combination of factors, including the price offered for keyword clicks and the ad's clickthrough rate.

Hypertext Markup Language (HTML)   The markup tagging system used to denote the precise document element of every piece of text on a web page. For example, all paragraphs are marked with a paragraph tag, and all headings are identified with heading tags. Web browsers interpret each tag to determine how to format the text on the screen when displaying that page.

impression   A term derived from banner advertising that denotes each time your ad is shown to someone. The number of clicks for your ad is divided by the number of impressions to derive the *clickthrough rate.*

inbound links   Also known as *back links*, the hypertext links from a page to your page. Inbound links to your page from outside your site are highly valued by search engines performing link analysis when they rank search results by relevance.

inclusion ratio   The percentage of your site's pages residing in a search index, calculated by dividing the number of pages found in a search index by the total number of pages you have estimated to be on your site.

index   The list used by the search engine of each word on the web, along with which pages each word is on. When a searcher enters a keyword, the search engine looks for the words in that keyword in the search index and locates the pages that contain those words. The search index is the primary database of a search engine, and no search engine can work without a very well-designed index.

indexing   The process by which the spider stores each word on the web, along with what pages each word is on. The search index is the primary database of a search engine, and no search engine can work if it does not have a very well-designed index.

information architect   1. The web specialist who decides the navigational structure of a website—how information is divided into separate pages, which pages link where, what nomenclature is used on a link to ensure people know what it is, and many other tasks. 2. The software specialist who determines the correct way to organize data fields in a database or a set of databases.

information retrieval   The name used by computer scientists to describe organic search technology.

informational searcher   A user who enters a search keyword looking for deep information about a specific subject. Informational searchers are looking for several top results that shed light on the subject, not one particular answer.

interactive advertising agency   A company that helps clients plan and purchase online promotional announcements, such as email ads, banner ads, search, and other electronic promotions.

interactive media   Electronic promotions such as email, banner ads, and search, that drive visitors to your website. Advertising agencies often handle client purchases of interactive media.

interior link   A hypertext connection to a page deep within your site, rather than one to the home page, for example.

internal link   A hypertext connection from one page of a website to another page within the same site, allowing visitors to move to the new page. Search engines do not treat these links with much importance.

Internet Yellow Pages   The online equivalent of a phone directory, which has become less important as local search has supplanted its monopoly of business listings.

IP address   A unique number assigned by a network when a device is connected to the Internet that allows identification of the device's geographic location.

IP delivery   A technique by which a site owner can deliver customized content based on the IP address of the visitor. When used within ethical standards, it allows a site to present local language or entitled content to specific visitors to reroute search engines around complex URL structures or give them exclusive access to databases that would normally require a keyword to retrieve the information. When used unethically, it is usually called *cloaking*—a spam technique, which, for the same URL, returns one page for human visitors and a different version of the page for a search engine's spider (one full of keywords designed to attain a high search ranking).

JavaScript   A programming language that can provide special effects inside a browser that cannot be performed in HTML. Search marketing success depends on certain standards about how and when JavaScript programming is used, because JavaScript, when misused, can prevent search spiders from indexing certain pages.

JavaScript redirect   A way of using a program to instruct web browsers to display a different URL from the one requested (such as `<script language="JavaScript" type="text/javascript">window.location="http://www.yourdomain.com/newURL"</script>`). JavaScript redirects, unfortunately, are usually ignored by search engine spiders, so this technique should be avoided.

keyword   A particular word or phrase that search marketers expect searchers to enter frequently as a query.

keyword demand   Also known as *keyword volume*, the number of times searchers enter a particular word into a search engine within a particular period of time. For example, if searchers enter *digital camera* into Google three million times each day, its daily Google keyword volume would be equal to three million.

keyword density Also known as *term density*, the ratio of a particular search query's terms to all terms on a page. Once an important part of organic search ranking algorithms, it is rarely used today.

keyword effectiveness index (KEI) A mathematical representation of the popularity of a keyword (the number of searches containing it) compared to its popularity in usage (the number of web pages it is found on).

keyword frequency A metric that identifies the number of times a keyword appears on the text. Once a critical part of the organic search ranking algorithm, it has been supplanted by more modern methods.

Keyword Insertion Google's name for a technique that allows a paid search advertiser to use placeholders in your ad copy that they will substitute with the actual keywords the searcher entered, allowing you to use the same ad for many keywords while still showing those keywords in the ad. Bing offers the same capability, calling it *Dynamic Text Substitution*.

keyword loading Also known as *keyword stuffing*, a spam technique by which keywords are overused in content merely to attract the search engines.

keywords metatag An HTML tag declaring the keywords the author believes the page to be relevant for. Because in practice these have been abused by spammers to attract search traffic for unrelated keywords, search engines now ignore this tag.

keyword models A structured way of analyzing keywords both for completeness and for segmentation. A keyword model helps you organize your keywords so that you see what's missing and so that you can identify categories of keywords that go together.

keyword placement Also known as *term placement*, a measurement of the value of the location of a word on a web page. All words do not have equal importance on a page. Words in a title or in a heading are more important than words in a body paragraph; these locations of keywords are their *placement*. Placement and position comprise *keyword prominence*.

keyword planning The process of deciding which words and phrases a search marketer should target in a search marketing campaign.

keyword position Also known as *term position*, a measurement of how close to the beginning of a web page element that a word appears. For example, words at the beginning of the body element are usually more important than those that show up later in that same element. Position and placement comprise *keyword prominence*.

keyword prominence A measurement that combines the *placement* and *position* of a term on a page to indicate its relative value to a search engine. The most *prominent* keyword location is the first word of the page's title because the title is the best placement and the first word is the best position. Pages with a keyword in prominent locations tend to be good matches.

keyword proximity Also known as *term proximity*, a measurement of the nearness of different search terms to each other within a matching page. Two words from the searcher's query that are adjacent to each other on a page have the highest proximity, and would tend to be ranked higher than pages where the terms were a paragraph apart, for example.

keyword ranking factor Any characteristic of an organic search match that is related to the terms in the search query. Keyword ranking factors—including prominence, frequency, and others—are used in the organic search ranking algorithm to sort the best results to the top of the list.

keyword rarity Also known as *term rarity*, a measurement of the frequency that a term is used on all pages across the web. In a multiple-word search query, some words might be very common, whereas others relatively rare. The search engines give higher weight to pages that contain rare terms than common terms when ranking the results.

keyword research The step in the keyword planning process during which search marketers discover all the possible words and phrases they should target.

keyword stuffing Also known as *keyword loading*, a spam technique by which keywords are overused in content merely to attract the search engines.

keyword suggestion A technique by which a search engine displays multiple keywords to a searcher that complete the few letters that the searcher has already typed. For example, if a searcher begins typing *digi* into the search box, Google might show a drop-down menu that includes *digital*, *digital camera*, *digital camera reviews*, and several more for the searcher to choose from.

keyword variant A different form of a search query in which the individual terms in a keyword are presented in a different order, or use different forms of the words. For example, *hotels in london* and *london hotel* are variants of the same essential search keyword, even though the word order and the form of the word *hotel* (singular or plural) is different in each case.

keyword volume Also known as *keyword demand*, the number of times searchers enter a particular word into a search engine within a particular period of time. For example, if searchers enter *digital camera* into Google three million times each day, its daily Google keyword volume would be equal to three million.

keyword weight A content metric that divides the number of keyword occurrences by the number of words in a body of text. Once an important part of organic search ranking algorithms, it is rarely used today.

landing page The URL on your website where visitors will go when they click a particular link. A *search landing page*, for example, is the URL a searcher is led to after clicking an organic or paid search result.

language metatag   An HTML tag declaring the language of the page (such as `<meta http-equiv="content-language" content="ja">` to indicate a page written in Japanese). Because in practice these tags are often syntactically incorrect or have the wrong language encoded, search engines never decide the language of the page based on this tag alone.

lead   A prospective customer passed from one business to another (or passed from one part of a company to another) who might eventually complete a transaction to become a customer. The number of leads passed is a critical measurement for businesses that cannot close a sale on the web; they must attract interest in their products on the web, but "pass the lead" to an offline channel to continue the process that might culminate in a sale.

lead management   A process by which companies process contact information for potential clients to nurture each opportunity into a potential sale.

lifetime value   A method quantifying what each new customer is worth, not just for the first purchase but for the lifetime of purchases from that customer.

link   A set of words, a picture, or other "hotspot" on a web page that, when clicked, takes the visitor to another web page. Search engines pay special attention to outbound links when crawling pages and to inbound links when ranking pages by relevance to respond to a search keyword.

link analysis   Also known as *link popularity*, the technique used by search engines to determine the authority of web pages by examining the network of connections between web pages. Search engines use link analysis when ranking search results by relevance—pages that have many inbound links from high-authority pages are ranked higher than other pages in the search results.

link auction   A method of buying a high-value hypertext connection to your site by outbidding other sites. Some websites, known as link auction sites, specialize in running the bidding for parties that wish to buy and sell links.

link audit   A procedure by which you analyze every hypertext connection to your landing page, or even to your whole site. Link audits help you to identify which pages have few or low-quality links and might be good targets for *link-building campaigns*.

link-building campaigns   A method by which you attract more hypertext connections to your site, often by contacting other websites and making a request.

link farm   A spam technique by which search marketers set up dozens or hundreds of sites that can be crawled by search engines just so that they can put in thousands of links to sites they want to boost in search rankings.

link landing page   The URL a searcher is led to after clicking a hypertext link from another website.

link popularity   Also known as *link analysis*, the technique used by search engines to determine the authority of web pages by examining the network of connections between web pages. Search engines use link analysis when ranking search results by relevance—pages that have many inbound links from high-authority pages are ranked higher than other pages in the search results.

link within the family   A hypertext link between two sites that search engines consider to be biased, perhaps because they have similar IP addresses, Whois information, or anchor text. Search engines seek to downgrade these links because they are not between neutral parties—the endorsement that the link provides is not as valuable as others.

local search   A technique that search engines use to display results from a particular geographic area. Searchers might actually enter the location as part of the keyword (such as *philadelphia restaurant*) or might have saved their location from a previous keyword. Local search is different from *geographic targeting*, in which paid placement results are selected based on the searcher's location, regardless of whether the keyword was intended to return results for a particular location.

local search engine   1. A search engine from a particular country or region, as contrasted with engines that attract searchers worldwide. 2. A search engine designed mainly to provide *local search*, such as Internet Yellow Pages providers.

log file   A file on your web server that serves as a record of every action the server has taken. Log files can be analyzed in complex ways to determine the number of visits to your site (by people and by search engine spiders) and the number of pages that they view.

machine learning   A technique in which a computer program (the *machine*) improves the performance of its algorithm (*learning*) by analyzing more and more patterns to classify new items properly. For example, search engines use machine learning to classify newly found pages as high quality or low quality based on the similarities of these pages to ones that have already been classified by human beings.

market segment   A group of customers with similar needs that receive the same marketing messages for your products. For your website, market segments are usually defined as audiences that include groups beyond your customers (stock analysts, press, and others). Your website messages are usually targeted to several market segments (audiences).

marketing manager   The leader of a team of people who are responsible for creating the demand for a company's offerings that can lead to sales.

marketing mix   The combination of ways in which you spend your marketing budget (TV, radio, print, and so on). Making a commitment to search marketing usually implies that some other expenditure must be reduced in your marketing mix.

markup   A publishing technique where text is *tagged* according to its meaning within the document so that computers can format and find the text more easily. Markup languages such as HTML allow content authors to "mark up" parts of their documents with tags denoting each document element. For example, a title tag (`<title>About Our Company</title>`) identifies the title of a web page.

match   A web page found by a search engine in response to a searcher's keyword. Search engines use various techniques to determine which pages match each keyword, and then rank the pages by relevance so the best matches are presented first.

match type   The way that paid search advertisers decide how their keywords correspond to searchers' queries. Paid search engines offer varying match types, providing control over how closely the keywords must match the queries before displaying the ad.

mega-keyword   A search query that is entered frequently by searchers.

merchant   Also known as an *affiliate program sponsor*, the company that launches the *affiliate program*, recruits the *affiliates*, and pays the commissions for sales.

merchant rating   A score assigned by shopping search engines to each company selling products, based on customer reviews of the company's service.

message board   Also known as a *forum* or a *news group*, a technique for multiple web visitors to ask questions and share opinions on a particular subject. Typically, broad subjects are broken up into smaller conversations, known as *threads*, for each specific question or comment.

meta refresh redirect   A metatag in the `<head>` section of your HTML that instructs a web browser to show a different URL from the one entered (such as `<meta http-equiv="Refresh" content="5; URL= http://www.yourdomain.com/newURL" />`). This tag flashes a screen (in this case for 5 seconds) before displaying the new URL. Unfortunately, search engine spiders usually ignore this technique, so you should avoid it.

metasearch engine   A search engine that sends the keyword entered by the searcher to several other search engines, collating the results from each into a single results list.

metatag   A particular kind of document element that is "about" the document rather than an intrinsic part of the document. HTML tagging standards specify numerous metatags, including titles, descriptions, dates, and many others. Metatags are especially important to search engines because they contain key clues about a page's overall relevance to a search keyword.

metrics specialist   The web specialist of the extended search team responsible for compiling and reporting statistics—how many visitors come to the site, customer satisfaction survey results, the number of sales, and many more.

microblogging   A form of blogging that allows *followers* to subscribe to short text updates akin to public instant messages. Twitter is the most famous microblogging service.

microconversion   The moment your buyer moves from step to step in the Buyer's Journey, allowing you to isolate successes and problems within each step so that small improvements lead to improvements in your overall conversion rate.

microdata   Also known as *microformats*, a form of markup that allows special objects, such as events and people, to be better recognized by search engines for retrieval.

microformats   Also known as *microdata*, a form of markup that allows special objects, such as events and people, to be better recognized by search engines for retrieval.

microsite   A small website, separate from your corporate site, designed to make web metrics easier to collect for your search campaigns.

missed-opportunity matrix   A table that enumerates the volume of searches that do *not* result in a visit to particular website.

monetize   To create revenue from a particular action.

multifaceted search   Also known as *faceted browsing* or *faceted search*, a search technique that allows searchers to restrict the search results by responding to choices offered by the search engine. Multifaceted search allows searchers to continually narrow down their results by choosing another constraint on their search.

multinational organization   A form of corporate organization in which the company is divided by country.

multivariate testing   A technique that allows thousands or even tens of thousands of possible approaches to be tested against each other automatically, to determine which approach seems to optimize the revenue provided from the customer.

natural language search engine   A search designed to accept natural language queries (such as *What is the capital of Florida?*) and get an answer, not just a list of documents containing the words.

natural search   Also known as *organic search*, the technique by which a search engine finds the most relevant matches for a searcher's keyword from all of the pages indexed from the web. Natural search contrasts with *paid search*, in which bidders vie for the highest rankings by topping each other's bids.

navigational searcher   A user who enters a search keyword looking for a specific website as a result. A searcher using the keyword *cornell university* is looking specifically for www.cornell.edu, and no other result.

negative keyword   A technique that allows a paid search marketer to indicate that a particular word should *not* be present within the searcher's keyword in order for an ad to match.

negative SEO   Also known as *Google bowling*, an unethical practice in which competitors pretend to be operating on your behalf and violate the search engines' terms of service, bringing spam violation penalties on your site. For example, spammers might create obvious link farms and point them to your website so that the search engines penalize your site, thereby raising the ranking of the spammer's site that was below yours.

negative site   Also known as a *hate site*, a website whose primary purpose is to discredit another organization or website. These sites frequently use the name of another site with the word *sucks* appended to the domain name, such as yourdomainsucks.com.

news group   Also known as a *forum* or a *message board*, a technique for multiple web visitors to ask questions and share opinions on a particular subject. Typically, broad subjects are broken up into smaller conversations, known as *threads*, for each specific question or comment.

<noframes> tag   An HTML tag designed to provide alternate content for (ancient) browsers that do not support frames. Search engine spiders use this alternate content to index your page, but you are better off eliminating frames altogether.

<noscript> tag   An HTML tag designed to provide alternate content for (ancient) browsers that do not support JavaScript. Search engine spiders also use this alternate content to index your page.

objective bidding   A style of paid placement auction bidding that relies on metrics to drive each bid.

offline sales   Revenue from product purchases in which customers began the sales process on the web but transacted the purchase on the phone, in person, or through some other off-web channel.

one-way link   A hypertext connection to a page with no corresponding reciprocal link back to the source.

online commerce site   A website that transacts sales of products, even though it might use offline distribution channels to ship the product to the customer. (Pure online sites, in contrast, need no physical shipment.)

optimizing content   A search marketing term for modifying the words and pictures shown on a web page so that search engines can more easily find that page for a relevant keyword.

organic search   Also known as *natural search* and *search engine optimization*, the technique by which a search engine finds the most relevant matches for a searcher's keyword from all of the content indexed from the web. Organic search contrasts with *paid search*, in which bidders vie for more advantageous ad placement.

origination page   According to the bow-tie theory of web pages, a page with numerous links into the core but relatively few from the core. Origination pages might be new or not terribly high quality, so they have not attracted the links back to them that would mark them as part of the core.

outbound link   A hypertext link from your page to a different page on the web, perhaps within your site, or maybe to another site.

page designer   The web specialist of the extended search team responsible for the visual appearance of the page, frequently handling the HTML templates and style sheets used. Search marketing often depends on the page designer optimizing the templates so that search engines can more easily find the page in response to relevant search queries.

page submission   A method of telling a search engine about the existence of a URL that you would like crawled. Search engines vastly prefer to find new sites by following links, but do offer ways to manually submit your home page's URL if your site is somehow not discovered.

page view   The web metrics term used to count how many web pages on a site have been viewed by individual visitors. If three people view a page once, and two people view that same page twice, that page is said to have seven page views.

paid inclusion   An service once offered by search engines that guaranteed a website's pages are stored in the search index in return for a fee.

paid link   A hypertext connection to a target site that has been purchased from the source site.

paid listing   An entry in a web directory. Directories contain hundreds or thousands of subjects (such as *fly fishing* or *needlepoint*) along with links to websites about those subjects. Yahoo! Directory is the most famous example.

paid search   Also known as *search engine advertising*, *pay per click* (PPC), or *cost per click* (CPC), the technique by which a search engine devotes advertising space on its search results page to display links to the advertiser's website based on the quality of the ad and the bid for each click. Paid search contrasts with organic search, for which no payment is made to the search engine for delivering traffic.

parameter   The name of a variable in a software program that displays dynamic web pages. The URL www.domain.com?product=45 contains a parameter named *product* and a value of 45. The software program uses the parameter and its associated value to decide which content to display on the page.

pay per click (PPC)   Also known as *paid search, search engine advertising*, or *cost per click* (CPC), the technique by which a search engine devotes advertising space on its search results page to display links to the advertiser's website based on the quality of the ad and the bid for each click. PPC contrasts with organic search, for which no payment is made to the search engine for delivering traffic.

penalty   An action taken by a search engine to lower the search rankings of a website that has been found to be violating the engine's terms of service (using spam techniques).

permanent redirect   Also known as a *301 redirect*, an instruction to web browsers to display a different URL than the one the browser requested, used when a page has undergone a lasting change in its URL. A permanent redirect is a type of server-side redirect that is handled properly by search engine spiders.

personalization   A technique by which a web or other end user experience is modified as it is being displayed based on attributes of the visitor. For example, Amazon shows different recommendations on the screen based on who has visited the site.

phoneme   The speech sound that corresponds to each syllable in a spoken word. Some search technologies use phonemes to help match text keywords to audio speech, but *speech recognition* is usually a stronger approach for any speech apart from proper names.

phrase   A search term within a search keyword consisting of multiple words enclosed in double quotation marks, indicating to the search engine that those words are found "as is" on any matching page. If words are not enclosed in double quotes, they are treated as individual words to search for rather than as a phrase to be found together.

phrase match   A paid search *match type* that specifies that an ad should match the searcher's keyword when those exact words (or their close variants) are present, although extra words might be present also.

podcast   An audio file downloaded from the web and played on demand using an Apple iPod or any MP3 media player.

pop-under window   A browser window that opens in the background on your screen, frequently containing an advertisement.

pop-up window   A browser window that overlays the web page on your screen, frequently containing an advertisement.

portal   The system software that manages the display of web pages for a website, often including the use of personalization rules that dynamically choose what content to display based on what is known about the visitor. Search marketing success often depends on proper standards for the operation of the portal software.

precision   A search metric that measures the number of "correct" organic search matches returned by the search engine for a keyword compared to the number of total matches returned. If the search engine returns ten matches, of which nine are judged "correct," its precision for that keyword is 90%. (Precision is a subjective measurement because it is based on someone's judgment of what is a "correct" match.)

primary demand   The name used by economists to describe the state of a prospective buyer in the very early stages of consideration of a purchase.

product feed   A method of sending updates of a company's eCommerce catalog to a search engine or other destination so that the destination may display entries from the catalog to send visitors to the company's website.

product-oriented organization   A form of corporate organization in which the company is divided by *product* so that each product or product line sold by the company is run by a semi-autonomous group, as if it were a standalone business.

profit margin   A financial term, the measurement of return on the sale per item. Profit margin is calculated as (Revenue – Cost) ÷ Price.

programmer   The web specialist of the extended search team responsible for developing the software that runs the website. Search marketing often depends on the programmer following certain standards so that search engines can more easily find pages in response to relevant search queries.

public relations   The professions of communicating between an organization and an external audience designed to persuade to a particular viewpoint, usually one that portrays the company in the best possible light.

pull-down navigation   A style of user interface in which a menu of links is hidden until the visitor clicks the exposed part of the menu—that action is referred to as "pulling down" the menu, because the links are then displayed underneath the area clicked.

pure online site   A website that not only transacts sales of products but also delivers products to customers without any physical shipment. Examples include stock purchases at Schwab.com and music downloads at iTunes.com.

qualified visitor   A person coming to your website that is within the targeted market segments for your product—a person who you are trying to attract because they are able to buy.

Quality Score   The measurement that a paid search engine applies in determining the value of ads and landing pages in a paid search campaign. The higher the Quality Score, the higher the ads will rank in the auction and the lower the per-click price required, compared to lower quality ads.

query   Also known as a *keyword*, the words that a searcher types into a search engine to identify which information should be searched for. Some queries are a single word, but others can consist of multiple words and might contain search operators.

ranking   The technique by which a search engine sorts the matches to produce a set of search results. Although some search engines can sort by the date of the web page, the most common ranking method is by relevance. The software code that decides exactly how the ranking is performed is called the *ranking algorithm*, and is a trade secret for each search engine.

ranking algorithm   The software instructions that control precisely how search matches are sorted into the order in which they are displayed on the search results page. Search matches are sometimes ranked by the date of the pages, but are most often ranked by relevance. A search engine's relevance ranking algorithm is one of the most proprietary parts of its secret sauce.

ranking checker   An automated tool that analyzes where a particular URL or set of URLs appear in the search results for a keyword.

ranking factor   Any characteristic of an organic search match that can be used by a ranking algorithm to sort the matches for presentation on the search results page. Relevance ranking algorithms use myriad factors, including the location on the page that matches the keyword, the authority of the page (based on link analysis), the proximity of different individual words in the keyword to each other on the page, and many more.

recall   A search metric that measures the number of "correct" organic search matches returned by the search engine for a keyword compared to the number of "correct" matches that exist in the search index. If the search engine returns nine "correct" matches, but ten "correct" matches exist in the search index, its recall for that keyword is 90%. (*Recall* is a subjective measurement because it is based on someone's judgment of what is a "correct" match.)

reciprocal link   Also known as a *two-way link*, a hypertext connection to a page that has a corresponding link back to the source.

redirect   An instruction to display a different URL from the one the browser requested. Redirects are used when the URL of a page has changed. They allow old URLs to be "redirected" to the current URL so that your visitors do not get a "page not found" message (known as an HTTP 404 error) when they use the old URL.

referral   The web metrics term for the event of a page being viewed after viewing a previous page. Web metrics systems capture the referrer URL for each page view so that referrals from particular places, such as search engines, can be counted and analyzed.

referrer   The URL of the page that a visitor came from before coming to the current page. Web metrics systems capture the referrer for each page view so that *referrals* from particular places, such as search engines, can be counted and analyzed.

relational link   An in-bound hypertext link to your site that you solicited based on an existing business relationship, such as the relationships your company has with suppliers, resellers, and customers.

relevance   The degree to which an organic search match is closely related to the keyword. A match with extremely high relevance is a candidate to be the #1 result for that keyword. Search engines typically sort the matches by relevance for presentation on the search results page using a relevance ranking algorithm. Relevance ranking algorithms use myriad factors, including the location on the page that matches the keyword, the authority of the page (based on link analysis), the proximity of different words in the keyword to each other on the page, and many more.

relevance ranking   The technique by which a search engine sorts the matches to produce a set of organic search results whose top matches most closely relate to the keyword. The software code that decides exactly how the relevance ranking is performed is called the *ranking algorithm*, and is a trade secret for each search engine. Relevance ranking algorithms use myriad factors, including the location on the page that matches the keyword, the authority of the page (based on link analysis), and many more.

remarketing   Also known as *retargeting*, a technique whereby visitors to your site are identified and shown your ads when they visit other sites. It's frequently used with *contextual advertising*.

result   A link to a matching web page returned by a search engine in response to a searcher's keyword. Search engines use various techniques to determine which pages match each keyword, and then rank the organic search matches by relevance so the best matches are presented first in the search results. Paid placement and directory results are typically governed by a mixture of relevance and the amount bid by the owner of the website listed.

results page   The web page containing the search engine's response to the keyword. Each search engine has a unique layout for its results page, but it is typically a mixture of organic and paid placement results, with directory listings also possible.

retargeting   Also known as *remarketing*, a technique whereby visitors to your site are identified and shown your ads when they visit other sites. It's frequently used with *contextual advertising*.

return on advertising spend (ROAS)   A financial term measuring the revenue impact of media expense using a formula such as Revenue ÷ Expense. Calculating the ROAS of several advertisements can help increase spending on the best ones.

return on investment (ROI)   A financial term measuring the monetary impact of an investment using a formula such as Profit ÷ Cost. Projecting the ROI of several possible investments can help you choose the best one.

reverse DNS lookup   Also known as *reverse IP lookup*, the technique by which a website examines the IP address of a visitor to determine geographic location, organization, and other information about that visitor at the time of the visit, usually for the purpose of personalization.

reverse IP lookup   Also known as *reverse DNS lookup*, the technique by which a website examines the IP address of a visitor to determine geographic location, organization, and other information about that visitor at the time of the visit, usually for the purpose of personalization.

rich snippets   A technique by which search engines show enhanced information about a piece of content on the search results page based on specialized markup contained within the page. For example, a web page about an event might be shown on the search results page with information about the schedule, price, and other information about that event.

ROAS Return on advertising spend, a financial term that measures the revenue impact of media expense using a formula such as Revenue ÷ Expense. Calculating the ROAS of several advertisements can help increase spending on the best ones.

robot A little-known name for a *crawler* or *spider*, the part of a search engine that locates and indexes every page on the web that is a possible answer to a searcher's keyword. Typically used only when discussing the robots HTML tag or the robots.txt file.

robots metatag An HTML tag found that controls whether a search engine spider indexes the page that the tag is found on, and whether the spider should follow any links found on that page to the linked pages.

ROI Return on investment, a financial term that measures the monetary impact of an investment using a formula such as Profit ÷ Cost. Projecting the ROI of several possible investments can help you choose the best one.

RSS Really Simple Syndication, a method of sending information to subscribers automatically, often used for blogs and product catalogs.

sandbox effect The informal name used by search marketing experts to describe the treatment of new sites by Google and other search engines when they discount the effect of a quick change in link popularity. Your page can play around all it wants, but it will stay in its "sandbox," without breaking into the top rankings for any queries. If its newfound popularity, over time, remains constant or even gradually grows larger, then the search engines begin to remove the discounts and give full weight to the link popularity, allowing search rankings to rise.

search engine advertising Also known as *paid search*, *Pay Per click* (PPC), or *cost per click* (CPC), the technique by which a search engine devotes advertising space on its search results page to display links to the advertiser's website based on the quality of the ad and the bid for each click. Paid search contrasts with organic search, for which no payment is made to the search engine for delivering traffic.

search engine marketing (SEM) The activities that improve search referrals to a website using either organic or paid search. Search engine marketing is also known as *search marketing*.

search engine optimization (SEO) The set of techniques and methodologies devoted to improving organic search rankings (not paid search) for a website.

search engine results page (SERP) The place that Google and other search engines show the links to web pages generated by organic and paid search ranking algorithms.

search filter   A constraint on a search that sets the scope of results, such as a country or language. Pages that are not included by the filters for a keyword do not appear in the results.

search index   A special database that stores every word found on every web page, along with the list of pages that each word was found on. When a searcher enters a search keyword, the organic search engine consults the search index to find the list of pages that match the keyword.

search landing page   The URL a searcher is led to after clicking an organic or paid search result.

search marketer   Someone who improves search referrals to a website using organic and paid search techniques.

search marketing   The activities that improve search referrals to a website using either organic or paid search. Search marketing is also known as *search engine marketing* (SEM).

search operator   A character with a special meaning to a search engine that controls the way the engine matches the keyword for organic search. Common operators include double quotation marks (treat enclosed words as a phrase), the plus sign (the following term is required), and the minus sign (the following term must not appear in any results).

search query   Also known as the *search keyword*, the words that a searcher types into a search engine to identify what information should be searched for. Some queries are a single word, but others can consist of multiple words and might contain search operators.

search referral   The web metrics term for the event of a page being viewed after viewing a search results page. Web metrics systems capture the referrer URL for each page view so that referrals from search engines can be counted and analyzed.

search result   A link to a matching web page returned by a search engine in response to a searcher's keyword. Search engines use various techniques to determine which pages match each keyword, and then rank the organic search matches by relevance so the best matches are presented first in the search results. Paid search results are typically governed by a mixture of relevance and the amount bid by the owner of the website listed.

search term   One word or phrase from the search keyword. Words enclosed in double quotation marks (the phrase operator) are treated as a single search term, but other words are treated as individual single-word terms.

search toolbar   A program used to enter search queries on your browser screen without first going to a search engine's website.

searcher   The web user who enters a keyword into the input box of a search engine and requests that a search be performed.

searcher context   The conditions under which a searcher enters a search keyword, including permanent or semipermanent characteristics (such as gender, job role, and marital status) and more ephemeral factors (such as current geographic location, the subjects of pages viewed recently, and recent search keywords).

searcher intent   The goals that a web user has when entering search queries, examining results, or choosing the result to click.

seed list   The enumeration of starting URLs for a spider to begin crawling web pages. Spiders examine each page to see what other linked pages it should go to next, but it requires a seed list of starting points when it begins crawling.

selective demand   The name used by economists to describe what a prospective buyer exhibits when weighing the purchase of a particular brand or model of a product.

sentiment analysis   A technique that allows a computer algorithm to determine whether text is positive or negative in tone.

server   A computer (or a program running on a computer) that responds to a client program's request. For example, a web server responds to its client, a web browser.

server-side redirect   An instruction from the web server to web browsers to display a different URL from the one the browser requested. Two common forms of server-side redirects are 301 (permanent) and 302 (temporary) redirects, named after the HTTP status codes they return to the browser. Server-side redirects are handled properly by search engine spiders.

session   Synonymous with a *visit*, a web metrics term for a single series of pages viewed from a single website. If a visitor comes to a website and views five pages before leaving to go to a new site, the metrics system logs five page views but just one session.

session identifier   Dynamic URL parameters (usually named ID= or Session= or some other similar name) used by a web metrics system to keep track of each unique visitor looking at a single page or at a series of pages in a visit to a site. Search engine spiders typically do not index pages with a session identifier.

shopping search   The means by which products can be found by searchers.

shopping search engine   A search engine specially designed to allow comparison of features and prices for a wide variety of products.

showrooming   The act of a consumer using a mobile device in a physical retail store to check pricing and other information on the Internet for a product they are looking at in the store.

sitelinks   Subsidiary links beneath the main organic search result link to the home page of a site that can take the searcher to other pages on that same website.

site map   A page consisting of spider-friendly links to the rest of your web domain. For a small site, your site map can have direct links to every page on your site. Medium to large sites use site maps with links to major hubs within the domain (which in turn allow eventual navigation to every page on the site).

sneezers   People with huge social networks who are constantly spreading ideas. Sneezers are ideal targets for viral marketers for ideas for their campaigns.

snippet   The short paragraph that a search engine generates under the title (on the results page) to display the relevant passages on the page for the keyword.

social bookmarking   Also known as *folksonomy* or *social tagging*, readers can categorize and vote for your content to alert other prospective readers of its quality, newsworthiness, or importance.

social computing   Sometimes known as social media, a way of using technology to enable connections between people. Blogs, wikis, social networks, and social bookmarking are all examples of social computing.

social tagging   Also known as *folksonomy* or *social bookmarking*, readers can categorize and vote for your content to alert other prospective readers of its quality, newsworthiness, or importance.

solicited link   A hypertext link to your site that you received by explicitly requesting the other site to link to yours.

spam   1. Unsolicited illegal email, usually containing a sales pitch or a fraudulent scheme offered to the recipient without permission. 2. Also known as *spamdexing*, unethical (but legal) techniques undertaken by a website designed to fool organic search engines to display its pages, even though they are not truly the best matches for a searcher's keyword.

spamdexing   Also known simply as *spam*, unethical (but legal) techniques undertaken by a website designed to fool organic search engines to display its pages, even though they are not truly the best matches for a searcher's keyword.

specialty search engine   A search engine that focuses on just one or two product categories or subject areas.

speech recognition   A software technique by which audio speech is converted into its equivalent text, allowing audio to be searchable just as ordinary text is.

spelling correction   A feature of most engines that suggest possible changes to the searcher's keyword when it appears to be finding relatively few matches and a different spelling yields many more matches.

spider   Also known as a *crawler*, the part of a search engine that locates and indexes every page on the web that is a possible answer to a searcher's keyword. Successful search engine marketing depends on crawlers finding almost all the pages on a website.

spider paths   Easy-to-follow navigation routes through your site, such as site maps, category maps, country maps, or even text links at the bottom of key pages. Spider paths include any means that allow the spider to easily get to all the pages on your site.

spider trap   A barrier that prevents spiders from crawling a site, usually stemming from technical approaches to displaying web pages that work fine for browsers, but do not work for spiders. Examples of spider traps include JavaScript pull-down menus and some kinds of redirects.

splog   A *spam blog* that is created for the sole purpose of fabricating links to other websites the spammer wants to improve in search rankings.

static web page   A web page whose HTML is stored in a file for display by a web server. Static pages typically do not change based on the visitor; they look the same to each person who views them—in contrast to *dynamic pages.*

stop word   Words that occur with very high frequency (such as *an* or *the*) and are ignored by search engines when entered by a searcher.

style guide   The rules governing the look and feel of the website, including page layouts, color schemes, information architecture, and many other areas.

style guide developer   The web specialist of your extended search team who maintains the style guide—rules governing the look and feel of the website.

style sheet   A set of formatting instructions for each tag in an HTML or XML file that can be customized so that the same tagged file can be formatted in different ways with different style sheets.

summarization   A text analytics technique whereby an entire document can be condensed into a short abstract of a few sentences.

syndication   A business arrangement by which results from one search engine are provided for display by another search engine. AOL, for example, shows Google's paid placement ads on the AOL search results page, and is thus a syndication partner of Google's.

tag   1. A method of marking text in a document with its meaning so that computers can format and find the text more easily. Markup languages such as HTML allow content authors to "mark up" parts of their documents with tags denoting each document element. For example, the title tag (`<title>About Our Company</title>`) identifies the title of a web page. 2. A social bookmarking label that identifies the subject of a piece of content. For example, readers of a web page about Cadillac automobiles might use del.icio.us to set and share bookmarks (links) named "Cadillac," "autos," or "cars."

temporary redirect   Also known as a *302 redirect*, an instruction to web browsers to display a different URL from the one the browser requested, used when a page has undergone a short-term change in its URL. A temporary redirect is a type of server-side redirect that is handled properly by search engine spiders.

term   One word or phrase from the search keyword. Words enclosed in double quotation marks (the phrase operator) are treated as a single search term, but other words are treated as individual single-word terms.

term density   Also known as *keyword density*, the ratio of a particular search keyword's terms to all terms on a page. Once an important part of organic search ranking algorithms, it is rarely used today.

term frequency   The search metric that describes the number of occurrences of a particular searcher's keyword term in a web page. Search engines use the term frequency as a ranking factor in the relevance ranking algorithm for organic search.

term placement   Also known as *keyword placement*, a measurement of the value of the location of a word on a web page. All words do not have equal importance on a page. Words in a title or in a heading are more important than words in a body paragraph—these locations of keywords are their *placement*. Placement and position comprise *keyword prominence*.

term position   Also known as *keyword position*, a measurement of how close to the beginning of a web page element that a word appears. For example, words at the beginning of the body element are usually more important than those that show up later in that same element. Position and placement comprise *keyword prominence*.

term proximity   Also known as *keyword proximity*, a measurement of the nearness of different search terms to each other within a matching page. Two words from the searcher's keyword that are adjacent to each other on a page have the highest proximity, for example.

term rarity   Also known as *keyword rarity*, a measurement of the frequency that a term is used on all pages across the web. In a multiple-word search keyword, some words might be very common, whereas others relatively rare. The search engines give higher weight to pages that contain rare terms than common terms when ranking the results.

term variant   Also known as word variant, a linguistic form of another word. *Mouse* is a variant of *mice*, and *will* is a variant of *be*. Search engines often treat variants interchangeably for matching purposes unless the searcher requests otherwise.

text analytics   A technique whereby software employs linguistics and pattern detection techniques to impute some larger meaning to the words in a document. Entity extraction and document categorization are two emerging types of text analytics.

thread   A specific question or conversation within a forum, message board, or news group.

<title> tag   An element of an HTML document that stores the main heading of the entire page, which will be used on the title bar or bookmarks for its page. Search engines pay more attention to what is in the title tag (`<title>About Our Company</title>`) than any other tag on the page.

toolbar   A program that adds a function on your browser screen you can execute without having to first navigate to a website. A search toolbar, for example, allows web users to enter search queries without first going to a search engine's website.

trackback   A comment a blogger makes about someone else's blog, except the comment is actually stored in the blogger's own blog, with a link to it from the blog commented on.

tracking code   A method of marking content so that visitors to your website from that content are measured by your analytics system and attributed to that content.

traditional advertising agency   A company that helps clients plan and purchase promotional announcements for TV, radio, and print media, but might cover interactive media, too.

traffic   The web metrics term to describe the number of visits to a website. Web metrics reports will frequently analyze increases or decreases in traffic, and they typically evaluate search marketing success in attracting visits from search engines.

transactional searcher   A user who enters a search keyword intending to complete a specific task, such as purchasing a product or downloading a file.

trusted feed   A way of sending your data to a search engine, instead of having the spider crawl your site. Some specialty search and almost all shopping search engines require the use of trusted feeds to load your data into their search indexes.

tweet   A short text update posted on the Twitter microblogging service.

two-way link   Also known as a *reciprocal link*, a hypertext connection to a page that has a corresponding link back to the source.

Uniform Resource Locator (URL)   The address of a web page that a visitor can enter into a browser to display that page. For example, bn.com is the URL of the Barnes & Noble home page.

unique visitor   Synonymous with *visitor*, a web metrics term for a person who visits a website at least once in a period of time. If the same person came to a website three times in 1 month, the metrics system would log three visits for that month, but just one unique visitor.

URL   Uniform Resource Locator, the address of a web page that a visitor can enter into a browser to display that page. For example, bn.com is the URL of the Barnes & Noble home page.

URL parameter   The name of a variable in a software program that displays dynamic web pages. The URL www.domain.com?product=45 contains a parameter named *product* and a value of 45. The software program uses the parameter and its associated value to decide which content to display on the page.

URL redirect   An instruction to display a different URL from the one the browser requested. Redirects are used when the URL of a page has changed. They allow old URLs to be "redirected" to the current URL, so that your visitors do not get a "page not found" message (known as an HTTP 404 error) when they use the old URL.

URL rewrite   A method of modifying the appearance of your URLs so that dynamic URLs look like static URLs. URL rewrite helps make your URLs more readable for your human visitors, but are also very important in getting spiders to crawl your site.

URL value   The number or character string assigned to a variable in a software program that displays dynamic web pages. The URL www.domain.com?product=45 contains a parameter named *product* and a value of 45, which the software program uses to decide which content to display on the page.

usability engineer   The web specialist of the extended search team responsible for the user experience. Search marketing often depends on the usability engineer's recognition that search is a critical user scenario that must be considered in all user experience strategy.

user agent   The name of the software program that made a request of your web server, as shown in your log file. Most browsers generate a user agent name with *Mozilla* in it, but search engine spiders each have unique names that allow you to see when they have visited.

user experience   The total environment a web visitor is exposed to that shapes satisfaction with each visit to a site, including content, visual design, navigation, and technology.

value   The number or character string assigned to a variable in a software program that displays dynamic web pages. The URL www.domain.com?product=45 contains a parameter named *product* and a value of 45, which the software program uses to decide which content to display on the page.

vertical search engine   As contrasted with a *horizontal search engine*, a search engine designed to return results of a particular type of content, such as all videos, images, blogs, or products.

viral marketing   A new term for *word-of-mouth* marketing on the web, which differs from traditional word of mouth only in the speed with which messages can be disseminated using technology.

visit   Synonymous with *session*, a web metrics term for a single series of pages viewed from a single website. If a visitor comes to a website and views five pages before leaving to go to a new site, the metrics system logs five page views, but just one visit.

visitor   Synonymous with *unique visitor*, a web metrics term for a person who visits a website at least once in a period of time. If the same person came to a website three times in one month, the metrics system would log three visits for that month, but just one visitor.

visitor behavior   The study of what web visitors think and do when using the web.

visual design   The appearance, often called the look and feel, of a web page, including page layouts, colors, fonts, images, icons, and buttons.

web   Known formally as the World Wide Web, an interlinked network of pages that display content or allow interaction between the web *visitor* and the organization that owns the *website*.

Web 2.0   A name made popular by Internet expert Tim O'Reilly to connote the next generation of web usage that provides more interaction and participation rather than passive consumption of information and products. Social media, *consumer-generated content*, and other trends are all considered part of the larger Web 2.0 trend.

web application server   The system software that executes the programs that run a website. Web application servers, also known as application servers, are typically used to display dynamic pages.

web conversion   Any measurable, successful outcome of a web visit—such as registering an account or donating to a cause—based on the behavior model developed for the website's specific goals.

web conversion rate   The ratio of website visitors to web conversions—how many people came to the site versus how many successfully achieved the goal (buy the product, sign up for a newsletter, fill out contact information, and so forth).

web developer   A web specialist who develops programs or HTML to display web pages in your visitor's web browser.

web feed   A technique that delivers subscribed information from an information provider (such as a marketer) to a feed reader. *Really Simple Syndication* (RSS) and *Atom* are two popular types of web feeds.

web governance specialist   The web specialist of the extended search team responsible for enforcing your website's operational standards.

web log   1. A file on your web server that serves as a record of every action the server has taken. Log files can be analyzed in complex ways to determine the number of visits to your site (by people and by search engine spiders) and the number of pages that they view. 2. Also known as a *blog*, an online personal journal, a kind of periodic column on the web. Some blogs are reminiscent of a private diary, but others resemble magazine columns focused on a particular subject of interest.

webmaster   The web specialist of the extended search team responsible for planning and operating the servers that display web pages when visitors arrive. Search marketing often depends on the webmaster understanding the importance of web search so that proper priority will be given to needed search marketing tasks.

web page   A combination of text and pictures, often augmented by software, that allows visitors to interact with the organizational owners of the *website*.

web server   The system software that displays *static* web pages from HTML files and can execute some programs to create *dynamic* pages.

website   A set of interlinked web pages managed by a domain team that allows interaction between visitors and the site's owner. For example, visitors speak of "going to Amtrak's website," which is at Amtrak.com. All pages whose URL starts with Amtrak.com are considered part of the Amtrak website.

widget   A small program embedded on a web page to perform a function, which some liken to a mini-website.

wiki   Derived from the Hawaiian word *wiki-wiki*, meaning "quick," a group word processor whose documents are always available for viewing and updating. The most famous wiki is Wikipedia, an encyclopedia created and maintained by the public.

within-the-family link   A hypertext link between two sites that search engines consider to be biased, perhaps because they have similar IP addresses, Whois information, or anchor text. Search engines seek to downgrade these links because they are not between neutral parties; the endorsement that the link provides is not as valuable as others.

word of email   An interactive form of *word-of-mouth* marketing in which customers pass along interesting information about products or services to other customers using electronic mail, thus spreading a marketing message.

word of IM   An interactive form of *word-of-mouth* marketing in which customers pass along interesting information about products or services to other customers using instant messages, thus spreading a marketing message.

word of mouth marketing   Also known as *viral marketing*, word-of-mouth marketing has traditionally referred to the way that customers talk to other customers about an interesting product or service, thus spreading a marketing message. Interactive marketing has expanded the pass-along possibilities beyond personal conversations to include *word of email*, *word of web*, and other formulations.

word of web   An interactive form of *word-of-mouth* marketing in which customers pass along interesting information about products or services to other customers using electronic means (message boards, news groups, and others), thus spreading a marketing message.

word variant   Also known as *term variant*, a linguistic form of another word. *Mice* is a variant of *mouse*, and *are* is a variant of *be*. Search engines often treat variants interchangeably for matching purposes unless the searcher requests otherwise.

World Wide Web Usually abbreviated as WWW, or simply "the web," an interlinked network of pages that display content or allow interaction between the web visitor and the organization that owns the website.

XML Extensible Markup Language, a standard for a markup language, similar to HTML, that allows tags to be defined to describe any kind of data you have, making it very popular as a format for data feeds.

Index

A

acronyms as keywords, 57

ad copy

    creating, 329-332

    keywords in, 330

Addesso, Patricia J., 31

Adobe Acrobat (PDF) files, 85

Adobe Flash, 294-295

ads as search result, 12

adult content filters, 68

affiliate marketing, 114-115

affiliate "spam," 36

AJAX (Asynchronous JavaScript and XML), 289, 295

always on keywords, 258

Amazon, 17

analyzing

    content

        different types of documents, converting, 85

        important, deciding which words are, 85-86

keywords

    antiphrases, detecting, 64

    common words, 65

    intent of searcher, identifying, 65-66

    operators, processing search, 65

    overview, 63

    phrases, detecting, 64

    spelling, correcting, 64

    stop words, detecting, 65

    word order, examining, 65

    word variants, finding, 63

links, 353-354

anchor text, 357

antiphrases, detecting, 64

App Store Optimization (ASO), 319

Asynchronous JavaScript and XML (AJAX), 289, 295

attracting links from other sites, 367-369

audiences

    as keyword category, 264-266

    multiple audience sites, 401-402

    multiple audiences and keywords, 56

auditing phase of search marketing campaign, 200

authority pages, 358

automated keyword management, 411

automatically submitting your site, 277

B

Back Azimuth Consulting Keyword Management tool, 59

back button, enabling, 342

Baidu, 10

Balzer, Evan, 118

banned or penalized

    activities to get you, 338

    verifying your site is not, 274-276